# CHRONICLE OF THE INDIAN WARS

By the same author:

*The War Between the Spies:*
*A History of Espionage During the American Civil War*

*Art of the Golden West: An Illustrated History*

*The Colonial Revival in America*

*Charles Brockden Brown: An American Tale*

# CHRONICLE OF THE INDIAN WARS

## From Colonial Times to Wounded Knee

### ALAN AXELROD

PRENTICE HALL GENERAL REFERENCE

NEW YORK • LONDON • TORONTO • SYDNEY • TOKYO • SINGAPORE

FOR ANITA AND IAN

PRENTICE HALL GENERAL REFERENCE
15 Columbus Circle
New York, New York, 10023

PRENTICE HALL and colophon are registered trademarks of Simon & Schuster, Inc.

Library of Congress Cataloging-in-Publication Data

Axelrod, Alan, 1952–
Chronicle of the Indian wars / Alan Axelrod.
p.    cm.
Includes bibliographical references and index.
ISBN 0-671-84650-7
1. Indians of North America—Wars.   2. Indians of North America—
History.   3. Indians of North America—Government relations.
I. Title.
E81.A9   1993                    92-20827   CIP

Designed by Rhea Braunstein

Manufactured in the United States of America

10   9   8   7   6   5   4   3   2   1

First Edition

# CONTENTS

# PREFACE

While writing this chronicle of protracted racial warfare, I have been assailed by a catalog of emotions about the subject itself as well as about the legion of scholars and historians who have studied it before me. Concerning the violently mingled destinies of Indian and white, I have felt simultaneously and by turns, admiration, reverence, outrage, sorrow, and shame. For the authors throughout five centuries who have written on the relationship of Indian and white, I have felt awe and gratitude. About my own work, which owes its every word to the writers who have witnessed, thought, and written before me, I can now feel only humility.

The bibliography of this book acknowledges the authors on whom I have drawn most often and most directly in writing *Chronicle of the Indian Wars*. Long as it is, that list hardly begins to suggest the multitude of works devoted to the Indian and to the relations between Indian and white. Yet for all its vastness, the literature available offers the merest handful of books that addresses the entire history of white–Indian warfare. I assume this lack is due less to a collective oversight among historians than to a conviction that few truly responsible scholars would risk a work doomed to certain superficiality, generalization, and distortion. Having completed this book, I must admit that I now share, in some measure, that conviction. Yet I am also convinced that *Chronicle of the Indian Wars* was worth the risk. Whatever the book omits or misrepresents, it does reveal—in one sweeping glance—the shape of four centuries of war. The contours of conflict are, in the main, ugly and dark, yet they also reveal bright details of heroism, humanity, and hope. I have learned and felt much in writing this book. Perhaps the reader will be rewarded similarly.

Although it begins in the late fifteenth century, almost three hundred years before the Declaration of Independence, *Chronicle of the Indian Wars* is solely about warfare between Indians and whites in the area occupied by the present continental United States. Where necessary, I have ventured briefly into Canada, Mexico, Central and South America, and the Caribbean; but I make no claim to covering any more of the New World than what is today encompassed by the United States.

For many Native American peoples, warfare was a traditional way of life, and combat among different tribes or among different bands within a tribe was, if anything, far more frequent than war between Indians and whites. Yet the story of war among Indians lies, for the most part, outside of recorded or even retrievable history. Francis Jennings, whose extraordinary works are listed in my bibliography, is among the very few scholars who have attempted to recover and interpret some fragments of the history of inter- (and intra-) tribal warfare. Except for a discussion of the intertribal Iroquoian Beaver Wars (Chapter 6), which were essential to the formation of evolving alliances and enmities between Indians and whites during the seventeenth century, I have devoted *Chronicle of the Indian Wars* almost exclusively to conflicts between whites and Indians. Having said this, I must observe that such conflicts very often also involved alliances between certain whites and certain Indians against other Indians, or other whites, or other whites and other Indians. In these cases, which are numerous, I have addressed inter- (and intra-) tribal conflict insofar as it was an aspect of warfare against whites or white interests.

As the focus of this book reflects Euro-American concerns, so its nomenclature—the names assigned to the various wars—is the product of history as written by whites. To Indians of the eighteenth and nineteenth centuries, "King George's War," "The French and Indian War," "The American Revolution," "The War of 1812," "The Civil War," and the like would have had little meaning—even to those Indians most intimately and urgently involved in the struggles on which whites have hung these labels. Likewise, the so-called Wars for the West are known to us chiefly by the nomenclature formulated by the United States Army in 1905 for purposes of authorizing campaign badges to be awarded to soldiers who had participated in actions against Indians between 1865 and 1891. To Indians of this period, the army's labels would have held little meaning, except, perhaps, as yet more symptoms of the white man's obsession with using words to carve up, divide, and claim whatever he wanted to take from the Indian.

Finally, there are the vagaries of the Euro-American calendar to deal with. The old Julian calendar, which was used in Great Britain and its colonies until 1752, overestimated the solar year by 11 minutes, 14 seconds a year. In 1752, Great Britain adopted the so-called New Style (or Gregorian) calendar, which adjusted errors in the former chronology by adding 10 days down through the year 1699 and 11 days beginning with 1700, and leaving 11 days out of the calendar in 1752 (September 3 became September 14). Under the Julian calendar, the New Year technically began on March 25; the New Style calendar restored New Year's Day to January 1. *Chronicle of the Indian Wars* follows New Style usage for all dates prior to 1752.

## ACKNOWLEDGMENTS

I began by akcnowledging my debt to the many authors whose books I have, I freely confess, plundered shamelessly. Those who have figured most centrally in *Chronicle of the Indian Wars* are listed in the bibliography.

It is also a pleasure to thank my literary agent, Bert Holtje of James Peter Associates, who encouraged the development of this book and found for it a great publisher in Prentice Hall General Reference. Kate Kelly, formerly senior editor at Prentice Hall, acquired the book, which has been faithfully shepherded by her successor, Deirdre Mullane. Deirdre's advice, criticism, encouragement, and sense of audience have greatly helped to shape the book. Vincent Janoski and Carol Blumentritt, acute and indefatigable copyeditors, made sense of certain stretches of nonsense and certainly saved me (and my readers) from an assortment of stupidities.

I am grateful to Thomas F. Cranmer, who produced the fine maps in this book, to Curtis Utz, who helped me research the illustrations, and to the individuals and institutions who have granted permission to reproduce them.

My partners in Zenda, Inc., Charles Phillips and Patricia Hogan, were, as usual, supportive beyond the call of duty and generous with their extremely useful insights.

My wife, Anita Arliss Axelrod, has endured patiently and with understanding a process that, as usual, has taken more time than either of us expected. Ian, my son, has also shown patience with his often preoccupied father—more patience than one has a right to expect from a boy about to enter kindergarten. I hope this book will repay his understanding by helping to inform, in some small way, the many decisions he will have to make in choosing between a world of intolerance, hatred, and death and one of generosity, love, and nurture.

# CHAPTER 1

# BLACK LEGEND, RED MEN
## New Spain (1492–1751)

Between 1492 and 1580 (when Philip II temporarily united Spain and Portugal, thereby consolidating the vast New World holdings of both nations), Spain established a virtual monopoly on American conquest and thereby came to control the largest empire the world had ever seen. Focused on the twin goals of propagating Christianity and mining gold, yet actually sustained by agriculture, it was an empire based on the availability of slave labor, Indian as well as African. And that meant it was an empire committed to conquest.

The subject of the Spanish in the New World is ample enough to fill many volumes. Here we will limit ourselves to chronicling the large-scale armed conflicts between the colonial Spanish and Indians within the boundaries of the present United States. Having said this, it is important to survey the Spanish conquests in Central and South America because those conquests created the base from which the Spanish struck out at the frontier of New World Indian civilization—the North American Southeast and Southwest.

In a celebrated journal passage for October 14, 1492, Christopher Columbus speculated on the need for quickly erecting a fortress at La Navidad, Hispañiola, near the site of his landing:

I do not see that it would be necessary, for these people are very simple as regards the use of arms [indeed, some cut themselves on the sharp Spanish swords, which they attempted to handle by the blade], as your Highnesses will see from the seven that I caused to be taken, to bring home and learn our language and return; unless your Highnesses should order them all to be brought to Castile, or to be kept as captives on the same island; for with fifty men they can all be subjugated and made to do what is required of them.

The passage not only suggests the highhanded cruelty that would characterize much of Spain's dealings with the natives of the Americas, but also shows how seriously the Spanish misjudged the Indians' temperament. When Columbus sailed back to Spain, he left behind a garrison, which, as soon as the admiral was safely departed, set about pillaging goods and raping women. One night, a band of Indians retaliated, killing ten Spaniards as they slept. The Indians hunted down the rest of the garrison and killed them as well, so that, when Columbus returned to La Navidad in 1493, no whites were left alive.

Yet the Spanish quickly built new settlements, moving on to the mainland and treating the Indians with a mixture of cruelty and profound (if wholly ethnocentric) concern for their spiritual well-being. Bartolomé de Las Casas, the first priest ordained in the New World, was a zealous but compassionate missionary who campaigned against the cruelty of his countrymen. He reported how Spanish soldiers overran

Cities and Villages, where they spared no sex nor age; neither would their cruelty pity Women with childe, whose bellies they would rip up, taking out the Infant to hew it in pieces. They would often lay wagers who should with most dexterity either cleave or cut a man in the middle, or who could at one blow soonest cut off his head. The children they would take by the feet and dash their innocent heads against the rocks, and when they were fallen into the water, with a strange and cruel derision they would call upon them to swim. Sometimes they would run both Mother and Infant, being in her belly, quite through at one thrust.

They erected certain Gallowses, that were broad but so low, that the tormented creatures might touch the ground with their feet, upon every one of which they would hang thirteen persons, blasphemously affirming that they did it in honour of our Redeemer and his Apostles, and then putting fire under them, they burnt the poor wretches alive.

The Spanish military, which came to the New World in the form of the *conquistador*—the conqueror—was well practiced in racial warfare. By the time Columbus first voyaged to America, Spain had been engaged in some eight centuries of brutal conflict with the Moors— like the "Indians" of Central America, a people of different religion and different race from the Spanish. Moreover, the conquistadors were themselves subject to a class system that was literally squeezing them out of Europe. Spain, like much of Europe, was dominated by primogeniture, which mandated that the first son in a family inherit all titles and property upon the death of the father, thereby severely limiting opportunities for second, third, and fourth sons. Among the lower classes, prospects were even more limited. For these reasons—and with the promise of gold, limitless slave labor, and a crop of souls ripe for conversion to Christianity—Spain *needed* a New World.

The occupation of Cuba and the southern Caribbean involved forced subjugation of native populations— Puerto Rico in 1508–09, Jamaica in 1510, and Cuba in 1511—but these were small-scale skirmishes and slave raids. The first large-scale war of conquest was fought on the mainland, in Mexico.

Hernan Cortés headed an expedition into the region of present-day Tabasco in March 1519, defeating the Tabascán Indians in a battle fought on March 25 and the Tlascalas on September 5. When he landed a small force at what is today Vera Cruz, he was cordially greeted by ambassadors of the Aztec king Moctezuma II. They bore gifts of great beauty and value—gems and objects wrought in gold—which only whetted the conquistadors' appetites. "Send me some [more] of it," Cortés declared, "because I and my companions suffer from a disease of the heart which can be cured only with gold." And so, on November 8, Cortés marched on the Aztec capital of Tenochtitlán (present-day Mexico City). He had taken some precautions beforehand, boring holes in the hulls of his own ships (he told his men it was the work of worms) so that there could be no turning back, and recruiting allies among the ever-warring city-states of the far-flung Aztec empire. Not that recruitment was a voluntary proposition. The people of Cholula were persuaded to help Cortés only after his men slaughtered some three thousand of them in the space of two hours. Perhaps at the news of this, Moctezuma lost any heart he may have had for a fight. Or perhaps he believed Cortés to be the incarnation of the birdlike god Quet-

*When Hernan Cortés and his conquistadors, having defeated the Tabascan Indians and the Tlascalas, landed at Vera Cruz in 1519, they were met by ambassadors of Moctezuma II, ruler of the Aztecs. The Indians presented the Spaniards with gems and objects wrought in gold. Cortés took the gifts and declared, "Send me some [more] of it, because I and my companions suffer from a disease of the heart which can be cured only with gold." By the end of the year, the conquistadors had taken the Aztec capital of Tenochtitlán. They were temporarily evicted from the city by a short-lived rebellion, crushed on August 13, 1521, after which all of the Aztec empire became part of New Spain. (Library of Congress.)*

Pictured in a fanciful seventh-century engraving, Moctezuma II, opulent ruler of the vast Aztec empire, opened his capital city to Cortés and his conquistadors, to whom he soon lost his empire and his life. (Library of Congress.)

zalcoatl, who created man out of his own blood. Whatever the reason, the Aztec emperor opened his city to Cortés and his army of conquest.

Tenochtitlán rivaled—indeed, surpassed—most European cities in magnificence, replete, as it was, with public buildings, temples, and aqueduct-delivered drinking water. It was the center of an empire that stretched from the Gulf of Mexico to the Pacific Ocean. And all of this seemed to Cortés ripe for the taking—all the more because Moctezuma appeared willing to give it up without a fight.

It is possible that the conquest of Mexico might have been accomplished, at least from this point on, without much bloodshed had another European not appeared on the scene. Panfilo de Narvaez was as inept as he was covetous, and he was most covetous of the conquests of Hernan Cortés. Narvaez conducted an expedition from Cuba to Mexico intending to arrest his rival for overstepping the authority granted him. Cortés did not quietly await the arrival of Narvaez, but set out from Tenochtitlán to meet him, leaving the imperial city in the hands of one Pedro de Alvarado.

Overcoming Narvaez proved to be no formidable task, but while European fought European in the Mexican countryside, Pedro de Alvarado and his men, according to an Aztec account, "were seized with an urge to kill the celebrants [it was the feast of the war god, Huitzilopochtli]. They all ran forward, armed as if for battle. . . .They posted guards so that no one could escape, and then rushed into the Sacred Patio to slaughter the celebrants." Alvarado's men seized the ritual drummer, hacking off his arms and then his head. Others they eviscerated. They pursued all who ran and killed everyone they possibly could.

The people who had so meekly submitted to conquest now rose up in rebellion, laying siege to the palace in which the soldiers had taken refuge, and in which Moctezuma was now held captive. Cortés returned in the midst of the rebellion, plundered what he could and, with his men, fought his way out of the palace and the city. During this evacuation on June 30, 1520—called by the Spanish the *Noche Triste*, Sad Night—Moctezuma was killed. Spanish accounts say that he had been assassinated by his own people; the Aztecs attributed his death to the Spanish.

Cortés had as his object more than the death of the emperor and the looting of the emperor's palace. Crushing a revolt at Otumba on July 7, the conquistador prepared to retake Tenochtitlán. Ten months after their evacuation from the city, the Spanish army returned to lay siege, destroying Tenochtitlán's aqueducts and choking off the supply of food. What thirst and starvation failed to do, smallpox—apparently carried to Mexico by

a black slave in the service of Narvaez—accomplished. Nevertheless, the people of the city held out for three months, before yielding on August 13, 1521. Tenochtitlán—and all Mexico—now belonged to Hernan Cortés and, of course, his Most Catholic Majesty, King Charles V.

The only conquistador to rival Cortés was Francisco Pizarro, who twice attempted to invade the Incas of Peru in the 1520s and succeeded upon a third try in 1531. He landed at Tumbez on the Pacific coast, just south of the equator, and marched to Cuzco, the Inca capital. The conquistador largely avoided clashes with the Indians by taking advantage of an ongoing civil war between factions allied to rival heirs to the chieftainship. Pizarro told each group he met along his way that he had come as an enemy of the other. At the town of Cajamarca, on the way to Cuzco, Pizarro captured Atahualpa, one of the contenders for the chieftainship, and began to plunder Inca treasure. While his soldiers were thus employed, Pizarro himself negotiated with Atahualpa's rival, even as Atahualpa secretly gathered a force to expel the Spaniards. But before Atahualpa could muster his army, Pizarro tried him for usurpation, idolatry, and polygamy; found him guilty; and had him executed. This, however, did not result in the kind of summary conquest Cortés had enjoyed in Mexico. Rival Spanish groups supported contending Inca factions, and Pizarro himself was murdered in 1541. Until royal Spanish forces defeated the conquistador's brother in 1548, the nation remained in a state of civil war. Indeed, while Peru henceforth yielded many riches to Spain, separatist Inca groups, centered in remote regions of the Andes, kept up an active resistance against the colonial government until 1572, when Viceroy Francisco de Toledo captured and killed Tupac Amaru, the last Inca heir.

The conquests of Cortés and Pizarro stimulated Spanish expeditions north into the borderlands—the area of the present United States. There was no civilization in this region as elaborate as that of the Aztecs or Incas, but there was a legend of gold—obscure references to the Seven Cities of Cibola—and that was enough for the conquistadors. A series of expeditions into the borderlands culminated in the 1540–42 explorations of Vásquez de Coronado, who traveled most extensively in the Southwest and even as far as present-day Kansas. In July 1540, he and his army rode into the Zuni pueblo of Hawikuh in Central New Mexico, demanding its surrender. In response, the Indians showered stones upon him and his men, knocking Coronado unconscious. Nevertheless, the conquistadors took the town in less than an hour.

In September, the main force of Coronado's army ventured into the pueblo region along the Rio Grande, taking

## TENOCHTITLÁN AND THE AZTEC EMPIRE

The Spaniards who entered Moctezuma's capital could justly boast of the magnificence of their own cities, cathedrals, and castles, as well as of the adminstrative complexities of their far-flung empire and the baroque subleties of their Catholic religion. Nothing in their European experience, however, prepared them for what they saw (and would soon destroy) in Tenochtitlán. It was a city as large as Cordova or Seville but situated entirely within Lake Texcoco, two miles from the mainland. Four artificial causeways gave magnificent entrance to it, constructed of immense beams that were perfectly hewn and fitted together. The city was watered by a system of aqueducts that rivalled anything produced by classical Rome, and the streets, which were lined with magnificent temples, issued onto great public squares affording market spaces. Here one could puchase gold, silver, jewels, game of every description, vegetables, rare herbs, pottery variously decorated, rich cloth—"everything which the world affords," according to one who traveled with Cortés. Tenochtitán offered barbershops, physicians' offices, and restaurants.

But most in evidence were the priests, legions of them, marching through the boulevards like black-robed soldiers. For, above all, Tenochtitlán was a capital of religion. More than this, it was the home of God himself—as incarnated in Moctezuma II. As far as can be ascertained from the accounts left by the conquistadors, Moctezuma occupied a complex of palaces at the center of the city. There is a description of one—"inferior to the rest"—built of marble and jasper, looking out onto a garden with ten pools, in which fish and water birds of every species in the empire were kept. The emperor seems to have maintained a private zoo, which included birds of prey, lions, wolves, foxes, and other animals, whose care was assigned to a staff of 300. Gold and jewel-encrusted sculpture abounded.

As for Moctezuma himself, his meals were served by 300 or 400 youths, and his clothes were changed four times a day, each costume being worn but once and then discarded. These were splendid garments worked with gold and silver and the plumage of rare birds.

What supplied such wealth? Remarkably, as far as anyone can tell, the empire as Cortés found it in 1519 was relatively new. Before the fourteenth century, the Aztecs appear to have been only one among several nomadic tribes wandering through Central America. As Spanish imperial ambitions claimed inspiration from the word of God, so the Aztecs claim to have heeded the word and commandment of the war god Huitzilopochtli, who enjoined the tribe to conquer all about them. Within the space of two centuries, the demands and the fruits of continual warfare created a vast, complex empire of dark beauty, extending from the Gulf of Mexico to the Pacific and from the Valley of Mexico south into Guatemala. It was an empire of slaves, whose work was supremely manifest in the capital.

Widespread slavery was perhaps the mildest aspect of the Aztec world. For all its magnificence, the empire was founded in blood for the very purpose of shedding blood. In Tenochtitlán, one temple was more spectacular than all the rest. It sprouted 40 towers and, in the fullness of its mass, was greater and taller than the cathedral of Seville. There were three main halls from which various windowless chapels branched. This was the temple where human sacrifice was practiced. The idols that lined its halls were molded of a paste of seeds and plants kneaded together with the blood of prisoners and slaves taken in battle. Blood was the fuel of Aztec government, economy, and culture. The very earth, according to some accounts, was dark with it.

Zuni and Hopi towns, one by one. Coronado's men seem to have admired the Hopi and Zuni—one soldier, Pedro de Castañeda, remarked on the absence among them of drunkenness, sodomy, sacrifice, cannibalism, larceny, and sloth. This notwithstanding, the conquistadors compelled the people into slavery, taking from them food, houses, and women. The Indians resisted as best they could, but the only organized revolt took place in the summer of 1541, after Coronado headed north into the Great Plains on his continuing search for the Seven Cities of Gold. An Indian named Texamatli in the town of Mixton took advantage of Coronado's absence to stage a rebellion. Niño de Guzmán, governor of New Spain, quickly called in additional troops to put down the rebels.

Coronado returned briefly to the pueblos for the winter of 1541–42, then departed, leaving behind two hapless missionaries. Nearly 40 years passed before more Spaniards visited the Hopis. The small band of missionaries and soldiers who arrived at that time learned that the original friars had been "martyred." Two more missionaries took up residence in the pueblos—and were also promptly killed.

In 1579, the English seafarer Sir Francis Drake entered a central California bay and laid claim to a land he called "New Albion." At this, the viceroy in Mexico City warned the royal court in Madrid that the Spanish colo-

## THE PUEBLOS BEFORE THE CONQUEST

When the Spanish encountered the Pueblo culture in New Mexico and Arizona, they saw the result of centuries of Native American civilization in this area. Three earlier cultures influenced the development of the Pueblo people: the Mogollon, the Hohokum, and the Anasazi.

The Mogollon seem to have emerged around 100 B.C. in the southern uplands along the present-day border of New Mexico and Arizona. They were an agricultural people who lived in pit-house villages and produced distinctive ceramics. They developed from a people today labeled the Cochise culture, the origins of which date back at least to 8,000 B.C. The Cochise people introduced agriculture to the area. The influence of the later Mogollon spread into the deserts of southern Arizona and, combined with cultural influences transmitted from tribes in Mexico, produced the Hohokum culture (a Pima word meaning "those who have vanished"). The Hohokum transformed the landscape in the drainages of the Salt and Gila rivers by building a system of canals and irrigation works.

The Anasazi, a Navajo word meaning "the ancient ones," developed from the Mogollon and the Hohokum. Since the earliest evidence of this people is found in elaborate woven baskets preserved in dry caves, the early Anasazi are called the Basket Makers. Around A.D. 700–800, the Basket Makers began a transition from the cave and pit house to multiroom masonry structures above ground and, even more characteristically, apartmentlike cliff dwellings, the so-called pueblos. The transition to life above ground coincided with and promoted the development of an increasingly complex agricultural society during A.D. 800–1100, the beginning of the Classic or Great Pueblo Period. During the eleventh through the thirteenth centuries, farming methods became highly sophisticated, employing elaborate and effective irrigation systems, and a market culture developed, along with religion and ceremony associated with agriculture and weather control. Artifacts from this period include beautifully wrought ceramics. Three great Pueblo population centers developed during these years: Mesa Verde, Colorado; Chaco Canyon, New Mexico; and Kayenta, Arizona.

At the height of the Classic Period, between 1276 and 1299, the three major centers of Pueblo population mysteriously declined. While researchers are still uncertain as to the cause, it is thought that a ruinous drought, aided by disease (infectious diarrhea) and the depredations of hostile nomadic tribes, brought about the precipitous decline. Some of the Pueblo people drifted south, founding new towns from which the modern Zuni and Hopi developed. Others migrated east to the Pajaritop Plateau and the valleys of the Rio Grande and its tributaries. The Pueblos who moved east, in particular, rebuilt their civilization rapidly. When the Spanish encountered these people in 1581, they were duly impressed with the architecture, agriculture, crafts, and what one conquistador called the "very remarkable . . . neatness . . . they observe in everything."

What the Spanish could not tolerate was Pueblo religion, which, centered on the underground ritual chamber called a kiva, emphasized the propitiation of favorable natural forces and the achievement of a oneness with the natural world. Uncomprehending, the conquistadors saw this as neither more nor less than the devil's work and sought to extirpate it.

Except for the Indians of the Acoma pueblo, the Pueblos offered no serious resistance to Spanish conquest. Perhaps this was the result of an almost total absence of central government among them. Each village constituted a politically independent entity, and within each village, social classes were unknown. As a result, coordinated resistance was virtually impossible. It took the efforts of an extraordinary leader, Popé, late in the seventeenth century, to unite the Pueblos in a revolt against the Spanish.

*The Acoma Pueblo as it appeared in 1936. When the pueblo resisted Spanish colonization, troops under Don Juan de Oñate killed most of Acoma's warriors in a battle fought during January 1599 and took captive 500 women and children. About 80 noncombatant men over the age of 25 were summarily sentenced to the loss of one foot and 20 years' enslavement. Women, as well as children over the age of 12, were also enslaved. (National Archives and Records Administration.)*

nies might soon be threatened. But Spain was busy with European wars, and the crown did nothing to protect the northern colonial frontier for about two decades. At last, in 1598 an expedition was dispatched north from Mexico. On April 30, Don Juan de Oñate reached present-day El Paso, Texas, and claimed all of "New Mexico," a province stretching from Texas through California. With 400 men, women, and children, 7,000 head of stock, and some 80 wagons, Oñate pressed farther north, aggressively colonizing the pueblo country.

Of all the pueblos, only Acoma, in western New Mexico, offered serious resistance. As he had with the other pueblos, Oñate sent squads of conquistadors to inform the Indians that they were now subjects of the Spanish crown and that they had to renounce their pagan ways and abide by Spanish law. The Acoma Indians killed 13 soldiers of this party, including three officers. Perched atop a steep-walled mesa, Acoma was a formidable objective; yet Oñate could not let the resistance go unpunished. In January 1599, his troops fought their way to the top of the mesa, killed most of Acoma's warriors, and took captive 500 women and children. About 80 noncombatant men over the age of 25 were summarily sentenced to the loss of one foot and enslavement for a period of 20 years. Women, as well as children over the age of 12, retained their extremities but were likewise sentenced to long terms of slavery. Children under 12 were consigned to the care of priests. Oñate seized two Hopis, innocent bystanders who had been visiting Acoma during the siege, and sent them to their home pueblo minus their right hands—as a warning about the consequences of rebellion.

The cruelty of Spanish governors such as Oñate forged the so-called Black Legend of Spain in the New World. While Oñate inherited the ruthless conquistador traditions, his cruelty had another motive. Oñate had financed the colonization of the pueblo country with his personal fortune in expectation of growing even wealthier from gold and silver. As it turned out, the country failed even to produce sufficient food for the colonists. In response, Oñate demanded more and more from the Indians in labor and tribute. His mistreatment of them was finally too much even for colonial authorities, who fined and stripped Oñate of all honors 15 years after he had first marched into the province.

The economic failure of Oñate and others in the northern borderlands might well have prompted Spain to abandon its colonization efforts in the region were it not for another Spanish "army" that had also been hard at work during this period. A determined band of priests had been zealously baptizing thousands of Indians, creating a population of Christian souls (the padres argued) who could not now be abandoned. Ironically, this concern for the Indians' spiritual welfare tended to perpetuate the horrors for which Oñate had been censured. For, like him, each succeeding governor had to buy his office and then had to devise a way to turn a profit from his investment. This inevitably meant working the Indians relentlessly. While slavery as such was outlawed, the *encomienda* system, central to the Spanish colonization program, was in fact a system of enslavement. In return for services rendered the crown, a colonist was granted designated Indian families—sometimes the inhabitants of several towns—from whom he could exact labor as well as commodity tribute. Technically, these Indians were not slaves, but wards.

For all practical purposes, however, the distinction between ward and slave was moot, and by the middle of the seventeenth century, after 50 years of Spanish tyranny, the Pueblo Indians were moved to form a desperate alliance with their hereditary enemies, the Apaches—the name itself is derived from the Zuni word for "enemy"—renowned and feared as avid makers of war. Despite the alliance, the early attempts at Pueblo rebellion were defeated. By the 1670s, however, the Apaches went on the warpath in earnest, terrorizing the Spanish Southwest. After two years of Apache and Pueblo guerrilla raids, during which colonial authorities were forced to stop sending supply caravans to their frontier outposts, Governor Antonio de Oterrmín arrested 47 Pueblo "medicine men," hanged three, and imprisoned the remainder in Santa Fe, the territorial capital. Among the prisoners was Popé, from the important Tewa Pueblo. Several years of imprisonment did nothing to endear the Spanish to Popé, who went into hiding in Taos after his release. There he secretly organized a major rebellion.

Coordinating a rebellion among the pueblos was a vast undertaking. Not only was it necessary to preserve secrecy, but since none of the pueblo towns would act without securing the unanimous consent of its council, Popé had to accomplish a complex task of persuasion. As it turned out, he was successful with all but the most remote pueblos along the Rio Grande. Next, however, was the matter of coordinating the strike among the widely dispersed pueblos. Popé dispatched runners to the various towns, each bearing a knotted cord designed so that the last knot would be untied in each pueblo on the day set for the revolt: August 13, 1680. Popé was ruthless in his effort to keep the revolt secret; he even had his brother-in-law killed because he suspected him of treachery. Somehow, however, word leaked, and the revolt had to be launched on the tenth.

Premature though it was, the action proved devastatingly effective. The major missions at Taos, Pecos, and Acoma were burned and the priests murdered, their bodies piled on the hated altars. Lesser missions throughout the frontier province also fell, and the outlying haciendas were destroyed along with their inhabitants. On August 15, Popé and his army of 500 advanced on Santa Fe, killing 400 settlers and 21 of 33 missionaries. The Santa Fe garrison consisted of only 50 men, but they were armed with a brass cannon, so the fighting lasted four days before the city was taken. The Pueblo leader installed himself in the palace Governor Oterrmín had hurriedly evacuated on August 21. Approximately 2,500 survivors of the invasion fled downriver, some as far as present-day El Paso, Texas, leaving behind all that they owned.

Unfortunately for the long-suffering Pueblos, Popé set himself up as a tyrant at least as oppressive as any Spaniard had been. For eight years he plundered and taxed his people, summarily executing anyone who resisted his rule. By the time of Popé's death in 1688, the pueblos were in a chronic state of civil war. The year after the dictator's death, the Zia Pueblo fell to the Spanish. Then, in 1692, Governor Don Diego de Vargas exploited the general confusion prevailing throughout the pueblos and laid siege to Santa Fe, cutting off its water and food supply until the inhabitants surrendered. Within another four years, all of the pueblos submitted once again to Spanish rule—except for the Hopis, whom the Spanish, it seems, simply overlooked.

In 1695, the Pimas of lower Pimeria Alta—present-day Sonora, Mexico, and southern Arizona—staged a short-lived revolt, looting and burning Spanish property and terrorizing missionaries. The uprising was quickly put down. However, half a century later, in 1751, the Pimas of upper Pimeria Alta, many of them descendants of earlier insurgents who had fled north, staged a more formidable uprising. Its leader was Luis Oacpicagigua, who had earlier served the Spanish as captain-general of the western Pimas. He had now come to believe that the incursion of ever greater numbers of Spanish settlers would force his people into slavery, working on ranches and in mines. Like Popé, Luis had a genius for coordinating action and secretly united many Pimas, Papagos, Sobaipuris, and Apaches.

On the night of November 20, 1751, Luis and some of his men killed 18 Spaniards whom he had been entertaining at his home in Saric. One, however, Padre Nentvig, escaped to Tubutama and spread the alarm. Nevertheless, during the following weeks, rebels attacked missions and ranches in Caborca, Sonoita, Bac, and Guevavi. While destructive, the raids failed to coalesce into the general uprising Luis had planned; the Sobaipuris and the Apaches backed out of the alliance at the decisive moment, and many Papagos and Pimas failed to participate as well. However, an army under Governor Parilla and several months of combat were still required to put down the rebellion. Luis escaped execution by pledging to rebuild the churches ruined during the violence. It was a promise he never fulfilled, and the Pimas never wholly submitted to Spanish rule, but lived through the next century and a half chronically waging guerrilla warfare—first against the Spanish, then the Mexicans, and finally the Americans.

A state of chronic, virtually institutionalized guerrilla warfare also reigned among the Apaches, Navajos, and Comanches, who also raided, plundered, and murdered Spanish colonists—and suffered from them the same in return—until the period of the Mexican Revolution, after which they continued to fight, this time with the Mexicans. When the United States defeated Mexico in the 1846–48 war, the Apaches, Navajos, and Comanches waged guerilla war against the Americans. It would not end until the final defeat of Geronimo in 1886.

# CHAPTER 2

---

# "TO SUBDUE THE WILDE SALVAGES"

## Jamestown and the Southern Settlements (1607–1671)

Unlike the Spanish, who came to the New World in military force as conquerors and with the backing of powerful sovereigns, the English came as traders, settlers, and religious dissidents in search of safe haven. This does not mean that they intentionally treated the Indians with more kindness than did the Spanish, but only that the English settlers lacked the military might—and turn of mind—that animated the conquistadors. Following Sir Walter Raleigh's disastrous expedition to Roanoke (1584–1602), the first arrivals in Jamestown, Virginia, in 1607 had come seeking gold, furs, sassafras (thought to cure syphilis), and a passage to India. Some 900 settlers arrived during the first three years of the colony; by 1610, sickness and starvation had killed all but 150. This early period was marked by few violent conflicts with local Indians. Perhaps the Indians believed the newcomers would quickly perish and, therefore, were not worth fighting. The English, burdened by disease and starvation, were hardly in a position to take the offensive.

The Indians living in the vicinity of the Jamestown settlement were members of a confederacy of 32 Algonquian tribes—about 10,000 people—distributed among approximately 200 villages and held together by a distinguished chief named Wa-hun-sen-a-cawh (or Wahunsonacock), whom the English dubbed Powhatan, which was also the name generally applied to the people the chief led. Captain John Smith, an English soldier of fortune who, as a member of the Virginia Company, was among the first 105 Jamestown settlers, was captured by some of Powhatan's men in December 1607 while scouting out provisions along the Chickahominy River. Taken to the chief, he was (so the venerable and possibly credible legend goes) saved from execution through the intervention of the chief's 13-year-old daughter Pocahontas

(a nickname meaning "frisky"; her real name was Matowaka). She later facilitated Smith's initiation into the tribe, a favored position used by the captain to obtain corn from the Indians.

Despite this contribution to the colony's survival, the colonists and the Indians did not form a close bond. They traded with one another, but always in an atmosphere of mutual distrust. On one occasion, for example, Smith was bartering for corn with the half-brother of Powhatan, Opechancanough, when he discovered that his small party was surrounded by a large group of Indians. Without missing a beat, Smith seized Opechancanough by his scalp lock, put his pistol to his ribs, and declared:

Here I stand, shoot he that dare. You promised to freight my ship ere I departed, and so you shall; or I mean to load her with dead carcasses. Yet if as friends you will come and trade, I once more promise not to trouble you, except you give me the first occasion. And your King shall be free and be my friend, for I am not come to hurt him or any of you.

Within a few years, when colonial tobacco cultivation created a need for more and more land, the English commandeered Indian fields, which had already been cleared, finding that easier than doing the work themselves. With this, the relationship between the two groups began to deteriorate. The Virginia Company, at one point, suggested taking Powhatan prisoner in order to bring his people under control. That was never carried out, but Sir Thomas Gates, who became the colony's governor in 1611, actually murdered some Indian priests, luring them out by having his soldiers beat a drum and dance. When the Indians showed themselves, they were killed. In 1613, Samuel Argall, mariner and colonist, kidnapped Pocahontas, whom Governor Dale then held hostage.

<hr>

## ROANOKE'S LOST COLONY

After the death of Sir Humphrey Gilbert, who twice attempted to colonize America before he was lost at sea in a storm off Newfoundland in 1583, Queen Elizabeth conferred what had been Gilbert's patent on her favorite, Sir Walter Raleigh. The 31-year-old courtier named the land he intended to colonize "Virginia" after his "virgin" queen. In 1585 he began colonization efforts, and a small group of explorers in Raleigh's employ landed on Roanoke Island in present-day North Carolina's Outer Banks. One year later, Sir Francis Drake called on them; starving, they were eager to return to England. In 1587, Raleigh tried again, sending 107 men, women, and children on a poorly planned expedition to the same swampy, inhospitable island, which was surrounded by hostile Croatan Indians. Back in England, Raleigh stocked additional ships with supplies for the fledgling colony, but the Spanish Armada's attack on England delayed their departure. It was 1590 before a shipload of additional settlers, with the supplies, arrived at Roanoke Island only to find that the village and its inhabitants had vanished. Some rusted debris and the word "CROATOAN" carved into a tree trunk was all that was left of the settlement.

What had happened? Perhaps the colonists had starved; more likely, in view of the carved message, they had fallen prey to the Croatans. The utter completeness with which Raleigh's colonists disappeared underscored the danger of colonization. Those settlers who survived in later colonies were not necessarily more determined but were lucky enough to experience in the first crucial years of settlement the relative goodwill of the Native Americans.

Perhaps it was her subsequent marriage to colonist John Rolfe that averted war over this and the earlier outrages; perhaps it was just that Powhatan wished to continue trading with the English. In any event, the chief preserved peace until his death in 1618. Opechancanough, who succeeded his half-brother, likewise pledged friendship with the colonists. Opechancanough, however, was not as committed to peace as was Powhatan, so it was not destined to last long.

Early in the spring of 1622, a planter named Morgan ventured inland to trade with the Indians and was never heard from again. In March, Morgan's servants determined—albeit hastily and on the flimsiest of evidence—that an Indian named Nemattanow (or Nematanou), prominent among the Powhatans, had ordered the death of their master. They summarily dispatched Nemattanow, for which Opechancanough vowed revenge. In response to the chief's threats, the colonists made bellicose noises, whereupon Opechancanough renewed his pledge of eternal friendship with the English. As if in proof of his pledge, on March 20, 1622, the chief served as a cordial guide to a group of planters traveling through the woods. Two days later, on Good Friday, in English settlements all along the James River, the Indians

as at other times . . . came unarmed into our houses with Deere, Turkies, Fish, Fruits, and other provisions to sell us, yea in some places sat downe at breakfast with our people, whom immediately with their owne tooles slew most barbarously, not sparing either age or sex, man woman or childe, so sudden in their execution, that few or none discerned the weapon or blow that brought them to destruction.

Opechancanough had coordinated these attacks carefully and deliberately. By the end of the day, 347 settlers had been killed—about one-third of the colony. Jamestown was saved by an Indian boy called Chanco, the Christianized servant of a colonist named Mr. Pace. The boy's brother had ordered him to murder Pace; instead, Chanco told his master of the plot. Pace alerted Governor Francis Wyatt, who proclaimed the English colony's new policy: "It is infinitely better to have no heathen among us, who were but as thornes in our sides, than to be at peace and league with them." As a result of these attacks, colonial patrols deliberately sought out and attacked Indians:

With our small and sicklie forces [for disease, far more than Indian violence, was the leading cause of death among the colonists] we have discomforted the Indians round about us, burnt their houses, gathered their corn and slain not a few; though they are as swift as Roebucks, like the violent lightening they are gone as soon as perceived, and not to be destroyed but by surprise or famine.

Violence persisted for 14 years, during which the colonists used various schemes to kill Indians. On one occasion, Governor Wyatt invited Opechancanough to a "peace conference" and served the chief and his men poisoned food. Two hundred Indians fell ill, and many, helpless, were slaughtered—though Opechancanough escaped. When the London-based administrators of the Virginia Company protested that the colonists had gone too

## POWHATAN AND HIS CONFEDERACY

According to Captain John Smith, the venerable (he was about 60 when the English first encountered him) Indian chief known as Powhatan was more properly called Wahunsonacock. *Powhatan*, which means "falls in a running stream," was originally the name of one small tribe, presumably led by Wahunsonacock, but was eventually applied to a large confederacy of eastern Virginia Algonquian tribes and to Wahunsonacock himself, the founder of the confederacy.

Native American history presents a handful of examples of Indian attempts to confederate for political, trading, or military reasons. Some time between 1400 and 1600 (probably circa 1560–70), the Huron mystic Deganawida and his Mohawk disciple Hiawatha (no relation to the Longfellow character) founded the most enduring of all intertribal confederacies, the Iroquois Confederation.

Toward the end of the seventeenth century, Popé successfully united many of the pueblos of the Southwest against the Spanish. Later Indian leaders, including most prominently Pontiac, Tecumseh, Black Hawk, and Osceola, would attempt to forge pan-tribal alliances. Generally, however, tribes rarely joined in politically effective unions, so Powhatan's confederacy is extraordinary. By 1607, after conducting a campaign of conquest, Powhatan controlled his own tribe plus 32 others, consisting of more than 200 villages.

Described as tall, well-proportioned, sour of expression, with a thin beard and graying head, Powhatan at first remained aloof from the English. As the first colonists languished in disease—of the 900 who arrived from 1607 to 1610, only 150 were alive in 1610—Powhatan could have destroyed the colony had he chosen to do so. Indeed, Spain sent official embassies to the chief, urging him to attack and destroy the English. While there were quarrels and skirmishes—including, most seriously, a 1610 massacre in Jamestown that has been attributed to Spanish scheming—peaceful relations prevailed between the English colonists and the confederacy during the reign of Powhatan, a situation strengthened by the marriage of colonist John Rolfe and Powhatan's celebrated daughter Pocahontas.

The historical significance of the Powhatan Confederacy is profound. Through Powhatan's influence, the tribes of New England allowed the struggling English colonists to survive. When the anti-English Opechancanough assumed leadership of the confederacy in 1618 on the death of his half-brother Powhatan, Indian-white violence increased dramatically. By this time, however, the colonies were firmly established, and the opportunity to destroy the English had passed.

---

far with such tactics, the Virginia Council of State replied:

Wee hold nothing inuiste [unjust] . . . that may tend to theire ruine. . . . Stratagems were ever allowed against all enemies, but with these neither fayre Warr nor good quarter is ever to be held, nor is there other hope of their subversione, who ever may inform you to the Contrarie.

A grudging truce, the product of mutual exhaustion, was finally declared in 1632. It lasted for 12 years, until April 18, 1644, when the aged Opechancanough again launched a coordinated assault along the James. It was devastating—400 to 500 colonists perished—but it was quickly over. The Indians attacked once and then withdrew. Perhaps they suddenly comprehended the futility of their action. For, although the attack was costly, the population of the Virginia colony now topped 8,000. The

Powhatans could well have wiped out the Virginia colony in 1622—or earlier—but not in 1644.

Virginia's Governor William Berkeley retaliated by declaring "perpetuall warre with the Indians" and issued orders to burn their crops and destroy their villages. The governor journeyed to England to obtain arms and ammunition, but with the country in the midst of civil war, his mission had little success, and a discouraged Berkeley returned in June 1645 to a colony still embattled. In March 1646, the Virginia assembly at last decided that further struggle was fruitless and dispatched Captain Henry Fleet, the colony's interpreter, to find Opechancanough and negotiate a peace. The governor, however, did not share the assembly's pacific sentiments and led a detachment of soldiers on a preemptive raid of the old chief's headquarters. Opechancanough, 100 years old and nearly blind, was taken captive and transported to Jamestown, where a crowd of gawkers offended him. He protested to Berkeley that, were the governor *his* prisoner, he would not expose him as a show before the people. Berkeley, abashed, ordered the chief to be treated with courtesy. The governor was hardly obeyed—one of the men guarding Opechancanough shot him in the back and killed him.

In October 1646, the assembly, this time with Berkeley's blessing, finally concluded a peace with Opechancanough's successor, Necotowance. The chief acknowledged his people's dependence on the king of England and agreed that future chiefs would be appointed, or at least confirmed, by the governor. Boundaries were formally set, and neither side was permitted to enter the other's land without permission from the governor. In token of their subjection, the Indians agreed to present the colony with an annual tribute of 20 beaver skins.

The peace was an uneasy one. As would be the case well into the early nineteenth century, frontier settlers obstinately refused to recognize any limit to settlement. The government could not regulate westward expansion, though Berkeley and Parliament tried. A fleet was sent out from England in January 1652 to compel obedience to Oliver Cromwell's government, including its desire to contain settlement. Not only did it fail, but Berkeley was forced out of office as the colony declared itself loyal to King Charles. With Berkeley out of the picture, a series

of interim governors refused to enforce the treaty with Necotowance, thereby spawning numberless skirmishes between colonists and Indians.

At last, in March 1656, the Virginia assembly dispatched Colonel Edward Hill with 100 militiamen to remove so-called foreign Indians—members of tribes not subject to English authority—from the vicinity of the Falls of the James. Chief Tottopottomoi of the Pamunkeys, a Powhatan tribe, allied himself with Hill, contributing 100 warriors to the expedition. The assembly explicitly ordered restraint in the removal. This notwithstanding, Hill executed five Indian chiefs who came out to parley with him. In the fight that followed, Tottopottomoi was killed. Later, the assembly censured Hill for his "crimes and weaknesses" and suspended him from office.

At about this time, the Virginia lawmakers made a further gesture in recognition of Indian rights by repealing an act that had authorized the killing of any Indian found trespassing. However, by the time Berkeley returned to Virginia and was restored to office in 1671, disease and warfare had decimated the Tidewater's Indian population. At the time of Jamestown's founding 60 years earlier, Powhatan led about 10,000 people. Now only 3,000 to 4,000 Indians remained, out of which a mere 750 might be classed as warriors.

# CHAPTER 3

## TROUBLE IN NEW CANAAN
### The Pequot War (1634–1638)

Farther north, by the 1630s increased migration of Dutch and English settlers into the Connecticut Valley was encroaching upon the territory of the Pequots, an Algonquian tribe related to the Mohegans and, like them, originally settled along the Hudson River. The Pequots first lashed out at Dutch traders who had established a post, called the House of Hope, on the Connecticut River. In an effort to oust the Dutch, Pequots killed some Indians—probably Narragansetts or members of a tribe subject to them—who were engaged in trade at the House of Hope. In retaliation, the Dutch killed the venerable Pequot sachem Tatobam, and the Narragansetts prepared for war against the Dutch.

As yet, the English were largely uninvolved in Pequot affairs. Then, in 1634, Captain John Stone entered the scene. He was a thoroughly disreputable trader—*pirate* is a more accurate word for him. He had tried unsuccessfully to hijack a vessel in New Amsterdam, had threatened the governor of Plymouth Colony with a knife, and had been hauled into a Massachusetts Bay Colony court on charges that included drunkenness and adultery. Banished from the colony on pain of death, he headed for Virginia. While his ship rode at anchor in the mouth of the Connecticut River, he fell victim to an Indian raid.

The only thing certain about the incident is that the raiders were not Pequots, but western Niantics, a tribe dominated by the Pequots. In other details, versions of the event, colored by special interest and prejudice, differ sharply. One Pequot version claimed that Stone had kidnapped a group of Indians, whom he took aboard his ship for the purpose of compelling them to show him the way up the Connecticut River (presumably, he would also later demand ransom for their release). Nine other Indians, who had witnessed the abduction, waited until Stone came ashore, pitched camp, and fell asleep. They

then killed Stone and two of his crew in order to free the captives. Another Pequot variant held that the raid had been a case of mistaken identity. The killers, commissioned by the Pequots, thought that they were attacking the Dutch traders who had killed Tatobam—they claimed they could not tell an Englishman from a Dutchman.

The version narrated by John Mason, English hero of the Pequot War, sidesteps the kidnapping issue, saying simply that Stone was trading with the Dutch and "procured" some Indians to guide two of his men, in a skiff, "*near twenty Leagues* up the River" to the Dutch trading house:

But being benighted before they could come to their desired Port, put the *Skiff* in which they went, ashore, where the *two Englishmen* falling asleep, were both Murdered by their *Indian* Guides: There remaining with the *Bark* about *twelve* of the aforesaid *Indians*; who had in all probability formerly plotted their bloody Design; and waiting an opportunity when some of the *English* were on Shoar and Capt. *Stone* asleep in his Cabin, set upon them and cruelly Murdered every one of them, plundered what they pleased and sunk the Bark.

The version related by Governor John Winthrop of the Massachusetts Bay Colony and retold by colonial historian William Hubbard was probably derived from the Narragansetts (traditional enemies of the Pequots) and handily glosses over the corrupt character of Captain Stone as it lingers on the Indians' barbarity:

The said Capt. *Stone* formerly belonging to *Christophers* in the *West Indies*, occasionally coming to these Parts, as he passed between this Place and *Virginia*, put in at that River [the Connecticut], where the *Indians* after they had been often on board

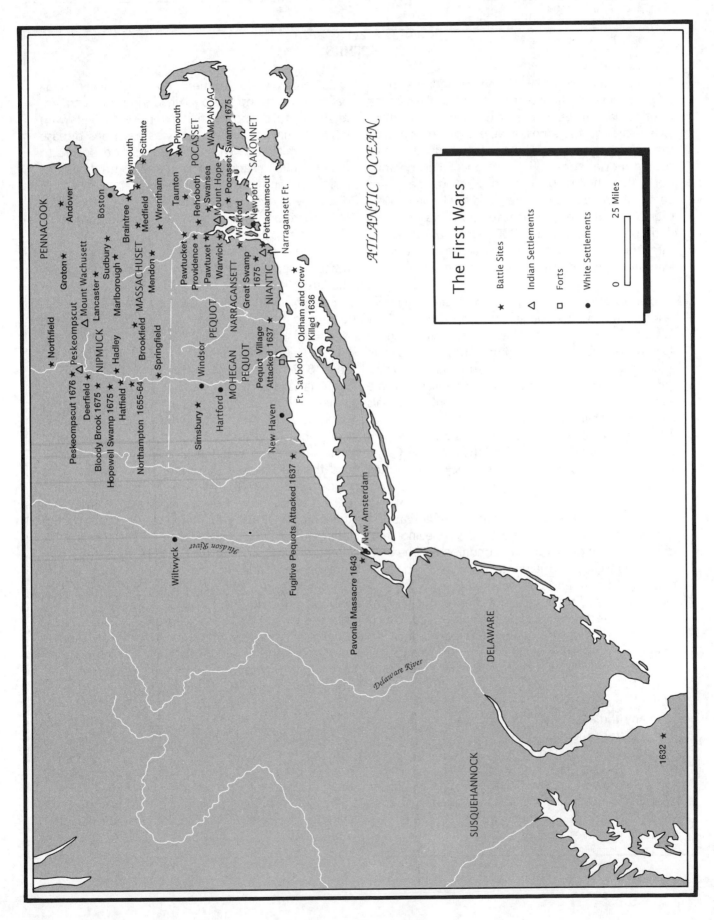

## The First Wars

| | |
|---|---|
| ★ | Battle Sites |
| △ | Indian Settlements |
| □ | Forts |
| ● | White Settlements |

0    25 Miles

ATLANTIC OCEAN

PENNACOOK

Plymouth

WAMPANOAG

POCASSET

SAKONNET

Scituate

Weymouth

Andover

Boston

Braintree

Medfield

Wrentham

Taunton

Rehoboth

Swansea

Mount Hope

Pocasset Swamp 1675

Wickford

Newport

Pettaquamscut

Narragansett Ft.

Groton

Mount Wachusett

Lancaster

Sudbury

Marlborough

MASSACHUSET

Mendon

Pawtucket

Providence

Pawtuxet

Warwick

NARRAGANSETT

Great Swamp 1675

NIANTIC

Northfield

Peskeompscut

NIPMUCK

Hadley

Brookfield

Springfield

PEQUOT

Peskeompscut 1676

Deerfield

Bloody Brook 1675

Hopewell Swamp 1675

Hatfield

Northampton 1655-64

Windsor

MOHEGAN

PEQUOT

Pequot Village
Attacked 1637

Ft. Saybook

Oldham and Crew
Killed 1636

Simsbury

Hartford

New Haven

Fugitive Pequots Attacked 1637

New Amsterdam

Wiltwyck

Hudson River

Pavonia Massacre 1643

Delaware River

DELAWARE

SUSQUEHANNOCK

1632

# EPIDEMICS

The most terrifying ally of the white man in his long war against the Indian in America was disease, chiefly smallpox. Between 1616 and 1619, smallpox swept through the tribes of New England, especially the Wampanoags and the Massachusets, "with such a mortal stroake," wrote one English chronicler, "that they died on heapes." A gauge of the destructiveness of the epidemic is a reliable modern estimate that the Massachuset tribe was reduced during these years from 10,000 souls to 1,000. William Bradford, governor and historian of Plymouth Plantation, recorded the horror of the disease:

A sorer disease [than smallpox] cannot befall them, they fear it more than the plague. For usually they that have this disease have them [pustules] in abundance, and for want of bedding and linen and other helps they fall into a lamentable condition as they lie on their hard mats, the pox breaking and mattering and running out into another, their skin cleaving by reason thereof to the mats they lie on. When they turn them, a whole side will flay off at once as it were, and they will be all of a gore blood, most fearful to behold. And then being very sore, what with cold and other distempers, they die like rotten sheep.

Bradford reported that the English, "though at first they were afraid of the infection, yet seeing their [the Indians'] woeful and sad condition and hearing their pitiful cries and lamentations, they had compassion of them, and daily fetched them wood and water and made them fires, got them victuals whilst they lived; and buried them when they died." Such compassion, however, was extraordinary. Other Puritan chroniclers fairly gloated over "The Wonderful Preparation the Lord Christ by His Providence Wrought for His People's Abode in this Western World," meaning by "preparation" the deaths of so many Indians, which providentially cleared the heathen from the path of the Chosen People. "The wondrous wisdom and love of God, is shewne, by sending to the place his Minister [i.e., smallpox], to sweepe away . . . the Salvages." One chronicler observed in particular that the smallpox had consumed "chiefly young men and children, the very seeds of increase."

Epidemics were frequent among Indians in all parts of the country, especially during the years immediately following the first extensive contacts with whites. Smallpox, of course, was a serious disease among whites as well, but centuries of exposure to the endemic malady had conferred some degree of resistance, and most whites survived the illness. The disease was unknown among Indians before contact; therefore, they were wholly unresistant to it. This was also the case with such "minor" ailments as measles, which proved deadly among some tribes, especially those in the Pacific Northwest in the late 1840s.

Epidemics of smallpox, measles, cholera, tuberculosis, and other maladies wreaked havoc on the New England tribes during 1616–19; on the Timucua of Georgia and Florida in 1613–17, 1649–50, and 1672; among the Pohoy of Florida in 1728; the Catawba of South Carolina in 1738 and 1759 (when half their number perished); the Bidai of Texas in 1776–77 (half of whom died); the Tonkawan tribes of Texas in 1779 (half died); the Pecos near Santa Fe during the late eighteenth century; and the Blackfeet of the upper Missouri during an epidemic in 1780–81. As the settlers advanced, epidemics plagued the Crees, Chipewayans, and other tribes of the Hudson Bay and westward during the late eighteenth century and in 1863; the Hidatsa along the Missouri River in 1837 (reduced from three major villages to one) and the Mandan in the same area and at the same time (of 1,600 villages only 31 survived the smallpox epidemic); various tribes of the Pacific Northwest, especially in the Columbia River Valley, who were ravaged by disease throughout the first half of the nineteenth century, culminating in a measles epidemic during the late 1840s and early 1850s; and the Cheyenne, who suffered cholera epidemics in 1849, 1860, and 1878. The tribes of the Kadohadacho Confederacy of northeastern Texas and southwestern Arkansas suffered from epidemics after the Civil War, and the Nez Percé were decimated by disease sweeping their Indian Territory reservation in 1885.

This list is hardly complete and does not touch on chronic, endemic diseases or on malnutrition and alcoholism.

his Vessel to trade with him, at the last came friendly on Board as they used to do, but finding the Captain asleep in his Cabin, took the Opportunity to Murther him as he lay, casting a Covering over him that he might not be discerned by the Rest, whom they presently after dispatched one after another, all but Capt. *Norton*, who made stout Resistance, for a long Time defending himself in the Cook-room of the Bark, till the Gunpowder which he had set in an open Vessel, to be more ready for his Use, accidentally took Fire, by which fatal Accident he was so burned, and his Eyes so blinded, that he could not make any longer Resistance, but forthwith fell into the Hands of these cruel and blood-thirsty Wretches, who after they had taken away his Life, made a Prey of all that was in the Vessel.

While the Pequots had not killed Stone, their tributary tribe had, and the Pequots were eager to placate colonial authorities. On October 23, they sent a messenger bearing gifts and the promise of tribute to Roger Ludlow, deputy governor of the Massachusetts Bay Colony. A second Pequot embassy, received on November 7, resulted in the Massachusetts Bay-Pequot treaty whereby the Pequots agreed to hand over those guilty of Captain Stone's murder, to pay an exorbitant indemnity, to relinquish rights to Connecticut land that the English might wish to settle, and to trade with the English "as Friends, which was a chief Thing aimed at, the said *Pequods* being at that Time in War with the Dutch, and the Rest of their Neighbours." The Pequots even asked the English to mediate their disputes with the Narragansetts.

Although a portion of the promised indemnity was paid, the amount demanded—£250 sterling in wampum, a lordly sum—remained a sticking point, and the Pequot council failed to ratify what the tribe's ambassadors had agreed to. In addition, the Pequots claimed that those of Stone's assailants who were still alive reported that all the guilty parties had died—one a victim of the Dutch, the rest of smallpox—except two, who had escaped beyond reach.

For two years, the English did not act upon what they later claimed was a breach of the treaty. Then, on June 16, 1636, a Plymouth trader named Jonathan Brewster conveyed a message that he had received from Uncas, chief of the Mohegans, a tribe friendly to the English. Uncas warned that the Pequots, fearful that the colonists were about to move against them, intended to strike first. A conference among Connecticut and Massachusetts Bay officials and representatives of the Western Niantics and Pequots was held in July at Fort Saybrook, an English fort on the Connecticut River. The colonists reasserted the demands of the 1634 treaty, again calling for the killers of Captain Stone and full payment of the wampum tribute. It is not clear what the Pequot response was to these demands. Sassious, sachem of the Western Nian-

## WAMPUM

Indian languages have contributed hundreds of words to the vocabulary of American English, including *tobacco, hominy, succotash, toboggan, moccasin, wigwam, tepee, squaw, papoose.* Another word is *wampum*, which has become a jocular and general synonym for money. To the various Indian tribes of the East Coast, *wampum*, an Anglicized version of the Algonquian word *wampompeag*, had a more precise meaning. It described cylindrical seashells strung on strings or beaded into belts, which were used in trade like money, but also served a more important diplomatic purpose as tokens of good faith. Wampum strings or belts were exchanged by tribes, by bands within tribes, or by Indians and whites to seal a variety of bargains and alliances. Especially elaborate belts of wampum served as "war belts," which were passed from tribe to tribe or band to band in preparation for large-scale warfare.

tics, however, left the conference with a pledge of loyalty and submission to the English (a pledge he would not keep during the ensuing war).

The agreements reached at the Saybrook conference were soon ignored. A few days following the meeting, word reached colonial authorities that another trading captain, John Oldham, and his crew had been killed by Indians off Block Island. This time, the perpetrators were Narragansetts or members of a tribe subject to them. The Narragansett sachems (or "chiefs") Canonchet (whom the English called Canonicus) and Miantonomo not only condemned the murder, they offered reparations (Miantonomo personally led 200 warriors to Block Island to mete out vengeance on behalf of the Massachusetts Bay Colony) and pledged not to ally themselves with the Pequots in any dispute the English had with that tribe.

In spite of the help offered by the Narragansetts, the colonists decided it was time to act and, on August 25, dispatched Captain John Endecott, with Captains John Underhill and William Turner and a force of 90 men (John Mason reports 120), to Block Island. Charged with apprehending the killers of Stone and Oldham, and with securing a "thousand fathoms" of wampum as reparation, Endecott was intent on slaughtering all the men he could find and capturing the women and children, who would be consigned to the West Indian slave trade at substantial profit.

Landing on the island, the well-armed colonists brushed aside the light resistance that met them. But most of the populace had withdrawn to the forest, thereby escaping death or capture, and in the deserted villages, the English found very little to plunder. The wampum had been well hidden.

Following this fiasco, Endecott and his troops sailed to Fort Saybrook, with the object of punishing the Pequots—despite their having had nothing to do with the death of John Oldham. The fort commander, Lieutenant Lion Gardiner, protested Endecott's mission: "You come hither to raise these wasps about my ears, and then you will take wing and flee away." Despite warnings and protests, Endecott proceeded to Pequot Harbor at the mouth of the Pequot (later called the Thames) River. The Pequots there greeted him and his men with blithe innocence: "What cheer, Englishmen, what cheer, what do you come for?" In answer, Endecott proclaimed his mission of retribution. The Pequots, in turn, responded with a request for a parley. Endecott refused and demanded that the Indians come out and fight like men— *English* men, that is, out in the open, in a formal, European-style battle. When the Pequots refused, the frustrated English troops turned to burning and despoiling the country. While this destruction hurt the Indians, it was hardly the massive punitive blow Endecott had been commissioned to deliver and, as Lion Gardiner had predicted, succeeded chiefly in provoking the Pequots to bloody war.

What was it that drove Endecott to such single-minded destruction? Clearly, the death of Stone, for all practical purposes an outlaw, had been an excuse to force the Pequots into a demonstration of subjugation. It is possible that the Massachusetts Bay Colony rejected the Indians' excuse for not finding and relinquishing Stone's killers and decided to include the Pequots in their plans for a punitive expedition that began with the bloody sweep through Block Island and Saybrook. But that does not explain the two-year delay between the putative breach of the Massachusetts Bay-Pequot treaty and the commencement of hostilities, a period during which the colonists and the Indians engaged in reasonably cordial trade.

Beyond motives of mindless hatred and racism, a more plausible explanation for the war provoked by Endecott is found in a contest for sovereignty between the Massachusetts Bay Colony and a group of Connecticut settlers. At stake was a large part of the Connecticut Valley. Whoever asserted dominance over the Pequots, whose country lay on either side of the Pequot River, squarely in the disputed territory, would have a strong legal claim

to the region. Moreover, a victory over the Pequots would render the other tribes in the region more pliable: the Western Niantics, who lived near the mouth of the Connecticut River and were subject to the Pequots; the Eastern Niantics, whose territory lay east of the Pequots, near the Pawcatuck River, and who were allied with the Narragansetts; and the Narragansetts, a large tribe on the bay named after them. Traditional rivals of the Pequots, they would be uneasily wooed to the English cause. A more solid and cordial English-Indian alliance was quickly forged with the Mohegans, really a Pequot splinter group whose leader, Uncas, desired to unseat Sassacus, the feared and mighty sachem of the Pequots proper. Indeed, it is entirely possible that Uncas's warning to the colonists, apprising them of Pequot war intentions, was a fabrication meant to provoke combat.

Sorely provoked, the Pequots soon laid siege against the Saybrook fort. The lieutenant ventured out with 10 or 12 soldiers, was surrounded, and barely made it back to the safety of the fort with the loss of two or three men. Another group of settlers was attacked next: Three were killed outright, one was captured and roasted to death, and the body of another was seen floating down the river, an arrow lodged in his eye. For his part, during a parley that punctuated the siege, Gardiner hinted at the English capacity for terrorist tactics as well. "They asked if we did use to kill women and children? We said they should see that hereafter."

The Fort Saybrook siege continued intermittently for month after miserable month. Some time in late winter or early spring, Captain John Mason briefly visited the fort, but his small contingent of seven men did not provide much relief. In April 1637, Captain Underhill was sent back to Saybrook with 20 men at the behest of the Saybrook Company, which held the charter for the Saybrook settlement, and Mason also reinforced the outpost briefly during April. There is evidence that the various commanders—Gardiner, Underhill, and Mason— quarreled among themselves more effectively than they repelled Indian harassment.

In the meantime, the Pequots were attempting to persuade the Narragansetts to break their promise of neutrality and join them as allies against the English. Fearing the sting of the wasps they had indeed raised, Massachusetts Bay officials sought aid from the Englishman recognized as most expert in negotiating with Indians, Roger Williams—whom the Bay colony had expelled to Rhode Island years earlier because of his heretical religious beliefs. He was now asked, at great personal risk, to persuade the Narragansetts to honor their neutrality pledge. Williams journeyed to the Narragansetts' headquarters, where they were then in counsel with the Pequot ambassadors. "Three days and nights my business forced me to lodge and mix with the bloody Pequot ambassadors, whose hands and arms, methought, wreaked with the blood of my country-men . . . and from whom I could not but nightly look for their bloody knives at my own throat also.'' In March, largely due to Williams's embassy, Miantonomo pledged the Narragansetts to an alliance with the English, solemnizing the treaty with a gift of wampum and the severed hand of a Pequot brave.

This alliance notwithstanding, the spring of 1637 was a bloody one. The settlers at Wethersfield, Connecticut, had ousted a sachem named Sowheag (or Sequin) from the land they had taken. He sought retribution from the Pequots, and on April 23, 1637, 200 warriors (Mason says 100) attacked settlers working a field near Wethersfield, killing seven to nine of them, including a woman and perhaps a child, and taking two girls captive. The raiders paddled past the fort at Saybrook, bearing the clothing of the dead on poles, as if in mocking imitation of English sailing vessels. The garrison men shot at the Indians ''with a Piece of Ordnance, which beat off the Beak Head of one of their *Canoes*, wherein our *two Captives* were,'' but they escaped, and the captives—no thanks to the garrison's precipitate action—were unhurt.

By this time, about 30 English colonists had fallen victim to the Pequots, and word was spreading throughout the increasingly alarmed and outraged colonies of acts of torture. The Plymouth, Massachusetts, and Connecticut colonies determined to unite in fighting the Pequots. This, however, was easier said than done, partly because of jockeying among the colonies for power and territory and partly because of more arcane issues. Massachusetts, for example, mustered a substantial force of 160. While 40 of that number were immediately dispatched under the command of Captain Daniel Patrick, the embarkation of the others was ''retarded by the most singular Cause that ever influenced the Operations of a military Force.'' It was discovered that some officers and private soldiers were not strictly orthodox in their religious convictions, ''and that the Blessing of God could not be implored or expected to crown the Arms of such unhallowed Men with Success. The Alarm was general, and many Arrangements necessary in order to cast out the Unclean. . . .''

While Massachusetts and Plymouth struggled to get under way, Captain Mason set out from Hartford, Connecticut, on May 10 with 90 colonists and 60 Mohegans under Uncas to attack the principal Pequot stronghold, the fort of Sassacus, on Pequot Harbor. The band reached Saybrook on the fifteenth, whereupon the impatient Mohegan chief led 40 warriors in a sortie against an equal number of Pequots and Niantics, killing four to seven and taking one prisoner. (One Mohegan was wounded.) They returned to Fort Saybrook with the cap-

tive, who answered English interrogation with mockery. Provoked at this, Mason's men tied one of the prisoner's legs to a post and pulled on a rope tied to his other leg, tearing him to pieces. Captain Underhill, who had been supplementing the Saybrook garrison since winter, appeared on the scene and, with a pistol shot, put the Indian out of his misery.

A day after this incident, Underhill placed his 19 men under Mason's command, freeing 20 of Mason's Connecticut troops to strengthen that colony's other embattled settlements. During the next two days, Mason contemplated his marching orders, which called for an immediate amphibious assault against Sassacus's fort in Pequot Harbor. He determined instead to sail past that stronghold, enter Narragansett territory, and recruit Indian allies before attacking. The combined forces of Mason and Underhill embarked on the eighteenth. Arriving in Narragansett territory on the twentieth, the two captains, together with Lieutenant Robert Siely, marched with their ''guard'' to a parley and during May 22–24, met with about 200 Narragansetts, who agreed to join forces against the Pequots. The English took on as allies a total of 500 Narragansetts (under Miantonomo) and Eastern Niantics (under Ninigret). These were added to the force of 60 Mohegans already marching with the colonial troops.

Accounts vary as to what occurred when the Englishmen and their Indian allies, on May 25, drew near to Sassacus's Pequot Harbor fort. Either at this time or earlier, a renegade Pequot named Wequash revealed the existence of another Pequot stronghold on the Mystic River. It was closer than the Pequot Harbor fort, and Mason (according to his own account), aware that his men were ''exceedingly spent in our March with extream Heat and want of Necessaries,'' determined once again to go against his orders and attack at Mystic—though ''the greatest and bloodiest *Sachem* [Sassacus] resided'' at the other stronghold. William Hubbard's 1677 account of the action ascribes the decision more to the cowardice of the Indian allies: ''We told them that we resolved to Assault *Sassacous* his Fort, at which they were all stricken, and as it were amazed with Fear.'' About 100 of the Indians deserted the company in dread of Sassacus, Hubbard reports, and when Mason announced the decision to attack the Mystic fort instead, his remaining allies ''very much rejoyced; for it was dreadful to them to hear the Name of *Sassacous*.''

At least one modern historian, Francis Jennings, offers a darker interpretation of Mason's strategy, suggesting that the decision to bypass Sassacus's fort and attack the Mystic stronghold instead was a deliberate choice to avoid a battle in favor of conducting a massacre. Jennings argues that Mason knew that the Mystic fort harbored women, children, and old men and was defended by few warriors, most of whom were with Sassacus. Whether the result of deliberate calculation or expediency of the moment, the assault on the fort at Mystic was indeed a massacre.

The approach to the stronghold was made at night. Apparently aware that the Narragansetts were still intimidated by the Pequots even in the absence of Sassacus, Mason deployed them in an outer circle around the fort while he brought his Englishmen up close. (Jennings ar-

gues that Mason kept the Narragansetts at this distance because he doubted they had the stomach for a massacre.) According to Mason's account, he and his men bedded down for the night within earshot of the Pequots' singing in celebration of the arrival of 150 reinforcements. (Jennings argues that Mason's report of Pequot reinforcements was a fabrication; there were none.)

At dawn on May 26, after firing a volley, the Englishmen stormed the fort through entrances at opposite ends: Mason on the northeast, Underhill on the south-

*This highly stylized woodcut depicts the assault on a Pequot "fort or Palizado" at Mystic, Connecticut, on May 26, 1637, by troops under Captains John Mason and John Underhill. The "fort" was really an Indian village, and the "battle" was really a massacre of women, children, and old men. (Library of Congress.)*

west. Surprised by the attack, the Pequot warriors nevertheless fought with such fury that Mason quickly abandoned his plan to seize booty and, instead, put the Indian camp to the torch, setting a fire so fierce that Underhill's men were forced to exit the fort as quickly as they had entered it. Eighty huts—housing some 800 men, women, and children—were set ablaze.

Within an hour, 600 to 700 Pequots died, while English losses amounted to two dead and 20 to 40 wounded. Mason records that only seven Pequots were taken captive, and another seven escaped.

The slaughter appalled even the colonists' Narragansett allies, who entreated: "*Mach it mach it*. It is naught [i.e., "wicked"], it is naught, because it is too furious, and slaies too many men."

Despite the magnitude of the victory, Mason was aware that he and his men were in hostile territory, exhausted by battle, lacking in provisions, and uncertain as to when their pinnaces would arrive to pick them up. As the commanders consulted over what course of action to take, the vessels, which carried Captain Daniel Patrick and his 40 men as well as fresh ammunition, were sighted. But so were 300 or more Pequots, arriving from Sassacus's harbor stronghold. Captain Underhill, with a detachment of Narragansetts and English troops, skirmished with them, but the Pequots failed to attack in force, and the English were able to begin their march toward the harbor and their vessels, burning wigwams along the way and exchanging sporadic gunfire with Indian snipers.

And as we came to any Swamp or Thicket, we made some Shot to clear the Passage. Some of them fell with our Shot; and probably more might, but for want of Munition: But when any of them fell, our *Indians* would give a great Shout, and then they take so much Courage as to fetch their Heads.

In late May or early June, Mason and Underhill's forces united with the Massachusetts troops under Captain Patrick and then with a larger body of Massachusetts soldiers commanded by Israel Stoughton. Shortly thereafter, news reached them that a large number of Pequots had been discovered near the Connecticut River. The English-allied Narragansetts, pretending to offer the Pequots protection, surrounded the warriors, making it easy for the colonial troops to capture

some hundreds of them, who were couped up as in a Pound; not daring to fight, not able to fly away, and so were all taken without any Opposition: The Men among them to the Number of thirty were turned presently into *Charons* Ferryboat, under the Command of Skipper [John] *Gallop*, who dispatched [drowned] them a little without the Harbour. The Females and

Children were disposed of according to the Will of the Conquerors; some being given to the *Narhagansets* and other *Indians* that assisted in the Service.

The rest of the Enemy being first fired out of their strong Hold, were taken and destroyed, a great Number of them being seized in the Places where they intended to have hid themselves, the rest fled out of their own Country over *Connecticut* River, up towards the Dutch Plantation. Our Soldiers being resolved, by Gods Assistance, to make final Destruction of them, were minded to pursue them which way soever they should think to make their Escape

Those Pequots who escaped death scattered, most making their way to Manhattan Island. When one fleeing group encountered three Englishmen in a shallop bound for Saybrook, the Indians killed them.

In July, Stoughton, commanding 120 Massachusetts troops, linked up again with Mason and 40 Connecticut soldiers to pursue the fugitive Pequots. The troops swept through the countryside, meeting "here and there with sundry of them [Pequots], whom they slew or took Prisoners; amongst whom were two Sachims, whom they presently beheaded," sparing the life of a third on condition that he ascertain and report the whereabouts of Sassacus. The Indian embarked on his mission, was discovered by Sassacus as a spy, and hunted down. He narrowly evaded his pursuers and faithfully reported back to the English after eight days. Hubbard's account suggests that by the time news of Sassacus's whereabouts reached the English, the sachem, with 20 or 30 others, had left the main body of survivors of the Mystic massacre and was seeking sanctuary among the Mohawks. Later historians believe that Sassacus was among the 20 Pequots who escaped slaughter during a subsequent pursuit, siege, and massacre.

On July 13, English forces ran the Mystic survivors to ground in a swamp near New Haven and surrounded them. Lieutenant Richard Davenport failed to hear—or heed—the general command to encircle the Indian camp and hold positions. Instead, he charged into the swamp with about a dozen men and, with two others, was wounded. The small force barely managed a retreat.

Despite this fiasco, the English still had the upperhand. Thomas Stanton, a skilled interpreter, volunteered for the hazardous mission of dictating surrender terms to the Indians. The English would allow old men, women, and children safe conduct out of the swamp and would extend the same courtesy to the non-Pequot Indians who regularly lived in the swamp and who were serving as the Pequots' unwilling hosts. "Near *Two Hundred old Men, Women and Children* . . . delivered themselves to the mercy of the *English*," Mason reports.

About 80 Pequot warriors welcomed Stanton's embassy far less cordially:

They were possessed with such a Spirit of Stupidity and Sullenness, that they resolved rather to sell their Lives for what they could get there; and to that End began to let fly their Arrows thick against him [Stanton], as intending to make his Blood some Part of the Price of their own; but through the Goodness of God toward him, his Life was not to be sold on that Account, he being presently fetched off.

The English troops cut through the swamp with their swords, closing in on the holdouts.

Twenty to 30 Indians (Mason says 60 to 70) were able to breach the English siege in the daybreak fog of July 14. Sassacus may have been among these, or he may have escaped earlier.

The Rest were left to the Mercy of the Conquerors, of which many were killed in the Swamp like sullen Dogs, that would rather in their Self-willedness and Madness sit still to be shot through or cut in Pieces, than receive their Lives for the asking at the Hand of those into whose Power they were now fallen. Some that are yet living and worthy of Credit do affirm, that in the Morning entering into the Swamp, they saw several Heaps of them sitting close together, upon whom they discharged their Pieces laden with ten or twelve Pistol-bullets at a Time, putting the Muzles of their Pieces under the Boughs within a few Yards of them; so as besides those that were found Dead (near twenty) it was judged that many more were killed and sunk into the Mire, and never were minded by Friend or Foe.

Sassacus and other Pequot fugitives sought refuge among neighboring tribes, but the terror tactics of the English had so intimidated the Indians of the region— few of whom were on friendly terms with the Pequots to begin with—that no tribe gave Sassacus sanctuary. Indeed, late in the summer, the English began to receive, as tribute from surrounding Indian groups, the severed heads of various Pequots. The Mohawks sent the head of Sassacus. Their motive for the execution is not entirely clear. Evidence suggests that the execution was a "contract killing" commissioned from the Mohawks by the Narragansetts.

The Treaty of Hartford, concluded on September 21, 1638, divided the survivors of the swamp siege as slaves among the Indian allies, with 80 apportioned to Uncas and his Mohegans; another 80 to Miantonomo and his Narragansetts; and 20 to the Niantics led by Ninigret.

The treaty also directed that no Pequot might inhabit his former country and that the very name *Pequot* was to be expunged; those enslaved had to take the name of their "host" tribe. Many who escaped death or enslavement fell prey to surrounding tribes, who had long been terrorized by the Pequots. *"Thus did the* LORD *scatter his Enemies with his strong Arm!"* Mason observes. Some survivors—perhaps as many as 200—voluntarily offered themselves as slaves to the English and other Indians. However, whether they were compelled into slavery or came voluntarily into it, the vanquished Pequots "could not endure that Yoke; few of them continuing any considerable time with their Masters." Perhaps the greatest beneficiary of the massacre was Uncas, whose renegade band of Mohegans, augmented by refugee Pequots, grew from 50 warriors to a few hundred.

Shortly after the treaty was signed, a number of Pequots violated the treaty by settling at Pawcatuck, in former Pequot country. Mason was dispatched with 40 colonials and 120 Mohegans, led by Uncas, to clear them out. As Uncas's men plundered the Pequot wigwams, 60 Narragansetts attacked—though to little effect—and seven of the attackers were captured. About 300 more, however, menaced Mason and his allies, proclaiming their friendship with the Pequots. The English challenged them to a fight, to which the Narragansetts replied:

*That they would not Fight with* ENGLISH MEN, *for they were* SPIRITS, *but would Fight with* ONKOS [Uncas]. *We replyed, That we thought it was too early for them to Fight, but they might take their opportunity; we should be burning* [Pequot] Wigwams, *and carrying Corn aboard all that Day*. And presently beating up our Drum, we Fired the *Wigwams* in their View: And as we Marched, there were *two Indians* standing upon a *Hill* jeering and reviling of us: Mr. *Thomas Stanton* our Interpreter, Marching at Liberty, desired to make a Shot at them; the *Captain* demanding of the *Indians, What they were*? Who said, *They were Murtherers:* Then the said *Stanton* having leave, let fly, Shot one of them through both his Thighs; which was to our Wonderment, it being at such a vast distance.

The English and Mohegans resumed their plunder unmolested, and with this anticlimax, the Pequot War ended. In June 1639, a Dutch traveler named David de Vries encountered an Indian dressed in a remarkable red mantle near the mouth of the Connecticut River. "I inquired how he came by the mantle," de Vries wrote in his *Voyages*. "He had some time ago killed one Captain Stone, with his people, in a bark, from whom he had obtained these clothes."

# CHAPTER 4

# NEW ENGLAND BLEEDS
## King Philip's War (1675–1676)

For more than three decades following the Pequot War, an unsettled peace reigned between the Indians and colonists of New England. The conflicts that occured during this time clearly were instigated by the English and served to heighten tension until war began again, this time with Philip, chief of the Wampanoags.

In 1661, the death of Massasoit, chief of the Wampanoags and longtime friend of the English, started a chain of events that culminated in war in 1675. His son Wamsutta, whom the English called Alexander, succeeded him as the tribe's principal sachem and continued the tradition of friendship with the English. However, under Wamsutta, the Wampanoags divided their loyalty between two English colonies, Rhode Island and Plymouth, which were perpetually engaged in competition for the purchase of Indian lands. In this case, both colonies sought to establish a protectorate over the Wampanoags in order to bolster their tenuous charters. (The Plymouth charter, for all practical purposes, was void because the colony had been founded in error. The settlers were authorized to plant a colony in Virginia but had landed too far up the coast. Rhode Island, a catch-all colony for those whose heterodoxy was unwelcome in Massachusetts and Plymouth, found its charter questioned not only by England's Restoration government, but by the colony of Massachusetts.)

Suspected by Plymouth Colony authorities of plotting war, Alexander was seized at gunpoint by Major Josiah Winslow (later governor of Plymouth). He was taken to Duxbury to answer conspiracy charges and—most important—to demonstrate his loyalty to Plymouth by selling land to that colony rather than to Rhode Island. During his captivity, Alexander contracted a fever. Winslow released him, but he died on his journey back home. Winslow and the Puritans claimed that Wamsutta's illness had

been brought on by a combination of hot weather and hot temper; others pointed out that the sachem had been forced to march too far and too fast and that he had been generally mistreated. His 24-year-old brother, Metacom or Metacomet, whom the English called Philip, succeed Wamsutta as sachem and, like a number of other Wampanoags, suspected that Winslow had not merely brutalized Wamsutta, but had poisoned him.

On August 6, 1664, Philip was summoned to Plymouth Town to answer charges of plotting against the colony. Although he denied the accusations, he agreed to sign a document pledging to seek permission from the colony before concluding any sale or exchange of land, and relations between colonists and Indians remained relatively peaceful until 1665, when a land dispute between Massachusetts and the Narragansetts threatened to erupt into war. A royal commission temporarily succeeded in assuaging hostilities.

Seeing an opportunity for exploiting the breach between the English and the Narragansetts, a rival tribe, Philip warned New York colonial authorities that the Narragansetts were plotting war against them. The Narragansett chief, Ninigret, in turn accused Philip of hostile designs, and the next year, 1667, Philip was summoned to Plymouth to answer these charges. Proud, even haughty, Philip resented this and other calls to bow to colonial authority. Over the succeeding two years, Philip's animosity toward the English was further aggravated by a dispute over land in the area of Wrentham, Massachusetts. And while Ninigret was accused in 1669 of joining with the French to stage a rebellion against the English colonies, this failed to vindicate Philip. On the contrary, the accusation served only to make the colonists generally more wary of Indian ''treachery.'' Early in 1671, Philip, outraged that the new Plymouth settle-

*The cataclysmic King Philip's War (1675–76) was a long time coming, preceded by decades of sporadic warfare following the Pequot War (1636–37). The battle depicted in this 1857 book illustration is a 1645 skirmish at Tiverton, Massachusetts. (Library of Congress.)*

ment of Swansea flagrantly encroached on his land, staged an armed display for the benefit of the town's citizens. On April 10, 1671, he was summoned to Taunton, to sign an agreement acknowledging and apologizing for such "plotting." The document compelled the Wampanoags to surrender their arms:

Whereas my Father, my Brother, and my self, have formally submitted ourselves and our People unto the Kings Majesty of England, and to the Colony of New Plimouth, by solemn Covenant under our Hand; but I having of late through my Indiscretion, and the Naughtiness of my Heart, violated and broken this my Covenant with my Friends, by taking up Arms, with evil intent against them, and that groundlessly; I being now deeply sensible of my Unfaithfulness and Folly, so desire at this Time solemnly to renew my Covenant with my ancient Friends, my Fathers Friends above mentioned, and do desire that this may testifie to the World against me if ever I shall again fail in my Faithfulness towards them (that I have now, and at all Times found so kind to me) or any other of the English Colonies; and as a real Pledge of my true Intentions for the Future to be Faithful and Friendly, I do freely engage to resign up unto the Government of *New Plimouth*, all my English Arms, to be kept by them for their Security, so long

as they shall see Reason. For true Performance of the Premises, I have hereunto set my Hand, together with the Rest of my Council.

| *In Presence of* | The Mark of *P. Philip*. |
|---|---|
| William Davis. | The Mark of *V. Tavoser*. |
| William Hudson. | The Mark of *Capt. Wisposke*. |
| Thomas Brattle. | The Mark of *T. Woonkaponchant*. |
| | The Mark of *Nimrod*. |

After signing the Taunton agreement, Philip cannily attempted to foment dissension between Plymouth and Massachusetts by suggesting that this retroactive pledge of submission to Plymouth posed a threat to the validity of land titles Massachusetts had earlier secured from the Wampanoags. Despite its political sophistication, Philip's strategy backfired, serving only to bring the two colonies closer together. By the end of September, he was haled to Plymouth, where he stood trial for failure to abide by the Taunton agreement. Fined £100, the sachem was further humiliated by a requirement that he henceforth obtain colonial permission in all matters involving the purchase or sale of land; he was also forbid-

*The Wampanoag chief Metacom or Metacomet, whom the English called King Philip, led his tribe and allies, including the powerful Narragansetts, in a war that was ruinous both to the Indians and the colonists of New England. (Library of Congress.)*

den to wage war against other Indians without authority from the colonial government.

For the next three years, Philip stayed in the background, quietly forging anti-English alliances with the Nipmuck Indians and with his tribe's former rivals, the Narragansetts. Then, in January 1675, came another revelation of Wampanoag designs against the English. John Sassamon, a "very cunning and plausible Indian, well skilled in the English Language, and bred up in the Possession of Christian Religion, imployed as a Schoolmaster at Natick [Massachusetts], the *Indian* Town, who upon some Misdemeanour fled from his Place to *Philip*, by whom he was entertained in the Room and Office of Secretary, and his chief Councellor, whom [Philip] trusted with all his Affairs and secret Counsels,'' left Philip and returned to the so-called Praying Indians of Natick, "where he was baptised, manifested publick Repentance . . . and made a serious Profession of Christian Religion.'' Evidence suggests that Sassamon was actively employed by colonial authorities against Philip as a spy. Whether this was true or not, he reported to Governor Josiah Winslow of Plymouth that Philip was plotting war against the English. He also told the governor

that he feared Philip would have him murdered for his revelation.

On January 29, the body of John Sassamon was found on the ice of a frozen pond. At first, the death was ruled an accident, but after some months, the body was exhumed, examined, and the death attributed to foul play. At this time, a Praying Indian—identified as William Nahauton (by Increase Mather) or Patuckson (in other contemporary sources)—told authorities that he saw Tobias (one of Philip's "chief Captains and Counsellors''), his son Wampapaquan, and Mattashunnamo kill Sassamon.

Despite the probably tainted nature of this testimony (Patuckson owed a gambling debt to the men he fingered), the accused murderers were apprehended and brought to trial before a jury of 12 colonists, to which were added four Indians—not as voting members but as consultants and advisors. Found guilty, all three at first protested their innocence, but (according to Increase Mather) Wampapaquan finally confessed that he had watched while his father and the other Indian killed Sassamon. Nevertheless, sentence was pronounced upon the three equally: death by hanging. Other sources record that Wampapaquan's confession was elicited only after the noose around his neck broke, at which time, vainly seeking a reprieve, he also accused Philip himself of complicity in the murder as part of yet another plot against the English.

None of the convicted escaped hanging, but the accusation did not go unheeded. Haled into court yet again, Philip behaved more haughtily than ever, nevertheless winning release for lack of evidence. On June 11, just three days after the executions, word of Wampanoags arming near Swansea and Plymouth Town reached authorities.

At about the same time, the authorities also heard of scattered incidents of cattle killing and house looting in outlying settlements. Already, settlers were beginning to desert some towns: Swansea, adjacent to Wampanoag country, was the first to be partially abandoned, and Indians began appropriating property left behind.

Apprised of the conflict's opening volleys, Benjamin Church, a 35-year-old Rhode Islander destined to emerge as the war's only distinct hero, called on Awashonks, squaw-sachem (female chief) of the Sogkonate Indians, who lived near him. Some historians have suggested a romantic, or at least sexual, attachment between Church and Awashonks. Regardless of the relationship, Church was one of those exceptional frontiersmen who respected the Native Americans among whom he lived, enjoying with Awashonks a friendship and trust rare between Indian and white. The squaw-sachem had been privy to Philip's war plans, which she now revealed to Church, who, in mid-June, reported to Plymouth's Governor Winslow. He, in turn, alerted Governor John Leverett of Massachusetts.

In an uneasy and mistrustful alliance, as the colonies jockeyed for possible territorial gains that might be tied to defeating the Indians, Massachusetts, Plymouth, and Rhode Island joined forces to mobilize an army, which was mustered during June 21–23 at Miles's Garrison, opposite Philip's base of operations at Mount Hope Neck. In the meantime, the Wampanoags raided Swansea, on the Sabbath, attacking townsfolk on their way to church. Seeing this and other Indian attacks as the "dreadful judgment" of God against a generation that had fallen away from the absolute piety of the colony's founders, Plymouth declared a day of "Public Humiliation" on June 24, the first of many fast days that would be proclaimed during the war. It was on this day, however, that Philip once again attacked Swansea—this time in force, and as worshipers *returned* from church. He burned half the town:

At the conclusion of that day of Humiliation, as soon as ever the people in *Swanzy* were come from the place where they had been praying together, the Indians discharged a volley of shot whereby they killed one man & wounded others. Two men were sent to call a Surgeon for the relief of the wounded, but the Indians killed them by the way; and in another part of the town six men were killed, so that there were nine english men murthered this day. . . . The Providence of God is deeply to be observed, that the sword should first be drawn upon a day of Humiliation, the Lord thereby declaring from heaven that he expects something else from his People besides fasting and prayer.

Four days later, Church and his troops fell under attack near beleaguered Swansea at Miles's Bridge, which led into Mount Hope Neck. Church was appalled by the poor showing of the English forces in this first military engagement of the war, "*The Lord have Mercy on us,* if such a handful of Indians shall thus dare such an Army!" During the next year and a half, he was frequently in the minority as he repeatedly suggested—usually in vain—aggressive strategies of attack that called for the abandonment of formal European battle tactics and the use of Indian battle practice. Again and again, the hastily mustered army proved ineffectual. Wampanoags staged lightning raids in the vicinity of Rehoboth, a Rhode Island settlement bordering Philip's territory, and Taunton on June 29, burning down eight Rehoboth farmhouses and killing 15 people—"eleven Men, two Maids, and two Youths"—at Taunton. The next day, troops from Massachusetts, Plymouth, and Rhode Island pursued Philip in Mount Hope Neck, but he and his forces handily evaded them by escaping to the swamps of Pocasset country in southern Rhode Island, which the English found impenetrable.

On July 1, Connecticut joined in the war effort, sending troops to aid Massachusetts, Plymouth, and Rhode Island. Philip, too, was forging an alliance at this time, with the Pocasset squaw-sachem Weetamoo. To forestall the spread of such alliances, Captain Edward Hutchinson marched the Massachusetts army out of Mount Hope Neck and into Narragansett country, in order to "overawe" that Rhode Island tribe with English might and thereby negotiate a promise of neutrality. With the Massachusetts contingent absent between July 5 and 15, however, the remainder of the army was effectively immobilized outside the swamp that harbored Philip's warriors.

In the meantime, Edmund Andros, powerful governor of the Duke of York's patent territories, was attempting to exploit the war crisis. His colony had substantial conflicting land claims with Connecticut, and on July 4, he dispatched troops to western Connecticut ostensibly to protect settlements there against Philip. Philip, however, was nowhere near western Connecticut, and the colony's governor, John Winthrop, understanding that Andros's real intentions were to seize that part of Connecticut, pulled soldiers from the Rhode Island front and sent them to Fort Saybrook to meet the threat from Andros. As a result the New York forces withdrew.

Back in Rhode Island, Benjamin Church recognized that feeble diplomacy with Narragansetts and intercolonial strife were siphoning energy from the real menace at hand. He persuaded the reluctant Rhode Island militia captain, Matthew Fuller, "to attempt to surprise the Indian forces in Pocasset swamp." Fuller and Church deployed their men at night and lay in wait to effect an ambush, "but Capt. *Fullers* party being troubled with the Epidemical plague of lust after Tobacco, must needs strike fire to Smoke it; and thereby discovered themselves to a party of the Enemy coming up to them, who immediately fled with great precipitation." Slenderly provisioned though he was, and not to be daunted, Church proposed to Captain Fuller that he would ask for volunteers to march with him in pursuit of the enemy.

Accompanied by about 20 of Captain Fuller's men, Church followed a fresh trail toward a pine swamp, but finding the trail infested with rattlesnakes, changed course toward Punkatees Neck. Church's men were briefly distracted by "a large Wigwam full of *Indian* Truck," which they set about plundering until the commander reminded them that they had come on other business. At Captain Almy's "pease field," the party divided in two. A pair of Indians was seen coming out of the field. Church and his group lay flat on the ground, and so escaped detection; the other detachment, however, was discovered, and the Indians began to run. Church called to them, asking for a parley, but to no avail. One of the Indians paused at the field fence, turned around, and fired. A member of Church's party returned fire, apparently wounding one of the Indians.

Realizing that his position was exposed, Church ordered his men to march "at double distance" in order to give the impression of a much larger force. But they soon found themselves "Saluted with a Volly of fifty or sixty Guns," and for the next six hours—short on powder and occupying a position that afforded scant cover—Church and his men endured an attack by about 300 Indians. An English river sloop finally arrived to rescue the party—but even that was a harrowing event. Since the sloop could not approach the shallows close to the riverbank, Church's men had to paddle to the vessel in a canoe, two at a time and under heavy musket fire.

In the meantime, Indians were attacking Middleborough and Dartmouth, two Plymouth towns. It is reported that they

barbarously murthered both men and women in those places, stripping the slain whether men or women, and leaving them

in the open field as naked as the day wherein they were born. Such is also their inhumanity as that they flay of[f] the skin from their faces and heads of those they get into their hands, and go away with the hairy Scalp of their enemy.

A few days later, Nipmucks attacked Mendon, Massachusetts, killing five or six people working in the fields. Settlers abandoned the town soon after, and it was destroyed.

By mid-July, with much of New England awash in blood, two diplomatic overtures were made. Captain Edward Hutchinson signed a treaty with some minor Narragansett leaders, who agreed to surrender to the English any Wampanoags they might have been harboring and to confirm certain English land rights. As with many white-Indian agreements, this one quickly proved unenforceable since the Indian signatories possessed negligible authority and influence. The Narragansetts for a time did, however, adopt a strategy of withdrawal, holing up in a swamp, hoping that the slaughter would pass them by.

Massachusetts militia Captain Ephraim Curtis attempted negotiation with the Nipmucks of eastern and central Massachusetts during July 16–24, but with far more disappointing results. On the twenty-eighth, Hutchinson marched in the company of cavalry under Captain Thomas Wheeler to another conference with Nipmuck chiefs near Brookfield, Massachusetts. When negotiations broke down, the Nipmucks solidly allied themselves with Philip. In general, colonial diplomacy, administered ineptly, arrogantly, with malice, and in bad faith, served only to prolong hostilities.

Equally clumsy and inadequate were the tactics the English customarily employed in fighting the Indians. The Battle of Pocasset Swamp, fought on July 19, 1675, demonstrates the impossibility of waging European-style war in the American wilderness. Between 7 and 15 English died in this vain attempt to dislodge the Wampanoags from the swamp. As Increase Mather relates, "The Swamp was so Boggy and thick of Bushes, as that it was judged to proceed further therein would be but to throw away Mens lives. It could not there be descerned who were *English* and who the *Indians*. Our Men when in that hideous place if they did but see a Bush stir would fire presently, whereby 'tis verily feared, that they did sometimes unhappily shoot *English men* instead of *Indians*."

Later in the war, Benjamin Church would recruit some Indian soldiers, of whom he inquired

*How they got such advantage often of the English in their Marches thro' the Woods?* They told him, That the *Indians* gain'd great advantage of the *English* by two things; The *Indians* always took care in their Marches and Fights, not to come too thick together. But the *English* always kept in a heap together, that it was as easy to hit them as to hit an House. The other was, that if at any time they discovered a company of *English* Souldiers in the Woods, they knew that there was all, for the *English* never scattered; but the Indians always divided and scattered.

Discouraged by their performance against the Indians in close combat—and over Church's vigorous objections—colonial authorities soon broke off pursuit of Philip and instead built a fort to besiege him in the swamp, intending to starve the enemy out.

Capt. *Henchman* and the *Plimouth* forces kept a diligent Eye upon the Enemy, but were not willing to run into the Mire and Dirt after them in a dark Swamp, being taught by late Experience how dangerous it is to fight in such dismal Woods, when their Eyes were muffled with the Leaves, and their Arms pinioned with the thick Boughs of the Trees, as their Feet were continually shackled with the Roots spreading every Way in those boggy Woods. It is ill fighting with a wild Beast in his own Den. They resolved therefore to starve them out of the Swamp, where they knew full well they could not long subsist. To that End they began to build a Fort.

This would prove to be a strategic error that only prolonged the war, for, the Indians did not starve easily. Mary Rowlandson, taken captive, witnessed firsthand the Indians' ability to subsist on almost nothing:

It was thought, if their corn were cut down, they would starve and die with hunger: and all their corn that could be found, was destroyed, and they driven from that little they had in store, into the woods in the midst of winter; and yet how to admiration did the Lord preserve them for his Holy ends, and the destruction of many still amongst the English! Strangely did the Lord provide for them; that I did not see (all the time I was among them) one man, woman, or child, die with hunger.

Though many times they would eat that, that a hog or a dog would hardly touch; yet by that God strengthened them to be a scourge to His people. . . . They would pick up old bones, and cut them to pieces at the joints, and if they were full of worms and maggots, they would scald them over the fire to make the vermin come out, and then boil them, and drink up the liquor, and then beat the great ends of them in a mortar, and so eat them. They would eat horse's guts, and ears, and all sorts of wild birds which they would catch: also bear, venison, beaver, tortoise, frogs, squirrels, dogs, skunks, rattlesnakes; yea, the very bark of trees; besides all sorts of creatures, and provisions which they plundered from the English.

While the English were occupied with fort building, Philip escaped from the Pocasset swamp on July 29 and headed for Nipmuck country to the northeast. Captain Daniel Henchman, with "six files" of Plymouth troops and aided by Mohegan allies, pursued Philip and engaged him on the thirty-first at Nipsachuck (present-day Burrillville, Rhode Island). Having exhausted his provisions in the chase, however, Henchman was forced to break off the attack, and Philip once again escaped.

In Massachusetts, Captains Hutchinson and Wheeler set out for Brookfield (Quabaog) at the beginning of August to attempt once again to treat with the Nipmucks. Failing to find the Indians at the appointed place of rendezvous, they rode on and were caught in an ambush. Hutchinson was fatally wounded, and Wheeler was shot through the arm. Eight other men were also killed, and the Nipmucks besieged the remainder of the company for 48 hours. One Brookfield settler recalled how the attackers "did roar against us like so many wild bulls, sending in their shot amongst us till towards the moon rising, which was about three of the clock; at which time they attempted to fire our house by hay and other combustible matter. . . .They continued shooting and shouting. . . scoffing at our prayers as they were sending in their shot upon all quarters." Captain (later Major) Simon Willard reached Brookfield with relief forces, but only after the town was in ruins. By the end of August, the theater of war had broadened into the upper Connecticut Valley, the Merrimac Valley, New Hampshire, and Maine.

Near Hadley, Massachusetts, colonials demanded that the local Indians surrender their arms as "Proof of their Fidelity." After some stalling, the Indians slipped away from their village on the night of August 25. Realizing that the Hadley Indians had absconded to join Philip, Captains Richard Beers and Thomas Lothrop (or Lathrop) marshaled their troops in pursuit and skirmished at Sugar Loaf Hill, ten miles above Hatfield, killing "about twenty-six" Indians and suffering the loss of nine or ten English.

A week later, Hadley was raided and Deerfield attacked, "leaving most of the Houses in that new hopeful Plantation in ruinous heaps." This was followed almost immediately by a devastating attack against Northfield (Squakeag). Beers, dispatched with 36 men to relieve the garrison there, was ambushed and slain with about 20 of his party. "On the *5th* of *September* Major *Treat* set forth for *Squakheag* [Northfield] with above an hundred men, next day coming nigh *Squakheag*, his men were much daunted to see the heads of Captain *Beers* Souldiers upon poles by the way side." This sight "daunted" Treat and his company sufficiently to stop their pursuit of the attackers. By mid-September, Northfield as well as Deerfield and Brookfield joined a growing list of devastated and abandoned towns.

Having already endured months of bloodshed, the colonies, now acting in concert as what they called the United Colonies, officially declared war on September 9, 1675, levying an army of 1,000, which was not actually mustered until November and December. Well before that time, war had engulfed Massachusetts, Plymouth, Rhode Island, Connecticut, and the more remote and sparsely settled "Eastern Colonies"—Maine and New Hampshire. During the autumn, several settlements in Maine were attacked, including Casco Bay, where a family was killed and three children taken captive; Falmouth, where five houses were burned, eight people slain, and three children taken captive; Saco, where 13 died and the settlement was effectively destroyed; Black Point, where seven were killed and 20 houses burned; and Kittery, which lost two men. Lieutenant Roger Plaisted (or Plaister), attempted to relieve Kittery but was driven back to his garrison at Salmon Falls. He dispatched an urgent message to Major Richard Waldron, in charge of forces at Quecheco:

*Salmon Falls, October 16, 1675*

*Mr.* Richard Waldern [Waldron] *and Lieut.* Coffin, *These are to inform you, that just now the* Indians *are engaging us with at least one hundred Men, and have slain four of our Men already,* Richard Tozer, James Burney, Isaack Bottes, *and* Tozer's Son, *and burnt* Benoni Hodsdens House; *Sir, if ever you have any Love for us, and the Country, now shew yourself with Men to help us, or else we are all in great Danger to be slain, unless our God wonderfully appear for our Deliverance. They that cannot fight, let them pray;* Nought else, but I rest,

Yours to serve you,
*Roger Plaisted,*
*George Broughton*

It is not known why Waldron did not dispatch troops to Plaisted's aid—or even if he received the message—but the siege must have lifted sufficiently, for the next day, Plaisted ventured outside the garrison with 22 men to bury Kittery's dead. One hundred fifty Indians attacked the burial detail, killing the lieutenant, one of his sons, mortally wounding another, and killing a fourth man.

During this time, repeated attempts at negotiating peace or a truce failed. A hopeful conference at Wickford, Rhode Island, between the English and Narragansetts broke down on September 22. Worse, previously friendly Indians now turned on the colonists. The town of Springfield, Massachusetts, having enjoyed cordial relations with the Indians for some 40 years, maintained no garrisons. On October 4–5, it was raided, and 32 houses—about half the town—were destroyed.

In October, the Narragansetts at last concluded a new treaty in Boston. Despite this gain, on November 2, Connecticut's colonial council resolved that the best way to prevent war with the Narragansetts was a peremptory strike against them. Plymouth and Massachusetts were in agreement on this. The army of the United Colonies, called for in September, was at last mustering, and would continue to do so throughout November and into December. Assembled at Dedham, Massachusetts; Taunton, Plymouth; and New London, Connecticut, the army united at Wickford, Rhode Island, where, under the command of Plymouth governor Winslow, it awaited provisioning during December 12–18.

The plan was not to move against Philip and his Wampanoags, who were wreaking havoc on the settlements and would have been a more formidable foe, but to attack the Narragansetts, who, so far, had offered no violence. The army's objective was a stronghold near Petenquanscut (Pettiquemscot), Rhode Island. However, the sudden fall on December 16 of Jeriah (Jerry) Bull's garrison house there, which was to have served as a base of operations, foiled this strategy. Instead, Winslow marched his thousand-man army—including a company under the redoubtable Benjamin Church—into a snowstorm on December 18 to assault another Narragansett fort, stronghold of the sachem Canonchet (whom the English called Canonicus) in a frozen swamp at Kingston, Rhode Island.

Marching through intense cold, the army reached the Indian fort the following day and found the stronghold formidable beyond expectation. The ensuing battle proved costly to the colonials, as two companies, noting an incomplete palisade at one corner, stormed the fortification prematurely before the arrival of the main company. Two captains were slain, and the few troops who did make it into the fort were quickly driven out. Benjamin Church led 30 soldiers in another assault and was hit by three bullets. Wounded in the hip and thigh, the frontiersman's only regret was that one shot had "pierced . . . and wounded a pair of mittens that he had borrowed from Capt. Prentis." In fierce battle, 80 of Winslow's army perished, including 14 company commanders, and about 600 Narragansetts—half of them women and children—were killed. Over the protests of the wounded Church, who pointed out that the battered English would need the shelter of the Indians' wigwams for the bitter winter night, the colonials torched the encampment—"hundreds of *Wigwams* (or Indian houses) within the Fort, which our Souldiers set on fire, in which men, women, and Children (no man knoweth how many hundreds of them) were burnt to death."

Bereft of so many of its commanders, its supplies depleted, the army retreated to Wickford, declining to pursue the surviving Narragansetts, who escaped to Nipmuck

## CAPTIVITY NARRATIVES

The first American "best-seller" was published in Boston in 1682. *The Sovereignty & Goodness of God . . . a Narrative of the Captivity and Restauration of Mrs. Mary Rowlandson . . .* went through two more editions in Cambridge and London that same year and continued to be popular for the next century and a half, with major reprints in Boston (1720, 1770 [two editions] 1771, and 1773), New London (1773), and then variously throughout the nineteenth century. A later narrative, John Williams's *The Redeemed Captive*, an account of an English minister's captivity among the French-allied Indians of Canada, was published in Boston in 1706 and sold 1,000 copies in a single week. It was reissued in Boston in 1707, 1720, 1758, 1774, and 1776 and in New London in 1773. Between 1680 and 1716, captivity narratives dominated the list of frontier literature published in America. Indeed, during this period, three of the four most popular narrative works in the colonies were captivity accounts (the fourth narrative was the perennial favorite *Pilgrim's Progress* by John Bunyan).

What were captivity narratives, and why were they so popular with colonial readers?

These works were usually first-person accounts of an individual's experience of being captured and held by hostile Indians. The pattern characteristic of this literary genre almost always included the suffering of hunger; pain; torture; the loss of a spouse, children (a frequent and heart-wrenching feature of these narratives is an episode in which an infant is snatched from its mother's arms and battered to death against a tree), and other relatives; and the patient endurance of all these things until the captive's "redemption" at the conclusion of the narrative.

Mary Rowlandson's 1682 narrative remains, to this day, the best-known of the New England captivity accounts:

On the tenth of February 1675, came the Indians with great numbers upon Lancaster: Their first coming was about sun-rising; hearing the noise of some guns, we looked out; several houses were burning, and the smoke ascending to heaven. There were five persons taken in one house, the father, and the mother and a sucking child, they knocked on the head; the other two they took and carried away alive. There were two others, who being out of their garrison upon some occasion were set upon; one was knocked on the head, the other escaped: another there was who running along was shot and wounded, and fell down; he begged of them his life, promising them money (as they told me) but they would not hearken to him but knocked him in the head, and stripped him naked, and split open his bowels. Another seeing many of the Indians about his barn, ventured and went out, but was quickly shot down. . . . At length they came and beset our own house, and quickly it was the dolefullest day that ever mine eyes saw. The house stood upon the edge of a hill; some of the Indians got behind the hill, others into the barn, and others behind any thing that could shelter them; from all which places they shot against the house, so that the bullets seemed to fly like hail; and quickly they wounded one man among us, then another, and then a third. About two hours (according to my observation, in that amazing time) they had been about the house before they prevailed to fire it (which they did with flax and hemp, which they brought out of the barn, and there being no defense about the house, only two flankers [projecting fortifications] at two opposite corners and one of them not finished) they fired it once and one ventured out and quenched it, but they quickly fired again, and that took. Now is the dreadful hour come, that I have often heard of (in time of war, as it was the case of others) but now mine eyes see it. Some in our house were fighting for their lives, others wallowing in their blood, the house on fire over our heads, and the bloody heathen ready to knock us on the head, if we stirred out. Now might we hear mothers and children crying out for themselves, and one another, Lord, what shall we do? Then I took my children (and one of my sisters, hers) to go forth and leave the house: but as soon as we came to the door and appeared, the Indians shot so thick that the bullets rattled against the house, as if one had taken an handful of stones and threw them, so that we were fain to give back. We had six stout dogs belonging to our garrison, but none of them would stir, though another time, if any Indians had come to the door, they were ready to fly upon him and tear him down. The Lord hereby would make us the more to acknowledge his hand, and to see that our help is always in him. But out we must go, the fire increasing, and coming along behind us, roaring, and the Indians gaping before us with their guns, spears and hatchets to devour us. No sooner were we out of the house, but my brother-in-law (being before wounded, in defending the house, in or near the throat) fell down dead whereat the Indians scornfully shouted, and holloed, and were presently upon him, stripping off his clothes, the bullets flying thick, one went through my side, and the same (as would seem) through the bowels and hand of my dear child in my arms. One of my elder sister's children, named William, had then his leg broken, which the Indians perceiving, they knocked him on the head. Thus were we butchered by those merciless heathen, standing amazed, with the blood running down to our heels. My eldest sister being yet in the house, and seeing those woeful sights, the infidels haling mothers one way, and children another, and some wallowing in their blood: and her elder son telling her that her son William was dead, and myself was wounded, she said, And, Lord, let me die with them; which was no sooner said, but she was struck with a bullet, and fell down dead over the threshold. I hope she is reaping the fruit of her good labors, being faithful to the service of God in her place. . . . The Indians laid hold of us, pulling me one way, and the Children another, and said, Come go along with us; I told them they would kill me: they answered, If I were willing to go along with them, they would not hurt me. . . . Of thirty-seven persons who were in this one house, none escaped either present death, or a bitter captivity, save only one, who might say as he, Job 1. 15, *And I only am escaped alone to tell the news.* There were twelve killed, some shot, some stabbed with spears, some knocked down with their hatchets. When we are in prosperity, oh the little that we think of such dreadful sights, and to see our dear friends, and relations lie bleeding out their heart's blood upon the ground. There was one who was chopped into the head with a hatchet, and stripped naked, and yet was crawling up and down. It is a solemn sight to see so many Christians lying in their blood, some here, and some there, like a company of sheep torn by wolves. All of them stripped naked by a company of hell-hounds, roaring, singing, ranting and insulting, as if they would have torn our very hearts out; yet the Lord by his almighty power preserved a number of us from death, for there were twenty-four of us taken alive and carried captive.

The word *redemption* (or *redeemed*) figures in the titles of many captivity narratives and is of particular significance. Captives were, usually "redeemed"—that is, ransomed—from the Indians in exchange for money or other valuables. The word is also a pun on the religious significance of "redemption." Characteristically, these narratives depict Indian captivity as a trial ordained by God to test the victim's faith (and thereby strengthen it). The redemption that comes at the end of a string of travails—a metaphor of the sufferings to which the world subjects all men and women—is the reward of faith sustained. Thus, captivity narratives were in large measure religious parables meant to teach and to inspire.

In addition, these narratives were also exciting tales about a subject of urgent importance to colonists clinging to the edge of a vast wilderness populated by "savages." Significantly, few of these narratives were about soldiers or solitary frontiersmen taken by Indians in combat. Most captivity narratives were written by or about women, who were taken from their homes by Indians. Throughout the most popular narratives—including that of Mary Rowlandson and Hannah Dustin (retold by Cotton Mather in his *Humiliations follow'd with Deliverances* of 1697)—there runs a strong sexual undercurrent of a woman threatened with violent rape by a "heathen" of a different race. All of these elements—religious edification and a confirmation of faith, the dramatization of a common colonial danger and fear, the excitement of adventure, and sexual titillation—contributed to the enormous popularity of the captivity narrative, hundreds of which were produced. The genre was America's first literature of mythic dimensions.

country. The Great Swamp Fight inflicted heavy losses on the Narragansetts and cut them off from their sources of supply. It also served to strengthen desperate anti-English alliances among the Wampanoags, Nipmucks, and Narragansetts.

With the new year, Philip attempted to extend his alliances beyond New England, taking many of his people to Mohawk country near Albany, New York, in search of ammunition, provisions, and supporters. Unfortunately for Philip, Governor Andros had reached the Mohawks first, persuading them not only to spurn the alliance, but to attack Philip, who was compelled to flee back to New England. The alliance Andros established effectively blocked the grand Indian confederacy so feared by the colonists.

The New England forces were not prepared to take

immediate advantage of Philip's rebuff. Winslow's army, crippled by its losses in the Great Swamp Fight (especially at the command level) and by a lack of provisions, was immobilized for more than a month. At the end of January, an Indian raid on Pawtuxet, Rhode Island, prompted Winslow to take his newly reinforced but still inadequately provisioned force on a so-called Hungry March into the country of the Nipmucks. After wholesale desertion, the expedition was aborted a week after it began.

With the principal English force in disarray, the Indians rallied and renewed their offensive. On February 10, 1676, Lancaster, Massachusetts, was raided a second time, and Mary Rowlandson, wife of the settlement's minister, was captured from Rowlandson Garrison. Although five additional garrisons remained, the panic-stricken settlers abandoned the frontier town, which the Indians then put to the torch. Mary Rowlandson's account of her ordeal, published in 1682, became a colonial "best-seller" and is the most vivid firsthand document of King Philip's War.

On February 21, in another crushing English defeat, 200 to 300 Indians overcame a 160-man militia force at Medfield, Massachusetts, about 20 miles from Boston, burning half the town and killing 20 people. Two days later, the citizens of Boston observed one of many desperate days of "Public Humiliation," entreating heavenly aid in their hour of need even as Philip attacked within ten miles of the city. Early in March, Major Thomas Savage wielded a cavalry troop in pursuit of Philip near Northampton, Massachusetts, but, as usual, he evaded capture as his allies managed a second raid on Pawtuxet, resulting in the burning of a dozen houses.

The colonies reeled under blow after blow. On March 12, Clark's Garrison, Plymouth, was raided and destroyed. The next day, Groton, Massachusetts, was abandoned after a raid. On March 14, following an attack on Northampton, colonial authorities, reacting to crisis with a siege mentality, drew up plans to erect a palisade around Boston, leaving the outlying towns exposed. About this time, too, various frustrated colonists turned against the friendly, Christianized "Praying Indians" in their midst. To protect the Indians from the mob, colonial authorities commissioned John Hoar of Concord to build a workhouse for the shelter of loyal Indians. This precaution quickly proved inadequate, and the Indians were next exiled to barren, bitter-cold islands in Boston Harbor. The largest concentration of refugees, about 400, suffered near starvation and froze on Deer Island. Even this awful place of refuge was not immune from attack: A band of 30 to 40 colonists unsuccessfully attempted an assault.

By mid-March, Warwick, near Providence, Rhode Is-

land, was all but deserted, after several attacks. The Indians finally burned it to the ground, killing the sole remaining inhabitant. On the twenty-sixth, worshipers were attacked on their way to church in Longmeadow, Massachusetts:

And although they [the colonists] were Armed, there were seven or eight *Indians*, who lying in Ambuscado, were so bold as to shoot at them. They killed a Man and a Maid that rode behind him, the English being surprised with fear, rode away to save their lives; in the mean while the Indians seized upon two women and Children, and took them away alive. . . .What shall be said when eighteen English-men well arm'd, fly before seven Indians?

On the same day, the town of Marlborough was badly mauled, though colonials gave chase to the retreating Indians and defeated their rear guard. In Connecticut, Simsbury was abandoned and burned. Near Rehoboth, Rhode Island, Captain Michael Pierce, leading a force of about 50 colonists and 20 friendly Indians, was ambushed as he pursued Philip's warriors. Although the Indians turned their pursuers back, killing several, including Pierce, it was reported that the battle had cost them 140 lives. It was also later learned that, before setting out after the Indians, Pierce, realizing he was likely to be outnumbered, had sent a letter to Captain Andrew Edmunds of Providence, requesting reinforcements. The messenger arrived in Providence after the lengthy forenoon church service was under way and decided to wait until it was concluded before delivering the letter. When Edmunds finally read the message, he pronounced Pierce's doom: "It is now too late."

The early spring of 1676 marked the low point of the war for the colonists. As a result of despair and frustration, soldiers under Lieutenant Richard Jacobs and citizens of Sudbury, Massachusetts, staged an unorthodox surprise nighttime attack against Indians camped near the town:

They discerned where the Enemy lay by their Fires, (near three hundred of them) and that within half a mile of a Garrison-house, near the Place where they had done so much Mischief the Day before. Such was the Courage and Resolution of the English, though but forty in Number, Townsmen and Soldiers, that they adventured to discharge [their weapons] upon them as they lay by their Fires, when it was so dark that an *Indian* could hardly be discerned from a better Man; yet God so directing, they discharged several Times upon them, wounded thirty, fourteen of whom either dyed of their wounds the same Day or soon after, which had been chief Agents in this present Mischief against the English.

Despite this action, raiding continued unabated. On March 28, the morning after the colonists' sortie, 30 barns and 40 houses were burned in Rehoboth, and on the day after that, Providence, Rhode Island, was destroyed. Although Connecticut soldiers operating in western Rhode Island succeeded in capturing the important Narragansett sachem and war leader Canonchet, whom they subsequently executed, by the middle of the month the English area of settlement had greatly contracted. Despite emergency laws forbidding the evacuation of towns without official permission, the outlying settlements around Boston were largely abandoned. To add to the misery—and the sense of visitation by God's wrath—epidemic disease began to take its toll among the colonists, killing John Winthrop among other important military officers.

On April 21, Indians repaid Sudbury for its earlier attack, sending as many as 800 to 900 warriors against the town. Militia from Sudbury and surrounding settlements responded and, in a fierce, daylong battle, repelled the attack. Following the battle, colonial forces at last began to take the offensive. By the end of April, Captain Daniel Henchman was sweeping through eastern Massachusetts. On May 1, the Waschusett Council was held, at which Indian hostiles finally agreed to negotiate ransom terms for English captives. This meeting resulted in the release of Mary Rowlandson (May 2–3) among numerous others.

In western Massachusetts, Captain William Turner, leading a force of 150 mounted men, attacked an Indian encampment at the Falls of the Connecticut above Deerfield, Massachusetts, on May 19. More a massacre than a battle, the soldiers poked their muskets into the wigwams and shot the Indians—including many women and children—as they slept. While the enemy was routed, the army failed to pursue, and the surviving Indians turned a retreat into a counterattack, killing about 40 men, including Turner. Yet the loss of many warriors (reportedly more than 100) and supplies made this a costly victory for the Indians and enabled the English to carry out a strategy of attrition—the kind of extended warfare alien to Indian culture and for which the loosely organized tribes were unprepared.

As Philip and his allies weakened, the colonists became more aggressive in attack and pursuit. Responding to reports of hostiles fishing in the Pawtucket River near Rehoboth, Captain Thomas Brattle led a combined force of colonists and Indian allies in attack, killing about a dozen of Philip's warriors, with the loss of only one colonial soldier. On June 2, Connecticut Major John Talcott, acting on orders to "kill and destroy [the Indians], according to the utmost power God shall give you," launched a combined Indian-English assault against Philip in western Massachusetts.

Early in the same month, Benjamin Church was au-

thorized to build a new army on behalf of the United Colonies, using white and Indian soldiers. While paddling in a canoe, on his way to recruit evacuees from Swansea, Dartmouth, and other destroyed towns, Church spied some Sogkonate Indians fishing from the rocks along the bank: "*He had a mighty conceit that if he could gain a fair Opportunity to discourse them, that he could draw them off from* Philip, *for he knew they never heartily loved him.*" At great risk, Church came ashore for parley and encountered an Indian known as "honest George," servant of the Sogkonate squaw-sachem Awashonks, Church's former ally who was now joined with Philip. Through George, Church arranged a meeting with Awashonks, and after tense negotiations, Church scored one of the few English diplomatic triumphs in King Philip's War, winning Awashonks over to the colonials' side.

Still, Philip fought on, launching a massive assault against Hadley, Massachusetts. Early on the morning of June 12, about 700 Indians descended on the town. In addition to the garrison, the town was defended by Connecticut forces, 500 strong, consisting of colonists and friendly Pequots and Mohegans. Positioned behind the town's palisades and equipped with some artillery pieces, the colonial army successfully repelled the attackers. On the nineteenth, Massachusetts colonial authorities offered amnesty to Indians who surrendered. By the end of the month, after the proclamation of many Days of Public Humiliation in the colonies, there was reason to celebrate a Day of Public Thanksgiving in Boston. On June 30, the squaw-sachem Awashonks, acting on her agreement with Benjamin Church, met with Plymouth forces under William Bradford and formally declared her new allegiance to the English.

On July 2, at Nipsachuck, Rhode Island, John Talcott dealt the Narragansetts two crushing blows when he attacked a band of 34 men and 137 women and children, killing all of the men and 92 of the women and children. At Warwick the next day, he killed 18 men and 22 women and children, taking 27 prisoners as well. At this time, too, war with the so-called North Indians—the Abnakis, Sokokis, and Pennacooks—came to an end when the Pennacook sachem Wannalancet signed a treaty with Major Richard Waldron, bringing peace to Maine.

On July 11, Taunton, Massachusetts, was attacked, but the town was prepared for it. Benjamin Church prevailed in skirmishes at Middleborough and Monponsett on the same day and, a week later, skirmished with Philip's men in and around Taunton. During this period, Major Bradford was pursuing Philip, narrowly missing the capture of the Indian leader on July 16.

By now, most of the warring Indians were beginning to realize that their cause was lost. On July 8, a Nipmuck whom the English called James sought amnesty and "affirm[ed] that very many of the Indians are dead since this *War* began; and that most have dyed by the hand of God, in respect of Diseases, Fluxes, and Feavers, which have been amongst them, then have been killed with the Sword." Confident of the growing Indian disaffection with Philip, Benjamin Church recruited into his army many of the Indians that he captured in the skirmish near Taunton:

If the [Church] perceived they look'd surly, and his [already allied] *Indian* Souldiers call'd them treacherous Dogs, as some of them would sometimes do, all the notice he would take of it, would only be to clap them [the captives] on the back, and tell them, *Come, come, you look wild and surly, and mutter,*

*but that signifies nothing, these my best Souldeirs were a little while a go as wild and surly as you are now; by that time you have been but one day along with me, you'l love me too, and be as brisk as any of them.* And it prov'd so.

Bowing at last to Church's success, authorities granted him a new commission on July 24, calling for a larger army of 200 men (of which 140 were to be friendly Indians) and ordering him to use that army "as you shall think fit: to discover, pursue, fight, surprise, destroy, or subdue our Indian enemies." The new army set out on the thirtieth in pursuit of the elusive Philip.

Closing in on King Philip, Church's troops killed his uncle on July 31 and, the next day, captured the sachem's wife and son. Philip, however, escaped, but when he

## THE TREATY PROBLEM

If the first four centuries of white-Indian contact in America produced almost continual warfare, they also produced a virtually uninterrupted stream of treaties and agreements. The continued warfare demonstrates a truth that surprises no one who has even a nodding acquaintance with American history: Treaties between whites and Indians were customarily violated almost as soon as they were signed.

It is all too easy to ascribe these violations to white perfidy. Indeed, this was often the case, as white governments, colonial or federal, sometimes entered into treaties in bad faith. More often, however, white treaty commissioners had reasonably good intentions and fully expected that their side would abide by the terms of the agreement. Unfortunately, neither colonial nor federal governments always had the means to compel the compliance of the people they governed. For example, the western limit to white settlement established by the Proclamation of 1763, pursuant to a central promise of the great treaty concluded at Easton, Pennsylvania, was immediately violated. Moreover, efforts to enforce it led to the discontent on the frontier that helped bring about the American Revolution. Even in the nineteenth century, federal treaties often proved impossible to enforce, as states, territories, individual military commanders, militia forces, or bands of settlers frequently took matters into their own hands and did as they pleased. Worse, within the federal government, Indian policy was administered with scandalous inconsistency and changed from one administration to the next. Res

ervations, Indian agencies, and those in charge of the disbursement of treaty funds were also notoriously inefficient and corrupt.

There were grave problems on the Indians' side as well. Tribal organization was characteristically loose and democratic to the point of anarchy. So-called chiefs were seldom sovereigns in the Euro-American sense, which meant that even though a particular chief might assent to a treaty, the decision was not necessarily binding on anyone else in the tribe. Tribes often splintered into "peace" factions and "war" factions, usually with the older men (those with whom colonial or federal authorities customarily treated) constituting the former, and the young warriors belonging to the latter. Sometimes, whites used this ambiguity of authority to their advantage, as when Andrew Jackson's administration chose to deal exclusively with the so-called Treaty party, unilaterally declaring that faction's agreements binding on all of the Cherokees, even though the Treaty party was outnumbered 17 to one by the "National party." More often, however, the ambiguity was accidental and created nothing but confusion and ill will.

Then there were the treaty ceremonies themselves. Some of these were relatively relaxed occasions solemnized by the presentation of gifts. Indians often signed a treaty simply to obtain the accompanying gifts, which were not the beads and trinkets of cliché and folklore but, more often, such sorely needed items as guns, ammunition, food, and clothing. Other treaty signings were tense af-

learned of the capture of his wife and son, he reportedly said, "My heart breaks; now I am ready to die."

On August 3, Connecticut's Major John Talcott chased, engaged, and defeated Indian forces retreating west to the Housatonic River in western Massachusetts. Three days later, Weetamoo, squaw-sachem of Pocasset and Philip's kinswoman and ally, was betrayed by an Indian who led the English to her encampment near Taunton. Some 20 colonists followed him and were able to surprise a party of 26 hostiles, capturing all except Weetamoo herself, who attempted to escape by floating across "a River or Arm of the Sea" on a makeshift raft or piece of wood. Colonists later found her naked and drowned body, from which they severed her head, in order to display it on a pole in Taunton.

A few days later, a deserter from Philip's camp approached Church, offering to lead him and his men to the camp. (Philip had killed the deserter's kinsman because he had dared to counsel surrender; the informant now sought revenge.) Church deployed his men around Philip's camp after midnight.

Our Souldiers came upon him, and surrounded the *Swamp* (where he with seven of his men absconded). Thereupon he betook himself to flight, but as he was coming out of the Swamp, an English-man and an Indian endeavoured to fire at him, the English-man missed of his aime, the Indian [known as Alderman] shot him through the heart, so as that he fell down dead. . . . And in that very place where he first contrived and began his mischief, was he taken and destroyed, and there

---

fairs presided over by a show of military might. The message of these was clear enough: sign—or else. Naturally, under duress, Indians assented with little or no intention of abiding by the terms to which they agreed. Finally, there were the grand treaty ceremonies, such as that marking the Treaty of Easton in 1763. The eastern Pennsylvania town was filled to overflowing with white and Indian dignitaries, government officials, traders, and trappers. Since no building was large enough to contain the treaty conference proper, negotiations were held "in the bower." Indian participants were generally disciplined by tribal custom to observe total silence in deference to the speaker, so the proceedings were most likely characterized by a superficial sense of orderliness. However, when the parties involved were not negotiating, they feasted and drank, and this after-hours aspect of the treaty conference came to resemble the institution that developed among fur trappers toward the beginning of the nineteenth century, the raucous "rendezvous." Whites negotiators frequently used the Indians' inebriation to coax agreement to terms favorable to white interests.

Treaties, like all aspects of Indian-white relations, were plagued by essential cultural differences, the most important of which centered on concepts of ownership and property. Most Indian cultures did not embrace concepts of private property and exclusive ownership. No one "owned" a particular parcel of land. A given tribe might claim the right to hunt or live on it and might defend that right by force of arms; however, most tribes were willing to make agreements allowing other tribes or individuals to hunt on "their" land. Such an agreement did not convey ownership of the land to the other party. Folklore has made much of the so-called sale of Manhattan to the Dutch for twenty-four dollars, calling it a great bargain. (Taking into account modern exchange rates, recent economists figure that 60 gulden worth of goods was probably closer to several thousands of dollars in value.) Indeed, it *was* a bargain—for the Wappinger Indians who made the "sale." They accepted the goods, but did not think that they had anymore power to convey exclusive title to the land than they had to convey the right to breathe the air. Elements of the natural world could neither be bought nor sold.

Treaties persistently ignored this profound cultural point, but not just because whites of the nineteenth century and earlier were incapable of overcoming their ethnocentrism. Colonial authorities sought from treaties not merely peace with the Indians, nor merely to acquire Indian lands for the sake of settlement, but also to establish their own legitimacy as political entities. Many nations and factions within nations laid claim to pieces of the New World. A good way to assert the precedence of one's claim over that of another was to demonstrate that one had acquired the land from those who owned it by "primitive right." Therefore, it became very important for colonists to purchase land or otherwise obtain cession of it from the Indians, and this assumed that the Indians *owned* the land to begin with. It was not an assumption in which most Indians shared, but it was nevertheless a key point in virtually all treaties. The great majority of treaties, therefore, were fundamentally flawed from their inception.

was he (Like as Agag was hewed in pieces before the Lord) cut into four quarters, and is now hanged up as a monument of revenging Justice, his head being cut off and carried away to Plymouth, his Hands were brought to *Boston. So let all thine Enemies perish, O Lord!*

With Philip's death, the war was all but over. On September 11, Church captured Annawon, identified as Philip's "chief captain," while the aged Indian lay sleeping in camp. Before he was led off to execution, Annawon fell upon his knees before Church and, "speaking in plain *English*, said *Great Captain, you have killed Philip, and conquered his Country, for I believe, that I & my company are the last that War against the* English, *so suppose the War is ended by your means; and therefore these things belong unto you*," whereupon the old Indian presented the Englishman with Philip's most prized possessions.

Except for sporadic skirmishes during August, September, and October, the war ended with this symbolic gesture.

The war was a catastrophe for New England's colonists and Indians alike. During the years 1675–76, half of the region's towns were badly damaged and 12 were completely destroyed, requiring the work of a generation to rebuild them. The fragile colonial economy suffered devastating blows, because of the direct cost of the war—some £100,000—and because of the disruption of the fur trade with the Indians and the virtual cessation of coastal fishing and the West Indies trade. The war siphoned off the manpower customarily devoted to these industries. Indeed, many workers never returned to their peacetime trades—one in 16 men of military age was killed. Many others—men, women, children—were also killed, captured, or starved. In proportion to New England's population of 30,000, King Philip's War was the costliest in American history, with at least 600 violent deaths and untold additional deaths from other causes related to the war. As for the Indians, at least 3,000 perished—Wampanoags, Narragansetts, and Nipmucks, mostly—and many of those who did not die were deported and sold into slavery.

As far as colonial chroniclers were concerned, the cause of this terrible conflict was simple: King Philip, haughty chief of the Wampanoag Indians, betrayed the traditional friendship between his tribe and the English by waging war against New England's settlers, hoping either to annihilate them or drive them out of the country. As with most white-Indian conflicts, however, the causes of King Philip's War were more complex.

Colonial land hunger and a rising population, combined with a racism sanctioned by Puritan religious doctrine that regarded the Indians as a benighted people ripe for spiritual conquest, met head on with Philip's growing resentment of English insults to his sovereignty and encroachments on his power. Indians were important to the colonists not only as a kind of spiritual crop waiting to be harvested, but as sources of trade, especially in fur. They were also the means by which the New England colonies might each legitimate a stake in America. New England colonial charters, granted as they were to religious and political dissidents, were chronically shaky. With the restoration of Charles II to the British throne, the Massachusetts charter, which had been secure under the Puritan reign of Cromwell, and that of Rhode Island, which had been granted by Cromwell's government, were most directly threatened.

To bolster their sovereignty in the New World, the colonies sought to associate themselves with those whose possession of the soil was acknowledged as a primitive right: the Indians. Colonial governments sought to purchase land from them and, even more important, to establish a protectorate over them. This led to complicated and strained relations between Indians and whites.

Such tribes as the Narragansetts and the Wampanoags were further alienated from the colonists by cultural differences in three areas: land ownership, political authority, and religion. Regarding land, the Indians, though they often fought among themselves for control of a particular hunting ground, did not share the English concept of ownership and private property. Complicating white-Indian relations yet further was a fundamental difference between the English and Indian concepts of government. Despite a recent civil war, Englishmen (like all Europeans) invested certain acknowledged individuals with the authority to govern and to enter into agreements with the sovereigns of other nations. The colonists projected this model of government onto the Indian groups with whom they dealt. Chiefs or sachems were usually influential or charismatic individuals who enjoyed no absolute political authority. Nevertheless, the English treated with them as they would with sovereigns of any European nation. To the Indians, therefore, white treaties often held little meaning, let alone authority.

Finally, the high-handed zeal of English missionaries threatened every aspect of Indian cultural identity. Converting to Christianity required not only submission to a particular doctrine, but removal from one's home village to a so-called Praying Town, where Indians were to live in English-style houses, wear English clothes, and speak the English language. Worse, Christianity (as it was preached to the Indians) abrogated the traditional bonds of family and kinship in absolute fealty to Christ. Culturally, politically, and spiritually, the stage was set for conflict in New England.

---

## PRAYING INDIANS AND PRAYING TOWNS

French as well as English colonial ventures in the seventeenth century had the conversion of the Indians to Christianity as one of their declared objects. At first, missionaries simply inculcated their beliefs into as many Indians as would listen, and then the missionaries sent these Indians back to their villages. Frequently, the result was not the spread of Christianity, but the "backsliding" of the converts, who returned to the ways of their people. To combat this trend, both the French and the English created "praying towns," special settlements for converted ("praying") Indians, who were segregated from the so-called heathen Indians. The missionary John Eliot established the first praying town in Natick, Massachusetts, in 1651, and by 1675, there were 14 such towns in Massachusetts and Connecticut.

In English practice, praying Indians were expected to sever all tribal and even familial ties, to adopt not only the English religion, but English manners, clothing, and names as well. Eliot scolded his converts for excessive lenience in disciplining their children and for overly passionate displays in mourning dead relatives. One of the praying Indians replied to Eliot: "Christ saith, he that loveth father, or mother, or wife, or Child better than me, is not worthy of me. Christ saith, I must correct my Child, if I should refuse to do that, I should not love Christ. . . . I am greatly grieved about these things, and now God tryeth me whether I love Christ or my Child best." The French tended to be more tolerant of Indian culture, even among the "converted."

To be a praying Indian meant great emotional and cultural sacrifice. As far as the English and French were concerned, the reward—a hope of salvation in Jesus Christ—was more than sufficient recompense. But there were worldly enticements to conversion as well. Praying Indians enjoyed more favorable status as trading partners, and they were entitled to protection against enemies. It is also true that many Indians coveted the effects of European technology—firearms, steel blades, convenient cooking utensils, warm and comfortable housing—and actively sought an education in white ways, hoping that, by acquiring the white man's knowledge, they would take on some of his power.

Obviously, praying Indians were confronted with many dilemmas of divided loyalty. For example, John Sassamon (or Saussamon), an Indian schoolmaster from Natick, reportedly served colonial authorities as a spy on King Philip. His murder helped touch off King Philip's War. More far-reaching questions of loyalty arose in connection with the French praying towns, particularly the two Jesuit mission villages near Montreal, which, during the late seventeenth century, harbored about 400 Indians, most of them Iroquois, and most of the Iroquois Mohawks. These French Mohawks—also called Caughnawaga Mohawks or simply Caughnawagas—were allied with France, putting them at odds with the bulk of the Mohawk tribe, which pledged allegiance to the English. The Caughnawagas and their English-allied Mohawk brethren tried to minimize combat between themselves, but they were frequently forced into confrontation.

In the English colonies as well as in the French, the greatest effect of the praying Indians and the praying towns was a weakening of what little political and strategic unity the Indians could muster. The English exploited this threat of disunity by attempting, with sporadic success, to persuade the Iroquois to evict the French Jesuits—and the French generally—from their midst, lest praying towns proliferate and the Iroquois Confederacy disintegrate.

---

A Frenchman who visited the English colonies a decade after the war reported "Nothing to fear from the Savages, for they are few in Number. The last Wars they had with the English . . . have reduced them to a small Number, and consequently they are incapable of defending themselves." That view was shortsighted. True, many of the war's Indian survivors were left demoralized and abject in their submission to the English. Others, however, fled to Canada, New York, and the Delaware and Susquehanna valleys, where they nursed a vengeance that exploded in a long series of raids and skirmishes culminating in the French and Indian War. As Governor Andros observed of King Philip's War, "the advantages thereby were none, the disadvantages very great."

# CHAPTER 5

---□---

# TRADE AND TYRANNY
## The Dutch–Indian Wars (1626–1664)

The Spanish marched into the New World as conquerors and treated the Indians as a conquered people. The English first arrived in smaller, more tentative numbers than the Spanish. They did not disport themselves as conquerors, but they nevertheless regarded the Indians with distrust and contempt. In contrast to the Spanish and the English attitudes toward the Indians, Dutch relations with Native Americans were characterized by ambivalence. They vacillated between belligerence and cruelty and timid defensiveness. It was an approach that also characterized their relations with other colonists. During the relatively brief Dutch tenure in the New World, they armed the Mohawks against the French and the French-allied Canadian Indians, but they did not openly use the Mohawks against their more formidable rivals, the English of New England. They laid claim to the Connecticut Valley, but submitted to dispossession of it without a fight. They displaced the Swedes along the Delaware River, but folded before the English in Chesapeake country.

Henry Hudson, sailing for the Dutch, discovered the river that bears his name in 1609. Five years later, Fort Nassau, a trading post, was built on Castle Island near present-day Albany. Here the Dutch were surrounded by 1,600 Mahican Indians, with whom they struck a trade agreement in 1618. The Indians at first declined to sell land to the Dutch, but they agreed to permit traders and trappers to live among them. That agreement illustrated another difference between the Dutch in the New World and the Spanish and the English. The latter came to conquer or, at least, settle; they required and demanded land. The Dutch came primarily as traders and, at first, had little interest in acquiring territory.

Fort Nassau was flooded out and abandoned in 1617, but the Dutch West Indies Company, formed in 1621, built Fort Orange on the site of Albany in 1624. The

first Indian crisis came two years later, in 1626, when the Mohawks launched a war against the Mahicans. The Dutch sent a small force under Daniel van Krieckebeeck to help their trading partners but were soundly defeated, with the loss of three men in addition to van Krieckebeeck. At this, the Dutch withdrew and concluded a truce with the Mohawks.

In 1628, Mohawk warriors once again trounced the Mahicans, but they did not press their advantage. Apparently the Mohawks were not interested in the annihilation of the Mahicans; rather, they wanted to take control of the much-desired trade with the Dutch. After 1628, however, the two tribes seemed to have reached an accord, since both conducted a profitable trade with the Fort Orangers. Not that the Dutch treated the Indians cordially. There were frequent bouts of cruelty and abuse as when, in 1660, Mohawk chiefs petitioned Fort Orange magistrates "to forbid the Dutch to molest the Indians as heretofore by kicking, beating, and assaulting them, in order that we may not break the old friendship which we have enjoyed for more than thirty years." Nevertheless, while New England was in a chronic state of war with the Indians, the Dutch were enjoying profitable, if not wholly pacific, trade.

The value the Dutch put on this trade is evident from their response to a 1632 incident in which a band of Delaware Indians massacred 32 settlers at Swaanendael on the western shore of Delaware Bay. Instead of launching a punitive expedition against the assailants, as the English would have done, the Dutch opened negotiations, appeasing the Delawares with gifts in order to maintain trade relations.

More serious rifts in Dutch-Indian relations began to appear as increasing numbers of colonists became farmers in addition to traders, a trend that resulted from the depletion of beaver (the Indians' principal trade commodity) along the coast. By 1639, when Willem Kieft replaced Wouter Van Twiller as governor of New Netherland, acquisition of territory had become more important to the Dutch than maintaining friendly relations with the Indians. Kieft imposed heavy taxes on the Algonquian tribes in the vicinity of Manhattan and Long Island, claiming that payment of such tribute was necessary to finance the cost of defending them against "hostiles."

In 1641, when Dutch livestock destroyed Raritan Indian cornfields on Staten Island, provoking retaliation, Kieft offered a bounty on Raritan scalps. The next year, a wheelwright named Claes Rademaker was murdered by an Indian in revenge for the killing of the Indian's uncle, who some settlers had assaulted for his beaver pelts. In response, Kieft marched a small army through the villages near New Amsterdam to intimidate the Indians. On its first foray, the army was anything but intimidating; marching at night, it got lost. When the governor consulted the patroons (landowners with manorial rights) on the advisability of war, they answered: "We were not prepared to carry on a war with the Indians until we had more people, like the English."

Nevertheless, Kieft plunged brutally ahead. In February 1643, the Mohawks—who were still active trading partners of the Dutch—traveled down the Hudson to extort tribute money from the Wappinger Indians. The terrified Wappingers fled to Pavonia (present-day environs of Jersey City, New Jersey) and New Amsterdam, where they appealed to Kieft for protection. The governor not only refused, but turned the Mohawks loose upon them. Mohawk warriors killed 70 Wappingers and enslaved others. Then, according to the recollections of David Pietersz. de Vries, a Dutch "artillery master," on

The 24th of February, sitting at table with the governor [Kieft], he began to state his intentions, that he had a mind to *wipe the mouths* of the Indians; that he had been dining at the house of Jan Caesz. Damen, where Maryn Adriaensz, Jan Caesz. Damen, together with Jacob Planck, had presented a petition to him to begin this work. . . . I answered him that there was not sufficient reason to undertake it; . . . he well knew that on account of trifling with the Indians we had lost our colony in the South river at Swanendael, in the Hoere-kil, with thirty-two men, who were murdered in the year 1630; and that in the year 1640, the cause of my people being murdered on Staten Island was a difficulty which he had with the Raritanese Indians, where his soldiers had for some trifling thing killed some Indians, and brought the brother of the chief a prisoner to the *Manates*.

But it appeared that my speaking was of no avail. He had, with his co-murderers, determined to commit the murder, deeming it a Roman deed, and to do it without warning the inhabitants of the open lands, that each one might take care of himself against the retaliation of the Indians, for he could not kill all the Indians.

Stop this work [deVries entreated]; you wish to break the mouths of the Indians, but you will also murder our own nation.

During the night of February 25–26, Kieft sent in Dutch soldiers to finish off the refugees, mostly women and children, whom the Mohawks had been reluctant to harm. The night of mayhem in Pavonia would become infamous as the Slaughter of the Innocents. The troops returned to New Amsterdam bearing the severed heads of 80 Indians, which soldiers and citizens used as footballs on the streets of New Amsterdam. Thirty prisoners also taken were tortured to death for the public amusement.

I remained that night at the governor's, sitting up [de Vries recalled]. I went and sat in the kitchen, when, about midnight, I heard a great shrieking, and I ran to the ramparts of the fort,

*The center of Dutch colonial activity in America was the small settlement of New Amsterdam, at the southern tip of Manhattan Island. Dutch relations with the Indians were ambivalent and inconsistent at best, and extraordinarily brutal at worst. During February 1643, Governor Willem Kieft directed a combined Mohawk-Dutch massacre of Wappinger Indians who had fled to Pavonia (vicinity of present-day Jersey City, New Jersey). Following this so-called Slaughter of the Innocents, Dutch troops returned to New Amsterdam bearing the severed heads of 80 Indians, which soldiers and citizens used as footballs on the town's streets. (Library of Congress.)*

and looked over to Pavonia. Saw nothing but firing, and heard the shrieks of the Indians murdered in their sleep. . . . When it was day the soldiers returned to the fort, having massacred or murdered eighty Indians, and considering that they had done a deed of Roman valour, in murdering so many in their sleep; where infants were torn from their mother's breasts, and hacked to pieces in the presence of the parents, and the pieces thrown into the fire and in the water, and other sucklings were bound to small boards, and then cut, stuck, and pierced, and miserably massacred in a manner to move a heart of stone. Some were thrown into the river, and when the fathers and mothers endeavoured to save them, the soldiers would not let them come on land, but made both parents and children drown,—children from five to six years of age, and also some decrepit persons. Many fled from this scene, and concealed themselves in the neighbouring sedge, and when it was morning, came out to beg a piece of bread, and to be permitted to warm themselves; but they were murdered in cold blood and tossed into the water. Some came by our lands in the country with their hands, some with their legs cut off, and some holding their entrails in their arms. . . . At another place, on the same night at Corler's Hook on Corler's plantation, forty Indians were in the same manner attacked in their sleep.

Not surprisingly, New Amsterdam and its outlying dependencies were now suddenly plunged into war with 11 Indian tribes. DeVries reported: "When now the Indians destroyed so many farms and men in revenge for their people, I went to Governor William Kieft, and asked him if it was not as I had said it would be, that he would only effect the spilling of Christian blood. Who would now compensate us for our losses? But he gave no answer." In March 1643, a panic-stricken Kieft parleyed with the Indians and offered them presents. "But now," de Vries observed, "it might fall out that the infants upon the small boards would be remembered. They then went away grumbling with their presents. . . . A chief of the Indians came to me, and told me that he was very sad. I asked him wherefore. He said that there were many young Indian youths, who were constantly wishing for a war against us, as one had lost his father, another his mother, a third his uncle."

The young men prevailed. On October 1, 1643, nine Indians came to a fort at Pavonia, where three or four soldiers were stationed to protect a local farmer. The Indians pretended to be friendly, then killed the soldiers and the farmer, sparing only the farmer's stepson, whom they took captive to Tappan. The Indians put the farmer's house—together with all the houses of Pavonia—to the torch. Soon, Indian tribes from the Delaware Bay to the Connecticut River were on the warpath. Terrorized settlers throughout New Netherland fled to New Amsterdam, which lay under siege for more than a year. Only

the Mohawks, still bound in a profitable trading alliance with the Dutch, remained aloof from the war. The Dutch hired Captain John Underhill, who had distinguished himself in New England's Pequot War, to lead Dutch and English soldiers in a sweep through the countryside, attacking Indians and burning their villages. By 1644, no longer able to endure the war of attrition directed against them, the Indian tribes lifted their seige of New Amsterdam and agreed to a peace.

Relative calm prevailed for a decade, until the so-called Peach War of 1655 begun when a Dutch farmer killed a Delaware Indian woman for picking peaches in his orchard. In retaliation, her family ambushed and killed the farmer. As word of the incident spread, other Delaware bands struck. Several settlers were killed at New Amsterdam, and 150 were taken captive. Governor Peter Stuyvesant called out the militia, which freed most of the captives and destroyed some of the Indians' villages.

After this, Dutch-Indian violence sporadically continued, debilitating Indians as well as settlers. In October 1658, the Dutch sought diplomatic aid from the Susquehannocks, who agreed to intervene in the "Esopus War"—an ongoing battle between the Dutch and the Esopus Indians, a stubborn Hudson River tribe. The Dutch had proven themselves no friend to Indians, but trade with them had become so important in Indian life that the Susquehannocks, in order to gain favored status with the Dutch, united with their bitter enemies, the Mohawks, to pressure the Esopus into concluding a peace.

Despite these diplomatic efforts, the Esopus, aided by Minisinks, moved up the Hudson to attack Wiltwyck (present-day Kingston, New York) and its environs in September 1659. During the struggle, Stuyvesant called for a parley, whereupon a delegation of Esopus chiefs entered Wiltwyck for a peace conference. These Indians were killed by Dutch soldiers as they slept after the first day of talks. By way of reprisal, the Indians took eight Dutch soldiers captive and burned them alive. Fitful warfare swirled about Wiltwyck until 1660, when Stuyvesant instituted a new tactic: rounding up Indian children as hostages to extort "good behavior" from the various Delaware tribes. The weaker tribes along the Hudson offered little resistance and yielded up their children. The Esopus, however, refused and, recalling what had happened at the last parley, refused even to negotiate. Stuyvesant responded by selling his Esopus prisoners into West Indian slavery.

It was 1664 before the Esopus finally yielded to the Dutch, and this was only after Stuyvesant called in his Mohawk allies to terrorize them. However, 1664 was also the last year of Dutch rule in New Netherland. On October 4, the English officially took possession of the province, which they renamed New York.

# CHAPTER 6

# IROQUOIAN IMPERIALISM
## The Beaver Wars (1638–1684)

The Beaver Wars—sometimes called the Iroquoian Beaver Wars—were a series of conflicts fought by member tribes of the Iroquois Confederation, the so-called Five Nations, against the Hurons, Tobaccos (also called the Petuns or Tionantati), Neutrals, Eries (or Cat People), Ottawas, Mahicans, Illinois, Miamis, Susquehannocks, Nipissings, Potawatomis, Delawares, and Sokokis during 1638–84. Even though whites did not participate in them as combatants, the Beaver Wars were an important passage in the complex development of white-Indian alliances and enmities and the means through which the Iroquois Confederation consolidated the power and influence that would make it a pivotal force in two great conflicts, the French and Indian War and the American Revolution.

The Iroquois Confederation is one of the few examples of an effective intertribal political confederation. Consisting of the Mohawk, Oneida, Onondaga, Cayuga, and Seneca tribes, whose territory extended from the Hudson Valley in the east to the shores of Lake Ontario in the west (much of present-day western New York State), the Confederation was founded some time between 1400 and 1600 (probably circa 1560–70) by the semilengendary Huron mystic Deganawida and his Mohawk disciple Hiawatha (no relation to the Longfellow character). The Five Nations became known as the Six Nations when the Tuscaroras, having suffered defeat in the Tuscarora War of 1712–13, left North Carolina, migrated northward, were adopted by the Oneidas, and, in 1722, joined the Iroquois Confederation.

The Iroquois Confederation figuratively occupied a "Longhouse," stretching from the Hudson Valley to Lake Ontario; the Mohawks were the Keepers of the Eastern Door, the Seneca were the Keepers of the Western Door. The body's guiding principles were codified in "The Great Law of Peace of the Longhouse People." Chief among the Confederation's tenets was a policy of conquest: "When the council of the League has for its object the establishment of the Great Peace among the people of an outside nation and that nation refuses to accept the Great Peace, then by such refusal they bring a declaration of war upon themselves from the Five Nations. Then shall the Five Nations seek to establish the Great Peace by a conquest of the rebellious nation." The early New York historian Cadwallader Colden was among those who observed that the Iroquois frequently adopted the tribes they vanquished.

The Confederation ethic of conquest was not born entirely of an abstract vision of destiny but, in large measure, was the result of competition for trade with European colonists. In the early seventeenth century, the Iroquois tribes aligned themselves with the Dutch as trading partners. When the English displaced the Dutch in New Amsterdam in 1664, they inherited the alliance. To the west, the Hurons (and several other western tribes) cleaved to the French. As the century progressed, the western hunting grounds remained rich in beaver—the Indians' chief article of trade—and Huron–French commerce flourished. The peltries of the eastern hunting grounds, however, were diminishing during this period, and the Iroquois trade with the Dutch and, later, the English suffered as a consequence.

Throughout the 1640s and as early as 1638, Huron and Iroquois war parties came to blows in raiding and guerrilla actions ranging from apparently random scalpings to the invasion and burning of villages.

An episode in 1638 illustrates the ferocious spirit of these peoples. A war party of 100 Iroquois met some 300 Hurons and Algonquins. It is a commonplace observation on Indian warfare that one party rarely attacks

*This French engraving depicts a "Sauvage Iroquois." While they were known as fierce warriors, the Iroquois were hardly simple savages. The original Iroquois Confederation consisted of five tribes: the Mohawks, Oneida, Onondaga, Cayuga, and Seneca, whose territory extended from the Hudson Valley in the east to the shores of Lake Ontario in the west. Founded some time between 1400 and 1600 (probably ca. 1560–70), the confederation was one of a few instances of effective intertribal alliance. Through much of the seventeenth and eighteenth centuries, the Iroquois were among the most powerful military and political forces—Indian or European—in America. (Library of Congress.)*

chief, unflinching, was roasted on a scaffold. When the Hurons thought him nearly dead, one of his tormentors scalped him—whereupon Ononkwaya leaped up, grabbed some burning brands, and drove the crowd back from the scaffold. They threw sticks, stones, and live coals at him until he finally stumbled. The Hurons seized him and threw him *into* the fire. But, again, he leaped out, a blazing brand in each hand, and ran toward the town, as if to set it ablaze. His captors tripped him with a long pole and then fell upon him, cutting off his hands and feet. Again, they threw him into the fire, and again he rolled off the pyre, crawling toward the crowd on elbows and knees. His gaze was fearsome enough that, even in his hopeless state, the crowd recoiled—only to rush forward upon him and, at last, cut off his head.

The fortified and palisaded Huron trading town of Saint Joseph was the focus of an attack in the summer of 1645. The Iroquois approached in force, and all through the night, the Huron defenders sang war songs intended to discourage the attackers. Two Iroquois crept up to the palisade and lay in wait until just before dawn. By that time, the Hurons, having vigilantly sung all night, had fallen asleep. One of the Iroquois climbed to the top of a Huron watchtower, sunk his hatchet into the slumbering head of one of the watchmen and tossed the other man down to his colleague, who scalped him. No general attack followed this two-man sortie. Twenty days later, three Hurons entered the Senecas' principal town. There was no night guard, but the doors to the houses were tied fast. The infiltrators cut a hole in the bark wall of one dwelling, tomahawked three Senecas, and slipped away.

By the spring of 1647, Huron harassment must have intensified, for on April 13, the Hurons dispatched an embassy on a two-month journey to the Susquehannocks, who lived along the Susquehanna River in New York, Pennsylvania, and Maryland. "We come from the Land of Souls," the ambassadors declared, "where all is gloom, dismay, and desolation. Our fields are covered with blood; our houses are filled only with the dead; and we ourselves have but life enough to beg our friends to take pity on a people who are drawing near their end." The Susquehannocks attempted to intervene diplomatically by negotiating treaties and establishing a fur-trading cartel (meant to counter Mohawk commercial dominance) with the central Iroquois tribes and the Senecas. An involved series of abortive embassies and negotiations ensued among the Susquehannocks, Hurons, Oneidas, Cayugas, Onondagas, and Senecas.

As the Susquehannock ambassadors discovered, however, the tribes of the Iroquois Confederation were hardly acting in concert. The Mohawks were by far the most aggressive (their tradition of warriorhood was perhaps

another unless the attacker enjoys substantial superiority of numbers. Nevertheless, Ononkwaya, an Oneida chief, refused to back down. "Look!" he is reported to have said, "the sky is clear; the Sun beholds us. If there were clouds to hide our shame from his sight, we might fly; but, as it is, we must fight while we can." All but four or five of the Iroquois warriors were killed or captured— and consigned to death by torture. The execution of Ononkwaya was related by a Jesuit missionary. The

## TRIBAL ADOPTION

In his *History of the Five Indian Nations* (1727), Cadwallader Colden observed of the Iroquois that "it has been [their] constant Maxim . . . to save the Children and Young Men of the People they Conquer, to adopt them into their own Nation, and to educate them as their own Children, without Distinction; These young People soon forget their own Country and Nation; and by this Policy the Five Nations make up the Losses which their Nation suffers by the People they lose in War." The brilliant modern scholar of the Iroquois Confederation, Francis Jennings, has gone so far as to identify an Iroquois "melting pot." By 1668, he points out, two-thirds of the Oneida village were fully assimilated Algonquins and Hurons. Five hundred to a thousand Hurons joined the Senecas in 1651, and another 400 subsequently joined the Mohawks and Onondagas. A Jesuit missionary, Father Paul LeJeune, reported in 1657 that at Onondaga, the "capital" city of the confederacy, there were Indians of seven different nations. Among the Senecas, LeJeune observed, no fewer than eleven nations were represented. Apparently, the assimilated individuals enjoyed full privileges of membership in the Iroquois Confederation and suffered none of the prejudices one would think might be the lot of a conquered people. Adoption was practiced by many tribes, but not on the scale and with the consistency evident among the Iroquois, who did not simply adopt individuals, but entire tribes.

strongest and their hunting grounds were the most seriously depleted); the central tribes had begun to resent the Mohawks' control over access to the Dutch trading post at Fort Orange; and the westernmost Senecas, still amply supplied with peltry and having no quarrel with the Hurons, were disinclined to war. It was the Europeans who forced the crisis. The directors of the Dutch West India Company, seeing a chance to usurp trade from the French, decided on April 7, 1648, to reverse their policy against trading arms to the Indians and sold the Mohawks about 400 rifles. In effect, the Dutch were arming their Indian allies against the French-backed Hurons.

Alliances between the French and Indians were based on trade and the work of Jesuit missionaries, who were based throughout Huronia. While the Indians derived important benefits from the missionaries, they also created dependence and dissension and brought disease, particularly devastating epidemics of smallpox. (See box on page 16) Indeed, during the 40 years of sporadic warfare between the Iroquois and Hurons, some Hurons were so embittered against the "Black Robes" that they willingly sided with the Iroquois to take revenge against the French.

One of the most important of the Jesuit Huron missions was Saint Joseph, in the Indian town of Teanaustayaé at the southeastern frontier of Huron country. Fortified with wooden palisades, it sheltered some 2,000 Indians and Father Antoine Daniel's mission. On July 4, 1648, after Daniel had just concluded mass, the alarm was sounded: "The Iroquois! The Iroquois!" Father Daniel seized the opportunity for saving souls. No one,

it seemed, was reluctant to receive baptism now. Hurons crowded around him, and, immersing his handkerchief in a bowl of water, he shook it out over them, baptizing the throng by aspersion. "Brothers," he declared, "today we shall be in Heaven."

Daniel urged his flock to make their escape as best they could, pledging himself to remain behind in order to rescue—from unsanctified death—whomever he could. He confronted the onrushing Iroquois attackers, who shot him with arrows and with musket balls from their Dutch weapons, hacking his body apart before throwing it on the flames that were even then consuming the town. The Iroquois marched off with about 700 prisoners and attacked a neighboring village.

At nine o'clock on the morning of March 16, 1649, priests at the Jesuit headquarters of Sainte Marie saw smoke to the southeast. It was, they knew, the Iroquois—a combination of Seneca and Mohawks—burning the outermost Huron settlements. They had descended first on Saint Ignace, a town surrounded on three sides by a deep ravine and further defended on all four sides by 16-foot-high palisades erected under the supervision of the missionaries. The town sheltered chiefly women, children, and old men, who were trapped by their own defensive measures when as many as 1,000 warriors burst through the palisade on the side without a ravine. Within a few minutes, the raid was over, and the attackers moved on to Saint Louis, about three miles distant.

Three Hurons who escaped from Saint Ignace warned the inhabitants of Saint Louis, about 700 in number. All fled, except 80 warriors and those too old, sick, or infirm to move. The town's two Jesuit missionaries, Fathers Brébeuf and Lalemant, remained behind to offer encouragement and baptism. Twice the small band of Huron warriors managed to turn back the Iroquois onslaught, killing about 30, but large numbers of warriors swarmed about the foot of the palisades, hacking through them with hatchets. The surviving Huron defenders—and the two Jesuits—were captured and the town set ablaze. The prisoners were sent back to Saint Ignace, where the Jesuits in particular were tortured and beaten.

The Iroquois divided themselves and launched further raids on smaller neighboring villages. Before them, the Huron fugitives fled toward the Tobacco (Tionantati) Indians west of Lake Ontario. On March 17, the Iroquois unleashed an assault on Sainte Marie, palisaded and defended by 40 well-armed Frenchmen augmented by perhaps 300 Huron warriors. A detachment of these warriors ambushed the Iroquois advance guard outside of Sainte Marie but were soundly defeated. The main body of Hurons came to the rescue, however, routing the Iroquois, who retreated to Saint Ignace before joining the main body of invaders at Saint Louis for a renewed assault against Sainte Marie. Cut in half by death and casualty, the defending Hurons fought fiercely, killing perhaps 100 of the Iroquois at a cost of all but 20 of themselves. Yet, the Iroquois were too badly shaken by the resistance they had met to capitalize on their victory. By the morning after the assault on Sainte Marie, they were in retreat (word was that they feared a Huron counterattack) though as a parting gesture, they bound a number of their prisoners—men, women, and children—to stakes at Saint Ignace and put the town to the torch.

A force of about 700 Hurons was gathering at Saint Michel, a short distance from Saint Joseph. They pursued the retreating Iroquois but, with no heart left for a fight, failed to engage them. Although the Iroquois had not taken Sainte Marie, the destruction they had wrought upon the other Huron towns was sufficient to send the survivors into flight. By the end of March, 15 Huron towns were abandoned. Some refugees fled to the Tobaccos, some to the Neutrals, who lived on the northern shores of Lake Erie. Others voluntarily sought adoption into the Iroquois tribes. A small body took refuge with missionaries on Isle Saint Joseph off the shore of Lake Huron, but essentially, the Huron nation had been extinguished. As for the French Jesuit missions, without Indians to convert, many were abandoned. As the Dutch had hoped, the French had suffered defeat alongside their Huron allies.

In November and December 1649, Mohawks and Senecas moved against the Tobaccos. When word of an impending attack came to the mission town of Saint Jean, the warriors there girded for combat with an enemy who,

day after day, failed to appear. At length, the Tobacco warriors decided to take the offensive and ventured out in search of the Iroquois.

The attackers were, indeed, nearby; but they were approaching Saint Jean from an unexpected direction and with a degree of caution that belies the myth of Iroquois—particularly Mohawk—invincibility. They happened to capture a straggling Tobacco and his squaw, who revealed that Saint Jean was at present without its warriors. At two o'clock on the afternoon of December 17, 1649, the Iroquois descended on the defenseless town. Father Charles Garnier, one of the missionaries there, hastily performed the requisite baptisms and absolutions, until he was cut down by three musket balls and brained with a hatchet. The surviving Tobaccos emigrated westward. During the opening years of the eighteenth century, they mingled with surviving Hurons to become the Wyandots of Detroit and Sandusky, Ohio country.

By the early spring of 1650, the party of Hurons who had escaped to Isle Saint Joseph was starving. In March, with the lake still frozen, they began to abandon the island, making their way to shore across the softening ice. Some fell through and drowned; others made it and survived by fishing. Their salvation was short-lived, however, as Iroquois bands fell upon them, pursuing small parties of refugees with a cruel persistence that stunned Jesuit observers. "My pen," wrote Father Superior Ragueneau, "has no ink black enough to describe the fury of the Iroquois. . . . Our starving Hurons were driven out of a town which had become an abode of horror. . . . These poor people fell into ambuscades of our Iroquois enemies. Some were killed on the spot; some were dragged into captivity; women and children were burned. . . . Go where they would, they met with slaughter on all sides. Famine pursued them, or they encountered an enemy more cruel than cruelty itself."

In late autumn of 1650, the Iroquois launched a furious campaign against the Neutral Nation, who, as their name (bestowed by the French) implies, had attempted to remain unallied in the ongoing combat between Iroquois and Hurons. In the initial attack, a large town of some 3,000 to 4,000 people was destroyed. In the spring of 1651, a second town was attacked with such savagery that the Neutrals abandoned all of their settlements and dispersed. It is likely that the Senecas, who made up a large part of the attacking force, adopted significant numbers of the defeated tribe—perhaps virtually all of the survivors. Whatever the details of their fate, the Neutrals had numbered about 10,000 at the beginning of the seventeenth century; in 1653, a mere 800 could be accounted for.

Between 1651 and 1653, the Iroquois habitually harassed the French and their Indian allies before four of the five nations, apparently in an effort to circumvent Mohawk domination of the Dutch trade, concluded a series of peace treaties at Montreal late in 1653. However, the following May an Onondagan delegate to the governor in Montreal declared: "Our young men will no more fight the French; but they are too warlike to stay at home, and this summer we shall invade the country of the Eries. The earth trembles and quakes in that quarter; but here all remains calm."

War was provoked when an Erie, who was a member of a treaty delegation visiting a Seneca town, quarreled with a Seneca and killed him. Enraged, the Senecas killed all 30 members of the delegation, touching off a series of reprisals and counterreprisals, until the Eries captured an Onondaga chief. They were on the verge of burning him, when he convinced them that to do so would provoke a war with all of the Iroquois. Following tribal custom, the Eries offered the Onondaga to the sister of a member of the slain delegation, expecting that she would adopt him as a surrogate for her dead brother. Instead, she bitterly rejected him, and he was put to death after all. This motive for war dovetailed neatly with the Iroquois grand strategy of conquest and usurpation of hunting and trapping grounds. The war was brief and costly to both sides, but like the Hurons, Tobaccos, and Neutrals before them, the Eries emerged from it no longer a nation.

The fall of the Eries in 1656 consolidated the power of the Five Nations, making them dominant from the Ottawa River in the north and the Cumberland in the south, into Maine in the east, and as far as Lake Ontario in the west. The Beaver Wars, however, did not end with the destruction of the Eries. During 1651–52, the Mohawks attacked a people known as the Atrakwaeronons. Information in Jesuit "relations"—firsthand missionary accounts—suggests that this may have been another name for the Susquehannocks; it is also possible that it referred to a tribe closely allied with the Susquehannocks. In either case, the Mohawk raid yielded 500 to 600 captives and brought the Susquehannocks into a quarter-century of sporadic warfare with the Five Nations.

In the spring of 1663, 800 Senecas, Cayugas, and Onondagas moved against the Susquehannocks' principal fort, only to find that the colonists of New Sweden had armed the Susquehannocks, whose well-palisaded stockade was defended not only by the Susquehannocks, but by Delaware Indian allies. The siege was lifted after a week. Similarly, Iroquois forces failed to displace the Mahicans of the upper Hudson Valley and the Sokokis of the upper Connecticut Valley. Like the Susquehannocks, these tribes had European guns and, unlike the Hurons, Tobaccos, Neutrals, and Eries, had not suffered the divisions and diseases brought by missionaries.

The Iroquois tribes were also unsuccessful in establishing hunting and trade monopolies in the west. In 1680, the Iroquois launched a major war against the French-allied Indian bands living along the Illinois and Mississippi rivers. After some initial victories, the Iroquois were defeated. They fared no better against the Miamis (in the present states of Wisconsin and Michigan) a few years later, during the final phase of the Beaver Wars. Thirty years of warfare established the Indian-Eurpoean alliances that would be active well into the eighteenth century and that would be crucial during the French and Indian War. For a time, 1649–55, the Beaver Wars consolidated the Iroquois' power, but ultimately, the wars gained much for the Europeans at the expense of the Indians, who were weakened by decades of ruinous combat.

## CHAPTER 7

# CLIENTS, ALLIES, ENEMIES, AND A DEMOGOGUE
## The Indian War of 1675–1676

The colony of Maryland declared war on the Susquehannocks on September 13, 1642. Its motives are obscure; perhaps it was to halt the incursion of Susquehannocks into territory occupied by Maryland's so-called client—that is, semi-dependent—Indians, the Piscataways (also called Conoys), Patuxents, and Yoamacoes. Whatever the cause, militiamen did not mobilize until some time between July 1643 and June 1644. The first campaign seems hardly to have involved any battles, as the Susquehannocks simply fled from the militia's guns. In a second confrontation, however, the colonists of Maryland's trading rival, New Sweden, aided the Indians, who prevailed against Maryland forces, capturing 15 prisoners, two of whom were tortured to death. Although there is little record of this Susquehannock victory, it must have been something of a rout, since the Marylanders fled the field in such haste that they abandoned arms, including two "field pieces"—precious artillery hard to come by in the colonies.

As is often the case with Indian-colonial conflicts, especially those involving alliances between Indians and "Christian" colonies fighting against each other, the records are virtually nonexistent. However, a relatively inactive state of war apparently continued from 1643 or 1644 to 1652, when the Susquehannocks, deeply embroiled in the Beaver Wars with the Five Nations, decided to make peace on the Maryland front and negotiated a treaty. Within ten years, the Maryland Assembly was calling the Susquehannocks a "Bullwarke and Security of the Northern parts of the Province" as the colony enlisted their aid in fighting the Five Nations.

The conflict between Maryland and the Iroquois was touched off in 1660, when a party of Oneidas killed five Pisicataway Indians "for being friends" with Maryland and the Susquehannocks. Maryland, either purposely or through ignorance, confounded the Oneidas with the entire Iroquois League and declared war on the Five Nations. As the Five Nations were closely allied with Maryland's trading rivals, the Dutch, it is doubtful that war was declared solely to defend the rights of the colony's "client" Piscataway tribe. Maryland wanted nothing so badly as to evict the Dutch from the Delaware Valley. For their part, the Susquehannocks wanted all the help they could get in prosecuting the ongoing Beaver Wars against the Iroquois.

Given the colonies' ever-increasing population and the growing hunger for land, such cordial relations could hardly endure. Maryland needed to make an accommodation with the Iroquois and, in 1674, notwithstanding the alliance with the Susquehannocks, made a separate peace with the Senecas, who pushed the Susquehannocks south to the Potomac. All that was needed to touch off a war between Maryland and its betrayed ally was a single spark.

That came in July–August 1675, when a group of Maryland Nanticoke (also called Doeg) Indians began a dispute with a wealthy Virginia planter named Thomas Mathew, who (they claimed) had failed to pay them for some goods traded. Unable to collect, the Indians appropriated some of Mathew's hogs, whereupon a party of the planter's men killed some of the Indians and recovered the hogs. The Nanticokes took their revenge by killing three Virginians, including Mathew's herdsman, a man named Hen.

George Brent and George Mason, captains of the local militia, gathered 30 Virginians and crossed into Maryland to confront the Nanticokes. Brent's party surrounded an Indian cabin and called for a parley. When the Indians emerged, Brent seized one chief by the hair and charged him with Hen's murder. The chief broke free, ran, and was shot. In the ensuing fight, ten more Nanticokes were killed. In the meantime, Mason's detachment had surrounded another cabin nearby. Roused by the sound of Brent's gunfire, the sleeping Indians ran out of the cabin—only to be shot down by Mason and his men. Fourteen were killed. But, Mason suddenly realized, these were not Nanticokes. "For the Lords sake Shoot no more," the captain shouted, "these are our friends the Susquehanoughs."

It was, of course, too late. Nanticokes, Susquehannocks, and allied tribes in both Maryland and Virginia began raiding. Virginia's Governor Berkeley attempted to meet the crisis rationally, instructing Colonel John Washington (great-grandfather of the president) and Major Isaac Allerton to convene the officers of the militia regiments between the Rappahannock and Potomac in order to conduct an inquisition into the raids and what had caused them. Only if the investigation yielded just cause, should the militia be called out to punish the Indians.

Washington and Allerton twisted Berkeley's commission into an order to raise a militia immediately. Seven hundred fifty Virginians were organized, and the colonel and major wrote to Maryland authorities, who sent an additional 250 cavalry and dragoons under Major Thomas Trueman. Late in September 1675, this combined force of 1,000 surrounded the place that had been appointed by the Maryland Assembly as the home village of the Susquehannocks. It was a stockaded settlement at the junction of the Piscataway Creek and the Potomac, sheltering at the time about 100 warriors and their families. Major Trueman called out the chiefs for a parley. Five emerged under a flag of truce, whereupon angry accusations were exchanged, and the chiefs were led away and killed.

Later, after the seige, both Maryland and Virginia authorities disclaimed responsibility for this act of treachery. The Marylanders blamed Colonel Washington for the order; the Virginians blamed Trueman. Trueman was impeached by the lower house of the Maryland General Assembly but was compelled only to forfeit a modest security bond. The upper house of the Assembly challenged this penalty as too light, pointing out that Trueman's "first Commands for the killing of those Indians were not obeyed and that he had some difficulty to get his men to obey him and that after [the chiefs] were put to death not at man would owne to have had a hand in it." The lower house refused to alter its decision, alleging that Trueman had been forced to the deed "to prevent a mutiny of the whole Army." As to Washington's role in the action, Berkeley conducted an investigation that exonerated him, though the governor righteously declared that "If [the chiefs] had killed my Grandfather

and Grandmother, my father and Mother and all my friends, yet if they come to treat of Peace, they ought to have gone in Peace."

For more than six weeks following the slaying of the five chiefs, the palisaded Susquehannocks withstood the militiamen's siege, until one night the warriors were able to slip out with their women and children. They managed to kill ten sleeping guards in the process, and general raiding was resumed. After 36 settlers had been killed along the Rappahannock and Potomac, the Susquehannocks sent a message to Governor Berkeley, declaring that with (approximately) ten common Englishmen killed for each of their chiefs slain, restitution had been made, and they were willing to conclude a peace. The offer was rejected, and the war continued.

Yet Governor Berkeley had no desire to anger the Indians more than necessary. He did not want Virginia to suffer the same general uprising that was currently engulfing New England in its war with King Philip. He espoused a defensive strategy, building a chain of fortifications around the settled parts of the colony. While this might have contained to some degree the wrath of the Indians, it also served to enflame the settlers of Virginia's frontier. Hard times had come to Virginia and the Chesapeake, including low tobacco prices and high taxes, which hit the dirt-poor frontiersmen especially hard. As was typical in the southern colonies, the interests of settled Tidewater and frontier Piedmont were often at odds, the westerners rightly feeling that they were poorly represented in the eastern centers of power. By 1675, Virginia had not had an election in 14 years. Now, in the midst of an Indian war, Governor Berkeley was leaving the outlying settlements to fend for themselves—or so it seemed. The beleaguered frontier was ripe for rebellion.

Into this state of affairs stepped Nathaniel Bacon. Cousin to Lord Bacon and to Lady Berkeley, "indifferent tall but slender, blackhair'd and of an ominous, pensive, melancholy Aspect . . . of a most imperious and dangerous hidden Pride of heart," Bacon had been expelled from Cambridge University for "extravagances." In 1673, he left for Virginia, armed with a bride and £1,800 from his father. He used the money to buy two plantations on the James River. Governor Berkeley welcomed his in-law, appointing him to the House of Burgesses. Despite his establishment credentials, Bacon was a fiery demagogue. While drinking with friends, he heard about a group of frontiersmen who had had enough of Berkeley's cautious policies and who were preparing to take Indian matters into their own hands. Bacon quickly became their leader.

In his first campaign, early in May 1676, Bacon and his men paid a call on the Occaneechi Indians, who lived

## COLONIAL FORTS

"Strong houses" were a fixture of frontier settlements. One settler among several in a particular area would build his cabin and fortify it with unusually thick walls and other defenses, such as a closely chinked log stockade and earthworks. The house would be well provisioned and supplied with powder and firearms. When word of an attack reached the settlement, a loosely organized militia made up of local settlers would hole up in the strong house and, so concentrated, attempt to fight off the assault. This strategy was born of some knowledge of Indian warfare and an understanding that Indians excelled at lightning raids but usually did not care to sustain a siege. With luck and nerve, even badly outnumbered settlers ensconced in a strong house stood a fair chance of surviving an Indian raid. Of course, while the inhabitants of the settlement might have escaped with their lives, frustrated Indians often burned down the homes they had abandoned.

As more settlers populated a frontier area, colonial authorities would establish and formally garrison a stockaded fort, complete with barracks, officers' quarters, storehouses, and powder magazines. A small number of artillery pieces were often provided for defense, but musket fire directed from behind the stockade was more common and usually more effective. The military forts ranged from crude, forbidding outposts to lively centers of social activity and commerce. Fort Pitt, for example, became the nexus of thriving Pittsburgh, and although soldiers stationed there were plagued by lice and other vermin (at best) and by cholera and smallpox (at worst), Simon Ecuyer, commanding during the period of Pontiac's Rebellion, authorized weekly dances and liberal rations of liquor. Although the post's garrison did not include an ordained minister, local traders were invited into the fort to attend regular sabbath services.

Military forts were sometimes laid out in a more or less rectangular pattern. In effect, they were little more than stockade-enclosed firing platforms. Other forts were built following more elaborate plans first developed and described in reniassance Europe. Fort Caroline, Florida, a French outpost, was one of these. A simplified bastion, Fort Caroline was triangular in form with each corner of the basic triangle fitted out with its own projecting stockade, which was shaped somewhat like an arrowhead. In this way, defenders had an unobstructed line of fire on all three sides of the fort, and any attacker would be caught in a crossfire between two of the fort's projecting corners. Moreover, the stockade was not a simple wall of log pilings, but a thick, sloping wooden palisade surmounted by a parapet from which musket fire could be effectively directed. The position of the fort was such that the "base" of the triangle fronted an ocean harbor, while the two "legs" were further protected by a moat filled with seawater.

Although Fort Caroline was essentially a military establishment, it also included a portion of a town within its walls. In New York, Fort Albany, as it existed during the 1680s, was another example of a fort encompassing a civilian settlement. The town sloped upward from the Hudson River to a palisaded fort. Surrounding the entire settlement, including the inner fort, was a wall of vertical stakes. Within the protected boundaries, 80 to 90 dwellings and two churches lined the town's few streets. Beyond the outer wall of stakes were groups of lodges built as living quarters for Indians, traders, and others who had come to buy and sell at what was then the principal fur-trading center of English-colonized America.

Some colonial towns were not built primarily as forts, but with the defensive function of a fort in mind nevertheless. The Pilgrims of Plymouth Bay, Massachusetts, built their first town, New Plymouth, in just this way. A visitor from New Amsterdam, Issack de Rasieres, described the town in about 1630:

New Plymouth lies on the slope of a hill stretching east towards the sea-coast, with a broad street about a cannon shot of 800 feet long, leading down the hill; with a [street] crossing in the middle. . . . The houses are constructed of hewn planks, with gardens also enclosed behind and at the sides with hewn planks, so that their houses and court-yards are arranged in very good order, with a stockade against a sudden attack; and at the ends of the streets there are three wooden gates. In the center, on the cross street, stands the governor's house, before which is a square stockade upon which four paterereos [artillery pieces] are mounted, so as to enfilade [flank and rake with gunfire] the streets. Upon the hill they have a large square house, with a flat roof, made of thick sawn plank, stayed with oak beams, upon the top of which they have six cannon.

along the Roanoke River, near the present Virginia-North Carolina state line. When Bacon announced that he was going to fight the Susquehannocks, the Occaneechis offered to do the fighting for him, as a token of their friendship with the English. Bacon accepted the offer, and when the war party returned in triumph, bearing Susquehannock prisoners and a captured stock of fur, Bacon attempted to appropriate the pelts for himself and his men. Worse, he proposed to seize as slaves a group of Manikin Indians who, working within the Susquehannock camp, had been instrumental in achieving victory. When the shocked Occaneechis refused to relinquish their fur and their allies, Bacon's men attacked them, making off with as many of the pelts as possible.

Returning to the English settlements, Bacon and his "boys" were welcomed as heroes. Berkeley, however, was furious. The governor posted him as a traitor on May 26, 1676, and had him arrested when he entered Jamestown to take his seat in the House of Burgesses. Bacon acknowledged his transgression and was pardoned by Berkeley, who released him on June 5.

While Berkeley was distracted by the actions of his in-law, Sir Edmund Andros, governor of the Duke of York's patent territories, was taking positive steps to forestall the kind of disaster that had beset New England. Captain Cantwell, of the New York militia, brought two Susquehannock sachems to Albany on June 2, where Governor Andros proposed an offer of refuge, within his colony, for the embattled tribe. (A number of the so-called North Indians of upper New England, fighting with Connecticut and Massachusetts, had agreed to a similar proposal just three days earlier.) Some accepted the offer and took refuge peacefully; others continued to raid Maryland settlers, periodically fleeing to the Iroquois—within New York—for protection. Because of this—and because the colony did not want to relinquish jurisdiction over even hostile Indians—Maryland protested Andros's policy.

As for Bacon, his atonement for treason was short-lived. He returned to Henrico County and raised an army of 500, which he led into Jamestown on June 23, demanding that the Burgesses commission him commander of all forces fighting the Indians. "God damne my Blood, I came for a commission, and a commission I will have before I goe," he declared in front of the State House. Reportedly, the 77-year-old Berkeley confronted the firebrand, bared his breast, and dared him: "Here! Shoot me, foregod, fair Mark, Shoot."

The confrontation became a standoff when Bacon's men aimed their guns at the burgesses, who were watching the proceedings from the windows of the State House. "Dam my Bloud, I'le Kill Governor Councill Assembly and all." One of the burgesses waved his handkerchief from the window: "You shall have it, You shall have it." And the burgess summarily commissioned him.

Thus legitimated, Bacon set out on another campaign—again against friendly Indians. He attacked the Pamunkeys of eastern Virginia. Their squaw-sachem, ever loyal to the British, led her people in a retreat through the Great Dragon Swamp, between the Rappahannock and Potomac. When Bacon discovered their hiding place, she told her warriors not to retaliate, but to escape as best they could. Many were killed or captured.

In the meantime, on July 29, Berkeley repealed Bacon's commission and again proclaimed him a traitor but failed to raise an army against him. Within a week of this declaration, a group of Virginia's most substantial planters took an oath to support Bacon, who continued his indiscriminate war.

At about this time, the Susquehannocks were seeking peace with Maryland. Authorities were inclined to accept, but the colony's Piscataway and Mattawoman allies insisted on fighting the rival tribe until they were fully neutralized as a threat. What had been convened in early August 1676 as a peace conference became a meeting for the purpose of renewing war against the Susquehannocks.

Back in Virginia, Bacon received word of his in-law's latest edict against him and broke off Indian fighting long enough to return to Jamestown on September 13, where he seized the wives of burgesses loyal to the governor, using them as shields while his men constructed siege lines, and forced Berkeley and his meager number of supporters out of Jamestown and into exile on the Eastern Shore. On September 18, the rebels burned Jamestown.

With Bacon's Rebellion at its apogee—he was master of all but the Eastern Shore of Virginia—New York's Andros turned his attention to Maryland, threatening to take the Susquehannocks *permanently* under his colony's jurisdiction "rather than hazard their being obliged to refuge with a grudge and rancour in their hearts, further off, if not wholly out of our reach"—that is, seek alliance with the Iroquois or, worse, the French. Hostilities cooled temporarily.

Bacon's ascendancy was short-lived. Berkeley rallied a force against him and, though the rebel spoke grandly of carving a free state out of Maryland, Virginia, and North Carolina to be allied with the Dutch or the French, Berkeley retook Jamestown, finally forcing Bacon to a stand at Yorktown. There he was cut down in October, not by Berkeley's musket balls, but by dysentery and the "Lousey Disease; so that the swarmes of Vermyn that bred in his Body he could not destroy but by throwing his shirts into the Fire as often as he shifted himself." With Bacon's death, so died his rebellion and his unauthorized war against the Indians of Virginia. An anonymous minister pronounced an epitaph recorded by Governor Berkeley:

Bacon is Dead I am sorry at my hart
That lice and flux should take the hangman's part.

The Indian War of 1675–76 solved little in any permanent way. A March 1677 conference and treaty at Shackamaxon (today part of Philadelphia) attempted to resolve the disposition of the Susquehannocks by removing them from the Delaware Valley—and thus (as Edmund Andros

wanted) beyond the reach of Maryland—and allowing their adoption by the Iroquois of New York. In actuality, while many Susquehannocks did accept removal and Iroquois adoption, 26 families remained in the Delaware Valley as adoptees of the Delaware tribe. Because the Iroquois continued to raid the Piscataways and Mattawomans in order to conquer them, Maryland and Virginia were involved in sporadic warfare against the Iroquois into the 1680s. The Iroquois made extensive use of adopted Susquehannocks in conducting raids, exploiting their desire for revenge against tribes allied to Maryland and Virginia.

# CHAPTER 8

# OLD WORLD ENMITIES, NEW WORLD BATTLES

### The Wars of King William and Queen Anne (1688–1713)

Developing hostilities between the English and French in Europe were, in part, an excuse to fight a trade war in America during the late seventeenth and early eighteenth centuries. After the Dutch yielded New York to the English in 1664, the Iroquois needed a new trading partner and turned to the colony's new masters, who offered better, more abundant, more varied, and cheaper goods than the French. Fearing an English-Iroquois monopoly of the fur trade and resentful of encroachments on territory they had claimed, the French continually pressured the Iroquois Five Nations into alliance with them or, at least, neutrality. For their part, British traders and settlers in northern New England were fearful of the menace presented by the French-allied Abnakis, a powerful tribe closely confederated with the region's Malecites, Penobscots, Pennacooks, and Micmacs.

Even before the European war broke out, Sir Edmund Andros, governor of Britain's northern colonies from New Jersey to Maine, acted on royal orders to put down French encroachments on English territory. He led a company of troops to Penobscot Bay, Maine, in April 1688. Their objective was the trading post of Jean Vincent de l'Abadie, baron de Saint Castin, which, Andros claimed, had been set up on land granted to the Duke of York. Baron Castin, who had married the daughter of an Abnaki chief, was loved and respected by the Abnakis, who were outraged when Andros's force plundered the trading post and demanded his submission to the British crown. Shortly after this incident, English settlers at Saco, Maine, took 16 Indians captive in retaliation for the killing of some cattle at nearby North Yarmouth. The Abnakis responded with raids in which they took a number of prisoners. This phase of hostilities, before the European war was declared, is sometimes referred to as the Abnaki War.

In September 1688, the English reacted to the raids in their usual manner. Soldiers began building fortlike stockades at North Yarmouth but abandoned these when they heard news of an approaching large party of Abnakis. In fleeing, they encountered another band of Abnakis, who had a good many English captives in tow. Neither side was particularly inclined to fight, but the English could hardly leave without attempting to free the prisoners. New England's early chronicler Cotton Mather, author of *Magnalia Christi Americana* (1702), described the battle that opened King William's War: "One Sturdy and Surly Indian held his prey so fast, that one Benedict Pulcifer gave the Mastiff a Blow with the Edge of his Broad Ax upon the Shoulder, upon which they fell to't with a Vengeance, and Fired their Guns on both sides, till some on both sides were Slain."

Abnakis raided northern New England settlements until winter. Andros responded with more forts, at Pemaquid and present-day Brunswick, Maine, and with about 1,000 troops. But he did not pursue the Indians into their winter refuges. Only when the raiding began anew in the spring, did Andros employ his army. By that time, Andros was deposed and returned to England as a result of the Protestant revolt that had dethroned King James II. Andros's patron James was replaced with William III.

## KING WILLIAM'S WAR

Soon after ascending the throne, William III joined the League of Augsburg and the Netherlands on May 12, 1689, to form the Grand Alliance in opposition to King Louis XIV's invasion of the Rhenish Palatinate (September 25, 1688). As a result of this action, war broke out not only in Europe, but intensified in North America as

OTTAWA

Quebec

NIPISSING

Montreal

ABNAKI

△ Caughnawaga

Saco

OJIBWA

Ft. Frontenac □

Ft. Wm.
Henry

Ft. St. Frederic
□ Ft. Ticonderoga
Ft. Number Four

WINNEBAGO

Ft. Oswego □

Ft. Stanwix □ Deerfield

POTAWATOMI

Ft. Niagara □

SAC

FOX

Bloody Run 1763 ★

IROQUOIS

MAHICAN

Cherry Valley Ft. Johnson
Albany

Boston

Galena ●

Detroit ● Ft. Malden
Point Pelee 1763 ★

Ft. Presque Isle □
□ Ft. Le Boeuf

Easton ●

New York ●

Ft. Dearborn □

Ft. Meigs □

MINGO

□ Ft. Venango

Saukenuk △ KICKAPOO

MIAMI

Ft. Sandusky □

DELAWARE

★ Bushy Run 1763
□ Ft. Pitt (Duquesne)

SUSQUEHANNOCK

KASKASKIA

Ft. Miami □

WYANDOT

△ Gnaddenhutten

Philadelphia ●

Keokuk △

Pickawillany △

△ Chillicothe

ILLINOIS

Ft. Greenville □

Ft. Washington □

PEORIA

□ Ft. Vincennes

SHAWNEE

St. Louis ●

△ Cahokia

Boonesboro ●

Richmond ●

*ATLANTIC
OCEAN*

TUSCARORA

CHEROKEE

New Bern ●

COREE

CHICKASAW

CATAWBA

Charleston ●

CREEK

△ ★ Horseshoe Bend 1814
Emuckfaw

YAZOO

YAMASEE

CHOCTAW

□ Ft. Rosalie

★ Fort Mims 1813

△ Fowl Town

NATCHEZ

Battle of Pensacola 1818

St. Augustine ●
Osceola's Capture 1837 ●

Mobile ●

★

Negro Fort 1816

Ft. King □

New Orleans ●

★

★ Gaines's Battle 1836

★ Dade's Battle 1835

*Gulf of Mexico*

## Wars of the East
## and Old Northwest

★ Battle Sites

△ Indian Settlements

□ Forts

● White Settlements

0          150 Miles

★ Big Cypress Swamp 1855-58

52

well. In Europe, the eight-year conflict was known as the War of the League of Augsburg; in America, it was called King William's War and pitted the French and Abnaki Indians (of Maine) against the English and their Iroquois allies.

In 1689, Louis XIV sent Louis de Buade, comte de Frontenac, to America as governor of New France, which then encompassed primarily Canada, the Great Lakes, and the Mississippi Valley. He had served in this capacity before, from 1672 to 1782, but had been recalled at the request of those he governed. Despite Frontenac's autocratic and quarrelsome nature, the French monarch knew that the 70-year-old leader was the best man for undertaking the mission Canadian officers had long recommended: not merely the defense of Canada, but the conquest of British New York. Frontenac's plan was to invade the colony, marching via Lake Champlain and Lake George into Albany. That accomplished, he would force an alliance with the Iroquois and sail down the Hudson to New York City.

The problem was, as Frontenac discovered when he arrived in Quebec, that New France was hardly in a position to take the offensive. During the night and early morning of July 25–26, 1689, the Quebec settlement of La Chine, just ten miles upstream from Montreal, had been attacked by 1,500 Iroquois warriors. Twenty-four civilians were killed and about 40 soldiers and French-Indian allies. Almost 100 people were captured, taken from their beds. About half of these would eventually be returned; the others were either killed or adopted by the attackers. Although the Iroquois withdrew from La Chine, the attack had badly demoralized the French, who abandoned their Lake Ontario fort at Catarqui. If a large offensive movement was now out of the question, Frontenac decided, he would conduct *"la petite querre"* against the English—what came to be called guerrilla warfare, the style of combat that would characterize most Indian-white conflicts in North America.

If the Iroquois were demoralizing the French, the Abnaki and allied tribes were terrorizing the English throughout Maine and New Hampshire. At Dover, New Hampshire, 30 settlers were killed, including Major Richard Waldron. At age 75, Waldron, a veteran of King Philip's War, traded in furs. Now, Pennacook, Ossipee, and Pigwacket Indians tortured him to death. He had customarily used his fist as a counterweight in trading goods for furs; now, cutting off one finger after the other, his tormentors asked him if his hand still weighed a pound. Each of his captors then slashed his chest, declaring, "See! I cross out my account." Through the summer of 1689, raiding intensified so that the English were forced to abandon their posts east of Falmouth, Maine. Boston authorities mustered and dispatched an army of

## LA PETITE GUERRE

The period of French and English conflict in America bequeathed to the lexicon of military history the word *guerrilla*, derived from *la petite guerre*, the phrase Louis de Buade, comte de Frontenac, governor of New France in 1689, used to describe the strategy he proposed to employ against the English. Frontenac's mandate from King Louis XIV was to defend New France and, even more, to extend its dominion southward by driving the English out of New York. Seventy years old, tough, and uncompromising, Frontenac intended to do just that, but soon concluded that New France, badly demoralized by unremitting pressure from English-allied Iroquois, was hardly in a position to take the offensive— at least by the methods of traditional warfare. If Frontentac lacked the means to wage war on a grand scale, he was determined to punish the English through a campaign of raids and terrorism on many fronts. It would not be a clash of one great army against another, but many little wars, characteristically involving small units of Indians led by one or two French commanders. In effect, Frontenac sought to institutionalize for strategic purposes the Indian-white violence that had long been endemic to the frontier. This pattern of "guerrilla warfare" would characterize white-Indian conflict for the next 200 years and would dominate the approaching French and Indian War.

600, but such a conventional military force had little effect against Indians fighting *la petite guerre*.

With the onset of winter, Frontenac assembled a combined force of 160 Canadians and about 100 Indian allies to exploit the weakness of the English position. His plan was to mount a three-pronged assault from Montreal into New York, New Hampshire, and Maine. After reaching the Hudson via a miserable, frozen trek down Lake Champlain to the southern tip of Lake George, the commanders of the assault force decided to attack Schenectady, which was closer than Albany. On the afternoon of February 8, 1690, after marching across bitterly cold, frozen swampland, they reached the vicinity of the settlement. Attacking after nightfall, they met with no resistance, for the village was "guarded" by two snowmen. In the span of two hours, the French and Indians did to

Schenectady what the Iroquois had earlier done to La Chine. Sixty men, women, and children, most taken in their beds, were slaughtered.

On March 27, another segment of Frontenac's forces attacked Salmon Falls, New Hampshire, where they killed 34 settlers, and in May, Fort Loyal (Falmouth, Maine) was attacked by a combined force of Canadians and Abnakis. The garrison surrendered on condition of a grant of safe conduct. As the defenders marched out of the fort, they were massacred; at least 100 died.

Amid these disasters, Mohawk representatives tried to encourage their panic-stricken and demoralized English allies by announcing: "Brethren, Doe not be discouraged. This is butt the beginning of the warr." They were right. On May 1, 1690, delegates from Massachusetts, Plymouth, Connecticut, and New York convened at Albany, where they determined to take the offensive by invading Canada with two land forces from New York and New England, joined by a naval force that would sail up the St. Lawrence River.

The assault was led by Sir William Phips. The twenty-first child of a Massachusetts farmer, Phips had become wealthy by recovering treasure from a Spanish ship sunk off the Bahamas. His luck held on May 11, 1690, when, with 14 vessels, he led a successful assault against Port Royal, Acadia (present-day Annapolis Royal, Nova Scotia). The hero of Port Royal was next assigned to command a larger expedition to invade Quebec. French defenses, however, easily overpowered the poorly organized force. By November, the army was also being decimated by smallpox. Phips withdrew.

Indeed, none of the plans projected at Albany came to fruition. In the course of 1690, French forces ousted the English from their Hudson Bay outpost at the mouth of the Severn River, and in 1691 the French retook Port Royal. Nevertheless, Frontenac's "little war" produced only little victories. To be sure, the guerrilla actions spawned much terror, but they accomplished little of enduring strategic value. Most significantly, the Iroquois remained loyal to the English, though they paid dearly for that loyalty. The Iroquois were the greatest sufferers in the war. Frontenac invaded the "capital" of their confederacy, Onondaga, destroying houses and badly needed crops, and continually incited western tribes to harass their settlements. In proportion to population, it is estimated that the Iroquois tribes lost far more than any other group participating in the war.

In September 1691, the superannuated hero of King Philip's War, Benjamin Church, was called out of retirement to lead 300 militiamen to the frequently harassed settlement of Saco, Maine. True to the tenor of this guerrilla war, he won no single decisive engagement, but he did sufficiently wear down the Abnakis to bring several sachems to peace talks in October that resulted in a formal treaty on November 29, 1691. The Abnakis agreed to release captives, to apprise the English of any French designs against them, and to refrain from hostilities until May 1, 1692.

Yet the dreary pattern of raid and counterraid continued The Abnakis violated their pledge, joining with Canadians to attack York, Maine, on February 5, 1692, killing 48 and taking 70 prisoners. In June, it was Wells, Maine, that fell under the hatchet. On June 6, Deerfield, Massachusetts, destined to suffer in war after frontier war, was raided. A widow, Hepzibah Wells, and three of her daughters were "knocked down and scalped, one of whom recovered from the terrific maiming. Thomas Broughton and his wife and three children were also killed at the same time." A casualty report like this is typical of the mean scale that usually characterized frontier warfare: no grand battles, no heroic charges of colorfully uniformed armies, no fanfares, no medals, just one murder after another in one isolated outpost after another. Although the records for them are more scant and less detailed than what survives for the English, the French and especially the Indians suffered similarly.

In January 1693, the French expedition against Mohawk villages in New York was exceptional only in size and strategic effect. Three hundred Mohawks, most of them women, children, and old men, were captured. Many others fled to Caughnawaga Mission in Canada. This was particularly significant in that the Caughnawagas were *Iroquois* Catholic converts allied with the *French*.

These attacks failed to accomplish much. The chronicles left to us from Deerfield, Massachusetts, provide a more typical picture of the war. On September 16, 1694, a band of Indians led by a Frenchman attacked the settlement, succeeding only in wounding two soldiers and killing a boy by the name of Daniel Severance. "A schoolmistress by the name of Mrs. Hannah Beaumont and her scholars were almost miraculously preserved; being fired upon by the Indians as they ran from the house to the fort, the bullets whistled about their ears, but not one of them was in the least injured, although the Indians were very near them." The next year, on August 18, a Mr. Joseph Bernard and a party of men were attacked by Indians who hid beneath a bridge. Barnard was mortally wounded (he died on September 6), and his horse was shot dead from under him. A year after this, on September 16, Thomas Smead and John Gillett were hunting when Indians attacked them. Gillett was captured, but Smead escaped. The raiding party advanced on the fort at Deerfield village, capturing, along the way, Daniel Belding and his son and daughter. They killed Belding's wife and three of his other children, and wounded two more of his children. ("They both recovered, although the son had his skull fractured by an Indian tomahawk, and a portion of brain issued from the wound.'')

On March 15, 1697, Abnakis raided Haverhill, Massachusetts. This incident, no different from the eight years of attacks that had preceded it, is remembered because the experience of one of the captives, Mrs. Hannah Dustin, was recorded and published in an early American best-seller, Cotton Mather's *Humiliations Follow'd with Deliverances* (1697). Having given birth to her eighth child the week before, Hannah Dustin was resting in her farmhouse when the attack came. Her husband, who had been working in the fields, sent his children to a "strong house"—one of the settlement's fortified houses. In the meantime, he tried to get to his wife, but was prevented by the attackers from reaching her. Warriors invaded the Dustin home and carried off Hannah, her newborn, and a nurse.

In a gesture recorderd with distressing frequency in accounts of Indian captivity, one of the captors seized the infant, who had begun to cry, and dashed its brains out against a tree. Later, some of the other captives were killed, and the remainder were divided up among the warriors and their families. Hannah and the nurse were handed over to a group of two warriors, three women, and seven children, who led their captives through the woods for many days. Catholic converts, the Indians paused twice daily to say a rosary. On the night of March 29, as their captors slept, Hannah Dustin and her nurse quietly rose, secured hatchets, and began murdering all but two Abnakis—an old woman and a boy, who fled. Mindful that Massachusetts offered a scalp bounty, Mrs. Dustin was not content merely to escape with her life. She set about scalping her victims, and then, she and her nurse made their way back to Haverhill. She returned to find that her husband and children had survived, and she collected £25 from Massachusetts for the scalps.

In September 1697, the Treaty of Ryswick ended the War of the League of Augsburg; consequently the conflict ended in America as well, although violence continued spasmodically on the frontier, especially between the French-allied western tribes and the Iroquois Five Nations. This culminated in a battle on the shores of Lake Erie during 1698 or 1699, between western tribes, including the Ojibwa (also known as Chippewa and whose tradition has preserved an account of the battle), and the Five Nations. The Iroquois were badly beaten, and by the close of the seventeenth century, the western Algonquian tribes had eroded much of the western territory formerly controlled by the Iroquois.

It is easy to assume that the French would have been jubilant over the defeats suffered by the English-allied Iroquois. Indeed, many Frenchmen were well pleased.

But, officially, the French had made peace—or, at least, concluded a truce—with the Iroquois. Officially, they did not wish to see the Five Nations destroyed. As Baron Louis-Armand de Lom d'Arce de Lahontan observed:

Those who allege that the destruction of the Iroquois would promote the interest of the Colonies of New-France are strangers to the true interest of that Country; for if that were once accomplish'd, the Savages who are now the French Allies would turn their greatest Enemies, as being rid of their other fears. They would not fail to call in the English, by reason that their Commodities are at once cheaper and more esteem'd than ours; and by that means the whole Commerce of that wide Country would be wrested out of our hands.

This statement is not only a measure of the futility of Frontenac's *petite guerre*, but of all wars between Indians and whites. Worse, it implies that reducing one group of Indians only necessitates doing the same to another—and another and another. It implies the developing philosophy of war that would be put into a single terrible phrase inspired by General Philip Sheridan more than a century and a half later: the only good Indian is a dead Indian.

## QUEEN ANNE'S WAR

Like King William's War, Queen Anne's War was the American theater of a larger European conflict. England, Holland, and Austria, fearful of an alliance between France and Spain, formed a new anti-French Grand Alliance in 1701 after King Charles II of Spain, a Hapsburg, died in 1700, having chosen a Bourbon as his successor. The French supported his nominee, Philip of Anjou, a grandson of Louis XIV, as his successor; England, Holland, and Austria gave their support to the second son of Hapsburg emperor Leopold I, the obscure Bavarian Archduke Charles. War was declared in Europe on May 4, 1702. The War of the Spanish Succession—called in its American phase Queen Anne's War—began in the colonies on September 10, 1702, when the South Carolina legislature authorized an expedition to seize the Spanish-held fort and town of Saint Augustine, Florida. First, a British naval expedition plundered the town, then, in December, a mixed force of 500 colonists and Chickasaws assaulted the fort. Failing to breach it, they turned to further pillaging and then burned the town instead.

A series of raids ensued until former South Carolina governor James Moore and a force of militia and Chickasaws swept through the territory of the Appalachees of western Florida during most of July 1704. Moore and

## CAPTURED BY INDIANS

Throughout the period of the Indian Wars—effectively from the earliest European settlements in America until the "battle" of Wounded Knee—captivity loomed in the darkest recesses of the frontier settler's consciousness. To be captured meant severance from all that was familiar, it meant being swallowed up in what the Puritans characteristically termed the "howling wilderness," it meant torture and an unspeakably cruel death.

The raid on Deerfield occasioned an extremely popular narrative—*The Redeemed Captive Returning to Zion*—written by the town's minister, John Williams:

They came to my house in the beginning of the onset, and by their violent endeavors to break open doors and windows, with axes and hatchets, awaked me out of sleep; on which I leaped out of bed, and, running towards the door, perceived the enemy making their entrance into the house. I called to awaken two soldiers in the chamber, and returning toward my bedside for my arms, the enemy immediately broke into the room, I judge to the number of twenty, with painted faces, and hideous acclamations. I reached up my hands to the bed-tester for my pistol, uttering a short petition to God. . . . Taking down my pistol, I cocked it, and put it to the breast of the first Indian that came up; but my pistol missing fire, I was seized by three Indians, who disarmed me, and bound me naked, as I was in my [night]shirt, and so I stood for near the space of an hour. Binding me, they told me they would carry me to Quebeck. . . .

I cannot relate the distressing care I had for my dear wife, who had lain in but a few weeks before; and for my poor children, family, and Christian neighbors. The enemy fell to rifling the house, and entered in great numbers into every room. . . . The enemies . . . insulted over me awhile, holding up hatchets over my head, threatening to burn all I had; but yet God, beyond expectation, made us in a great measure to be pitied; for though some were so cruel and barbarous as to take and carry to the door two of my children and murder them, as also a negro woman; yet they gave me liberty to put on my clothes, keeping me bound with a cord on one arm, till I put on my clothes to the other; and then changing my cord, they let me dress myself, and then pinioned me again. Gave liberty to my dear wife to dress herself and our remaining children.

There began a hellish, 300-mile winter march to Quebec, which the reverend's wife did not survive:

I asked each of the prisoners (as they passed by me) after her, and heard that, passing through [a river], she fell down, and was plunged over head and ears in the water; after which she travelled not far, for at the foot of that mountain, the cruel and bloodthirsty savage who took her slew her with his hatchet at one stroke, the tidings of which were very awful.

It is a fact that Indians were often cruel to their captives. The weak, the old, the infants, and the wounded—prisoners who would impede flight from the scene of a raid—were often summarily dispatched. Children were killed before the eyes of

his men killed or captured the inhabitants of seven villages and destroyed 13 of 14 Spanish missions in the country, virtually annihilating the Appalachee. The strategic significance of this action was to open a path into the heart of French Louisiana territory and the settlements along the Gulf of Mexico. The French, however, had been working on the Choctaws, Cherokees, Creeks, and Chickasaws, using every means of bribery to gain their support. The Chickasaws remained pro-English, and the Cherokees managed to maintain a neutral stance. Some bands of Creek Indians sided with the French, but that nation's most powerful ally was the Choctaw, who successfully blocked Moore's advance into Louisiana.

In the North, the French had more extensive Indian alliances. As would be the case even as late as the French and Indian War half a century later, English colonial authorities tended to treat the Indians with contempt, provoking and angering them even as French authorities courted them. In June 1703, Massachusetts governor Joseph Dudley, charged with maintaining peaceful relations with the powerful Abnakis, remarked, "I value them not, no more than the paring of my nails." In Northampton, Massachusetts, the Reverend Solomon Stoddard urged fellow colonists to use their dogs to "hunt Indians as if they were bears," and, shifting similes, declared that since the Indians "act like wolves [they] are to be dealt with like wolves."

their parents. Elderly parents were killed in front of their children. But contrary to what many popular captivity narratives implied, captive women were seldom in danger of rape. Among most Indian groups, forcible rape was seen as deviant and unacceptable behavior, and in any case, Indian men often professed a disdain of white women, whom they claimed to find unattractive. Male prisoners were often subjected to torture, in which the tormentors, including warriors, women, and children, seemed to exalt. Cutting, flaying alive, dismemberment, piercing, beating, and burning were common. One usual torture was to cut off an ear, a strip of flesh, or a finger and force the victim to eat it—a fate the missionary Father Isaac Jogues almost suffered among the Mohawks during the 1630s. His thumb was amputated and presented to him. He

offered it to Thee, my true and living God, calling to mind the sacrifice which I had for seven years [as a priest administering the holy eucharist] constantly offered Thee in Thy Church. At last, warned by one of my comrades to desist, since they might otherwise force it into my mouth and compel me to eat it as it was, I flung it from me on the scaffold and left it I know not where.

The famed frontiersman Simon Kenton was captured by Shawnees in 1778 and subjected to many weeks of cruel beatings, including running the gauntlet on several occasions. This combination of torture, ritual, and sport placed the captive at the head of parallel rows of club-wielding warriors (and often women and children as well); the captive had to run from one end of the "gauntlet" to the other as blows rained down on him. If he stumbled and fell, he was placed at the starting point again—or he was beaten to death.

Kenton endured many tortures, which, in the end, earned him the respect of his captors, who adopted him into the tribe. This, too, was a common outcome of Indian captivity—and it did not necessarily follow a period of abuse. In some tribes, widows were given the option of "adopting" prisoners as replacement husbands. Bereft mothers might adopt a child. Or the tribe might simply induct a captive into its society as an equal or as a semislave. The vast contemporary literature of captivity rarely makes note of the significant number of whites who resisted or declined "rescue." Many captives, including Rev. Williams's own daughter Eunice, did not wish to return to the settlement, preferring to stay with their adoptive tribe. Eunice married the warrior who saved her life during the terrible march; although she later visited Deerfield, she chose to return to the Indian village with her husband. Stephen W. Williams, author of a "Biographical Memoir" appended to John Williams's narrative, notes that "many of the prisoners became very much attached to the Indians and their mode of life, and some of them were very loath to leave them after they were redeemed." For many, captivity among the Indians was a liberation from the brutal life of the white frontier. While French and Spanish colonists readily accepted intermarriage of whites and Indians, the English remained resistant to it and often forcibly "redeemed" captives.

Given their attitude toward the Indians, it is not surprising that the colonists unleashed the fury of the Abnakis. On August 10, 1703, a party of settlers broke into and plundered the Maine house belonging to the son of Jean Vincent de l'Abadie, baron de Saint Castin. The baron's trading post had been similarly attacked in April 1688, during King William's War, provoking bloody conflict with the Abnakis. Because his mother was the daughter of an Abnaki chief, the younger Saint Castin was likewise a chief, and the attack on his house touched off raids along 200 miles of northern New England frontier. Governor Dudley, who had boasted at an earlier conference held in Casco, Maine, that he commanded a militia of 1,250 men, mustered a mere 360. They marched on Saco, Maine, a center of Abnaki activity, but failed to engage the Indians, who nevertheless continued their guerrilla-style raids.

Among the towns hardest hit was Deerfield, Massachusetts, a prosperous village of 41 houses and 270 people at the time, which had borne the brunt of numerous raids during King Philip's War and King William's War. In the present conflict, the townspeople had taken the precaution of posting a night sentry, but on the night of February 29, 1704, he was absent or asleep. Fifty French colonists and 200 Abnakis and Caughnawagas (French-allied Mohawks) descended on the village two hours before dawn, killing many settlers as they slept. Militia Sergeant Benomi Stebbins managed to muster seven men to barricade the windows of his house, which, though lacking a formal garrison, did have bulletproof brick walls. Stebbins fell in battle, but the militiamen drove off an attack of about 50 Indians. Except for this single stand, panic was general in Deerfield. Fifty villagers died; 100 were taken captive.

Farther north, in Nova Scotia, Benjamin Church, now so old that he had to be helped over fallen logs in his path, marched 550 men into Acadian French territory, terrorizing two settlements, Minas and Beaubassin, in July 1704. He warned the inhabitants that he would return with 1,000 Indians to avenge the loss of any more English lives. The old commander wanted to seize the valuable Acadian fisheries and to attack the staunchly fortified Port Royal, but he was restrained by his own officers. To the north, in Newfoundland, between the eighteenth and twenty-ninth of August, a mixed force of French and Indians operating out of Placentia destroyed the English settlement at Bonavista in a series of retaliatory raids.

In the north and south, the war dragged on in a succession of murders, raids, and counterraids. The English again attempted to take Port Royal, Nova Scotia, in 1706 but failed. The French and Spanish launched a seaborne assault on Charleston, South Carolina, but also failed. The French, however, captured Saint Johns, Newfoundland, on December 21, 1708.

In 1710, the colonies sent a contingent of English-allied Mohawk chiefs to England and the court of Queen Anne. The visit was carefully orchestrated to garner sympathy and support for the plight of the colonies; the Indians were carefully arrayed in "savage" attire—by a London theatrical costumer!—and made a sensation. Moved by the show and opinion, Queen Anne sent to the colonies badly needed troops under Colonel Francis Nicholson and a naval fleet under Sir Francis Hobby, who together reduced Port Royal on October 16, 1710. The following summer, all Acadia fell.

Another naval expedition, aimed at Quebec and led by Sir Hovendon Walker, was shipwrecked at the mouth of the Saint Lawrence River with the loss of 1,600 men. The next year, another move against the French Canadian capital was badly mismanaged and had to be aborted. By this time, King Louis XIV, war-weary and burdened by debt, was ready to end the war, both in the New World and the Old. The original source of the conflict—the succession to the Spanish throne—had in any case become a moot point. In the course of the 11-year war, Archduke Charles, the Bavarian candidate supported by the Grand Alliance, died, and Louis's grandson Philip of Anjou ascended the throne by default. The French monarch signed the Treaty of Utrecht on July 13, 1713, ceding Hudson Bay and Acadia to the English, but retaining Cape Breton Island and other small islands in the Saint Lawrence. The Canadian boundaries, however, remained unsettled. As to the Abnakis and other French-allied Indians, they signed a treaty with the New Englanders, pledging to become loyal subjects of queen Anne. The treaty was destined soon to be broken as Indians resisted English incursions into their territory.

# CHAPTER 9

---□---

# DESPERATE RESISTANCE
## The Tuscarora and Yamassee Wars (1710–1716)

The Tuscaroras, who lived along the coastal rivers of North Carolina, were inclined to be friendly to their colonist neighbors, but by the second decade of the eighteenth century, they were suffering indignities and abuses, especially at the hands of local white traders. Plying the Tuscaroras with liquor, traders cheated them out of goods and territory—in the case of the latter, there was rarely even the semblance of a business transaction; settlers simply squatted on the Tuscaroras' best land. Worse, traders began kidnapping Tuscaroras and selling them into West Indian slavery. If this were not misery enough, Iroquois raiding parties from the north were ambushing isolated groups of Tuscarora hunters.

After enduring this situation for some years, the Tuscaroras, still desirous of averting war, petitioned the government of Pennsylvania for permission to migrate there. Authorities were willing to grant the permission only if the Tuscarora settlers could secure a note from the government of North Carolina attesting to their good conduct. The Tuscaroras had shown great forbearance under terrible pressure, but the North Carolinians refused to furnish the required certificate. This was hardly a surprise, since allowing the Tuscaroras to leave would mean relinquishing a valuable inventory of slaves.

About a year later, in 1710, a band of Swiss colonists organized by an entrepreneur named Baron Cristoph von Graffennried settled on a tract of North Carolina land at the confluence of the Neuse and Trent rivers. They proudly and hopefully christened the settlement New Bern. The problem was that it was already occupied by a Tuscarora village. Instead of attempting to negotiate with the Indians, von Graffenried complained to North Carolina's surveyor general, who affirmed that, as far as the government was concerned, the von Graffenried settlers held clear title to the land. The surveyor general

told the Swiss promoter that he was perfectly within his rights to drive the Indians off without payment. And so he did.

At dawn, on September 22, 1711, Tuscarora patience at last gave way to violence. A raiding party attacked New Bern and other settlements in the area, killing 200 settlers, including 80 children. Von Graffenried was captured but secured his release, as well as the Indians' pledge not to attack New Bern again, by promising not to make war on the Tuscarorras. Unfortunately, one of his settlers, William Brice, thirsting for revenge, was unwilling to abide by von Graffenried's promise. He captured a local chief of the Coree tribe, allied with the Tuscaroras, and roasted him alive. This provoked the Tuscaroras, Corees, and other, smaller tribes to renewed raids.

With the situation badly out of hand, North Carolina officials sought aid from South Carolina, which dispatched Colonel John Barnwell, an Irish-born commander, leading 30 militiamen and 500 Indian allies, many of them Yamassees. This force took a great toll on Tuscarora settlements and those of their allies. Heartened by his victory, and with forces augmented by a contingent of North Carolinians, Barnwell directed an attack against the stronghold of the Tuscarora "king" Hancock in March 1712. The North Carolina men proved to be unreliable assets. Meeting fiercer opposition than they had anticipated, the North Carolina ranks broke in a panic, and the assault failed. The Indians, wanting a peace parley but meeting with refusal, began to torture their captives in full view of Barnwell's men. Finally, Barnwell agreed to withdraw in exchange for the release of the captives. This granted, he returned to New Bern.

Upon his return, the North Carolina assembly angrily ordered him back to the front. Nothing less than the

## A SOUTHERN *LAST OF THE MOHICANS*: WILLIAM GILMORE SIMMS'S *THE YEMASSEE*

Largely forgotten today, South Carolinian William Gilmore Simms (1806–70) was regarded in his own time as a worthy rival of his senior nothern colleague, James Fenimore Cooper. In his historical novels—"romances," he called them—Simms dramatized the history of early white-Indian relations in the Carolinas in the way that Cooper used the history of upstate New York. As with Cooper, the historical impulse behind Simms's novels was greatly tempered by an allegiance to the conventions of nineteenth-century romantic fiction; however, Simms's 1835 *The Yemassee: A Romance of Carolina* reveals much not only about the Yemassee War but about ambivalent white attitudes toward the Indians of the Southeast who, when Simms was writing his novel, were in the midst of forced "removal" to the West.

Like many well-educated whites of his day, Simms recognized the justice of Indian claims to the land they occupied. In one passage of *The Yemassee*, Simms admires the classical nobility of the Indians:

The elements of all uncultivated people are the same. The early Greeks, in their stern endurance of torment, in their sports and exercises, were exceedingly like the North American savages. The Lacadaemonians went to battle with songs and dances; a similar practice obtained among the Jews; and one particularly, alike of the Danes and Saxons, was to usher in the combat with wild and discordant anthems.

Sanutee, a Yemassee chief is the principal Indian character in the novel. He is portrayed as a figure of stoic courage, whose son, Occonestoga, is transformed into an alcoholic through contact with the whites. Despite his understanding and admiration—patronizing though it may be—Simms, like so many white Americans of his time, concluded that the reign of the Indian was *necessarily* finished. In the book, Hugh Grayson, a young colonist, argues with Reverend Matthews over the fate of the Yemassees. Grayson speaks for Simms and prevailing white attitudes when he declares:

"[I]t is utterly impossible that the whites and Indians should ever live together and agree. The nature of things is against it, and the very difference between the two, that of colour, perceptible to our most ready sentinel, the sight, must always constitute them an inferior caste in our minds."

The "nature of things" included, as Simms saw it, the Indians' absolute devotion to cruelty and torture as a way of life. Simms has South Carolina governor Charles Craven (disguised as one Gabriel Harrison) witness the capture and torture of "a poor labourer, named Macnamara":

He was a fine-looking, fresh, muscular man—not more than thirty. Surrounded by howling savages, threatened with a death the most terrible, the brave fellow sustained himself with the courage and firmness which belongs so generally to his countrymen. His long, black hair, deeply saturated and matted with his blood, which oozed out from sundry bludgeon-wounds upon the head, was wildly distributed in masses over his face and forehead. His full, round cheeks, were marked by knife-wounds, the result also of his fierce defence against his captors. His hands were bound, but his tongue was unfettered; and as they danced and howled about him, his eye gleamed forth in fury and derision, while his words were those of defiance and contempt.

"Ay! ye may screech and scream, ye red divils—ye'd be after seeing how a jontleman would burn in the fire, would ye, for your idification and delight. But

---

reduction of Hancock's "fort" was acceptable. Barnwell marched back in greater force, bullied Hancock into signing a peace, then, marching back to New Bern, summarily violated his own treaty by seizing a party of Tuscaroras and selling them as slaves.

War was renewed in the summer of 1712, and North Carolina again appealed to South Carolina for help. This time, the neighboring colony sent Colonel James Moore with a force of 33 militiamen and 1,000 Indians. They arrived in November 1712, combined with North Carolina troops, and in March 1713 struck at the principal concentration of Tuscarora warriors. Hundreds of Tuscaroras died in this battle and about 400 were captured. The proceeds from their sale into slavery, at £10 each, helped defray the cost of the campaign. Many Tuscaroras who escaped death or enslavement migrated northward,

it's not Teddy Macnamara, that your fires and your arrows will iver scare, ye divils; so begin, boys, as soon as ye've a mind to, and don't be too dilicate in your doings.''

He spoke a language, so far as they understood it, perfectly congenial with their notion of what should become a warrior. His fearless contempt of death, his haughty defiance of their skill in the arts of torture—his insolent abuse—were all so much in his favour. They were proofs of the true brave, and they found, under the bias of their habits and education, an added pleasure in the belief, that he would stand well the torture, and afford them a protracted enjoyment of the spectacle. His execrations, poured forth freely as they forced him into the arena, were equivalent to one of their own death-songs, and they regarded it as his. . . . Under a shower of kicks, cuffs, and blows from every quarter, the poor fellow, still cursing them to the last, hissing at and spitting upon them, was forced to a tree; and in a few moments tightly lashed back against it. A thick cord secured him around the body to the overgrown trunk, while his hands, forced up in a direct line above his head, were fastened to the tree with withes—the two palms turned outwards, nearly meeting and so well corded as to be perfectly immovable. . . . ''Ay, ye miserable red nagers,—ye don't frighten Teddy Macnamara now so aisily. He is none of yer spalpeens, honies, to be frightened by your bows and your painted sticks, ye red nagers. It isn't your knives, nor your hatchets, that's going to make Teddy beg yer pardon, and ax for yer marcies. I don't care for your knives and your hatchets, at all at all, ye red divils. Not I—by my faith, and my own ould father, that was a Teddy before me.''

They took him at his word, and their preparations were soon made for the torture. A hundred torches of the gummy pine were placed to kindle in a neighbouring fire—a hundred old women stood ready to employ them. These were to be applied as a sort of cautery, to the arrow and knife-wounds which the more youthful savages were expected, in their sport, to inflict. It was upon

their captives, in this manner, that the youth of the nation was practised. It was in this school that the boys were prepared to become men—to inflict pain as well as to submit to it. To these two classes,—for this was one of the peculiar features of the Indian torture,—the fire-sacrifice, in its initial penalties, was commonly assigned; and both of them were ready at hand to engage in it.

They began. A dozen youth, none over sixteen, came forward and ranged themselves in front of the prisoner.

''And for what do ye face me down after that sort, ye dirty little red nagers?'' cried the sanguine prisoner.

They answered him with a whoop—a single shriek, and the face of the brave fellow paled then, for a moment, with that sudden yell—that mere promise of war—the face which had not paled in the actual conflict. . . . The whoop of the young savages was succeeded by a simultaneous discharge of all their arrows, aimed, as would appear from the result, only at those portions of his person which were not vital. This was the common exercise, and their adroitness was wonderful. They placed the shaft where they pleased. Thus, the arrow of one penetrated one palm, while that of another, almost at the same instant, was driven deep into the other. One cheek was grazed by a third, while a fourth scarified the opposite. A blunted shaft struck the victim full in the mouth and arrested, in the middle, his usual execration—''Ye bloody red nagers!''—and there never were fingers of a hand so evenly separated one from the other, as those of Macnamara, by the admirably-aimed arrows of those embryo warriors.

The torture—and Simms's scene—continues until Macnamara makes an implausible dash for freedom (after a hurled tomahawk cuts through his bonds) and is killed. However accurate or fanciful, Simms's depiction of the Yemassee War suggests much about the dynamics of racism, settlement, and white-Indian warfare.

eventually as far as New York, where they were given asylum among the Iroquois and, in 1722, were admitted into the Iroquois League as its ''sixth nation.'' A smaller faction, led by a chief the English called Tom Blount, remained in North Carolina, signing a peace treaty on February 11, 1715.

Brief and terrible, the Yamasee War followed hard upon the Blount treaty. Like the Tuscaroras of North

Carolina, the Yamasees of South Carolina had freely associated with their white neighbors. And, like the Tuscaroras, they suffered abuses at the hands of traders and squatters, ranging from insults, to land fraud, to debauchment with liquor, to enslavement. On Good Friday, April 15, 1715, the Yamasees, Catawbas, and other smaller tribes, probably encouraged by the French, attacked settlements north of present-day Savannah, Georgia (then under the jurisdiction of South Carolina). Cabins were burned, and more than 100 were killed; others fled to Charleston, where South Carolina's governor, Charles Craven, quickly mustered his militia. By June, he had managed to drive the Yamasees from their villages. In the fall, he pursued them as they fled to Spanish Florida and harried them to the point of tribal extinction. The land vacated by the Yamasee was appropriated for James Edward Oglethorpe's new proprietary colony of Georgia.

With so much interior land now opened to white settle-ment, Governor Craven still feared the powerful Creek nation. English victories against the Tuscaroras and the Yamasees, however, gave his colony sufficient prestige to entice the Cherokees into the English fold. Their presence counterbalanced that of the Creeks. In 1716, Cherokee allies were employed to drive out remaining Yamasees and members of the Lower Creek tribe from territory northwest of Port Royal, which South Carolina settlers had attempted to occupy. Casualties on both sides were heavy, but the Cherokee-English alliance prevailed, making this the final battle of the Yamassee War.

# CHAPTER 10

□

# AN EAR AND AN EMPIRE
## THE FOX RESISTANCE, KING GEORGE'S WAR, AND THE CHICKASAW RESISTANCE (1712–1748)

Following Queen Anne's War (in Europe, the War of the Spanish Succession), Great Britain concluded a treaty in 1713 with France's ally Spain that included the "Assiento," a contract permitting—but regulating—English trade in slavery and goods with the Spanish colonies. English abuses of the Assiento and other trade conflicts in the West Indies provoked Spanish officials to deal harshly with British merchant sailors in the region. Robert Jenkins, master of the ship *Rebecca*, claimed that Spanish coast guards had cut off his ear while interrogating him. When word of this—and other incidents—reached Great Britain, hostilities flared into the open.

These hostilities led to the so-called War of Jenkins' Ear in 1739 between Great Britain and Spain. Reflecting the European hostilities, James Oglethorpe, principal founder of Georgia, invaded Florida in January 1740. Aided in the west by the Creeks, Cherokees, and Chickasaws, none of whom had any love for the Spanish, Oglethorpe captured Fort San Francisco de Pupo and Fort Picolata, both on the San Juan River. He besieged Saint Augustine from May through July but was compelled to break off when Spanish forces threatened him from behind. His troops successfully repulsed a Spanish counterattacked on Saint Simon's Island, Georgia, in the Battle of Bloody Marsh, June 9, 1742, but after Oglethorpe's second attempt to capture Saint Augustine failed, in 1743, the Georgia governor withdrew from Florida.

The War of Jenkins' Ear did not so much end as it dissolved into the larger conflict fought in Europe as the War of the Austrian Succession (1740–48) and known in the colonies as King George's War. The death of the Holy Roman Emperor Charles VI in 1740 touched off several challenges to the succession of his daughter Maria Theresa as ruler of the Austrian (Hapsburg) lands. Amid threats to carve up Austria, King Frederick the

Great of Prussia pushed his own claim to a piece of the empire by invading Silesia. France, Spain, Bavaria, and Saxony aligned themselves with Prussia. Britain came to the aid of Maria Theresa. With the signing of the Second Family Compact on October 25, 1743, France joined Spain in its fight with England, declaring war on March 15, 1744.

## THE FOX RESISTANCE

Events preceding 1744 laid the groundwork for war in the colonies. In 1722, New York's governor William Burnet vigorously vied with the French for the profitable trade with the Senecas and other Iroquois tribes. When Louis-Thomas Chabert de Joncaire, Indian agent for the French, persuaded the Senecas to permit enlargement of the French fortifications at Niagara, Burnet secured permission to build Fort Oswego on the eastern shore of Lake Ontario. In response, Canadian governor Vaudreuil convinced the Senecas to allow him to strengthen Niagara further, replacing the wooden palisades of the fort with stone. Except for the Mohawks, the easternmost Iroquois tribe steadfastly allied with the English, the Iroquois generally struggled to remain neutral in the contest between France and England. By the 1720s, however, they strove more actively to play one side against the other in order to achieve a balance of power. Then, in 1729, a combination of French and Indians, chiefly Ojibwa, attacked the Foxes, whose territory was the eastern shore of Lake Michigan in the present states of Illinois and Wisconsin. This was the first of three events that pushed the Iroquois into the English camp.

The Foxes were far western allies of the Iroquois, who, in their disintegrating effort to monopolize inland

*Sir William Johnson, an influential New York landowner, forged an enduring Mohawk–English alliance. During the French and Indian War, the Mohawks were often the only allies the English could depend on. Their loyalty to the English put them at odds with other Iroquois tribes, who were generally neutral or sided with the French, and greatly weakened the Iroquois Confederation. (Library of Congress.)*

trade, needed all the western allies they could get. Since at least the late seventeenth century, the Foxes had been sporadically at war with the Ojibwa tribe, also called Chippewa, who were concentrated in present-day northwestern Wisconsin. The French, who established profitable trading relations with the Ojibwa, aided that tribe in its ongoing contest with the Foxes. In response, the Foxes repeatedly harassed French traders and raided frontier outposts. In 1712, they planned an attack on the French fort at Detroit, which nearly succeeded. This was the start of the Fox Resistance, which lasted from 1712 until approximately 1733.

By the 1720s, Fox raiding had become so frequent that not only was trade between New France and the Ojibwa disrupted, but the lifeline connecting New France in the north with Louisiana in the south—Lake Michigan, the upper Mississippi, and the portages connecting them—was threatened. The French met among themselves and with their Ojibwa allies in a series of councils to decide how best to deal with the Fox menace. The most ambitious solution suggested was extermination, but foreshadowing the method of handling recalcitrant Indians predominant in the early nineteenth century, it was decided to round up the Foxes and move them to Detroit, where the armed garrison of the fort could monitor and control their activities. Several French-Ojibwa campaigns were mounted with little success. By 1729, the attacks against the Foxes became more fierce, and the next year, French-Ojibwa policy veered toward extermination. Despite aid from Sac allies, Foxes fled east to territory controlled by the Iroquois in an effort to escape what had become relentless slaughter. Most who attempted the flight were caught and killed.

With the collapse of the Foxes, the only Algonquian-speaking tribe not allied with the French, the Iroquois lost an important western ally. Without the Foxes, the Iroquois' most formidable trading opponent, the Potowatamis of the Michigan-Chicago-Green Bay region, would end any Iroquois pretension to a trade monopoly in the west. The Fox massacre of 1730 was the second event that prompted the Iroquois to look increasingly to the English for alliance.

The English-Iroquois alliance was further strengthened by a third event. In 1731, responding to the English presence as manifested at Fort Oswego and claiming that the fort was, in fact, on French territory, the French built Fort Saint Frédéric at Crown Point, on the southern narrows of Lake Champlain.

For their part, the English had an equally significant stake in the outcome of this western war. English colonial charters, such as that of Virginia, often granted territory from sea to sea. The trouble was that France and Spain had preempted by claim of discovery much of the western territory encompassed in these charters. Even Sir William Johnson, New York's commissioner of Indian affairs, admitted that "in a political Sense our Claims . . . include lands we never saw, and over which we could not Exercise full Dominion with 10,000 of the best Troops in Europe." The English hope of a claim to the western territories was inextricably bound to the fortunes of the Iroquois. In a series of treaties, some more dubious than others, the English attempted to define the Iroquois tribes as subjects of the British crown. This relationship was never wholly or unambiguously acknowledged by the Iroquois (indeed, a 1756 royal commission issued to Sir William Johnson fudges absurdly, defining the Iroquois as "subjects and allies"). That hardly mattered to the English, who included in the 1713 Treaty of Utrecht an acknowledgment of the Iroquois' subjection to the crown. The traveler and naturalist John Bartram explained as well as anyone the significance of this relationship:

The honour of first discovering these extensive fresh water seas [the Great Lakes] is certainly due to the French, who are at this time in possession of settlements at Fort Ponchartrain, on the strait between Lake Erie and the Lake Huron and at Misilimahinac [Michilimackinac] between the latter and the upper lake, but as these can give them no title against the original inhabitants or the five nations [i.e., the Five Iroquois Nations], Conquerors of all the adjacent [Indian] nations, so it is difficult to conceive by what arguments these small posts, inhabited by no subjects of France but soldiers, can be extended to mark any possession beyond the reach of their gun's, or land actually cultivated, except by such as must intitle the crown of Great Britain to all North America, both as prior discoverers and prior planters, without a subsequent desertion.

In short, the Iroquois possessed the Ohio country by right of conquest; the Iroquois were subjects of the English crown; therefore, England had legitimate claim to the western lands, which claim it might perfect by treaty with and/or purchase from the Iroquois. If the Iroquois lost control of the West, English claims to it, questionable as they were, would simply dissolve.

## KING GEORGE'S WAR

With these alliances and territorial claims and counterclaims in place, and with a war already under way in Europe, the stage was set for armed conflict in America. Fort Saint Frédéric became a staging area for repeated raids into New York and New England, though neither side prosecuted the American phase of the war vigorously until the French made an unsuccessful assault on Annapolis Royal (Port Royal, Nova Scotia) late in 1744. This was followed by the war's only major battle, the British siege of Louisbourg on Cape Breton Island, Nova Scotia.

On June 16, 1745, after a siege of 49 days, the fort fell to William Pepperell, who commanded 4,200 Massachusetts militiamen. Boasting the greatest concentration of cannon in North America and guarding the approach to the vital Saint Lawrence River, Louisbourg was a significant prize.

Most of King George's War, however, did not consist of sieges or formal battles. The French and the English attempted to enlist the aid of Indian allies for guerrilla actions and raids. Lieutenant Governor George Clinton of New York attempted something more organized when he set about recruiting and arming Indians for an invasion of Canada, and William Johnson rallied Mohawk allies for an assault on Montreal in June 1747. Lack of coordination with other colonial forces and wrangling in Albany over appropriations for frontier defense contributed to a debacle at Fort Saint Frédéric, which cost the Mohawks heavy casualties and forestalled the attack on Montreal. Johnson was more successful, however, financing smaller Mohawk raids against French supply lines and similar objectives throughout the balance of the war.

Incited by their French allies, Indians made lightning raids on a number of New England settlements. Typical were the engagements in the Connecticut Valley, north of Springfield, Massachusetts. It is not known how many settlers or Indians, if any of either, were killed in the initial assault on the Connecticut River fort at Great Meadow in July 1745, but it is recorded that one William Phips was "captivated" and, after marching half a mile, "killed one of his captors, and knocked down another, when he attempted to escape, but three of the enemy overtook and killed him. Josiah Fisher was killed and scalped about the same time, near Upper Ashuelot." On October 11, 1745, the Indians returned and again attacked Great Meadow, succeeding only in capturing Nehemiah How, who was carried off to Quebec, where he died.

From August 1745 until the conclusion of the war, French provincials and Abnaki Indians raided remote settlements in Maine. The war intensified by the end of 1745; on November 28–29, the French, with Indian allies, captured and burned Fort Saratoga, New York.

Throughout the next year, Indians—mostly Abnakis—attacked many New England towns. The northernmost settlement on the Connecticut River, a fort called "No. 4," at Charlestown, New Hampshire, was subjected to repeated assault. In April 1746, three settlers were captured and carried off to Canada. In May, No. 4 was again attacked, and Seth Putnam was killed. However, 30 militiamen managed to drive off this assault, killing two of the Indians. On June 19, the fort withstood yet another attack, with the loss of one man and three wounded. Fiercer still was the attack on August 3, which resulted in the death of Ebenezer Phillips, the burning of a number of houses, and the destruction of cattle. On April 7, 1747, the fort was assaulted again, but the attackers were repulsed. Two militiamen were slightly wounded.

Frontier "forts" like No. 4 were not generally the tightly constructed log palisade-and-stockade structures depicted in romantic historical paintings and movies.

Usually, they were ordinary houses that had been reinforced to some extent and supplied with weapons and provisions. Nevertheless, they afforded a degree of protection. While No. 4, for example, withstood attack after attack, those who ventured outside of its walls were not always so fortunate. On October 24, 1747, 12 settlers passing down the Connecticut River from the fort were attacked by Indians. Nathaniel Gould and Thomas Goodell were killed and scalped; Oliver Avery was wounded; John Henderson captured. On March 15 of the next year, 20 Indians attacked about eight settlers "who were out a few rods from No. 4." One man was killed, one wounded, and another captured. On June 28, Captain Hobbs marched out of the fort and ventured into the woods with about 40 men. Attacked by a large body of Indians, with "much coolness, judgment, and deliberation, he arranged his men in order, and fought the enemy four hours with great bravery, and dispersed them. Captain Hobbs lost three men [killed and another three wounded]."

Fort Massachusetts, at the western foot of Hoosac Mountain, 30 miles west of Deerfield, did not fare as well as No. 4. It fell to an attack by a combination of French and Indians on August 20, 1746. Bereft of the fort's protection, Deerfield was once again exposed to attack, and on August 25, the Barrs Fight occurred in the southwestern part of Deerfield Meadows. Like most of the engagements of King George's War, the Barrs Fight was anything but a formal battle, and it is no more significant than any other similarly brutal skirmish that convulsed the frontier at this time. It was witnessed, however, by Eunice Allen, who was tomahawked during the fight, and survived. At age 80, she recalled the encounter for a nineteenth-century local historian. Her account paints a vivid picture of the nature of frontier warfare during the years before the French and Indian War:

After the capitulation [of Fort Massachusetts], a party of Indians, meditating an attack upon Deerfield, came down upon the borders of the meadows, and reconnoitered them. They first examined the North Meadow, and then the South. Finding a quantity of hay in the South Meadow, two miles south of the Street [in Deerfield town], and supposing that our people would be there at work the next day, they concealed themselves in the brush and underwood upon the borders of the adjoining hills. The next day, ten or twelve men and children, the men armed with guns, which they always carried with them, went into the field and commenced labor. A Mr. Eleazer Hawks was out hunting partridges on the hills, where the Indians lay, that morning. He saw a partridge, and shot it. This alarmed the Indians, who supposed they were discovered. They immediately killed and scalped Mr. Hawks, and then proceeded to attack the workmen. They fought some time, which gave some of the children an opportunity to escape. Mr. Allen, father of Miss [Eunice] Allen, resolutely maintained his ground in defence of three children, who were at work with him in the field, until he killed one or two of the enemy. When he was overpowered, he fought them with the breech of his gun, but was finally shot, and horribly mangled. The shirt which he wore on that day, torn with many balls and gashed with tomahawks, is still to be seen [in 1853], as a curiosity, either in the Museum in Deerfield Academy, or at the house of his grandson, at the Barrs. In this engagement three men and a boy were killed, one boy was taken prisoner, and Miss Allen was wounded in the head, and left for dead, but not scalped. In endeavoring to make her escape, she was pursued by an Indian with an uplifted tomahawk and a gun. She was extremely active, and would have outrun him, had he not fired upon her. The ball missed her, but she supposed that it had struck her, and in her fright she fell. The Indian overtook her, and buried his tomahawk in her head, and left her for dead. The firing in the meadows alarmed the people in the Street, who ran to the scene of action, and the Indians made a hasty retreat, and were pursued for several miles by a body of men under the command of Captain Clesson. Miss Allen was passed by a number of people, who supposed her to be dead. At last an uncle came to her, discovered signs of life, and conveyed her home. Her wound was dressed by Dr. Thomas Williams, who took from it considerable quantities of brain.

Samuel Allen, Jr., was the boy captured during the assualt on Mr. Allen. Like many prisoners taken in northern New England, Samuel was conveyed to Canada. Also like many other prisoners, his experience with the Indians was not horrific. After a year and nine months among them, Samuel was "redeemed" by Colonel John Hawks, "a celebrated partisan officer in Indian warfare." Samuel was extremely loth to see Colonel Hawks, who was his uncle, and when he came into his presence refused to speak the English language, pretending to have forgotten it; and although he was dressed most shabbily, fared most miserably, and was covered with vermin, he was very much opposed to leaving the Indians. Threats and force were finally employed to make him consent to quit them, and he asserted to the day of his death, that the Indian mode of life was the happiest.

Most of the war's engagements involved small numbers of combatants. On July 14, 1748, 120 Indians ambushed a party of 17 militiamen on their way to Fort Dummer; two militiamen were killed, two wounded, four escaped, and the remainder were taken prisoner in what amounted to one of the war's larger actions. The Indians killed the wounded men after they had traveled with them about a mile. On August 2, about 200 Indians "were hovering'' around Fort Massachusetts. When the Indians opened fire on a scouting party sent from the fort, commandant Captain Ephraim Williams led 30 men against the attackers—but prudently retreated.

Only in Nova Scotia was the fighting on a grander, more European scale. Not only had Pepperell taken Louisbourg in 1745, but in 1746 a French fleet dispatched from Europe under the command of the Duc d'Anville attempted a grand assault against Port Royal. It was not the English military presence, but the rugged, fogbound coast of Nova Scotia that foiled this attempt. The next year, however, a French land force marching out of Beaubassin under the command of Coulon de Villiers, captured the English fort at Grand Pré.

Not all Indians were fighting on the side of the French. In the northeast, the Mohawks were solidly allied with the English. Officially, the other Iroquois tribes struggled to maintain neutrality, but they, too, leaned toward the English. Although Iroquois neutrality nominally extended to ''dependent'' tribes in the Ohio country, preeminent among which were the Shawnee, a delegation of Ohio warriors came to Philadelphia in November 1747 asking for arms to fight the French. The *Pennsylvania Council Minutes* does not identify the Ohio speaker:

The old men at the [council] Fire at Onondago are unwilling to come into the War, [so] the Young Indians, the Warriors, and Captains consulted together and resolved to take up the English Hatchet against the will of their old People, and to lay their old People aside as of no use but in time of Peace. This the Young Warriors have done—provoked to it by repeated Applications of our Brethren the English.

The principal English provocateurs among the Ohio tribes were not official agents of any government, but traders such as the wily, rapacious, and resourceful George Croghan. Toward the end of King George's War, during August and September 1748, Pennsylvania and Virginia officially commissioned Conrad Weiser, a trader and Indian interpreter, to treat with the Ohio tribes. As a result of his efforts, the Wyandots, whose territory lay just above that of the Shawnees, joined Pennsylvania's celebrated Chain of Friendship. A few months earlier, on July 20, 1748, the Miamis (also called Twightwees, a name derived from the cry of the crane), from present-day Indiana and western Ohio, had joined the chain.

## THE CHICKASAW RESISTANCE

In addition to these northern and northwestern allies, the English had support in the South from the Chickasaws and Cherokees, who were warring with the French and French-allied Creeks and Choctaws. The Chickasaw Resistance had begun in 1720, when the Chickasaws defied French authority by maintaining trade relations with the English and by allowing English traders to ''invade'' territory claimed by France along the Mississippi River. In an attempt to enforce control, the French incited their Choctaw allies to raid Chickasaw settlements. The Chickasaws retaliated with raids of their own, not only against Choctaw villages, but against French shipping on the river, effectively creating a trade blockade. French authorities redoubled their recruitment of Choctaw allies, fixing a bounty on Chickasaw scalps and supplying firearms and ammunition. Raids and counterraids were exchanged for about four years, until a 1724 treaty effected an armistice.

On November 28, 1729, the Natchez Indians, centered a little east of the present Mississippi city that bears their name, rose up against Fort Rosalie, a French settlement and military outpost, killing about 200 whites and staging scattered raids throughout the lower Mississippi Valley. Relations between the French and the Natchez had been marked by violence in the past, but open warfare had been averted largely through the efforts of Tattooed Serpent, brother of the Natchez principal chief, known as the Great Sun. After Tattooed Serpent died, however, the governor of Louisiana, Sieur Chepart, foolishly ordered the removal of the Natchez from their sacred Great Village, opposite Fort Rosalie on the bluffs of the Mississippi. Despite the counsel of the tribal ''queen mother,'' Tattooed Arm, the Natchez took up the hatchet. Among those taken captive in the attack on Fort Rosalie was the governor. The Natchez regarded him with such contempt that no warrior would defile his weapon by taking his life. That job was consigned to a Stinkard, a member of the lowest caste in the hierarchy of Natchez society, who beat him to death with a club.

The French retaliated vigorously, sending out invasion forces from New Orleans. The Natchez and the Yazoo Indians, who had joined in the uprising, were badly beaten in battle. Those captured were sold into West Indian slavery. Those who evaded death or captivity made their way to the Chickasaws.

Peace endured only a few years when in 1732, the French renewed their demands that the Chickasaws expel English traders from their villages—along with refugees from the Natchez Revolt of 1729. Other tribes were also rebelling against the French. Augmenting their Choctaw allies with Indians brought down from Illinois country, the French backed a series of raids against the Chickasaws, who, by 1734, had once again blocked shipping on the Mississippi.

In an effort finally to shake free of the Chickasaw stranglehold, Governor Jean Baptiste le Moyne, Sieur de

## THE COVENANT CHAIN AND THE CHAIN OF FRIENDSHIP

The Covenant Chain was an extraordinary bisocietal confederation between the British colonies and various Indian tribes. New York and the Iroquois League dominated the chain, with New York generally representing the colonial consensus and the Iroquois speaking for the Indians. After the English conquered the Dutch in 1664, the Mohawks, who had enjoyed profitable trade relations with the Dutch, eagerly allied themselves with the new government of New York. In 1677, the Five Iroquois Nations joined in the Covenant Chain with New York, Massachusetts Bay, Connecticut, Maryland, and Virginia. The Shawnees joined a few years later. Pennsylvania, by means of a 1736 treaty, forged a special place for itself in the chain by creating a separate alliance with the Iroquois in what became known as the Chain of Friendship. Subsequently, the Shawnees and Miamis joined this chain as well. The more allies—in effect, client tribes—a colony could claim, the more powerful it was.

The language of the treaties and declarations that solemnized these alliances was full of grand and hopeful eloquence. Pennsylvania welcomed the Shawnees with a speech recorded in the minutes of a council meeting of July 22, 1748:

At the Intercession of our good Friends and Allies the Six Nations [of the Iroquois League, whose original five member tribes had become six with the addiction of the Tuscaroras in 1722] we have granted you a Council Road, whereby you have free access to any of His Majestie's Provinces; we admit you into our Friendship and Alliance, and, therefore, now call you Brethren, an appelation which we hold sacred, and in which is included everything that is dear. It obliges us to give you assistance on all occasions, to exercise unfeigned affection toward you, to take you into our Bosoms, to use our Eyes and Ears

and Hands as well for you as for ourselves. Nothing is put in competition by an Englishman with the Faith and Honour due to those whom our Gracious King pleases to take into his Protection, admit into his Chain of Friendship, and make them our Fellow Subjects. From that Moment they become our own Flesh and Blood, and what hurts them will equally hurt us. Do you on your parts look upon this Important Name of Brethren in the same Light; You must no more think of Onontio [the Indian name for the French governor] and his Children, all that sort of Relationship now ceases—His Majesty's Friends are your Friends, and his Majesty's Enemies are your Enemies. On these Conditions we accept your Calumet Pipe . . . [and] we present you with this Double Belt of Wampum as an Emblem of Union.

Thus, New York, Pennsylvania, and the other English colonies jockeyed with the French and with one another for Indian allies. For their part, the Iroquois used the two chains as the means of consolidating their own power and influence.

The Covenant Chain and the Chain of Friendship were grand and ambitious schemes of alliance; however, the realities of culture and nationality soon intervened. The Iroquois Confederacy, which had been losing power since the end of the seventeenth century, was being torn apart by divided loyalties between the French and the English. The Iroquois also proved incapable of controlling the Shawnees, who left the two chains before the outbreak of the French and Indian War. As for the English, despite the fine language associated with the chains, their attitude and actions toward their Indian allies were contemptuous at best and treacherous at worst. By the time the French and Indian War began, the Covenant Chain and the Chain of Friendship were, as the Indians put it, "rusted" and "broken."

Bienville, of Louisiana launched a full-fledged military campaign against the Indians. Under the command of Major Pierre d'Artaguette, a force of 400 French regulars augmented by Indian allies approached along the Mississippi from the north. The governor commanded another army, consisting of 600 regulars and 1,000 Choctaws, which converged from the south along the Tombigbee River. Despite the impressive numbers, the maneuver lacked coordination, and the two armies failed to meet. Divided, they were defeated in separate Chickasaw attacks.

Three years later, in 1739, Bienville attempted to field an army of 3,000. This time he was defeated not by Chickasaws, but by torrential rains, which forestalled attack. Chickasaw pressure was unrelieved throughout the course of King George's War.

## STRENGTHENED ALLIANCES

King George's War and the Indian resistances associated with it accomplished little for the colonial powers except to establish or solidify certain white-Indian alliances. Broadly speaking, the Iroquois tribes (especially the Mohawks) tended to side with the English, and the Algonquian tribes tended to ally themselves (often more enthusiastically) with the French. The peace brought by the Treaty of Aix-la-Chapelle on October 18, 1748, was no more than an armistice in prelude to the French and Indian War. The futility of King George's War in the colonies is symbolized by one of the conditions of the treaty. Although the war resulted in nominal British control of Nova Scotia (the founding of Halifax in 1746 strenghtened the English presence there), the English agreed to return to France the one indisputable strategic prize, Louisbourg. It would figure importantly—and bitterly—in the next war.

# CHAPTER 11

## PATHS OF GLORY
### The Period of The French and Indian War (1749–1763)

The treaty of Aix-la-Chapelle, which ended King George's War on October 18, 1748, brought to the American frontier a fleeting peace, but no lasting stability. On March 16, 1749, King George II granted huge western tracts to the Ohio Company, a powerful syndicate of British traders and speculators, stipulating that, within seven years, the company must plant a settlement of 100 families and build a fort for their protection. This grant and its stipulation renewed enmity with the French and Indians, who felt that the new charter would encroach on their lands.

### THE FERMENT OF ALLIANCE

They were right. Throughout 1749, an influx of British traders "invaded" territories that had been the exclusive trading province of the French. About this time, the Wyandot chief Memeskia (whom the English called Old Briton and the French, La Demoiselle) led a band of his people from Detroit, where they had been under the direct supervision of the French, to Sandusky, in present-day Ohio. In open defiance of French authority, they welcomed Pennsylvania traders there and even plotted to overthrow the French.

Although French agents discovered and defeated the plot, unrest in the area continued. On June 15, 1749, Roland-Michel Galissonière, marquis de La Galissonière, governor of New France, dispatched Captain Pierre-Joseph Céleron de Blainville with 213 men to the Ohio country. By November 9, Céleron had made a round trip of 3,000 miles, sinking at intervals lead plates inscribed with France's claim to sovereignty over the territory. No number of lead plates, however, could convince the Ohio Indians to forsake cheaper, better, and more-varied En-

glish trade goods for the inferior and more costly wares the French had to offer. The English traders remained in the territory.

The ineffectual La Galissonière was replaced as governor by Jacques-Pierre de Jonquière, marquis de La Jonquière, who assumed office in August 1749 and began to take more aggressive military steps, building Fort Rouillé (Toronto) to cut off trade between the northern Great Lakes and Oswego, on the south shore of Lake Ontario in New York. The new governor strengthened the fortifications at Detroit and took measures to stop the lively smuggling trade between Caughnawagas—"French Mohawks" attached to Jesuit missions—and Albany. In the West, La Jonquière launched a raid against the Shawnees, most powerful and flagrant among the tribes who traded with the English in the Ohio country. This action succeeded only in driving the Shawnees deeper into the English camp.

In the meantime, from September 11, 1750, to March 29, 1752, the trader Christopher Gist, commissioned by Virginia as a provincial agent-envoy, traveled the Ohio country to scout out suitable tracts for settlement and to offer peace and friendship with the Indians. Gist was not the first to offer peace and friendship in return for land.

From June 16 to July 7, 1744, commissioners from Virginia and Maryland and a delegation from Pennsylvania met with representatives of all six nations of the Iroquois Confederacy in Lancaster, Pennsylvania. Their object was to negotiate a cession of territory in the Ohio country, which the Iroquois Six Nations claimed by right of conquest. The Iroquois ceded the territory for a price—£300 in Pennsylvania currency from Maryland; £200 in the same currency from Virginia, plus £300 in gold; and £300 in currency from Pennsylvania. It seemed a great bargain, especially for Virginia, whose deed with the Iroquois stipulated that the Indians "renounce and disclaim not only all the right [to the territory] . . . , but also recognize the right and title of our sovereign the King of Great Britain to all the lands within [Virginia] as it is now or hereafter may be peopled and bounded." Most likely, no one troubled to point out to the Iroquois that Virginia's charter boundaries stretched "from sea to sea." Within three months of the treaty, Virginia was granting petitions for western lands totaling 300,000 acres. The French, whose traders were already working much of the Ohio country, justifiably felt threatened.

From May to July 1752, Gist conducted a major treaty conference at Logstown (Ambridge, Pennsylvania) between the Iroquois Six Nations, the Delawares, Shawnees, and Wyandots and Virginia and the Ohio Company.

Amid a muddle of cross-purposes and conflicting interests, the goal of Virginia and the Ohio Company was to secure from the Indians a quitclaim to the Ohio country—to reiterate, reinforce, and expand agreements made in 1744 at Lancaster. "Brethren," declared a Virginia treaty commissioner on July 10, "be assur'd that the King, our Father, by purchasing your Lands, had never any Intention of *taking them from you*, but that we might live together as one people, and *keep them from the French*, who wou'd be bad Neighbours."

The situation in the Ohio country at this time was one of seething ferment. Pennsylvania traders occupied the territory in question, and the Ohio Company (whose investors were Virginians) intended to seize and settle it. The French were trying to evict English traders of any kind and prevent English settlement. The Indians of the country were pressured by all factions. The Iroquois, who had once represented the closest thing to centralized, coordinated government the customarily independent Indian tribes had ever known, were rapidly losing their influence in the West by appeasing the French while treating with the English.

The Logstown treaty accomplished its purpose, securing for Virginia and the Ohio Company deeds to Ohio lands, reaffirming the 1744 Lancaster treaty, and apparently reconciling rival Delaware and Iroquois claims to authority. This part of the treaty was especially important since the Delawares were embittered against the English because of a swindle perpetrated by the sons of William Penn, proprietors of Pennsylvania, in the notorious Walking Purchase.

In 1735, the financially strapped Penn brothers, John and Thomas, needed to sell large tracts of land in order to satisfy massive debts. Unfortunately, they lacked the funds to purchase sufficient territory from the Delaware Indians for resale. The brothers produced a fragmentary,

unsigned draft of a document apparently drawn up early in the century and persuaded the illiterate Indians that it was a binding deed stipulating the cession of lands bounded by a walk of a day and a half from a certain starting point. The paper did not specify the direction of the walk, so the brothers hired a man to walk in the direction they desired. He made 64 miles in the time allotted.

Through a further exercise in sleight-of-topography, the Penns figured out a way to make the walk encompass a vast tract of Pennsylvania. Directly after the walk, the "original" scrap of paper disappeared, and only a "copy," retained by the Penns, remained. The Delawares protested, but the Penns' agent James Logan persuaded a delegation of Iroquois in 1742 to evict the Delawares on the basis of a further (and equally fraudulent) claim of former conquest. The Delawares realized they had been cheated but had no legal recourse, since an Indian could not bear testimony against an Englishman in colonial courts. As directed by the Iroquois, some of the Delawares reluctantly settled along the Wyoming Valley of Pennsylvania, and others unwillingly removed to the Ohio country.

Key components of the Logstown treaty began to unravel almost instantly. While Miami (Twightwee) delegates were engaging in preliminary negotiations at Logstown, news reached them that Pickawillany (present-day Piqua, Ohio), their "capital" and the center of English trade in the Ohio country, had been raided and largely destroyed. The attack was led on June 21, 1752, by Charles Langlade, a half-breed French Indian agent who commanded Ojibwas (also known as Chippewas), Potawatomis, and Ottawas. Thirteen Miami warriors perished, as well as one trader; three other traders were taken captive. Chief Memeskia was killed and ritually devoured by his assailants. George Croghan's politically crucial trading post was also destroyed.

Reacting to the raid, Tanaghrisson, chief of the Senecas, westernmost of the Iroquois tribes, requested of the Virginia Logstown delegates that their government build a "strong House, at the Fork of the Mohongalio [the juncture of the Monongahela and the Allegheny; the site of present-day Pittsburgh], to keep such Goods, Powder, Lead and necessaries as shall be wanting, and as soon as you please." Although this request for an arsenal and trading post was for the Seneca's use to defend themselves against the French and their Indian allies, the Virginians made it an excuse to establish a garrisoned fort for themselves two years later. For the present, the English did nothing in response to Pickawillany, and the Miamis quickly returned to the French fold. For the English, this had dire consequences: Essentially, their trade had been driven out of the Ohio Valley.

Ange Duquesne de Menneville, marquis Duquesne, who replaced La Jonquière as governor of New France on July 1, 1752, seized the moment by commencing the construction of new forts to secure the Ohio country and protect the thin French lifeline extending from Montreal to New Orleans. At Fort Niagara, Duquesne assembled an army of 2,200 men, complete with artillery—the largest European force thus far mustered in North America. The Iroquois—famed for their invincible ferocity—were intimidated. The council at Onondaga sent a delegation of *matrons*—not warriors, let alone chiefs— to Captain Paul Marin de La Malgue, the leader of Duquesne's expedition, to ask his intentions. Marin, with some contempt, told them that the Iroquois were not his objective, but that they had better not interfere with him. They did not.

Similarly, the Delawares of Venango (which the French called Rivière aux Boeufs, present-day French Creek, Pennsylvania) asked after the expedition's purpose, but they did not obstruct it. Indeed, when Marin began construction of Fort Venango at Rivière aux Boeufs in July 1753, Delawares came from the surrounding country in search of work—mostly as bearers of burdens across the Niagara portage—after a punishing winter. The Oneida chief Scarouady had responded similarly when, in June 1753, he led a delegation of Delawares, Shawnees, and Mingo Senecas to Fort Presque Isle (Erie, Pennsylvania), then under construction. His followers sought work, not trouble.

Construction of Fort LeBoeuf (Waterford, Pennsylvania) did not go so smoothly, but the enemies were neither the English nor the Indians. Disease and drought, which made downstream passage impossible, as well as corrupt profiteering on the part of certain French officials, greatly impeded progress. Meanwhile, early in September 1753, in defiance of Iroquois neutrality (the Iroquois held nominal sway over the Mingos, whose origin was part Seneca and part Cayuga), Tanaghrisson led a delegation of Mingo warriors to challenge Marin at Presque Isle. "The river where we are," he declared, "belongs to us warriors." He presented Marin with a wampum belt: "With this belt we detain you and ask you to have them cease setting up the establishments you want to make. . . . I shall strike at whoever does not listen to us." Marin replied: "I shall continue on my way, and if there are any persons bold enough to set up barriers to hinder my march, I shall knock them over so vigorously that they may crush those who made them." The chief and his warriors withdrew; as Thomas Penn's treaty commissioner wrote to his employer: "This Chief who went like a Lyon roaring out Destruction, came back like a Sheep with Tears in his Eyes, and desired the English to go away, for that the French who were coming down the River Ohio in two hundred Canoes, would hurt them and make Spoil of their Goods."

On September 11, 1753, following his confrontation with Marin, Tanaghrisson dispatched Chief Scarouady with a delegation of 98 Ohio Indians, including Delawares and Shawnees, to Winchester, Virginia, to seek aid from the Virginians against the French. The Winchester conference was torn with dissension. All treaty commissioner William Fairfax could promise was that southern Cherokees, Catawbas, and Chickasaws would march to the aid of the Ohioans. The problem with this, Scarouady pointed out, was that these tribes were enemies of the Iroquois. Virginia would have to work out a peace between them.

Chief Scarouady moved next to Carlisle, Pennsylvania, on October 4, 1753, for another treaty conference, this time with Pennsylvania. This meeting hardly proved more satisfactory. Because of bad judgment and intrigue, the Pennsylvania commissioners decided to withhold the £800 worth of presents that were to be given to the Indians as part of the treaty.

The result of these two treaty conferences was anything but what the English had hoped for. The Delaware and Shawnee revoked the year-old Logstown treaty and threw their support behind French claims to the Ohio, and Iroquois enthusiasm for an English alliance cooled drastically.

Even as English colonial bumbling was contributing to the disintegration of Indian alliances, Lord Halifax, in August 1753, was pushing the British cabinet toward a declaration of war with France. Using as his basis the 1713 Treaty of Utrecht, which stipulated an acknowledgment that the Iroquois were British subjects, and bolstering his claims by allusions to Iroquois deeds from 1701 and 1726, Halifax asserted English rights to Iroquois lands, including those the Iroquois claimed by conquest—that is, the Ohio country. Halifax argued before the cabinet that the French, in trading throughout the Ohio Valley, had invaded Virginia.

In this climate, Governor Robert Dinwiddie of Virginia received authorization from the crown to evict the French from territory under his jurisdiction. He commissioned 21-year-old George Washington to carry an ultimatum to Captain Legardeur de Saint-Pierre, commandant of Fort LeBoeuf after Captain Marin's death. Washington set out from Williamsburg on October 31, 1753, and attempted to pick up a substantial allied Indian escort along the way. In the wake of the Winchester and Carlisle conferences, however, the Delaware and Shawnee warriors declined to accompany him. Only Tanaghrisson and three Mingos reluctantly escorted Washington and his party. Understandably, when the delegation reached Fort LeBoeuf on December 12, 1753, Captain Legardeur was less than impressed. Thirty years older than Washington, he treated him courteously, but he rejected Virginia's demand to vacate.

Dinwiddie next ordered Captain William Trent to build a fort at the "forks of Ohio," the junction of the Ohio, Monongahela, and Allegheny rivers. Construction began in January 1754 and proceeded without interference from the French, not only because the harshness of the winter made campaigning impossible, but because the Indians, suffering terribly from the weather, blamed the French for the inadequacy of their provisions. Now was not a time to seek Indian allies. The fort completed, Ensign Edward Ward was left in charge of its small garrison.

In the meantime, with the approach of spring, British authorities in Nova Scotia decided to tighten their hold on the region by demanding that its Acadian residents— French-speaking Roman Catholic farmers and fishermen who freely intermarried with the Micmac and Abnaki Indians—swear loyalty to the British crown. The Acadians, who had the misfortune of occupying the most important fishery in the world, waters used and coveted by all the nations of Europe, were caught in a crisis. While the British demanded the loyalty oath, under pain of dispossession and expulsion, the French, operating from Fort Beauséjour, pressured them to refuse the oath. Using Fort Beauséjour as headquarters, Abbé Jean-Louis Le Loutre, a Spiritan missionary operating in Nova Scotia, led the French resistance, instigating Micmac converts to raid British settlers. He explained his operations in a letter to the French minister of Marine:

As we cannot openly oppose the English ventures, I think we cannot do better than to incite the Indians to continue warring on the English; my plan is to persuade the Indians to send word to the English that they will not permit new settlements to be made in Acadia. . . . I shall do my best to make it look to the English as if this plan comes from the Indians and that I have no part of it.

Le Loutre also used the threat of Indian raids as a cudgel against his flock, the Acadians, warning that he would unleash the Micmacs upon them if they took the oath of loyalty. Tensions mounted steadily.

## WAR BEGINS

Spring also brought French action against the fort at the forks of Ohio. While the winter delayed attack, French spies had observed construction. Captain Claude-Pierre Pécaudy de Contrecoeur, latest commandant of Fort Le-Boeuf, sent 600 men to the English fort, at the time defended by Ensign Ward and a garrison of 41. Ward

prudently surrendered on April 17, 1754, and was allowed to march off with his men the next day. Contrecoeur renamed the stronghold Fort Duquesne.

Having secured £10,000 from the Virginia assembly, Governor Dinwiddie set about raising troops and promoted Washington to lieutenant colonel. On the day that the Ohio fort fell, Dinwiddie sent Washington with 150 men to reinforce the position. On May 28, having been warned by Tanaghrisson that the French were nearby, Washington, with 40 provincials and a dozen of Tanaghrisson's warriors, surprised a 33-man French reconnaissance party. In the ensuing combat, ten of the Frenchmen were killed, including Ensign Joseph Coulon de Villiers de Jumonville, a French "ambassador." The remaining 23 men surrendered. Later, the French would accuse Washington of murdering innocent men in a time of peace, and specifically of "assassinating" Jumonville. Most likely, Jumonville was dispatched by Tanaghrisson's hatchet; as to the other deaths, Washington explained that he and his party should not have been subject to hostile reconnaissance.

This encounter was the first real battle of the French and Indian War, and knowing that the French would retaliate in strength, Washington asked Tanaghrisson to summon Delawares for help—not all of them, after all, were pro-French. They were, however, hardly enthusiastic allies of the English; only 40 answered the call. Washington made an unconvincing speech to them: "The only motive for our conduct is to put you again in possession of your lands, and to take care of your wives and children, to dispossess the French, to maintain your rights and to secure the whole country for you; for these very ends are the English arms now employed."

When it became painfully apparent to the young commander that his force would not stand a chance against the French, he attempted to organize a full-scale retreat. But it was too late; the French were too close, and his own troops were exhausted. At Great Meadows, in northwestern Pennsylvania, near Fort Duquesne, Washington ordered the hasty erection of a makeshift stockade, dubbing it Fort Necessity. Tanaghrisson protested that the structure was useless. But, as the chief later explained, the lieutenant colonel

would by no means take Advice from the Indians . . . he lay at one Place from one full Moon to the other and made no Fortifications at all, but that little thing upon the Meadow, where he thought the French would come up to him in open Field; . . . had he taken the Half King's [Tanaghrisson's] advice and made such Fortifications as the Half King advised him to make he would certainly have beat the French off; . . . the French had acted as great Cowards, and the English Fools in that Engagement; . . . he (the Half King) had carried off his Wife and Children, so did other Indians before the Battle begun, because Col. Washington would never listen to them, but was always driving them on to fight by his Directions.

On July 3, Major Coulon de Villiers, the brother of the man Washington's small detachment had killed, led a mixed force of 900—French soldiers, Delawares, Ottawas, Wyandots, Algonquins, Nipissings, Abnakis, and "mission" Iroquois—to Great Meadows. Vastly outnumbered, inadequately fortified, and fighting in driving rains that melted entrenchments and rendered swivel guns useless, Washington surrendered Fort Necessity on July 4, 1754. Half of his men had been killed. The survivors were permitted to leave, save for two held as hostages, who were taken back to Fort Duquesne.

There, the easy-going French, elated with their victory, gave the prisoners free run of the fort. Captain Robert Stobo used this liberality to advantage, making careful observations of its defenses and pacing off the fort's interior dimensions. Using friendly Delaware visitors, including Chief Shingas, his brother Delaware George (Nenatchehunt), and a Mingo called Moses the Song, he managed to smuggle plans of the fort to Philadelphia. Stobo's document revealed how weakly the French held Fort Duquesne and even suggested that allied Indians might be employed to take it:

The Indians have great liberty here; they go in and out when they please without notice. If 100 trusty Shanoes [Shawnees], Mingoes and Dillaways [Delawares] were picked out, they might surprise the Fort, lodging themselves under the platform behind the palisades by day, and at night secure the guard with the Tomahawks. The guard consists of 40 men only and five officers.

Stobo's suggestion, however, was not heeded. Throughout the first four years of this long and miserable war, the English showed a remarkable contempt for Indians as allies, even as the French used them to devastating advantage. Not only was there dissension between the colonies and potentially invaluable Indians, there was great bitterness between the crown and the colonies, some of which resisted war. In New York, for example, powerful mercantile interests, which had long engaged in a profitable smuggling trade with Montreal, refused to cooperate with attempts to meet the French threat.

With the fall of the Ohio fort and the defeat of Washington, the English were expelled from the Ohio country. In the wake of this defeat, the Iroquois, the only Indian allies remaining to the English, wavered. To bring colonial factions into line and to bolster the Iroquois alliance, a congress was convened at Albany from June 19 to July 10, 1754.

The congress produced a plan for colonial unity, which managed to please no one. The crown rejected it on the grounds that it gave too much power to the individual colonies; the colonies rejected it on the grounds that it conceded too much power to the crown. A treaty was concluded with Iroquois representatives but was greatly vitiated by the land grabs "negotiated" by Pennsylvania's Conrad Weiser and Connecticut's John Lydius. Through underhanded means, they obtained massive cessions from the Iroquois chiefs present, including tracts in western Pennsylvania and in the Wyoming Valley along the north branch of the Susquehanna River. This territory was occupied by Delawares and Mahicans who had been converted by Moravian missionaries; in effect, the Iroquois Confederation was their landlord. At the time, the French were wooing them into their fold, and the events at Albany pushed them closer to the French camp. As Concochquiesie, sachem of the Oneida, another tribe dependent on the Iroquois and affected by the land grab, declared to colonial superintendent of Indian affairs William Johnson:

Brother. You promised us that you would keep this fire place clean from all filth and that no snake should come into this Council Room. That Man sitting there (pointing to Coll: Lyddius) is a Devil and has stole our Lands. He takes Indians slyly by the Blanket one at a time, and when they are drunk, puts some money in their bosoms, and perswades them to sign deeds for our lands upon the Susquehanna which we will not ratify nor suffer to be settled by any means.

Amid dissension and double dealing, the Six Iroquois Nations proclaimed their official neutrality in the war between the English and the French, while several tribes nominally dependent on the Iroquois actually went over to the French.

These early events would prove typical of much of the French and Indian War. There were some formal battles fought by regular European armies, but most of the war was conducted guerrilla fashion, using provincial troops and Indians. And among both French and English, regular troops and provincials were constantly at odds. The provincials were appalled at the cruelty of the regular army, where flogging was the chief punishment for even the most petty of offenses, and regular army commanders were contemptuous of the provincials. British commander Major General James Wolfe observed that

there never was people collected together so unfit for the business they were set upon [as the provincials]—dilatory, ignorant, irresolute and some grains of a very unmanly quality and very unsoldier-like or unsailor-like. . . . The Americans are in general the dirtiest, the most contemptible, cowardly dogs you can conceive. There is no depending on 'em in action. They fall down dead in their own dirt and desert by battalions, officers and all.

Nevertheless, it would be provincial forces that won the only British victories of the war's first four years. As to the importance of Indian allies, the British won battles only when the Indians abandoned the French, or the British managed to muster Indian allies themselves, or when Indians were not involved on either side.

While the English forces either failed to use Indian allies effectively or only spurned them, the French, in contrast, exploited them, though the European commanders found doing so distasteful. Louis Antoine de Bougainville, comte de Bougainville, observed: "The cruelties and the insolence of these barbarians is horrible, their souls are as black as pitch. It is an abominable way to make war; the retaliation is frightening, and the air one breathes here is contagious of making one accustomed to callousness." He wrote to his mother that her "child shudders at the horrors which we will be forced to witness" in combat employing these most "ferocious of all people, and great cannibals by trade." Europeans had

long been horrified—and fascinated—by tales of New World cannibalism. To his brother, Bougainville wrote that the western Indians had been "drawn from 500 leagues by the smell of fresh human flesh and the chance to teach their young men how one carves up a human being destined for the pot."

Despite his professed scruples, Bougainville understood that Indian allies were crucial to the French cause. "What a scourge!" he wrote in his journal. "Humanity shudders at being obliged to make use of such monsters. But without them the match would be too much against us." And Pierre Rigaud de Vaudreuil de Cavagnial, marquis de Vaudreuil, who replaced Duquesne as governor general of New France, reported to the French minister of war that the Indians he had sent out in the winter of 1755–56 "to harass the enemy" had been responsible for the loss of "one hundred [English] men for our one."

## TOTAL WARFARE

Vaudreuil did not point out that most of the losses (on both sides) were civilian. For the French and Indian War

---

## CANNIBALISM

In *The Tempest,* a play set in a fictional quarter of the New World just then being explored by Englishmen and others, Shakespeare makes reference to its native population of "anthropophagi"; for Elizabethan explorers carried home many tales of cannibalism. These reports were both exaggerated *and* true. There is no evidence that any American Indian tribe practiced cannibalism as a means of regular subsistence. However, ritual cannibalism was widespread and was reported among Indians well into the nineteenth century. One recent scholar, Richard Slotkin, has declared that cannibalism was practiced as a ritual by almost all tribes, and the anthropologist Harold E. Driver reports its occurrence "in a continuous area from the Iroquoians in the Northeast to the Gulf tribes in the Southeast, thence south through northeast Mexico to Meso-America and the Carribean."

In some ways, cannibalism was just one of many war-related tribal tortures. Puritan sources report New England Indians tying captives to trees and gnawing their flesh from their bones. Yet the ritual significance of the practice went far beyond mere

cruelty. In *The Present State of New-England . . .* (1676), Nathaniel Saltonstall details a telling instance:

[The] Executioners (for there were many) flung one End [of the rope] over the Post, and so hoised him up like a Dog, three or four Times, and with his Knife made a Hole in his Breast to his Heart, and sucked out his Heart-Blood.

The whites present asked one of the Indians "his Reason therefore," to which he replied: "Me stronger than I was before, me be so strong as me and he too, he be very strong Man fore he die." This was no different from the common practice among Indian hunters of eating a piece of a just-killed bear or wolf in order to partake of the former's strength or the latter's cunning. Eating one's enemy—or a part of him—was the consummation of conquest. The *killing* had taken his life; the *eating* took something of his identity, his strength, courage, cunning, all that is most effectively summed up in the Latin term *vertus*: manliness, strength, capacity.

was "total war." It was war waged not only by one army against another, but by armies, militia, and other groups of whites and Indians against civilians as well. It was war brought home. In 1755, Robert Rogers, a New Hampshire commander of a crack outfit of provincial "rangers"—woodsmen who fought with the skill of Indians—was instructed by Massachusetts governor William Shirley to "distress the French and their allies by sacking, burning, and destroying their houses, barns, barracks, canoes, battoes, &c. and by killing their cattle of every kind; and at all times to endeavour to way-lay, attack, and destroy their convoys of provisions by land and water, in any part of the country." These instructions describe the policy of both sides throughout the war. Even during the more conventional battles fought by European generals leading regular troops, civilians were hardly immune from terror and destruction. During the siege of Quebec, British general James Wolfe deliberately laid waste the surrounding country and trained his artillery on civilian targets within the city. For their part during the siege, General Montcalm and Governor Vaudreuil prevented the citizenry from capitulating by threatening to turn Indians loose upon them.

Indians, too, were subject to the horrors of total war. Pennsylvania offered scalp bounties, as did New England. In 1756, Pennsylvania's John Armstrong surprised the Delaware settlement of Kittanning and burned its inhabitants in their houses. Robert Rogers, and his Rangers massacred the men, women, and children of the Abnaki mission village of Saint Francis. Of course, the Indians suffered in a more enduring way as well. The battles in which they participated as "allies" of one side or the other were all fought at their expense, regardless of whether the French or the English side claimed victory. Whatever side ultimately prevailed, it prevailed against the Indians, for the French and the English were fighting one another over *Indian* land. When the English, after seven bitter and most often inept years of combat, finally forced the surrender of New France, they were free to turn the full force of their rapacity against the Indians.

## INDIAN ALLIANCES

Many Indian leaders were well aware that, French or English, the white men intended to take their lands. But they could not ignore the struggle in their midst. The Iroquois for the most part, with the exception of the pro-English Mohawks, struggled to remain neutral, though Governor Vaudreuil, in October 1755, threatened that "should any of the Five Nations be found next spring among the English, I will let loose all our Upper [western] and domiciliated Nations on them; cause their vil-

lages to be laid waste and never pardon them." Most of the other tribes, however, sided in varying degrees with the French, hoping to eke out some advantage thereby, or hoping merely to survive. Indeed, during the first three years of the war, the English could count only on the Mohawks as allies.

The Delawares and other eastern tribes, having good reason to fear dispossession from their lands at the hands of the English, were fairly reliable French allies—though, later in the war, when the English bothered to negotiate with them, they showed a willingness to stop raiding. The Delawares were generally supported in the West by the Shawnees. In the Northeast, the Abnakis proved to be extremely reliable allies. Loyal to the French missionaries among them, they fought at their behest. Also reliable were the Ojibwas, Ottawas, and Potawatomis, Ohio country tribes known collectively among themselves as the Three Fires. Their links to French interests included a long tradition of trade and intermarriage. Closer to home, the "domiciliated" Indians of the Jesuit mission reserves near Montreal and Quebec could be counted on, except when loyalties to the Iroquois Six Nations conflicted with allegiance to New France.

In contrast to the arrogant and parsimonious attitude of the English in Indian affairs, the French were more respectful of Indian culture—intermarriage was common—and far more liberal with presents. The Moravian missionary Christian Frederick Post, carrying a peace proposal to the Ohio tribes in 1758, recorded how one of his Indian companions, Shamokin Daniel, "went over to [Fort Duquesne] . . . and counselled with the governor, who presented him with a laced coat and hat, a blanket, shirts, ribbons, a new gun, powder, lead &c. When he returned he was quite changed, and said, 'See here, you fools, what the French have given me. I was in Philadelphia, and never received a farthing.' " When such positive measures failed, the French used their western allies as menaces to bring the eastern Indians into line. In general, the Ohio country became a staging area for many eastern raids. While the Micmacs, who harried the English in Acadia, and the Abnakis, who raided them in northern New England, were locals, New York, for example, was often assaulted by tribes brought in from the West.

Many raids on Pennsylvania, Maryland, and Virginia involving Shawnees, Delawares, and some Iroquois were staged from Fort Duquesne. Such French-instigated operations generally consisted of one or two Frenchmen leading a group of Indians. Other raids were motivated more directly by Indian interests, as when the Delawares devastated the German settlers of Pennsylvania's Tulpehocken Valley in revenge for their having driven out the tribe's "royal family." Fighting styles varied. The Jesuit mission Indians, accustomed to taking orders from the French, were the most reliable fighters from a strategic point of view. The so-called Far Indians—Potawatomi, Ojibwa, and Ottawa—were also particularly effective. Usually raiding far from home, they tended to stay on the job after an action rather than simply running off with booty. Tribes raiding locally, such as the Abnaki and the Canadian Algonquins, tended to hit and run, making them less useful in executing larger-scale strategies. The Ohio Indians—Delaware, Shawnee, Mingo—grew less reliable as the war, ever so slowly, turned against the French. They, after all, had enjoyed trade with the English and moved into the French camp largely because the French, in pushing the English out of the Ohio country, had become necessary trading partners. Alliances with the Iroquois were even more tenuous, since the Six Nations were officially neutral, and the Mohawks, one of their leading tribes, were openly allied with the English.

## BRADDOCK TAKES COMMAND

In December 1754, the crown authorized Massachusetts governor William Shirley to reactivate two colonial regiments—about 2,000 men. These regiments were joined by two of the British army's worst regiments, which set out for America in January 1755 from Cork, Ireland, under Major General Edward Braddock, a tough, blustering, thoroughly mediocre commander. When the French responded the next month by dispatching 78 companies to Canada, British forces were expanded to seven regiments—about 10,000 men—assigned to take Fort Duquesne, Fort Saint Frédéric, Fort Niagara, and Fort Beauséjour.

It was now apparent to all concerned that what had started as a brushfire war in the vicinity of Fort Duquesne was escalating rapidly and would soon be a continental conflict. Indeed, the French and Indian War soon became part of an even greater struggle, the Seven Years War (1756–63), which came to involve much of Europe and the European colonies. Before it was over, Britain, Austria, Prussia, and Hanover would square off against France, Austria, Russia, Saxony, Sweden, and Spain. Recognizing that France's position as a world power was at stake, the French government in North America embraced escalation by openly authorizing Indian hostility against the British colonies on February 17, 1755.

On February 23, Braddock arrived in Williamsburg, Virginia, and on April 14, in Alexandria, he convened a council of war at which he laid out his plan of attack. Brigadier General Robert Monckton would campaign against Nova Scotia, while Braddock would take Forts Duquesne and Niagara. Governor Shirley would strengthen and reinforce Fort Oswego and then proceed to Fort Niagara—in the unlikely event that Braddock was detained at Fort Duquesne. William Johnson was slated to take Fort Saint Frédéric at Crown Point.

In the meantime, on April 23, 1755, Admiral Edward Boscawen set sail for the colonies on a mission to intercept an anticipated French troop-transport fleet (which actually sailed from Brest on May 3). Bad weather hindered Boscawen, and he only managed to seize two ships, the *Lys* and the *Alcide*, carrying one-tenth of the troops between them, on June 8, 1755. While the remainder of the army was able to land, Boscawen's actions did delay reinforcements from reaching Fort Beauséjour, the Nova Scotian center of guerrilla resistance against the English.

By May 19, 1755, when Massachusetts rangers set sail from Boston to attack the forts of Nova Scotia, Fort Beauséjour had already been compromised by a British agent provocateur, Thomas Pichon, who busied himself counseling the garrison to surrender. Morale at the fort was low, commanded as it was by the thoroughly corrupt profiteer Louis DuPont Duchambon de Vergor. Two thousand Massachusetts provincials under John Winslow, and a few British regulars commanded by General Monckton easily took the fort on June 16, after a "velvet siege" of four days. Fort Gaspereau, across the Chignecto peninsula, surrendered the next day without a shot. By the end of the month, the British held Nova Scotia—though Louisbourg, the important naval base at Cape Breton that guarded the Saint Lawrence, was still firmly in French hands.

In July, Acadian representatives refused to submit to the loyalty oath the victorious British demanded. Threatened with deportation, many of them relented—but Governor Charles Lawrence was no longer willing to accept a mere oath. On July 28, 1755, he ordered the deportation of Nova Scotia's Acadians. On October 13, 1,100 were sent into exile; many others followed—6,000 to 7,000—distributed throughout the colonies, especially Louisiana. With their customary blundering brashness, the British destroyed the Acadians' homes and the improvements they had made, including the dikes that held back the tidal waters of the Bay of Fundy. Due to saltwater floods, a great deal of land was rendered useless, and years later, the British colonial government would summon far-flung Acadians to return to restore the dikes. After the expulsion of the Acadians, the Micmac Indians, their neighbors, fought a war of resistance against the British—though some attempted to remain neutral. Eventually, they, too, were dispossessed of their lands.

While General Monckton and, more to the point, the

Massachusetts provincials were achieving success in Nova Scotia, General Braddock was struggling to get his expedition to Fort Duquesne under way. He faced two major problems. His battle plan called for the recruitment of Indian allies, but they failed to materialize. Governor James S. Glen of South Carolina was supposed to win the Choctaws from French alliance but failed so miserably that he actually provoked a Choctaw uprising. Virginia governor Dinwiddie, who had promised to deliver 400 Indian troops from the southern tribes, tangled with Governor Glen on this matter in a dispute that discouraged any Indian alliance at all. William Johnson was supposed to deliver Iroquois allies, but in the midst of a dispute with Governor Shirley, managed to discourage potential allies among them and succeeded only in getting the trader George Croghan to lead 50 Mingo warriors to Braddock's headquarters at Fort Cumberland, Maryland. The warriors, refugees from the French, brought their families along, including women, whose presence wreaked havoc in the English camp. On May 20, Braddock ordered the women out; when the women left, the warriors followed them, except for eight who remained to serve as scouts. Then Braddock decided to mend fences with the Delawares and asked George Croghan to bring before him some Delaware chiefs. They met with the general in a council later recalled by Chief Shingas:

He [Shingas] with 5 other Chiefs of the Delaware, Shawnee, and Mingo Nations (Being 2 from Each Nation) had applied to Genl Braddock and Enquired what he intended to do with the Land if he Could drive the French and their Indians away. To which Genl Braddock replied that the English Shoud Inhabit and Inherit the Land, on which Shingas asked Genl Braddock whether the Indians that were Friends to the English might not be Permitted to Live and Trade Among the English and have Hunting Ground sufficient To Support themselves and Familys as they had no where to Flee Too But into the Hands of the French and their Indians who were their Enemies (that is Shingas' Enemies). On which Genl Braddock said that No Savage Should Inherit the Land. On receiving which answer Shingas and the other Chiefs went that night to their own People—To whom they Communicated Genl Braddock's Answer And the Next Morning Returned to Genl Braddock again in hopes he might have Changed his Sentiments, and then repeated their Former Questions to Genl Braddock again and Genl Braddock made the same reply as Formerly, On which Shingas and the other Chiefs answered That if they might not have Liberty To Live on the Land they would not Fight for it. To which Genl Braddock answered that he did not need their Help and had no doubt of driveing the French and their Indians away.

Braddock succeeded in cementing an alliance—between the Delawares and the *French*.

Oneida Chief Scarouady later declared of Braddock: "He was a bad man when he was alive; he looked upon us as dogs, and would never hear anything what was said to him. We often endeavoured to advise him of the danger he was in with his Soldiers; but he never appeared pleased with us and that was the reason that a great many of our Warriors left him and would not be under his Command."

As inept as Braddock was with Indians, he was also unpopular with the colonists. Contemptuous of the provincials, he failed to consult the governors on his plan of attack. As a result, the colonies resisted war levies and generally refused to cooperate, except for Pennsylvania, which, at the urging of Benjamin Franklin, who was Postmaster General of the colony at this time, obtained wagons for Braddock's army and built him a road. In his *Autobiography*, Franklin recalled how he had cautioned Braddock against the dangers of Indian ambush: The General "smil'd at my Ignorance, and reply'd 'These Savages may indeed be a formidable Enemy to your raw American Militia; but upon the King's regular and disciplin'd Troops, Sir, it is impossible they should make any Impression."

Braddock finally led two regiments of British regulars and a provincial detachment (under George Washington) out of Fort Cumberland, Maryland, an unwieldy force of 2,500 men laden with heavy equipment. Along the way, French-allied Indians harried English settlements; in July 1755, Governor Dinwiddie reported that Indians "had murdered and taken off about eighty of our frontier Settlers, burning and destroying their Houses." After some weeks of hacking through virgin forest, Braddock, acting on the advice of Washington, detached a "flying column" of 1,500 men to make the initial attack on Fort Duquesne, which Braddock believed was defended by 800 French and Indians. By July 7, the flying column set up a camp ten miles from their objective.

Fort Duquesne's commandant, Claude-Pierre Pécaudy de Contrecoeur, had been observing Braddock's clumsy advance through Potawatomi and Ottawa scouts. What he saw discouraged him, and he contemplated surrender; but Captain Liénard de Beaujeu convinced Contrecoeur not to wait for siege, but to send him at the head of his available force—72 regulars of the French Marine, 146 Canadian militiamen, 637 assorted Indians—in an attack on Braddock as he approached the fort. On the morning of July 9, 1755, Beaujeu deployed his forces in ravines on either side of Braddock's line of march. Disdainful of the techniques of wilderness warfare, Braddock did not so much as dispatch scouts in advance of his great red-coated column.

The attack fell swiftly upon the van of the British army. At first, the soldiers reacted well, the grenadiers returning French fire effectively; one shot killed Beaujeu. At his fall, second-in-command Jean-Daniel Dumas rallied his men and set them about new tactics. Rather than continuing to confront the British in the open, he regrouped and deployed his Indians in the trees on either side of the road and on a height overlooking the road. The result was utter confusion among the British ranks because no one could see the enemy, whose fire was now devastating. Troops fired wildly—or at each other. It is said that many of the British regulars huddled in the road like flocks of sheep. Braddock had five horses shot from under him. He set about rallying his troops, but to no avail. The small body of Virginians, who had been holding their own by fighting like the Indians, were mustered by Braddock into European-style platoons that were quickly mowed down. Finally, Braddock was mortally wounded and carried off the field by two provincial soldiers.

The rout was crushing for the British. Of 1,459 officers and men who had engaged in this battle—called Battle of the Wilderness—only 462 returned. Two-thirds of the enlisted men had been killed or wounded, as were three-quarters of the officers, a good number of whom may have been victims of their own men. Washington, though unhurt, had had two horses shot from under him, and his coat had been pierced by four bullets. The French had lost a mere 60 men.

In their panic, the British troops flung away a fortune in arms and ammunition and abandoned their artillery. They also left behind Braddock's well-stocked money chest and, worst of all, papers revealing the campaigns proposed against Forts Niagara and Saint Frédéric. The

*This 1808 engraving depicts the burial of Major General Edward Braddock. His arrogance and bluster outstripped only by his thorough mediocrity as a commander, Braddock led his troops to disaster against the French and Indians in the Battle of the Wilderness (July 9, 1755). Of the almost 1,500 British and colonial soldiers engaged, nearly 1,000 were killed. Stunned by the spectacle of this rout, the mortally wounded Braddock uttered his last words: "Who would have thought it? We shall better know how to deal with them another time." (Library of Congress.)*

defeat was the more humiliating because Braddock had commanded a force twice the strength of the French. Braddock's dying words were poignant: "Who would have thought it? We shall better know how to deal with them another time."

The ramifications of the defeat went far beyond humiliation, as many Indians, hitherto neutral or even inclined to side with the English, now took up with the French and attacked English settlements along the length of the frontier, where panic reigned. In the wake of Braddock's defeat, his successor, Colonel Thomas Dunbar, simply ran away, taking with him not only his own troops, but three independent companies nominally under Governor Dinwiddie's command.

Acting on the information found in Braddock's abandoned papers, Governor Vaudreuil altered his own plan of attack. He had intended to move against Fort Oswego on the south shore of Lake Ontario. Now, learning that Forts Niagara and Saint Frédéric would be the objects of attack, he reinforced these positions, using the cannon the English had left behind.

In the depths of this crisis, the English were still bungling Indian relations. A group of Wyandots and Delawares offered an alliance with Pennsylvania, only to have Governor Robert Hunter Morris ineffectually defer their offer to the Iroquois Grand Council. Delaware Chief Shingas later explained the situation to an English captive:

After the French had ruined Braddock's Army they immediately compelled the Indians To join them and let them know that if they refused they wou'd Immediately cut them off, On which the Indians Joined the French for their Own Safety—They However sent [the Delaware Indian called] Capt Jacobs with some other Indians to Philadelphia to hold a Treaty with the Government.

Chief Scarouady of the Oneidas was even more emphatic:

Brethren, the English, We let you know that our Cousins the Delawares, as well as our Brethren the Nanticokes, have assured me that they were never asked to go to war against the French in the late Expedition, but promised in the strongest Terms that if their Brethren the English (especially those of Pennsylvania) will give them their Hatchett they would make use of it, and would join with their Uncles [the Iroquois] against the French. So we assure you by this belt of Wampum that we will gather all our Allies to assist the English in another Expedition. One word of Yours will bring the Delawares to join You; . . . any Message you have to send, or answer you have to give to them, I will deliver to them.

When Morris failed to embrace the Delaware offer of alliance, which meant that he declined to supply the

weapons and ammunition the Delaware needed to defend themselves against the French and their Indian allies, the Indian representatives returned home from Philadelphia and, as Shingas explained

. . . agreed To Come out with the French and their Indians in Parties To Destroy the English Settlements. The French having appointed 1400 French and Indians to come out in Small Parties for that Purpose—the First Breach was made on the South Branch of Patowmack near Fort Cumberland from which they carried a number of Captives and Scalps with Considerable Plunder, Immediately on the return of this Party to Fort Du Quesne Capt Jacobs, King Shingas, Capt John Peter and Capt Will a Delaware Chief were sent out by the French Commander at Fort Du Quesne against Pennsylvania and accordingly they went out. Divideing themselves into two Parites, one of which under Capt Jacobs went against the Canallaway, and the other Party under Shingas with the two other Chiefs, Capt John Peter and Capt Will Fell upon the Great Cove—Thus began the War between the English and the Indians and Such have been the Consequences thus far.

In response to these widespread raids, the Pennsylvania assembly voted £1000 not to raise a militia, but to furnish arms to backwoods settlers, letting them make their own defense as best they could. Governor Morris demanded that the assembly place an organized militia under his command, but the legislators ignored him.

## BATTLE OF LAKE GEORGE

While the Pennsylvania, Maryland, and Virginia frontiers were convulsed by Indian raids, William Johnson was encamped at the southern tip of Lake George, preparing, as Braddock had ordered, to move against Fort Saint Frédéric. As a result of the information contained in papers captured at the Battle of the Wilderness, Jean-Armand, Baron de Dieskau, had been sent with a mixed force of 3,000 French and Indians (many of them mission Iroquois) to reinforce the fort. Johnson had received erroneous intelligence placing the French numbers near 8,000. In reality, Johnson's forces were about equal to Dieskau's, but he thought he would be fighting a desperate defensive battle rather than the offensive assault originally planned.

Baron Dieskau, however, made a mistake of his own. Acting against Governor Vaudreuil's instructions, which were simply to reinforce Fort Saint Frédéric against the anticipated English attack, he detached about 1,400 of his regular and Indian troops, moved out of the fort, and launched an assault on Johnson's camp.

News of Dieskau's approach reached Johnson late on

the night of September 7, 1755. Instead of consolidating his forces in camp, Johnson commanded 1,000 militiamen and 200 Mohawks to reconnoiter the approach. Hendrick (Theyanoguin), chief of Johnson's Mohawk allies, pronounced their doom: "If they are to be killed, they are too many; if they are to fight, they are too few." Nevertheless, the party left camp at sunrise, while the balance of the troops remained behind to fortify the camp as best they could with a breastwork of logs. The reconnaissance column marched into an ambush. Its commander, Colonel Ephraim Williams, was shot dead, as was Chief Hendrick. (His companion in this campaign was the 14-year-old Joseph Brant [Thayendanegea], who, narrowly missing death in this battle, would become an important Iroquois leader during the American Revolution.) The party, under withering fire, retreated toward the camp and was met by reinforcements who managed to check Dieskau's pursuit. The baron then retreated to regroup for a final assault on the camp itself.

Fortunately for Johnson's forces, now all collected in the rudely fortified camp, Dieskau did not attempt a final, overwhelming thrust. Instead, he set up a line of fire that had minimal effect. Johnson's return fire, in contrast, was devastating, especially from the two cannon, which sent balls crashing through the thick forest. The battle went on for more than four hours, until the French lines wavered and finally broke. The English charged, wounded Dieskau, and took him captive. The baron subsequently blamed his Iroquois allies for the defeat at the Battle of Lake George, saying that the Canadian Iroquois had warned their Mohawk kinsmen.

Instead of advancing to Fort Saint Frédéric following Dieskau's defeat, Johnson began construction of Fort William Henry on the south end of Lake George. George Washington, returned from the debacle at the Battle of the Wilderness, persuaded authorities to build even more forts between the Potomac and James and Roanoke rivers, down into South Carolina. And for his part, Governor Vaudreuil did not accept Dieskau's criticism of his Indian allies. The Battle of Lake George convinced him of the strategic necessity of fighting Frontenac's *la petite querre*, "I apply myself particularly to sending parties of Indians into the English Colonies," Vaudreuil declared. "Nothing is more calculated to disgust the people of those Colonies and to make them desire the return of peace. . . . the English have lost one hundred men for our one."

*The Mohawk chief Theyanoguin, whom the English called Hendrick, was Sir William Johnson's ally during the French and Indian War. He was killed in September 1755 in a desperate battle against a mixed French and Indian force led by Jean-Armand, Baron de Dieskau. (Library of Congress.)*

## FORT BULL AND THE SUPPLY OF FORT OSWEGO

An abstract of dispatches from Canada for the winter of 1755–56 reported that "the French and Indians have, since Admiral [sic] Braddock's defeat, disposed of more than 700 people in the Provinces of Pennsylvania, Virginia and Carolina, including those killed and those taken prisoner." New York was similarly ravaged, though New England, perhaps more accustomed to Indian warfare, seems to have suffered less.

Meanwhile, early in 1756, having failed to take Forts Frontenac and Niagara as prescribed in Braddock's battle plan, Governor Shirley retreated to Albany to regroup and, on March 17, dispatched Lieutenant Colonel John

Bradstreet to reinforce Fort Oswego, on the southeast shore of Lake Ontario and one of the most important English bases. It was too late, for the French were already well on their way to cutting the supply line to Oswego. On March 27, 1756, 360 Indians, Canadians, and French regulars under the command of Lieutenant Gaspard-Joseph Chaussegros de Léry attacked Fort Bull at the west end of the portage between the Mohawk River and Wood Creek, which feeds into Lake Oneida. Great quantities of munitions and stores, all intended for Fort Oswego, were destroyed. The massacre at Fort Bull was terrible. Léry himself reported that he directed all of his men to rush into the fort "and put every one to the sword they could lay hands on. One woman and a few soldiers only were fortunate enough to escape the fury of our troops."

Bradstreet responded to this disaster with a speed and determination that astounded the French. In Albany, he built 100 new bateaux (boats) and, with 1,000 men and a total of 350 bateaux he delivered food and supplies over 160 miles from Albany to Oswego by the end of May, narrowly averting collapse of the fort due to starvation. On July 3, as Bradstreet and his men were returning from Oswego, a combined force of about 700 Canadians and Indians ambushed his advance group of about 300. Bradstreet rallied his badly outnumbered troops and charged the attackers, using Indian hatchets as well as European firearms. Stunned by the ferocity of this response, the larger force retreated to the banks of the Oswego River. Cornered, they could fight or swim. They chose the latter and made easy targets for Bradstreet's men. Bodies were carried downstream so swiftly, it is said that many more were shot than could be counted.

But such British triumphs were rare during the first three years of the war. By June 1756, British settlers in Virginia had withdrawn 150 miles from the prewar frontier, and George Washington moaned to Governor Dinwiddie that "the Bleu-Ridge is now our Frontier . . . there will not be a living creature left in Frederick-County: and how soon Fairfax, and Prince William may share its fate, is easily conceived."

## BRITISH DISASTERS

On May 11, 1756, Louis Joseph, Marquis de Montcalm arrived in Canada to take charge of French and provincial forces. Less than a week later, on May 17, England officially declared war on France. After successfully supplying Oswego and defeating the ambush, Bradstreet, on July 12, warned his commanders that the vital fort was in grave danger. But Governor Shirley, who respected

Bradstreet, had been relieved of command of the provincial forces. Major General James Abercromby, a British regular, was put in charge of the colonials, and rather than heed the words of another provincial officer, not only excluded Bradstreet from a council of war held on July 16 but, impatient with the lack of conventional military discipline shown by the "bateaumen" (riverborne frontiersmen) who had fought so brilliantly under Bradstreet, discharged 400 of them. These were the best fighting men the English had.

Abercromby did order Major General Daniel Webb to prepare his regiment for departure to Oswego. But no one perceived any need for haste. On July 23, 1756, John Campbell, fourth earl of Loudoun, arrived in the colonies to take overall charge of all British forces, regular and provincial. He reached Albany on the twenty-eighth and managed to get Webb moving—as far as Schenectady, some 15 miles away. There Webb spent more than two weeks arguing about contracts for provisions, stubbornly refusing to accept supplies from the "wrong" contractors. By August 14, his regiment had reached German Flats (Herkimer, New York), still 100 miles from Oswego. On that date, Fort Oswego fell.

Montcalm, with 3,000 French and Indian troops, had invested the fort on August 11. The demoralized garrison put up a feeble resistance, and when its commander was killed by a random cannon shot, surrendered on the fourteenth. A jubilant Montcalm wrote: "The success has been beyond all expectation." Montcalm appropriated all of the provisions and equipment Bradstreet had delivered to Oswego, including six vessels and 100 pieces of artillery. The fall of Oswego meant that the British had yielded Lake Ontario to the French, thereby strengthening French communication with Fort Duquesne and the West. It was now out of the question to attack Fort Niagara, and the Iroquois, still officially neutral, inclined more sharply to the victors. It was a blow even more severe than the defeat of Braddock, and one made more bitter by the massacre that followed the garrison's capitulation. Promised safe conduct by Montcalm, the garrison issued from Oswego only to be set upon by the general's Indian allies. Perhaps 100 soldiers were killed, including 30 in the fort hospital. No accounting of civilian deaths exists.

Despite the awful lessons of Oswego, which should have taught the British commanders the value of Indian allies and of provincial troops, who, like the Indians, knew how to fight in an American wilderness, Loudoun alienated provincials by trying to force their incorporation into the regulars. The highest provincial commanders were to be outranked by any captain of regulars. General Edward Winslow, in command of provincials, tried to explain that enlisting his men into the regular forces would violate the resolutions of colonial assemblies. Weary of wasting time in argument, he moved his troops to Lake George to attack Fort Ticonderoga, only to have Loudoun recall his forces to protect Albany—which was in no danger. On their arrival in the capital, Loudoun decried the "mutiny" among the provincials, discharged and disbanded them, and relieved Winslow of command.

In the meantime, on August 20, having received word of Oswego's fall, General Webb advanced to the portage known as the "great carrying place." There Major Charles Craven was rebuilding some forts, but Webb, noting that Craven's troops were undisciplined and the forts far from completed, panicked. Fearing the advance of the French, he ordered the forts burned and withdrew—without even seeing the enemy—to German Flats.

Thus, 1756 went very badly for the British: Oswego fell, and Webb ran from its defense; Winslow was forced by his own commander to relinquish Lake George; Loudoun spent more time and energy fighting provincials than he did the French; Iroquois neutrals, once inclined toward the English, turned increasingly to the French. The only gain for the English came late, on November 8–17, when Pennsylvania commissioners met with the Delaware chief Teedyuscung in an attempt to conclude a peace between the colony and his tribe. The resulting treaty redressed Delaware grievances stemming from the "Walking Purchase" land grab.

Despite this gesture of conciliation, 1757 began with the French accumulating Indian allies in greater and greater numbers as tentative British alliances with Iroquois as well as Delawares faltered or failed. The English now had virtually no control over any Indians; most were hostile to them. Though the British had superior numbers, the regular army was remarkably and pathetically ineffectual against the Indians. During raids, the troops often folded, huddling together for protection. Israel Pemberton, a Quaker negotiator for Pennsylvania, was shocked during treaty talks at Lancaster in the spring of 1757 when six to fifteen Indians seized a well-inhabited area nearby and drove out 200 families while an army of 500 regulars never offered aid. "Within eighty rods of a fort where the guns could be heard, but not a man went to help. Can such an Instance be produced in the English annals?" Pemberton exclaimed.

## NEW DIRECTION FOR THE BRITISH

In December 1756, William Pitt became British secretary of state for the southern department, with direct charge of American colonial affairs. Despite half-hearted support from the king and outright opposition from the powerful Duke of Cumberland, within three weeks of taking office Pitt ordered 2,000 additional troops to Halifax, Nova Scotia, intending to bring the war into Canada, through the Saint Lawrence Valley and against Quebec. The first objective was the French naval base at Louisbourg. With its defeat, Acadia would fall, cutting off New France from communication with Europe.

While this plan was sound, its execution suffered from the usual British bumbling. By the time transports were hired to bring troops and supplies from England, it was already June. Cargo was neatly divided among the vessels—cannon in one ship, ammunition in another, powder in yet another—which meant that the sinking of any one ship would render the cargo of the other two useless. Although the ships arrived safely, the gunpowder had been purchased without having been tested and on its arrival, proved to be bad. Loudoun's American troops gathered in New York at the end of April and waited until late June for transportation to Halifax. The fleet from London, under Admiral Holburne, did not arrive in colonial waters until July. By the time English and American forces converged at Halifax, the French had assembled a superior fleet at Louisbourg. Once in Halifax, Loudoun drilled his men incessantly. Disease racked the camp: Two hundred men died, and an additional 500 required hospitalization. On August 4, 1757, Holburne and Loudoun concluded that the season was too late and the enemy now too strong to attempt an assault on Louisbourg. They withdrew to New York.

Between July 21 and August 7, 1757, 159 of Teedyuscung's Delawares and 119 Senecas and others of the Iroquois Confederation once again met with Pennsylvanians at Easton and managed to cobble together a tenuous peace on the Pennsylvania frontier. Back east, General Webb was camped with 4,000 troops near Fort William Henry. Since April he had been receiving intelligence of a massing of French troops at Fort Ticonderoga, but did nothing. July brought further information that made it clear Montcalm was preparing for an assault on Fort William Henry. Still, Webb failed to act.

Montcalm began his advance against Fort William Henry on July 29. In taking the fort, he hoped to gain control of the so-called Warpath of Nations, the link connecting the ocean, Hudson River, Lake George, Lake Champlain, and the Richelieu River, which leads into the Saint Lawrence. The link between Lake George and Lake Champlain was a vital part of this system; the French had built Forts Ticonderoga and Saint Frédéric on Lake Champlain, at the north end of Lake George; the British had built Fort William Henry at the south end of Lake George and, south of that, Fort Edward, on the headwaters of the Hudson. For much of the war, armies fighting in the eastern theater faced one another between these sets of forts.

Even with the information he had been receiving, General Webb, according to a contemporary historian of the war, was "struck . . . with such panic, that he resolved to retire to Fort Edward that same night; but with much persuasion was prevailed upon to stay till next morning: when he marched off early, with a strong artillery, leaving the defence of the fort to [Lieutenant] Colonel [George] Monro and Colonel Young with 2,300 men." To be more precise, Webb decamped on August 4, refusing to reinforce the fort and advising Monro "to make the best terms left in your power." Of Monro's 2,372 men, only 1,100 were fit for duty at the time. Opposing him, Montcalm commanded 7,626 men, including 1,600 Indian allies.

Remarkably, Monro held out for one week, capitulating on August 9, 1757. As he had at Fort Oswego, Montcalm promised the defeated commandant safe conduct for his garrison. As at Oswego, the Indians ambushed them while their French allies, having promised the warriors plunder, stood by. Montcalm had been particular about granting special protection to the sick and wounded, who were unable to march; but instead of posting guards at the hospital as ordered, the French officers deliberately withdrew them. It was at the hospital that the massacre began. With horrible irony, the Indians paid a heavy price for this. They scalped smallpox patients, acquired the disease themselves from the infected scalps, and carried it home to their people, where it certainly caused more deaths than English bullets.

Perhaps as many as 1,500 soldiers, women, and children were massacred or taken prisoner; certainly, more than 200 were killed. Père Roubaus, missionary to the Abnakis, ordered his charges not to participate in the ritual cannibalism the Ottawas practiced on their victims. He also tried to save some individuals, including an infant, which he reunited with its mother. And Montcalm himself supposedly rose up among the "savages," bared his own breast, and exclaimed: "Since you are rebellious children who break the promise you have given to your Father and who will not listen to his voice, kill him first of all." The massacres at Oswego and Fort William Henry strongly suggest that the French deliberately used their Indian allies as instruments of terror. "Savages," they could perform acts from which a European soldier would shrink (at least until the twentieth century).

The fall of Fort William Henry and the subsequent massacre were the nadir of British fortunes in the French and Indian War. As William Pitt's policies began to take effect, however, the tide slowly turned. Pitt reversed crown policy by cooperating with the colonists rather than dictating to them, and he ensured that colonial assemblies had a voice in managing funds used to prosecute the war. in response, Massachusetts, which Loudoun had accused of mutiny, raised a large and effective army. On December 30, 1757, Pitt recalled Loudoun and appointed General James Abercromby as commander in chief of American operations. Abercromby was no prize, it is true, but Pitt reduced his office so that abler commanders nominally serving under him were given more freedom of movement and decision. Pitt also sought, rather than shunned, Indian allies, promising them that, after the war, Great Britain would enforce a boundary line to restrict white encroachment on their lands.

Pitt selected Brigadier General John Forbes, one of his best commanders, to assault—for the third time—Fort Duquesne. In contrast to the bull-headed and imperious Braddock, Forbes willingly worked with the Pennsylvania governor and assembly to obtain the supplies and recruit the men he needed for the campaign. Initially, he was also more successful in recruiting Indian allies. The Iroquois were reluctant and unreliable, but in return for presents, 700 Cherokee and Catawba warriors joined Forbes. Unfortunately, Pitt had not managed to transform the English military establishment overnight. Quartermaster Sir John St. Clair, who had bungled the supply of Braddock's army, now did the same for Forbes. Colonial troops were poorly trained and at odds with one another. Maryland sent a contingent, but its assembly failed to vote the funds necessary to pay them; Forbes himself negotiated pay. There was much political wrangling about where Forbes would cut his road through the wilderness to reach Fort Duquesne; after all, the road would survive the war and become an artery of commerce that promised to enrich land speculators who owned parcels along it. Finally, Forbes was ill; he would have to be carried to battle on a litter suspended between two horses.

Delay made the Indian allies restless. On May 29, 1758, Forbes wrote: "The Cherokees are now no longer to be kept with us, neither by promises nor presents. . . . They begin to grow extremely licentious, and have gone so far as to seize the presents designed for them, and divide it among themselves according to their own Caprice." Five hundred Indians abandoned Forbes at this time, and the rest trickled off throughout the long, achingly slow progress toward Fort Duquesne. In September, the army of 5,000 provincials, 1,400 elite Scottish Highlanders, and ever-diminishing numbers of Indians bogged down in the quagmire of Loyalhanna (Ligonier, Pennsylvania). More Indians deserted the expedition; by October, only 50 remained. Worse, the Indians did not simply leave. Forbes was obliged to provide them with a guard to prevent fighting between them and settlers along the way. William Byrd III of Virginia and former

Governor Glen of South Carolina were able to recover 200 Cherokee allies led by Chief Little Carpenter. The trader George Croghan promised 50 Ohio Indians, but delivered only 15 to Forbes's camp on November 20, which was, in any case, too late to join the long-delayed final advance on Fort Duquesne.

During this time, Forbes was also aware that the terms of enlistment among his provincial troops were due to expire. Yet he had to bide his time. One of his commanders, Colonel Henry Bouquet, could stand waiting no longer. On September 11, he ordered 800 Highlanders under Major James Grant to reconnoiter in the vicinity of Fort Duquesne. The troops arrived near the fort on September 14 in the dead of night. At dawn on the fifteenth, Major Grant ordered the drums to beat; he thought they would inspire his men; what they did was alert the French to Grant's presence. A sortie of French and Indians poured from the fort and overran the Highlanders, killing one-third of them, including Grant.

To Forbes, literally stuck in the mud, his Indian allies deserting him, his provincial forces soon to leave as well, Grant's defeat came as a terrible blow. Yet the English defeat was not really a triumph for the French. Indian losses were also heavy and made them reconsider their alliance with the French. Seizing their plunder, most deserted the fort. With the desertion of the Far Indians (Potawatomis, Ojibwas, and Ottawas), only the Ohio allies were left. These, however, were about to be neutralized by yet another treaty concluded at Easton, Pennsylvania, in October 1758. Pennsylvania returned to the Iroquois western lands the Six Nations had earlier ceded to the colony, but prevailed upon the Iroquois to grant the Delaware—hitherto French allies—the right to hunt and live on these lands. The Iroquois thus became landlords to the Delaware, a position of power that pleased them while providing the Delaware with land west of the Appalachians and Alleghenies. Furthermore, it was agreed at Easton that European settlement was not to encroach on this territory—a treaty provision that would be violated almost instantly. The Easton treaty, Colonel Bouquet proclaimed, "knocked the French on the head."

During Forbes's interminable progress toward Fort Duquesne, there were many developments on other fronts, some diplomatic, some military. Christian Frederick Post, the remarkable Moravian missionary who had lived many years among Indians (he was twice married to Indian women), undertook a hazardous mission among the western tribes, reassuring them that the English had no intention of seizing their lands. The Delaware chief Shingas challenged Post, telling him that "We have great reason to believe you intended to drive us away; or else, why do you come to fight in the land that God has given

us? . . . This was told us by the chief of the Indian traders . . . the French and English intended to kill all the Indians, and then divide the land among themselves." Post replied: "I am your flesh and blood, and sooner than I would tell you any story that would be of hurt to you, or your children, I would suffer death. . . . I do assure you of mine and the people's honesty." Ultimately, he was believed.

In August, Post and Pisquetomen, a Delaware, traveled to the Delaware Indian town of Kuskuski, near Fort Duquesne. While the French intrigued to capture and, presumably, kill Post, the intrepid missionary pleaded the English cause before his Indian hosts. Next, Post set off for a village called Sankonk, where (he recorded in his journal) he was "received in a very rough manner."

They surrounded me with drawn knives in their hands, in such a manner that I could hardly get along; running up against me with their breasts open, as if they wanted some pretence to kill me. I saw by their countenances they sought my death. Their faces were quite distorted by rage, and they went so far as to say, I should not live long; but some Indians, with whom I was formerly acquainted, coming up and saluting me in a friendly manner, their behavior to me was quickly changed. . . .

In the afternoon, all the captains gathered together in the middle town; they sent for us, and desired we should give them information of our message [proclaiming a desire for peace and pledging not to take the Indians' land]. . . . We read the message with great satisfaction to them. . . . In the evening, [French] messengers arrived from Fort Duquesne, with a string of wampum from the commander; upon which they all came together in the house where we lodged. The messengers delivered their string, with these words from their father, the French king:—

"My children, come to me, and hear what I have to say. The English are coming with an army to destroy both you and me. I therefore desire you immediately, my children, to hasten with all the young men; we will drive the English and destroy them. I, as a father, will tell you always what is best." He laid the string before one of the [Indian] captains. After a little conversation, the captain stood up, and said, "I have just heard something of our brethren, the English, which pleaseth me much better. I will not go. Give it to the others; maybe they will go." The messenger took up again the string, and said, "He won't go; he has heard of the English." He then threw the string to the other fireplace, where the other captains were; but they kicked it from one to another, as if it was a snake. [Indian] Captain Peter took a stick, and with it flung the string from one end of the room to the other, and said, "Give it to the French captain, and let him go with his young men; he boasted much of his fighting; now let us see his fighting. We have often ventured our lives for him; and had hardly a loaf of bread when we came to him; and now he thinks we should jump to serve him.'' Then we saw the French captain mortified to the uttermost; he looked pale as death.

With the defection of the Delawares to the English camp, the French at Fort Duquesne proposed to their Ottawa allies a joint move against them: ''Now all their chiefs are here, and but a handful, let us cut them off, and then we shall be troubled with them no longer.'' The Ottawas refused ''No, we cannot do this thing; for though there is but a handful here, the Delawares are a strong people, and are spread to a great distance, and whatever they agree to must be.''

## ASSAULTS ON FORTS TICONDEROGA, LOUISBOURG, FRONTENAC, AND DUQUESNE

While these diplomatic maneuverings were taking place, General Abercromby assembled 16,000 troops at Lake George for a march on Fort Ticonderoga, which the French called Fort Carillon. Abercromby sent Bradstreet ahead. After overpowering the fort's outer defenses, Bradstreet asked permission to attack the fort itself before Montcalm could call up reinforcements. Abercromby, however, insisted on waiting until the main body of his troops had arrived. It was a fatal decision. For it bought Montcalm the time he needed to bring up reinforcements from Fort Saint Frédéric and to construct highly effective entrenchments and fascines that used fallen trees and branches in the way that later armies would use barbed wire.

Thus Montcalm, with only 3,000 men, came to occupy a formidable position. Even so, the British held a position above it, Mount Defiance, which made these defenses vulnerable to artillery. Abercromby, however, did not put his artillery there, but stationed William Johnson and his detachment of 400 Mohawks on Mount Defiance instead. It turned out to be a position from which they could never even be committed to battle.

From Mount Defiance, Johnson *did* have a splendid view of the debacle Abercromby suffered when he attacked on July 8. Having fatally delayed while waiting for his forces to assemble, Abercromby now moved prematurely. Instead of waiting for the bulk of his artillery to arrive (even poorly placed, ordnance could have blasted away at the French lines), he sent his regulars against Montcalm's defenses in a series of bayonet charges. The woefully outnumbered French general had been prepared to retreat. Instead, he easily mowed down the charging Highlanders: 464 killed, 1,117 wounded. Provincial forces lost 87 with 239 wounded. The French lost 112 officers and men, with 275 wounded. Aber-

cromby retreated with his large stunned and battered army to Albany.

Ticonderoga was to be the last major French triumph, however. On July 26, 1758, Major General James Wolfe and Brigadier General Jeffrey Amherst, transporting a force of 9,000 regulars and 500 provincials in a fleet of 40 ships, at long last took Louisbourg, Nova Scotia. At the end of the next month, Bradstreet assembled a provincial task force—1,112 men from New York, 675 from Massachusetts, 412 from New Jersey, and 318 from Rhode Island, supplemented by 300 bateaumen, 135 British regulars, and 70 Iroquois—to seize Fort Frontenac, near present-day Kingston, Ontario. The objective seemed so formidable that, when they learned of it, the Iroquois contingent deserted.

Actually, Fort Frontenac was nearly defenseless. Governor Vaudreuil and General Montcalm had withdrawn most of its garrison to Fort Ticonderoga, anticipating a renewed assault there. Bradstreet's 3,000 men surrounded a mere 110, including men, women, and children. Fort Frontenac fell on August 27, after a token resistance of two days. Bradstreet captured 60 precious cannon and 800,000 livres' worth of provisions. With the loss of Frontenac, the French lifeline to Forts Niagara and Duquesne was severed. The French now relinquished control of Lake Ontario to the English, and Bradstreet took possession of a nine-vessel French fleet, loading two ships with booty and burning the rest. Prisoners seized were sent to Montreal in exchange for British captives. Finally, Bradstreet burned Fort Frontenac and returned with his army to Oswego. He had not lost a single man.

Fort Duquesne, to which General Forbes was drawing slowly closer, was now without a source of artillery and supplies. Francois-Marie Le Marchand de Lignery, the fort's commandant, aware that he would soon be forced to release his militiamen from Illinois and Louisiana, as well as his dwindling Indian allies, launched a desperation raid on Forbes's position at Loyalhanna, October 12, 1758. Repulsed, Lignery retreated to the fort, his few remaining Indian allies now badly shaken. One month later he launched another raid. While chasing this force off, Forbes captured three prisoners, who revealed just how weakly Fort Duquesne was held. On November 24, as Forbes's army was preparing to move out of Loyalhanna, they heard a distant explosion. Sending what remained of his garrison downriver to Illinois country, Lignery had blown up Fort Duquesne and retired to Fort Machault (present-day Franklin, Pennsylvania) to plan a counterattack. When Forbes's army at last marched into Fort Duquesne, they found it gutted and deserted. The heads of Highlanders captured earlier had been skewered atop stakes, the soldiers' kilts tied below.

The nation that controlled the ''forks of Ohio''—the

confluence of the Monongahela, Allegheny, and Ohio rivers—controlled the gateway to the West. That was the prize represented by Fort Duquesne. However, having taken the fort, which he renamed Fort Pitt, Forbes faced serious problems. Troop desertion soon left Fort Pitt with a garrison of only 200 men, far too few to withstand a counterattack. Indian allies also would melt away, unless Forbes could fortify their resolve with gifts. Through the good offices of Israel Pemberton, a Philadelphia Quaker pacifist, Forbes received £1,400 worth of presents in the nick of time; another £3,000 soon followed.

In order to hold Fort Pitt, the English needed the cooperation not only of the Iroquois (especially the Senecas and Onondagas) but also that of the Shawnees and Delawares. These western tribes, however, were now fearful that the British, having taken their lands out of French control, would not leave themselves. Indeed, English settlers took the fall of Fort Duquesne as a signal to travel the "Forbes Road" and take out claims in the Ohio country.

In January 1759, a delegation of 40 Indians—Senecas, Onondagas, Shawnees, and Delawares—met with the British at Fort Pitt to enforce what had already been agreed to at Easton, that no permanent forts nor settlements would be established west of the Alleghenies. The Indian position, though, was not united. Five of the Iroquois met with the garrison commander, Colonel Hugh Mercer, to tell him that the Delawares and Shawnees were not to be trusted. Maneuvering to reassert the Six Nations' political dominance over the western tribes, the Iroquois delegates agreed to a charade. In front of the other delegates, they would demand that the English leave Fort Pitt. Actually, they committed the Iroquois to cooperation with the English at Fort Pitt to help them reduce the Delawares and Shawnees.

By no means were the Iroquois unanimous in their collaboration with the English. The westernmost Iroquois tribe, the Senecas, drifted closer to the Delawares as English intentions to maintain Fort Pitt and settle in the Ohio country became increasingly evident. A Delaware named Kittiuskund told missionary Christian Frederick Post that

all the nations had jointly agreed to defend their hunting place at Allegheny, and suffer nobody to settle there; and as these Indians are very much inclined to the English interest, so he [Kittiuskund] begged us very much to tell the Governor, General, and all other people not to settle there. And if the English would draw back over the mountain, they would get all the other nations into their interest; but if they staid and settled there, all the nations would be against them; and he was afraid it would be a great war, and never come to a peace again.

Thus was laid, at the turning point of the French and Indian War, the foundation for another century and a half of Indian-white warfare.

*Brigadier General John Forbes succeeded where Braddock had failed, taking the French-held Fort Duquesne (present-day Pittsburgh), except for Quebec, the single most strategically significant military prize of the French and Indian War. Situated at the confluence of the Monongahela, Allegheny, and Ohio rivers, it controlled access to the West. The road Forbes built to get his army to Fort Duquesne became a principal postwar avenue of western migration. (Library of Congress.)*

## THE YEAR OF FRENCH DISASTER

The year 1759 proved disastrous for the French. Pitt proposed a three-pronged campaign that included the capture of Fort Niagara and reinforcement of Oswego in order to sever the west from the Saint Lawerence; a strike through the Lake Champlain waterway into the Saint Lawrence Valley; and an amphibious assault on Quebec itself. Early in the year, the Fort Pitt garrison was expanded to 350 as Brigadier General John Stanwix assembled 3,500 men to operate in the Ohio country using the fort as their base. In February, William Johnson proposed an expedition against Fort Niagara via the country of the Six Nations. Indian allies could be acquired along the way. In April, the Seneca, the Iroquois tribe most inclined toward the French, at last become disgusted with the failure of their white allies to provide satisfactory trade goods. In April, they proposed to assist the English in reducing Fort Niagara. That same month, the Oneida chief Conochquieson told William Johnson that all the Six Nations were ''ready to join and revenge both Your Blood and ours upon the French.''

While Johnson was gathering allies for the assault on Niagara, General Wolfe was preparing to take Quebec. On May 28, 1759, Rear Admiral Philip Durrell landed a detachment on the Ile-aux-Coudres. His troops advanced to Ile d'Oreleans to await the main amphibious force under Wolfe and Vice Admiral Charles Saunders, which landed at Ile d'Orleans on June 27. By July, Wolfe's army of 9,000 men was in possession of the north shore of the Saint Lawrence above Quebec. Montcalm attempted to burn the British fleet at anchor by chaining rafts together, setting them ablaze, and sending them downriver. British seamen in small boats managed to repel these assaults. But for the next two and a half months, Wolfe probed Quebec's defenses without success. Failing to penetrate, Wolfe turned to terrorism against the civilian population, bombarding the city day and night with his artillery, concentrating his fire on residential rather than military targets. He also ordered his troops to lay waste the surrounding countryside, in the meantime warning Montcalm that should any more fire ships be sent against the British fleet, he would make them fast to the two transports that held all the French and Canadian prisoners. For his part, Montcalm was no less ruthless. When, after weeks of siege and bombardment, the citizens of Quebec expressed their desire to surrender, the general threatened to turn his Indians loose upon them. It was the same terror tactics Abbe Le Loutré had employed against the Acadians early in the war.

While the siege of Quebec continued, General Amherst decided to put the Niagara command in the hands of a regular army officer, Brigadier General John Prideaux, with William Johnson as his second in command. Troops and Indian warriors mustered at Oswego, from which they were transported to a position before Fort Niagara on July 7. The next day, Prideaux presented Niagara's commandant, Captain Pierre Pouchot, with a demand for his surrender. Pouchot pretended not to understand English, and the siege commenced.

Pouchot appealed to Lignery, now at Fort Machault, for reinforcements. Lignery had been assembling a force of 1,000 for a counterattack on Fort Pitt. He was ready to begin his march when two Iroquois warriors, ostensibly his allies, forced a delay of one day. That was enough time for Pouchot's plea to reach him. Lignery now abandoned his assault against Fort Pitt in order to

relieve Niagara. The delay undoubtedly saved the undermanned British fort, and some historians have suggested that it was a deliberate maneuver on the part of the Iroquois.

In the meantime, at Fort Niagara, the Seneca chief Kaendaé, allied to the French, held discussions with Iroquois allied to the English. William Johnson, in an effort to maintain the goodwill of his Iroquois allies, permitted the discussions to take place. The result was the withdrawal of the English-allied Iroquois to a place called La Belle Famille. This seemed a blow to the English, but then the withdrawing Iroquois attempted to persuade the French-allied warriors to join them at La Belle Famille. At this point, Commandant Pouchot cut off negotiations between the tribes, figuring that this was an English-inspired attempt to siphon off his Indian allies.

As the British forces prepared for the assault, an accidental shot from one of his own guns killed Prideaux on July 19. Over the protest of Lieutenant Colonel Eyre Massey, a regular army officer, William Johnson assumed command. At this point, news of Lignery's approach reached Johnson. Whether by Johnson's order or of his own volition, Massey took charge of a position held by New York captain James De Lancey, who had erected barricades against Lignery's approach. While Indian allies (600 Mohawks under the command of 19-year-old Joseph Brant), apparently operating independently of Johnson and Massey, attacked from the sides of the road, De Lancey led a bayonet charge against Lignery as Massey ordered a volley of fire. ''We killed 200 and took 100 prisoners,'' De Lancey reported. Among the prisoners were five senior officers. Pouchot capitulated, and Niagara fell to the British on July 23. The Iroquois were jubilant, but then, they had their own agenda. They were happy that, in defeating the French, they had taken the first step toward ridding their land of all Europeans. Mary Jemison, a settler who had been captured earlier by the Senecas, reported that she heard them plotting to oust the British within a month.

On July 26, Colonel Frederick Haldimand reinforced Oswego, and the French, outnumbered by Jeffrey Amherst, unceremoniously abandoned and blew up Fort Ticonderoga. Amherst moved against Fort Saint Frédéric next, taking it on July 31. The French retreated down the Richelieu River.

Quebec, however, remained unbreached. By July 9, 1759, Brigadier General Robert Monckton occupied Point Lévis, opposite the city, and Brigadier General George Townshend occupied the north shore of the Saint Lawrence. On July 31, General Wolfe attempted to storm the French position at Quebec. Covered by a barrage of English ships and land-based artillery, the troops attempted a frontal assault. But, badly timed and poorly coordinated, the attack collapsed before withering French fire. More than 400 English troops were slain.

Wolfe formulated another plan. On August 25, General James Murray was dispatched to attack French positions above Quebec. As for the small army gathered before Quebec, Wolfe decided to divide it, with one portion making false attacks before the city while the other, under cover of darkness, ascended the Plains of Abraham—the plateau above Quebec—and attacked from there. On September 12, Wolfe, with 1,600 soldiers, set off in 30 small vessels down the river toward Quebec. They approached their landing. *"Qui vive?"* a French sentinel called out. To which a Highlander captain, fluent in French, answered: *"La France!"* The sentinel returned: *"A quel règiment?"* The Highlander, who happened to know the names of the Comte de Bougainville's regiments, replied, *"De la Reine!"* The sentry was deceived; a little later, the French-speaking Scotsman would dupe another sentinel, and the party would disembark.

There were still the heights to scale and more sentinels to pass. When a sentry challenged Captain Donald MacDonald as he was climbing in advance of his men, the officer replied in fluent French that he was the relief guard and ordered the sentry to leave—which he did. By the time the sentinel realized that he had been duped, a sufficient number of Highlanders had scaled the heights to overpower the additional guards summoned by the Frenchman. Strangely enough, having secured a position, Wolfe ordered a halt to the landing of more men. His adjutant, General Isaac Barré, ignored the order, however, and continued to land troops. For his part, Montcalm committed uncharacteristic errors. Expecting that Wolfe would attack downstream at Beaumont (which Wolfe had wanted to do but was dissuaded from it by his officers), Montcalm had fortified that position.

At daybreak, Montcalm, his troops, and the citizens of Quebec were astonished to see an army forming battle lines on the Plains of Abraham. The French commander could have attacked while Wolfe's mustering forces were still relatively small. But he waited until he could bring his men up from their position at Beaumont. However, he did not wait for Bougainville's reinforcements from Cap Rouge. Thus, Montcalm ordered a charge that was both too late and premature, committing 4,500 troops—mostly provincials—to battle.

For once, the discipline of European-trained fighting men triumphed over a provincial militia. The British held their fire until the last possible moment. Then they delivered it into the poorly organized French ranks with devastating effect. The battle was over in a quarter of an hour, leaving 200 French troops dead and another 1,200 wounded; the British lost 60, with 600 wounded. Among the fatalities were the two commanders, Mont-

On May 11, 1756, Louis Joseph de Montcalm-Gozan, Marquis de Montcalm arrived in Canada to take charge of French and provincial forces. Almost always outnumbered by the British, he fought brilliantly throughout much of the French and Indian War. In defending Quebec, however, his skill as a tactician seemed to desert him, and the city fell to British general James Wolfe. Both commanders were mortally wounded in the action, which effectively brought an end to French power in North America. (Library of Congress.)

calm and Wolfe. By the time Bougainville arrived, the British forces were securely ensconced on the high ground, and the reinforcements were compelled to withdraw. Quebec formally surrendered on September 18, 1759, effectively bringing an end French power in North America.

The war had been decided, but the fighting was not yet over. The French still held Montreal and the Richelieu River as far as Isle-aux-Noix, at the bottom of Lake Champlain. Commander-in-chief Jeffrey Amherst could have pushed his advantages, but, always cautious, he chose instead to consolidate his positions, and the winter passed without event.

In the meantime, all was not well in Quebec. While fewer than 250 English soldiers died in the siege of the city, 1,000 succumbed to disease while garrisoning it, and another 2,000 became unfit for service. After the long siege and Wolfe's policy of laying waste the country-

## MONTCALM AND WOLFE

Louis Joseph de Montcalm-Gozon, Marquis de Saint-Veran, and James Wolfe are probably the best-remembered names from the French and Indian War. Commanding, respectively, the forces of the French and the English, they perished together in the war's climactic battle for Quebec City.

Montcalm, who had served in the French military since boyhood, fought in the War of the Polish Succession and the War of the Austrian Succession before coming to North America in 1756 to take command of French forces in Canada. Montcalm proved to be a ruthless and skillful commander. His capture of Fort Oswego not only deprived the British of a strategic Great Lakes outpost, but convinced wavering members of the Iroquois Confederation—all except the Mohawks—to abandon any idea of alliance with the British and either declare neutrality or join in the fight on the side of the French.

In contrast to most of his British counterparts, Montcalm fully exploited Indian allies, deliberately using them as weapons of terror against English settlements. At times, it seems that the practices of his Indian forces exceeded even what Montcalm was willing to tolerate, as when Indian allies captured and killed the garrison at Fort William Henry, despite Montcalm's guarantee of safe passage for the prisoners of war. Historians are divided over the question of the French commander's complicity in this event.

Montcalm continued to triumph during 1758, when he successfully defended Fort Ticonderoga (Fort Carillon) against an offensive led by General James Abercromby. An array of western Indian allies, including Ojibwas, Sacs and Foxes, Ottawas, Hurons, Illinois, and Miamis proved invaluable in the defense of the fort.

Despite Montcalm's brilliance and the activity of his Indian allies, the British began steadily to strengthen their position in North America, so that by 1759, Montcalm found himself desperately defending Quebec City against a long siege by water and land led by Vice Admiral Charles Saunders and General James Wolfe.

Like his French adversary, Wolfe had entered the military at an early age. He was 14 when he joined a regiment of Royal Marines commanded by his father. Wolfe distinguished himself in actions fought in the Low Countries during the 1740s and 1750s and in the brutal Battle of Culloden (April 16, 1746) that brought the Jacobite Rebellion to an end.

Wolfe did not join the fighting in North America until 1759, when, promoted to brigadier general, he led the long and frustrating siege against Quebec City. After three months, Wolfe put himself at the head of troops that finally managed to infiltrate the city's defenses, and in a battle fought on September 13, 1759, he succeeded in taking Quebec. Although mortally wounded, he lived long enough to witness the victory.

side, there was little left in Quebec to sustain an occupying force. Hauling parties, sent to gather precious firewood, were subject to attack from Indians still faithful to the French. General James Murray, commanding the garrison, made attempts to foil the mounting French effort to retake the capital and, in May 1760, was badly beaten in a battle before the city. One thousand of his men—a third of his troops fit for service—were killed before he finally retreated back into Quebec, where he and his men now suffered siege until the arrival of the British fleet relieved them.

### INDIAN TROUBLES

From this point on, the British steadily gained ground, as William Haviland, marching from Crown Point (Fort Saint Frédéric), captured Chambly on September 1, 1760, and Amherst and Murray joined forces in an assault on Montreal. On September 8, 1760, Governor Vaudreuil surrendered the province of Canada. Still, the French fought on, in hopes of salvaging something they could bring to the peace table.

Much of the action throughout the remainder of the war was less between the English and the French, aided by their Indian allies, than between the English and various groups of Indians. During 1760, having promised the Delawares and Shawnees that the English had no intention of occupying their lands, Amherst nevertheless built more and more forts in the West. The Senecas had come over to the English side in order to rid themselves of the French. Now Amherst began granting land—Seneca land—to his officers as a reward for faithful service.

The Ottawas, Potawatomis, and Ojibwas also had rea-

*Moody and brooding, Major General James Wolfe was passionately fond of the poetry of Thomas Gray (he was given to recite from memory the "Elegy in a Country Churchyard") and suicidally reckless in battle. After a long siege, he succeeded in taking Quebec, only to fall, mortally wounded, in the attempt. (Library of Congress.)*

son for alarm, first over the ever-augmenting presence of the English at Fort Pitt and then at Detroit. On September 12, 1760, Amherst ordered Major Robert Rogers, celebrated as the heroic guerrilla leader of his famous Rangers, to take *actual* possession of Detroit, Fort Michilmackinac (on Michigan's upper peninsula), and other western outposts *formally* ceded to the English after the fall of Montreal. Rogers left Montreal on the 13th, with 200 rangers in 15 boats and ascended the lakes to Detroit.

The party reached Niagara on October 1, carrying their boats over the portage and reaching Presque Isle by the end of the month. At the mouth of the Chogage River, in November, Rogers and his party were confronted by an Ottawa chief named Pontiac. He demanded that Rogers and his men leave the country. The major responded that, having defeated the French, the English were now in possession of Detroit, and he intended to occupy it. Pontiac declared that he would stand in Rogers's path until the morning. After a tense night, Pontiac returned

to the English encampment and told Rogers that he was willing to live in peace with the English in his country as long as they treated him with deference and due respect. The white commander and Indian chief smoked a calumet, the traditional "peace pipe."

The rangers resumed their journey on November 12 and, within a few days, had reached the western end of Lake Erie, where they received word that the Indians of Detroit were prepared to attack. Four hundred warriors, they were told, lay in ambush; but Pontiac persuaded them to disperse. As he approached Detroit, Rogers sent a young lieutenant ahead to deliver a letter to Captain Belètre, the French commandant there, informing him of the capitulation of Canada and instructing him to relinquish Detroit. The Frenchman not only refused to acknowledge the authority of the letter, he attempted to rally the local Indians to the French cause.

The Indians wanted nothing to do with either side, and Rogers and his rangers entered the mouth of the Detroit River unopposed. Another messenger was sent to Bel-

*In November 1760, Robert Rogers, on his way to occupy Detroit, now fallen to the British, encountered the Ottawa chief Pontiac, who declared that he would live in peace with the English as long as they treated him with deference and due respect. Thereupon the white commander and Indian chief smoked a calumet, the so-called peace pipe. Within three years, Pontiac would be one of the leaders of a general Indian uprising among the Ottawa, Delaware, Iroquois (principally the Seneca), and the Shawnee along the western frontier. (Library of Congress.)*

ètre, bearing surrender orders from Governor Vaudreuil himself, and the French commandant at last yielded. Detroit was officially conveyed to Robert Rogers on November 29, 1760. From Detroit, a detachment was sent south to forts Miami and Ouatanon, which guarded communication between Lake Erie and the Ohio. Rogers embarked for Michilimackinac, to relieve the garrison there, but early winter storms prevented his departure, so for the time being, this fort remained in French hands. The Royal Americans, a regiment of regulars, took possession during the next season.

As the British took over Detroit, the local Indians os-

tensibly renounced their loyalty to the French. The Senecas, however, resentful of the continued and increasing British presence at Niagara, consulted with other Iroquois Confederation chiefs at Onondaga to plan a coordinated uprising. Indian discontent was aggravated by Amherst's decree on February 22, 1761, ending the policy of giving gifts to the Indians. This step was all the more inflammatory because of the commander's high moral tone. He declared that taking the Indians off the government dole would force them to be self-subsistent; yet his decree deprived them of the ammunition they required for hunting.

On July 3, encouraged by local Frenchmen, two Seneca chiefs bore a war belt to Indians in the vicinity of Detroit, inviting the western tribes to join them in resisting the English. The Detroit Indians rejected the belt and disclosed the planned rebellion to the commandant of Fort Detroit. At this point, William Johnson, long a supporter of the Iroquois Six Nations, decided that, with the French defeated, the Indians had become a threat rather than an asset. He set about stirring up intertribal discord, explaining to Major General Thomas Gage that "The Six Nations on the one side and the Indians of [eastern] Canada on the other may be made an usefull barrier and Check upon the Western Indians, and the fomenting a Coolness between them and Jealousy of each others power will be the surest means of preventing a Rupture [with British interests], dividing them in their Councils, and rendering an union impracticable which cannot be too much guarded against."

*New Hampshireman Robert Rogers, depicted in a British engraving of 1776, led his celebrated band of Rangers in numerous guerrilla-style raids in the western theater of the French and Indian War and during Pontiac's Rebellion. (Library of Congress.)*

About the time that Quebec was taken, trouble began to erupt in the South. The Cherokees had been English allies since South Carolina Governor Charles Craven had concluded a treaty with them, by which they supplied warriors in exchange for a commitment from the colonials to defend, in their absence, their families against the Creeks and Choctaws. With this commitment came frontier forts and outposts, so that the promise of defense now became a threat of encroachment. The sequence seemed inevitable: Forts were built and settlers followed, creating an unresolvable tension.

The situation erupted in 1758 when a group of Cherokee warriors, slowly making their way home after abandoning General Forbes's interminable campaign against Fort Duquesne, appropriated some wild horses. A group of Virginia frontiersmen encountered the Indians, claimed the horses were theirs, and attacked the party. Twelve Cherokees were killed. The frontiersmen not only sold the horses, they collected bounties on the Cherokee scalps, claiming that they had been taken from *hostile* Indians. The Cherokees retaliated, killing 20 to 30 settlers.

Soon, the southern frontier was embroiled in a full-scale uprising that would require two armies and two years to put down. Colonel Archibald Montgomery and his Scottish Highlanders conducted the first campaign, which met with heavy—and highly effective—guerrilla resistance led by the Cherokee war chief Oconostota. By early April 1760, Amherst was building more forts on the Virginia frontier, but they were not sufficient defense against guerrilla tactics. Oconostota expelled some 1,500 Highlanders from his territory and laid siege to Fort Loudoun on the Little Tennessee River. The garrison surrendered, and many were killed as they fled Fort Loudoun for Fort Prince George.

A larger army, consisting of Carolina Rangers, British light infantry units, Royal Scots, and Indian allies next swept through Cherokee country, bringing total war to warriors as well as their families. After a relentless round of crop and village burning, the Cherokees capitulated in the winter of 1762, when they ceded much of their eastern land and agreed to a boundary separating them from the English settlers. The boundary did not endure long.

In the meantime, the British had concluded a treaty with the pro-French Micmac Indians in Nova Scotia. Negotiated in June 1761 with chief Joseph Shabecholou, the treaty guaranteed friendship with the English, but did not make mention of territorial cessions. Indeed, a December 1761 directive from Lord Halifax via the crown's board of trade instructed colonial governors to respect Indian lands and prevent their seizure contrary to treaties. This attempt to woo Indian allies failed in the case of Nova Scotia's Micmacs when the colony's governor, Jonathan Belcher, Jr., figured out a way to feign compliance with the crown's directive while summarily usurping the Micmacs' land. The governor issued a proclamation in accordance with the board of trade's instructions, but he did not issue it "at large," but, in effect, kept it secret. Publicly, he announced that the Micmac treaty was invalid. The French, he argued, who had acquired title to the lands in question from the Micmacs, ceded their title to the English pursuant to the 1713 Treaty of Utrecht; therefore, the land was rightfully English. Thus Micmacs came to know English justice: Their rights to the land were officially recognized, but also officially denied; they were dispossessed, yet allowed to remain in the country.

Next, Connecticut's Susquehannah Company encroached on land in Pennsylvania's Wyoming Valley assigned to the Delaware chief Teedyuscung by the last treaty at Easton. The chief threatened war, and the Iroquois, including the pro-English Mohawks, promised to support him. In June 1762, William Johnson convened a hearing at Easton, which was heavily weighted in favor of the Susquehannah Company's claims. In return for gifts, Teedyuscung relented and returned peacefully to the Wyoming Valley. Settlers, however, came in larger numbers, drove his people off the land, and assassinated the chief by burning him in his cabin. It became obvious

to the Indians of the Ohio country, regardless of their alliances, that the English, having driven off the French, were not about to leave.

In the meantime, Spain came into the Seven Years War in Europe on the side of France, and England declared war on the new combatant on January 2, 1762. British sea power rapidly prevailed against Spain. On February 15, 1762, Martinique fell to the English, followed by Saint Lucia and Grenada. On August 12, 1762, Havana yielded to a two-month siege, and Manilla fell on October 5. On November 3, France concluded the secret Treaty of San Ildefonso with Spain, in which it ceded to that country all of its territory west of the Mississippi and the Isle of Orleans in Louisiana. These cessions were by way of compensation for the loss of Spain's Caribbean holdings. With the Treaty of Paris, concluded on February 10, 1763, France ceded all of Louisiana to Spain and the rest of its North American holdings to Great Britain.

The treaty at last ended both the American and European phases of the Seven Years War. But, within a few days of the Treaty of Paris, the Ottawa, led by Chief Pontiac, together with other tribes, most notably the Delaware, Iroquois (principally the Seneca), and the Shawnee, began a series of attacks on the western outposts the French had just officially relinquished to the English.

# CHAPTER 12

# CODA AND PRELUDE

## The Epoch of Pontiac's Rebellion, the Paxton Riots, and Lord Dunmore's War (1760–1774)

## PONTIAC'S REBELLION

Since the influential, if often fanciful, nineteenth-century historian Francis Parkman published his two-volume *Conspiracy of Pontiac* in 1870, the general Indian uprising in the Old Northwest that followed as an unwelcome coda hard upon the French and Indian War has been called Pontiac's Rebellion. In reality, the Ottawa chief was only one among several Indian leaders who cooperated in an attempt to resist English encroachment on their land. The so-called rebellion, spanning 1763 to late 1764, included Delawares, Iroquois, (principally the Senecas), and Shawnees in addition to the Ottawas.

The rebellion can be traced to the fall of Detroit to the British on November 29, 1760, and General Jeffrey Amherst's decision to abolish the custom of giving gifts to the Indians. He was particular about cutting off their supply of ammunition, which made it difficult for the Indians, long accustomed to the use of firearms, to hunt. The French had always been liberal with gifts, and the sudden loss of arms and ammunition would likely mean starvation and death. Colonel Henry Bouquet, commanding forces in Pennsylvania, protested to Amherst that the action would have disastrous effect. Amherst's reply was that of a bureaucrat: "As to appropriating a particular sum to be laid out yearly to the warriors in presents, &c., that I can by no means agree to; nor can I think it necessary to give them any presents by way of *Bribes*, for if they do not behave properly they are to be punished." British Indian superintendent William Johnson, long accustomed to meeting Indians half-way, clear-headedly reported the situation to Lieutenant Governor Cadwallader Colden of New York in a letter of December 24, 1763:

I shall not take upon me to point out the Originall Parsimony &c. to w$^h$ the first defection of the Indians can with justice & certainty be attributed, but only observe, as I did in a former letter, that the Indians (whose friendship was never cultivated by the English with that attention, expense & assiduity with w$^h$ y$^e$ French obtained their favour) were for many years jealous of our growing power, were repeatedly assured by the French (who were at y$^e$ pains of having many proper emissaries among them) that so soon as we became masters of this country, we should immediately treat them with neglect, hem them in with Posts & Forts, encroach upon their Lands, and finally destroy them. All w$^h$ after the reduction of Canada, seemed to appear too clearly to the Indians, who thereby lost the great advantages resulting from the possession w$^h$ the French formerly had of Posts & Trade in their Country, neither of which they could have ever enjoyed but for the notice they took of the Indians, the presents they bestowed so bountifully upon them, w$^h$ however, expensive, they wisely foresaw was infinitely cheaper, and much more effectual than the keeping of a large body of Regular Troops, in their several Countrys.

In the wake of Amherst's edict, a prophet arose among the Delawares, counseling the Indians to reject all the ways of the white man and return to a pure Indian life, the way of the ancestors. Although the prophet charged his listeners to keep the peace, traders and agents in the vicinity of Detroit were worried. The Delaware Prophet was one more instance of Indian discontent and "conspiracy." Captain Donald Campbell, commandant of Fort Detroit, learned in the summer of 1761 that a delegation of Senecas had visited the nearby Wyandot village to enlist its inhabitants in a campaign to destroy the garrison. Investigating further, Campbell discovered similar plots against Forts Niagara and Pitt, as well as other outposts. Campbell wrote to Amherst as well as the com-

95

## THE DELAWARE PROPHET

Several major Indian military or political movements were promoted with the aid of charismatic and influential men of religion. Pontiac's Rebellion is a case in point. Little is known about the so-called Delaware Prophet, except that he was a Delaware, most active in the 1760s, who preached a powerful message to the Delawares and other tribes of the Old Northwest. He enjoined his followers to renounce all customs of and contacts with whites, including trade goods, liquor, and firearms. He called for a return to ancient Indian ways, with one important difference: Intertribal warfare should be abandoned in favor of pan-tribal unity. The Delaware Prophet's most famous convert was the Ottawa chief Pontiac, who eagerly embraced the anti-white message and the call for tribal unity, but who tempered the goal of racial purity with the practical compromises necessary for fighting against whites. Pontiac accepted alliance with the French, and he cultivated the use of firearms.

mandants of the other English forts, including Major Hugh Walters at Fort Niagara:

I have sent You an Express with a very Important piece of Intelligence I have had the good fortune to Discover. I have been Lately alarmed with Reports of the bad Designs of the Indian Nations against this place and the English in General; I can now Inform You for certain it Comes from the Six Nations; and that they have Sent Belts of Wampum & Deputys to all the Nations, from Nova Scotia to the Illinois, to take up the hatchet against the English, and have employed the Messagues to send Belts of Wampum to the Northern Nations. . . .

Their project is as follows: the Six Nations,—at least the Senecas—are to Assemble at the head of French Creek, within five and twenty Leagues of Presqu'Isle, part of the Six Nations, the Delawares and Shanese, are to Assemble on the Ohio, and all at the same time, about the latter End of this Month, to surprise Niagara & Fort Pitt, and Cut off the Communication Every where; I hope this will Come time Enough to put You on Your Guard and to send to Oswego, and all the Posts on that communication, they Expect to be Joined by the Nations that are come from the North by Toronto.

In response to Campbell's intelligence, Amherst dispatched Major Henry Gladwin, a hardened veteran of

Braddock's disastrous campaign against Fort Duquesne, with reinforcements to Detroit. This step and Campbell's timely warning to other outposts were apparently sufficient to forestall the planned raids. In the summer of 1762, similar "plots" were discovered, but these also failed to materialize.

In 1763, however, as soon as France had capitulated in the French and Indian War, ceding virtually all of its territory to Britain—without consulting any Indian allies—the Indians in the vicinity of Detroit were roused to rebellion again. Pontiac called a grand council on April 27, 1763, urging the Potowatomis and Hurons to join his Ottawas in a pan-tribal attack upon Detroit. Four days later, Pontiac visited the fort with a group of his warriors, ostensibly to entertain the garrison with a ceremonial dance. His real purpose in going was to size up the outpost's defenses. On May 5, Pontiac outlined his plan of assault: The Indians would conceal muskets, tomahawks, and knives under their blankets. Once they were inside the fort, the attack could begin. Other Indians would surround the fort in order to prevent escape and blockade any attempt at reinforcement.

The operation was scheduled for May 7 but was thwarted by an informant whose identity is unknown. Some have speculated that it was an Indian woman called Catherine, who was in love with Major Gladwin. Fort Detroit's garrison of 120 Royal Americans and Queen's Rangers was prepared for Pontiac's entrance on the appointed day. The chief came with 300 warriors, each with a blanket thrown over his shoulder, but he quickly realized that he had lost the element of surprise. Though he outnumbered the garrison two to one, Pontiac aborted his plan and withdrew from the fort. Knuckling under to pressure from some of the warriors, who accused him of cowardice, Pontiac tried to enter the fort again on May 8, but Gladwin told him that he would admit only the chiefs, no warriors. Wishing to create an aura of innocence, the chief organized an intertribal game of lacrosse just outside the fort. At the game's conclusion, Pontiac told Gladwin that he and his warriors would be back the next day for counsel, whereupon the commandant announced again that he would admit only the chiefs.

Frustrated again, and again pressured by his warriors, Pontiac began raiding the settlers in the vicinity of the fort. Next, Pontiac's Ottawas, joined by Wyandots, Pottowatomis, and Ojibwas, began firing into the fort. After some six hours, the attackers, exhausted, backed off. Five of Gladwin's men had been wounded; few of the Indians had been hurt.

Following this battle, on May 10, Pontiac conferred with other Indians and local Frenchmen. The French counseled a truce, and Pontiac allowed that he, too, desired peace. Pontiac dispatched some of the Frenchmen and four Indian chiefs to the fort with a request that Captain Donald Campbell be sent out to negotiate. Gladwin did not trust Pontiac and refused to order Campbell to go; the captain, however, volunteered, reassured by the French that he would be treated as an ambassador. No sooner was Campbell outside of the fort than he was seized by the Indians and held hostage. A day later, Pontiac conferred with Wyandot chiefs at a nearby village and enlisted their warriors as allies. On May 11, Pontiac ordered Gladwin and his garrison out of Fort Detroit, telling him that it would be stormed by 1,500 warriors within an hour. Gladwin refused, and about 600 Indians opened fire on the fort, maintaining the assault until after seven in the evening. Again, Pontiac demanded surrender; again, Gladwin refused. He declined to discuss any terms of settlement until Campbell was released. In the meantime, Indian parties continued to ambush and raid settlers in the vicinity of the fort, and Pontiac sent war belts to the Miamis and to the French in Illinois country, inviting their support.

The French, however, were no longer confident of Pontiac's ability to control his warriors. Reports were being received from French farmers, who complained of harassment at the hands of Indians allied to Pontiac. In an eloquent speech to a delegation of French settlers, the chief apologized for the actions of some of his followers and pledged his undying loyalty to France. He managed to win enough support to make war in earnest.

On May 16, 1763, some Ottawa and Huron chiefs requested Ensign Christopher Pauli to admit them into Fort Sandusky for a conference. Pauli did so and was seized by the warriors, who killed the small fort's 15-man garrison. Pauli escaped death because, following tribal custom, a widowed Indian adopted him to replace her dead husband. On May 25, Fort Saint Joseph fell. Two days later, Fort Miami (near present-day Fort Wayne, Indiana) was breached when its commandant, Ensign Robert Holmes, was lured outside the fort by his mistress, a Miami. He was killed and, threatened with massacre, the 11-man garrison surrendered.

On May 28, Lieutenant Abraham Cuyler, commanding 96 Queen's Rangers out of Niagara and bound for Detroit with badly needed supplies, was attacked at Point Pelee on the western end of Lake Erie. Eight of Cuyler's ten bateaux were taken and most of his men killed or captured. At the same time, a smaller group of 18 soldiers out of upper Michigan's Fort Michilimackinac was taken prisoner.

The first day of June saw the fall of Fort Ouiatenon (at present-day Lafayette, Indiana) when its commander, Lieutenant Edward Jenkins, was approached by a group of Indians who asked him to meet with several chiefs in a cabin outside of the fort. Jenkins complied, entered the cabin, and was seized. His 20-man garrison surrendered shortly afterward.

The forts fell so easily, in part, because the attacks followed one another with such speed that they outran word of the hostilities. Fort Michilimackinac's commandant, Captain George Etherington, and his 35-man garrison left the fort to watch a game of lacrosse between Ojibwas (Chippewas) and Sacs. The attack had been carefully plotted: One of the players threw the ball into the stockade, and all the Indians rushed in. They dropped their lacrosse sticks and picked up weapons that their women had smuggled in earlier. Twenty soldiers and one trader perished. Some soldiers who managed to escape were sheltered by sympathetic French families nearby as the warriors wreaked havoc on the surrounding countryside.

During early June, after the fall of Michilimackinac, attacks began farther east, Forts Pitt, Ligonier, and Bedford in Pennsylvania were all besieged, but they held out. About June 16, 1763, Senecas killed the entire 15- or 16-man garrison at Fort Venango (Franklin, Pennsylvania), except for the commandant, a Lieutenant Gordon, whom they forced to write (from dictation) a list of grievances addressed to the king of England. Following this, after three days of torture, Gordon died. On June 18, the Senecas moved on to Fort LeBoeuf (present-day Waterford, Pennsylvania) and burned it, killing about half the 13-man garrison. Joined by Ottawas, Hurons, and Ojibwas, the Senecas attacked Fort Presque Isle (Erie, Pennsylvania) on June 20. The Indians put the fort to the torch, and 30 soldiers surrendered on a pledge that they would be given safe conduct to Fort Pitt. Despite their promise, the Indians divided up the defeated men among the four tribes as prisoners.

When a group of Delawares demanded the surrender of Fort Pitt on June 24, Simon Ecuyer, commanding in the absence of Colonel Henry Bouquet, refused. General Amherst ordered Bouquet to commit an act of germ warfare by disseminating smallpox among the Indians. Bouquet ordered Ecuyer to summon Delaware chiefs to the fort for a parley and present them with a handkerchief and two blankets from the fort's smallpox-ridden hospital. Not only did the attackers soon retreat, a rescued white captive of the Delawares later reported that the disease was epidemic in the tribe.

Fort Niagara endured a Seneca siege and was never taken, but 72 soldiers were ambushed outside the fort at the Devil's Hole road.

Detroit also survived siege—five months of it, from May to September, at the hands of the Ottawas, Ojibwas, Potawatomis, Hurons, Shawnees, Delawares, and Eries. The fort was not entirely cut off during this time, as sloops cruised the Detroit River and Lake Erie, bringing in supplies and reinforcements. Major Gladwin was not content with a passively defensive policy, but periodically launched sorties against the attackers. One on July 4, 1763, resulted in the deaths of two Indians, including the nephew of Wasson, an important Ojibwa chief. Wasson demanded that Pontiac turn over to him Captain Donald Campbell. Pontiac did so, and Wasson summarily killed and scalped the soldier, throwing his body into the river so that it floated past the defenders of Fort Detroit. As a result of other sorties, however, prisoners were exchanged, at the rate of one Indian for three Britons, and the fort's band played regularly throughout the ordeal of the siege. The local French were not universally opposed to the British; some cooperated with the Indians, some with the garrison. Traders did a brisk business supplying both sides—though, not infrequently, a trader came to grief when Indians plundered his wares.

In the meantime, Colonel Bouquet was leading Fort Pitt's relief column, about 460 men, including Highlanders of the famous Black Watch regiment. On August 5, when they were within 30 miles of Pittsburgh, at a spot called Edge Hill, a party of Delawares, Shawnees, Mingos, and Hurons ambushed the column's advance guard. Bouquet's forces held the high ground throughout the long afternoon of battle, but they were surrounded.

Bouquet, however, had a plan. He planted a thin line of men along the crest of Edge Hill, so that, when the sun came up on August 6, the Indians would be tempted by the sight of a weakly held position. The Indians were tempted and made an unorthodox change in fighting style. They abandoned the guerrilla tactics of forest warfare and rushed into the open to charge the position, breaching the line with little trouble. Then they discovered that Bouquet had hidden in reserve two full companies, which now smashed into the attackers. Losses were probably equal in numbers—for Bouquet it was 50 men killed and 60 wounded—but the Delawares also lost two chiefs and, having failed to stop the relief column from reaching Fort Pitt, gave up a decisive battle. History would record it as the Battle of Bushy Run, after the stream beside which Bouquet was camped.

The siege at Detroit was lifted in September, and on October 3, 1763, Pontiac at last agreed to a peace. While a key participant in the rebellion, Pontiac was not the "supreme commander" of a centrally controlled movement. So, while he agreed to peace, other Indians involved in the uprising sporadically continued hostilities for another year.

Roundly criticized for his inability to put down the rebellion more expeditiously, General Amherst was recalled to England on November 17, 1763. General Thomas Gage replaced him as commander in chief of the American forces. Gage carried out two punitive expeditions, previously authorized by Amherst, sending Colonel Bouquet through Delaware and Shawnee country and Colonel Bradstreet from Niagara to Detroit.

At Detroit, Bradstreet engineered a sweeping treaty with a large number of Indians on September 7, 1764, compelling them to acknowledge the king of England as their *father* rather than their *brother*, thereby asserting royal sovereignty over them. The British, for their part had already addressed the major grievance behind the uprising—white incursion into Indian land. With the Proclamation of 1763, issued on October 7, The British government reasserted the earlier agreement made at Easton, Pennsylvania, which established a westward limit to white settlement. This proclamation did much to conciliate the Indians; however, like the earlier Easton agreement, it was honored more in the breach than in the observance. The remaining Indians involved in the uprising surrendered on November 17, 1764, at the Muskingham River in Ohio territory.

*General Jeffrey Amherst went up against Pontiac and, in his desperation, even authorized germ warfare against him—a successful attempt to disseminate smallpox among some hostile Delawares. Criticized for failing to defeat Pontiac expeditiously, Amherst was replaced as commander of British forces in America by General Thomas Gage. (Library of Congress.)*

The rebellion was costly, mostly in civilian lives. According to a contemporary estimate, 2,000 civilians and more than 400 soldiers were killed. No one knows how many Indians died, especially when the effects of smallpox are taken into consideration.

## THE PAXTON RIOTS

Noncombatant Indians were also victims of the violence associated with Pontiac's Rebellion. On December 14, 1763, a mob of 57 Scotch-Irish Presbyterians from Paxton and Donegal, on the raid-racked Pennsylvania frontier, shot and hacked to death a party of six innocent Conestoga Indians in Lancaster County. Governor John Penn issued a proclamation of arrest for the mob, but it was ignored. Thirsting for revenge against the Indians—*any* Indians—most frontier Pennsylvanians were in sympathy with the "Paxton Boys."

The magistrates of Lancaster County decided to gather the remaining Conestogas into a public workhouse in order to protect them. Given the prevailing mood of hatred, thus concentrating them only made them more vulnerable. The Paxton Boys struck again on December 27 and killed the 14 Conestoga workhouse inmates while they knelt at prayer. "Men, women and little children were every one inhumanly murdered in cold blood!" colonial statesman and Pennsylvania postmaster general Benjamin Franklin wrote. At this time, too, the people of the Irish Settlement in the Delaware Valley were menacing and even killing their converted Moravian Delaware Indian neighbors. Authorities removed the Indians to Province Island, Philadelphia. The Paxton Boys now marched on Philadelphia, where they were met by a band of young citizens who had rallied to the Indians' defense. Benjamin Franklin intervened and averted violence, persuading the badly outnumbered Paxton Boys to go home. Colonel Bouquet chided them:

After all the noise and bustle of our young men on the Frontiers, Every body expected that they [the Paxton rioters] would have offered their Services, as soldiers or Volunteers, for the defence of their Country, as being the fittest men for an Expedition against Indians, and as the best way to wipe off the Reproaches cast upon them for the violences committed, and offered to defenseless Indians;

Instead of such honourable conduct . . . they [returned to their homes] as Pack Horse Drivers and Waggoners, Employs for which a Coward is as fit as a brave man;

Will not People say that they have found it easier to kill Indians in a Gaol, than to fight them fairly in the Woods?

In the meantime, confined to the barren little island in the middle of the windswept Delaware River, 56 Indians

*This late nineteenth-century book illustration romanticizes the death of the Ottawa chief Pontiac, who was shot or clubbed and stabbed, but not tomahawked, by a Kaskaskia Indian named Black Dog as he was leaving a trading post in Cahokia, Illinois. Most likely, the assassin had been hired by an English trader who was fearful of the presence of the legendary chief. (Library of Congress.)*

sickened and died. Later, after peace was ostensibly restored, the survivors returned to the Delaware Valley, only to find that their villages had been destroyed. Some sought refuge farther west, in the Ohio country. Others met with death at the hands of ever-vengeful frontiersmen.

After peace was declared, Pontiac visited French settlements in Illinois country, for the next two years, and it was said that he was stirring up another "rebellion." However, with the English presence increasing in the interior (despite the Proclamation of 1763), Pontiac signed a treaty with William Johnson at Oswego on July 24, 1766, and pledged loyalty to the English. He kept his word until 1769, when he was assassinated as he was leaving a trading post in Cahokia, Illinois, by Black Dog, a Kaskaskia Indian who was with him. Evidence suggests that the assassin had been hired to do the job by an English trader, who, most likely, felt threatened by the presence of the legendary chief.

## LORD DUNMORE'S WAR

During the early 1770s, Lord Dunmore, the governor of Virginia, announced that he would issue patents for land on both sides of the Ohio River in territory claimed by his colony. In April 1773, he commissioned a survey party under Michael Cresap and John Floyd. In May, Captain Thomas Bullitt arrived in the camp of the Shawnee chief Black Fish to tell him that Lord Dunmore intended to settle land explicitly reserved for the Shawnee by the Fort Stanwix treaty of 1768. Black Fish responded that he would attack anyone who crossed the river into Kentucky. He sent braves to observe the surveying party, and when some of them did cross the river on May 29, 1773, a Shawnee named Peshewa—Wild Cat—went down to them, unarmed, to warn them back. He was shot and killed. In retaliation, Shawnees killed some of the suveyors but sent one back to Wheeling, West Virginia, to tell his compatriots that they would kill all the Virginians who attempted to cross the Ohio. Furthermore, the Shawnee would be aided in this by the fur trader George Croghan. Dr. John Connolly, Dunmore's magistrate of western Pennsylvania, concluded that a conspiracy existed among the Shawnees, fur traders, and Pennsylvanians (the latter bitterly disputed Virginia's claim to the Ohio country) and, in effect, declared war.

Like Black Fish, Chief Cornstalk, principal leader of the Ohio Shawnees, wanted to prevent a white invasion. He realized the futility of warfare with the whites. At the invitation of George Croghan, he journeyed to Fort Pitt (recently renamed Fort Dunmore) to negotiate a peaceful resolution to the conflict. Angry frontiersmen assaulted Cornstalk, his brother Silverheels, and another Shawnee, Non-hel-e-ma, as they returned from the fort. Silverheels was fatally wounded, and all hope of peace was thereby shattered. Cornstalk sought aid from the Miamis, Wyandots, Ottawas, and Delawares, all of whom declined. The Mingos, Senecas, and Cayugas who had removed to southern Ohio, also wished to remain neutral, but were driven to war when the family of one of their principal chiefs, known to the whites as John Logan, was slaughtered by a party of Cresap's men led by Daniel Greathouse. Greathouse murdered 13 women and children, which incited Logan and eight Mingo and Shawnee war-

riors to kill 13 Virginians. Fearing a general Indian uprising, Lord Dunmore officially declared war on June 10, 1774, raised a militia, and got under way on September 8.

Leading 1,500 men, Dunmore was to journey to Fort Pitt, then descend the Ohio to its juncture with the Kanawha River, where he would rendezvous with Andrew Lewis, who was to recruit an additional 1,500 militiamen. The combined force would then cross the Ohio and destroy the Shawnee villages.

For all his bluster, however, Lord Dunmore proved to be a timid commander. Fearful that his boats would be ambushed, he abandoned his plan to rendezvous with Lewis on the Ohio and instead proceeded slowly overland to the Scioto River in central Ohio. In the meantime, Lewis, with about 1,000 men, had reached Point Pleasant, the appointed rendezvous, on October 6. On October 9, Simon Girty arrived at Lewis's camp to tell him of the change in plans. He conveyed Dunmore's new order for Lewis to cross the Ohio and meet Dunmore near the Scioto.

The movements of both Dunmore and Lewis had been observed by Shawnee scouts. Cornstalk had gathered about 700 warriors—Shawnees and Mingos (including John Logan), as well as some Wyandots and Delawares. Cornstalk determined to attack Lewis on the morning he was to leave Point Pleasant to unite with Dunmore. Unfortunately for Cornstalk, an unauthorized hunting party from Lewis's camp discovered the Indians lying in wait and alerted Lewis, who sent out two companies to attempt an ambush. This failed, but the action did buy Lewis some time to erect crude breastworks of fallen trees. The battle on October 10 was fierce, and at its conclusion, the Indians were pushed back. But the cost was high: 222 of Lewis's men (including his brother, Charles) had been killed or badly wounded; about half as many Indians died.

All commanders emerged from the engagement enraged and disgusted. Cornstalk was appalled by the half-hearted performance of his Mingo, Delaware, and Wyandot allies; even his own people urged him to seek peace. The chief, who had not wanted war in the first place, now reasoned that, hostilities having commenced, it was foolhardy and disgraceful to seek quarter. But since his warriors lacked the stomach to continue fighting, he had no choice. Meanwhile, Lord Dunmore's army was near mutiny, his men itching to press the campaign. Lewis openly defied Dunmore's order to halt his march on the Shawnee towns and was stopped by Dunmore—at sword point—only a half mile from the villages. Despite urgings on both sides for revenge, a truce was concluded on October 26, 1774, among all hostile parties except for John Logan, who refused to attend the negotiations.

CHAPTER 13

# WHITE WAR, RED BLOOD
## The Revolutionary Period (1774–1784)

In fighting the American Revolution, both the British and Americans courted Indian allies. For the Indians, the colonial struggle for independence was a struggle to hold on to their homeland. Most Indians sided with the British, not because they perceived the British and Loyalist (or Tory) interests as more powerful, but because they saw a British victory as their only hope for containing white settlement. The British argued—quite accurately—that colonial victory would mean a steady push westward that would drive the Indians before it. Defeat of the revolutionaries, however, would result in enforcement of the Royal Proclamation of 1763, which prohibited settlement west of the Alleghenies. Clearly, in wooing Indian support, the British had learned something from the French and Indian War. Fortunately for the Americans, however, they had not learned quite enough. The British-allied Indians wreaked much havoc, especially in upstate New York, the back counties of Pennsylvania, and the fledgling settlement of Kentucky, but if the British had treated them with more trust and respect, equipped them better, and used them more, their alliance might well have won the war.

Since 1764, the British had been dealing with Indians through their Indian Department, divided into northern and southern jurisdictions. In 1775, the Americans organized their own Indian Department, divided into northern, middle, and southern districts. But it was personal relationships, not bureaucracies, that won allies. For example, well before the battles of Lexington and Concord formally began the revolution in April 1775, William Johnson, a British hero of the French and Indian War, and Thayendanegea, a Mohawk better known to the English as Joseph Brant, had forged a powerful personal and political alliance. Johnson had come to America from Ireland at age 15, settled in the Mohawk Valley

northwest of Albany, and quickly became friendly with the Mohawks. The tribe adopted Johnson, naming him Warraghiyagey, The Man Who Undertakes Great Things—for Johnson, who had become a powerful landowner with significant influence in the colony of New York, served not only as an official British Indian agent, but as the Mohawks' chosen "ambassador" to the colonial government.

Johnson's colonial and tribal affiliations became more personal when, after the death of his wife, he married Degonwadonti—Molly Brant—daughter of his friend Nichus Brant and Nichus's Indian wife, Owandah. Molly was at least 25 years younger than Johnson and had an even younger brother, Joseph. The young man became as a son to Johnson, who saw to his education at the Rev. Dr. Wheelock's Indian school. By age 15, Brant had seen action, on the British side, in the French and Indian War. His prestige grew among the Mohawks as well as the colonists, after he led successful raids against the Delaware towns of Kanastio and Kanaughton during Pontiac's Rebellion in 1764. It was Joseph Brant who captured the important Delaware chief Teedyuscung. Subsequently, Brant married the daughter of an Oneida chief, which added to Brant's standing not only within his own tribe, but in the Iroquois Confederation, since the Oneidas, like the Mohawks, were tribal members of the Six Nations. He was chosen as ambassador to the important 1768 grand council held at Fort Stanwix. Attended by 3,200 Indian representatives, it was the largest treaty conference ever convened and established the Fort Stanwix Treaty, which reiterated and elaborated on the boundary proclamation of 1763.

Thus, in February 1774, when the always-seething boundary question erupted into open resistance on the frontier, Brant knew that he could rely on Johnson to

*Thayendanegea, a Mohawk chief better known as Joseph Brant, was the brother-in-law, ally, and protégé of Sir William Johnson. He was a skillful and charismatic military leader and a valuable British ally during the American Revolution. (Library of Congress.)*

support Indian territorial rights, and Johnson knew that the Mohawks—and, he hoped, the rest of the Iroquois Confederation—would side with the Loyalists in the coming rebellion.

Nevertheless, in 1774, the crown proved unable to hold the proclamation line. When colonial governors were instructed to enforce the policy, Pennsylvania defiantly responded by declaring a scalp bounty, attracting a horde of bounty hunters who raided the Indian borderlands, pushing back Indian settlement. "Everywhere on the frontier is found new encroachment by our people as cabins are being built on Indian lands beyond the established white limitations," Johnson protested to the Lords of Trade. "Worse, they abuse and maltreat the Indians at every meeting. It seems as if the people are determined to bring a new war, though their own ruin may be the consequence." The two major centers of conflict at this time were Pennsylvania's Wyoming Valley and New York's Tryon County, with settlements along the Mohawk Valley. In the midst of this, during July 1774, William Johnson, after settling a land dispute between Mohawks and a particularly unscrupulous white settler, collapsed while addressing an assembly of some 600 Indians. "Brothers!" he gasped, mindful of the far greater crisis to come. "Whatever may happen, you must not be shaken out of your shoes!" The 59-year-old Johnson died a short time later, leaving his son Guy to assume the position of superintendent of Northern Indian Affairs. While Brant was able to pledge to him the loyalty of the Mohawks in whatever war was to come, he could not speak for the rest of the Iroquois Confederation, which was on the verge of its own revolution. He accurately predicted that the Oneidas and the Tuscaroras would side with the Americans.

The Oneidas' allegiance to the Americans was largely due to Samuel Kirkland, a teacher and Presbyterian minister among the Oneidas, who was beloved of that tribe. Guy Johnson, hoping to stem Kirkland's influence, officially removed him as missionary to the Oneidas, but that merely angered the tribe, driving them squarely into the American camp. They were joined in their support for the American cause by the Mahicans—also called the Stockbridge Indians—the remnants of a tribe, once quite powerful, that had been decimated by the Mohawks. Through the efforts of American Indian agent James Dean, the Tuscaroras also sided with the Americans. Colonel Ethan Allen worked the backwoods of New York, less successfully, attempting to attract additional Indian allies.

Although the Oneidas promised the Americans that they would attempt to convince the other members of the Iroquois Confederation that it was a mistake to side with the British, the Mohawks, Senecas, Cayugas, and Onondagas—all members of the confederation—determined at a council on June 12, 1775, to take up the hatchet on behalf of the British. Joseph Brant was named war chief, in effect making him second in command of the entire Iroquois Confederation. The earl of Dartmouth, who was British secretary of Colonial Affairs and Board of Trade, wrote to Guy Johnson, authorizing his enlistment of Indian allies:

White Hall, July 24th, 1775

Sir,

I have already, in my letter to you of the 5th Instant, hinted that the time might possibly come when the King, relying upon the attachment of his faithful allies, the Six Nations of Indians, might be under the necessity of calling upon them for their aid and assistance in the present state in America.

The unnatural rebellion now raging there calls for every effort to suppress it, and the intelligence His Majesty has received of the Rebels having excited the Indians to take part, and of their having actually engaged a body of them in arms to support their rebellion, justifies the resolution His Majesty has taken requiring the assistance of his faithful servants, the Six Nations.

It is, therefore, His Majesty's pleasure that you do lose no time in taking such steps as may induce them to take up the hatchet against His Majesty's rebellious subjects in America, and engage them in His Majesty's Service, upon such plan as shall be suggested to you by General Gage, to whom this letter is sent, accompanied with a large assortment of goods for presents to them upon this important occasion.

Whether the engaging of the Six Nations to take up arms in defence of His Majesty's government is most likely to be effected by separate negotiations with the chiefs, or in a general council assembled for the purpose, must be left to your judgment; but in all events, as it is a service of very great importance, you will not fail to exert every effort that may tend to accomplish it and to use the utmost diligence and activity in the execution of the views I have now the honor to transmit to you.

I am, &c.,
DARTMOUTH

In October 1775, acting on this authorization, Johnson commissioned Colonel John Butler to recruit allies among the Senecas and other Indians of the lower Great Lakes while he went to Montreal to gather additional Indian allies. By the late fall of 1775, the crown had accumulated an auxiliary army of 3,280 warriors.

Joseph Brant did not wait for the gathering of these forces. On September 5, 1775, he led 100 Mohawks, together with a small body of soldiers under Captain Gilbert Tice, in an attack on the American army under General Philip Schuyler near the Richelieu River as it was advancing on Montreal. Eight Americans were killed and another eight were wounded. Under bombardment from nearby Fort Saint Johns, Schuyler was forced to retreat. Another assault on Montreal, led by Colonel Ethan Allen on October 24–25, 1775, also failed because of desertions and the botched coordination of forces. A detachment of 40 regulars and 200 Canadians and Indians under Brant captured Allen and his men just outside the stockaded city's gate.

After these victories, Guy Johnson took Joseph Brant to London in November, where he created a sensation. He returned to America on July 29, 1776, more steadfastly pro-British than ever. Upon his return, New York City was besieged by General George Washington's army, so he fought briefly in the Battle of Long Island before he slipped northward into Iroquois country, where he set about calling his fellow tribesmen to arms against the rebels.

## FRONTIER WARFARE

By September 1776, the frontier populace of Virginia, Pennsylvania, and New York was in a state of panic. Sporadic Indian raids had already resulted in a number of deaths and disappearances. Throughout New York's Mohawk Valley, various Loyalists, dispossessed by the Rebels of house and lands, disguised themselves as Indians and raided settlers. In Pennsylvania's Wyoming Valley, the Continental Congress authorized raising two companies of militia, each with 82 men. Both companies, however, were almost immediately summoned to fight elsewhere, leaving the valley more vulnerable than ever. This was also the case in the Cherry Valley of New York, 12 miles south of the Mohawk River. There Captain Robert McKean raised a company of rangers, only to have them called away for action elsewhere. Captain William Winne raised another company of rangers, which was installed in the house of Samuel Campbell. Occupying a hill, it was fortified with an embankment of logs and earth and was the closest thing to a fort Cherry Valley could boast of. These frontier areas would endure repeated hit-and-run Indian raids, though more devastating, highly coordinated action was yet some two years off.

In the meantime, by June 1777, Joseph Brant and his followers were participating in Major General John Burgoyne's grand plan (as Burgoyne worded it) for "Conducting the War from the Side of Canada." The strategy called for splitting the rebel forces in two. After assembling his army at Montreal, Burgoyne would proceed up the Richelieu River and Lake Champlain, take Crown

Point, Ticonderoga, and Skenesborough, then continue by boat down the Hudson River, pushing General Philip Schuyler's army before it. The final objective was Albany.

Simultaneously, General Sir William Howe, supreme commander of the British forces in North America, would move up from the south, up the Hudson, in order to catch Schuyler's force in a pincers. A smaller third force, under French and Indian War veteran Lieutenant Colonel Barry St. Leger, was given a diversionary mission to the frontier. St. Leger would leave Montreal, proceed up the Saint Lawrence River to Lake Ontario and Fort Oswego. From the fort, the force would move up the Oswego River to the headwaters of the Mohawk River, then progress down that river in order to destroy the forts of the Mohawk Valley before meeting up with Burgoyne at Albany.

British Secretary of State Lord George Germain outlined the plan to the Canadian governor:

It is the King's determination to leave about three thousand men under your command and to employ the remainder of your army upon two expeditions, the one under command of General Burgoyne, who is to force his way to Albany, and the other under command of Lieutenant Colonel St. Leger, who is to make a diversion on the Mohawk River.

As this plan cannot be advantageously executed without the assistance of Canadians and Indians, His Majesty strongly recommends it to your care to furnish both expeditions with good and sufficient bodies of those men; and I am happy in knowing your influence among them so great that there can be no room to apprehend that you will find it difficult to fulfill His Majesty's expectations.

Unfortunately for Burgoyne's plan, Howe felt that he had insufficient numbers of troops to allow him to detach an army for service up the Hudson. He suggested, however, that Loyalist sentiment would prove strong enough in upstate New York to supply aid and reinforcement to Burgoyne. In fact, as the details of Burgoyne's plan were leaked and then highly publicized, Loyalist residents of the Mohawk Valley, fearing peremptory attack from their Rebel neighbors, defected to Canada. Officials in Tryon County, New York, issued orders for the arrest of Joseph Brant and Loyalist leaders. Even worse, the Canadians proved difficult to recruit; about 1,000 volunteers had been expected, but only 150 were finally mustered. In Burgoyne's force, the Indian auxiliaries—about 400 warriors—outnumbered the combined Canadians and American Loyalists (a complement of about 250). In addition, Burgoyne mustered 3,700 British regulars, 3,000 Hessians and Brunswickers, and 470 regular artillerymen. Additional Indian warriors were picked up on the shores of Lake Champlain. There Burgoyne met with chiefs and principal warriors of the Algonquin, Iroquois, Abnaki, and Ottawa tribes, inviting them to attack the Americans, but cautioning them that "Aged men, women and children must be held sacred from the knife or hatchet," and that scalps were to be taken only from the dead, not from the wounded or dying. Despite these instructions, by late June 1777, Burgoyne deliberately brandished his Indian allies as a weapon of terror, issuing an intimidating proclamation to the Americans:

Let not people consider their distance from my camp provides them safety. I have but to give stretch to the Indian forces under my directions—and they amount to thousands!—to overtake the hardened enemies of Great Britain. If the frenzy of hostility should remain, I trust I shall stand acquitted in the eyes of God and man, in executing the vengeance of the British government against the willful outcasts.

In the meantime, Lieutenant Colonel St. Leger had mustered 675 regulars and 700 to 900 Indians for his diversionary expedition into the frontier.

As Loyalists were deserting the Mohawk Valley, Rebel settlers were leaving settlements in and around Oquaga, Unadilla, and Cherry Valley, along the Susquehanna, and seeking refuge to the north, in the Mohawk Valley. Late in February 1777, New York militia colonel John Harper, commanding the fort at Schoharie, on the Schoharie Creek, about 25 miles due west of Albany, was directed by the New York Congress to investigate the activities of Joseph Brant. Harper interrogated Indians at Oquaga, accusing them of planning an invasion. They denied this, but on his way back from Oquaga, Harper encountered 15 warriors whom he believed were on their way to attack Johnstown. With 14 militiamen, Harper sneaked up on the Indians as they lay sleeping in camp; he disarmed them and marched them off to Albany as prisoners. In response, Brant led 80 warriors to Unadilla, a settlement of perhaps 20 to 30 houses, and complained that not only had 15 warriors been imprisoned without just cause, but the Rebels had appropriated provisions rightfully belonging to the Mohawks. Brant warned the settlers that Unadilla was now a dangerous place for anyone disloyal to the king. His threat was sufficient to send two-thirds of the population packing for the Mohawk Valley.

This was not the only American retreat. By the end of June 1777, Burgoyne had reached the American-held Fort Ticonderoga, opposite which was Mount Independence, a well-fortified American position controlling the water passage between Lake Champlain and Lake George. The Americans had deemed a third position, Sugar Loaf Hill, too steep to fortify, even though it overlooked both Fort Ticonderoga and Mount Independence. Burgoyne's engineers managed to haul cannon up Sugar Loaf, which they had dubbed Mount Defiance. In view of this development, Arthur St. Clair, the commander of Fort Ticonderoga, realizing that both the fort and Mount Defiance were indefensible, ordered a retreat. As both American positions were virtually surrounded by British forces, the evacuation, on the night of July 5, had to be accomplished very quietly. St. Clair left four artillerymen on Mount Independence with instructions to fire grapeshot on the British troops when they started to pursue the retreating Americans. Instead, the soldiers decided to drown the sorrows of battle with a cask of Madeira, failed to follow orders, and were later captured, stuporously drunk. One of the British-allied Indians, however, apparently curious about the artillerymen's still-smoldering wick, touched it to a cannon fuse, and, indeed, a load of grapeshot flew across the line of march of the British Ninth Regiment. No one was injured.

The British, under Brigadier General Simon Fraser, chased the retreating Americans until they themselves were attacked by reinforcements under General Philip Schuyler. The British Ninth Regiment was actually in jeopardy until some of their Indian allies set up a volley of war whoops that thoroughly dispirited the Americans, who retreated to Fort Anne. Such was the awe in which both sides held the Indian warrior. Indeed, Fraser used the threat of Indian savagery to control Patriot prisoners of war, assigning a very small guard to one group, but warning them that, should they try to escape, "no quarter would be shown . . . and those who might elude the guard, the Indians would be sent in pursuit of, and scalp them."

Valuable as they were, the Indian auxiliaries were virtually impossible to control. After the fall of Ticonderoga, they overran the fort, pillaging everything, leaving the British soldiery nothing. Worse, as Burgoyne's army was advancing toward Fort Edward, on the Hudson above Saratoga, Indians led by Wyandot chief Panther captured Jane McCrea, a young woman who was engaged to one of the Loyalists attached to the army. The warriors fell to disputing just who had captured her, and in the course of the argument she was tomahawked to death, stripped naked, and scalped.

Burgoyne and his men were, of course, outraged, but the general's hands were tied. To execute the guilty braves would alienate the Indians. To let the matter pass would incur the contempt of his own men and give the Patriots powerful moral ammunition. In the end, fearing Indian reprisals, Burgoyne chose the latter course—but he could not restrain himself from delivering a monitory speech on self-restraint in time of war. At this, a large number of warriors deserted Burgoyne, angry at being told how to wage war. One Hessian officer attached to Burgoyne's command observed: "It did not make any difference to the Indians, if they attacked a subject loyal to the king, or one friendly to the rebels; they set fire to all their homes, took away everything, killed the cattle. . . . It would certainly have been better, if we had not had the Indians with us."

## FORT STANWIX AND THE BATTLE OF ORISKANY

In the meantime, on June 18, 1777, one of the colonels attached to St. Leger's force, Daniel Claus, dispatched a dozen Iroquois braves—mostly Cayugas—under the Mohawk Odiseruney and the Cayuga chief Hare to scout out the Rebel stronghold at Fort Stanwix and to capture some prisoners to be brought back for questioning. They ambushed a tree-cutting party and a sod-cutting party outside of the fort, killing eight men and capturing five. Under interrogation several days later, the prisoners painted a picture of Fort Stanwix as formidably garrisoned. This was enough to give St. Leger pause, and he delayed his attack on the fort.

In truth, Fort Stanwix was in a state of disrepair, and its 29-year-old commandant, Colonel Peter Gansevoort, feverishly urged his 750-man garrison to improve the fortifications. As these preparations were under way, militia general Nicholas Herkimer unsuccessfully attempted to assassinate Joseph Brant, the best and most dangerous pro-British Indian leader. At Herkimer's invitation, Brant met him, to talk peace, in an open square in Unadilla, at the junction of the Unadilla and Susquehanna rivers, about 60 miles south of Fort Stanwix on the Mohawk River. Four men were to have drawn pistols hidden in their cloaks and shoot Brant. As it turned out, only one tried—the weapon became entangled in the folds of his garment—a war whoop went up from the Indians with Brant, *their* weapons were levelled, and both sides—at a standoff—parted.

Gansevoort was more fortunate in his undercover dealings. At the end of June, he dispatched Ahnyero, a prominent Oneida warrior known to the Americans as Thomas Spencer, to infiltrate the large Indian council convening at Oswego toward the end of July. As a result of this mission, Ahnyero was able to warn Gansevoort of the impending attack on Fort Stanwix, supplying details of troop strength.

St. Leger decided it was prudent to detach 30 riflemen, commanded by Lieutenant Harleigh Bird, and 200 Iroquois under Chief Hare to intercept a supply party to Fort Stanwix. That party, however, under Lieutenant Colonel Robert Mellon, reached the fort before Bird and unloaded the supplies. Only as Mellon was returning from this mission did Hare and his Indians attack, killing one bateauman and capturing four more. Bird's mission was not a total disappointment, since he was able to assess the strength of Fort Stanwix; contrary to what the prisoners had reported, he found it quite weak.

On August 3, 1777, St. Leger began his advance on Fort Stanwix with full military pomp, aiming to impress the outpost's defenders with the might of the British army. He set up his position just out of range of the American artillery and demanded Gansevoort's surrender. The American commander ignored the demand, and on August 4, St. Leger commenced artillery bombardment. This assault resulted in the death of one man and the wounding of six—far less effective than the work of Indian snipers, who picked off soldiers desperately working to cover the fort's interior roofs and parapets with sod. One sharpshooter, a Mohawk named Ki, killed three Americans and wounded seven others before he himself was felled by grapeshot from the fort.

During this siege, on August 6, three messengers managed to penetrate the Indian lines with a dispatch from General Herkimer, who was at the Indian town of Oriskany, ten miles southwest of Fort Stanwix, with 800 militiamen. The letter asked Gansevoort to join in a combined assault on St. Leger's lines. As the letter requested, Gansevoort fired three cannon shots as a signal that he had received the message and would comply. Immediately, Gansevoort sent out 200 men under Lieutenant Colonel Marinus Willett. They quickly encountered one of St. Leger's encampments and attacked, killing 15 to 20 British and Indians and taking four prisoners. But this minor Patriot victory came at the expense of alerting St. Leger to Willett's presence. He would now be unable to join forces with Herkimer.

Wisely, General Herkimer insisted on waiting for a sortie from Fort Stanwix before he attacked. His officers, however, were impatient, accused their general of cowardice and of harboring Loyalist sympathies (one of his brothers was fighting on the side of St. Leger), and demanded an immediate advance. Facing the prospect of mutiny, Herkimer had no choice but to proceed. When St. Leger's Indian scouts brought the British commander word of the advance, he sent Joseph Brant with 400 Indians and an equal number of Loyalist troops—John Butler's Tory Rangers and John Johnson's Royal Greens—to ambush Herkimer's force. Herkimer also employed Indian scouts—some 60 Oneidas—but, in this case, they failed to detect the ambush. Six miles from Fort Stanwix, where a wide ravine was crossed by a log causeway, Brant, Butler, and Johnson struck at 10:00 A.M. on August 6.

Most of the American officers were killed in the first few minutes of the Battle of Oriskany. Herkimer's leg was shattered by a musket ball, and it was reported that, propped up against a saddle, smoking a pipe, and bleeding to death, he calmly tried to direct the chaos that passed for a battle. One entire American regiment turned tail and ran; the others fought in vicious hand-to-hand combat in which the Americans were not the only sufferers. The Tory forces were also taking a beating, and Brant's Indians incurred serious losses, including the deaths of the Cayuga chief Hare and Chief Gisu-gwatoh of the Senecas, and the wounding and capture of another Cayuga chief, Ghalto.

Fortunately for the Americans, a sudden thunderstorm interrupted the battle, providing sufficient time for the forces to regroup on some moderately defensible high ground. John Butler succeeded briefly in breaching the Patriots' defensive positions by ordering his men to turn their green coats inside out, so that they resembled the American uniforms, and advancing. But even this attack was beaten off. At last, the Indians, discouraged by their own heavy losses, retreated, and with that desertion, Butler and Johnson also had to withdraw. The American forces were in no shape to pursue them.

The Battle of Oriskany was a disaster for all concerned. Half of the American forces were killed, wounded, or captured. The able militia commander Herkimer died of his wounds. The British lost 33, with 41 wounded. And, as was so often the case when they fought in white men's wars, Indian losses were the heaviest: 17 Senecas killed—including their chief warriors—and sixteen wounded; 60 to 80 Indians from other tribes were also killed or wounded. At least 23 of the Indian casualties were chiefs. It was said that British officers had given the warriors liberal doses of rum to buck them up before the battle. As a result, many fought drunk—and poorly.

Although Oriskany was not a victory for either side, the battle did halt Herkimer's attempt to reinforce Fort Stanwix, and St. Leger again demanded Gansevoort's surrender, sending two officers to the fort for a parley. One of them declared to Gansevoort and Willett that

If the terms are rejected, the Indians, who are numerous and much exasperated and mortified from their losses in the action against General Herkimer, cannot be restrained from plundering property and probably destroying the lives of the greater part of the garrison. Such indeed is their ire at the loss of several of their chiefs who were killed, that unless the surrender is agreed to, they threaten to march down this country on both sides of the Mohawk River, destroying the settlements and not sparing even the women and children.

To which Willett indignantly replied:

Do I understand you, Sir? I think you say, that you come from a British colonel . . . and by your uniform, you appear to be an officer in the British service. You have made a long speech on the occasion of your visit, which, stript of all its superfluities, amounts to this, that you come from a British colonel, to the commandant of this garrison, to tell him, that if he does not deliver up the garrison into the hands of your Colonel, he will send his Indians to murder our women and children. You will please to reflect, sir, that their blood will be on your head, not on ours. We are doing out duty; this garrison is committed to our charge, and we will take care of it. After you get out of it, you may turn around and look at its outside, but never expect to come in again, unless you come as a prisoner. I consider the message you have brought, a degrading one for a British officer to send, and by no means reputable for a British officer to carry. For my own part, I declare, before I would consent to deliver this garrison to such a murdering set as your army, by your account consists of, I would suffer my body to be filled with splinters, and set on fire, as you know has at times been practiced, by such hordes of women and children killers, as belong to your army.

General Schuyler, encamped at Fort Dayton, 50 miles from Fort Stanwix, dispatched General Ebenezer Learned and a Massachusetts brigade to the relief of the fort; a short time after this, he also sent the First New York Regiment under General Benedict Arnold. An advance party from Learned's brigade happened to meet Major Walter Butler (the brother of Tory Ranger commander John Butler) and Hon Yost Schuyler, a prominent Tory, and took both men captive. Arnold promised Hon Yost Schuyler pardon and restoration of his property if he agreed to return to St. Leger's camp and tell the Indians that Walter Butler—who was Joseph Brant's close friend and, therefore, a friend and military leader to the Indians—had been captured and would be hanged; Hon Yost Schuyler agreed and also greatly exaggerated reports of the strength of Arnold's force. The ruse worked. As many as 500 to 600 Indian warriors, many of them under the Seneca chief Gu-cinge, deserted St. Leger, who, alarmed by the report of Arnold's strength, hastily lifted the siege of Fort Stanwix on August 22, and withdrew, leaving behind a large store of equipment and artillery.

The ultimate failure of St. Leger's siege convinced Gu-cinge and Joseph Brant that if this was fighting in the style of the whites, they would have no more of it. Henceforth, they would pursue the hit-and-run tactics of lightning raids that had served them well in the past. As for the British, in the wake of St. Leger's failure, they found a new use for their Indian allies; Burgoyne's poorly provisioned army was plagued by desertions, and the general gave his Indian auxiliaries leave to kill and scalp any deserters they found.

In mid-August 1777, with his army in straitened circumstances, Burgoyne decided to raid Bennington, Vermont, where the Patriots had a large store of provisions. Indian auxiliaries were assigned to round up much-needed horses, which they did—but then demanded to be paid for them. When they were refused, the Indians cut their hamstring muscles, rendering them useless. The German mercenary commander of the assault on Bennington, Colonel Frederick Baum, complained bitterly of these so-called allies.

Although the initial engagement at Cambridge, New York, on August 12, resulted in the rout of 40 to 50 Americans, the Battle of Bennington went badly for the British and their German mercenaries. Instead of the small company of militiamen Baum expected to find at Bennington, the Americans had assembled a substantial force of Continental troops. When Baum's Indian auxiliaries realized this, they deserted. The battle, on August 16, 1777, resulted in the deaths of 207 from among the British-German forces and the capture of 600. Forty Americans were killed and an equal number wounded.

Still, the Indians' reputation for ferocity was such that (at least by one account) the Battle of Freeman's Farm, near Saratoga, began on September 19 with a skirmish between Colonel Daniel Morgan's famed corps of riflemen and a combine of Tories and Canadians *disguised* as Indians—the disguise intended to intimidate the enemy and to discourage attack. Reportedly, Benedict Arnold remarked, ''Colonel Morgan, you and I have seen too many redskins to be deceived by that garb of paint and feathers; they are asses in lions' skins, Canadians and Tories, let your riflemen cure them of their borrowed plumes.'' Not only did this battle result in an American victory (albeit with very heavy losses), but it discouraged the relatively few Indian auxiliaries who remained with Burgoyne. Most of these now decamped. The Battle of Saratoga, which followed, forced Burgoyne to surrender his army.

## HAVOC IN THE BORDERLANDS

While Britain's Indian allies quit fighting as auxiliaries in conventional battles after Oriskany and Saratoga, they did—as Joseph Brant and Gu-cinge had already decided—continue to raid the border country with increased ferocity. Early in 1777, the Tory governor of New York, William Tryon, openly urged British military authorities to ''loose the savages against the miserable Rebels in order to impose a reign of terror on the frontiers.'' While British prime minister Lord Chatham thought this tactic ''unconstitutional, inhuman, and unchristian! . . . Such horrible notions shock every precept of religion, divine or natural, and every generous feeling of humanity,'' the use of Indians as instruments of frontier terror became unofficial British policy.

By the end of 1777, hit-and-run raids were increasing in frequency throughout the New York and Pennsylvania frontier, particularly in the Cherry Valley, Mohawk Valley, and the Wyoming Valley. Soon, a pattern of raids and counterraids developed. In March 1778, General Philip Schuyler warned Congress that the western frontiers were about to erupt, and by April 1778, a major build-up of Tory and Indian forces was well under way along the upper Susquehanna.

Colonel John Butler, commanding 400 Rangers and Tories, was joined at the Indian town of Tioga by some 900 Senecas and Cayugas, led by the two important Seneca war chiefs, Gu-cinge of Kayingwaurto. Their objective was the Wyoming Valley of northern Pennsylvania. While Butler and his Indian allies constructed boats for the trip down the Susquehanna, Gu-cinge took 400 warriors in advance to attack settlements among the west branch of the river. In the meantime, Joseph Brant, with 450 Indians and Tories, was planning an attack on New York's Cherry Valley at the headwaters of the Susquehanna.

While Cherry Valley had been suffering raids since 1776 and anticipated more massive assaults, fortifications were crude and the militia garrison weak. Colonel Samuel Campbell, commanding the small force, outfitted 26 boys with wooden rifles and pointed hats made of paper and set them to drilling outside of the stockade. Brant, observing the fort from a distance, took these counterfeit soldiers for the real thing. Campbell also sent a rider with phony dispatches thanking commanders at Albany for the reinforcements provided and for the entire regiment whose arrival was anticipated. Brant captured the rider, read the dispatches, and decided to attack nearby Cobleskill instead of Cherry Valley. This small settlement of 20 houses, defended by 20 local militiamen under Captain Christian Brown and a 37-man detachment from Colonel Ichabod Alden's Seventh Massachusetts Regiment of Continental troops, was set upon by Brant's 450 men. Thirty-one Americans were killed and six wounded; Cobleskill was burned.

On June 2, after escaping capture by the Seneca warchief Red Jacket, Lieutenant John Jenkins warned the Wyoming Valley of an impending assault. Nevertheless, little could be done on June 28, 1778, when Butler's Rangers—400 disguised as Indians—and 800 to 900 Delawares and Senecas (including Gu-cinge and 400 warriors fresh from a savage raid on the West Branch) descended on the valley. On that day, they burned a mill, capturing—and subsequently torturing to death—three prisoners. On the thirtieth, Butler's scouts over-

whelmed some men working in the cornfields. John Gardner, who was taken captive, revealed in detail just how defenseless Wyoming was.

There was a collection of wilderness forts—most of them little more than fortified houses—including Wintermoot's (or Wintermot's), Forty Fort, Jenkins' Fort, Wilkes-Barre Fort, and Pittston Fort. The Wintermoots were Tory sympathizers, who readily ''surrendered'' their fort to Butler and provisioned his men. The weakly defended Jenkins' Fort fell to the Tory-Indian force on July 2. The next day, under a flag of truce, John Butler proceeded to Forty Fort, garrisoned by 450 Continental troops and militiamen (including boys and old men) commanded by Colonel Zebulon Butler (no relation to John), a Continental Army officer, and Nathan Denison, a colonel of the militia. He demanded the fort's surrender, but Denison and Zebulon Butler refused.

Although the militia was badly outnumbered, John Butler realized that, without artillery, it would still be difficult or impossible to take Forty Fort and, subsequently, Pittston and Wilkes-Barre. He decided on a ruse to lure the defenders out into the open. At five in the afternoon of July 3, he burned down Wintermoot's Fort (over the horrified objections of Helmut Wintermoot) in order to give the impression that he and his raiders were retreating. Zebulon Butler argued with Denison and the other militiamen in an attempt to dissuade them from leaving the fort in pursuit of the apparently retreating enemy. But, at last, he was overruled. The entire garrison sallied forth—and was promptly ambushed.

Of the 450 Americans involved, 300 died or were wounded. Of the 1,200 Tories and Indians, only 11 were lost. Battle casualties were not simply killed, but mutilated, scalped, and burned; captives were tortured and committed to the stake. Those who had survived the ambush, known as the Wyoming Valley Massacre, retreated to Forty Fort. Colonel Zebulon Butler escaped with his wife and family, and remarkably, the remaining defenders, including Colonel Denison, who surrendered the next day, were not harmed. However, the Wyoming Valley, now defenseless, was burned and looted. John Butler, aware of what little control he exercised over his Indian allies, retained his military prisoners but released the women and children, who fled into the wilderness, preferring to take their chances there than trust to the tender mercies of the Indians. Some fled to Wilkes-Barre Fort, but news of the fall of Fort Pittston—like Wilkes-Barre, on the east bank of Susquehanna—sent them back into the woods.

To the northeast, Joseph Brant again turned his attention to Cherry Valley. He began on July 18 by raiding Andrustown, seven miles west of Cherry Valley. With 50 warriors and a few Tories, he captured 14 settlers and killed 11 before burning the town. On September 12, Brant, commanding a much larger party of Indians, attacked German Flats on the Mohawk River. Most of the town's inhabitants had fled to refuge in nearby forts, so Brant destroyed a virtually deserted village. This, indeed, was the kind of fighting he preferred. Unlike his more bloodthirsty Indian brethren—and, for that matter, sadistic Tory counterparts—he concentrated his efforts on destroying property and hitting military objectives rather than murdering noncombatants. There are many stories of his efforts to spare women and children.

In September and October 1778, while Brant and about 600 warriors were attacking settlements in the valleys of the Neversink and Mamakating, Delaware River tributaries in the area where New York, New Jersey, and Pennsylvania meet, the militias of New York and Pennsylvania—quite independently of one another—retaliated against principal Indian towns.

Pennsylvania's Colonel Thomas Hartley (who was subsequently joined by Colonel Zebulon Butler) set out on September 21 with 217 men and, over the next two weeks, moved up the Susquehanna destroying Sheshaquin, village of the Seneca chief Eghobund, and Queen Esther's Town and Tioga, Seneca settlements that served as the so-called "southern door" of the Iroquois Confederation and that also served Brant and John Butler as a staging area for their raids. The expedition continued up the Chemung River to the Indian village of Chemung but was stoutly resisted there and turned back. Nevertheless, the campaign had been successful: In the course of a 300-hundred-mile march, Hartley's force had recovered 50 head of cattle, appropriated 28 canoes and other items of Indian property, killed 11 Indians, took 15 prisoners, and burned three major Indian towns. Hartley lost two men killed, and two were wounded.

Colonel William Butler, of New York (not to be confused with the Tory John Butler, to whom he was not related), left Fort Defiance at the town of Schoharie, due west of Albany, with 260 men on October 2. They made a circuit up the Schoharie Creek, then to the west branch of the Delaware River, then overland to the Susquehanna and downstream to Joseph Brant's headquarters town of Oquaga, where they burned 40 wooden houses. They also destroyed five other small Indian towns nearby before burning a Tory village called Scotch Settlement and a large Indian town, Conihunto. Then they burned the major Indian settlement of Unadilla. Only one of their party was wounded.

Doubtless, the sight of so much destruction when Brant and his party returned to their villages later in October stirred them to a particularly fierce retaliation against Cherry Valley. In July, Lieutenant Colonel Ichabod Alden and the 250 Continental soldiers of the Seventh Massachusetts Regiment had been sent for the defense of that settlement. A dull and obtuse officer, Alden ignored warnings from friendly Indians in November 1778 that a large body of Indians and Tories was planning to attack Cherry Valley. Worse, although he had spent the last several months supervising the building of a new fort, he refused to allow settlers to take refuge within it—protesting that, with his large garrison, the fort would be overcrowded—and denied them permission to store their valuables there—arguing that his soldiers would thereby be tempted to theft. Besides, no one seriously believed that the Indians would attack in winter.

Tory Ranger Captain Walter N. Butler (son of John Butler) infiltrated the sleeping camp of Sergeant Adam Hunter near the fort on the night of November 10. Facing 800 Tories and Indians, Hunter revealed the strength of Fort Alden (as Ichabod Alden had christened Cherry Valley's stockade) and, even more importantly, revealed that Alden and other principal officers were quartered *outside* the fort, at the house of Robert Wells. Consequently, the first objective on November 11, when Brant and Seneca chiefs Little Beard and Gu-cinge began their attack, was to surprise and cut off the Wells house. At 10:30 A.M., they stormed the house, killing the Wells family as well as Colonel Alden. Brant tried to intervene in order to save the family, with whom he was acquainted, but he was too late. Indeed, although the Indians had promised Walter Butler that they would refrain from unnecessary cruelty, the Senecas and some of the Mohawks ran amok, scalping, dismembering, even indulging in ritual cannibalism. Some of the Tory soldiers were even more bloodthirsty. Lieutenant Rolf Hare participated in the brutal stabbing of a woman named Sarah Dunlop and watched as a halfbreed named William of Canajoharie ate chunks of her flesh.

By two in the afternoon, Cherry Valley was virtually destroyed, with every building outside the stockaded fort ablaze—except for the house of Joseph Brant's friends, the Shanklands. Major Daniel Whiting, who had taken command of Fort Alden after the death of Ichabod Alden, dispatched a remarkably cool plea for aid to Colonel William Butler at Schoharie:

Cherry Valley, Nov 11th, 1778

Dear Col:—

This day at 11 o'clock I was attacked by a large body of Indians, who still keep up a steady fire. I would, therefore, have you do what you can for our assistance.

I am your humble servant,
D. Whiting, Major

P.S. Col. Alden is dead.

By the day's end, the death toll reached 74, including 42 military men and 32 civilians. Thirty-two of 33 houses were burned, in addition to 231 barns, two mills, and a blacksmith's shop. Not one of the attackers was killed, and only one was injured—by the unfortunate Sarah Dunlop, who struck William of Canjoharie with a frying pan before he killed her.

Even Captain Walter N. Butler was appalled by the slaughter, yet was not above using it as a continued threat. Via the Reverend Samuel Dunlop, he sent a letter to General Philip Schuyler that is a remarkable blend of self-exoneration in the matter of the Cherry Valley Massacre and an attempt to exploit it:

near Cherry Valley, Nov. 12th, 1778

Sir,

I am induced by humanity to permit the prisoners, whose names I send you herewith, to remain, lest the inclemency of the season, and their naked and helpless situation, might prove fatal to them; and expect that you will release an equal number of our people in your hands, amongst whom I expect you will permit Mrs. Butler and family to come to Canada. But if you insist upon it, I do engage to send you, more over, an equal number of yours taken either by Rangers or Indians, and will leave it to you to name the persons.

I have done everything in my power to restrain the fury of the Indians from hurting women and children, or killing the prisoners who fell into our hands; and would have more effectually have prevented them, but they were so much enraged by the late destruction of their village Oquaga, by your people. I shall always continue to act in the same manner. I look upon it as beneath the character of a soldier to wage war with women and children. I am sure that you are conscious that Colonel [John] Butler or myself have no desire that your women or children shall be hurt. But be assured that if you persevere in detaining my father's [John Butler's] family with you, that we shall no longer take the same pains in restraining the Indians from making prisoners of women and children, as we have heretofore done.

I am, Sir, your humble servant,
Walter N. Butler
Captain of the Rangers

Major Samuel Clyde, a resident of Cherry Valley, addressed a letter to New York governor George Clinton, who used it to help convince General George Washington to send food and clothing to relieve Cherry Valley.

To His Excellency, George Clinton, Esq.,
Governor of the State of New York, at Poughkeepsie.

Sir:—

The unhappy circumstances that we are reduced to, by the late massacre and destruction by Butler and Brant at Cherry Valley, I cannot help acquainting you of, and of the hard struggle and difficulty we have had these two years past to maintain our settlement. Being a frontier, with the disaffected amongst us doing their endeavors to disappoint all our measures by giving the enemy intelligence and robbing us of our horses and cattle, we could scarce lay down one night in fear of our lives.

This last spring when we found that the enemy were collecting at Unadilla, and that they intended to cut off the frontier settlements, we immediately informed our generals at Albany that we must either quit the settlement or they must send us some troops to help us; which, if they could not do so, to give us notice, that we might move away. But they seemed to make light of our intelligence and sent us word that we must by no means quit the post, that they intended to protect it; but that they did not think we should be disturbed either by Indians or Tories that summer. This was about twelve days before Cobleskill was burnt.

Then we assembled together and fortified our meeting house, brought in our provisions and effects and, with the assistance of the militia, maintained the post until Colonel Alden arrived with the Continental troops. He immediately ordered us out of the garrison which we had made ourselves. He would not allow us the liberty to keep one chest in it—that he would protect us. Few of us having wagons to ride our effects away, we were obliged to carry them back to our houses again and so continued there, in fear, till we were drove out by the enemy.

General [Edward] Hand being in Cherry Valley a few days before the attack, recommended us to move our effects into the fort but, when he was gone, Colonel Alden would not allow it, saying that he had out good scouts and that he would give us timely notice when to move in. It was not in our power to convince him that the enemy would attempt to come there; which has occasioned us the loss of our all. The greater part of us have neither provisions, body clothes nor bed clothes to cover us in this cold season of the year. If we cannot get some relief to help us through the winter, we must suffer either by cold or hunger. We cannot get either clothing or grain to buy for money if we had it.

We are mostly moved out to the River, but we can get no farther. The inhabitants here are in general riding down their grain and effects and storing them. They hold themselves in readiness to move as soon as they hear of the approach of the enemy, and those that can't help themselves must fall a sacrifice to the enemy.

This, Sir, is real fact.

From your Most Obedient and
Most Humble Servant,
Sam Clyde.

Washington did more than send relief to the beleaguered valley; he authorized a massive campaign of retaliation—even extermination—against the Iroquois Confederation.

The campaign was authorized early in 1779, but it was June 18 before General John Sullivan, an officer notorious for his excessive caution, began marching his force of 2,500 men—the New Jersey, New York, and New Hampshire brigades—from their rendezvous at Easton, Pennsylvania, to the Susquehanna. Washington had laid out a three-pronged strategy: Sullivan would cut a swath through the valley of the Susquehanna, up to the southern border of New York; General James Clinton, commanding 1,500 troops, would move through the Mohawk Valley to Lake Otsego and then proceed down the Susquehanna; and Colonel Daniel Brodhead would lead 600 men from Fort Pitt up the Allegheny. At Tioga, Pennsylvania, Sullivan and Clinton would join forces, move north to Niagara, and meet Brodhead at Genesee.

Despite Washington's exhortations to travel light and move fast, the obsessively cautious Sullivan had burdened his expedition with 120 boats, 1,200 packhorses, and 700 cattle. Average progress during the first month of the campaign was a mere six miles a day. Moreover, Sullivan had ordered Clinton to travel with similar baggage, so he was equally slow. Even before Sullivan had gotten under way, however, Clinton had launched a six-day raid from his base of operations at Canajoharie on the Mohawk River.

Five hundred fifty-eight of Clinton's command, under Colonel Goose Van Schaik, combined with 60 Oneidas led by Chief Hanyerry, left Fort Stanwix to attack Onondaga, the traditional capital of the Iroquois Confederation. On April 21, 12 Onondagans were killed and 34 captured; 50 houses were destroyed, and food and supplies plundered. The longhouse, in which representatives of the Iroquois Six Nations met to debate the confederation's policy, was burned. The significance of the raid extended beyond the immediate destruction. Because the Oneidas, an Iroquois tribe, participated in the raid, it signalled the dissolution of the Iroquois Confederation.

Still, the progress of the main column was heartbreakingly slow. An advance guard dispatched from Easton—200 men under Major John Powell—sent out a small hunting party near Wyoming Mountain. They were ambushed and killed. The passage of the overloaded army through wilderness and, especially, the Shades of Death Swamp, was agonizing. Sullivan's army endured a number of mutinies. Worse, on June 30, Clinton wrote to Sullivan that

we had with us a fortnight some two hundred Oneida Indians under Chief Hanyerry. Only two days ago these Indians received a very threatening letter from the British commander, General Sir Frederick Haldimand, Governor of Quebec, which threatened the destruction of their towns if they joined our force. At this most of them deserted us and we are left now with only 25, but these include Hanyerry, who is angered at the threats.

In the meantime, on July 22, 1779, Brant hit the Mohawk Valley town of Minisink, about 20 miles above the juncture of New York, New Jersey, and Pennsylvania. Sixty Indians and 27 Tories disguised as Indians torched the settlement in the dead of night, as the settlers, mostly women, children, and men too old for militia duty, slept. Minisink's small fort, its mill, and 12 houses were destroyed, along with orchards and farms. A few settlers were killed or taken prisoner.

The attack spurred Colonel John Hathorn and Lieutenant Colonel Benjamin Tusten (or Tustin) to launch a militia assault from nearby Goshen. Tusten mustered 149 men, and Hathorn joined him with an additional detachment. Hathorn assumed command of the combined force and attempted to ambush Brant at the confluence of the Delaware and Lackawaxen rivers, cutting off his line of retreat. Brant, however, perceived Hathorn's intention and maneuvered his force behind Hathorn, springing an ambush upon him before he could ambush Brant. Accounts vary. Out of 170 Americans, anywhere from 40 to 140 were lost in the attack by a combined Indian-Tory force of 87. Subsequently, 300 Indians and Tory Rangers led by Gu-cinge and Captain Robert McDonald attacked Forts Freeland and Sunbury on the West Branch of the Susquehanna. The 37-man garrison of Fort Freeland surrendered after a brief fight. Colonel Thaddeus Cook, commanding Fort Sunbury, dispatched Captain Hawkins Boon with 80 men to the aid of Freeland. His force, however, was surrounded and overwhelmed, with the loss of 40 men, including Boon.

At last, on August 7, Sullivan's column entered Indian country. Sergeant Thomas Roberts recorded in his journal the devastation of the country at the mouth of the Lackawanna River:

Incamped at Lackenwanney whear the Land is the Best that Ever I see Timmothy as high as mu head and the Bildngs ar Burnt by the Saviges the Warter is but Poor the Wild turkes very plenty the young ones yelping throug the Woods as if it Was inhabbited Ever So thick.

On August 9, Sullivan reached Newtychanning, a deserted Seneca village, and put its 28 buildings to the torch. Sullivan reached Tioga—where he would rendezvous with Clinton—erected Fort Sullivan, and posted General Orders:

As the army will soon be called upon to march against an enemy whose savage barbarity to our fellow citizens has rendered them proper subjects of our resentment, the General assures then that though their numbers should not be equal, which he is sensible cannot be the case, yet it is his firm opinion they cannot withstand the bravery and discipline of the troops he has the honor to command. Nevertheless, it ought to be remembered they are a secret, desultory and rapid foe, seizing every advantage and availing themselves of every defeat on our part. Should we be so inattentive to our own safety as to give way before them, they become the most dangerous and most destructive enemy that can possibly be conceived. They follow the unhappy fugitives with all the cruel and unrelenting hate of prevailing cowards, and are not satisfied with slaughter until they have totally destroyed their opponents. It therefore becomes every officer and soldier to resolve never to fly before such an enemy, but determine either to conquer or perish, which will ever insure success. Should they thus determine and thus act, nothing but an uncommon frown of Providence can prevent us from obtaining that which will insure peace and security to our frontiers and afford lasting honor to all concerned.

Although Newtychanning was the first in a long line of towns destroyed, few of the enemy were actually encountered. Clinton burned Otego on August 11; Unadilla on August 12; Conihunto and its cornfields on the thirteenth; Chemung on the fifteenth; the Tuscarora town of Shawhiangto on the seventeenth; Ingaren and the crops in its adjacent fields on the eighteenth; Otsiningo, with 20 hewn log houses, on the same day; two villages named Cohoconut on the nineteenth; and Owego on the evening of the same day. The occupants of these towns had already fled before the raiders arrived.

On August 26, Sullivan's and Clinton's forces combined to advance toward Newtown, where Walter N. Butler and Joseph Brant had prepared an ambush. Sullivan sent as a scout Major James Parr, leading a detachment of Morgan's riflemen. He spied the ambush and reported it: The enemy was in a semicircular bend of the Susquehanna, deeply entrenched and also occupying two plots of strategic high ground. Prepared, Sullivan and his officers defeated the ambush, though with difficulty and with the loss of three men and 39 wounded. After the battle an entire day was consumed in destroying the large Indian village at Newtown. It was a bitter defeat for John and Walter Butler, and for Joseph Brant.

Throughout September 1779, Sullivan devastated almost completely deserted towns: Catherinetown, Kendaia, Canadasaga—capital of the Senecas—and Canandaigua. As Sullivan's army approached Chenussio, an important Seneca town, Brant and John Butler planned an ambush at Conesus. At this point, the Indians and Tories could muster a force of no more than 200—insufficient to attack Sullivan's whole army, but enough to wreak havoc on the advance guard. On September 13, between Chen-

ussio and Conesus, Brant and Butler lured a 26-man scouting party led by Lieutenant Thomas Boyd into ambush. Fifteen men were killed outright, including the pro-American Oneida chief Hanyerry, whose dead body was hewn to pieces, the scalped head impaled on a branch. Boyd, wounded, was taken captive, whipped, his fingernails pulled out one by one, his nose and tongue cut off, an eye gouged out, his genitals cut off, his body pierced with spears in numerous places, and his head cut off.

But this attack was nothing more than a gesture of vengeance. The main body of Sullivan's army continued on to Gothsegwarohare on September 14, destroying it, and Chenussio on the fifteenth, destroying it as well. Next came Genesee, a town of 128 houses, ample fields, and large orchards—all of which the army destroyed. Sullivan's mission was to proceed to Niagara, the major source from which the British supplied their Indian allies, but pleading a shortage of supplies, the cautious commander launched a less ambitious—and strategically far less significant—campaign of destruction against Cayuga towns.

At the end of September, the expedition was concluded. "I flatter myself that the orders with which I was entrusted are fully executed, as we have not left a single settlement or field of corn in the country of the Five [i.e., Six] Nations, nor is there even the appearance of an Indian on this side of the Niagara," Sullivan observed in his report to Congress. Indeed, the roll of devestation is formidable: fifty towns destroyed, comprising some 1,200 houses, each of which sheltered two or three inhabitants; vast amounts of corn destroyed; two hundred thousand bushels of grain destroyed; ten thousand fruit trees felled or girdled.

While this destruction caused great hardship for the Indians in the country, winter, starving many, and while the campaign tore the Iroquois Confederation apart, the Indians were still at large after the long campaign. As Major Jeremiah Fogg observed in his journal when the army returned to Fort Sullivan at Tioga on September 30:

The question will naturally arise, what have you to show for your exploits? Where are your prisoners? To which I reply that the rags and emaciated bodies of our soldiers must speak for our fatigue; and when the querist will point out a mode to tame a partridge, or the expedience of hunting wild turkey with light horse, I will show them our prisoners. The nests are destroyed, but the birds are still on the wing.

The winter of 1779–80 was calm, with no raids, but with spring came renewed Indian warfare fueled by desperation, a thirst for vengeance, and a sense that there was nothing more to lose.

## THE OLD NORTHWEST, KENTUCKY, AND THE SOUTH

While raids, counterraids, and a campaign of vengeance were being waged on the borderlands of Pennsylvania and New York, terror also visited the thinly settled Old Northwest—the Ohio country—and Kentucky.

Around July 2, 1775, chiefs and subchiefs of the five Shawnee septs (bands) met at Chillicothe on the Little Miami River in Ohio to deliberate a response to white incursions into Kentucky. Chief Cornstalk, a principal Shawnee leader, preached a policy of neutrality in the Revolution, but by fall 1775, Shawnees began raiding the new Kentucky settlements, which, however, did not stem the tide of immigration. In June 1776, George Rogers Clark organized a meeting of settlers at Harrodsburg to decide how to resist the Indian attacks. The meeting sent Clark and John Gabriel Jones to Williamsburg—Kentucky was under the jurisdiction of Virginia—to secure aid against the Indians. In the meantime, a Shawnee subchief named Pluck-kemeh-notee, known to the whites as Pluggy, renewed attacks on Kentucky settlements and particularly menaced Harrodsburg, the best-established village and supply center for fledgling settlements. On his way to Harrodsburg, Pluggy attacked the house of John McClelland, and, though McClelland died in the fight, Pluggy was also killed. His death incited Chief Black Fish to organize 200 warriors in a campaign meant to annihilate white Kentucky once and for all.

On or about July 4, 1776, at a grand Indian council among the Shawnees, Iroquois, Delawares, Ottawas, Cherokees, Wyandots, and Mingos held on Muscle Shoals on the Tennessee River, Cornstalk abandoned neutrality and threw in with the British: "It is better for the red men to die like warriors than to diminish away by inches. Now is the time to begin. If we fight like men, we may hope to enlarge our bounds."

By the end of January 1777, Indian depredations had driven large numbers of settlers from the country, so that only Harrodsburg and Boonesboro could muster a body of men—103, to be exact—capable of opposing Black Fish. The chief moved against Harrodsburg on March 18, 1777, but had to withdraw because of a severe snow, ice, and rain storm. After ten days of inclement weather, he returned on the twenty-eighth—just as the temperature began to plummet, again making an attack impossible. On April 24, however, Black Fish laid siege to Boonesboro, which was more thinly manned than Harrodsburg. During a four-day siege, one settler was killed and seven wounded, including Daniel Boone, founder of the settlement. Yet the settlement endured, and Black Fish withdrew, though his warriors remained in the area through much of May, occasionally ambushing hunting and for-

aging parties. On May 23, he attacked the settlement yet again, broke off the engagement at nightfall, resumed the next day, and then withdrew from the vicinity of Boonesboro on May 25. Black Fish turned next against Saint Asaph, weakest of the Kentucky forts in that it was held by only eleven men. On May 30, the Indians attacked a milking party of three women and four men, killing all. Nevertheless, the remaining settlers held out for two days until Black Fish finally withdrew.

By this time, George Rogers Clark had persuaded Virginia authorities to make Kentucky a county of that state and was commissioned to raise and command a Kentucky militia. Clark laid out a plan to attack the British western forts—at Kaskaskia, Cahokia, and Vincennes, all deep in Ohio country—with the object finally of taking Detroit. These outposts of the Old Northwest, Clark reasoned, were the real sources of threat to Kentucky. They served as Indian sanctuaries and points of supply.

Early in June 1777, Clark dispatched two woodsmen, Samuel Moore and Benjamin Linn (or Lyon), to assess the strength of Vincennes and Kaskaskia. They returned from their mission at the end of August, reporting that the British garrison at Kaskaskia had been withdrawn to Detroit and that the surrounding settlements up to Cahokia were virtually defenseless. Clark reported the intelligence to Virginia governor Patrick Henry and began to assemble a force at Fort Pitt, from which they would journey down the Ohio to Corn Island, at the Falls of the Ohio, join up with militia men from Kentucky and Tennessee, and move against Kaskaskia and Cahokia.

While Clark was formulating his plans and assembling his force, Cornstalk, the Shawnee chief, was talking neutrality with the Americans even as he was preparing to war against them. The young Shawnee warriors were impatient, however, to act on the bellicose sentiment Cornstalk had expressed in July 1776. In concert with Wyandots, Mingos, and Cherokees, a group of Shawnees raided the area of Wheeling (in present-day West Virginia) during midsummer 1777. This moved Congress to dispatch General Edward Hand to recruit Pennsylvanians, Virginians, and Kentuckians for an attack on a British-Indian supply depot on the Cuyahoga River, near present-day Cleveland.

Hearing of this plan, Cornstalk, under a flag of truce, went to Fort Randolph at Point Pleasant on the confluence of the Ohio and Kanawha to warn the Americans that, if Hand attacked, all the Shawnee and allied nations would retaliate. Captain Matthew Arbuckle, commandant of the fort, ignored both the warning and the flag of truce. He imprisoned Cornstalk, his son Silverheels, and another warrior, intending to hold them hostage to ensure the good behavior of the Shawnees. On November 10, 1777, a party of white hunters, having heard that the

## DANIEL BOONE (1734–1819)

The invasion of the American West by White settlers was triggered by a massive immigration of Scottish-Irish fleeing oppression, poverty, and starvation in Ireland's Ulster plantation. By 1770 more than 400,000 Scottish-Irish, joined by other European immigrants, spread through Pennsylvania and trekked south down the valleys of the Appalachians to the foothills of the Carolinas. As good eastern land became scarce, they moved into the forests farther west. Armed only with an ax and a flintlock, they knew great hardship and almost constant strife with the Indians.

For these pioneers, Daniel Boone became the first of many western heroes, a deerslayer and Indian fighter whose story was so emblematic of life on the frontier that he became their uncrowned king. Born of a lapsed Quaker in 1734 in southern Pennsylvania, he moved with his family to Yadkin County, North Carolina when he was 19. He first heard about a place called Kentucky from one of his fellow volunteers under George Washington at Fort Duquesne during British General Edward Braddock's disastrous assault. After the French and Indian War, Boone left his home to wander the game-rich wilds of Kentucky for months, sometimes years, at a time, seeking enough deerskins to allow him to make ends meet. Plagued by debt like most pioneers, uneasy with the growing number of new neighbors he found each time he returned home, Boone developed the burning conviction that there was a fortune be to made beyond the mountains.

In Kentucky, his legend spread. Though he had been fighting Indians since he was a teenager—during the fierce Yadkin Valley raids from 1758 to 1760, again in the French and Indian War, and in sporadic wilderness encounters—it was a Shawnee siege of Boonesboro (the settlement he founded on April 6, 1774) at the beginning of the American Revolution that became the most celebrated of his many battles.

Later, in 1778, Boone was captured by the Shawnee chief Blue Jacket. Boone pretended to turn traitor, accepted adoption into the Shawnee tribe, and offered to cooperate with Henry Hamilton, England's brilliant liaison with the Indians and, perhaps, the most hated man in the West. (The Indians called him Hair Buyer because he paid bounties on Patriot scalps.) As the Shawnees' captive, Boone managed to delay an attack on vulnerable Fort Pitt at the forks of the Ohio and to gather information on an attack planned against Boonesboro. Boone escaped in time to mount a successful resistance at his settlement. Some accused him of cowardice and collaboration, but a postwar court martial exonerated Boone and credited his strategem with the salvation of the frontier during the American Revolution.

After the Revolution, Boone's fame grew in a fashion that would become standard for many a western legend: He became a hero in the popular literature read primarily by easterners. His "press agent" was a Pennsylvania schoolteacher turned land promoter named John Filson, who traveled to Kentucky in 1782 and wrote *The Discovery, Settlement, and Present State of Kentucke*, which included a section subtitled "The Adventures of Col. Daniel Boone," a purported autobiography.

But, by the time of Filson's book, Boone had suffered considerable misfortune. His son Israel died in an Indian ambush during the last major frontier conflict of the Revolution. In 1780, Boone headed for Virginia with $50,000—most of it belonging to his friends—to buy the land warrants necessary to preempt eastern speculators from gobbling up the "Bluegrass"; the money was stolen along the way. The incident was characteristic. Though he had become a successful surveyor, trader, and landowner, he lost everything through his own carelessness and the legal chicanery of land speculators.

In the 1790s, bitter as a result of his business dealings, Boone swore he would never live within 100 miles of a "damned Yankee." He packed up his belongings and his family and moved west again, along with a flood of immigrants, to present-day Missouri. There he died in 1819, just as Missouri was applying for statehood.

chief was being held under light guard, decided to take vengeance on Cornstalk for previous depredations. They shot, killed, and mutilated all three Shawnees.

The death of Cornstalk drove the Shawnees openly into the British camp. In February 1778, General Hand, with 500 militiamen, began to march against the Cuyahoga supply depot but, ignorant of the country, failed to find the Cuyahoga River and engaged no warriors. They did kill a small boy, two women, and one old man, and they captured two women before returning to Fort Pitt. Hand's campaign was mockingly christened the "Squaw War," and the general resigned as western commander to return to more conventional combat in the East.

While Hand was thrashing about in the wilderness, Black Fish, Black Hoof, and Blue Jacket, all Shawnee chiefs, were raiding the frontier. On February 8, 1778, Blue Jacket, with 102 warriors, captured a salt-making party of 27 at Blue Licks, Kentucky. Among the captives was Daniel Boone, who was adopted by Black Fish, and who did not escape—or choose to leave—the Shawnee until May. He made it back to Boonesboro in time, however, to warn of an impending raid on the settlement and prepare for it. (On September 8, 1778, 444 warriors under Black Fish laid siege to the settlement for almost two weeks before finally giving up and returning to Chillicothe.) In May, Black Fish and 400 warriors laid siege to Fort Randolph, where Cornstalk had been imprisoned and killed. As was commonly the case in Indian warfare, the siege proved unsuccessful, and, after several weeks, Black Fish withdrew and divided his forces for scattered raids along the Kanawha River, east into Virginia, and into the Shenandoah Valley. Throughout the west, Shawnee, Wyandots, Mingos, Delawares, Miamis, and some Kickapoos were making raids. Perhaps as many as 3,500 warriors were involved.

By the end of May 1778, George Rogers Clark managed to recruit only 175 men—rather than the 350 he had hoped for—to march against Kaskaskia and Cahokia. On June 26, 1778, Clark embarked from Corn Island in flatboats, shot the rapids, and reached the mouth of the Tennessee River in four days. At Fort Massac, he and his men proceeded overland to Kaskaskia. With great stealth, Clark captured a farm near the Kaskaskia River, collected boats, and ferried his troops across the river. Dividing his band in two in order to give the impression of greater numbers, he surrounded and surprised the fort, which surrendered without a shot. From this new base, Clark easily took Cahokia—also without combat.

Vincennes was more difficult. Clark realized that Lieutenant Colonel Henry Hamilton, British commander at Detroit, would soon retaliate and easily overwhelm his diminutive army if he did not take the initiative and attack first. On February 5, 1779, Clark began the 150-

*George Rogers Clark organized an effective western strategy against the British and British-allied Indians during the American Revolution, systematically attacking and taking the forts of the Old Northwest, including Detroit.*

## GEORGE ROGERS CLARK (1752–1818)

Brother of William Clark, who served as co-captain of the Lewis and Clark expedition, George Rogers Clark began his own career in the 1770s as a surveyor in the western frontier territory of Virginia (present-day Kentucky). He fought against the Shawnee chief Cornstalk during Lord Dunmore's War and against the Shawnees and British in Kentucky and the southern Ohio Valley during the American Revolution. In 1778 he led a spectacular militia action against the western forts of the British and their Indian allies, and between 1780 and 1782 he was the chief American defense on the Ohio frontier, also leading offensives against the Indian villages of Chillicothe and Piqua.

After the Treaty of Paris ended the revolution in 1783, Clark patrolled the Ohio country, helping to establish and maintain U.S. sovereignty over the region. By the time he mounted a major offensive against the Shawnees in 1786, however, he was aging and inclined to drink; after three weeks of marching without encountering the enemy, his 2,000-man Kentucky militia dissolved. That same year, Clark lost his appointment as Indian Commissioner for the Old Northwest Territory, largely through the manipulations of the treacherous (and finally treasonous) James Wilkinson. This began a period of great bitterness and disappointment for Clark, who was particularly distressed over the refusal of Virginia and the federal government to pay for his long service on the western frontier. Disgusted, he became involved in Spanish and French colonization schemes in the Mississippi Valley and accepted a commission as French commander on the Ohio. When these schemes collapsed, Clark's reputation suffered as his countrymen questioned his loyalty, and in 1794, he retired to private life in Jefferson County, Kentucky, where he ran a mill. Ill health plagued his final years, especially after 1808, when a crudely performed amputation of his right leg left him partially paralyzed.

mile march to Vincennes through a hostile wilderness in the dead of winter. He and his men reached Vincennes on February 23 and took a few prisoners in the settlement, from whom they learned that Fort Sackville (the British outpost at Vincennes) was now defended by only a few hundred men. Lieutenant Colonel Hamilton had released most of his Indian allies, whom, he reasoned, he would not need until the spring offensive against Kaskaskia. Like other British commanders, Hamilton found that his Indian allies were restive and troublesome between battles.

Nevertheless, Clark figured that he was outnumbered and that a prolonged siege would bring British reinforcements. He sent one of his prisoners back into town with a letter announcing his intention to take and occupy Vincennes and inviting those loyal to the king to repair to the fort, as no mercy would be shown them. To give the impression of greater numbers, Clark signed the letter with the names of several officers who were not, of course, present; he also paraded some of his men in the fading light with counterfeit regimental colors and generally deployed his troops to make it look as if there were far more of them. As soon as the attack began, many of the remaining British-allied Indians deserted Vincennes, and the Kickapoo and Piankashaw Indians, who had remained, ventured out to *help* Clark. With bluff confidence, Clark pressed unconditional surrender terms on Hamilton, who, after a brief resistance, capitulated.

The fall of the forts of the Old Northwest made life harder for the raiding Indians. At least one important Delaware clan, the Rabbit, led by Chief Running Fox, withdrew entirely from the Ohio country. The Shawnee nation split over the new incursion of Americans into their country. Like the Rabbit Delaware, some moved west; others remained to fight ever more desperately.

On July 10, 1779, Colonel John Bowman, of the Continental Army, led about 250 regulars and militiamen in an inept attack on Chillicothe, the Shawnee "capital." At the time, most of the warriors were out raiding, and the town was defended by about 35 men and boys. Bowman's men rushed into the all-but deserted town, fired the buildings and looted whatever valuables came to hand, whereupon Indians began sniping, killing ten of this vastly superior force. Bowman withdrew as Indians continued to snipe at his rear, killing a total of 30 men. Bowman's men succeeded in wounding one important warrior, Chief Black Fish. But that and the destruction of Chillicothe served only to enflame the Shawnees and incited their closer cooperation with the British. After Black Fish died of his wounds in October, a grand council of Shawnees, Wyandots, Hurons, Ottawas, Tawas, Tuscaroras, Ojibwas, Delawares, and Miamis met with

British representatives, including the famous Tory-allied frontiersman Simon Girty, to plan a vengeance invasion of Kentucky.

The early spring of 1780 was marked by frequent hit-and-run raids, especially in the vicinity of Lexington, Kentucky, a new and weak settlement. In June, 300 Delawares, Hurons, Wyandots, Ottawas, Mingos, Ojibwas, Tawas, Miamis, and Potawatomis joined forces at the mouth of the Auglaize River with 100 British regulars and an additional 70 Canadian Greens under Captain Henry Byrd to begin the invasion. As they traveled downriver, they were joined by Shawnees and by the Girty brothers, Simon, James, and George, as well as the British Indian agent Alexander McKee.

By the time he established a staging area at the conflu-ence of the Licking and South Licking rivers, on June 22, 1780, Byrd had assembled a force of almost 1,200 and was prepared to attack Ruddell's Station on the South Licking. After an artillery bombardment, John Ruddell surrendered, securing Byrd's promise that his people would not be harmed. As was often the case, the Indian auxiliaries proved impossible to restrain. The stockade gates were opened, the Indians rushed in, and a massacre ensued.

Byrd, sickened by the slaughter, threatened to break off the campaign if such an atrocity were repeated. He moved on to Martin's Station and took 100 prisoners, who were not harmed. The Indians wanted to continue on to Bryant's Station, but the British officer had had enough of frontier combat and demurred. Despite the enraged contempt of his Indian allies, Captain Byrd withdrew.

## SIMON GIRTY (1741–1818)

In his influential *Letters from an American Farmer* (1782), Michel-Guillaume Jean de Crèvecoeur (who wrote under the name of Hector St. John de Crèvecoeur) described the class of settlers who occupied the farthest frontier as "a kind of forlorn hope, preceding by ten or twelve years the most respectable army of veterans which came after them." *Forlorn hope* is military jargon for the advance guard or shock troops who are calculatedly sacrificed in order to secure a position for the main force that follows them. These first pioneers, Crèvecoeur argued, separated from white civilization and thrust into intimacy with Indian civilization, emerged from the experience neither white nor Indian, but lost between two identities, sacrificed, as it were—forlorn.

Such precisely describes the Girty brothers, Simon, James, and George, who in 1756, during the French and Indian War, were captured by Indians. Simon, aged 15, was traded to a band of Senecas, with whom he lived for the next three years. Released to the British at Fort Pitt in 1759, he did not, unlike many youthful captives, resist return to white society, but he did retain a strong identification with the Indians. For almost two decades, through the end of the French and Indian War and in Lord Dunmore's War, Simon Girty served the Ohio country militia and British regulars as a scout and interpreter (he was fluent in the Iroquoian language). At the start of the American Revolution, Girty enlisted in the Virginia militia, but in 1778 he defected to the Tory cause and worked closely with Alexander McKee in Detroit as an interpreter and a liaison with Great Britain's western Indian allies.

A master of Indian battle tactics and eagerly embracing the culture of the Indian warrior, Girty led various Indian sorties against the Americans. It was he who ordered Colonel William Crawford to be burned alive when Shawnee and Delaware Indians captured him during the Continental Army's unsuccessful Sandusky campaign in 1782. And it was Girty who led combined Indian and Tory assaults on the frontier settlements of Kentucky.

Although Simon Girty, who became known as the "Great Renegade," was a wanted man after the revolution, he continued to serve as a go-between and interpreter in the Ohio Valley, which was still controlled in large part by British trading interests and hostile Indians. During Little Turtle's War (1790–94), Girty firmly sided with the Indians, participating in the disastrous defeat of Arthur St. Clair's forces on November 4, 1791. After "Mad Anthony" Wayne decisively defeated Indian forces at the Battle of Fallen Timbers (August 20, 1794), Girty attempted in vain to dissuade the Indians from signing the 1795 Treaty of Greenville, by which they ceded vast tracts to the Americans. With the Americans firmly in possession of Detroit, Girty fled to Ontario. When the War of 1812 broke out and Canada was threatened with invasion, Girty took refuge among a band of Mohawks. In 1818, he died in Ontario, in the village of Amherstburg.

## A FRONTIER CAMPAIGN

Fighting Indians on the frontier was a matter of long marches, hunger, and cold punctuated by "battles" more closely akin to murder and wanton vandalism than to military operations.

In an August 22, 1780, letter to Virginia governor Thomas Jefferson, George Rogers Clark summarized his retaliatory campaign and what it had accomplished:

"By every possible exertion . . . we completed the number of 1000, with which we crossed the river at the mouth of the Licking on the first day of August and began our March on the 2nd. Having a road to cut for the artillery to pass, for 70 miles, it was the 6th before we reached the first [Shawnee] town, which we found vacated, and the greatest part of their effects carried off. The general conduct of the Indians on our march, and many other corroborating circumstances, proved their design of leading us to their own ground and time of action. After destroying the crops and buildings of Chillecauthy we began our march for the Picaway settlements, on the waters of the Big Miami, the Indians keeping runners constantly before our advanced guards. At half past two in the evening of the 8th, we arrived in sight of the town and forts, a plain of half a mile in width lying between us. I had an opportunity of viewing the situation and motion of the enemy near their works.

I had scarcely time to make those dispositions necessary, before the action commenced on our left wing, and in a few minutes became almost general, with savage fierceness on both sides. The confidence the enemy had of their own strength and certain victory, or the want of generalship, occasioned several neglects, by which those advantages were taken that proved the ruin of their army, being flanked two or three different times, drove from hill to hill in a circuitous direction, for upwards of a mile and a half; at last took shelter in their strongholds and woods adjacent when the firing ceased for about half an hour, until necessary preparations were made for dislodging them. A heavy firing again commenced, and continued severe until dark, by which time the enemy were totally routed. The cannon playing too briskly on their works they could afford them no shelter. Our loss was about 14 killed and 13 wounded; theirs at least triple that number. They carried off their dead during the night, except 12 or 14 that lay too near our lines for them to venture. This would have been a decisive stroke to the Indians, if unfortunately the right wing of our army had not been rendered useless for some time by an uncommon chain of rocks that they could not pass, by which means part of the enemy escaped through the ground they were ordered to occupy.

By a French prisoner we got the next morning we learn that the Indians had been preparing for our reception, moving their families and effects: that the morning before our arrival, they were 300 warriors, Shawnees, Mingos, Wyandots, and Delawares. Several reinforcements coming that day, he did not know their numbers; that they were sure of destroying the whole of us; that the greatest part of the prisoners taken by Byrd, were carried to Detroit, where there were only 200 regulars, having no provisions except green corn and vegetables. Our whole store at first setting out being only 300 bushels of corn and 1500 of flour; having done the Shawnees all the mischief in our power, and after destroying the Picaway [Piqua] settlements, I returned to this post [Fort Jefferson, Louisville], having marched in the whole 480 miles in 31 days. We destroyed upwards of 800 acres of corn, besides great quantities of vegetables, a considerable portion of which appear to have been cultivated by white men, I suppose for the purpose of supporting war parties from Detroit. I could wish to have had a small store of provisions to enable us to lay waste part of the Delaware settlements, and falling in at Pittsburgh, but the excessive heat, and weak diet, shew the impropriety of such a step. Nothing could excel the few regulars and Ketuckyans, that compose this little army, in bravery and implicit obedience to orders; each company vying with the other who should be the most subordinate.

I am, sir, your most humble
and obedient servant,
George Rogers Clark,
Colonel"

In response to these raids, George Rogers Clark tabled his planned assault on Detroit and secured a militia of 1,000 mounted men, which he assembled at the mouth of the Licking River for an attack on Byrd and his Indian allies, especially the Shawnees. Although Byrd evaded Clark, the Shawnees, led principally now by Black Hoof, retreated westward before his advance. On August 8, 1780, a combined force of Shawnees, Mingos, Wyandots, and Delawares took a stand at Piqua Town. The battle was hotly contested at first, but Clark's men succeeded in outflanking the Indians, concentrating them, and pinning them down where they would be vulnerable to artillery bombardment. By the battle's end, 14 Americans had been killed and 13 wounded; Indian losses were about three times that number.

While Clark had been organizing his campaign, a British trader named Emmanuel Hesse was carrying out a plan to seize control of Saint Louis, at the time under the jurisdiction of Spain, which, in 1779, had announced its alliance with France and America against Britain. Hesse persuaded Patrick Sinclair, British governor of Fort Michilimackinac, that he could recruit a large army of Indians with whom he would float down the Mississippi from its confluence with the Wisconsin River to Saint Louis, which he would seize, establishing a base there from which he would launch attacks on Natchez and New Orleans. Hesse embarked with 300 regular troops and 900 Indians, including Menominis, Sacs, Foxes, Winnebagos, Ottawas, and Sioux. Captain Don Fernando de Leyba, the Spanish commander at Saint Louis, reinforced the town's fortifications with five tower-mounted cannon in preparation for the attack, which came on May 26, 1780. Although de Leyba's 29 regular soldiers and 281 town residents were vastly outnumbered, the attack failed. The Indians, disappointed, turned away from the fortified settlement and raided the surrounding countryside instead.

After Clark's campaign against the Shawnees, Congress commissioned him a brigadier general and sent him on an expedition west of the Ohio and, ultimately, to Detroit. It was August 1781 before he finally gathered 400 regulars and volunteers (he *had* hoped to muster 2,000 men) and started down the Ohio. The new brigadier was diverted from his objective, however, by a need to strengthen Vincennes and the surrounding frontier against an impending British attack. Indeed, bolstered by British claims that they were planning a grand offensive, the Shawnees had rebuilt Old Chillicothe and Piqua Town and began raiding Kentucky again. Virginia, its treasury strained, could no longer support the Kentucky militia. Soldiers deserted their frontier posts. By the time General Cornwallis had surrendered to General Washington at Yorktown in 1781, virtually ending the revolution,

military discipline on the frontier had disintegrated, white raiding continued.

Elsewhere in the South, campaigns against Indians were more decisive. At the outbreak of the revolution, Cherokees, acting on the encouragement of the Shawnees, launched a series of devastating raids on the frontiers of Georgia and South Carolina. In August 1776, General Andrew Williamson led 1,800 troops—guided by Catawba scouts—against the Cherokees, wreaking havoc on their villages and cornfields. The next month, Williamson was joined by North Carolina's General Griffith Rutherford commanding 2,500 militiamen. Together they drove the Indians southeastward, toward Florida. An additional 2,000 Virginia and North Carolina militiamen, under Colonel William Christian, attacked from the Holston River. Overwhelmed, and receiving no aid from the British or from their Creek allies, the Cherokees sued for peace and, from May to July 1777, ceded vast lands east of the Blue Ridge Mountains and north of the Nolichucky River. James Robertson was appointed Indian agent for North Carolina and, operating out of the principal Cherokee town of Echota, kept the peace until he left in 1779.

The Creeks, initially reluctant to war against the Americans, were recruited to the British cause late in 1778 by John Stuart, the British Indian superintendent installed at Pensacola, Florida. Stuart's plan was to use the Indians to support a British invasion of the south. But lack of coordination between him and the commander of the fleet that landed redcoats at Savannah rendered the alliance ineffective. Still, many of the Creeks were actively hostile toward Americans, and with a Cherokee splinter group that had moved to Chickamauga Creek, they conducted hit-and-run raids throughout the revolution. Later, additional Cherokees joined their Chickamauga and Creek brethren in more extensive combat until October 7, 1780, when John Sevier and Andrew Pickens, after defeating the Tories at Kings Mountain, on the border of the two Carolinas, once again devastated the Indian settlements.

Generally, the British badly mishandled their potential Indian "assets" in the South. The Cherokees, Creeks, Choctaws, and Chickasaws could have fielded about 10,000 warriors—by far the largest body of Indian allies—who might well have turned the tide of the war. But, poorly paid and poorly supplied, they could not be relied upon. General John Campbell called upon the Choctaws to help him defend Mobile on the Gulf of Mexico against an attack by the Spanish fleet. The warriors showed up, but when the attack did not materialize, they deserted. By the time Admiral Bernardo de Gálvez arrived, on February 10, 1780, only 18 Indians were left, and the town fell to the Spanish. In contrast, when Gálvez moved on to Pensacola in March, 2,000 Creeks were there to aid the British. Gálvez postponed the attack for six weeks, when the Indians left—though, by that time, the British fleet had arrived, and Pensacola was saved.

## THE FRONTIER WAR: LATE PHASE

Back in upstate New York, settlers were learning that General Sullivan's massive campaign of destruction had only served to make the Indians more desperate. Raiding was general throughout the spring and summer of 1780. Colonel Daniel Brodhead, leading 500 to 600 men in a month-long campaign along the Allegheny River and deep into Indian territory, retaliated by destroying ten Mingo, Wyandot, and Seneca towns as well as some 500 acres of corn. Despite this, Mohawks, Senecas, and Cayugas launched a devastating attack against the Americans' principal ally, the Oneidas, pushing them back to Schenectady. In March 1780, the militia garrison at Skenesboro, near Lake George, was overrun and captured. Harpersfield fell a few weeks later to Joseph Brant. From Canajoharie to the northern end of the Wyoming Valley, small parties of Indians terrorized the frontier.

Then, on May 21, 1780, Sir John Johnson organized a massive assault on the forts and strong houses of the Mohawk Valley. With 400 Tories and 200 Indians, he burned Johnstown on May 23 while brant hit Caughnawaga. Brant, leading a mixed force of 500 Indians and Tories, overran Canajoharie on August 1 and 2. From there Brant started down the Ohio, where he intercepted and ambushed a Pennsylvania militia force under Archibald Lochry. Out of 100, 5 officers and 35 men were killed and 48 men and 12 officers captured.

Triumphant, Brant and his men turned back north and rejoined Johnson for a continued assault on Tryon County, New York. Johnson, Brant, and a Seneca chief named Cornplanter met at Unadilla. As a force of 1,800, they descended upon the Scoharie Valley on October 15 and then progressed up the Mohawk River, burning everything they encountered. A small militia force of 130 men led by Colonel John Brown out of Fort Paris, near Stone Arabia, was cut to pieces by the far superior Tory-Indian force at Fort Keyser, an abandoned outpost. Johnson then burned Stone Arabia.

Finally, on October 19, General Robert Van Rensselaer, with a militia force augmented by Oneidas, forced Johnson to a stand at Fox Mills and succeeded in driving him out of Scoharie. In the course of a five-day raid, Johnson and his Indian allies had destroyed as much as General Sullivan had in a month-long campaign.

Wounded during Johnson's raid, Joseph Brant was out of action until early 1781, when he returned to the Mohawk Valley with a vengeance—though few families

(and no militia) remained in the area. In April he attacked Cherry Valley, capturing two detachments of Continental soldiers, who were attempting to provision the perpetually besieged Fort Stanwix—which, at long last, was abandoned.

American fortunes were at low ebb in New York when Colonel Marinus Willett was assigned command of the region. By this time, only 2,000 settlers remained in and about the Mohawk Valley. Willett had at his disposal a mere 130 Continental troops and a vastly diminished pool of militia recruits. Willett made the most of his resources, circulating them throughout the countryside. Shortly after Willett took up his new command, his scouts reported fires near Corey's Town. The commander dispatched men to investigate and extinguish the blazes while he mustered as large a militia as he could—about 170 men. With this force, Willett attacked a combined detachment of 200 Indians and Tories under Donald McDonald, killing at least 40 of them while sustaining losses of only five men, with nine wounded. This effectively quelled raiding in western New York for the balance of the summer of 1781.

In October, however, 800 Tories and British regulars plus 120 Indians under the command of Captain Walter N. Butler were reported at Warrens Bush, 20 miles from Willett's headquarters at Canajoharie. The Americans could muster no more than 400 men, mostly militia. Nevertheless, Willett marched to Johnstown, where he divided his force in two for a combined frontal and rear assault. The men assigned to the front, directly under the command of Willett, panicked and broke ranks—despite their commander's exhortations. But the detachment attacking from the rear, led by a Major Rowley, carried out their attack so fiercely that the British forces scattered, leaving much of their equipment behind. Despite the failure of the frontal assault, the combined British and Indian force had 50 men killed or wounded and yielded another 50 prisoners. Willett's losses were also considerable, 40 dead or badly wounded.

Willett then withdrew to German Flats, a position between Butler's scattered troops and their boats, which had been left at Oneida Creek. At the Flats, Willett was joined by 60 Oneidas and waited for Butler to make his move. Two days passed; clearly, Butler had given up on his boats and, Willett guessed, was heading overland to Oswego. With 400 men, Willett set off after him at a forced march, in part through heavy snow. He first encountered a detachment of 40 soldiers and Indians. After attacking them, Willett reached the main body of Butler's troops, who, exhausted and demoralized, fled. Willett, his own men spent, pursued.

At last, at Canada Creek, Butler made a stand. He was fatally wounded in the fight, and 20 of his men were killed. The remainder fled once again. With his own rations running short, Willett was compelled to break off the chase. In any case, he reasoned, the Tory-Indian force, without provisions and a full week's wilderness march from Oswego, was doomed in the gathering winter. Indeed, after Willett's victory, western New York was still occasionally subject to isolated raids, but the death of Walter Butler and the defeat of his raiders meant the end of the major assaults.

On October 19, 1781, Joseph Brant, representing the Mohawks, and Pimoacan and Pipe, chiefs of the Delaware, met with Abraham, chief of the Moravian Indians—Delawares who had been christianized by Moravian missionaries. Brant and the others tried to persuade Abraham to unite with them in attacking the settlers of western Pennsylvania, but Abraham refused, arguing that the Americans would surely leave peaceful Christian Indians alone. Captain Matthew Elliott, in charge of British forces at Detroit, then ordered the Moravian Indians to leave western Pennsylvania "for their own safety." Accordingly, they set out for the banks of the Sandusky River in Ohio country. By early 1782, however, a harsh winter famine compelled the Moravian Indians to seek permission to move back temporarily to their western Pennsylvania mission towns on the Tuscarawas River. They arrived just after the Mohawks and Delawares had conducted a series of particularly brutal raids in the area. In February, Colonel Daniel Brodhead, commander of the Continental Army's Western Department, dispatched Colonel David Williamson to "punish" the hostiles. Tragically, Williamson's campaign coincided with the Moravian Indians' return.

In March Williamson and 100 men marched into Gnaddenhutten, where he announced to Abraham and the 48 men, women, and boys gathered there that he had been sent to take them back to Fort Pitt, where they would be protected from all harm. At Williamson's request, Abraham sent runners to a neighboring missionary-Indian town, Salem, to fetch the Indians there and bring them back to Gnaddenhutten. No sooner was this done than Williamson had the wrists of each Indian bound behind him; when the 50 or so people from Salem arrived, he had them likewise bound. And so they were all confined until morning, when Williamson announced that they would be put to death as punishment for the depredations of the Delawares. During the night, each of the captives—90 men, women, and children—was killed by a mallet blow to the back of the head. Two boys managed to escape.

Although the Gnaddenhutten massacre was roundly condemned, even by the Pennsylvania legislature, Williamson was not punished. When the massacre triggered acts of vengeance from the Delawares, Colonel William Crawford was sent on May 25 to undertake what was called the second Moravian campaign—the destruction of the Moravian, the Delaware, and the Wyandot towns along the upper Sandusky River, including the principal village of Sandusky. One of the 480 volunteers Crawford commanded was John Rose, whose real name was Baron Rosenthal, a Russian nobleman self-exiled because of a duel. Rose recorded his impressions of Colonel Crawford and left a picture of what a frontier citizen army was really like:

[Crawford was] kind and exceedingly affectionate . . . Brave, and patient of hardships. . . . As a Commanding Officer, cool in danger, but not systematical. Like others in the same stations, he wanted to be all in all: by trusting everything to the performance of his own abilities only, everything was but half done, and Everybody was disgusted. . . . Jealous of his military Knowledge & Superiority, but a mere quack in the profession of a Soldier. No military Genius; & no man of Letters.

As to the men of Crawford's command:

Upon these Volunteer Expeditions, every Man allmost appears on Horseback; but he takes care to mount the very worst horse he has upon the farm. This horse he loads with at least as much provisions as he is well able to carry. No man calculates the distance he is going, or how long he can possibly be absent. As he has provisions enough to maintain at least three Men on the Campaign, he does not stint himself to a certain allowance. Lolling all day unemployed upon his horse, his only amusement is chewing, particularly as all noise in talking, singing & whistling is prohibited.

The horses, Rose observed, were actually an impediment to a wilderness campaign, loaded down, as they were, with provisions and having to negotiate thickets and swamps. "Add to this that every Man hangs upon his horse to the very moment of attack. Then instead of being disencumbered & ready to defend himself, his first care is his horse. Him, he must tye and look after during an engagement, because all his dependence is in his horse & his horses burthen." Furthermore, Rose complained, order—"regularity and precaution"—was "looked upon as . . . mere Moonshine."

Lack of discipline and their commander's want of skill promised disaster. Simon Girty, under a flag of truce, attempted to warn Crawford to turn back, telling him that he was surrounded by Shawnees and *real* Delawares, not the pacific, christianized kind. But it was to no avail. On June 4, near Sandusky, the Indians began to pick off members of Crawford's force. On June 5, they encircled the militiamen until an additional 150 Shawnees arrived. Crawford attempted a retreat, but all was confusion.

Many men simply deserted. Others wandered off into the woods. At least 40 to 50 were killed or captured and 28 were wounded. Among the captives was Colonel Crawford, who was slowly tortured to death.

Crawford's defeat touched off a new spate of Indian raids along the upper Ohio, and the call went out for another expedition against the Sandusky villages. Joseph Brant, who had been planning an attack against Wheeling, in present-day West Virginia, decided to turn his force of 1,100 Indians back to the Ohio to head off the Sandusky expedition. On the way, on August 16, 1782, a detachment of 300 Wyandots and Tory rangers—including Simon Girty—surrounded Bryant's (or Bryan's) Station, five miles north of Lexington, Kentucky. After a brief siege, Girty withdrew, destroying crops, killing livestock, and stealing horses as he went. As Girty retreated, reinforcements from Lincoln and Fayette counties (the latter group led by Daniel Boone) arrived.

One hundred-eighty mounted riflemen set out after Girty's party. At lower Blue Licks, they caught sight of a few Indians—whereupon Boone suspected a trap and argued that they should await reinforcements before proceeding. But militia major Hugh McGary prevailed on the small force to press the attack. Presently, they were flanked by Wyandots and Tories—a classic ambush—and in the ensuing battle (August 19), 70 Americans were killed and 20 captured or wounded. It was the worst defeat the Kentucky militia had yet suffered.

With the looming possibility of abandoning the Kentucky frontier, General William Irvine, who replaced Brodhead as commander of the Western Department, assembled 1,200 Continental soldiers and militiamen for an assault on Sandusky to burn the Shawnee, Wyandot, and Delaware towns there. In November 1782, George Rogers Clark assembled 1,050 Kentuckians on the Ohio shore opposite the mouth of the Licking River. His objectives were the rebuilt towns of Chillicothe and Piqua. On November 9, he issued general orders:

As an action with the Enemy may be hourly Expected the Officers are Requested to pay the Strictest attention To their duty as Suffering no man to Quit his Rank Without leave as Nothing is more dangerous than Disorder. If fortunately any prisoner Should fall in to our hands they are by no means to be put to Death without leave as it will be attended with the Immediate Masseerce of all our Citizens that are in the hands of the Enemy and Also deprive us of the advantage of Exchanging for our own people, no person to attempt to take any Plunder until Orders Should Issue for that purpose under penalty of Being punished for Disobedience of orders and to have no share of Such plunder himself. The Officers in perticular are requested to Observe that the Strictest Notice be paid to this Order, as much Depends on it all plunder taken to be Delivered to the Quarter Master, to be Devided among the Different Batallions in proportion to their Numbers any person Concealing Plunder of any kind Shall be Considered as Subject to the penalty of the Above Order.

Clark was on the move well before Irvine, but, as with Sullivan's campaign in western New York, the Indians eluded him. He burned Chillicothe and other Shawnee towns, and he destroyed 10,000 bushels of corn, but killed only ten Indians and captured another ten. This was at least sufficient to stave off additional Indian raids. In any case on November 30, 1782, the preliminary articles of peace between the United States and Great Britain were signed in Paris, and the British agreed to cede the Old Northwest to the new nation. This hardly brought an end to Indian-white warfare in the area, but for the time being, Clark was recalled—and Irvine never even got under way.

# CHAPTER 14

# AFTER THE REVOLUTION
## Little Turtle's War (1786–1795)

Despite the provisions of the Treaty of Paris, which ended the American Revolution, British garrisons, administrators, and traders did not vacate Detroit and other outposts of the Old Northwest. They realized that the new nation lacked the military might to enforce its treaty rights and continued to court Indian alliance against American settlers. However, the postwar influx of settlers into Kentucky and the Ohio country outran even the combined Indian and British efforts to stem it. Moreover, United States policy, while it regarded the Indians of the Old Northwest as a conquered people without civil rights, did contain the merest modicum of conciliation. The federal government attempted to regulate white settlement and did offer to buy—albeit cheaply—territory rather than simply appropriate it.

This policy worked, for a time, with the Wyandots and Delawares, who agreed, for a price, to relinquish their holdings in eastern and southern Ohio and move west of the Cuyahoga River. Farther east, the Iroquois fared less well. The Six Nations were the Indians hit hardest by the revolution. Their confederation torn asunder, their lands thoroughly occupied, they were, in fact, largely a conquered people and had little choice but to accept confinement to small areas of central New York and northern Pennsylvania. (Although the first Indian reservation, Edge Pillock in New Jersey, was established in 1758, the term *reservation* and the institutional, political, and administrative concepts associated with it would not come into existence until the next century.)

While the United States might regard the western Indians—especially the Shawnees—as a conquered people by virtue of victory over their British allies, this was not the case in fact. If anything, during the revolution, the Shawnees had defeated the Americans in the West. They were, understandably, reluctant to negotiate any land

treaties with American commissioners and declined for many months to answer Commissioner William Butler's request that they send representatives to a treaty conference at Fort Finney, at the confluence of the Ohio and Greater Miami rivers.

Finally, in January 1786, 300 Shawnees did show up. Their chief, Kekewepellethe—known to the Americans as Tame Hawk—adamantly declared that the land in question was Shawnee and would always be Shawnee. Just as adamant, Butler declared the land was the sovereign territory of the United States, and he and George Rogers Clark threatened war. With his people suffering the effects of a bad winter and wartime destruction of crops and shelter, Kekewepellethe agreed to relinquish the entire Miami Valley. Immediately, other Shawnee bands and the Miamis repudiated the agreement and, led principally by the war chiefs Blue Jacket (Shawnee) and Little Turtle (Miami), intensified the campaign of hit-and-run raids that had not stopped with the end of the revolution.

Despite the bluster of Commissioner Butler, the United States was not prepared to prosecute a major Indian war. Realizing this, British interests intensified their aid to the Shawnee. At last, during the fall of 1786, George Rogers Clark raised a 2,000-man militia in Kentucky and marched toward the Wabash Valley, where Shawnees, Miamis, and Ottawas were meeting with British agents. But the Clark of 1786 was not the same man who had fought so effectively in 1778. Aged and inclined to drink, he was often confused, and the portion of the militia under his command suffered massive desertions. After three weeks without encountering the enemy, the militia dissolved and returned home.

Eight hundred other militiamen, under Colonel Benjamin Logan, attacked Shawnee villages on the Miami River. Many of these villages were deserted, and all were

## LITTLE TURTLE (1752–1812)

Little Turtle (Michikinikwa, Michikiniqua, Meshikin-noquah, Mishekunnoghwuah), born near present-day Fort Wayne, Indiana, was the son of a Miami chief (Acquenacke) and a Mahican mother. His position within the Miami tribe was hereditary, but he also earned on his own merits great esteem among the Mahicans. Little Turtle allied his people with the British during the American Revolution, but it was after the Treaty of Paris that he became most aggressive—and effective—against the hordes of white settlers pouring into the region. Between 1783 and 1790, he and his allies were responsible for the deaths of about 1,500 settlers. When President George Washington responded to the crisis on the frontier by sending Josiah Harmar with a band of militiamen and a small number of regulars, Little Turtle, Blue Jacket, and other Indian leaders countered the threat with great skill. A brilliant strategist, who used the wilderness itself as an ally, drawing soldiers far from their bases of supply and hitting them when they were at their weakest and most fatigued, Little Turtle routed not only Harmar but Arthur St. Clair as well, dealing that general the worst single beating the U.S. Army has ever suffered.

Not much is known about Blue Jacket, the chief to whom Little Turtle yielded general command, except that he was highly respected by the British and, while more aggressive than Little Turtle, did not possess the latter's skill either in political manipulation or in combat tactics.

left defenseless while warriors were out hunting or raiding. In October, at Mackachack, a Miami River village friendly to the whites, Logan's force was greeted by the aged and infirm Moluntha, who had been one of the signers of the Fort Finney peace treaty. One of Logan's party, Hugh McGary, challenged the old Indian, demanding to know if he had been at Blue Licks, scene of a massacre four years earlier. Moluntha failed to understand the question, but—apparently in an effort to be polite—cheerfully answered yes. McGary seized Moluntha's own hatchet, and brained and scalped him with it. Mackachack and other villages were burned. The effect of the slaying and the destruction was to solidify Shawnee hatred of the Americans; worse, it brought Indians of many tribes to a council near Detroit, where they vowed all-out war on whites in the Ohio country.

Logan's raid destroyed about 15,000 bushels of corn, and in the summer of 1787, most of the Shawnees migrated from the Miami River region to Kekionga, in the upper Maumee River valley—near present-day Fort Wayne, Indiana—where they formed a strong bond with the Miami Indians. From this base, and with the Ottawas, Ojibwas (Chippewas), Kickapoos, and Potawatomis, the Shawnees and Miamis continually raided the surrounding frontier. Shawnee warriors, including the young Tecumseh, also joined forces with Chichamaugas and Cherokees to fight in the middle basin of the Cumberland River during 1788.

Despite a degree of Indian alliance unprecedented since the great days of the Iroquois Confederation and despite almost continual raiding, whites continued to move into Kentucky and the Ohio country at an astonishing rate. The federal government abetted this by granting large tracts of land to Revolutionary War officers as payment for service. By 1790, the West was agitating for the commencement of a general Indian war. Secretary of War Henry Knox calculated that 2,500 men and $200,000 would be required to prosecute such a war in the Ohio Valley, but only $15,000 would be needed to buy Indian cooperation and cession of territory. Refused military aid, the westerners became increasingly restive.

In 1787, Congress passed the Northwest Ordinance, federalizing the area encompassed by the present states of Ohio, Indiana, Michigan, Illinois, Wisconsin, and upper Minnesota in an effort to impose order on discontented frontiersmen. In 1785, Congress had authorized a 700-man militia, the 1st American Regiment, under Josiah Harmar, and charged it with the hopeless task of keeping white squatters off public lands. It was not until 1790 that a regular federal army of 1,216 was established. Augmented by an authorized militia of 1,500, this army was to police the federal lands, keeping order not only among the whites, but among the Indians as well. In accordance with Knox's policy, President George Washington cautioned Harmar and Arthur St. Clair, governor of the territory, to avoid igniting a major Indian conflict. Unfortunately, neither of these western leaders was practiced in the art of restraint and soon deliberately provoked confrontations with the Shawnees.

Fewer militiamen than anticipated—1,133 instead of 1,500—joined 320 regulars at Fort Washington (present-day Cincinnati) and set off for the Miami and Maumee region on September 30, 1790. Unruly, untrained, and uncooperative, Harmar's command reached Kekionga on October 15. The villages had been abandoned, and the men began to burn the buildings.

Little Turtle's and Blue Jacket's scouts, however, were spying on the army. Moreover, the Indians were well informed of Harmar's plan of attack. Secretary Knox, fearful that the British in the area would interpret the movements of the army as an attack on them, had St. Clair alert Major Patrick Murray, the British commandant at Detroit, telling him that the Indians, not His Majesty's subjects, were the target. Murray, in turn, conveyed the information to the Indians.

On October 19, Harmar dispatched 150 mounted militiamen under John Hardin in hopes of ferreting out a few Indians. Little Turtle and his Miami warriors ambushed Hardin's company, which panicked, withdrew, and collided with a detachment of infantry sent to reinforce them. The infantry also cut and ran. Only 30 regulars and nine militiamen stood their ground against the attack. While they killed perhaps a dozen warriors, all but eight of the soldiers died. Harmar had no choice but to withdraw, and on October 21, he sent a small body of regulars and 400 militiamen back to Kekionga as a rear guard, which again encountered ambush.

This time Blue Jacket and his Shawnees carried out the attack. As before, the militia fled—though not before 108 of them had been killed; 75 regulars also were slain. While it was another stunning defeat for the army, the Indians also suffered heavy losses—perhaps 100 warriors. Nevertheless, Harmar's force was thoroughly panicked and beat a disorderly retreat, which would have made them easy game for the Indian attackers had they given chase. Fortunately, a total lunar eclipse took place the night following the engagement, which the Ottawa warriors took as an evil omen. Although Blue Jacket vehemently protested, the Indians decided against pursuit.

In the wake of Harmar's defeat, the Shawnees and allied tribes staged a series of unorthodox winter raids. Early in January 1791, Blue Jacket and 200 Shawnees laid siege to Dunlap's Station near Cincinnati. There 75 settlers and 13 members of the garrison held out against Blue Jacket for a week until they were reinforced by 36 regulars from nearby Fort Washington. Other outposts were similarly attacked, and even flatboat traffic on the Ohio was routinely ambushed. In one such action early in the spring of 1791, a raiding party captured Daniel Greathouse, the leader of the men who had wantonly slain the family of the Mingo chief John Logan, igniting Lord Dunmore's War. Greathouse and his wife were hideously tortured to death.

At the height of violence in 1791, the British in the area suddenly volunteered to play a peace-making role.

Their motive was fear that the incessant raiding would unleash a massive American force, which would not only drive out the Indians, but the British as well. The Shawnees and other Indians listened to the British proposal with interest but without commitment. The Americans— represented by Alexander Hamilton—summarily rejected the proposal. Rather than treat with "savages" as sovereign nations, the United States would punish (a favorite word in white-Indian relations) them once and for all. This time, a force of 2,300 men—half of them temporary soldiers (enlisted for a period of six months)—convened at Fort Washington under the command of Governor St. Clair, with Richard Butler as his second in command. The expedition advanced to the Great Miami River and built Fort Hamilton. On October 4, 1791, the punitive expedition got under way.

Progress was painfully slow, and the army was poorly supplied. By October 19, the force was still 100 miles from the Maumee River, its objective. St. Clair erected Fort Jefferson, but during a spell of miserably wet weather, suffered substantial desertions. Fearing that his army would dwindle if he delayed, St. Clair left behind a 120-man garrison at Fort Jefferson (most of these were ill or totally unreliable), sent a 300-man patrol to capture deserters, and set off with 1,400 troops to seek out Little Turtle, Blue Jacket, and their warriors. A full month passed without an encounter.

On November 3, 1791, the army made camp on a plateau above the upper Wabash, which was a particularly vulnerable position. Little Turtle and Blue Jacket, with 1,000 warriors, took advantage of it.

At dawn on November 4, the Indians rushed the camp from three directions. Once again, the Americans were gripped by panic. Many soldiers dropped their weapons and simply ran about or cowered in prayer. The artillery, positioned too high to be of use, fired without effect, and Blue Jacket led a party of Shawnees against the gunners. Richard Butler attempted to rescue the artillerymen, but his detachment of the 2nd American Regiment was quickly cut down and Butler mortally wounded. After three hours, those who could—about 500 men—fled back down the road they had cut through the wilderness. They were fortunate, for the triumphant Indians, celebrating their victory with looting and whiskey, were too engrossed to give chase. Six hundred twenty-three officers and men died, along with 24 civilian teamsters; 271 soldiers were wounded. The Indians lost 21 warriors and had 40 wounded. In proportion to the number of men fielded that day, it stands as the worst loss the U.S. Army has ever suffered.

When news of the defeat was conveyed to President Washington, he vented his wrath before Tobias Lear, his private secretary:

HERE on this very spot [the President's study], I took leave of him [St. Clair]; I wished him success and honor; you have your instructions, I said, from the Secretary of War, I had a strict eye to them; and will add but one word—BEWARE OF A SURPRISE. I repeat it, BEWARE OF A SURPRISE—you know how the Indians fight us. He went off with that as my last solemn warning thrown into his ears. And yet!! O God, O God, he's worse than a murderer! how can he answer it to his country;—the blood of the slain is upon him—the curse of widows and orphans—the curse of Heaven!

In the wake of his defeat, Arthur St. Clair resigned as head of the army but retained his post as governor of the Northwest Territory. The defeat also convinced President Washington to abandon any hope of a conciliatory Indian policy. Although a still war-weary public was inclined toward peace, in 1792 the House of Representatives authorized a larger army—with the proviso that an earnest attempt first be made to conclude a treaty. Washington used this proviso to buy the time necessary to reorganize his shattered western forces, which had been reduced to a mere 750 men. Iroquois agents, including Chief Red Jacket (though the revolution had sundered the Six Nations, the Iroquois were still highly esteemed as inter-tribal and Indian-white diplomats), were hired to present an American peace proposal at a meeting with the Shawnees and other tribes on the Auglaize River during the summer of 1792. The American government proposed a boundary line along the Muskingum River, beyond which whites agreed not to settle (tracts already settled would remain unmolested).

*When white-Indian violence erupted along the western frontier following the American Revolution, Major General Arthur St. Clair, governor of federal lands, organized forces for a "punitive expedition" against the Shawnees and others. St. Clair led 2,300 men out of Fort Hamilton on October 4, 1791, only to be attacked and routed by warriors under Little Turtle and Blue Jacket on November 4. More than 600 officers and men perished, and almost 300 more were wounded. In proportion to the number of men fielded that day, it stands as the worst loss the U.S. Army has ever suffered. (Library of Congress.)*

The Shawnees responded contemptuously, insisting that all of the land north of the Ohio River was theirs, that all Americans settled on it must move, and that restitution must be made for the usurpation and spoliation of Kentucky hunting grounds. In reporting this rebuke to the American commissioners, Red Jacket, perhaps reluctant to admit diplomatic defeat, put the response in its best light and announced that the Shawnee, Miami, and other western tribes were willing to *consider* peace at a conference next year. In the meantime, however, Tecumseh and other Shawnees sporadically raided the Ohio country, and President Washington sought and found a new general.

He chose a former Revolutionary commander, Anthony Wayne, who bore the nickname "Mad Anthony." Legend has interpreted this sobriquet as homage to the commander's fearless impetuosity. In fact, it was the product of a fairly irrelevant set of circumstances. A neighbor of Wayne's who was serving in the Continental Army deserted, was arrested, and told the military police to contact General Wayne, who would vouch for him. Wayne not only refused to help, he denied any knowledge of the man. "He must be mad," the deserter responded. And the name stuck.

Wayne accepted the commission in April 1792 and set about recruiting his army, which he first mustered at Pittsburgh in the summer of 1792. After he gathered 1,000 men, he christened the force the Legion of the United States and moved his headquarters 20 miles downstream from Pittsburgh to a campsite he named Legionville. As he recruited more troops, he set about carefully training and disciplining them while he, unlike previous commanders, learned all he could about the lives and military tactics of the western Indians. He concluded that it was best to pursue a strategy of sustained conflict, to fight the kind of war of attrition that the Indians were least well suited to prosecute.

By the spring of 1793, Wayne moved his growing army to Fort Washington, then set up camp—called Hobson's Choice—just outside of town. While these preparations were under way, a final peace commission offered considerable concessions, which were presented on July 31, 1793. The commissioners recanted the previous position of the United States, that the western Indians were a conquered people by virtue of their alliance with the defeated British; they also announced that the government would relinquish all claim to lands north of the Ohio except in the immediate vicinity of Cincinnati and the Scioto and Muskingum rivers. For these lands, the government would pay the Indians. The Shawnees replied on August 15, 1793, through the British agent Alexander McKee:

You agreed to do us justice, after having long, and injuriously, withheld it. We mean in the acknowledgment you now have

made, that the King of England never did, nor ever had a right to give you our County, by the Treaty of peace, and you want to make this act of Common Justice a great part of your concessions, and seem to expect that, because you have at last acknowledged our independence, we should for such a favor surrender to you our country. . . . Money, to us is of no value . . . and no consideration whatever can induce us to sell the lands on which we get sustenance for our women and children; we hope we may be allowed to point out a mode by which your settlers may be easily removed, and peace thereby obtained. . . . We know these settlers are poor, or they would never have ventured to live in a country which has been in continued trouble ever since they crossed the Ohio; divide, therefore, this large sum of money [$50,000 plus a $10,000 annual annuity], which you have offered to us, among these people . . . and we are persuaded, they would most readily accept of it, in lieu of the lands you sold them. . . . If you add also, the great sums you must expend in raising and paying Armies, with a view to force us to yield you our Country, you will certainly have more than sufficient for the purposes of repaying these settlers for all their labor and improvements.

On September 11, 1793, Big Tree, an Iroquois hired by the Americans as a secret agent and courier, informed Wayne of the breakdown of peace talks. Although the general himself had warned against doing battle with the Indians during the fall, when they were at their greatest post-hunt strength, he determined to attack immediately. The corruption, however, that had plagued the supply of St. Clair's army came back to haunt Wayne. Worse, the army's second in command, Brigadier General James Wilkinson, deliberately sabotaged supply lines, inadequate as they were, in order to overthrow Wayne. (Wilkinson proved an inveterate traitor: A secret agent in the employ of the Spanish and perhaps even the British, he later conspired unsuccessfully with Aaron Burr to force the secession of the western territories from the United States.)

During the delay, Wayne built a fort at Greenville, Ohio, and then, farther west, erected Fort Recovery, on the site of St. Clair's defeat. While the American commander solidified his position, many of the allies of the Shawnees and Miamis, disgruntled in their idleness, began to desert the cause. When Wayne, still impeded by lack of supply, failed to get his campaign under way by May 1794, Little Turtle and Blue Jacket decided to strike the first blow. Their plan was to attack the army's already tenuous supply line, thereby drawing soldiers out of their forts to defend the baggage trains. Once exposed, the Legionnaires could be ambushed and, it was hoped, the entire army would follow those of Harmar and St. Clair into ignominious retreat.

Twelve hundred warriors under Blue Jacket and Tecumseh set out from the Maumee River to blockade Fort

*After Major General St. Clair resigned his command following the terrible defeat he suffered at the hands of Little Turtle and Blue Jacket, President George Washington replaced him with "Mad Anthony" Wayne, an able Revolutionary War commander, who formed the "Legion of the United States" and forged it into an effective fighting force. His victory over Blue Jacket at the Battle of Fallen Timbers (August 20, 1794) brought relative peace to the Old Northwest for the next 40 years, a hiatus that promoted western settlement. (Library of Congress.)*

Recovery and were spotted on June 29 by a scout, one of the 60 Chickasaws—traditional enemies of the Shawnees—fighting on the American side. Unfortunately, the Chickasaw knew little English, and the Legion captain to whom he reported, Alexander Gibson, knew no Chickasaw. The June 30 attack on the pack train and its escort of 140 Legionnaires was therefore a total surprise and a rout. Blue Jacket and Tecumseh, victorious, tried to call off their warriors, but the Ottawas and other allies insisted on advancing to Fort Recovery itself. There they were turned back by artillery (ordnance recovered from the site of St. Clair's defeat), with the loss of 20 to 30 warriors.

At this point, the Indian alliance suffered when some of the Shawnees' Great Lakes allies raped and robbed a number of Shawnee women. The alliance with the British also faltered when promised aid, including two pieces of artillery, failed to materialize. In the meantime, on July 28, the bulk of the American forces—2,200 regulars and 1,500 Kentucky militiamen—arrived at Fort Recovery. Wayne ordered the construction of a more advanced post, Fort Adams, which the army reached on August 8. Yet deeper in country hastily abandoned by the Indians, Wayne built Fort Defiance.

Just downstream from this newest fort, Little Turtle

was counseling the leaders of his 1,500 warriors that victory over Mad Anthony Wayne was impossible. It was time, he said, to negotiate peace. Both Blue Jacket and Tecumseh refused to yield, and overall command of the forces passed to Blue Jacket; Little Turtle would lead only his 250 Miamis.

Blue Jacket decided to intercept the Legion at a place opposite the rapids of the Maumee. Pocked with deep ravines and strewn with the trunks of trees that had been blown down by a tornado, the site was known as Fallen Timbers. Not only would the rugged terrain provide cover and concealment, the battleground was only five miles from Fort Miamis, a British stronghold that the Indians hoped would provide sanctuary and succor if the battle went badly.

Wayne, whose scouts had informed him of the Indians' position, halted on August 17 a few miles from it to build Fort Deposit. There he cached all that was unnecessary for combat. It was August 20 before he advanced against Blue Jacket. Perhaps this delay was a brilliant stroke of strategy gained from his study of Indian customs; perhaps it was just good luck. Whichever, it exploited the warriors' custom of fasting before battle in order to put an edge on reflexes and ferocity. The Indians had expected an encounter on the eighteenth, so had advanced to Fallen Timbers without rations on the seventeenth. By the twentieth, they had gone without food for three days. On that day, some warriors had absented themselves to look for food; many of the others who remained waiting for the Americans were weak from hunger.

Blue Jacket's plan was to entrap Wayne in a vast, half-moon-shaped line, but an Ottawa commander acted prematurely, leading his men in a charge against the advance guard of 150 mounted Kentucky militia, who panicked, broke, and incited the front line infantry to do the same. It looked like another rout, but Wayne was no St. Clair. He rallied his men—in part by the effective expedient of shooting those who ran—and ordered an attack on the Indians' line, which had been cut up by the hasty action of the Ottawas. Although Brigadier Wilkinson failed to obey the command to charge (he later claimed he had not heard it; many historians believe he deliberately ignored it in order to sabotage the attack), two

regiments under the command of Colonel John Hamtramck attacked vigorously, mainly with bayonets. It was now Blue Jacket's turn to suffer a rout.

Retreating to Fort Miamis, Blue Jacket and his warriors received yet another blow. British commandant Captain William Campbell, under orders not to get involved in the battle, refused to admit the Indians to the fort.

After taunting both the Indians and the British, Wayne withdrew on August 23, destroying abandoned Indian towns in his path. At Kekionga, chief village of the Miami, he built Fort Wayne.

In January 1795, his warriors defeated and many of his people refugees, Blue Jacket came to Fort Greenville, in western Ohio near the present Indiana state line, to negotiate a treaty with Anthony Wayne. Formally signed in August, the Treaty of Greenville secured white occupancy of lands northwest of the Ohio River, established yet another "permanent" boundary of white settlements west of the present state of Ohio, and instituted a program of compensation for territory lost ($20,000 as a lump sum and an annual payment of $9,500). For their part, the British agreed at last to vacate the Old Northwest.

In the wake of Fallen Timbers, Little Turtle was resigned to accommodation with the whites, whose dominance he came to see as inevitable. The destroyer of two armies traveled to Philadelphia in 1797, where President Washington greeted him as a respected *former* foe, and Thaddeus Kosciuszko, the Americans' invaluable Polish ally during the revolution, presented the Indian with a gift of fine pistols. Gilbert Stuart, the nearest thing to a court painter the young republic could boast of, executed a portrait of Little Turtle, and the government paid the chief to help Indiana's territorial governor, William Henry Harrison, negotiate treaties entailing massive cessions of land from the Indians who had once been Little Turtle's allies in mortal combat against the whites. Tecumseh vainly attempted to win Little Turtle back to the cause of resistance. Harrison had supplied Little Turtle with a house on the Maumee River, and the aging chief set about attempting to transform his people into peaceful farmers. He died from complications of the gout, a disease common to many well-fed white men of the period.

# CHAPTER 15

# FORLORN PROPHECY
## The Period of Tecumseh and the War of 1812
## (1805–1814)

After the Battle of Fallen Timbers, the Old Northwest was generally quiet for the first time in 40 years. Yet two forces were at work that would once again tear the frontier apart. First, Tecumseh had moved west to the present area of Indiana, but he returned regularly to Ohio to hunt. During the last five years of the eighteenth century and into the first few years of the nineteenth, he earned the admiration, respect, even affection of the Indians and whites with whom he came into contact. Throughout the Old Northwest, he was becoming a one-man political power. Second, Thomas Jefferson, who succeeded John Adams as president of the United States in 1801 was eager to foster expansion into the Ohio country. His plan was not to wage war against the Indians, but to transform them culturally. While the Indians of the southern frontier—the Choctaw, Chickasaw, and Creek in particular—were essentially agricultural people, those of the Old Northwest were hunters who moved with their game. As a consequence, they did not own defined plots of land as individuals but, communally, claimed vast ranges of hunting ground. Jefferson wished to compel them to forsake their hunting culture for a sedentary agricultural life. Individuals would then own defined plots of land, which they could sell in an orderly fashion to incoming whites, obligingly removing themselves west to the newly purchased Louisiana Territory.

As a first step toward this policy, Jefferson directed his new governor of the Indiana Territory, William Henry Harrison, to obtain "legal" title to as much Indian land as possible through purchase. As white communities developed on these lands, Jefferson reasoned, more Indians would sell out—in part because they would become dependent on white trade, running up debts so large that they could be discharged only by the sale of land. Between 1803 and 1806, Harrison acquired 70 million acres

west of the "permanent" Greenville Treaty boundary, trading or negotiating for it with the Sac and the Fox and various smaller tribes, most of which had been broken and impoverished by years of white–Indian warfare.

The land cessions from the Sac caused some of the most immediate as well as longest-lasting conflicts. In 1804, a group of Sacs attacked and killed three settlers along the Cuivre River, just north of Saint Louis. Governor Harrison summoned five chiefs under the Sac and Fox leader Quashquame to Saint Louis, demanding they deliver those guilty of the murders. They brought one warrior, whom Harrison imprisoned, promising to set him free after the Sacs made restitution to the families of the slain and ceded certain lands. Plying the chiefs with liquor and gifts, Harrison soon wheedled from them all tribal lands east of the Mississippi, a huge tract encompassing parts of three present-day states, in exchange for $2,234.50 in gifts and an annuity of $1,000 in goods. Ma-ka-tai-me-she-kia-kiak, a Sac chief better known as Black Hawk, considered the cessions fraudulent and incited his followers in the village of Saukenuk (Rock Island, Illinois) to attack Fort Madison, near Saint Louis, several times between 1808 and 1811.

Despite Black Hawk's resistance, settlers continued to rush in with remarkable speed, and with speed equally remarkable, the Indians in their proximity degenerated. The Miamis, for example, a numerous and proud people in the eighteenth century, had become a diseased, drunken group of 1,000 by 1810. As Bil Gilbert observes in *God Gave Us This Country: Tekamthi and the First American Civil War*, "civilization created a desperate need for a red resistance leader." Tecumseh realized that the terrible dilemma his people, the Shawnee, faced was common to Indians everywhere. Indian culture could sur-

## TECUMSEH (c.1768–1813)

Elder brother of Tenskwatawa, the so-called Shawnee Prophet, Tecumseh (whose name is more properly transliterated as Tekamthi) was born near present-day Springfield, Ohio. As a youthful warrior, he attained renown for fighting Kentucky's early settlers. In the struggle for the southern Ohio Valley, Tecumseh's father and two older brothers were killed, and as Tecumseh watched the Indians relinquish more and more land, he became an implacable enemy of the whites.

Yet the life of Tecumseh is hardly a simple story of bitterness and revenge. While he worked toward attaining a degree of intertribal alliance that would liberate the Indians from the necessity of white contact, he studied white customs; it is even reported that he read history books and the Bible, which were furnished him by Rebecca Galloway, a frontier schoolteacher. While he and Tenskwatawa preached abstinence from all dealings with whites, he carefully cultivated an alliance with the British during the War of 1812. And while no Indian more fiercely opposed accommodation to white customs and demands, his opposition did not extend to gratuitous hatred. Most feared and respected among Indian military leaders, he nevertheless earned white respect, even gratitude, by his efforts to curb strategically unnecessary violence and cruelty on the part of his warriors.

Tecumseh and Tenskwatawa began their campaign for pan-tribal unity in 1805, as William Henry Harrison, territorial governor of Indiana, was buying up vast tracts of Indian land. Tecumseh traveled the Ohio Valley, preaching the doctrine of Indian unity and his unalterable opposition to the white man.

The Prophet imparted to Tecumseh's political message the added force of a religious crusade. It was, more than anything, the religious zeal of Tecumseh's message that alarmed Governor Harrison, who was appalled when Tecumseh and his brother established a bustling headquarters—Prophet's Town—with provocative defiance at the abandoned site of Fort Greenville. As the United States and Great Britain drifted toward the War of 1812, Tecumseh built up a large following among the Shawnees, Potawatomis, Ottawas, Winnebagos, Ojibwas, and Wyandots, significant numbers of whom gathered at Prophet's Town, Tecumseh and Tenskwatawa's new headquarters at Tippecanoe, Indiana Territory. Taking note of Tecumseh's growing power, British and Canadian authorities courted an alliance. And through all of this, with consummate diplomatic skill, Tenskwatawa continued discussions with Governor Harrison, always pledging peace.

After defeat at the Battle of Tippecanoe, Tecumseh broke with his brother. With the commencement of the War of 1812, he accepted a commission as brigadier general in the British army.

Tecumseh proved a valuable ally to the British, bringing many Indians to their cause and participating in the capture of Detroit, the siege of Fort Meigs, and other battles. However, he never fully trusted his English colleagues, and his hopes of defeating the Americans were soon dashed. When Harrison defeated the combined British and Indian forces on October 5, 1813, at the Battle of the Thames, Tecumseh was among the casualties.

---

vive neither prolonged peace under the influence of white civilization nor prolonged war against it.

Tecumseh's strategy, therefore, was to buy time with the *threat* of war, time in which he could travel the length and breadth of the Ohio country and beyond; west to the Sioux; and south to the land of the Chickasaws, Choctaws, and Creeks, preaching not only the urgent need of severing ties to the white man but, more importantly, of forging a red union stretching from the Great Lakes to the Gulf of Mexico. Only as a unified, sovereign state, Tecumseh reasoned, could the Indians resist displacement and death or absorption and death. To white audiences, Tecumseh argued in legal and moral terms, holding that the Treaty of Greenville was solemn

and binding and that William Henry Harrison's purchases, acquired from minor chiefs and disparate bands who had no authority to grant land, were illegal.

Tecumseh's program of oration took on a religious dimension with the rise of his brother Tenskwatawa, called the Prophet, who claimed to be imbued with the Great Spirit, and who commanded his ''children'' to cleanse themselves of the influence of the unclean white race. A side effect of Tenskwatawa's fervor was a series of witch hunts among various Indian communities, which resulted in trials and executions. Alarmed by the intensity of the religious movement, Governor Harrison intervened in the case of the Delawares, urging them to drive the Prophet from their midst. He challenged Tenskwatawa to prove his favored connection with the Deity. The Prophet obliged by announcing that on June 16, 1806, he would cause the sun to stand still and darken. On that day, a solar eclipse occurred. It is likely that Tecumseh had learned of the event from an almanac and counseled his brother to exploit it. In any case, William Henry Harrison's challenge only helped to solidify the Prophet's reputation. Tenskwatawa and Tecumseh established their headquarters at the abandoned site of Fort Greenville. By 1807, Shawnee, Potawatomi, Ottawa, Winnebago, Ojibwa (Chippewa), and Wyandot leaders and warriors were assembling there.

Meanwhile, as tensions mounted between the United States and Great Britain in the years and months preceding the War of 1812, British and Canadian authorities began courting Tecumseh. Francis Gore, royal administrator in Ontario, appointed William Claus, the part-Mohawk grandson of the late, powerful British superintendent of Indian affairs Sir William Johnson, to head a new Indian department. In April 1808, Tecumseh, Tenskwatawa, and their followers moved their headquarters to the confluence of the Wabash River and Tippecanoe Creek, calling it Prophet's town. A month later, Gore invited Tecumseh and approximately 1,500 other Indian chiefs and warriors to a conference at Amerherstburg, site of Fort Malden on the Canadian side of Lake Erie. Cautiously, a British-Indian alliance was forged, the British promising to supply military aid and ordnance.

Even as this dangerous alliance was being formed, Tenskawatwa was conferring with Governor Harrison, promising him that he and his brother intended nothing but peace and securing from him provisions for the winter. Thus assured, Harrison set about acquiring yet more Indian land, three million acres in the Wabash Valley. In the spring of 1809, he convened a conference at Fort Wayne with selected Miami, Delaware, and Potawatomi leaders to negotiate the purchase. The resulting Treaty of Fort Wayne enraged many Indian groups, especially the large Potawatomi faction led by Chief Main Poc, who commenced a bitter series of raids on white communities and farms in the area. The treaty also validated Tecumseh's warning, that the whites would violate the provisions of the Treaty of Greenville at every opportunity. The Sac and Fox tribes, hitherto hesitant to ally themselves with Tecumseh, now joined his "brotherhood" wholeheartedly, as did about half the Miami tribe, who broke with Little Turtle—the former war chief who now lived complacently in a government-supplied house. Except for followers of Chief Roundhead, the Wyandots had also been reluctant to join Tecumseh's union; now they, too, were ready. In July 1810, Harrison had no choice but to inform the president that a general Indian uprising was in the making.

Hazardous as the situation was, Governor Harrison was nevertheless led to believe that it was even worse. Michael Brouillette, a French-Canadian spy in the governor's employ, reported the presence of 3,000 warriors in the vicinity of Tippecanoe. In actuality, Tecumseh could muster only about 600. Harrison called Tecumseh to a conference at Vincennes on August 15–16, 1810, during which the Indian leader demanded repudiation of the Fort Wayne treaty. Harrison at first bitterly refused, then told Tecumseh that he would report the Indians' objections to President Madison, who had succeeded Jefferson the year before. "As the great chief [Madison] is to determine the matter," Tecumseh replied, "I hope the Great Spirit will put sense enough into his head to induce him to give up this land: it is true, he is so far off he will not be injured by the war; he may sit still in his town and drink his wine, whilst you and I will have to fight it out."

That autumn, still more tribes joined Tecumseh's brotherhood: Kickapoo, Menominee, and Winnebago. The frontier, subject to sporadic raids, was in a panic. From July 27 to 31, 1811, Tecumseh and the governor again met at Vincennes without resolving their differences—though Tecumseh did take pains to outline for Harrison his campaign of Indian unity. He did not wish to provoke a war, but he did want to impress upon the governor that, this time, the tribes would not be divided and conquered.

Late summer of 1811 was the high-water mark of Tecumseh's confederacy. He undertook a recruiting expedition among the Chickasaws, Choctaws, and Creeks—together, a vast body of some 50,000 and a potential source of many warriors—but was largely rebuffed, except by a militant faction of Creeks known as the Red Sticks. Worse, William Henry Harrison decided to take advantage of Tecumseh's absence by now moving against the confederacy.

Using the pretext of demanding that Tenskwatawa surrender any warriors at Prophet's Town who had participated in raids, Harrison planned to wipe out the brotherhood's "capital" once and for all. The governor assembled a ragtag force of 1,000 men—350 regulars and the balance in raw Kentucky and Indiana militiamen—and a few friendly Delaware and Miami scouts at the newly created Fort Harrison, near present-day Terre Haute. On November 6, 1811, Harrison's command took up a position two miles from Tippecanoe. That night, Tenskwatawa encouraged his warriors by telling them they would go into battle protected by a magical fog, that the Great Spirit was urging them to fight.

The Indians attacked before dawn on November 7 with such ferocity that the Americans at first fell back. But Harrison rallied his men, who at last held their ground.

*As governor of Indiana Territory, William Henry Harrison earned the hatred of the Shawnee leader Tecumseh by engineering the sale or cession of millions of acres of Indian land. Harrison and Tecumseh became principal adversaries in the western theater of the War of 1812. (Library of Congress.)*

Losses on both sides were heavy—50 Americans killed and at least 120 wounded, with casualties approximately the same on the Indian side—but the Indians withdrew. Because of this, Tenskwatawa was the single most significant casualty. Having held himself apart from the fighting, he was uninjured, but he was now the object of angry derision, and his credibility as a seer had suffered a crippling blow. When Tecumseh returned from his largely unsuccessful recruiting expedition in the South, he, too, publicly rebuked his brother. After the Battle of Tippecanoe, the Potawatomis, Winnebagos, and Sacs and Foxes, though shaken, remained loyal to Tecumseh. The Wyandot followers of Roundhead likewise adhered to the cause. But among the Delawares, Miamis, and even the Shawnees, there were wholesale defections.

It was at this point that the War of 1812 officially began. Ostensibly, the conflict was triggered by the British policy of waylaying American ships in international waters, boarding them, and seizing any sailor deemed a British subject for forced service in His Majesty's Navy. But the declaration of war came on June 19, 1812, three days *after* the British government had agreed to suspend the objectionable practice of seizure and impressment and only four days before that agreement was scheduled to go into effect. Actually, the War of 1812 was brewed in the West. In 1812, Spain was allied with Britain against Napoleon. War with Britain would entail war with Spain, and victory would mean the acquisition of Florida. Moreover, it was well known that the English Canadians were arming Indians and inciting them to harass western American settlers.

Westerners were eager to invade Canada, and William Hull, a superannuated hero of the Revolutionary War, now governor of Michigan Territory, was placed in command of American forces north of the Ohio—300 regulars and 1,200 Kentucky and Ohio militiamen (when substantial numbers of these deserted, Hull picked up some Michigan men). With the object of taking Fort

Malden, which guarded the entrance to Lake Erie, Hull crossed the Detroit River into Canada on July 12, but the old man, mistakenly believing himself outnumbered, had no stomach for a fight.

Repeatedly, he delayed the assault on Fort Malden—long enough for the British, under the able Major General Isaac Brock, and their Indian allies to reinforce their positions. When Hull sent out a force of 120 men to reconnoiter in the vicinity of Amherstburg, Tecumseh and 150 warriors ambushed them on the Canard River. This confirmed Hull's belief that he was surrounded by a vastly superior force. In reality, only Tecumseh and 300 warriors were nearby.

Meanwhile, on July 16, Captain Charles Roberts, commander of the British garrison on Saint Joseph's Island, in the Saint Mary's River between Lake Huron and Lake Superior, assembled a force of 50 regulars, 400 Indians, and some North West Company traders to invade Fort Michilimackinac. The invaders, complete with two six-pound cannon, landed on Michilimackinac Island undetected about three o'clock on the morning of July 17. The American garrison of 61 men surrendered without a fight.

On August 2, Tecumseh crossed the Detroit River with 24 warriors and, three days later, ambushed 150 Ohio militiamen—sent to escort a supply train—at Brownstown Creek. Seventeen whites were killed, twelve wounded, and two captured. Hull sent 600 more men to escort the pack train, and again, the party was ambushed at Brownstown Creek—this time by a force of 200 warriors (led by Roundhead) and 150 British regulars. Hull lost 20 men, and 50 wounded, but held his ground. However, the American commander decided to withdraw his troops from Sandwich—present-day Windsor—Ontario and return to Fort Detroit. In the meantime, Isaac Brock, the British commander, united his 600 men with about 700 warriors Tecumseh had mustered and moved on Detroit. Hull surrendered the fort and his 1,500 men on August 16. He had not fired a shot.

For the Americans—especially the bellicose westerners—the war was hardly going as planned. The day before Hull caved in, the garrison at Fort Dearborn (present-day Chicago) surrendered. As the troops, together with settlers, their wives, and children, evacuated the fort, Potawatomi Indians attacked, killing 35, many by torture.

Again, as during the revolution, the West was now laid open to Indian massacre and British invasion. Yet neither the British nor their Indian allies were able to capitalize decisively on their advantages. The Potawatomis attacked Fort Wayne on September 5 but were driven off by Zachary Taylor, the commandant. Other war parties, responding to Tecumseh's call, attacked Fort

Madison near Saint Louis, Fort Harrison on the Wabash River, and the town of Pigeon Roost in southern Indiana. By September, most of the Old Northwest was effectively under Indian control, except for Ohio territory south of the Maumee River. Yet the anticipated, fully coordinated British-Indian assault never materialized, in part because Isaac Brock was killed in an October 13 engagement and was replaced by a far less imaginative, aggressive, and effective man named Henry Procter.

Procter demonstrated his shortcomings in a second assault on Fort Wayne. Throughout August 1812, war parties were assembling at Amherstburg. Tecumseh and Roundhead were to lead 800 of the 1,000 gathered there in a joint action with Procter's 200 British regulars and—crucial to taking a fort—three cannon. When they reached the junction of the Maumee and Auglaize rivers on September 25, Procter heard that 2,000 men under William Henry Harrison had left Fort Wayne and were on an intercept course with his forces. (This information, it turned out, was faulty.) Procter wanted to halt the advance against Fort Wayne, dig in, and fight it out. Tecumseh and Roundhead advised an ambush—and at a more advantageous site. Procter refused, withdrew his men and, more important, withdrew his cannon to Amherstburg. Realizing that it was futile to assault a fort without artillery, Tecumseh and Roundhead also withdrew, whereupon many of their warriors dispersed.

Late in 1812, Harrison turned his attention to the non-combatant Miamis—followers of Little Turtle, who had died in July—in the vicinity of Fort Wayne. Harrison's men burned their homes and crops, forcing them to move west. In December, at what amounted to a series of refugee camps near present-day Peru, Indiana, 600 militiamen fought 100 warriors, killing 50 of them. Most of the women and children were taken prisoner.

The fighting, however, was not going terribly well for Harrison. In January 1813, he decided to move against Fort Malden by advancing across frozen Lake Erie. One of his generals, James Winchester, started off early, ill-prepared and unsupported, to the Raisin River, just south of Detroit. Five hundred British regulars and 600 Indians (including a contingent of Red Stick Creeks led by the infamous Little Warrior) under Henry Procter attacked Winchester's unguarded encampment at Frenchtown (present-day Monroe, Michigan) on January 21, 1813, and annihilated it. Of 960 Americans engaged, approximately 400 were killed and some 500 captured. Only 33 escaped.

As a result of this crushing defeat, Harrison had to buy time to rebuild an army and so was put on the defensive. Beginning on April 30, Procter laid a two-week siege against Fort Meigs at the Maumee Rapids of the Ohio River, which Harrison defended at great cost. On May

7, Procter finally broke off the siege, after many of his Canadian militia and Indian allies had drifted off.

By late June 1813, Sioux and other far western tribes had arrived at Amherstberg, swelling the number of warriors to 2,000. Between July 21 and 23, now fielding a combined army of 3,000, Procter attacked Harrison's principal supply depot, Fort Stephenson, on the Sandusky River but was held off spectacularly by Major George Croghan and only 150 men.

In the wake of these defeats, the British-Indian alliance soured. On the face of it, the Americans were the big losers, with 4,000 men either killed or captured in the course of the war's first year. Combined British and Indian casualties were only about 500, but the Indian victories were pyrrhic, and the losses—houses burned, crops destroyed, populations displaced—were terrible. By the end of 1813 the American position seemed to improve. Benjamin Howard, governor of the Missouri Territory,

*Tecumseh made a bold and imaginative effort to unite the tribes of the Old Northwest against the advance of white settlement. He allied himself and his followers with the British during the War of 1812 and was among the casualties of the British defeat at the Battle of the Thames (October 5, 1813). (Library of Congress.)*

led a successful invasion of the Illinois country, and William Clark, who succeeded him as governor, mounted an offensive against Prairie du Chien (in present-day Wisconsin) in 1814. By the end of August 1813, William Henry Harrison had finished rebuilding—and even enlarged—the western army, fielding some 8,000 men.

While Harrison fashioned a new army, an officer named Oliver Hazard Perry cobbled together an inland navy. Since the end of March 1813, the 27-year-old U.S. Navy captain had been building an armed flotilla at Presque Isle (present-day Erie), Pennsylvania. By August, he moved his vessels out onto Lake Erie and, on September 10, engaged the British fleet. The message he sent to General Harrison entered instantly into history: "We have met the enemy and they are ours." In a single, brilliant stroke, Perry had cut off Procter's waterborne support, and the British general abandoned Fort Malden. With 3,000 men, Harrison pursued the retreating British and the Indians, including Tecumseh, who persuaded Procter to take a stand at the Thames River. There Harrison defeated him on October 5, 1813. No one knows who actually killed Tecumseh, but he died that day, and with him died the Indians' last real hope of halting the northwestward rush of white settlement.

# CHAPTER 16

## WARS OF THE REMOVAL
### The South (1812–1858)

Even for admirers of the seventh president of the United States, the name of Andrew Jackson is forever linked to the inequitable, immoral, and inhumane Federal policy of Indian "removal." It is true that the Indian Removal Act of 1830 was the work of the Jackson administration and that Jackson, as well as his Indian agents and treaty commissioners, shamelessly manipulated the law and interfered with internal Indian affairs well beyond the point of fraud in order to compel tribal cession of eastern land and the removal of tribes to the West. The notion, however, of transferring the Indians beyond the limits of white settlement, even beyond the United States proper, did not originate with Jackson.

George Washington imagined a western "Chinese wall" to separate whites and Indians. Thomas Jefferson saw the Louisiana Purchase, in significant part, as a means of acquiring a vast reserve of vacant land for Indian resettlement. In order to pacify Indians after the War of 1812, James Madison considered exchanging newly acquired areas in the West for Indian lands in the East. James Monroe followed the advice of his Secretary of War, John C. Calhoun, in adopting a policy of Indian removal in 1825.

Finally, John Quincy Adams responded to an impending constitutional crisis by laying the groundwork for the removal legislation enacted during Jackson's administration. On December 20, 1828, the Georgia state legislature decreed that all Indian residents would come under state jurisdiction within six months. Other southern states contemplated similar legislation, which was aimed at circumventing federal protection of Indian lands and rights. Not only did the southerners covet agriculturally valuable and, in some cases, mineral-rich Indians lands, they were alarmed by the flight of fugitive slaves into Indian territory. The Seminoles and others repeatedly re-fused to return the fugitives, and the federal government was unwilling to compel them to do so. President Adams consistently turned down southern requests for the summary removal of the Indians, and he even threatened to call in the army to *protect* the Indians against the depredations of the state. Facing a showdown between state's rights and federal authority, Adams agreed that a plan for removing the eastern tribes to the trans-Mississippi West was the only viable solution to the crisis. It fell to Jackson's administration to enact and implement the plan.

On the face of it, the Indian removal Act of 1830 seemed fair enough, not sanctioning removal by fiat or fort force, but by land exchanges. In practice, however, Jackson's government, both officially and unofficially, was ruthless and devious. The Indians that Jackson proposed to move west of the Mississippi were primarily the Choctaws, Chickasaws, Cherokees, Creeks, and Seminoles living in Georgia, Alabama, Mississippi, and the territory of Florida (which Spain had ceded to the United States in 1819). Alabama and Mississippi followed Georgia in passing legislation that abolished tribal government and placed Indians under state jurisdiction. When the Indians protested to the federal government that such state laws violated treaties made with the United States, Jackson replied that he was unable to enforce the treaty provisions on the states. Exercising the hydra-headed logic generally employed in negotiating with Indians, Jackson then tried to persuade the tribes to make *new* treaties with this apparently powerless federal government, agreeing to removal west of the Mississippi to a vaguely defined "Indian Territory" that first corresponded with present-day Oklahoma and portions of Kansas and Nebraska, but later was reduced to the territory now encompassed by Oklahoma alone.

## THE INDIAN REMOVAL ACT

At the urging of the administration of Andrew Jackson, Congress, following bitter debate, passed *"An Act to provide for an exchange of lands with the Indians residing in any of the states or territories, and for their removal west of the river Mississippi,"* which was signed into law on May 28, 1830:

*Be it enacted . . . ,* That it shall and may be lawful for the President of the United States to cause so much of any territory belonging to the United States, west of the river Mississippi, not included in any state or organized territory, and to which the Indian title has been extinguished, as he may judge necessary, to be divided into a suitable number of districts, for the reception of such tribes or nations of Indians as may choose to exchange the lands where they now reside, and remove there; and to cause each of said districts to be so described by natural or artificial marks, as to be easily distinguished from every other.

SEC. 2. *And be it further enacted,* That it shall and may be lawful for the President to exchange any or all of such districts, so to be laid off and described, with any tribe or nation of Indians now residing within the limits of any of the states or territories, and with which the United States have existing treaties, for the whole or any part or portion of the territory claimed and occupied by such tribe or nation, within the bounds of any one or more of the states or territories, where the land claimed and occupied by the Indians, is owned by the United States, or the United States are bound to the state within which it lies to extinguish the Indians' claim thereto.

SEC. 3. *And be it further enacted,* That in the making of any such exchange or exchanges, it shall and may be lawful for the President solemnly to assure the tribe or nation with which the exchange is made, that the United States will forever secure and guaranty to them, and their heirs or successors, the country so exchanged with them; and if they prefer it, that the United States will cause a patent or grant to be made and executed to them for the same: *Provided always,* That such lands shall revert to the United States, if the Indians become extinct, or abandon the same.

SEC. 4. *And be it further enacted,* That if, upon any of the lands now occupied by the Indians, and to be exchanged for, there should be such improvements as add value to the land claimed by any individual or individuals of such tribes or nations, it shall and may be lawful for the President to cause such value to be ascertained by appraisement or otherwise, and to cause such ascertained value to be paid to the person or persons rightfully claiming such improvements. And upon the payment of such valuation, the improvements so valued and paid for, shall pass to the United States, and possession shall not afterwards be permitted to any of the same tribe.

SEC. 5. *And be it further enacted,* That upon the making of any such exchange as is contemplated by this act, it shall and may be lawful for the President to cause such aid and assistance to be furnished to the emigrants as may be necessary and proper to enable them to remove to, and settle in, the country for which the may have exchanged; and also, to give them such aid and assistance as may be necessary for their support and subsistence for the first year after their removal.

SEC. 6. *And be it further enacted,* That it shall and may be lawful for the President to cause such tribe or nation to be protected, at their new residence, against all interruption or disturbance from any other tribe or nation in the country to which they may remove, as contemplated by this act, that he is now authorized to have over them at their present places of residence: *Provided,* That nothing in this act contained shall be construed as authorizing or directing the violation of any existing treaty between the United States and any of the Indian tribes.

SEC. 8. *And be it further enacted,* That for the purpose of giving effect to the provisions of this act, the sum of five hundred thousand dollars is hereby appropriated, to be paid out of any money in the treasury, not otherwise appropriated.

As the Indians continued to protest and Jackson continued to plead powerlessness, the states systematically violated the civil rights of Native people, prosecuting them under state laws while barring in court Indian testimony against white men, including testimony presented in *defense* of charges brought against Indians by whites. Squatters and land speculators waited for neither the state nor federal government to resolve disputed claims, but overran Indian lands at will and, whenever possible, swindled Indians out of their property.

One year after passage of the removal act, the Choctaws were the first to give in to state pressure and federal promises. In 1831, they left Mississippi and western Alabama for the West, suffering through a terrible winter

WARS OF THE REMOVAL

and the corrupt inefficiencies that would prove the tragic hallmark of the government's handling of Indian affairs throughout the entire nineteenth century. Next followed the Chickasaws, who signed removal treaties in 1832 and 1834 providing for the federal government to sell on their behalf the lands vacated and hold the proceeds in trust for Chickasaw use. Surprisingly, at least sometimes, this trust was honored.

## THE CREEK WAR

The Creeks had a longer, more complex, and more violent history of removal. The Battle of the Thames had dramatically and decisively reversed the course of the War of 1812, but it by no means ended white-Indian hostilities. In Georgia, Tennessee, and the Mississippi Territory, the Creeks were engaged in an intratribal war between those who advocated cooperation with the white man—the Lower Creeks, or White Sticks—and those bent on driving the whites out of their land—the Upper Creeks, or Red Sticks. Little Warrior, of the Red Sticks, had fought against the Americans in the War of 1812, taking part in the massacre of James Winchester's command on the Raisin River (near present-day Monroe, Michigan) and raiding settlers along the Ohio on his way home. The tribe's peace faction, led by Big Warrior, had arrested and executed Little Warrior, thereby widening the gulf between the two tribal factions.

Equipped by the Spanish in Pensacola, Florida, Red Sticks led by a half-breed known as Peter McQueen attacked a party of settlers at Burnt Corn Creek in present-day Alabama. But the worst catastrophe for the settlers came on August 30, 1813, when William Weatherford (Red Eagle), a half-breed adherent of Tecumseh, attacked Fort Mims, on the lower Alabama River. Major Daniel Beasley, commanding the fort's garrison of Louisiana militia, ignored the warnings of black slaves, who reported seeing Indians in the tall grass outside the stockade. At noon, 1,000 Red Sticks attacked, using, among other weapons, flaming arrows. When it was all over, more than 400 settlers were dead. Thirty-six whites escaped, and most of the black slaves were spared. It was to be the last Indian attack on a settlement east of the Mississippi, and it brought down a terrible vengeance.

In response to this attack, the Tennessee legislature authorized the substantial sum of $300,000 to outfit a large army under Major General Andrew Jackson. He marched into Red Stick country with 5,000 Tennessee militiamen, 19 companies of Cherokee warriors, and 200 White Sticks. Early in November 1813, a detachment under Colonel John Coffee (including Davy Crockett among its number) ambushed a large contingent of Red Sticks at Tallashatchee, killing 186 Indians with the loss of five and 41 wounded. Later in the month, Jackson relieved Talladega, a White Stick fort that had been held under siege. It was reported that 290 Red Sticks died in this engagement, with the loss of 15 whites and 85 wounded.

Jackson and General William Claiborne unsuccessfully pursued Red Eagle for the next two months, but Jackson was hampered by desertions and the departure of short-term enlistees. It was not until January 1814 that, with 800 new troops, Jackson's army was fighting again, engaging the enemy twice that month, at Emuckfaw and Enotachopco Creek and destroying every Red Stick town in its path. In March, with his militiamen augmented by 600 regulars from the U.S. 39th Infantry, Jackson attacked Horseshoe Bend, a peninsula on the Tallapoosa River. After a daylong battle on March 27, 1814, in which Jackson's army besieged and bombarded the Red Sticks' breastwork-defended position, about 750 of the 900 Red Stick warriors lay dead. The Americans lost 32 soldiers, and 99 were wounded; the Cherokees lost 18, with 36 wounded; the White Stick Creeks counted 5 dead and 11 wounded. William Weatherford—Red Eagle—appeared in Jackson's camp a few days after the battle and formally surrendered. Afterward, Jackson allowed him to depart.

But that was the general's only magnanimous act following the defeat of the Red Sticks. The Cherokees, Jackson's own allies, were also abused, as Tennessee militiamen stole their horses, destroyed their property, took their food, and generally harassed their women, children, and old men. Colonel Return J. Meigs, whom the Cherokees called White Eagle, reported to the secretary of war on May 5, 1814:

I received a letter from an officer of high rank in the army, in which he says, "The return of the Horse [mounted militia] thro' their country has been marked by plunder & prodigal, unnecessary and wanton destruction of property: their [Cherokee] stocks of cattle & hogs have been shot & suffered to rot untouched—their horses in some instances shared the same fate; their cloathing intended to defend them from the wet & cold in the present campaign has been stolen and in some instances where they remonstrated their lives have been threatened."

The Treaty of Horseshoe Bend, which ended the Creek War, extorted 23 million acres not from the Red Sticks alone, but also from the friendly White Stick Creeks. This represented two-thirds of Creek tribal lands, the cession of which pushed the tide of American settlement from the Tennessee River to the Gulf of Mexico.

## THE FIRST SEMINOLE WAR

At this point, the fortunes of the Creeks merged with those of a closely related tribe, the Seminoles. As the War of 1812 drew to a close, the British built a fort in Florida (still a Spanish colony at the time) at Prospect Bluff, 15 miles up the Apalachicola River. When the British withdrew from the fort during the summer of 1815, they left it to Seminoles and a band of fugitive slaves. "Negro Fort," as it soon became known, posed a threat to navigation on the Apalachicola, the Flint, and the Chattahoochee rivers, all important water routes into Florida, Georgia, and Alabama. It also stood as an affront to southern slaveholders by sheltering their escaped "property." Responding to the pleas of the states involved, Major General Andrew Jackson dispatched Brigadier General Edmund P. Gaines in the spring of 1816 to build Fort Scott on the Flint River fork of the Apalachicola in Georgia. In July, Jackson ordered Lieutenant Colonel Duncan Lamont Clinch to take 116 regulars together with 150 white-allied Coweta Creeks under William McIntosh (half-breed Creek cousin of Georgia's governor) downriver from Fort Scott to attack Negro Fort. The land assault would be combined with a naval attack from a force of two supply vessels and two gunboats under the command of Sailing Master Jarius Loomis arriving upstream from the Gulf of Mexico.

Clinch's mission was to take the fort and recover as many fugitive slaves as possible. The attack that came on July 27, 1816, however, proved more devastating than Clinch had intended. The skipper of Gunboat 154, a man named Basset, decided that his cannonade would be more effective against the wooden fort if he heated a ball red hot and fired it with an extra-heavy charge. The missile landed in Negro Fort's powder magazine, which it set off in an explosion that has been described as the biggest bang on the American continent to that date. About 300 African Americans, including men, women, and children, died along with about 30 Seminoles.

The deaths outraged the Seminoles to the brink of war. Clinch pushed them over that brink when he appropriated the spoils of the assault—2,500 muskets, 1,000 pistols, 500 swords, and a quantity of powder that had escaped the conflagration—and gave them to his Coweta allies. Aware of the cache of arms involved, the Seminoles avoided an immediate confrontation with Clinch and his allies. However, the succeeding months were marked by frequent incidents between Indians and white Georgians.

The situation became increasingly tense until, in November 1817, a Seminole chief named Neamathla, who occupied a village called Fowl Town, 14 miles east of Fort Scott, issued a stern message to Brigadier General Gaines, protesting white incursions into his village: "I warn you not to cross, nor to cut a stick of wood on the east side of the Flint. That land is mine. I am directed by the powers above and the powers below to protect and defend it. I shall do so." Not one to be affronted, Gaines dispatched a force of 250 men under Major David E. Twiggs to arrest Neamathla at Fowl Town. Twiggs attacked the town, and although Neamathla escaped, the soldiers killed four warriors and a woman and burned the town.

The villagers, including Red Stick Peter McQueen, retaliated nine days after the attack, falling upon 40 soldiers, seven soldiers' wives, and four children as they made their way to Fort Scott by boat. All but four men (who escaped) and one woman (a Mrs. Stuart, who was taken captive) were killed in the attack. The United States, now formally engaged in what would become the First Seminole War, sent Andrew Jackson back to Fort Scott, where he organized a force of 800 regulars, 900 Georgia volunteers, and a large number of friendly Creeks, led by William McIntosh and Major Thomas Woodward. In March 1818, they rebuilt Negro Fort as Fort Gadsden and used it as a base from which to launch a ruthless attack against the Seminoles. Jackson pushed through the Mikasuki Seminole villages in the vicinity of present-day Tallahassee and pursued the Indians to Saint Marks, a Spanish fort and town in which the fugitives sought refuge. Having heard of Jackson's approach, however, the Indians abandoned the place. This did not stop Jackson from taking possession of it on April 7, 1818, in total disregard of Spanish sovereignty.

Two days after taking Saint Marks, Jackson set off for Suwannee Town, 107 miles to the east, where an important chief the Indians called Boleck (a name the whites corrupted to Billy Bowlegs) was ensconced with warriors and fugitive slaves. On the way, Creek scouts or spies reported that McQueen was hiding in a swamp near the Econfina River with 150 warriors—Seminoles and Red Stick Creeks—and 100 women and children together with 700 head of cattle, a variety of hogs and horses, and a supply of corn. Jackson and his allies attacked McQueen's camp on April 12. The uneven battle lasted for three hours, after which 37 of McQueen's warriors lay dead, and six were captives, along with 98 women and children, including the future Creek and Seminole leader Osceola, aged 14 at the time. McQueen and at least 100 warriors escaped.

Jackson, anxious to get to Suwannee Town, had no desire to burden himself with prisoners. He struck a deal with Ann Copinger, a Red Stick Creek and the sister of Peter McQueen, who agreed to betray her brother in exchange for the release of the women and children. Jackson gave Copinger a letter addressed to the commandant of Saint Marks confirming the deal they had made:

Ann Copinger and the women would persuade McQueen's braves to turn their leader in. Of course, the Indian woman had no intention of carrying out the bargain; released, she and the other captives headed not for Saint Marks, but for the swamp. When Jackson's force was safely out of the way, Copinger led the fugitives to a Mikasuki Seminole camp at the southern boundary of the Okefenokee Swamp.

Jackson, in the meantime, pressed on to Suwannee Town, fighting several skirmishes along the way. When he finally reached his objective, however, he found that it had been deserted and burned. Jackson captured two Englishmen, Lieutenant Robert Armbrister of the Royal Marines and Peter Cook and returned with them to Saint Marks. There, after a mockery of a trial, he executed Armbrister and Alexander Arbuthnot, an old Scottish trader captured at Saint Mark's Fort, for aiding and abetting the Indians. Next, with consummate arrogance, Jackson captured Spanish Pensacola on May 26, 1818. Although this rash act caused the United States temporary diplomatic embarrassment, it prompted Spain to abandon Florida and cede its territory to the United States, which resulted in a rapid influx of white settlers, who grabbed as much land as possible. With the cession, Jackson left Florida, and the First Seminole War came to an end. The surviving Mikasuki Seminoles remained in the inland portion of northern Florida, while the Alachua Seminoles moved to central Florida, near present-day Orlando. The Red Stick Creeks, including Peter McQueen, moved to the area around Tampa Bay, far from Alabama and Georgia. McQueen, aging and exhausted, died a few years later—no one knows exactly when.

Following the First Seminole War, William McIntosh sought to solidify his position with white officials by concluding a series of treaties in 1821, 1823, and 1825 that ceded to the whites some 25 million acres. The 1823 agreement—called the Treaty of Tampa—also specified that the Seminoles would move to a reservation inland from Tampa Bay. Few actually did; for the overwhelming majority of Creeks, including a council of 36 chiefs, repudiated the McIntosh treaties as illegal. The tribal council, acting upon Creek law, condemned McIntosh to death; accordingly, a party of Creek warriors led by Menewa shot him and his son-in-law, and Menewa went to Washington to conclude a new treaty securing the Creeks in the territory that remained to them. But Georgia's governor, George Troup, cousin of William McIntosh, was bent on driving the Creeks out of the state, despite the federal treaty. He increased his state's customary persecution of the Indians by encouraging squatters, speculators, and purveyors of liquor to move in. Jackson, as usual, claimed powerlessness to enforce the

provisions of the treaty and urged the Indians to seek relief by moving west of the Mississippi. After participating briefly in armed resistance, the Creeks at last complied with removal, amid fraud, theft of land, and impoverishment.

## THE TRAIL OF TEARS

The Cherokees, who lived primarily in northwestern Georgia and northeastern Alabama (as well as the southeastern corner of Tennessee and the southwestern corner of North Carolina), took a different approach. After resisting unrelenting pressure from the state of Georgia, including seizure of property and grossly unjust treatment in state and local courts, the tribal council successfully laid its case before the United States Supreme Court. In his 1832 decision in the case of *Worcester* v. *Georgia*, Chief Justice John Marshall found in favor of the Cherokees, declaring Georgia's persecution of the Indians unconstitutional. It proved, however, a hollow victory, as President Jackson refused to enforce the decision of the court.

During the period of negotiation, pressure, and persecution, two factions emerged among the Cherokees. In favor of compliance with removal was a minority "Treaty party," led by Major Ridge (who had served with Andrew Jackson in fighting the Creeks during the War of 1812), his son John Ridge, and his nephew Elias Boudinot, as well as Boudinot's brother Stand Watie (who would serve as a brigadier general during the Civil War in command of the last Confederate unit to lay down arms after Appomattox). A majority "National party," led by John Ross, son of a Scots immigrant and mixed-blood Cherokee mother, opposed removal. Unlike most nationalist Indian groups, however, Ross's party did not advocate a desperate armed conflict against inevitably superior white forces. If resistance to removal should fail, they wanted at least to be in position to secure the most favorable terms possible for the sale of the ceded lands, so that they could purchase land somewhere beyond the territorial limits and jurisdiction of the United States.

The Jackson administration decided to deal solely with the Treaty faction, arbitrarily investing in them the authority to represent the Cherokee nation, even though the party represented a mere 1,000 of the 17,000 Cherokees living in the South. A treaty was concluded on December 29, 1835, calling for the completion of removal by 1838, and following Senate ratification of the agreement, Jackson effectively abolished the National party by forbidding it to hold meetings to discuss the treaty or alternative courses of action. Furthermore, Jackson warned John

Ross that the United States would recognize no Cherokee government prior to removal west of the Mississippi and that any attempt to resist removal would be met by force of arms. Brigadier General John E. Wool, in charge of expediting the removal, declared that any recalcitrant Cherokees would "be hunted up and dragged from your lurking places and hurried to the West."

Despite Jackson's threats, the National party worked during the period 1835–38, albeit to no avail, to expose the fraud that had been perpetrated. During this period, too, the state of Georgia and various individuals did their worst to cheat the Cherokees out of their removal funds. By the 1838 deadline, only 2,000 Cherokees had emigrated. Martin Van Buren, who succeeded Jackson as president, replaced Brigadier General Wool with Major General Winfield Scott, who approached the task of removal with far more vigor. To begin with, Scott constructed stockades—what the twentieth-century world would call concentration camps—to house Cherokees in preparation for their removal. The round-up and interrment were carried out swiftly and brutally; Indians had to abandon property, ponies, and other livestock, and the soldiers charged with overseeing the stockades indulged in every manner of abuse, including rape and murder. "I fought through the civil war," one Georgia soldier later recalled, "and have seen men shot to pieces and slaughtered by thousands, but the Cherokee removal was the cruelest work I ever knew."

Except for a handful who managed successfully to hide in the mountains, the Cherokees of the South were penned into the camps during the long, hot summer. In the fall and winter of 1838–39, they were marched off to Indian Territory along what came to be called the Trail of Tears. Fifteen thousand followed that 1,200-mile route, always cold, always short of food and other supplies. Four thousand died along the way.

## THE SECOND SEMINOLE WAR

With Cherokees subdued and removed, the government again turned its attention to the Seminoles. As with the other tribes, the Seminoles were persecuted and subjected to unremitting pressure to accept removal. As if depredations suffered at the hands of the whites were not enough, a devastating drought in 1831 brought great hardship to the tribe. Faced with annihilation, Seminole leaders signed a provisional removal treaty on May 9, 1832, which stipulated that removal was conditional on tribal approval of the site selected for resettlement. Accordingly, a party of seven Seminoles was dispatched to the site. Before they returned with their report, however, an Indian agent named John Phagan coerced tribal representatives into signing a final treaty binding the Seminoles to leave Florida by 1837 and to unite with the Creeks, who were already lodged beyond the Mississippi. The tribe at large rescinded the signatures and protested that the "final" treaty was fraudulent. Indeed, Phagan was removed from office for repeatedly defrauding the Indians. However, President Jackson dismissed any challenge to the legitimacy of the treaty and passed it on to the Senate for ratification.

The report of those who had seen the proposed site of resettlement did nothing to make Seminoles more willing to give up their familiar lands. Secretary of War Lewis Cass decreed that all tribes removed to Indian Territory be lumped into a single political unit—an expedient that would facilitate the government's dealing with them, but an idea most tribes found abhorrent. Certainly, the Seminoles did not want to merge their identity with the Creeks or any other tribe. This was not entirely an ethnic issue. In fact, many Creeks and Seminoles had long enjoyed a close association, but the Creeks had been compelled to compensate Georgia planters for fugitive slaves they had harbored, and the Seminoles feared that the Creeks would, in turn, appropriate their slaves. As for the African Americans, they recognized that their treatment by Seminole masters was far more generous than they would experience at the hands of whites or Creeks. Since the African Americans enjoyed considerable influence among the Seminoles, they reinforced the Indians' resolve not to be removed.

Evidence of the essential bond between Creek and Seminole is the fact that Osceola, who emerged during this tumultuous period as the central leader of the Seminole resistance, has been variously identified as a Red Stick Creek and a Seminole. Early in the winter of 1835, the infantry company at Fort King (near present-day Ocala, Florida), was reinforced by four companies of mixed artillery and infantry under the command of Brevet Colonel A. C. W. Fanning. Fort Brooke—at Tampa—was also reinforced at this time with three artillery companies under Major Richard A. Zantzinger. Twenty miles north of Fort King, General Duncan Lamont Clinch, now in command of all Florida troops, owned a plantation he called Auld Lang Syne. It was now occupied by a company of soldiers under Captain Gustavus Drane. It was clear to Osceola that the whites were gearing up for a war intended to force the Seminoles west. He negotiated with federal Indian agent Wiley Thompson and General Clinch to put off emigration until January 15, 1836. Osceola's object was not to delay the inevitable, but to buy time for his people to prepare for war.

Soon after this negotiation, Thompson decided that it was prudent to suspend the sale of powder to the Indians.

## THE TRAIL OF TEARS

During the fall and winter of 1838–39, Major General Winfield Scott conducted the roundup of Cherokees to be removed to Indian Territory (present-day Oklahoma) along what came to be called the Trail of Tears. Fifteen thousand Indians were compelled to follow the 1,200-mile route. Four thousand died in concentration camps preparatory to the removal or along the way.

On May 10, 1838, shortly after arriving in Cherokee country, Scott addressed the Indians:

*Cherokees!* The President of the United States has sent me, with a powerful army, to cause you, in obedience to the Treaty of 1835, to join that part of your people [about 2,000 souls] who are already established in prosperity, on the other side of the Mississippi. Unhappily, the two years which were allowed for the purpose, you have suffered to pass away without following, and without making any preparation to follow, and now, or by the time this solemn *address* shall reach your distant settlements, the emigration must be commenced in haste, but, I hope, without disorder. I have no power, by granting a farther delay, to correct the error that you have committed. The full moon of May is already on the wane, and before another shall have passed away, every Cherokee man, woman and child, in those States, must be in motion to join their brethren in the far West.

*My Friends!* This is no sudden determination on the part of the President, whom you and I must now obey. By the treaty, the emigration was to have been completed on, or before, the 23rd of this month, and the President has constantly kept you warned, during the two years allowed, through all his officers and agents in this country, that the Treaty would be enforced.

I am come to carry out that determination. My troops already occupy many positions in this country that you are to abandon, and thousands, and thousands are approaching, from every quarter, to render resistance and escape alike hopeless. All those troops, regular and militia, are your friends. Receive them and confide in them as such. Obey them when they tell you that you can remain no longer in this country. Soldiers are as kind hearted as brave, and the desire of every one of us is to execute our painful duty in mercy. We are commanded by the President to act towards you in that spirit, and such is also the wish of the whole people of America. . . .

This is the address of a warrior to warriors. May his entreaties be kindly received, and may the God of both prosper the Americans and Cherokees, and preserve them long in peace and friendship with each other!

The Cherokees were cruelly abused by the soldiers, who beat, robbed, and raped their charges. By far the worse enemy, however, was sickness. In the filth of makeshift trail camps, the heat of summer claimed many lives, and during the summer of 1838, 100 prominent Cherokees petitioned Scott not to send any more summer detachments of "emigrants," but to wait until cold weather:

We your prisoners wish to speak to you. We wish to speak humbly for we cannot help ourselves. We have been made prisoners by your men, but we do not fight against you. We have never done you any harm. Sir, we ask you to hear us. We have been told we are to be sent off by boat immediately. Sir, will you listen to your prisoners. We are Indians. Our wives and children are Indians and some people do not pity Indians. But if we are Indians we have hearts that feel. We do not want to see our wives and children die. We do not want to die ourselves and leave them widows and orphans. We are in trouble, Sir, our hearts are very heavy. The darkness of the night is before us. We have no hope unless you will help us. We do not ask you to let us go free from being your prisoners, unless it should please yourself. But we ask that you not send us down the river at this time of the year. If you do we shall die, our wives will die or our children will die. Sir, our hearts are heavy, very heavy. We want you to keep us in this country until the sickly time is over.

A traveler from Maine encountered a "detachment of the poor Cherokee Indians" enroute to the West:

About eleven hundred Indians—sixty waggons—six hundred horses, and perhaps forty pairs of oxen. We found them in the forest camped for the night by the road side . . . under a severe fall of rain accompanied by heavy wind. With their canvas for a shield from the inclemency of the weather, and the cold wet ground for a resting place, after the fatigue of the day, they spent the night . . . many of the aged Indians were suffering extremely from the fatigue of the journey, and the ill health consequent upon it. . . . Several were then quite ill, and an aged man we were informed was then in the last struggles of death.

And an old Cherokee, many years after he made the journey, recalled the experience:

Long time we travel on way to new land. People feel bad when they leave Old Nation. Womens cry and made sad wails. Children cry and many men cry, and all look sad like when friends die, but they say nothing and just put heads down and keep on go towards West. Many days pass and people die very much.

Osceola took offense at this and openly threatened the Indian agent in his own office:

Am I a Negro? Am I a slave? My skin is dark, but not black! I am an Indian—a Seminole! The white man shall not make me black! I will make the white man red with blood, and then blacken him in the sun and rain, where the wolf shall smell of his bones, and the buzzard live upon his flesh!

The Indian leader stormed out of Thompson's office, more than ever resolved to fight.

Early in June 1835, Osceola again called on Thompson, apparently to discuss some minor fighting between whites and Seminoles and the confiscation of some liquor. Once again, Osceola exploded at the Indian agent, who directed Colonel Fanning to arrest him. "I shall remember the hour!" Osceola shouted in Creek as he was being dragged to a cell. "The agent has his day, I will have mine!"

Confined overnight, Osceola had time to reflect. He decided to apologize and to sign a document affirming earlier treaties that mandated removal. For these acts, he would be set free—free to commence the war for which his people had been preparing. Thompson accepted Osceola's contrition as sincere, but Colonel Fanning was not taken in. "You've made a mistake, General," Fanning told Thompson. "That man should never have been turned loose. He's your enemy for life—yours or his."

"Oh, I don't think so," Thompson replied. "He's learned his lesson." Suddenly, Fanning and Thompson heard a shrill cry from the woods beyond the fort. "As you very well know, General," Fanning remarked, "we have just heard the Seminole war cry. May I respectfully

*Among the many Indians the artist and author George Catlin painted was Osceola, a Seminole (sometimes identified as a Red Stick Creek) known to whites as Billy Powell, who led the Red Stick Creeks and the Seminoles in a strong resistance against Andrew Jackson's efforts to "remove" these Florida tribes to Indian Territory. (Library of Congress.)*

## OSCEOLA (1804?–1838)

Osceola, variously identified as a Red Stick Creek and a Seminole, emerged as a leader of the Seminole tribe during the Second Seminole War. Born on the Tallapoosa River in Alabama, Osceola was probably the son of a Creek mother and an English father, William Powell. Whites generally called Osceola Billy Powell or simply Powell. (Some historians believe that William Powell was Osceola's stepfather and that his natural father was a Creek. Osceola himself claimed to be a full-blooded Indian.)

Osceola was introduced to warfare during the First Seminole War. He was among those Andrew Jackson captured in an attack on the camp of Red Stick leader Peter McQueen. Young Osceola, probably about 14 years old at the time, was held only briefly. His band of Red Sticks moved to Tampa Bay, and it is probable that Osceola served for a time as an Indian agency policeman, responsible for apprehending Indians who strayed from the reservation.

By 1833–34, as tribal debate over the mandated removal to Indian Territory grew heated, Osceola emerged as a powerful voice in the resistance movement. In an 1834 council with Indian agent Wiley Thompson, Osceola was the principal spokesman for the cause. He was at the forefront again in April 1835, when President Jackson convened a large council to settle the matter of removal once and for all. It is said that, at this council, 16 Seminole chiefs signed a document reaffirming their agreement to remove to Indian Territory, but that Osceola pinned the paper to the table with his knife, declaring that *this* would be the only mark he would make. (No official record of his incident exists.) In November 1835, Osceola committed his now sizable following to action when he murdered Charley Emathla, a Seminole chief who had agreed to move west. Late the next month, in a raid on Fort King, Osceola and his warriors killed Agent Wiley Thompson and four others.

Against regular troops as well as militia, Osceola proved to be a skillful strategist and tactician who used the impenetrable swamplands of Florida as a powerful ally in a grim guerrilla war. He also exercised a combination of powerful verbal persuasion and ruthless strong-arm tactics to keep the various chiefs loyal to the resistance. Osceola repeatedly eluded capture and was taken, at last, only by treachery.

suggest that your former prisoner hasn't learned any damn lesson at all.''

Yet Osceola did return as promised and signed a document affirming the treaties. All was quiet through the balance of the summer. In the fall, during October, the Seminoles held a secret council of war. By this time, only six chiefs, Charley Emathla, Holata Emathla, Conhatkee Mico, Enconchatimico, Fuch-a-Lusti-Hadjo, and Otulkechala, remained in favor of removal. Osceola announced that anyone who wanted to go west would be killed. The war chief Micanopy agreed.

Late in November, Osceola and two other resistance leaders, Holata Mico and Abraham, led 400 warriors to the village of Charley Emathla, near Fort King. The party demanded that the chief renounce his agreement to go west. ''I have agreed to go west,'' Charley Emathla replied. ''I've lived to see the Seminoles degraded and almost ruined. The only hope of being saved from total destruction depends on going west. I've made arrangements to go, and I *will* go.''

''You must die if you don't join us. You know of this decision of the nation,'' Osceola declared.

''If I must die, I die,'' Charley Emathla replied.

Osceola and his party gave Charley Emathla a matter of hours to reconsider his decision. Reportedly, he went to the Indian agency office to collect some money due him. As he was leaving the agency with his two daughters and a black man, Osceola and 12 warriors ambushed him. Charley Emathla was hit by 11 bullets. Osceola seized the gold and silver coins the chief had wrapped in a handkerchief and threw them in the air. ''This is made of red man's blood!'' he exclaimed. With this gesture, the Second Seminole War began.

Indian Agent Thompson, Colonel Fanning, and General Clinch scrambled to reinforce their positions. In the meantime, the Seminoles named Osceola war chief, with the warriors Jumper and Alligator as his seconds in command. His first act was to coordinate with Philip (called King Philip), leader of the Seminoles east of Saint John's River, an assault on white plantations in the vicinity of his land. Osceola's people, meanwhile, hid themselves in the impenetrable swamp lands near the Withlacoochee River, southwest of Fort King.

Beginning in December 1835, Osceola launched a series of guerrilla raids on farms and settlements. A skillful strategist, he also attacked what today would be called the area's infrastructure, destroying the bridges that were essential to transporting troops and artillery. Repairing them, Osceola knew, would cost the whites valuable manpower at a critical time. Osceola was also one of the few Indian leaders who, without abandoning Indian guerrilla tactics, successfully instilled Anglo-style military discipline among his warriors.

The first real engagement of the Second Seminole War—the Battle of Black Point—took place on December 18, 1835, west of the town of Micanopy (near present-day Gainesville). Osceola with 80 Seminoles raided and plundered a wagon train. When 30 mounted militiamen happened on the scene, their commander, Captain John McLemore, ordered a charge. Only 12 men obeyed, however, and were quickly forced to retire. In all, McLemore lost eight men, and six were wounded.

Osceola made effective use of reconnaissance and seemed to be aware of every movement of the white forces. While King Philip drew off white strength by raiding plantations along the Atlantic coast, Osceola turned his attention to Fort King. He ordered a war party under Chief Micanopy to ambush a relief column that had left Fort Brooke under the command of Major Francis L. Dade to come to the relief of Fort King.

On December 28, 1835, about three o'clock in the afternoon, Osceola and a small band of warriors raided a sutler's store just outside Fort King, killing the sutler—a Mr. Rogers—and three others. Osceola also encountered the Indian agent, Wiley Thompson, and killed him. On the same day, Micanopy, Alligator, and Jumper, with a contingent of 300 warriors, ambushed Dade's relief column of 110 men, killing 107 at a cost of three Seminoles killed and five wounded. (The three whites who escaped did so by feigning death.)

Having learned that General Clinch intended to attack Seminole villages near the Withlacoochee River, Osceola and Alligator set out with 250 warriors to intercept him. It was a bold move, since the Indian leader was well aware of Clinch's strength: 550 mounted Florida militiamen and 200 regulars. He also knew, however, that the army was encumbered with the usual heavy wagons and equipment that made moving through the swamp painfully slow—about 12 miles a day—noisy, and conspicuous. Osceola ascertained that the column was headed for a ford across the Withlacoochee River and planned to ambush it there. However, by December 30, it became clear that the column was moving below the ford. When Osceola's scouts found a good position for an ambush south of the originally anticipated point, the chief planted an old canoe at that place. Clinch took the bait and commenced crossing the river there, sending his soldiers across in the canoe a few at a time, while a makeshift bridge was under construction. On the far side of the river, the gathering troops were instructed to stand down and stack arms. They were sitting ducks.

Osceola and Alligator attacked at noon on New Year's Eve, killing four men and wounding 52 (one mortally) before withdrawing. More importantly, outnumbered almost three to one, Osceola had succeeded in driving off Clinch's force, causing him to abort his offensive campaign.

These clashes, at the outset of the war, proved to be the only decisive battles during the seven long years of the Second Seminole War. A series of white commanders successively tried and successively failed to win the war: Edmund Gaines, Duncan Clinch, Winfield Scott, Robert Call, Thomas Jesup, Zachary Taylor, Alexander McComb, Walker Armistead, and William Worth. General Jesup succeeded in capturing Osceola on October 21, 1837, but not through military skill. He requested a conference at Osceola's camp, over which the chief raised a white flag of truce. Despite the flag, Jesup had the chief seized and consigned him to a prison cell at Fort Moultrie, South Carolina. Although he was treated reasonably well in prison, Osceola fell ill and died on January 30, 1838. The fort's doctor diagnosed the malady as "acute quinsy," but many who knew Osceola believed that he had actually *willed* his own death. "We shall not write his epitaph or his funeral oration," *Niles Weekly Register* reported:

yet there is something in his character not unworthy of the respect of the world. From a vagabond child he became the master spirit of a long and desperate war. He made himself—no man owed less to accident. Bold and decisive in action, deadly but consistent in hatred, dark in revenge, cool, subtle, and sagacious in council, he established gradually and surely a resistless ascendancy over his adoptive tribe, by daring of his deeds, and the consistency of his hostility to the whites, and the profound craft of his policy. In council he spoke little—he made the other chiefs his instruments, and what they delivered in public, was the secret suggestion of the invisible master. Such was Osceola, who will long be remembered as the man that with the feeblest means produced the most terrible effects.

In a gesture of peculiar military sentiment, Osceola was buried at Fort Moultrie with full honors. Alligator and Billy Bowlegs continued to lead the resistance after Osceola's death, but between 1835 and 1842, about 3,000 Seminoles submitted to removal and were shipped to Indian Territory. The cost to the Americans was high: For every two Seminoles who were sent West, one soldier died—1,500 in all. The war cost the federal government $20 million, and it ended in 1842 not through any victory on either side, but because the government sim-

*Delegates from 34 "removed" tribes pose with Indian agents before the Creek Council House in Indian Territory about 1880. The Creeks, who were removed from their southeastern homelands during 1836, adjusted well to reservation life and became influential leaders in Indian Territory. (National Archives and Records Administration.)*

ply stopped trying to flush out the remaining Seminoles who had hidden themselves deep in the Everglades.

Thirteen years after the Second Seminole War petered out, a party of surveyors working in the Great Cypress Swamp stole or vandalized some crops belonging to followers of Billy Bowlegs. The Indians approached the whites, demanding compensation or, failing that, an apology. Neither was given, and from 1855 to 1858, a pattern of Indian raiding was again established, as settlers, traders, and trappers fell under sporadic attack. The regular army and militiamen were called in, but as in the Second Seminole War, their efforts were largely ineffective against Indian guerrillas whose knowledge of the dense swamplands made them virtually undetectable.

This third Seminole conflict was brought to an end when Seminoles who had earlier moved to Indian Territory were brought back to Florida to negotiate on behalf of the whites. Accepting a cash settlement, Billy Bowlegs and his followers at last immigrated to Indian Territory. A significant number of Seminoles, however, never left the Florida Everglades and their descendants remain there today.

# CHAPTER 17

□

# WARS OF THE REMOVAL
## The Old Northwest (1812–1833)

The end of the War of 1812 and the death of Tecumseh failed to bring peace to the Old Northwest, for white settlement of the region relentlessly pressed the Indians farther west. The many veterans of the war who had been granted land warrants as payment for their services added to the pressure. The practice of "removal," coaxing or compelling cession of Indian lands and resettling the displaced Indians on western lands "reserved" for them, became increasingly institutionalized until the Indian Removal Act of 1830 made it official government policy. In the South, the Creeks, Cherokees, and Seminoles offered the greatest resistance to the policy. While a number of tribes in the Old Northwest, most notably the Peoria and the Kaskaskia, ceded territory and accepted removal, the policy incited two significant uprisings and one brief but bloody war.

## KICKAPOO AND WINNEBAGO UPRISINGS

By the beginning of the nineteenth century, the Kickapoos occupied lands in central Illinois and in Indiana, especially the Illinois and Wabash rivers. The easternmost band of the tribe established its principal village on the banks of the Vermilion River and became known as the Vermilion band. Another division, the Prairie band, headed farther south in Illinois, settling on the Sangamon River. Although they ceded some lands to the United States in 1809, both of these bands fought on the side of the British during the War of 1812. However, in 1819, by signing the Treaty of Edwardsville, most of the Kickapoos ceded the remainder of their Illinois lands to the federal government and moved west to Missouri (eventually, by 1852, a large band would move first to Texas

and then to Mexico, where they became known as the Mexican Kickapoos). Two factions, one led by Mecina and the other by Kennekuk, refused to join in the 1819 exodus.

Mecina's braves launched a small-scale guerrilla war against white settlers, destroying or stealing property. After some months of military pressure from state militia and federal regulars, Mecina's faction crossed the Mississippi River into Missouri.

Kennekuk, who combined the roles of chief and prophet, was a more charismatic leader then Mecina. As Indian prophets before him had and after him would, Kennekuk preached a withdrawal from contact with whites and a return to "pure" Indian ways. His tactics had less to do with guerrilla warfare than with passive resistance. Though he preached avoidance of whites, Kennekuk maintained a dialogue with federal authorities for 12 years, promising to move westward, but always finding an excuse for delay. At last, in 1831, many of his warriors joined forces with the Sacs and Foxes under their dynamic leader Black Hawk in open warfare against the whites.

The Winnebago Indians, like the Kickapoos, were strongly pro-British during the War of 1812 and vigorously resisted white incursion into their lands, which lay between the Rock and Wisconsin rivers in northern Illinois and southern Wisconsin, thence eastward toward Lake Michigan. A conflict with the Fox Indians, however, drove them to seek aid from the United States during the war, in return for which the Winnebagos pledged neutrality.

The pressures of white settlement following the war of 1812 again drove the Winnebagos to active resistance, and this time their situation was more urgent than that of the Kickapoos. Whereas the Kickapoos had the cus-

*Like Tecumseh before him, Black Hawk, leader of the closely allied Sack and Fox tribes, attempted to forge an effective multi-tribal alliance against the ceaseless incursion of white settlement. (Library of Congress.)*

tomary farmers and homesteaders to confront, the Winnebagos faced lead miners who came in large numbers to work the rich ore in the vicinity of Galena, Illinois, on the Mississippi River. Friction between Winnebagos and whites intensified as the Indians began to compete with white miners by selling lead to traders at lower prices. Bowing to mining interests, the federal government ordered its Indian agents to pressure the Winnebagos to stop trading in lead. It was becoming apparent

that the Winnebagos felt not only the strong emotional attachment to their homeland that was common among Indians of almost all the tribes, but that they were also acutely aware of the mineral-rich land's monetary value.

The actions of the miners and the Indian agents incited numbers of Winnebagos to acts of violence. The most serious came in 1826, when several Indians killed a family of sugar-maple farmers living near Prairie du Chien, Wisconsin. This incident emboldened the Winnebago

## KEOKUK (1783 or 1788–1848)

Keokuk—the "Watchful Fox"—was a Sac and Fox chief who, advocating accommodation with the Americans, was the most powerful rival of Black Hawk. Born in the Sac and Fox "capital" of Saukenuk, Keokuk was not a hereditary chief, since his mother was half French, but he gained his position through the courage he demonstrated in combat against the Sioux and through his great skill as a diplomat and orator.

Keokuk broke with Black Hawk during the War of 1812, when he declined to support the British. Moreover, he deliberately courted the favor of U.S. officials, and as a result, the government recognized Keokuk as sovereign representative of the Sacs and Foxes. When Keokuk, along with two other leaders of the Sac and Fox peace faction, Powasheek and Wapello, ceded the Rock River country in exchange for an annuity (which Keokuk administered) and land west of the Mississippi, the Black Hawk War erupted in full force.

In the history of white-Indian relations, Keokuk is a controversial figure. He made further land cessions in 1845, which finally resulted in his tribe's removal to Kansas. His administration of tribal annuities was questionable, and he was prone to heavy drinking (which may have contributed to his death in middle age, from dysentery). Yet he also represented his people well in Washington, D.C., especially over the issue of Sioux claims to Sac and Fox lands in Iowa, and while Black Hawk finally offered his people nothing more than a fugitive life and a violent death, Keokuk was able to trade land for survival.

chief Red Bird and two braves to kill a farmer and his hired hand. Miners and settlers agitated for an increase in the garrison at Galena, which only served to exacerbate the situation. In June 1827, two Mississippi keelboats, bearing supplies for the augmented garrison, stopped at a Winnebago village near Prairie du Chien. One of the Indians' principal grievances against the miners and traders was their practice of deliberately fostering the abuse of alcohol. It was no surprise, then, that the boatmen drank rum and encouraged the Winnebago men to indulge as well. The Indians were soon incapacitated, whereupon the keelboatmen abducted several women and

raped them. As the warriors came to their senses, they set out after the boats, catching up to them after several days. The braves attempted a nighttime assault on the boats, and although they failed to capture the vessels, they did manage to free the captive women. A number of Indians as well as boatmen were killed in the fight.

A combination of federal regulars and territorial militamen, led by General Lewis Cass, Henry Atkinson, Samuel Whiteside, and Colonel Henry Dodge, pursued the Winnebagos. This would have been bad enough for the Indians, but their situation was made even worse when the Sacs and Foxes turned down their appeal for aid. General Atkinson had wisely negotiated with the Sac and Fox chief Keokuk, who pledged the cooperation of the Sacs and the Foxes. Atkinson did not actively employ the Sacs and Foxes against the Winnebagos, but Thomas Forsyth, a U.S. Indian agent, did use Sacs and Foxes as spies to report on Winnebago activity.

In the face of overwhelming odds, Chief Red Bird surrendered to the forces arrayed against him on condition that his people should suffer no reprisals. This granted, Red Bird was imprisoned and, spiritually broken, died in captivity while awaiting trial for murder and inciting rebellion. As in the case of Kennekuk's Kickapoos, the defeat of Red Bird prompted other Winnebagos—most notably White Cloud (the so-called Winnebago Prophet)—to ally themselves with Black Hawk in the war of 1832.

## THE BLACK HAWK WAR

Black Hawk, chief of the separate but intimately allied Sac and Fox tribes, was a most skillful commander, but less adept at negotiating with the white man. Black Hawk unwittingly affirmed a treaty of 1804 by which the Sacs and Foxes ceded some 50 million acres to the government. His understanding of the treaty was that it conveyed nothing more than hunting rights. When he discovered that he had actually consented to give away his village—and much else—he became embittered toward the increasing numbers of white settlers and, when the opportunity came, fought alongside Tecumseh during the War of 1812.

As settlers flooded in with the end of the war, they pillaged Sac and Fox villages, fenced cornfields, and even plowed up cemeteries. Black Hawk protested to the U.S. Indian agents at Rock Island, who told him to move west, across the Mississippi. In 1829, Black Hawk returned from a hunt to find that a white family had settled in his lodge. Through an interpreter, he told them to leave, explaining that there was plenty of unsettled land available. They ignored his demand. Soon, more whites were settling in Black Hawk's village. Next came an announcement from the General Land Office that the area would be offered for public sale.

Black Hawk spent his summers on his usurped land, and his winters west of the Mississipppi. Finally, in April 1832, he crossed the river and marched eastward with 2,000 men, women, and children, the so-called British Band of the Sacs and Foxes, followers dedicated not only to himself but to his supporter, the charismatic Winnebago Prophet. Not all of the Sacs and Foxes were hostile to the whites, however. Keokuk led a faction that opposed Black Hawk's defiance of the whites and had alerted Indian agent Felix St. Vrain to Black Hawk's approach. Keokuk also spoke to General Henry Atkinson, who commanded a small force of about 220 men. "If Black Hawk's band strikes one white man," Atkinson warned Keokuk, "in a short time they will cease to exist." Whereupon Keokuk renewed his pledge to attempt to persuade Black Hawk and the British Band to recross the Mississippi. Atkinson convened a second council, directing Keokuk to invite the British Band. Black Hawk refused Keokuk with indignation and threats.

General Atkinson was sufficiently alarmed to appeal to Illinois governor John Reynolds for militiamen to supplement the small number of regulars in the region. Although the general had hoped for 3,000, only 1,700 men answered the governor's call—among them a lanky youth named Abraham Lincoln. On April 28, the militia force set off for Yellow Banks on the Mississippi, where they expected to confront Black Hawk and his British Band.

In the meantime, on April 24, Atkinson had again dispatched emissaries to Black Hawk, offering him a final opportunity to withdraw with impunity west across the Mississippi. These representatives were treated with the same contempt as was Keokuk's. But, for all his bravado, Black Hawk realized that he was playing a dangerous game. Earlier, Winnebagos and Potawatomis had promised to aid the British Band. Black Hawk must have been disconcerted by the presence of the Winnebago chiefs among the emissaries Atkinson had sent—even though these chiefs secretly informed him that they were only pretending to be friendly to the Americans in order to assess their strength. Black Hawk did not know what to believe. As the militiamen were reaching the Rock River, Black Hawk decided to retreat farther up the Rock in hopes that the Potawatomis would prove less ambiguous allies than the Winnebagos.

On May 1, Atkinson mustered into federal service 1,500 mounted militiamen and 200 infantry volunteers, who joined 340 infantry regulars—the latter under Colonel Zachary Taylor. On May 9, Atkinson ordered the mounted militia, under General Samuel Whiteside, to march up the Rock River via the village of the Winnebago Prophet. In the meantime, Atkinson himself would transport the volunteer and regular infantry by boat and join Whiteside as fast as he could.

Atkinson was a far more capable commander than Whiteside, and it was a mistake to relinquish to Whiteside command of raw, undisciplined, and undependable militiamen. The 1,500 proceeded to the Prophet's village, which they burned and then, learning from a captured Indian that the British Band was but two days' march upriver, Whiteside decided to pursue. Abandoning their baggage wagons for the sake of speed, the volunteers moved up the Rock River, reaching Dixon's Ferry—where Black Hawk and the British Band were last seen—on May 14.

But Black Hawk and his people were nowhere to be found. Disappointed and short of food, Whiteside halted at Dixon's Ferry to await resupply from Atkinson, who was laboring up the river. In the meantime, two additional, battalion-strength milita units were also patrolling the area. Major Isaac Stillman's command was ranging east from the Mississippi, and Major David Bailey's men were combing the territory between the Rock River and settlements along the Illinois. Without consulting Atkinson, Governor John Reynolds acceded to these two officers' request to scout ahead of the main force. Stillman set out with 275 men (in the words of the governor's orders) "to the head of 'Old Man's Creek' [the Kyte River], where it is supposed there are some hostile Indians."

Stillman camped just north of the mouth of the Kyte on May 14. The militia, eager for a fight but wholly undisciplined, shared out its whiskey ration. At the same time, Black Hawk, encamped with about 40 warriors in advance of his British Band, having learned of the presence of the troopers and well aware that he could expect no help from the Winnebagos, was now visited by Potawatomi envoys, who told him that their tribe would not supply his people with the corn they so badly needed. Determining that further resistance was futile, Black Hawk sent three warriors under a white flag to Stillman's camp. As a precaution, Black Hawk sent an additional five warriors to follow the first three as observers.

The three representatives entered the camp and announced that Black Hawk wanted a parley. While this was going on, one of the militiamen sighted the five Indians out on the prairie. Alarm spread throughout the whiskey-charged battalion, and with neither orders nor order, men charged willy-nilly after the five Indians. Shots were fired, and two of the five warriors were killed. Back at the camp, two of the three emissaries managed to escape. The surviving Indian scouts ran back to Black Hawk's camp and told him of the treacherous violation of the truce. Valiantly mustering his 40 warriors, Black Hawk set his men up in ambush, preparing for a stand he had every reason to believe would be suicidal.

What he had not counted on was the drunken disarray of the raw militia. When the warriors leaped out of ambush, the panic-stricken whites wheeled about and ran. Worse, the retreating militia troopers spread the alarm to those who remained at Stillman's camp on the Kyte, and the retreat turned into a rout. Thus, 40 Sac and Fox braves defeated 275 well-armed Illinois militiamen in a "battle" that quickly became known as Stillman's Run.

The hysterical reports of surviving militiamen placed casualties first at over 100, then at 52—the most widely circulated figure. In fact, as stragglers wandered back to Dixon's Ferry, it became apparent that only 11 men had been killed. That was bad enough, as young Abraham Lincoln, who saw the aftermath of Stillman's Run, recalled. He remembered "the red light of the morning sun . . . streaming upon them as they lay heads toward us on the ground. And every man had a round, red spot on the top of his head, about as big as a dollar, where the redskins had taken his scalp. It was frightful, but it was grotesque; and the red sunlight seemed to paint everything all over. I remember that one man had on buckskin breeches.''

As was often the case in Indian-white combat, the demonstration of a failure of skill and courage escalated the magnitude of the defeat beyond the actual numbers of killed and wounded. Emboldened by the opposing army's incompetance, Black Hawk and his warriors terrorized the frontier. On May 20, 40 braves, mostly Potawatomis allied with the British Band, attacked the Davis farm at Indian Creek. Fifteen men, women, and children were murdered and mutilated. Two girls, Rachel and Sylvia Hall, were abducted, but later ransomed for horses— though not before they saw the Indians dance in triumph, brandishing their parents' scalps.

Stillman's Run and the Indian Creek Massacre disrupted the Illinois frontier as much as any major strategic Indian victory could have. "The alarm and distress of the frontier, cannot be described," one of Atkinson's officers reported, "it is heart rending to see the women and children in an agony of fear, fleeing from their homes and hearths, to seek what they imagine is but a brief respite from death." Farming and lead mining were suspended, and the editor of Galena's newspaper called for a "war of extermination until there shall be no Indian (*with his scalp on*) left in the north part of Illinois."

Atkinson mustered additional militia forces, together with auxiliaries drawn from the Sioux and Menominees, to pursue Black Hawk and the British Band, which was taking evasive action in a retreat toward the headwaters of the Rock River. At the Kishwaukee River, Black Hawk encountered a band of Winnebagos, who, now that the British Band had tasted triumph, offered themselves as guides to refuge near the Four Lakes in present-day Dane County, Wisconsin. To cover his escape, Black Hawk dispatched more war parties into the settlements. Thirty Winnebagos encountered a party of seven whites carrying messages from Dixon's Ferry to General Atkinson at Galena. Among the four slain was the Indian agent Felix St. Vrain, who had been sympathetic to the Sacs and Foxes.

While Black Hawk continued to evade the white soldiers, militiamen frequently skirmished with scattered war parties, almost always acquitting themselves poorly. "The more I see of the militia," Colonel Zachary Taylor lamented, "the less confidence I have in their effecting any thing of importance; and therefore tremble not only for the safety of the frontiers, but for the reputations of those who command them." At last, on June 16, Colonel Henry Dodge led 29 miners-turned-militiamen against 11 marauding warriors, engaging them at the Pecatonica River. Though three of his men were severely wounded in the initial exchange of gunfire, the miners charged and killed the Indians. Colonel William S. Hamilton, who came on the scene about an hour later, turned his party of Sioux, Menominees, and friendly Winnebagos on the corpses of the slain warriors. They hacked the bodies to bits. The whites celebrated the whole bloody episode as a great victory.

Still, Black Hawk and his followers continued their raiding, until, after mid-June, white-allied Potawatomis and Winnebagos reported that the war chief was lodged above Lake Koshkonong. By this time, Atkinson had managed to muster into the federal service three brigades of militia, together with a battalion of regulars and a company of spies. But, even with 3,000 militiamen and 400 regulars, Atkinson remained so hesitant that President Andrew Jackson and the War Department called in Major General Winfield Scott with 800 regulars, six companies of rangers, and assorted militia to coordinate with Atkinson a strike against Black Hawk. While this force was gathering at Chicago, Black Hawk and 200 warriors attacked a fort on the Apple River, about 14 miles from Galena. For 12 hours, 25 men held off the Indians, who finally withdrew, plundering livestock and property on the way.

By the end of June, Atkinson's forces were at last on the move in pursuit of Black Hawk, who continued to prove elusive. By the second week in July, Atkinson's command had failed to encounter Indians, and was running low on supplies. Militiamen, whose enlistments were coming to an end, began dropping out of the campaign—among them Abraham Lincoln, who later recalled: "If General Cass [the Michigan territorial governor who became Andrew Jackson's secretary of war] went in advance of me in picking whortleberries, I guess I surpassed him in charges upon wild onions. If he saw any live fighting Indians, it was more than I did, but I had a good many bloody experiences with the mosquitoes; and although I never fainted from loss of blood, I can truly say I was often very hungry." Scott's army, still in Chicago, was likewise beginning to disintegrate as the result of a cholera epidemic. General Atkinson despaired of ever overtaking Black Hawk.

But Black Hawk and his people were also in dire straits, subsisting on a starvation diet of bark and roots. They were too far from the white settlements to raid them, but they dared not approach more closely. Ironically, this chief who had embarked on the warpath because he did not want to move west, now saw the West as his only possible salvation. He decided to head for the Wisconsin River and then to the Mississippi, which he would cross to safety on the Great Plains. As the Indian leader was pondering this move, on July 11, Colonel Dodge encountered a party of Winnebagos who claimed that Black Hawk was camped on the rapids of the Rock River. Dodge pulled together 600 weary men and set out. When they reached the rapids on July 18, they were once again disappointed. But, this time, the Winnebagos of a local village were able to tell the American commander that the British Band was now camped just 20 miles north. Sending word to Atkinson, Dodge pressed on, following what was now a clear trail—the trees stripped here and there of bark, the earth pocked with holes where roots had been dug up.

On July 21, some of Dodge's men killed an Indian who was mourning beside the grave of his wife, a victim of starvation. This was the first of numerous contacts that day, which resulted in skirmishes with the rear guard of the British Band. By day's end, almost 70 of Black Hawk's followers lay dead. On the twenty-second, Neapope, Black Hawk's right-hand man, appeared at Dodge's camp with what amounted to a surrender offer. Tragically, white and Indian interpreters had left after the battle of the previous day, and Dodge could not comprehend what was being proposed. The grim pursuit continued.

On July 24, Atkinson, in command of some regulars and part of a militia brigade, met with Dodge's forces at the Blue Mounds, 65 miles east of Prairie du Chien. Atkinson picked 1,300 men to press after Black Hawk through country previously untraveled by whites.

On August 1, 1832, when Black Hawk convened a council at the junction of the Bad Axe and Mississippi rivers, the British Band had been reduced by desertion, starvation, and battle deaths to 500 people. The chief

advised continuing up the Mississippi and seeking refuge among the Winnebagos. His people resisted this, having lost all faith in these supposed allies. Most set about hastily constructing canoes or rafts in order to cross the Mississippi. Some made it across, but the majority were still on the east bank as the steamboat *Warrior* hove into sight loaded with soldiers and a six-pounder gun.

When the boat anchored near the shore, the Indians raised a flag of truce. Yet again, there was confusion and misunderstanding. Lieutenant James W. Kingsbury, commander of the *Warrior*, refused to send his men ashore as requested, but insisted that two Indian representatives come aboard. For some reason—probably because of faulty communication—the Sacs and Foxes did not comply. To the men aboard the steamboat, it looked as if the Indians were priming their weapons and seeking cover. The nervous lieutenant ordered his men to open fire.

A two-hour battle ensued, before Kingsbury broke off the engagement because of lack of fuel. Twenty-three of the British Band were killed, others were delayed crossing the river, and only a few of Black Hawk's closest followers went with him northward.

On August 3, Atkinson's and Dodge's 1,300-man command arrived. The Indians who had remained on the east bank of the Mississippi attempted to surrender, but the troops, frustrated by weeks of fruitless pursuit and months of general panic, stormed their position in an eight-hour frenzy of clubbing, stabbing, shooting, and—despite General Scott's explicit ban against the practice—scalping. During this, the *Warrior*, having gone downstream to collect wood for fuel, returned to train her six-pounder on what remained of the British Band. Although about 200 Sacs and Foxes did make it to the west bank, white-allied Sioux intercepted most of them there, capturing or killing them.

As for Black Hawk, who had fled north, the Winnebagos among whom he had sought refuge proved yet again treacherous. In exchange for a reward of 100 dollars and 20 horses, they betrayed the chief to white authorities. He was in prison when General Scott concluded a treaty on September 19, 1832, with the surviving Sacs and Foxes who had failed to escape. The treaty called for the cession of a strip of land, 50 miles wide, running virtually the entire length of Iowa's Mississippi River frontage—about six million acres, which was in addition to the many more millions of acres ceded in the 1804 treaty. This time, however, Scott and the treaty commissioners sought to improve upon the 1804 agreement by stipulating the absolute removal of the Indians by June 1, 1833. The Sacs and Foxes further pledged never to return, to live, to hunt, to fish, or to plant on the land. For this enormous cession the Indians were paid $660,000.

Black Hawk languished in prison for a year before federal officials decided that, rather than bring him to trial and execute him, they would exhibit him as a trophy of battle. He was, accordingly, packed off on a tour of the United States, where he was greeted in some places with hatred and in others as a celebrity, almost a hero—or, at least, a respected former enemy. Black Hawk dictated his autobiography to a trader named Antoine Le Claire, and in 1837, he sat for the great painter of Indian portraits, Charles Bird King. Black Hawk was permitted to return to his people in Iowa on the humiliating condition that he submit to Keokuk's authority and no longer act as chief. He died in Iowaville, on the Des Moines River. Grave robbers exhumed his bones, which were put on display at a local historical society.

# CHAPTER 18

# THE WARS FOR THE WEST

## Overture (1840s–1850s)

Many whites deplored and protested against the Indian "removal." A significant number of even these people, however, believed that, though the policy was cruel and immoral, it served the purpose of separating white from red, thereby promising to bring peaceful Indian-white relations. It is a profound understatement to say that this proved a fond hope.

## CONTINENTAL EXPANSION

Thomas Jefferson had made the Louisiana Purchase in large part to acquire seemingly endless space into which white settlement, always moving west, could push the Indian. Andrew Jackson's policy of removal was also a matter of pushing tribes westward. Neither Jefferson, Jackson, nor the other presidents who contemplated or enacted removal considered the possibility that the white settlement of the American West might also someday proceed *from* the west as the United States rapidly evolved into a continental nation.

Americans began settling in fertile, richly forested Oregon in the mid-1830s. By the 1840s, many in the United States were prepared to go to war with Great Britain over possession of the territory. ("All Oregon or None," ran one of presidential candidate James K. Polk's campaign cries, and, more famously, "Fifty-four Forty or Fight!"—a reference to the parallel [54 degrees, 40 minutes] that the most militant U.S. faction proposed as the northern boundary of Oregon Territory.) A compromise between the two nations was reached on June 15, 1846, and white Americans began to enter Oregon in large numbers.

About the time that the Oregon question was being settled, the matter of annexing Texas, which had won its independence from Mexico, was also becoming more urgent, as both France and Britain worked to block U.S. expansion in that quarter. Both nations saw an independent Texas as a profitable market for export goods. Britain also envisioned Texas as a potential ally against the United States should some future conflict develop. The British foreign secretary, Lord Aberdeen, proposed an alliance of Britain, France, Mexico, and Texas to guarantee the independence of Texas (Mexico would benefit by the allies' promise to protect its boundaries "forever"). France demurred, not wishing to fight a war to defend the independence of a country so remote. At this, Lord Aberdeen retreated—but too late. News of an impending Anglo-French alliance against the United States prompted outgoing President John Tyler to urge Congress to adopt an annexation resolution. On June 16, 1845, the Congress of the Republic of Texas accepted, and President Polk admitted Texas to the Union on December 29.

Next came California, which was held so feebly by Mexico that it was ripe and ready to fall into the hands of whomever was there to catch it. Again, both the British and the French were interested and made diplomatic moves that prompted President Polk to offer Mexico $40 million for it. When Mexican President José Joaquin de Herrera refused to see Polk's minister John Slidell, Polk commissioned the U.S. consul at Monterey, Thomas O. Larkin, to organize California's small but powerful American community into a separatist movement sympathetic to annexation.

The movement never had time to get off the ground. John Charles Frémont, intrepid western explorer surveying potential transcontinental railroad routes for the U.S. Bureau of Topographical Engineers, was camped with 60 armed men near the "fort" John A. Sutter had built in Northern California. Sutter, a Swiss immigrant, would

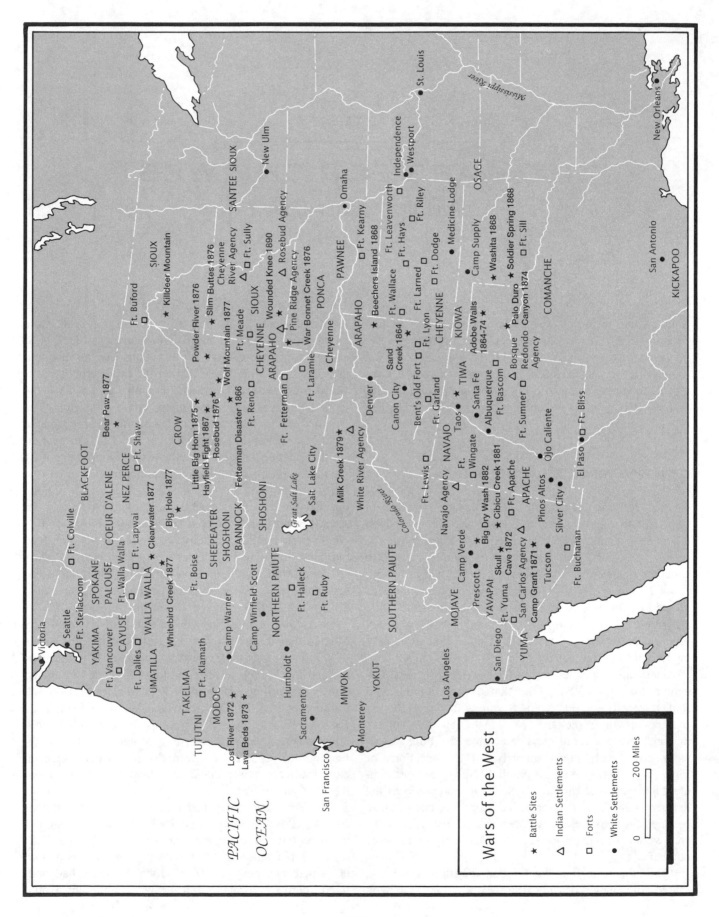

## Wars of the West

- ★ Battle Sites
- △ Indian Settlements
- ☐ Forts
- ● White Settlements

0 ___ 200 Miles

*PACIFIC OCEAN*

*Mississippi River*

New Orleans

St. Louis

San Antonio

KICKAPOO

Independence
Westport

Medicine Lodge

OSAGE

Soldier Spring 1868
Washita 1868
Ft. Sill
COMANCHE

Palo Duro
Redondo Canyon 1874

Ft. Riley
Ft. Dodge
Camp Supply
CHEYENNE
KIOWA

Ft. Leavenworth
Ft. Hays
Ft. Larned
Ft. Wallace
Beechers Island 1868
Ft. Lyon

Ft. Kearny

Omaha

New Ulm

SANTEE SIOUX

Ft. Sully
Rosebud Agency
Cheyenne River Agency
Wounded Knee 1890
Pine Ridge Agency
War Bonnet Creek 1876
CHEYENNE
SIOUX
ARAPAHO
PONCA
PAWNE

Ft. Buford

SIOUX
Killdeer Mountain

Powder River 1876
Slim Buttes 1876
Wolf Mountain 1877
Ft. Meade

Bear Paw 1877
BLACKFOOT
Ft. Shaw
CROW
Little Big Horn 1875
Hayfield Fight 1867
Rosebud 1876
Fetterman Disaster 1866
Ft. Reno

COEUR D'ALENE
NEZ PERCE
Ft. Walla Walla
Ft. Lapwai
Clearwater 1877
Big Hole 1877
WALLA WALLA
Whitebird Creek 1877

SPOKANE
PALOUSE
YAKIMA
Ft. Colville
Ft. Steilacoom
Seattle
Victoria

Ft. Vancouver
CAYUSE
Ft. Dalles
UMATILLA
Ft. Boise
SHEEPEATER
SHOSHONI
BANNOCK
Camp Warner
Camp Winfield Scott

TAKELMA
TUTUTNI
MODOC
Lost River 1872
Lava Beds 1873
Ft. Klamath

NORTHERN PAIUTE
Ft. Halleck
Ft. Ruby

Humboldt

Sacramento
Monterey
San Francisco

MIWOK
YOKUT
SOUTHERN PAIUTE

Los Angeles
San Diego

MOJAVE
YAVAPAI
Prescott
Camp Verde
Ft. Yuma
YUMA
Skull Cave 1872
Big Dry Wash 1882
Cibicu Creek 1881
San Carlos Agency
Camp Grant 1871
APACHE
Ft. Apache
Tucson
Ft. Buchanan
Silver City
Pinos Altos
Ojo Caliente
El Paso
Ft. Bliss

NAVAJO
Navajo Agency
Ft. Lewis
Ft. Wingate
Ft. Sumner
Bosque Redondo Agency
Ft. Bascom
Albuquerque
Santa Fe
TIWA
Taos
Ft. Garland
Bent's Old Fort
Canon City
Sand Creek 1864
Denver
Ft. Fetterman
Ft. Laramie
Cheyenne
ARAPAHO

*Colorado River*

Milk Creek 1879
White River Agency
*Great Salt Lake*
Salt Lake City
SHOSHONI

156

soon gain fame for the gold discovered in his millrace, which triggered the rush of 1848–49. José Castro, governor of Northern California, ordered them to leave California. Frémont responded by helping to provoke the Bear Flag Rebellion, through which California won its independence, and Californians quickly chose annexation to the United States. The rebellion soon dissolved into the Mexican War of 1846–48, through which not only California, but New Mexico and Arizona became U.S. territories.

The stage was set for the situation that Maine's Senator Lot Morrill described in a speech before the 40th Congress in 1867: "As population has approached the Indian we have removed him beyond population. But population now encounters him on both sides of the continent, and there is no place on the continent to which he can be removed beyond the progress of population." The enveloping net of white settlement, with its ramifying systems of trails, then roads, then railroads, caught up Indians and whites in almost continual war for two-thirds of a century.

## GOVERNMENT POLICY AND INDIAN CULTURE

Contrary to the claims of some Indian as well as white activists in the twentieth century, it was never the federal government's official policy to practice genocide against the Native peoples of the West—though there was no shortage of individual racists and fanatics who advocated just that. If any single approach to the Indian can be identified as the nation's official policy, it was "concentration," the gathering together and installation of Indians on lands "reserved" for them. Theoretically, once consigned to a reservation, Indians became wards of the federal government, which pledged to provide them with rations and other necessary goods. In practice, one of the many tragedies that beset the U.S. Indian policy was the almost universal corruption among the agents entrusted with the administration of the reservations. Many reservation Indians suffered varying degrees of starvation and abuse, which provoked rather than discouraged further warfare.

Corruption and calculated deceit were only two evils in what the crusading nineteenth-century novelist Helen Hunt Jackson called "A Century of Dishonor." Even when treaties between the United States and Indians were drawn up in good faith, war, dispossession, and death were most frequently the result. As they had during the "removal" of the Creeks and Seminoles, federal authorities not only treated with the various tribes as if they were sovereign foreign powers, but treated only with those factions within a tribe that were most willing to

see things the government's way. Tribal organization was far too loose, too organic for such an approach to have real meaning. Tribal decisions were characteristically reached by highly democratic means, often through innumerable meetings—councils—which frequently came to no unanimous conclusion at all. Moreover, individuals, if they disagreed with a so-called tribal decision, were usually not bound by it. In short, tribes could rarely enforce treaties on their own people.

There were, of course, many other cultural differences between the westering whites and the Indians, and none more profound than those involving the culture of warfare itself. While whites waged war principally to acquire and control territory, the Indians often fought from more diverse motives: for the honors of war (which carried religious significance), or for plunder (a way of life for some tribes), or for revenge. For many of the Plains tribes, war, along with hunting, was the male's principal activity.

Compounding the complexity of white-Indian relations was the fact that by no means were all Indians hostile, and even hostile Indians were not hostile all of the time. Also, the culturally diverse tribes warred with one another far more frequently than they fought against whites. The problem was that whites rarely took the time and trouble to distinguish enemies from allies, enemies from neutrals, and neutrals from allies. The result was a chronic state of provocation and confusion.

## U.S. ARMY

If the United States did not officially seek to exterminate the Indians, it did mean to coerce them into obedience and onto reservations. For the most part, before the Civil War, campaigning against Indians was conducted largely by locally organized bands of settlers or locally raised bands of militia. After the Civil War, the regular army took on most of the responsibility for the twofold mission of policing hostile Indians and impressing upon them the invincible majesty of the government of the United States of America. Thus impressed (the theory went), the Indians would have no choice but to submit meekly to obedient lives on the reservations.

The trouble was that, to accomplish this dual task, a less majestic instrument than the mid-nineteenth-century U.S. Army can hardly be imagined. Following the Civil War, the army rapidly mustered out men—almost a million of them—leaving about 30,000 regular troops in 1866. Congress acted to increase manpower, and the size of the "peacetime" army peaked at 56,815 in September 1867. But fully one-third of these troops were needed in the South to conduct the work of Reconstruction, and as

## THE RESERVATION SYSTEM

The first Indian reservation in North America, Edge Pillock, in New Jersey, was established in 1758 and became home to about 100 Unamis. The concept of the reservation did not come into its own, however, until the beginning of the nineteenth century when the Louisiana Purchase opened up vast tracts of land that (government officials believed) whites would never want. By 1817, the area encompassing present-day Oklahoma and part of Kansas and Nebraska was designated Indian Territory, and state and federal governments began pressuring the Five Civilized Tribes of the Southeast to "remove" to it. With passage of the Indian Removal Act of 1830, the policy of removal became federal law.

During the period of roughly 1870 to 1920, reservations became the strictly regulated but poorly administered places that make them seem, in retrospect, little better than concentration camps. The following is from a visitor to the Crow Creek Agency in South Dakota and indicates the mindset of those who administered the reservation:

Some time about the middle of the winter a large vat was constructed of cotton-wood lumber, about six feet square and six feet deep in connection with the steam sawmill, with a pipe leading from the boiler into the vat. Into this vat was thrown beef, beef heads, entrails of beeves, some beans, flour and pork. I think there was put into the vat two barrels of flour each time, which was not oftener than once in twenty-four hours. The mass was then cooked by the steam from the boiler passing through the vat. When that was done, all the Indians were ordered to come there with their pails and get it. . . . The Santees and Winnebagos were fed from this vat; some of the Indians refused to eat it, saying they could not eat it, it made them sick. . . . The Indians reported several deaths from starvation.

The reservations of this period were administered by the Bureau of Indian Affairs, which had its origin in 1789, when Congress created the War Department, assigning to it all duties relating to Indian affairs. In 1824, the War Department created a separate bureau for Indian affairs, headed by Thomas L. McKenney. In 1832, Congress established the office of commissioner of Indian affairs, to be appointed by the president and confirmed by the Senate, but to report to the secretary of war. An 1834 law further defined and refined the bureau. As white-Indian violence subsided east of the Mississippi during the 1840s, it no longer seemed appropriate for Indian affairs to be administered by the War Department, and in 1849 the Bureau of Indian Affairs was transferred to the Department of the Interior.

The Bureau of Indian Affairs was regarded more as a cache of political favors than as a committed policy-making body. Between 1834 and 1907, no fewer than 21 men served as commissioner of Indian Affairs. Almost to a man, they were political hacks for whom the job was a patronage reward—an opportunity for profits both legal and illegal. Between 1834 and 1890, according to one authoritative estimate, 85 percent of all Congressional appropriations for Indian subsistence, education, and land payments were diverted by the Bureau of Indian affairs to defray padded administrative costs, overpriced supplies, as well as unvarnished graft and fraud. Even well funded and honestly administered, the reservations would have been cruel, hard places, but coming at

this was completed, a war-weary and economy-minded Congress put into effect a series of cutbacks. In 1869, troop strength was reduced to 37,313; in 1870 the limit was set at 30,000; in 1874 a ceiling of 25,000 enlisted men was set (with officers, the total came to 27,000). As these mandated limits included casualties, deserters, even dead men who had not yet been officially discharged, the actual strength of the army throughout much of the 1870s was closer to 19,000. These forces were apportioned into 430 companies to man about 200 posts—more than 100 of which were widely dispersed and isolated western forts—which meant that companies were often seriously undermanned.

Though small, the army did not attract the elite. Quite the contrary. Pay was miserable—$13 a month for privates, $22 for sergeants—and was made in currency, quite useless on the frontier, which demanded gold and silver. Converting one to the other slashed the paltry salary even further. Food was terrible and poorly prepared, not by trained commisary personnel but by men detailed to ten-day tours as cooks. Tainted rations were common, as was scurvy. Barracks accommodations were

the end of a pipeline choked by corruption, they were hellholes that bred violence and despair.

By the middle 1880s, there were 187 reservations in the United States, some 181,000 square miles of land, harboring—for the most part miserably—243,000 Indians. In 1850, the Bureau of Indian Affairs consisted of 300 officials; by 1880, it had 2,500, the overwhelming majority of whom were incompetant, corrupt, or a combination of the two. While the physical conditions of the reservations were inhumane and immoral, perhaps even more insidious was the policy implicit in the very idea of the reservation: to destroy tribal organization and replace tribal customs and beliefs with the ways of the white man. This policy was not merely the result of abstract ethnocentricism or out-and-out racism, but was due even more to the greed that had poisoned 400 years of Indian-white relations. By undermining tribal identity, the government sought to break up the reservations into individual homesteads, returning any "surplus" lands to the public domain for white settlement. Furthermore, once a piece of reservation land had become an individually owned homestead, it could be sold—or forfeited for debt. Thus the Indians were confined wholesale to reservations, which were then, whenever possible, retailed out from under them.

Reform would come to the reservation system after the 1920s and would be intensified during the years of the Indian Power movement, which coincided with the African American civil rights movement of the 1960s. But the reservation system had done terrible damage by making the Indians wholly dependent wards of an ungiving state, and for many Indians, tribes as well as individuals, neither the present nor the future seems bright.

*This unidentified Indian delegation, posed on the White House lawn, was one of many that visited the "Great White Father" throughout the nineteenth century. The National Archives dates the photograph before 1877; the style of the officials' clothing suggests mid-century or somewhat earlier. (National Archives and Records Administration.)*

*A Kaivavit Paiute arrowmaker and his daughter, photographed in northern Arizona on October 4, 1872. (National Archives and Records Administration.)*

deserted, and reenlistment was generally low, so that the pool of experienced soldiers was always shallow. Perhaps 5,000 to 6,000 men at any given time could be described as veterans—soldiers with at least five years' experience. The rest were raw recruits who received little or no combat training, as economy measures meted out precious few practice rifle cartridges. Horsemanship was no better than marksmanship. For example, the men of the Second Cavalry at Fort Phil Kearny along the Bozeman Trail in 1866 could not mount their horses without help.

The officer corps was also plagued by low salaries ($1,400 for a second lieutenant, $3,500 for a colonel in 1870), subject to reduction at the annual whim of Congress, and dismal prospects for promotion. A stodgy seniority system meant that a second lieutenant could look forward to reaching the rank of major after a quarter-century of service; a colonelcy might take 33 to 37 years. Not only was this discouraging to able men considering a military career, it made for senescence at command level. As General Oliver O. Howard reported in 1890, "almost all the captains of infantry and artillery are too old for duty involving marching on foot or even drill requiring continous movement."

Undermanned and poorly trained, the U.S. Army in the West faced the Plains Indians (among others), whose culture exalted warfare, warriors, and combat-effective horsemanship. Indian warriors were experts in guerrilla tactics, well suited to much of the western landscape, but a branch of warfare the regular army persistently refused to acknowledge.

In addition to the tactical advantages they enjoyed, the Indians also possessed the less tangible, but not less significant, advantage of indigenous warriors pitted against "foreign" invaders. Menaced with impoverishment, dispossession, and death, Indians had little choice but to believe in their fight. The army, however, was beset with ambivalence over its mission. Soldiers familiar with Indian acts of brutality—torture and mutilation—might be able to think of their enemy as beasts to be hunted down. But many soldiers came to respect the Indians and to despise the injustice and abuse to which poorly conceived and indifferently, incompetently, or maliciously executed federal policy had subjected them. Ambivalence reigned at the highest levels of government as well. Numerous legislators openly condemned military activity in the West.

Although the Indian warriors in any one place usually outnumbered the white troops arrayed against them and were generally more skilled and more dedicated than their adversaries, the Indians of the West were doomed. For all their physical and spiritual advantages, Indians were fatally handicapped in warfare by the very aspects of their culture that elevated individual strength, cunning,

dirty, dark, vermin-infested, and overcrowded; each enlisted man shared his straw-stuffed pallet with a "bunkie." Sanitary conditions were poor enough that disease was responsible for far more casualties than Indian hostility. During the 1860s through 1880s, army "surgeons" annually treated about 1,800 cases per 1,000 men, of which 1,550 were for disease and 250 for injuries due to accidents *and* combat. (Thirteen out of 1,000 died—eight from diseases, five from injuries—and 30 out of 1,000 were mustered out with disability discharges.)

Fully half the enlisted men between 1865 and 1874 were poorly educated immigrants, who were unlikely to get a better job, if any job at all. Even so, statistics for 1871 reveal that almost one-third of the enlisted men

## HORSES OF THE PLAINS

Nothing was more central to the Plains Indian culture than buffalo hunting and warfare, and nothing more essential to either of these pursuits than the horse. Although wild horses were idigenous to North America and were widely distributed until about 15,000 years ago, they disappeared entirely over a period of some 7,000 years. It was the Spanish who reintroduced the horse onto the continent. Those brought by Columbus, Cortés, de Soto, and Coronado did not survive to produce progeny, but the Spanish colonists who followed did breed the animals. They also employed Pueblo Indians to help them tend their herds of cattle and horses, and it is likely that a significant number of these servants, discontented, ran off, taking some horses with them. The runaway Pueblos took up life among the tribes of buffalo hunters who inhabited the Plains and introduced to them both the horses and the methods for breaking, handling, and riding them. By the mid-seventeenth to late eighteenth centuries, horses were common to all the Indians of the Plains, and horse culture spread from the Plains tribes to the Navajos, Utes, and Shoshonis and then to the Nez Percés and Crows.

The horse revolutionized Plains life, making the buffalo hunt and warfare more efficient and more demanding of skill and daring. The gain in efficiency allowed the hunter-warriors more leisure time, and by the end of the eighteenth century, when horse culture was at its early height, Plains tribes developed elaborate war games and religious rites. The horse had, in effect, liberated the Plains culture.

During the nineteenth century, most western horses stood from 14 hands (one hand equals four inches) to 15 hands, two inches. Animals smaller than this were called ponies, and most of the mounts raised by Plains Indians fell into this category; characteristically, their growth was stunted by scant feed. Hunter-warriors particularly prized semi-wild or rough-broke animals, which were especially swift, strong, and agile.

Horse herds also served the Indians as valuable trade goods. Fur traders bought hundreds of animals each year, and later, wagon trains and freighting and coaching companies routinely replenished their stock by purchasing mounts from Indian herds. Horse stealing was common among Indians and was often the cause of conflict with whites. Realizing the importance of the horse to the Indians' way of life and their ability to make war, military commanders often planned operations with the objective of destroying Indian pony herds.

skill, endurance, courage, and honor. War chiefs were not the equivalents of generals; they did not command their braves so much as they "led" them through charisma and personal influence. Truly coordinated military action was usually impossible. On a larger scale, the exaltation of individual virtue meant that so-called tribes did not often act with unity, and one tribe rarely formed a strategically effective alliance with another. Even if this were not the case, after the Civil War, white population in the West outnumbered Indian population by a factor of ten. Against such odds, no warriors, regardless of skill and committment, could long prevail.

## THE SOUTHWEST

Indian-white conflict in the West did not resolve itself into a set of neatly defined wars. For the Indians involved, much of their experience with white contact was uninterrupted war. For soldiers, Indian "warfare" usually consisted of much exhausting and fruitless pursuit punctuated by episodes of bloody violence. More for the sake of clarity of exposition than anything else, the conflicts described in the following chapters have been labeled with the names given by either the Anglo military or Anglo historians. Even such marginally adequate labels are lacking for the sporadic but chronic violence that ensued between the mid-1830s, particularly in the Southwest—when the greatest number of eastern Indians were resettled west of the Mississippi—and 1850–51, the outbreak of the Mariposa War in California.

For as long as anyone could remember, the Apaches and Navajos had been raiding Mexican frontier settlements in New Mexico and Arizona. In 1847, the United States, so far victorious in the war against Mexico, proposed to change all that. "From the Mexican government you have never received protection," General Stephen Watts Kearny declared in the plaza of Las Vegas, New Mexico, as his army of the West hoisted the Stars and Stripes. "My government . . . will keep off the Indians."

## THE APACHES

The name *Apache* is probably derived from the Zuni word *ápachu*, signifying "enemy." The Zunis applied this to the Navajos (a tribe closely related to the Apaches), who were their traditional enemies and whom the early Spanish settlers called *Apaches de Nabaju*. (*Apache* has also been applied to some Yuman tribes, including the Apache Mohave [Yavapai] and the Apache Yuma.) The Apaches of southern New Mexico and Arizona, western Texas, southeastern Colorado, and northern Mexico are so closely associated with the Navajos and the Kiowas that some authorities classify these latter groups as part of the Apache tribe. The Jicarilla and Lipan are most often regarded as Apache subdivisions, but some authorities (notably John R. Swanton, in his standard *The Indian Tribes of North America* [1952]) classify the Jicarilla and Lipan as distinct tribes. The Jicarilla encompass the following bands, all of which live in New Mexico:

Apatsiltlizhihi
Dachizhozhin
Golkahin
Ketsilind
Saitinde

Three bands are recognized within the Lipan group, which lived in New Mexico and western Texas during the early nineteenth century:

Lipanjenne
Lipanes de Arriba
Lipanes Abajo

By the mid-nineteenth century, they had moved to Mexico. Nineteen individuals—apparently all that remained of the Lipans—were brought back to the United States in 1905 and placed on the Mescalero Reservation (New Mexico).

The major body of Apaches is usually classified into the following subdivisions (according to Swanton; all groups are located in Arizona unless otherwise noted):

1. San Carlos Group
    San Carlos proper:
        Apache Peaks Band, in the Apache Mountains, northeast of Globe.
        Arivaipa Band, on Arivaipa Creek.
        Pinal Band, between Salt and Gila rivers in Gila and Pinal counties.
        San Carlos Band, in the region of San Carlos River between Gila and Salt rivers.
    White Mountain Group:
        Eastern White Mountain Band, in the region of the upper Gila and Salt rivers in southeastern Arizona.

---

At first, it actually seemed possible to make good on this bold promise. The Mexican states of Chihuahua and Sonora had been so plagued by Apache raids that the Mexican government began offering generous bounties for Apache scalps. "Backyard barbering" became a kind of gruesome industry. Not only Mexicans, but Americans, runaway slaves, and even Indians engaged in the government-sponsored scalp trade, which became so lucrative that its practitioners did not limit themselves to Apache warrior scalps, let alone warriors caught in the act of raiding. Scalp hunters would storm whole villages and kill every man, woman, and child. A special examination committee had been established to certify the authenticity of the scalps, but it soon became evident to the bounty hunters that there was no way to distinguish between the scalps of friendly Indians and those of hostiles. So the harvest of death widened.

Soon all Indians looked upon all whites as potential murderers, and a cycle of raids and counterraids ensued. (No one was safe from the scalper's knife. Many bounty hunters discovered that the examination committee was incapable not only of distinguishing friendly scalps from hostile, but could not tell the difference between Indian hair and Mexican. Remote Mexican villages, accustomed for years to enduring Apache raids, now fell victims to raids by the bounty hunters as well.)

Although hatred of whites had become intense, the remarkable Apache chief Mangas Coloradas—Red Sleeves—was able and willing to distinguish between whites with whom he could ally himself and those he wanted to annihilate. In 1846, he pledged friendship to Kearny and proposed an alliance against their common enemy, the Mexicans. Although the general gladly accepted Mangas Coloradas's promise to stop raiding New Mexico, he declined his invitation to join him in the invasion of Chihuahua, Sonora, and Durango; for Kearny

Western White Mountain Band, in the same region between the Eastern Band and the San Carlos Band.

Cibecue Group:

Canyon Creek Band, centering on Canyon Creek in Gila and Navajo counties.

Carrizo Band, on Carrizo Creek in Gila County.

Cibicue Band, on Cibecue Creek between the Canyon Creek Band and the Carrizo Band.

Southern Tonto Group:

Mazatzal Band, about the Mazatzal Mountains.

Six semibands: north of Roosevelt Lake; on the upper Tonto Creek; between upper Tonto and the East Verde; north of the East Verde; and from Cherry Creek to Clear Creek.

Northern Tonto Group:

Bald Mountain Band, about Bald Mountain, south of Camp Verde.

Fossil Creek Band, on Fossil Creek between Gila and Yavapai counties.

Mormon Lake Band, centering on Mormon Lake, south of Flagstaff.

Oak Creek Band, about Oak Creek south of Flagstaff.

2. Chiricahua-Mescalero Group:

Gileños Group:

Chiricahua Band, about the Chiricahua Mountains in southeastern Arizona.

Mimbreño Band, centered in the Mimbres Mountains in southwestern New Mexico.

Mogollon Band, about the Mogollon Mountains in Catron and Grant counties, New Mexico.

Warm Springs Band, at the head of the Gila River.

Mescalero Group:

Faraon or Apache Band of Pharaoh, a southern division of the Mescalero.

Mescalero Band, mainly between the Rio Grande and Pecos rivers, New Mexico.

It should be noted that the Mimbreño, Warm Springs, Mogollon, Chiricahua, and Mescalero, together with a group sometimes called the Copper Mine Apaches, were assigned to the Ojo Caliente (Warm Springs) Agency in southwest New Mexico. For this reason, these groups were often referred to collectively as the Warm Springs Apaches. The Apache leader Victorio, a Mimbreño, exercised great influence on all of these bands and is, therefore, often called a leader of the "Warm Springs Apaches."

---

was under orders to march to California to prosecute the war against Mexico there.

The proposed alliance was a greatly missed opportunity, for Red Sleeve's active friendship might have averted later violence in the Southwest. Born at the end of the eighteenth century, the chief grew into a giant of a man, standing six feet, six inches, and was consistently 18successful at out-maneuvering Mexican soldiers and volunteers. Largely through his influence, relations between the Chiricahua Apaches and the Americans were relatively peaceful during the 1840s and 1850s—despite the outrageous and galling fact that a number of Forty-Niners financed their westward trek to California by selling Apache scalps to the Mexicans.

Conflict with the Utes and the Jicarilla Apaches broke out in the summer of 1853 after Commissioner of indian Affairs George W. Manypenny compelled New Mexico territorial governor William Carr Lane to discontinue the

federally promised supply of rations. Brigadier General John Garland, commanding the army's Department of New Mexico, authorized military action. After Jicarillas and Utes rustled some cattle belonging to an army beef contractor, Lieutenant Colonel Philip St. George Cooke, commandant of Fort Union, sent out 30 men from the 2nd Dragoons to engage Jicarillas led by Lobo Blanco (White Wolf). The troops defeated the chief's band in the breaks of the Canadian River on March 5, 1854, and killed Lobo Blanco. Three weeks after this, Major George A. H. Blake, commanding an outpost called Cantonment Burgwin, sent a company of 1st Dragoons under Lieutenant John W. Davidson to investigate Apache activity along the road from Taos to Santa Fe. Davidson's command was ambushed by warriors under the Jicarillas' head chief, Chacón. This, the Battle of Cienguilla, left 22 troopers dead and 36 wounded. Outraged, Garland ordered Colonel Cooke to "give them neither rest nor quarter until they are humbled to the dust."

Into a snowy late March day, with the famed Kit Carson as his guide, Cooke led 200 dragoons, an artillery company serving as riflemen, and 32 Pueblo and Mexican auxiliaries. They pursued Chacón until April 8, when a Pueblo spy spotted an ambush. In the brief Battle of Rio Caliente that followed, one trooper was killed and another wounded; the Indians lost five, and six were wounded, but they were forced to scatter, leaving their supplies, ponies, and a number of women and children. Cooke's command continued to pursue Chacón and his band for five days until, on June 4, they surprised a Jicarilla camp of 22 lodges at the base of Fisher's Peak in the Raton Range. The skirmish was brief, the Apaches losing a small number of men before they fled the camp, leaving behind ponies and supplies. In the fall, Chacón surrendered with most of his followers—except for a small handful of renegades who continued raiding with the Utes.

A mixed Ute and Jicarilla party of 100 warriors descended on Pueblo, Colorado, on Christmas Day 1854, killing 15 settlers, wounding two more, taking a woman and two children captive, and stealing 200 horses. Throughout the next several weeks, Utes and Jicarilla renegades raided travelers and stole large numbers of livestock. In response, General Garland gathered five companies of volunteers led by trapper Céran St. Vrain, and put them together with four companies of regulars under the command of Colonel Thomas T. Fauntleroy. These 500 men combed the San Luis Valley in search of Utes. After two months of fruitless patrol, on March 19, they engaged a small number of Utes and killed eight of them. Finally, on April 28, they fell upon 150 warriors, killing 40 in a hail of lead. Smaller engagements followed, but the Battle of Poncha Pass essentially put an end to Ute violence in the region. St. Vrain, who had detached from the main force to engage renegade Jicarillas, found them on April 25 on the banks of the Purgatorie River. Of the 60 Jicarillas encountered, St. Vrain's command killed six, captured seven, destroyed supplies, and appropriated horses.

Just as the Utes were settling into a discouraged acquiesence, bands of Mescalero Apache intensified raiding during 1854, hitting wagon trains as they traversed West Texas. A patrol of 80 1st Dragoons under Captain Richard S. Ewell rendezvoused with a column of 50 infantry and 20 dragoons under Captain Henry W. Stanton on January 13, 1855, on the Pecos River. Together, the troopers traveled to the Peñasco River and made camp. On January 17, the combined force was attacked by Mescaleros, with whom the troopers skirmished into the next day. On the eighteenth, Captain Stanton and a dragoon were killed, and the remainder of the soldiers withdrew toward the Rio Grande.

At about the same time, on January 16, Lieutenant Samuel D. Sturgis led 18 dragoons and 6 civilians in pursuit of another band of Mescaleros who had raided a ranch near Santa Fe. On the nineteenth, the whites caught up with the Mescaleros, who offered to surrender. Claiming that he could not understand their words, Sturgis ordered his men to open fire. The Indians broke and ran as the troopers gave chase. Three Mescaleros perished and four were wounded; three dragoons and Captain Eaton were wounded; one of the dragoons subsequently died.

The Mescaleros, having lost heart for further fighting, approached the Fort Thorn agency on the Rio Grande in southern New Mexico with an offer of peace. General Garland would hear none of it. He ordered Lieutenant Colonel Dixon S. Miles and 300 troopers of the 3rd Infantry to march through the country of Mescaleros. They discovered about 400 warriors, who quickly offered to surrender. Reluctantly—for Garland and Miles were spoiling for a fight—the officers granted the Mescaleros terms, and the campaign against them was officially concluded in May 1855. Other Apache tribes, including the Mimbres and Gilas, followed suit and pledged to live in peace with the whites.

Under Mangas Coloradas, however, some of the Gila Apaches, suffering through a hungry year, conducted raids through 1855–56. Two columns of infantry and dragoons, a total of about 200 men, led by Lieutenant Colonels David Chandler and John H. Eaton, marched into the Mogollon Mountains of New Mexico, where they harassed Gila and Mogollon Apaches and inadvertently attacked friendly Mimbres as well. Despite Chandler and Eaton's campaign, the Mogollons raided sheep herds along the Rio Grande during the summer and fall of 1856.

When, in November, the Navajo agent Henry L. Dodge disappeared and was presumed dead, the Mogollons were blamed. Garland, on leave, had been replaced by the aged Benjamin Bonneville, who gathered troops from all over New Mexico to embark on a punitive expedition against the Mogollon Apaches. Unable to locate these Indians, Bonneville vented his wrath against whatever Apache bands he encountered, including Mimbres, who had earnestly taken up the agricultural life white Indian agents had promoted among them. In a May 25 attack, six Mimbres were killed, including Chief Chuchillo Negro, a strong advocate of peace and accommodation.

Bonneville had detached 600 men under Dixon S. Miles to comb the territory along the Gila River. Again no Mogollons were located, but Miles did encounter some Coyotero Apaches, whom he engaged on June 27, killing or wounding 40 warriors and capturing 45 women and children. While the Coyoteros were not as conspicuously peaceful as the Mimbres, neither had they done anything manifestly hostile. As for the Mogollons, the ostensible object of the campaign, only one had been killed. For the next few years, the country of the Apaches—Apacheria—was generally quiet.

Whereas the Apaches and Navajos in the far Southwest discriminated—for a time, at least—between Mexicans and Americans, directing most of their raids against the former, the Kiowas and Comanches plundered Mexicans and Americans alike throughout the 1830s and, less intensely, the 1840s, especially in Texas. As with the Apaches and Navajos, raiding was a way of life for the Kiowas and Comanches. Indeed, through the mid-nineteenth century, raiding was the engine that drove Indian-white relations in Texas. The southern Comanche tribes preyed upon Texans, while Comanches in the north and west enjoyed a peaceful trading relationship with Americans, especially those living in New Mexico. They traded stolen goods—even captive women and children—taken from Texas in return for arms, ammunition, and liquor. As early as the 1820s, this commerce had become a regular feature of southwestern life. Annual caravans of traders known as Comancheros trafficked in the goods Indians desired. Poor New Mexicans and Pueblo Indians, the Comancheros occupied the lowest rung of New Mexico society. "Dirty filthy looking creatures," one traveler described them; another was horrified by their nasty habit of catching the lice that infested their bodies and eating them.

Immediately following victory in the Mexican War in 1847 (the final treaty was signed on February 2, 1848), the American administration in New Mexico found itself in a quandary. Should it ignore, condone, or condemn the Comanchero trade? It was a terrible fact that the Comancheros rewarded Indians for their depredations in Texas, but it was also true that they helped keep the peace in New Mexico—something the Mexicans had been unable to do and the American army was certainly incapable of. The Commancheros also regularly ransomed white captives, purchasing them in Texas and selling them in New Mexico—although this was hardly a humanitarian service. The Commancheros were in the *business* of ransoming white captives; if they didn't ransom them, most likely, the Comanches would not take them captive in the first place. While Indian Superintendent James S. Calhoun was appalled by the Comanchero "system," he frequently resorted to the Comancheros as the only viable means of recovering captives. The delicate, if thoroughly distasteful, economy of Texas-New Mexico-Comanche-Comanchero relations endured from the 1820s through the mid to late 1850s, when Comanches were caught in a pincers between Texas Ranger campaigns that drove them west and increasing white settlement of New Mexico, which pushed them east.

The Texas Rangers, organized by the colonist and entrepreneur Stephen F. Austin in 1826 when Texas was still a province of Mexico, had as their mission the engagement and suppression of hostile Indians. In 1839, acting in concert with various militia groups, the Texas Rangers applied sufficient pressure to the Comanches in the western borderlands that they ceded large tracts of land and at least reduced, if not desisted in, their raiding activity. (That, however, would be resumed with vigor in the later 1840s and early 1850s.) In east Texas, the rangers and militia were more enduringly effective in expelling Cherokees (unwillingly pushed west in the first place) across the border into Arkansas.

## THE NORTHWEST

In California, the first major clash came, predictably enough, with the influx of prospectors during the Gold Rush of 1848–49. Much of gold country was inhabited by poor bands of Indians whom whites collectively called "Diggers" because they eked out a meager subsistence digging roots and picking berries. To whites, the Diggers seemed contemptible; worse, they were simply in the way. California's governor blandly stated that "a war of extermination will continue to be waged until the Indian race becomes extinct." This, he said, "must be expected." In a remarkably short time, prospectors killed 10 percent of the Digger population—although, as was often the case, white diseases (as well as malnutrition and outright starvation) felled even more. Before the gold rush, California was home to perhaps 100,000 Indians. By the end of the gold era, the population was about 30,000.

Farther up the coast, in Oregon country, the Indians were not as feckless as California's Diggers. In 1835, Marcus Whitman, a physician and Presbyterian minister, scouted a location for a mission to the Cayuse Indians. After finding a site near Walla Walla in present-day Washington state (then part of Oregon country), he returned east briefly to marry the beautiful Narcissa Prentiss, whom he brought back with him to the mission. Whitman looked to the spiritual as well as physical well-being of Indians and whites alike. In a short time, his mission became a vital way station for mountain men and incoming settlers, who came to rely on his courage and medical skill. The legendary mountain man Jim Bridger, who had taken a Gros Ventre arrow in the back during the Battle of Pierre's Hole (in present-day Wyoming) on July 17, 1832, came to Dr. Whitman in 1835 to have the long-imbedded arrowhead removed.

## THE GOLD RUSH

By the early 1840s, white settlement of the West was no longer simply a movement from the East. Oregon and California were being settled, and the population was expanding eastward from these points. It was, however, a gradual process—until January 24, 1848, when James Wilson Marshall, a 35-year-old carpenter from New Jersey, made a discovery while he was building a mill on the south fork of the American River in Northern California. The partner of rancher and trader John Sutter, Marshall recorded the event in a notebook: "upon the rock about six inches beneath the water I discovered the gold."

News of the discovery leaked out slowly. It was one of Sutter's mill hands, a Mormon named Henry Bigler, who shared the revelation with his fellow Saints. Soon, the news gathered momentum, yet "gold fever"—as it soon would be called—did not take fire until another Mormon, Sam Brannan, spread the word. Brannan had led 238 Saints to California in 1846, a year before Brigham Young made his way to Salt Lake, and he had tried to persuade Young's group to follow him back to his settlement. Brannan visited what had become known locally as the "Mormon Diggings," decided to open a store to serve prospectors near Sutter's mill, filled a quinine bottle full of gold dust, and ran through the streets of San Francisco (then also called Yerba Buena), shouting "Gold! Gold! Gold from the American River!" *That*, he reasoned, should bring plenty of business to his new store—especially coupled with a well-timed story in his own fledgling newspaper, the San Francisco *Star*.

The effect was electric. San Franciscans abandoned their work, closed up shop, walked off the fields, dropped their tools, and went out in search of gold. (Brannan made a fortune—not from the nuggets directly, but by supplying grossly overpriced provisions and equipment to hordes of prospectors. Most Gold Rush fortunes would be amassed in this way. Collis P. Huntington, for example, left a life as an itinerant peddlar of watches and watch parts and then as a small store owner in upstate New York to join the 1849 rush. He prospected for just one day. Then he opened up a miners' supply store in Sacramento, built a fortune, and became one of the principal financiers of the Central Pacific portion of the transcontinental railroad.) By the end of 1848, about 10,000 prospectors were at work in California and had already extracted a quarter of a million dollars' worth of yellow metal. Two men extracted $17,000 in gold dust and nuggets from a single canyon. Five men at Mormon Diggings split a profit of $1,800, garnered from five day's work. A solo prospector earned over $5,000 in two months of work. More usual, however, was an average take of $20 a day—still a handsome return in an era when common labor paid a single dollar a day.

Then, in the summer of 1848, Colonel R. B. Mason, military governor of California, purchased samples of the American River gold, a little over 230 ounces of it, packed it in a tea caddy, and put it in the care of Lieutenant Lucien Loeser for delivery to Washington, D.C. Loeser traveled by sea, crossing the Isthmus of Panama overland and via a jungle river, took ship again and touched port at New Orleans, whence he took a stagecoach to the capital. By the time of his arrival it was late in the year, but news of the tea caddy had reached President Polk by telegraph in time for his opening message to the 30th Congress. "The accounts of the abundance of gold in that territory," the president declared, "are of such extraordinary character as would scarcely command belief were they not corroborated by the authentic reports of officers in the public service." The caddy itself arrived two days after the address, on December 7, and was put on public display.

Gold fever reached epidemic proportions virtually overnight. Gold was the subject of countless newspaper articles and popular lectures, all touting the ease with which a $1,000 a day could be washed from rivers or plucked from the ground. One guidebook—typical of the hundreds that seemed to materialize out of nowhere—reported riverbeds "paved with gold to the thickness of a hand," promising that "twenty to fifty thousand dollars worth of gold" could be "picked out almost instantly."

Of course, such claims were unfounded—and yet, for the firstcomers, prospecting really was quite easy. The Mother Lode in Northern California presented a good deal of gold close to the surface. In earlier geological times, volcanic activity had pushed magma up from the interior to the surface, where the molten magma gradually hardened into rocks veined with gold and other ores. Over the eons, erosion carried the metals into rivers and streams, depositing heavier pieces farther upstream than the lighter bits. The farther upstream a prospector went, the more gold he could find. The dust and nuggets, there for the taking, were called placer gold. At first, one needed only to work the dry gulches and ravines—places where the water had deposited gold in superficial crevices that could be excavated with nothing more elaborate than a knife or spoon. If one dug deeper, one might find larger pockets of gold. Heaps of promising earth were shoveled onto a blanket and tossed, winnowing away the dirt and leaving the heavier gold dust behind—or, at least, some of it. In those early days, when the Mother Lode appeared to be limitless, losing some gold dust to the wind did not seem overly wasteful.

As the surface gold dwindled, prospecting became a more elaborate and sustained affair. One could no longer hope simply to arrive in California, endure a brief period in a miserable mining camp, take out gold by the sackful, and leave. Mining camps developed into rude settlements, some even of a permanent nature. As the coastal gold deposits waned, miners and their camps moved inland, warring with whatever Indians happened to get in the way.

The major *eastward* movement of miners began in 1854, when a servant at Fort Colville, in Washington Territory, discovered gold in the Columbia River. The influx of California miners to this area helped fuel the Rogue River and Yakima wars, which effectively caused the suspension of prospecting operations until about 1859. Mining resumed, but the Colville strike soon petered out, and miners moved farther north for a time. Then, late in the summer of 1860, gold was discovered in the Oro Fino Creek on the western slope of the Bitter Root Mountains in Idaho (at the time part of Washington Territory). Soon, additional strikes were reported in Montana, and miners and mining settlements followed.

During the 1850s, the Southwest attracted California miners, who had heard stories of "lost mines" abandoned by the early Spanish settlers. The miners were easy prey for the Apaches of Arizona, and the army built Fort Yuma (the present-day city of Yuma) and Fort Buchganan (near Tucson) in response. Placer gold had been found in Nevada's Washoe Mountains as early as 1848, but had run out by the early 1850s. In January 1859, however, James "Old Virginny" Finny and three friends struck gold near a shanty settlement called Johntown. Henry T. P. Comstock bought out Old Virginny's share of the claim for the price of a blind horse, and as it turned out, the so-called Ophir vein emerged as the richest lode of gold and silver ever discovered. The hordes of miners who rushed into the region called it the Comstock Lode, and the town of Virginia City, Nevada, soon grew up around it.

Even farther east, in Colorado, news of gold and silver strikes brought a rush of gold seekers in 1859. They were disappointed in the short run, but the Rockies finally proved very rich in ore, and Denver became a major western town. Nevada continued to produce gold and silver in the 1860s and 1870s, and a rush comenced to Leadville, Colorado, when gold was discovered there in 1877. In that same year, Tombstone, Arizona, became the focus of a rush when Ed Schieffelin found silver in that region, and in 1883, the Northern Pacific Railroad trumpeted a gold discovery in the Coeur d'Alene region of Idaho.

Starting with the 1849 California gold rush, all of this mining activity put tremendous pressure on white-Indian relations. The worst crisis began on July 30, 1874, when Horatio N. Ross, a miner attached to a military expedition George Armstrong Custer led into the Black Hills of Dakota Territory, discovered gold. The resulting influx of miners quickly led to the Sioux War.

Zealous, indefatigable, and high minded, Whitman was also a bigot who demanded that his Cayuse converts sever themselves utterly and completely from their former beliefs. Over the years, Indian resentment of his arrogant insensitivity simmered until it boiled over in 1847, when the Cayuses were devastated by an epidemic of measles. As they watched half their number die of the disease, many among the Cayuses attributed the origin of the sickness to the presence of the new white settlers, and to the evil influence of Whitman in particular. Alarmed by the mounting hostility around him, and wishing to direct it away from himself, one settler, a French Canadian from Maine named Joe Lewis, spread the word among the Cayuses that the epidemic was part of Dr. Whitman's plot to steal the Indians' land. When some pointed out that Whitman tried to heal sick Indians as well as sick whites, Lewis replied that the whites Whitman treated recovered from the measles, while the Cayuses died. As the epidemic continued, Whitman's days were numbered.

On November 28, 1847, Whitman traveled 30 miles south of his mission at Waiilatpu to treat sick Indians in the Umatilla Valley. After ministering to them, he returned directly home—for 11 of the 42 mission children were also ill—reaching his house about midnight. There Narcissa was watching two girls, Helen Meek and Louise Sager (one of the Whitmans' adopted daughters), both very ill. Although profoundly fatigued, the minister-physician sent his wife to bed while he continued to watch the two sick girls. After breakfast on a foggy, dark morning, he supervised the butchering of some beef. He returned to the kitchen, where 17-year-old John Sager was winding twine. Whitman sat reading and, for a time, dozed.

About noon, an Indian came to tell Whitman of three more measles deaths among his tribe. The missionary officiated at the burials. Later in the afternoon, when Whitman had returned home, two more Indians, Tomahas and Chief Tiloukaikt (whose daughter had been among those who had died that day), came to the doctor's door. Tiloukaikt spoke to Whitman, and as he did, Tomahas struck him from behind with a bronze toma-

*An imaginative illustration of the death of Marcus Whitman. Popular nineteenth-century depictions of Indians often bore little relation to reality. Not only is Tomahas incorrectly costumed for a Northwest Indian, Whitman attired in the clothes of an easterner, and the missionary's hearth too fancy for a frontier outpost, it is also difficult to believe that anyone could be quite so absorbed in a book.*

## INDIAN WARS OF THE WEST

Already in the throes of the chronic white-Indian violence, the American West by the end of the 1840s was on the verge of widespread, full-scale warfare. White historians have named, summarized, and divided the major wars as follows:

*Mariposa War*—California, 1850–51, with the Miwoks and Yokuts.

*Yuma and Mojave Uprising*—Arizona and California, 1851.

*Rogue River War*—Oregon, 1855–56, with the Takelmas and Tutunis.

*Yakima War*—Washington, 1855–56, with the Yakimas, Walla Wallas, Umatillas, and Cayuses.

*Coeur d'Alene War (Spokane War)*—Washington, 1858, with the Coeur d'Alenes, Spokanes, Palouses, Yakimas, and Northern Paiutes.

*Paiute War (Pyramid Lake War)*—Nevada, 1860, with the Southern Paiutes.

*Apache Uprising*—Arizona and New Mexico, 1861–63.

*Navajo War*—New Mexico and Arizona, 1863–64.

*Santee Sioux Uprising*—Minnesota and North Dakota, 1862, Santee and Teton Sioux.

*Shoshoni War (Bear River Campaign)*—Utah and Idaho, 1863, with the Western Shoshonis.

*Cheyenne–Arapaho War*—Colorado and Kansas, 1864–65.

*Civil War*—In addition to the major Indian wars of the 1861 to 1865 period, whites recruited various Indian allies—Comanches, Kiowas, Mexican Kickapoos, Cherokees, Chickasaws, 18Choctaws, Creeks, Seminoles, Caddos, Wichitas, Osages, Shawnees, Delawares, Senecas, Quapaws—to fight in the western theater of the Civil War. Most Indians fought on the side of the Confederacy. But despite the number of tribes involved, Indian involvement in the Civil War was not extensive.

*War for the Bozeman Trail*—Wyoming and Montana, 1866–68, with the Teton Sioux, Northern Cheyennes, Northern Arapahos.

*Hancock's Campaign*—central plains, 1867, Southern Cheyennes, Southern Arapahos, and various Sioux.

*Sheridan's Campaign (Southern Plains War)*—southern and central plains, 1868–69, with Cheyennes, Arapahos, Sioux, Comanches, and Kiowas.

*Snake War*—Oregon and Idaho, 1866–68, with the Yahuskin and Walpapi bands of Northern Paiutes.

*Modoc War*—California, 1872–73.

*Red River War*—southern plains, 1874–75, with the Comanches, Kiowas, and Southern Cheyennes.

*Sioux War for the Black Hills*—South Dakota, Montana, and Wyoming, 1876–81, with the Sioux, Cheyennes, and Arapahos.

*Pursuit of the Nez Percé*—the Northwest, 1877.

*Bannock War*—Idaho and Oregon, 1878, Bannocks, Northern Paiutes, and Cayuses.

*Pursuit of the Northern Cheyennes*—central plains, 1878.

*Sheepeater War*—Idaho, 1879.

*Ute War*—Colorado, 1879.

*Apache Wars*—Southwest, 1872–1873, 1877–80 ("Victorio's Resistance"), 1881–86 ("Geronimo's Resistance").

At best, this listing serves as a set of signposts in what was really a half-century of chronic and barely differentiated white-Indian violence. The list is incomplete and, certainly, one-sided. The chapters that follow correspond to the list at many points, but they include some conflicts not accounted for here. It was a half century distinguished from the two decades that preceded it (1830–50) only in the pace and intensity of the conflict.

hawk and then hacked his face. Another Indian entered, pressed a rifle against Whitman's neck, and fired. When young John Sager leaped up to get a gun that was hanging on the wall, he, too, was shot—dead. Astoundingly, the preacher was still breathing as he was dragged outside. He would, however, expire soon. Narcissa, who had been in another room, ran to the window. A bullet hit either her arm or lodged in her breast. She apparently staggered upstairs to the attic bedroom, where (it is said) she prayed for the children—and the Indians.

More Indians attacked the mission's miller, teacher, tailor, and the three men who had been butchering beef, but other whites inside the house held off a final assault. At last, one Indian, an old friend of the Whitmans, warned those inside that the house was about to be put to the torch. He promised them safe conduct out. Narcissa, unconscious from loss of blood, was put on a wooden settee and carried out the door, whereupon the Cayuses opened fire. The missionary's wife, riddled by bullets, rolled off the settee. An Indian seized a fistful of her long, blonde hair and beat her across her face with a quirt.

Accounts vary as to the final death toll. Either 12 men in addition to Whitman were massacred, or 11 men and one woman in addition to Narcissa. Louise Sager, Helen Meek, and probably another sick girl died from lack of care. It is known that at least one brave raped some of the women and girls, which was highly unusual behavior; even in the most brutal Indian attacks, rape rarely played a part.

Six other settlers escaped, though one of them subsequently drowned in the Columbia River. Thirty-four children, eight women, and five men were captured and held as hostages until Peter Skene Ogden, of the Hudson's Bay Company, ransomed them for $500 worth of shirts, firearms, blankets and tobacco.

To be sure, the Cayuses had secured temporary vengeance on Whitman and the white community, but the Whitman massacre finally served to hasten the displacement of the Indians by white settlement. The famous mountain man Joe Meek (whose daughter died as a result of the raid) led a party of Oregon settlers back to Washington, D.C., to petition his cousin-in-law, President Polk, to make Oregon, at last, a territory of the United States, entitled to the full protection of the federal government.

Meek saw Polk on May 28, 1848; on August 14, the Oregon Territory was formed. Even more immediately, after Skene ransomed the white prisoners, a zealot named Colonel Cornelius Gilliam led 550 Oregon militiamen on a punitive expedition, without pausing to determine just whom he was going to punish. The Cayuses had by no means been unanimous in their support of Chief Tilokaikt, who had conducted the Whitman raid. But Gilliam made no attempt to separate the guilty from the innocent. Instead, he launched an attack on the first Indian camp he could find, killing more than a score of apparently peaceful Indians and suffering five casualties himself.

While Gilliam was running amok among the Cayuses, Joel Palmer, appointed by the territorial governor to head a three-man peace commission, was attempting to calm neighboring tribes, especially the Nez Percés and Palouses. In a manner both infantile and tragic, Gilliam stubbornly sabotaged all peace efforts. "Col Gilliam left the [peace] council in a huff," wrote one of the men on Palmer's commission, "and declared he has come to fight and fight he will." The next week 250 Palouse warriors attacked Gilliam and his men, who were "appropriating" cattle they assumed belonged to Cayuses. Ten militiamen were wounded. Gilliam died, not at the hands of the Indians, but through his own blundering clumsiness. He was trying to tether his horse, caught the rope on the trigger of his rifle, and was killed.

Despite their colonel's demise, the militia continued to stalk the Cayuses, though with little success. Their hostile meanderings managed to rouse the ire of Walla Wallas, Umatillas, Palouses, and Nez Percés. Fortunately, the militia retired before full-scale warfare erupted. But, as for the future of Indian-white relations in the Northwest, the die had been cast.

# CHAPTER 19

─────────────── ☐ ───────────────

# EARLY WARS IN THE FAR WEST

## (1850–1859)

## MARIPOSA WAR AND YUMA AND MOJAVE UPRISING

The so-called Diggers, bare-subsistence people who lived in California's gold country, were brutally swept aside by the ore-mad miners of 1848–49. Those who did not succumb to violence, died from disease, either contracted as a direct result of contact with whites or, indirectly, due to the many hardships of dispossesion and disruption whites wrought upon them. By the end of the Gold Rush era, the Digger population was reduced by two-thirds.

In 1850, however, the Miwoks and Yokuts, who lived in the foothills of the Sierra Nevada and the San Joaquin Valley, rose up against the miners who had invaded their country. Led by Chief Tenaya, warriors attacked prospectors and burned trading posts belonging to James D. Savage. In retaliation, Savage led a militia force, called the Mariposa Battalion (after Mariposa County), against them in 1851. Tenaya and approximately 350 warriors evaded Savage's first campaign. A second campaign resulted in the capture of the chief and many warriors, and the Mariposa War came to an end.

More formidable was resistance from the Yumas and Mojaves, who lived in southwestern Arizona and southeastern California. Although the Forty-Niners did not prospect in Yuma and Mojave country, many of them traveled through it along the Southern Overland Trail (later called the Butterfield Southern Route, when it was used by the Butterfield Overland Mail). The Yumas and Mojaves raided the travelers, an activity they had been engaged in since 1827, when the legendary guide and mountain man Jedediah Strong Smith first led a trapping expedition through the area.

The Yumas, in particular, controlled a strategic position known as Yuma Crossing, a natural ford across the Colorado River near the mouth of the Gila River. Partly in protest of the abuses they had suffered at the hands of invading whites, Antonio Garra, leader of a Yuma tribe called the Cupanga-kitoms, notified San Diego County authorities that his people would not pay the taxes assessed them. By November 1851, Garra, Chief Gerónimo of the New River Kamias (not to be confused with the far more famous Geronimo of the Chiricahua Apaches); Captain Alleche of Cahuillas; and Chief Fernando of the Chemehuevis called on Yuma leaders and laid plans for a revolution among them and the Mojaves and Yokuts of the San Joaquin Valley, as well as various tribes in Baja California.

On November 10, 1851, a party of sheep drovers, led by William J. Ankrim, with some 1,500 animals reached the Colorado. The next day, the party divided, five men continuing on with the sheep, the remainder making camp with a battle-hardened, one-armed veteran of the Mexican War, Lieutenant Thomas "Fighting Tom" Sweeny and his small command. Presently, about 100—and soon 400—Yumas surrounded the camp but retired when Sweeny threatened them with a 12-pounder howitzer. Another party of Indians attacked the drovers who had remained with the sheep, killing four of the five. On November 12, Sweeny's troops were augmented by the arrival of reinforcements. However, Camp Independence—as Sweeny's garrison was called—was continually besieged throughout November and into early December. Sweeny and a garrison now numbering about 100 men withdrew from the camp on December 6.

Elsewhere in California, the most serious Indian attack on whites occurred November 23 at Warner's Ranch. This raid prompted California whites to organize effective militia forces. Antonio Garra, however, was captured not by militiamen but by a band of Cahuilla

Indians, who refused to take part in the rebellion. He and other rebels (including a Mexican and an Anglo, in addition to Indians) were tried and executed. Next, army major H. P. Heintzelman mobilized 80 troopers and, on Christmas Day 1851, attacked and defeated a rebel Indian band near the Cahuilla villages in Coyote Canyon. Treaties were summarily concluded.

Along the Colorado, however, the Yumas maintained control until February 1852, when 500 soldiers arrived in San Diego, half of whom were sent to the Colorado, led by Major Heintzelman. California recruits were added to this number until Heintzelman commanded 400 troops, who were matched against about 500 less well armed and supplied Indian warriors. Operating out of Fort Yuma, on the California side of the Colorado, Heintzelman's men raided villages during March and April to relatively little effect in terms of warriors killed (about 16), but with considerable impact on the Indians' shelter and provisions. Sweeny was more successful in Baja California, where he burned two Cocopas villages on April 12, leading to the surrender of some 150 warriors, who agreed to help fight the Yumas.

In August 1852, a group of Mexican sheep drovers learned that the Yumas and neighboring tribes were planning an all-out attack on Fort Yuma at the end of the month. Heintzelman and Sweeny prepared for the onslaught, which, however, failed to materialize. Instead, the Yumas expressed their desire to talk peace. Sweeny arranged truce talks, and the Indians assembled near the Colorado. Rather than approaching the warriors peacefully, however, Heintzelman ordered three companies of regulars to fix bayonets and charge. The Indians promptly retreated and, once again, requested a parley, which was granted on August 27, when a ten-day truce was concluded. This stretched into several weeks of inconclusive peace, during which time the Indians evaded white attempts to pin them down to definitive terms. On September 23, Heintzelman lost patience and embarked on a renewed campaign. On September 29, he surprised a band of Yumas near present-day Blythe, California, who fled without offering battle. Finally, on October 2, 1852, the Yumas held a grand council with the army in which they asked for forgiveness and permanent peace terms.

## ROGUE RIVER AND YAKIMA WARS

The early Indian wars in Oregon Country—the area encompassed by the present states of Oregon and Washington—were considerably more serious than those in California. Following the Whitman Massacre of 1847 and the reprisal led by Cornelius Gilliam, Indian-white relations in the Northwest steadily deteriorated until, by 1854, according to the local Indian agent, hostility between whites and Indians had become a kind of reflex "almost impossible to realize, except from personal observation." Indians and whites fell into the habit of shooting each other on sight.

Fearful and outraged settlers called for aid from the regular army. General John Ellis Wool, who commanded the army's Department of the Pacific, was charged with policing the Indian situation in the Northwest. One of the few whites who favored reason and moderation in dealing with Indians, Wool soon faced not only an Indian "situation" but a white "situation" as well. The general not only refused to annihilate the Indians, as the settlers loudly demanded, he also repeatedly and publicly excoriated the citizenry of Oregon for their lust after Indian extermination. By the autumn of 1855, the army found itself caught between Indians and settlers.

Settlers called the Takelma and Tututni—who lived near the Oregon-California border—"Rogue" Indians because of their incorrigible habit of attacking travelers along the Siskiyou Trail. In August, drunken Rogues killed 10 or 11 miners along the Klamath River. In retaliation, whites killed about 25 Indians—though not the individuals who had actually killed the miners; they had fled. The Rogue River War was now under way, and in September 1855, the local violence was intensified by rumors of a developing war between Yakimas and whites east of the Cascades.

As whites began to menace all Indians, hostile or not, Captain Andrew Jackson Smith, commanding Fort Lane, just north of the present California-Oregon state line found it necessary to offer Indian men, women, and children the protection of the fort. Before Smith could admit all of the endangered Indians into this haven, however, a band of settlers raided a nearby camp, killing 23 Rogue Indians, including old men, women, and children. The next day, October 17, Indian war parties took revenge, killing 27 settlers in the Rogue Valley and burning the hamlet of Gallice Creek. With the bulk of General Wool's regulars off fighting the Yakimas, Walla Wallas, Umatillas, and Cayuses in what was now being called the Yakima War, Captain Smith could do little with his small garrison except try to keep it from being overrun.

The fuse that touched off the Yakima War had been lit in May 1855 when Isaac Stevens, the youthful and aggressive governor of Washington Territory, was hastily concluding treaties binding the Indians to relinquish their lands in exchange for life on a reservation. He promised the tribes east of the Cascades—the Nez Percé, Cayuse, Umatilla, Walla Walla, and Yakima—homes, schools, horses, livestock, and generous annuities. He also pledged that removal to the reservation would be delayed two or three years after they signed the treaty. The majority of the tribal representatives believed that resistance was ultimately useless and that Stevens's offer and pledge were the best treatment they were likely to secure at the hands of the whites. Accordingly, they signed.

A stubborn minority, including the Yakima chief Kamiakin, revered among the tribes of the Columbia River basin, refused to add their assent, for they believed they could not take Isaac Stevens at his word. Kamiakin and his fellow holdouts were proven right when, 12 days later, Governor Stevens summarily declared the Indian country open to white settlement.

Kamiakin was stalwart, but he was not stupid. Distressed by the growing population of miners in the Colville region, he forged an alliance that included the Walla Wallas, Umatillas, and Cayuses, as well as his own Yakimas. Even thus allied, he thought it best to bide his time, organize, and plan before confronting superior white forces. As often happened when Indians contemplated war, hot-headed young warriors acted independently and rashly. A group of five braves led by Kamiakin's nephew, Qualchin, attacked and killed six prospectors in mid-September 1855. A. J. Bolen, the local Indian agent, was sent to investigate the incident; he, too, was killed.

Although dismayed by the precipitate act, Kamiakin made the most of it, issuing a warning that a similar fate would befall all whites who ventured east of the Cascades. In October, a small force of regulars—84 men and a howitzer—under Major Granville O. Haller out of Fort Dalles (at the Dalles, on the south bank of the Columbia River) reconnoitered the east face of the mountains with the intention of coordinating a pincers attack against the Indians with 50 men from Fort Steilacoom (far to the north, just below Seattle) under Lieutenant W. A. Slaughter. Five hundred of Kamiakin's warriors ambushed Haller's column, killing five of their number, forcing the abandonment of the howitzer, and driving the remainder back to the fort. Fortunately for Slaughter's command, the lieutenant had been warned of the action and escaped the area by making a night march back to Puget Sound.

With few troops now in the area, local Indians raided a settlement along the White River above Seattle, killing nine people. The survivors of the attack fled in panic to Seattle, where they hastily erected a stockade in anticipation of a siege. At this point, Lieutenant Slaughter reappeared and engaged the Indians repeatedly until they gradually broke off the attack on Seattle. This action cost the lieutenant his life; he was shot through the heart one night when he made the mistake of approaching too near a campfire, thereby providing a clear silhouette target.

Governor Isaac Stevens, who was busy making treaties in Montana, received a greatly exaggerated account of the Rogue River and Yakima "wars" and immediately dashed through hostile territory back to Washington. He hastily organized a militia company of friendly Spokane Indians (the "Spokane Invincibles") and personally directed a white militia he called the Stevens Guards. Combined, the forces numbered only 50 men, who were understandably fearful of making their way to Fort Dalles. Fortunately for them, they encountered no hostiles, as Major Gabriel Rains, with a mixed force of regulars and volunteers, was keeping the Yakimas amused by his inept attempts to ambush them.

At about this time, Colonel James Kelley led a unit of militiamen into the Walla Walla homelands along the Walla Walla and Touchet rivers. Encountering the Walla Walla chief Peo-Peo-Mox-Mox, who had just burned Fort Walla Walla (an abandoned Hudson's Bay Company facility), Kelley agreed to a peace parley with him. Kelley stated his terms, and Peo-Peo-Mox-Mox sent one of his men back to the village, ostensibly to communicate the terms to the people there. As a precaution, Kelley held Peo-Peo-Mox-Mox and six other chiefs as voluntary hostages. Apparently, the message Peo-Peo-Mox-Mox had sent was an order to attack, for Kelley and his men soon found themselves charged by what was described as "hordes" of Indians. Kelley ordered Peo-Peo-Mox-Mox and the other hostages tied, the principal chief protesting, "No tie men; tie dogs and horses." According to Kelley's men, a struggle ensued between Peo-Peo-Mox-Mox and those who were trying to tie him down. The chief produced a dagger, whereupon a militiaman brained him with a gun barrel. After a four-day battle, the attacking Indians at last withdrew, and the triumphant Oregon volunteers brazenly displayed to fellow settlers the chief's ears and scalp ("a beauty," one who saw it reported, "the hair about eighteen inches long, all braided in with beads and eagle feathers").

Whatever feelings the trophy may have stirred in the hearts of Oregonians, it roused the Umatillas and Cayuses to rage and sent them raiding outlying white settlements. On February 23, raids along the lower Rogue destroyed more than 60 homes and left 31 settlers dead. One hundred thirty survivors of the raids took refuge near Gold Beach, where they were besieged for almost a month. Seaborne rescue efforts were repeatedly foiled by a heavy surf that prevented landing. Eventually, however, the Indians withdrew.

Seventy-one-year-old General Wool did not approve of "amateur" and "illegal" volunteer actions by Kelley and his ilk. Washington's governor Isaac Stevens and Oregon's governor George Curry persistently argued with him over the conduct of the war, pushing him to mount a winter campaign. "I have neither the resources of a

## SCALPING

No feature of Indian warfare is better known than scalping, or subject to more folklore and misunderstanding. Traditionally, whites have pointed to scalping as evidence of the Indian's incorrigible barbarity. Others have attributed to it special religious significance, claiming that the act of taking a scalp was intended to release the "spirit" or "soul" of the slain. Still others assert that scalping was unknown among Indian tribes before the arrival of Europeans.

Scalping was, in fact, practiced among North American Indians before the advent of the Europeans. Jacques Cartier reported it in 1535, Hernando de Soto in 1540, Tristán de Luna in 1559, and others subsequently. It was not, however, universal among Indians, and it spread generally from east to west with the migration of eastern tribes and contact with whites, who had adopted the custom from eastern Indians. Thus, while whites did not introduce scalping to the Indians of North America, they did contribute to the proliferation of the custom, both by pushing eastern Indians westward and by their own example.

There is no evidence that scalping was meant to be of spiritual benefit to the victim. Quite the contrary, the act of scalping was meant as an insult, and the scalp served as a battle trophy. Colonial and later authorities added a profit motive to the practice by offering scalp bounties, rewards paid for the scalps of "hostiles."

Different tribal groups practiced various methods of actually taking the scalp. Some tribes took the whole skin of the upper head, ears included; others removed only the crown. After Europeans introduced sharper, sturdier steel knives and hatchets among the Indians, many tribes practiced a faster method of scalping, which involved grasping the forelock, making a single gash in the front of the head, and popping the "scalp lock" trophy out with a sharp tug. As the "scalp lock" method was an abbreviated technique for taking scalps, so the practice of scalping seems to have originated in the first place as a substitute for decapitation. The scalp trophy stood for the head even as the head represented the entire person of the victim. In some tribes, particularly among certain Plains groups, decapitation persisted, and a severed head was considered a greater trophy than a scalp or scalp lock.

---

Territory nor a treasury of the United States at my command," Wool protested. "Still . . . I think I shall be able to bring the war to a close in a few months, provided the extermination of the Indians, which I do not approve of, is not determined on, and private war prevented, and the volunteers withdrawn from Walla Walla country." Accordingly, in the early spring of 1856, Wool released reinforcements to the beleagured Captain Smith at Fort Lane and assembled an additional 500 regulars under George H. Wright to march against Chief Kamiakin.

By the time relief was scheduled to arrive at Fort Lane, the Rogue River War seemed to be winding down. Weary of fighting, the Takelma and Tututni chiefs, known to the whites as Limpy, Old John, and George, agreed to surrender to Captain Smith at a place called Big Meadows. Apparently at the last minute, the chiefs thought better of it and instead mustered about 200 warriors for an attack on Smith's 50 dragoons and 30 infantrymen. The element of surprise was lost when two Indian women informed Smith of the planned attack. Outnumbered, the captain did the best he could, deploying his men on a hilltop that offered a good defensive position.

When the attack came, it was fierce and unremitting. The soldiers dug in the night after the first day of fighting. Morning revealed that 25 men had been killed or wounded, and by the afternoon of May 28, 1856, the Indians were massing for a final assault. At that moment, with the good timing of a bad adventure novel, the promised reinforcements arrived, commanded by Captain Christopher C. Augur. Overjoyed, Smith rallied his men for a downhill charge as Augur's infantry charged up from the rear. It was one of the few times that a classic military charge was effective against Indians, as Smith and Augur played out the cliché situation in which victory is snatched from the jaws of defeat. Indeed, the Rogues were so utterly routed that, within the month, all had surrendered and meekly submitted to life on a reservation.

In the meantime, Wright and his 500 regulars went on the hunt for hostiles. By this time, however, Chief Kamiakin had retreated eastward, and all Wright found were Indians peacefully fishing for salmon. Wright spoke with these Yakimas, who convinced him that they intended no further harm. When the colonel reported this to General Wool, the old commmander declared the Yakima War over. The general's declaration notwithstanding, a final engagement was yet to be fought—though the regular army would not participate. In July, as Wright was hearing talk of peace, militia colonel Benjamin Franklin Shaw and a force of volunteers engaged Walla Wallas and Cayuses in the Grande Ronde Valley and soundly defeated them, so that they, too, sued for peace. And Governor Stevens had opportunity to savor his own private victory, as the War Department at last agreed to the removal of old General Wool as commander of the Department of the Pacific, citing (to the governor's delight) his lack of initiative in "punishing" the Indians. In May 1857, Wool was replaced by Newman S. Clarke.

Though the Yakimas that Wright had encountered were peaceful enough, Kamiakin, now active east of the Columbia River, was not finished. During 1857 and 1858, he worked to foment a general uprising against settlers and gold seekers who were overrunning the country. The Coeur d'Alene and Spokane Indians became a ready audience for Kamiakin's exhortations as word spread among them that a white man's road—the Missouri-to-Columbia road—was to be built through their lands. The whites had not even bothered to inform the Indians, let alone negotiate a treaty to allow passage of the road, and the Indians were ready for a fight. The resulting hostilities would be called the Coeur d'Alene (or Spokane) War.

## COEUR D'ALENE WAR

Late in 1857, beset by sporadic raiding, a number of prospectors at Colville petitioned for the protection of U.S. troops. In May 1858, 158 regulars out of Fort Walla Walla and under the command of Lieutenant Colonel Edward J. Steptoe, were marching to the gold camp of Colville with the intention of impressing the Palouse, Spokane, and Coeur d'Alene Indians with the prowess of the U.S. Army. Steptoe, who was unaware of the Indians' rage over the proposed Missouri-to-Columbia road, thought he was marching out principally to satisfy a handful of distressed miners. The regulars carried inferior and obsolescent arms and were so poorly provided with pack animals that ammunition boxes were discarded in order to make room for baggage.

More than 1,000 warriors intercepted the column about 20 miles south of the present-day city of Spokane. They told him to go home, and while Steptoe had been foolish

enough to march out poorly prepared, he was not an idiot. He agreed to turn back. Through the rest of the day and into the next, the warriors followed the retreating regulars, taunting them with jeers. On May 17, the Indians suddenly attacked the column, killing two officers. Steptoe made for a defensive hilltop position, arranging the now burdensome baggage as breastworks and alotting from the niggardly supply only three rounds of ammunition per man. Steptoe brought his only major asset to bear, some howitzers, and managed to hold the warriors at bay during the remainder of the day.

But by nightfall it was clear to the regulars that they were in a very desperate situation. For his part, Steptoe resolved to fight to the finish, to go down in honor and a blaze of glory. His officers were less than enthusiastic, however, and successfully argued for the alternative of escape. Leaving their artillery and other supplies behind, the regulars crept in darkness down the hill, circled behind the dozing Indian camp, and slinked back to the safety of Fort Walla Walla.

Outraged by this humiliation, General Clarke ordered Colonel George Wright to conduct a vigorous campaign against the hostiles. "Make their punishment severe," the general admonished, "and persevere until the submission of all is complete." In a rare act of overconfident stupidity, the Indians gave Wright a perfect opportunity to carry out his orders. About 600 warriors met Wright's force (which was augmented by friendly Nez Percés) in the open on two battlefields—Spokane Plain (September 1, 1858) and Four Lakes (September 5)—suited to the kind of conventional warfare the army had been trained to fight. Wright not only commanded a superior force, but a better-armed one; each man had been issued brand-new long-range repeating rifles.

Deeming his decisive victories insufficient "punishment," Wright sent a Major Garnett and a detachment of men from Indian camp to Indian camp to demand delivery of those who had led the attack on Steptoe and his men. Fifteen braves were hanged, and others were made prisoner. Chief Kamiakin, although he had been injured by artillery fire in the Battle of Spokane Plain, escaped to British Canada. The chief's brother-in-law, Owhi, approaching Wright to make peace, was seized and forced to summon his son, the war leader Qualchin. Wright summarily hanged the young man in the presence of his father. In a subsequent escape attempt, Owhi was shot and killed. Thoroughly dispirited, the tribes of the Columbia Basin waged no more war, but resignedly marched to the reservations prescribed by Governor Stevens's treaties, which the Senate hurriedly ratified on March 8, 1859.

# CHAPTER 20

# ON THE EVE OF CIVIL WAR
## (1851–1860)

As the nation drifted toward civil war, the political and military focus concentrated on the East. But Indian–white conflict in the West continued and, in some cases, was intensified, as Indians took advantage of an increasingly unstable situation. In New Mexico and Arizona, two culturally related tribes, the Navajo and the Apache, went to war with the whites at the same time.

## THE NAVAJOS

The Navajos, as well as the Apaches, had consistently raided their white (as well as Indian) neighbors before 1861. Even more feared than the Apaches, the Navajos provoked an earlier and more focused military response. Having eluded the attempts of late eighteenth-century missionaries to Christianize them and the efforts of every authority thereafter to "pacify" them, the Navajos raided farms and settlements, including the Hopi village of Orai-bi in 1837, nearly wiping it out. Mexican troops were powerless against them, but Americans thought they were faring better when, in 1846, during the Mexican War, Lieutenant Colonel Alexander Doniphan encountered a party of 500 Navajos near Bear Springs, New Mexico, and negotiated what was intended as an enduring treaty of peace. Between the signing of that treaty and 1849, when Lieutenant Colonel John Washington negotiated another, the United States launched no fewer than five expeditions against marauding Navajo bands.

On July 19, 1851, Lieutenant Colonel Edwin V. Sumner assumed command for the Ninth Military Department, which was responsible for much of the Southwest. Sumner had earned the sobriquet "Bull-head" when (reportedly) a musket ball struck him in the head and bounced off. The nickname also described his obstinate determination to prevail. He pulled his troops out of the towns in which they had been garrisoned and set them to building a chain of forts, including Fort Defiance (on the Arizona side of the present New Mexico state line, southeast of Canyon de Chelly), which hampered Navajo raiding activity and brought the Indians in for peace talks.

The Navajos saw that the Americans were determined to make a stronger military committment to the region than the Mexicans had, so Sumner was presented with an opportunity to negotiate from a position of strength and even mutual respect. The situation appeared more promising because of the presence of New Mexico's excellent territorial governor, James S. Calhoun, who was as level headed as Sumner was bull headed. Whether willingly or not, Sumner stepped aside as Calhoun began negotiating a workable peace.

But such a peace was not to be. Before the treaty was consolidated, Calhoun became desperately ill. Forced to appoint John Greiner, acting superintendent of Indian affairs, to stand in for him, he left Santa Fe to return home, dying en route. Sumner had no patience with Greiner and summarily—as well as illegally—assumed the post of acting governor, overruling most of what Greiner did. Despite Sumner's interference, peace generally prevailed until the summer of 1852, when William Carr Lane arrived to serve as the new territorial governor. His attitude toward the Navajo, which was very different from Sumner's, could be put succinctly: "it is better to feed the Indians, than to fight them." Accordingly, Lane negotiated generous treaties with the Navajos and with the Jicarilla Apaches.

Besides the cruelty, rapacity, indifference, and incompetence with which the white government customarily treated the Indian, there was inconsistency. As in the case of Sumner and Calhoun/Greiner, military policy was frequently opposed to civil policy. Even worse, Washington's civil policy was often inconsistent with the policy of the territorial authorities and the Indian agents in the field. Governor Lane's treaty efforts failed because the United States Congress failed to vote the modest $20,000 appropriation needed to make good on the promise of the treaties. The Jicarillas, disappointed by the failure of their treaty, vigorously raided the countryside. Remarkably, though, the Navajos, except for an occasional raid, remained generally quiet for several years, even after a band of Utes asked them to unite in an alliance against the whites.

The spring of 1856 brought renewed Navajo raids followed by punitive expeditions against them, escalating tensions on the frontier over the next two years until, one spring day in 1858, some Navajos argued with soldiers from Fort Defiance who had been grazing their horses on land claimed by the Apache chief Manuelito. A few months later, Manuelito defiantly set his stock to graze on the land claimed by the fort for that purpose. Major Thomas H. Brooks, commander of Fort Defiance at the time, ordered his men to slaughter 60 of Manuelito's animals as a warning to clear off the disputed land.

In retaliation, on July 7, Navajos shot volleys of arrows into a soldiers' camp, and, on the twelfth, a Navajo warrior murdered Brooks's black servant, Jim. The major demanded that the Navajos produce the murderer and prepared a substantial punitive expedition made up of volunteers and Ute Indians in addition to regulars. General John Garland, who had replaced Sumner as commander of the Ninth Military Department, not only approved Brooks's plans but, deciding they were too important to be left to a major, dispatched Lieutenant Colonel Dixon S. Miles to Fort Defiance to put them into operation.

Miles summoned a Navajo leader named Sandoval to Fort Defiance, telling him that unless he produced Jim's murderer by 8 A.M. on September 9, the war would begin. On September 6, Sandoval informed Miles that the murderer had been captured and would be brought in. The next day, however, Sandoval told Miles that the prisoner had died of wounds sustained during capture. One day before the deadline, the Navajos brought the body into Fort Defiance. It was that of an 18 year old, whereas the murderer was known to have been at least 40; it was also a freshly killed corpse, whereas Sandoval said the man had been dead four days. A nameless war commenced with a punitive expedition to Canyon de Chelly, Arizona, where soldiers burned fields of corn and a peach orchard; they killed six Indians and appropriated 6,000 sheep. The army next conducted a raid on the

village of another Navajo leader, Zarcillos Largos, wounding him at least three times and capturing 40 warriors. The Navajos conducted retaliatory raids and even attacked Fort Defiance.

By the next month, the Ninth Military Department had yet another new commander, Colonel Benjamin Bonneville, the celebrated western explorer, who, unlike General Garland, was not hungry for war. Old and tired, he was nevertheless a good soldier and, accordingly, dispatched Lieutenant Colonel Miles and Major Electus Baccus to lead assaults against the Navajos. Little was actually accomplished—except for the burning of what Miles mistakenly believed to be Manuelito's village—but the show of force was enough to prompt the Indians to sue for peace.

In treating with the Navajos, it is apparent that white negotiators did not learn from the failure of previous treaties. As usual, the terms of peace were dictated in the kind of punitive spirit destined to leave one side feeling self-righteously complacent and the other side cheated, disgraced, and outraged. In this case there was no talk, no negotiating. The commissioners simply read to the assembled chiefs a unilaterally composed treaty that compelled the Navajos to accept all blame for everything that had occurred; that set the boundary of their land farther west and forbade the crossing of that boundary for any reason; that required payment of $14,000 damages for livestock losses; that required all white captives to be released; that asserted the United States' right to send soldiers through Navajo country at any time and to build forts there; and that proclaimed that the entire Navajo nation would be held culpable for the actions of any individual Navajo. Finally, if anticlimactically, the treaty made the Indians promise they would not harbor the murderer of poor Jim.

Remarkably, the Navajos tried to comply with the unreasonable "Bonneville Treaty," as it was called. Some of the $14,000 indemnity was paid—in the form of livestock—and some captives were returned. But by the middle of 1859, Ute Indians had begun raiding the Navajo, who retaliated and, while they were at it, stole some New Mexican sheep. New Mexico Indian superintendent James L. Collins ordered that the Navajo's "chastisement must be more severe, they must be well punished and thoroughly humbled." A new offensive was prepared and put into execution, which again brought the Indians to a peace conference. This time, however, the Navajo chief Huero refused to sign a treaty, claiming that such pieces of paper bound the Indians, not the whites. The treaty "conference" collapsed.

By the beginning of 1860, Navajo raids were almost a daily occurrence. Far from administering a severe chastisement, the army was powerless to stop the unremitting

## THE WESTERN FORT

Western forts ranged from the makeshift misery of hewn-log, mud-daubed huts—the worst was Fort Ruby, midway between Salt Lake City, Utah, and Carson City, Nevada—to well-built facilities boasting clean barracks and neat officers' quarters, as well as houses for married officers arranged along tree-lined avenues. Fort Shaw, called the "Queen of Montana forts," was an example of such refinement.

Contrary to twentieth-century Hollywood depictions of western forts, most forts built after 1860 lacked the outer wall or the log stockade. As one officer remarked, "It is better for troop morale to depend on vigilance and breechloaders for protection than to hide behind palisades." Generally, the only stockaded area in a regular army post was built inside the fort, to protect the goods of sutlers (private merchants licensed to travel with a regiment) from thieving soldiers. Indeed, most frontier forts were little more than a distinctively arranged group of buildings made of lumber, stone, or adobe, depending on the availability of local materials. Enlisted men's barracks faced officer's quarters across the dusty expanse of a parade ground. Depending on the size of the fort, other buildings included an administrative office, warehouse, workshops, corrals, the sutler's store, and "suds row," the home of noncommissioned officers married to post laundresses.

Unfortunately, the quality of most western forts, especially those on the far frontier, was closer to that of Fort Ruby than that of Fort Shaw. General Sherman frequently lamented their condition, calling the forts "mere collections of huts made of logs, adobes, or mere holes in the ground . . . [they] are about as much *forts* as prairie dog villages might be called *forts*." They were commonly overcrowded and dirty. An enlisted man usually had to share his bunk with another man—his "bunkie"—and while regulations prescribed a weekly bath, more often than not, the fort offered neither bathhouse nor sufficient surplus water for bathing. In 1878, one officer remarked that, during 30 years of service, he had never seen a bathhouse on *any* western post. In the excerpt below, Lieutenant Frederick E. Phelps described Fort Bayard, New Mexico, a typical frontier outpost:

18The locality was all that could be desired; the Post everything undesirable. Huts of logs and round stones, with flat dirt roofs that in summer leaked and brought down rivulets of liquid mud: in winter the hiding place of the tarantula and the centipede, and ceilings of "condemned" canvas; windows of four and six panes, swinging, door-like on hinges (the walls were not high enough to allow them to slide upward): low, dark and uncomfortable. Six hundred miles from the railroad . . . with nothing to eat but government rations—beef, bacon, coffee, sugar, rice, pepper, salt, and vinegar—together with a few cans of vegetables divided pro rata, old Fort Bayard was the "final jumping off place" sure enough.

Indian violence. On April 30, 1860, 1,000 warriors attacked Fort Defiance, which was ordered abandoned on May 4. By the end of 1860, the Santa Fe *Gazette* estimated that the Navajos had killed 300 people during the first six months of the year and had destroyed or stolen property worth $1.5 million. Colonel Thomas T. Fauntleroy was sent to replace Bonneville, but he was ordered to concentrate his undermanned forces against the Comanches and Kiowas, who were raiding mail routes in Texas. The outraged governor of New Mexico territory called for a volunteer force. Before such a force could be assembled, Fauntleroy received reinforcements and announced that he would launch a full-scale expedition against the Navajos.

More than 500 regulars were joined by 470 civilian volunteers in an expedition led by one of the regular army's more competant officers, Colonel Edward R. S. Canby. While the regulars killed few Navajos, the volunteers burned enough crops and captured enough cattle to prompt the Indians, yet again, to seek peace. The Canby treaty was signed by 54 Navajo leaders—more than had signed any previous document—which gave the army reason to hope that this peace, at long last, would be an enduring one. Unfortunately, the Navajos were prepared to sign anything in order to gain some respite from the destruction of their crops and the appropriation of their cattle. The peace turned out to be little more than a tenuous truce. The so-called Navajo War spanned 1863–64, but nameless warfare actually continued through 1866, as the army attempted to force the Navajos onto a singularly unlivable reservation called the Bosque Redondo.

Army policy in its war against the Indian was offensive rather than defensive. Soldiers spent most of their time in the field, in pursuit of bands of warriors. The fort, therefore, was principally a place of refuge and supply. There was a prescribed routine for life on the fort: reveille at 5:30, first drill at 6:15, "fatigue duty" (routine maintenance, repair, woodcutting, etc.) commenced at 7:30, guard mount at 8:30, afternoon fatigue began at 1:00, afternoon drill at 4:30, and taps was sounded at 8:15. Drilling did not mean combat training or target practice, which, due largely to the cost of ammunition, was rare. Rather, the object of drill was strictly to maintain order and discipline.

Life on the frontier fort did afford some time for relaxation, which included card playing and gambling (against regulations, of course), singing, and story swapping. At some larger forts, traveling minstrel shows entertained on occasion, and if the fort were a regimental headquarters, the regimental band performed for an hour each evening. Sometimes, soldiers staged amateur theatricals. Reading was also popular—for those soldiers who could read—and some forts even had libraries (the one at Fort Sully, on the Cheyenne River in present-day South Dakota, boasted 800 volumes). Sutlers set up their stores on the post and offered the kind of "delicacies" that were not part of government-issue rations: tobacco, canned fruit and meat, whiskey, and beer.

Drinking was a popular diversion, as well as the cause of fights and disease; in the 1880s, no fewer than 4 percent of American soldiers were hospitalized as alcoholics. When the sale of alcohol was prohibited on forts in 1881, saloons opened up outside post property, and, if anything, the rate of alcohol consumption and alcoholism increased.

On larger posts, the sutler's store also offered backroom lounge space, separately for officers and enlisted men. The officers' facility functioned rather like the present-day officers' club, providing a place to converse and to read the newspapers, while the enlisted men's room was frequently a place of illicit gambling. The sutler also served as the soldier's banker—or, more accurately, loan shark.

Finally, there were women. The saloons (the men called them "hog ranches") that sprouted in the vicinity of larger posts usually purveyed prostitution in addition to liquor, and by the 1880s, about 8 percent of the soldiers were being treated for venereal disease. Some commanders even turned a blind eye to prostitution within the fort itself. The army allowed one on-post laundress for every nineteen and one-half men in the garrison. Often, laundresses were nothing more or less than women who were paid to do the soldiers' wash. Often, they married noncommissioned officers. But some were also prostitutes, and one officer, Colonel R. I. Dodge, declared in 1876: "Get rid of them! It is an absurd continuation of a custom which grew out of other wants of the men of the company than washing clothes." General Tasker Bliss disgustedly observed that army surgeons had "nothing to do but confine laundresses and treat the clap."

## THE SIOUX

Up north, on the central and northern plains, 40 years of warfare were about to begin because of an arrow shot into the hindquarters of a hapless beast of burden. On August 18, 1854, High Forehead, a Brulé Sioux, shot an arrow into the flank of an ox belonging to a wagon train passing through the North Platte valley of Wyoming, near Fort Laramie. The Mormon owner of the ox put in a complaint at the fort, and the next day, Lieutenant John L. Grattan, eager to show the Sioux what the U.S. Army could do, was dispatched to the Indian camp of Chief Brave Bear (sometimes translated as Conquering Bear) with 27 privates and two noncoms, together with a 12-pounder howitzer and a 12-pound mountain gun. When a 45-minute parley resulted in High Forehead's refusal to give himself up, Grattan rashly opened fire on the village, fatally wounding Brave Bear.

Unfortunately for the thoughtless lieutenant and his command, the two artillery pieces had been set too high to do any more damage. The next shots caused little harm, but incited the fury of the Brulé warriors, who, joined by some Oglala Sioux, turned against Grattan's small band. One trooper survived long enough to return to Fort Laramie, where he later died of his wounds. Seizing upon the "Grattan Massacre" as sufficient cause, Secretary of War Jefferson Davis ordered General William S. Harney to "punish" the Brulé. Leading 600 men out of Fort Kearny, Nebraska, Harney was heard to declare, "By God, I'm for battle—no peace."

Not that what happened could be called a battle. Chief Little Thunder, successor to Brave Bear, gathered his band of 250 about him and simply waited for Harney's approach. For, although his camp harbored those who had participated in the Grattan massacre, he considered himself peaceful. He gave an old fur trapper named Louis Vasquez a message to deliver to Harney. The general could have peace or war, whichever he wished; apparently Little Thunder had intended the proffered choice as rhetorical, assuming that any rational man would want peace. Little Thunder was tragically mistaken. Harney chose war.

On September 3, 1855, Harney's infantry approached from the south, and his two companies of dragoons and two mounted infantry companies, under Colonel Philip St. George Cooke, moved in from the north. Under a flag of truce, Little Thunder approached Cooke. Cooke did not want to talk. Instead, he offered a stark ultimatum: Give up those responsible for the Grattan massacre or die. The chief and his party rushed back to their people. Neither Harney nor Cooke waited for any further reply. They opened fire and charged. A rout followed amid murderous fire, and the mounted troops, too far advanced to hear Harney's bugler sound recall, mercilessly cut down survivors from the initial onslaught. By the time it was over, 85 Indians had perished and 70 women and children were taken captive. The Sioux would learn to call Harney "The Butcher."

Harney continued his march into the heart of Sioux country, the Black Hills, but no Indians offered a fight. At Fort Pierre, a former fur-trading post, he held a peace conference with chiefs of the Teton Sioux, who signed a peace treaty that actually endured for a number of years.

## THE CHEYENNES

In contrast to the Apaches, Navajos, and the Sioux, the Cheyennes, through the early 1850s, were regarded as largely compliant. This perception changed as they came into more frequent contact with whites in the form of army surveyors laying out roads. Although the Cheyennes had agreed in an 1851 treaty not to raid the Pawnees (their traditional enemies) in the vicinity of Fort Kearny, by the mid-1850s, many of their young warriors began doing just that. The army saw this activity as a danger to the emigrant road. In 1856, General Harney issued a stern warning to the Cheyennes as well as the Arapahos: Stop the raids or he would "sweep them from the face of the earth." In reality, he could do little to back up his threat, since the slavery issue was causing widespread civil violence throughout "Bleeding Kansas" on the eve of the Civil War.

In April 1856, a small group of Cheyennes came to the Upper Platte Bridge to trade with local whites. They fell into an argument over the ownership of a horse, whereupon Captain Henry Heth attempted to arrest three Indians. In a scuffle, one was killed; the other two were taken to prison. The nearby Cheyennes, fearing an outbreak against themselves, abandoned their lodges and retreated to the Black Hills, killing a trapper along the way. Two months later, Cheyennes in pursuit of Pawnees killed a white emigrant near Fort Kearny. They made matters worse by then defiantly riding into the fort, where Captain Henry W. Wharton attempted to arrest them, but they escaped. In August, another Cheyenne party, also in search of Pawnees, stopped a mail coach to beg for tobacco. The driver, aware of the earlier incidents and traveling in country aflame with violence and the rumor of violence, panicked, drew his revolver, but took an arrow in the arm before he could shoot. Thus wounded, he made for Fort Kearny.

Wharton immediately dispatched Captain George H. Stewart and a company and a half of the First Cavalry to find the Cheyennes. Discovering a camp of about eighty Indians, the troopers attacked, killing ten, wounding another ten, and "appropriating" an assortment of goods and livestock.

This action was sufficient to trigger the usual retaliatory raids along the Platte Road. Secretary of War Davis issued the customary order for a campaign of punishment, which was set for the spring of 1857. During late May and June, Bull-head Sumner patrolled the Cheyenne country of Nebraska and western Kansas but found no Indians to fight. It was not until July 29, 1857, that scouts reported a band of 300 Cheyennes along the Solomon River. The cavalrymen and the Indians were pretty equally matched. Since Indians rarely fought unless they enjoyed substantially superior numbers, Sumner expected them to scatter, and he was prepared to pursue. But, this time, things were different. These warriors had washed their hands in a magic lake whose waters, according to a medicine man, would protect them from white bullets.

About to attack, Bull-head Sumner gave an unusual order: "Sling—carbine. Draw—saber. Gallop—march! *Charge!*" Seeing the drawn sabers, the Indians broke and ran—the water's magic was against bullets, not sabers. Sumner's troops pursued the fleeing band for seven miles.

In September, Sumner was ordered to break off his Cheyenne campaign to join an expedition to Utah. The Indians conducted a few retaliatory raids but the fight had largely gone out of them, and, after brooding on the situation during the winter of 1857–58, the Cheyennes generally sued for peace during the summer of 1858. They remained relatively peaceful until Colonel John M. Chivington brutally provoked war with them in 1864.

## SUPERIORITY OF ARMS: WEAPONS OF THE BLUECOATS

Much has rightly been made of the inadequacy of the U.S. Army in the West. It was undermanned, poorly trained, badly supplied, and miserably paid. Until 1873, when the frontier forces received their first standardized issue of arms, soldiers were indifferently furnished with a variety of firearms, often obsolete muzzle-loading muskets of Mexican War vintage. During and immediately after the Civil War, western troops were usually given leftover weapons, a grab bag of small arms, some repeating rifles (fast but prone to jam or misfire), and muskets that had been converted from muzzle loaders to breech loaders. After testing 108 shoulder arms, the Army issued Springfield rifles to infantrymen in 1873 and was sufficiently pleased with the weapon to maintain it as the standard until 1892. Although this rifle was highly dependable, not all Indian fighters were happy with it. An efficient breech loader, the Springfield rifle was nevertheless a single-shot weapon that could not match for speed the seven-shot Spencer rifle, which many troops had carried during the later 1860s. The Springfield was, however, more accurate, and its 3,500-yard range was about twice that of the Spencer. This was of great significance because it also outdistanced Indian weapons, bows and arrows as well as rifles, sometimes making it difficult or impossible for Indians to make effective attacks.

Cavalrymen were issued the Springfield carbine, a shorter and lighter version of the rifle, meant to be carried easily by mounted troops. The shorter barrel did exact a price in accuracy and range, however, as the carbine used a 55-grain cartridge while the rifle used a 70-grain.

To infantrymen and cavalry personnel alike, the Army issued Colt .45-caliber revolvers, a weapon so popular that it became virtually synonymous with *handgun* in the West. The 1873 standard arms issue also included 1860-model sabers for cavalry troops. This light weapon was largely worthless in combat against Indians, who seldom got close enough for swordplay, and its function was principally ceremonial. The notable exception to this was Edwin V. "Bull-head" Sumner's engagement against Cheyennes along the Solomon River on July 29, 1857 (page 180).

Large columns also hauled Gatling guns and 12-pounder howitzers. The Gatling gun, a ten-barrel, crank-revolved weapon capable of firing (in theory) 400 shots a minute, was a formidable precursor of the twentieth-century machine gun. However, its black-powder ammunition frequently fouled the barrels, and the gun could rarely be counted on for anything approaching its full specification of 400 rounds a minute. The 12-pounder was cumbersome to haul, and was always the first piece of equipment abandoned when it came time for a fast getaway. But it could lob two shells a minute, raise a lot of dirt, and kill anything it happened to hit. Frontier artillery troops were not known for their accuracy, but howitzers often served to drive off—or frighten off—attacks even by superior numbers of Indians.

## THE PAIUTE WAR

The last significant Indian-white conflict before the Civil War was between Nevada miners and the Southern Paiutes. Williams Station was one of two trading posts in the Carson Valley along the California Trail. The station served the Central Overland Mail and the Pony Express and was a vital link to the outside world for the miners of Carson City, Virginia City, Gold Hill, and Genoa. Early in May, traders at Williams Station abducted and raped two Indian girls. The Southern Paiutes, already resentful of white intrusion into their land, were moved to revenge. A party of warriors rode to the station, rescued the two girls, then burned the station and killed five whites.

Word of the "massacre" reached Virginia City's Wells Fargo office on May 8. Anticipating a major Indian attack, a large and rowdy "army" of miners—perhaps as many as 2,000 men—immediately assembled. The miners telegraphed the governor of California asking for arms. As quickly as they had banded together, the miner army, wholly undisciplined and disorganized, dissolved. A miner named Henry Meredith organized and armed a new force drawn from the Nevada mining towns. At Dayton, Nevada, Meredith's men were joined by Major William M. Ormsby and a group from Carson City. Ormsby now assumed command of the combined force of 105 men, which made its way to Pyramid Lake in Paiute country—not merely to defend the mining towns, but to exact revenge.

The Paiute chief Numaga had hoped to avoid further

violence, but he realized that the miners would be satis-fied with nothing less than blood. He set up an ambush at the Big Bend of the Truckee River Valley. In the narrow pass, about four in the afternoon of May 12, the trap was sprung. It was deadly effective. The Paiutes' poison-tipped arrows accounted for some 46 fatalities—almost half the force that had been sent against them.

The Comstock country was thrown into a panic, but the governor of California responded with troops under the command of Colonel Jack Hays (or Hayes), a former Texas Ranger. A small body of U.S. Infantry regulars out of the Presidio at San Francisco, together with some local volunteer groups, brought the force to about 800 men, who headed toward the Truckee at the end of May. The force encountered a few Paiutes near the site of the original ambush and, after a skirmish, pursued the Indians to Pinnacle Mountain, killing about 25 warriors. The short-lived Paiute War was over, but to ensure the peace and keep the California Trail open, the U.S. Army established Fort Churchill near Buckland Station.

Peace, of course, was always an ephemeral condition in the West. In 1860 it was a forlorn hope. There would be no peace, not in the West or the East; not for red man or for white. The North and the South were going to war.

# CHAPTER 21

# BLUE, GRAY, AND RED
## The Apache Uprising and Navajo War (1861–1864)

With the outbreak of the Civil War, Unionists in the West feared that the Confederates would actively cajole or purchase Indian allies in the struggle. In fact, the Confederacy did find some recruits among the Caddos, Wichitas, Osages, Shawnees, Delawares, Senecas, and Quapaws. Both the North and the South recruited some troops from tribes who had been removed to Indian Territory, including the Cherokees, Chickasaws, Choctaws, Creeks, and Seminoles. The Cherokee leader Stand Watie became a Confederate general of considerable tenacity; his command was the last Rebel unit to lay down arms, fully a month after Appomattox. It is also true that, for a time, the Confederates armed the Comanches and Kiowas on the southern plains.

For the most part, however, Indian-white conflict from 1861 to 1865 had little to do directly with the white man's war against himself except—and this was, indeed, very significant—insofar as the Civil War siphoned off troops from the West and, therefore, provided an opportunity for Indians to conduct raids against settlers without the intervention of the regular army. Not all Indian-fighting troops were withdrawn from the West, however. In a number of cases, regiments raised in the western states for the purpose of fighting in the eastern theater of the Civil War were diverted to do battle with Indians. In this indirect, but important way, Indian warfare affected the Civil War.

## COCHISE

Cochise, chief of the Chiricahua Apaches, was taller than the average Apache, a handsome man, except that his body had been scarred by buckshot. His father, also a Chiricahua chief, had led the band in horse-stealing raids against the Mexicans, but Cochise was inclined to like the Americans. He struck a profitable contract with the Butterfield Overland Mail to supply wood to the station at Apache Pass and lived in peace and accommodation with the whites for some years. But, almost inevitably, the tensions of racial hatred simmered and then boiled over.

About 12 miles from Fort Buchanan, Arizona, lived a thoroughly disreputable rancher named John Ward. His common-law wife, Jesusa Martinez, had been captured by Pinal Apaches and, during her captivity, had conceived and borne a son. She was subsequently released, but late in 1860, a Pinal band raided Ward's place and recaptured the child, rustling some cattle as well. Ward, who had been too drunk at the time of the raid to offer much resistance or even to identify the raiders correctly, went to Fort Buchanan to tell its commander, Lieutenant Colonel Pitcairn Morrison, that Chiricahua Apaches, led by Cochise, had taken his stepson and his cattle. Morrison did not, however, spring into action. Indeed, no one knows why he let three months pass before he dispatched Second Lieutenant George N. Bascom with 60 men to recover the boy and the stock. Bascom set up camp in Apache Pass on February 4, 1861, and Cochise, together with his brother, two nephews, and a woman and child, came voluntarily to talk with him. (Some sources say that Cochise was accompanied by six or seven others.)

Bascom was all bluster and demanded the return of Ward's cattle and stepson. When Cochise protested his innocence, Bascom announced that he and his party would be held captive until the boy and property were returned. Cochise drew his knife, slit the canvas of the conference tent, and escaped. The other five hostages remained behind. (Some sources say that one warrior followed his chief out the hole, but was clubbed by one soldier and lethally bayonetted by another.)

Seething with rage, Cochise gathered his warriors and raided the Butterfield station, killing one employee and taking another, James F. Wallace, prisoner. When a small wagon train passed by the station, Cochise captured it, along with eight Mexicans and two Americans who had been riding with it. The Mexicans he ordered bound to the wagon wheels and burned alive. The Americans—the two from the wagon train and the station employee—he offered to exchange for the captives Bascom held.

Bascom refused—though he realized that the position of his camp, in the middle of Apache Pass, was thoroughly vulnerable to attack by the Chiricahuas who now surrounded him. He dispatched runners who sneaked through the Indian lines and summoned reinforcements from Fort Buchanan. Seventy dragoons under Lieutenant Isaiah N. Moore arrived on February 14, only to find that Cochise and his braves had vanished. The soldiers scouted the area and found the bodies of the three American hostages, pierced by lances and mutilated. Bascom took his own prisoners, as he explained in his official report, "to the grave of [the] murdered men, explained through the interpreter what had taken place, and my intentions, and bound them securely hand and foot, and hung them to the nearest trees."

Cochise responded with a vow to exterminate all Americans in Arizona Territory. The drunken rancher's false accusation could not have come at a worse time, and for that matter, Bascom could not have handled the incident more ineptly. With the country on the brink of civil war and western garrisons about to be reduced as a result, warfare with the Apaches was bound to be bloody and protracted. While the army defined the "Apache Uprising" as spanning 1861–63, Apache-white violence would actually endure for a quarter of a century. (As for Ward's stepson, he was held captive by the Pinal Apaches for about four years, when he gained his release. Calling himself Mickey Free, he became an army scout, tracker, and interpreter.)

## CIVIL WAR IN THE SOUTHWEST

The outbreak of the Civil War wreaked havoc on the U.S. Army, especially its officer corps. In the West, 313 officers, one-third of the army's officer corps, left western commands to take up arms on the side of the Confederacy. "We are practically an army without officers," one federal soldier complained. In the Southwest, Confederate Lieutenant Colonel John Robert Baylor took advantage of the Union's weakened position to sweep through the southern New Mexico Territory, from the Rio Grande to California. Fort Bliss in El Paso fell to him in July 1862, and he marched into the Mesilla valley of New Mexico, taking Fort Fillmore and Fort Stanton, whereupon Baylor proclaimed the Confederate Territory of Arizona (which included all of present-day Arizona and New Mexico south of the thirty-fourth parallel) and named himself governor. Baylor's efforts were followed during the winter of 1861–62 by a larger Confederate invasion led by General Henry Hopkins Sibley, whose mission was the capture of all of New Mexico, the seizure of the Colorado silver mines, and possibly the occupation of Southern California. Sibley moved up the Rio Grande, intent on taking Fort Union, at the time the best-provisioned Union post in the Southwest.

Fort Union was the headquarters of Colonel Edward R. S. Canby, commander of the Department of New Mexico under whom Sibley—his brother-in-law—had served as a major just a few months before. As Sibley's invaders threatened, Canby had his hands full with Navajo raids in New Mexico and unauthorized, highly provocative New Mexican counterraids. Indeed, the people he was trying to protect, the citizens of New Mexico, repeatedly provoked the Navajos by raiding them and taking captives who were subsequently sold as slaves. In retaliation, the Navajos, joined by Mescalero Apaches, Utes, Comanches, and Kiowas, ravaged the countryside.

Learning that the majority of New Mexicans were loyal to the Union, Canby hastily sought to organize them as the First and Second Regiments of New Mexican Volunteers. This gesture, however, failed to bring the volunteers under Canby's control. Lieutenant Colonel Manuel Chaves, second in command of the Second Regiment, was placed in charge of Fort Fauntleroy (soon renamed Fort Lyon because Colonel Fauntleroy defected to the Confederacy) at Ojo del Oso on August 9, 1861, with a detachment of 210 officers and men. As the Canby treaty of February 1861 promised, Chaves's men began distributing rations to the Navajos in August and September. In addition they provided alcohol and set up gambling. A series of horse races were run, with a featured event between Chief Manuelito on a Navajo pony and an army lieutenant on a quarter horse. Many bets were laid.

Early in the race it was apparent that Manuelito had lost control of his mount, which soon ran off the track. The horse's reins and bridle, the Indians claimed, had been slashed with a knife. Despite Indian protests, the "judges"—all soldiers of the Second New Mexican Regiment—declared the quarter horse the winner. The soldiers formed a victory parade into the fort, as the angered Navajos stormed after them, only to have the gates shut in their faces. One Navajo tried to force his way in. A sentinal shot and killed him. Then Colonel Chaves turned his troops on the 500 or so Navajos gathered outside the fort. One New Mexican, Captain Nicholas Hodt, disgusted by what was happening, depicted the carnage in a memorandum read into the Congressional Record:

The Navahos, squaws, and children ran in all directions and were shot and bayoneted. I succeeded in forming about twenty men. . . . I then marched out to the east side of the post; there I saw a soldier murdering two little children and a woman. I halloed immediately to the soldier to stop. He looked up, but did not obey my order. . . . Meanwhile the colonel had given orders to the officer of the day to have the artillery brought out to open upon the Indians. The sergeant in charge of the mountain howitzers pretended not to understand the order given, for he considered it an unlawful order; but being cursed by the officer of the day, and threatened, he had to execute the order or else get himself in trouble.

Thirty or 40 Navajos were killed. The rest fled and began a campaign of raiding. After relieving Chaves and arresting him, Canby ordered John Ward, the Indian agent, to attempt to persuade the Indians to gather at Cubero, where they could be given the "protection" of the government during the impending Confederate invasion. Canby's primary aim, of course, was to concentrate the Indians where they could be watched and kept from alliances with Rebel forces. Canby dispatched the celebrated Kit Carson, commander of the First New Mexico Volunteer Cavalry, to move vigorously against any Navajos who persisted in raiding. He was ordered to take no prisoners.

On the Confederate side, Baylor was having his own problems with the Indians. While his troops were suffering through an epidemic of smallpox, Chiricahua and Mimbreño Apaches, convinced that the Union soldiers had permanently withdrawn from the region, intensified their raids in the new Confederate territory. Blue-clad or gray, the white men who had invaded their country were all fair game. Confederate authorities organized a company of Arizona Rangers to punish the Indians. This unit was soon augmented by a volunteer group calling itself the Arizona Guards. Neither was effective at halting the raids.

If soldiers ostensibly under Canby's command had created an outrage at Fort Faunteleroy/Lyon, Baylor soon proved that the Confederates could be equally vicious. Angered by the poor showing of the Arizona Guards, Baylor sent their commander a letter announcing that "The Congress of the Confederate States has passed a law declaring extermination of all hostile Indians. You will therefore use all means to persuade the Apaches or any tribe to come in for the purpose of making peace,

*Manuelito, an important Navajo chief, was cheated in a horse race against a U.S. Army lieutenant at Fort Fauntleroy (Fort Lyon), New Mexico. The resulting dispute became a massacre and then a war. (National Archives and Records Administration.)*

and when you get them together, kill all the grown Indians and take the children prisoners and sell them to defray the expense of killing the Indians.'' It was so ghastly a document that it soon reached the public, causing great embarrassment to the Confederacy and, of course, setting back southern efforts to win allies among the tribes.

Deep in the heart of Apache country, Tucson, Arizona, came into existence in the decade before the Civil War as a mining boom town and depended for its survival on a garrison of federal troops. When these men were withdrawn at the outbreak of the war, the town and its strongly pro-Confederate miners were virtually besieged by raiding Apache bands. Late in January 1862, General Sibley sent a small detachment of 54 men under Captain Sherod Hunter to Tuscon, which greeted them as saviors.

Sibley, in the meantime, turned his attention not to the Indians, but to his brother-in-law, Colonel Canby, engaging his forces at Valverde, New Mexico, on February 21, 1862. Victorious there, Sibley next took Santa Fe and pressed on toward Fort Union. En route, at La Glorietta Pass, the Confederates encountered a Union force under the command of Colonel John Slough. On March 26–28, in a battle sometimes called "the Gettysburg of the West," Slough's regulars, reinforced by Colorado volunteers rushed to the scene by Governor William Gilpin, defeated the Confederates. Major John M. Chivington—soon to become infamous for his unbridled policy of Indian extermination—led a flanking party that destroyed the Confederates' supply train. Sibley's invaders, who had seemed unstoppable, were forced to retreat from New Mexico.

Simultaneously with the victories of Slough and Chivington, Colonel James Henry Carleton was sweeping through the Southwest with his "California Column" of Union regulars newly authorized by the War Department. They pushed the Confederates out of Arizona—fighting the westernmost battle of the Civil War at Picacho Peak on April 15, 1862—and southern New Mexico. By the end of 1862 the short-lived Confederate Territory of Arizona was no more, and both Arizona and New Mexico were securely in Union hands.

But Carleton's work was hardly finished. With the Rebels out of the way, he turned his attention to the raiding Apaches and Navajos. A New Englander, born in Lubec, Maine, in 1814, James Henry Carleton first saw action as a militiaman in 1838, during the so-called Lumberjack War between his home state and New Brunswick, Canada. Discharged from the militia in 1839, he collected letters of recommendation from his commanding officers, passed a test in Washington, D.C., and was commissioned a second lieutenant of dragoons. He served in several western posts and fought in the Battle of Buena Vista during the Mexican War.

He next turned his attention to the Mescalero and Jicarillo Apaches as well as Navajos, becoming a disciple of total warfare against the Indians and advocating a scorched earth policy. To hone his skills, he went east briefly in 1856, to Philadelphia, where he studied European cavalry methods—including those of the Cossacks. But, unlike so many officers of the regular army, Carleton was not a slavish student of European warfare. He carefully studied Indian tactics and battle traditions, and he learned from them. To the degree that it was possible,

he trained his army to fight like Indians. "The troops," he told a subordinate in 1863,

must be kept after the Indians, not in big bodies, with military noises and smokes, and the gleam of arms by day, and fires, and talk, and comfortable sleeps by night; but in small parties moving stealthily to their haunts and lying patiently in wait for them; or by following their tracks day after day with a fixedness of purpose that never gives up. . . . If a hunter goes after deer, he tries all sorts of wiles to get within gunshot of it. An Indian is a more watchful and a more wary animal than a deer. He must be hunted with skill; he cannot be blundered upon; nor will he allow his pursuers to come upon him when he knows it, unless he is stronger.

In 1858, Carleton took 700 recruits to California, where he served under his longtime friend, Edwin V. Sumner. With the outbreak of the Civil War, Major Carleton was promoted to colonel and given command of a volunteer outfit, the First California Regiment of Infantry, which, mustered into the federal army, became known as the California Column.

## APACHE UPRISING

Ever since the "Bascom Affair," the false arrest of Cochise and the killing and reprisals that followed it, settlements and trade routes between El Paso and Tucson had felt the wrath not only of Cochise's band of Apaches, but those led by his older ally, the Mimbreño Apache chief Mangas Coloradas. The federal abandonment of Forts Buchanan, Breckinridge, Stanton, and Fillmore in the face of the Confederate invasion of New Mexico was interpreted by the Apaches as a sign that the "bluecoats" feared *them*. Beginning in July 1861, the Mescaleros vigorously raided the subsistence herds of local settlers. The Indians were not afraid, in July 1862, when they saw more bluecoats approaching from the west. The soldiers had run before; they would run again. The Apaches were ready to fight.

What they saw approaching was the van of Carleton's California Column—119 infantrymen and seven cavalrymen equipped with two howitzers—led by Captain Thomas L. Roberts. On July 15, they marched into Apache Pass and were promptly ambushed by 700 warriors under Cochise. As on previous occassions, the soldiers were reprieved by their howitzers, and Roberts sent six of the cavalrymen back to warn the wagon train that was following him. Apaches pursued the messengers, hitting the horse of one. Private John Teal used the carcass of his mount as a breastwork and fired rapidly with his modern breach-loading carbine. These Apaches were apparently familiar only with the old muzzle loaders and, instead of attacking Teal, merely circled his position, taking an occasional potshot. The private returned fire, hitting what he called "a prominent Indian," after which the others retreated.

That "prominent Indian" proved to be none other than Mangas Coloradas, who made a tall target. His men took him to Mexico, where they forced a physician in Sonora to extract the bullet, and the chief recovered, resuming his raids against settlers and miners and skirmishing with Carleton's troops. For some reason, on January 17, 1863, Mangas Coloradas agreed to meet with Captain E. D. Shirland, who was serving under Brigadier General Joseph R. West, commander of the southern sector of the Department of New Mexico. Despite his flag of truce, the chief was seized and delivered to West's camp.

Two stories relate the death of Mangas Coloradas under West's jurisdiction. The official story was that West promised the Apache chief that he would not be executed because he had come voluntarily, but that he would be imprisoned for life. Any attempt to escape, he was warned, would mean death. According to the official report, he made three escape attempts and was shot and killed on the third. An American prospector named Connor, who was present at West's camp, told a different story. According to the prospector, West told his troopers, "Men, that old murderer has got away from every soldier command and has left a trail of blood for five hundred miles on the old [Butterfield] stage line. I want him dead or alive tomorrow morning, do you understand. *I want him dead.*" According to Connor, guards heated their bayonets in the campfire and applied them to the chief's feet. When he rose up in pain to protest, the guards emptied their weapons into him pointblank, then shot him another four times in the head with their revolvers.

Canby, who had been promoted to brigadier general, temporarily transferred to an eastern command on September 18, 1862, and was replaced by Carleton, who now assumed command of the Department of New Mexico. As Canby had done earlier, Carleton called upon the services of the redoubtable Indian fighter Kit Carson. Born in the backcountry of Kentucky, Carson learned the ways of the wilderness early. His mother apprenticed him to a saddlemaker in 1825, from whom the young man bolted the following year to join a Santa Fe trading caravan as a herder. He remained in New Mexico, becoming a trapper, Indian fighter, and trailblazer. He served with distinction in the Mexican War, after which he settled with his Mexican wife near Taos, to farm. In 1853, he was appointed Indian agent for the Utes, a post he held for the next seven years, by all accounts serving with honesty, intelligence, and compassion—qualities

very rare in the generally corrupt and inept Indian agency system. Having resigned as agent at the outbreak of Civil War, Carson was not wholly prepared to follow General Carleton's order to pursue Mescalero Apaches and hold no "council . . . with the Indians, nor any talks. The men are to be slain whenever and wherever they can be found. The women and children may be taken as prisoners, but, of course, they are not to be killed."

Carson and his First New Mexico Volunteer Cavalry pursued the Mescalero, but he also arranged for five chiefs to visit Santa Fe for talks with Carleton. En route, two of the chiefs met a detachment of soldiers commanded by Captain James (Paddy) Graydon, in civilian life a saloonkeeper. Graydon offered them beef and flour for the journey, and the two parties went on their separate ways, only to meet again a short time later. This meeting turned into one of those incidents of senseless brutality that were repeated with nauseating regularity throughout the history of Indian-white relations. Graydon went into the chiefs' camp, shared with them the customary libation, and then shot them dead. Three other chiefs reached Santa Fe and informed General Carleton that they no longer had the heart to fight. "Do with us as may seem good to you," the chiefs told Carleton, "but do not forget we are men and braves."

What Carleton proposed to do with them—and, shortly, with the Navajos as well—was to round them up and send them to a 40-mile-square reservation at the Bosque Redondo on the Pecos River in New Mexico. It was not an act of deliberate cruelty. Carleton knew the history of this region all too well: how raiding was a way of life for the Apaches, and how no military administrator had ever been able to halt the cycle of raid and counterraid. Removal to the Bosque, Carleton believed, was the best way to bring years of warfare to an end at last. However, Carleton's own board of officers, dispatched to inspect the Bosque Redondo, reported negatively on it. Yet Carleton, intoxicated by the prospect of ending the Apache wars once and for all, saw only that the site was 50 miles from any white settlement (except for Fort Sumner, which would guard it), but close to sources of water and game, including buffalo plains. To him it seemed ideal. He told the Mescalero chiefs that there would be no peace unless they and their people marched to the Bosque. Many Mescaleros fled to Mexico; others marched to Bosque Redondo.

## NAVAJO WAR

While Kit Carson dealt with the Mescaleros, four companies of his First New Mexico Volunteer Cavalry, commanded by Lieutenant Colonel J. Francisco Chavez,

## KIT CARSON (1809–1868)

Christopher Houston "Kit" Carson was born near Richmond, Kentucky. The family moved to Missouri in 1812, where Carson had his only formal schooling—three years' worth—before the death of his father in 1818 made it necessary for him to stay at home to tend to the farm. His mother apprenticed the 14-year-old Carson to saddlemaker David Workman in 1825, but the young man yearned for adventure and joined a Santa Fe trading caravan as a herder. He remained in New Mexico, settling near Taos, the gathering place of trappers, and he teamed up with famed trapper Ewing Young, traveling between 1828 and 1831 through southern Arizona and California. Unlike most "mountain men," who were solitary, irresponsible figures, Carson quickly acquired a reputation for great courage and character. His friend and in-law Tom Tobin said that Carson "wasn't afraid of hell or high water," that his personal life was "clean as a hound's tooth," and that his word "was as sure as the sun comin' up." By all accounts a quiet and dignified man ("Kit never cussed more than was necessary," Tobin recalled), he earned the respect of whites and Indians alike.

For the next several years, Carson continued to trap throughout the Rockies and the Far West, gaining intimate and thorough knowledge of the country. At a trappers' rendezvous in 1835, he impressed the legendary Jim Bridger—and practically everybody else in the region—by fighting a duel with a belligerent and unpopular French trapper known to history only as Captain Shunar.

After working as a hunter at Bent's Fort on the Arkansas River from 1841 to 1842, he returned to Missouri to visit his relatives. Enroute, he met John C. Frémont, who was organizing the first of his western expeditions. Frémont hired Carson as a guide, and the two undertook a series of three expeditions, becoming fast friends in the process. Be-

tween the first and second expeditions, Carson married (February 6, 1843) 15-year-old Josefa Jaramillo of Taos. She was actually Carson's third wife, since he had earlier wed an Arapaho girl (who died) and then a Cheyenne (who divorced him, Indian style, by throwing his belongings outside the tepee).

Carson's travels with Frémont made him nationally famous, especially his involvement in the California Bear Flag Rebellion, which faded into the Mexican War. Carson served Frémont as a courier and also guided the army of Stephen Watts Kearny from New Mexico to California. After the Mexican War, Carson settled down to life as a rancher east of Taos, earning a substantial profit from driving a large flock of sheep to California in 1853. In that year, Carson was appointed Indian agent for the tribes of northern New Mexico. Unlike most Indian agents, Carson was caring, honest, and efficient, earning the friendship and respect of the Indians he served.

Carson relinquished his position as Indian agent in 1861 to serve as colonel of the First New Mexico Volunteer Cavalry at the outbreak of the Civil War. He distinguished himself at the Battle of Valverde (February 21, 1862) and was breveted a brigadier general. Throughout the balance of the Civil War, acting under orders of General James Carleton, Carson campaigned vigorously against the Mescalero Apaches, the Navajos, the Comanches, and the Kiowas. He was highly successful as an Indian fighter, but it was a role that deeply disturbed him, for he had great fellow feeling for this "enemy."

Following the Civil War, Carson served briefly as commander of Fort Garland in southern Colorado, then settled with his family at Boggsville, near Las Animas, Colorado. There his wife died in April 1868. Carson suffered a hemorrhage and died on May 23 of the same year.

established Fort Wingate near Mount Taylor, on the border of Navajo country. Ever since the slaughter at Fort Fauntleroy/Lyon, Navajos had been raiding Rio Grande settlements. The new fort, together with the campaign against the Mescaleros, prompted 18 important Navajo chiefs, including the renowned Delgadito and Barboncito (but not the always recalcitrant Manuelito), to come to

Santa Fe seeking terms of peace. Carleton replied to them harshly, protesting that he had no faith in their promises and talk of peace. In April 1863, Carleton sent word to Delgadito and Barboncito—most prominent among the "peace" chiefs—that "we have no desire to make war upon them and other good Navajoes; but the troops cannot tell the good from the bad, and we cannot nor will tolerate their staying as a peace party among those upon whom we intend to make war." Their only alternative to war, Carleton told them, was to take their people to the Bosque Redondo reservation. He set a deadline of July 20, 1863, after which "every Navajo that is seen will be considered as hostile and treated accordingly . . . after that day the door now open will be closed." Barboncito replied: "I will not go to the Bosque. I will never leave my country, not even if it means that I will be killed."

Carleton did not deal in idle threats, for he knew that the Indians respected strength and preyed upon weakness. On June 15, he concentrated Kit Carson's regiment at Fort Wingate. When July 20 came and went, Carson set out with 736 men and officers—nine companies—to make war on the Navajos. While Lieutenant Colonel Chavez remained at Fort Wingate with two companies, Carson's men established Fort Canby at Pueblo Colorado (Red Town) Wash, in New Mexico, southwest of the now-abandoned Fort Defiance. Ordered to prosecute his campaign "until it is considered, at these headquarters, that [the Navajos] have been effectually punished for their long-continued atrocities," Carson succeeded in killing 13 warriors before the end of the month, taking eleven women and children captive.

Far more significant was the widespread destruction of Navajo fields and orchards. Carleton offered a $20 bounty for each horse or mule captured and a dollar for each sheep. Although Navajo raiding continued—10,000 sheep were stolen in August alone—the Indians began to surrender to confinement at the Bosque Redondo: 51 at the end of September, 188 in November, more than 500 in January. By March, a total of 2,138 Navajos were sent from Fort Canby, New Mexico, to the Bosque.

Not satisfied, however, until every Navajo had been consigned to the reservation, Carleton pressed his campaign relentlessly. He repeatedly admonished Carson and his officers that they were to negotiate nothing with the Navajos, for the Indians' choice was as simple as it was absolute: Either go to the Bosque or be destroyed. On December 31, 1863, Carleton issued an order for the kind of hard winter campaign soldiers dreaded almost as much as the Indians did. "*Now*, while the snow is deep, is the time to make an impression on the tribe."

On January 6, 1864, Carson and 389 officers and men set out from Fort Canby to strike the Navajos' ancient stronghold, Canyon de Chelly, from the west. Two more companies, commanded by Captain Albert H. Pfeiffer,

approached from the east. On January 12, a patrol in advance of Carson's main body, under Sergeant Andreas Herrera, engaged a party of Navajos, killing 11. No other Navajos were encountered that day. Instead, on January 15, 60 Navajos surrendered to Carson, complaining that the ceaseless warfare was starving them. After destroying dwellings and orchards, Carson declared the Canyon de Chelly Expedition ended, and yet more Navajos dejectedly marched off to the Bosque Redondo. By late 1864, three-quarters of the Navajo tribe had accepted concentration on the reservation.

The Bosque Redondo was a place to be dreaded. Although government wagons were furnished to transport the very young, the old, and the infirm, the remainder took the infamous "Long Walk." Conditions at Fort Canby, the jumping-off point for the Bosque, were deplorable, and 126 Navajos died there of dysentery. More died en route to the Bosque. Reportedly, some, no longer able to march, were shot by their soldier escorts. The entire deplorable affair was reminiscent of the Cherokees' Trail of Tears. Eventually, 8,000 Navajos crowded the reservation, but with an inefficiency and inhumanity that had become routine, the government failed to supply sufficient rations to feed this population. To his credit, General Carleton was unremitting in his pleas for 2,000,000 pounds of food, 13,000 yards of cloth for clothing, 7,000 blankets, 20 spinning wheels, 50 mills for grinding corn, farm implements, and seeds. Lastly—perhaps it was his special nod toward the amenities of white civilization—Carleton asked for 600 cotton handkerchiefs.

Congress did appropriate funds, but the amount fell short of what was needed. Attempts to teach the traditionally peripatetic Navajo and Apache Indians sedentary farming techniques likewise failed. By 1864, conditions at "Fair Carletonia"—as the soldiers sardonically christened the reservation—were desperate. After enduring through 1868, Manuelito, Barboncito, and other chiefs were permitted to journey to Washington, D.C., to inform President Andrew Johnson of conditions on the reservation. A month later, peace commissioners visited the Bosque Redondo and concluded that the Navajos "had sunk into a condition of absolute poverty and despair." A treaty was concluded on June 1, 1868, returning the Indians to their homeland and declaring it their new reservation. By this expedient, the grim Navajo war was ended, its final victim the grandiose, but tragically misguided plan of Brigadier General James H. Carleton.

# CHAPTER 22

□

# BLUE, GRAY, AND RED

## The Santee Sioux Uprising, the Shoshoni War, and the
## Cheyenne–Arapaho War (1862–1865)

### SANTEE SIOUX UPRISING

The Santee Sioux of Minnesota (a division of the Sioux often called the Dakota, consisting of the Mdewakantons, Wahpekutes, Sissetons, and Wahpetons) initially accepted the policy of "concentration" that the Apaches and Navajos had so vigorously resisted. Resentment, however, smoldered among them, as, confined to a narrow strip of land along the upper Minnesota River, they suffered the effects of a crop failure, were hemmed in by growing numbers of Scandanavian and German immigrants and, as usual, were prey to a corrupt Indian agency system that diverted funds and supplies guaranteed them by an 1851 treaty.

As if the corruption were not enough, the Indians, on the verge of starvation, were told that the cash and food annuities to which their treaty entitled them would be delayed by a month. The government, it seems, could not decide whether to pay the annuity in gold or Civil War greenbacks, and, therefore, delayed shipment of the money. The Indians, though reluctant, were willing to be patient. The food, after all, was already stored in a warehouse at the Yellow Medicine Agency, and that could now be distributed. Faced with about 3,000 hungry Indians, Major Thomas J. Galbraith, the local Indian agent, incredibly declared that "bookkeeeping problems" and "reservation custom" dictated that the provisions had to be distributed at the same time as the money. He told the Indians to go off and hunt and come back in a month.

With remarkable forebearance, the Sioux did just that, returning to Galbraith on July 14. The reservation's money had not yet arrived, and, once again, the agent refused to distribute the food. On August 4, a band of mounted warriors broke into the warehouse and began carrying away sacks of flour. When a garrison detachment under Lieutenant Timothy J. Sheehan threatened the looters with a howitzer, they temporarily withdrew. Realizing that this was only a respite, Sheehan argued Galbraith into releasing some provisions, and in the meantime, he contacted Captain John S. Marsh, commander of the garrison at Fort Ridgely, on the Minnesota River, near New Ulm, requesting that he attend a council with local traders and the Indians.

Little Crow, chief of the Mdewakanton villages and highly influential among the Santee Sioux generally, forcefully but reasonably represented the Indians at the council. "We have no food," he explained, "but here are these stores, filled with food. We ask that you, the agent, make some arrangements by which we can get food from the stores, or else we may take our own way to keep ourselves from starving. When men are hungry they help themselves." Agent Galbraith put the question to the assembled traders, who had it in their power to distribute provisions on credit. They all deferred to the most prominent among them, Andrew J. Myrick, who, offended by what he took as Little Crow's threat, declared: "So far as I am concerned, if they are hungry, let them eat grass." Myrick's thoughtless reply sealed his fate and that of many settlers in the area.

Captain Marsh managed temporarily to defuse the tension by ordering Galbraith and the traders to commence food distribution at once. The Indians, thus provided for, returned to their villages, and, on August 11, the troops left the agency to return to Fort Ridgely.

In the presence of Captain Marsh, Galbraith had promised to distribute food and annuity money to the tribes of the Lower Agency. Galbraith called on Little Crow at the Lower Agency on August 15. Observing that the harvest there seemed to be abundant, he announced to

190

## THE SIOUX

The name *Sioux*, an abbreviation of Nadouessioux, is an Ojibwa word transliterated by the French. The Ojibwa name reflects that tribe's hostile relations with the Sioux; it signifies "adders"—meaning, by extension, "enemies." The Sioux generally refer to themselves as the Dakota, a word meaning "allies" in the Santee Sioux dialect. Yankton and Assiniboin Sioux use the name Nakota, and the Tetons use Lakota. By the nineteenth century, the large Sioux nation was divided as follows:

Mdewkanton
Wahpeton
Wahpekute
Sisseton
Yankton
Yanktonai (Includes Upper Yanktonai, Lower Yanktonai or Hunkpatina, from whom the Assiniboin separated.)
Teton (Includes Upper Brulé, Lower Brulé, Hunkpapa, Miniconjou, Oglala, Oohenonpa or Two Kettle, San Arcs, and Sihasapa or Blackfoot.)

Collectively, the Mdewkanton, Wahpeton, Wahpekute, and Sisseton constitute the Santee or Eastern division of the Sioux.

the chief that he had changed his mind about making the distribution, and that he would, after all, wait until the annuity money arrived.

On Sunday, August 17, four young Mdewakanton men were returning dejectedly from a fruitless hunting trip. At the settlement of Acton, one of them stopped to steal eggs from the nest of a hen belonging to a white man. Another of the young hunters cautioned against taking the eggs, warning that it would cause trouble. The three youths ganged up on the fourth, accusing him of cowardice, whereupon he replied that he was not afraid to kill a white man. This declaration had to be put to a test. The young men started an argument with the owner of the hen, following him to his stepson's house. There the Indians' anger seemed suddenly to melt away. They invited the whites to do some target shooting together. Without warning, the Indians turned their guns on the whites, killing five, including two women.

When they rode back to the village on stolen horses and announced what they had done, Little Crow was in despair. At first, he declared that he wanted nothing to do with the consequences of so rash an act. But the other members of his village prevailed upon him. Finally, with a resignation typical of many Indian leaders, Little Crow addressed the assembled braves: "You are little children," he said. "You are fools. You will die like rabbits when the hungry wolves hunt them in the Hard Moon. Taoyateduta [Little Crow] is not a coward; he will die with you!" Without consulting the so-called farming Indians—those who had adopted white ways—Little Crow and a band of warriors attacked Myrick in his store on the morning of August 18. They shot him as he tried running away into the woods. Into his dead mouth they stuffed a tuft of grass.

At the same time, additional war parties were sweeping across the countryside. Refugees began arriving at Fort Ridgely by ten o'clock in the morning. Captain Marsh commanded a garrison of only 76 men and two officers. He dispatched a messenger to Lieutenant Sheehan, who was taking 50 men to Fort Ripley on the Mississippi River. In the meantime, Marsh left Fort Ridgely with a detachment of 46 men, headed for the Lower Agency. What they saw along the way should have caused them to turn back: the smoldering ruins of settlers' houses and mutilated corpses.

At the Redwood Ferry, which crossed the Minnesota River to the Lower Agency, Marsh and his men found the body of the ferryman, still warm. White Dog, a farming Indian, friendly to the whites, told Marsh that things were not as bad as they looked. The majority of the Indians, he said, wanted no fight. Accordingly, Marsh made preparations to cross the ferry. At that moment, Marsh's men found themselves engulfed in an ambush. The captain's command was quickly routed, and Marsh ordered the survivors to swim across the river. Marsh himself drowned. Twenty-five of 46 men died, and five were wounded.

The survivors reached Fort Ridgely, now commanded by Lieutenant Thomas P. Gere, who could muster only 22 able-bodied men—the rest, including himself, were sick with the mumps. He sent a messenger to Fort Snelling (Minneapolis), asking for reinforcements; the messenger also managed to overtake Galbraith and his volunteer Renville Rangers, who rode back to Fort Ridgely. Even augmented by Galbraith's men, the fort was in a poor position to withstand an Indian attack. An unstockaded collection of wooden buildings, its only real defense consisted of two 12-pounder mountain howitzers, a 24-pounder of the same type, and a 6-pounder field gun.

The first onslaught came on August 19, led by Little Crow, Mankato, and Big Eagle. Surprisingly—and unnervingly—the Indians halted just before reaching the

## LITTLE CROW (c.1810–1863)

Called by his people Taoyateduta ("his red people") or Cetan Wakan Mani ("the sacred pigeon-hawk which comes walking"), Little Crow, a Mdewakanton chief, was born in the band's village on the east bank of the Mississippi, about 14 miles below the mouth of the Minnesota River. His father, Chetanwakanmani, also called Little Crow, had signed the first treaty between the Sioux and the U.S. government in 1805, but allied his band with the British during the War of 1812. The younger Little Crow became chief of the Mdewakantons around 1834, when Chetanwakanmani died.

Little Crow signed a cession treaty in 1837; in 1851, he ceded more territory; and in 1857, he volunteered his warriors to campaign with the whites against the Wahpekute renegades of Inkpaduta, who led an uprising at Spirit Lake, Iowa, the year before. With good reason, younger Mdewakanton warriors regarded Little Crow as a weak leader. To be sure, in his personal life, he hardly fit the stereotype of the stoic Indian. In early youth he had acquired a reputation as a scapegrace, and he was given to heavy drinking. When, however, he injured his hands in a drunken fight in 1846, he asked the Indian agent at Fort Snelling (present-day Minneapolis, Minnesota) to send a missionary among his people to discourage the sale of alcohol. A devotee of the pleasures of the flesh, Little Crow had 22 children by six wives.

If it was his cooperation with the whites that most infuriated the younger warriors, his reward from the government was betrayal and starvation. When four young Mdewakanton warriors murdered five white settlers on August 17, 1862, a tense situation exploded. Little Crow counseled that war against the white man was futile, but warriors among the Santee Sioux pressured him into attack, and the Santee Sioux Uprising—the worst Indian uprising in American history—commenced.

The orgy of raiding that Little Crow (against his own best judgment) led ended on September 23, 1862, at the Battle of Wood Lake. Little Crow fled west, and sought aid from the British at Fort Garry (Winnipeg, Manitoba) in May 1863. Turned away from there, he reentered Minnesota to steal horses. On July 3, 1863, he was picking raspberries with his 16-year-old son Wowinapa, when he was ambushed and killed near the village of Hutchinson by settlers seeking to collect a $25 bounty on Sioux scalps. (His son escaped. Subsequently captured, he was sentenced to hang, but the sentence was commuted to imprisonment. He converted to Christianity in prison and assumed the name of Thomas Wakeman.)

Little Crow's body was discarded on an offal heap behind a slaughterhouse, but the Minnesota Historical Society rescued his skeleton, which, along with his scalp, was put on display. Eventually, the historical society returned the remains to the Sioux for a proper burial.

fort and, in full view of the soldiers, held a lengthy council, which concluded with the Indians turning away from Fort Ridgely and heading off to the nearby settlement of New Ulm. It was a reprieve for the fort, which was soon reinforced not only by Galbraith, but by 50 men under Lieutenant Sheehan. There were now about 180 armed defenders—soldiers as well as civilians—at the fort.

At three in the afternoon on August 20, a war party of about 100 began firing into New Ulm. Militiamen under the command of a settler named Jacob Nix, augmented by 23 volunteers from Nicollet County, held the warriors off until a sudden and severe thunderstorm compelled the Indians to break off the attack. Seventeen townspeople had been killed. That night, reinforcements from the surrounding countryside began to arrive at New Ulm, and the town hunkered down for the next anticipated attack.

In council, however, Little Crow, whose war party had been joined by an additional 400 braves, decided to turn his attention back to Fort Ridgely. On August 21, he led about 400 warriors against the fort. Though badly outnumbered, Ridgely's defenders trained their artillery on the attackers, thereby staving off annihilation. After cannister grapeshot had felled 100 warriors, and with the onset of more heavy rains, Little Crow withdrew. ("With a few guns like that," remarked one Santee, "the Dakotas could rule the earth.") Joined by yet more allies— another 400 Sisseton and Wahpeton Sioux warriors—Little Crow attacked Fort Ridgely again on August 22. This time, the 180 defenders faced more than 800 Sioux, who tried to set fire to the fort buildings with flaming arrows.

The heavy rains of the day before prevented a wholesale conflagration, however, and again the artillery drove the attackers off.

Disappointed, Little Crow launched 400 warriors against New Ulm on August 23. At first, the town's defenders, commanded by Judge Charles Flandrau, gave way before the onslaught. But the judge was able to rally his men into putting up a stout defense that finally caused the Indians to withdraw. Thirty-six townspeople died, and about 23 were wounded. One hundred ninety buildings—the better part of the town—lay in smoldering ruins. Although the Indians had withdrawn, the town was unlivable, and 2,000 citizens evacuated to Mankato.

New Ulm was not alone in producing refugees. By August 27, it was evident that virtually the entire Sioux nation in Minnesota was on the warpath. Between 350 and 800 settlers had been killed, and about half the state's population were essentially fugitives from Indian wrath. The opening phase of the uprising would stand as the worst Indian massacre of whites in the nation's history. Rumor had it that the depredations had been provoked by Confederate interests—as if Agent Galbraith had needed any help in causing trouble. While it is unlikely that Confederate sympathizers had had anything to do with the uprising, it did delay Minnesota from sending its quota of enlistees to fight the Civil War in the East. Though badly in need of men, President Abraham Lincoln replied to Governor Alexander Ramsey's request for an extension of the deadline for enlistment: "Attend to the Indians. If the draft cannot proceed of course it will not proceed. Necessity knows no law."

At the end of August, after a period of training and preparation many critics found excessive, a relief column of Minnesota volunteers, led by militia colonel Henry Hastings Sibley (no relation to the Confederate general Henry Hopkins Sibley) marched into the Minnesota River valley. On August 31, Sibley dispatched 150 men under Captain Hiram P. Grant to reconnoiter the Redwood Agency and also to bury any bodies they found. They found and buried 80.

At dawn on September 2, a large party of warriors under Big Eagle, Mankato, and Gray Bird attacked Grant's camp at the head of a deep gulch called Birch Coulee. In the initial onslaught, 22 troopers were killed and 60 wounded; nevertheless, the remainder managed to stave off utter annihilation long enough for a relief column under Colonel Samuel McPhail to reach them. The rescuers, however, soon found themselves surrounded as well. A howitzer was brought to bear, which drove off the Indians and enabled McPhail's command to reach a defensible position, which they held until September 3, when the main body of Sibley's force arrived. Grant had withstood a 31-hour siege.

The Battle of Birch Coulee provoked harsh criticism of Sibley's lack of aggressiveness in the face of an emergency that now reached beyond the borders of Minnesota into Wisconsin and Dakota Territory, as Indians raided throughout the region. In the midst of a civil war that was going badly for the Union, Lincoln responded to the crisis by creating a new Military Department of the Northwest, headquartered in St. Paul and commanded by Major General John Pope, who was stinging from ignominious defeat at the Second Battle of Bull Run (August 29–30, 1862). Pope was determined to do better in the West—though he soon learned that the resources available to him were severely limited. In the meantime, for his part, and to his credit, Sibley resisted the temptation to cave into criticism and act rashly; he knew that he needed more troops and that the militiamen he presently commanded were raw and required further training. It was not until September 19, with the addition of officers and men from the Third, Sixth, Seventh, and Ninth Minnesota Infantry and a mounted company of Renville Rangers, that Sibley, now commanding 1,619 soldiers, felt ready to move.

But the Indians decided to move first. At dawn on September 23, about 700 warriors took up positions in ambush along the road that Sibley's column would take out of its camp near Wood Lake. This time, his volunteer troops' lack of discipline would serve Sibley well. At seven in the morning, a small band of soldiers from the Third Minnesota sneaked out of camp, without permission, to forage for potatoes or pumpkins. As luck would have it, the men did not follow the road, but cut across the field, precisely in the direction of the waiting warriors. Seeing the soldiers, about 200 warriors rose up and opened fire. The noise alerted Sibley's main camp, and Major Abraham K. Welch rushed to the foragers' aid with the balance of the Third Minnesota. In the confusion of battle, however, the Third was soon surrounded, only to be extricated by the Renville Rangers and elements of the Sixth and Seventh Minnesota. The Battle of Wood Lake resulted in the deaths of 7 troopers and about 30 Indians; 30 troopers were wounded, as well as 30 Indians. Most of the 700 warriors assembled never engaged in this prematurely fought battle after which, they drifted away in discouragement. Little Crow's army rapidly dissolved, and beginning on September 26, Sibley accepted the surrender of about 2,000 hostiles and the release of about 370 captives.

The commander who had been slow and deliberate in committing his men to action now moved swiftly and heedlessly to punish those found guilty of participating in the uprising. By November 3, a military tribunal had sentenced a total of 303 Santees to be hanged. The remaining 1,700 prisoners were transferred to Fort Snelling—a hellish march, as angry whites stoned and clubbed many; a baby was snatched from the arms of its mother and beaten to death. In the meantime, President Lincoln, doubting the justice of Sibley's tribunal, personally reviewed the 303 death sentences. On December 6, the president notified Sibley that he should "cause to be executed" 39 of the 303 convicted, the balance to be held "subject to further orders." Nevertheless, the 38 hangings (one Indian was given a last-minute reprieve) at Mankato constituted the largest mass execution in American history. Because of an administrative error, two Indians not on Lincoln's death list were hanged. Only after the lapse of nine years was this fact admitted. "It was a matter of regret that any mistakes were made," declared an official. "I feel sure they were not made intentionally." It is said that one of those hanged had saved a white woman's life during the raiding.

While the Battle of Wood Lake was a severe blow to the uprising, it hardly brought an end to hostilities on the Plains. Indeed, the battle marked the beginning of eight years of warfare with the Sioux. The theater of war shifted from Minnesota to Dakota Territory after Sibley (who, despite his request that he be allowed to retire to his home, was commissioned a brigadier of the U.S. Volunteers) and another general, Alfred Sully, succeeded in stirring to war Santee Sioux refugees and the Teton Sioux, as well as the Cheyenne. In the spring of 1863, General John Pope ordered Sibley to travel up the Minnesota River, crossing into Dakota Territory to Devil's Lake, while Sully went up the Missouri and turned northeast to meet him. It was intended as a show of force that would discourage Santee and Yanktonai Sioux from massing for another uprising. Neither Pope, Sibley, nor Sully was aware that Little Crow had repeatedly failed in efforts to garner renewed support for the war against the whites. In June, a disappointed Little Crow and his son disappeared into Canada, where, near the town of Hutchinson, Little Crow was shot and killed while picking berries. The Indians who were gathered near Devil's Lake were Sisseton Sioux led by Standing Buffalo, who considered himself at peace. Not far from them were Indians of the same tribes who were followers of Inkpaduta, a hostile chief, as well as Teton Sioux (including Hunkpapas and Blackfeet), who were potentially hostile.

Between them, Sibley and Sully commanded about 4,200 troopers. Hampered by supply problems—riverboat traffic was snarled by low water in the Missouri—the columns made slow progress. By the time Sibley reached the Devil's Lake area, Standing Buffalo had left, joining Inkpaduta's people in search of buffalo. On July 24, 1863, Sibley at last made contact with Standing Buffalo and Inkpaduta's followers and ar-

ranged a parley near Big Mound, northeast of present-day Bismarck, North Dakota. Clearly, Standing Buffalo wanted no war, but at the start of the parley, a young partisan of Inkpaduta shot and killed the surgeon of the Minnesota Rangers.

At this, Sibley's artillery opened on the Indians, whom the cavalry routed from one defensive position to the next until nightfall. On July 26, Sibley pressed the pursuit, burning villages and using his artillery to counter Sioux attacks. On July 28, at Stony Lake, a large body of Sioux charged for a head-on attack, which was successfully parried, and Sibley resumed the pursuit until the next day when he decided that 150 Indians killed (at a cost of a dozen Minnesota casualties) was sufficient.

Sully, who had been more seriously delayed than Sibley, met up with Sibley's command in August, long after the action was over. Sully dispatched elements of his command to search for Inkpaduta, who was found on September 3 near Whitestone Hill (northwest of present-day Ellendale, North Dakota) by four companies of the Sixth Iowa Cavalry under Major Albert E. House.

Badly outnumbered, House seemed destined for certain destruction—and would have been annihilated had he not managed to get a message to Sully, who brought the rest of the brigade to his rescue. A savage battle ensued, in which 22 soldiers fell, 50 were wounded, and some 300 warriors died. Two hundred fifty women and children were taken captive. What had begun as certain triumph for Inkpaduta ended in disaster for the Sioux. Yet it prompted few Indians to seek peace. When the spring of 1864 brought rumors of Sioux resistance along the Missouri and the routes of Montana-bound prospectors, the army's general-in-chief Henry Wager Halleck warned Pope that the exigencies of the Civil War in the East left him few resources with which to prosecute an Indian campaign. He urged Pope to seek peace.

Peace, however, was far from Pope's mind. He ordered Sibley to establish forts on Devil's Lake and the James River. Sully would also increase the military presence in the Dakotas and was directed to hunt for Sioux. Between them, Sibley and Sully mustered about 3,400 troops, though the entire command for this campaign would be under Sully, since Sibley secured Pope's permission to remain in Minnesota. Despite the number of troops, conditions were hardly ideal for undertaking a campaign of pursuit and punishment. One of the volunteer groups assigned to Sully's command arrived with 123 emigrant wagons in tow. Close behind this unit was another train of gold prospectors. Not only would these civilians get in the way of military operations, the officers and men deeply resented the prospectors, whom they regarded either as draft evaders or Rebel sympathizers.

Sibley was compelled to detach 400 of his men to escort the wagons. "I am damn sorry you are here," he told his civilian charges, "but so long as you are, I will do my best to protect you."

On July 28, the remaining 3,000 of Sully's troops reached Killdear Mountain, site of hostile Indian camps. Sully estimated the enemy's strength at 6,000 warriors, while the Indians claimed no more than 1,600. The wooded, hilly terrain made a cavalry assault impractical, so Sully dismounted his men and formed them into a hollow square that enclosed artillery and horses. Remaining in formation, the men advanced on the Indian camp. The advancing troops continuously exchanged fire with the Indians. When the Indians appeared to be gaining the howitzers were used. On one occasion, Major Alfred E. Brackett led an effective cavalry charge into the woods, but with two killed and eight wounded. Sully decided that it was safer simply to bombard the Indians with the howitzers. Sully's total losses were light—five killed and ten wounded—and he estimated that he had killed 150 warriors (the Indians put the figure at 31). The Battle of Killdeer Mountain resulted in something even worse for the Sioux, however. Forced to run, they abandoned a vast store of food and provisions, which the soldiers promptly destroyed.

After the battle, Sully turned to escorting the emigrant train west to the Yellowstone River, crossing the Little Missouri Badlands and enduring the early August heat as well as thirst, hunger, and repeated Indian attacks. After depositing the emigrants on the banks of the Missouri River, Sully marched far and wide in a fruitless search for more Sioux. This was the character of the Indian wars throughout the balance of the century: interminable marches and empty-handed searches punctuated by brief, sharp, bloody battles. At Fort Rice (in present-day North Dakota), Sully was called to rescue a group of emigrants who were under Indian attack. Colonel Daniel J. Dill led a detachment of 850 men, who successfully lifted the siege.

## SHOSHONI WAR

Despite Sibley's and Sully's campaigns, the Plains were fairly quiet through much of 1863 except for Shoshoni and Ute attacks on the emigrant and mail routes west and south of Fort Laramie. Brigadier General James Craig, operating out of Forts Laramie (in Wyoming at the junction of Laramie and North Platte rivers) and Halleck (in northeastern Nevada), had fewer than 500 troops to patrol thousands of miles of trails. Fortunately for him, Colonel Patrick Connor's California troops—the Third California Infantry and a portion of the Second California Cavalry, a total of 1,000 men—had arrived to garrison the forts of Utah and Nevada late in 1862.

In Utah, the Shoshonis, Bannocks, and Utes were hitting the mail and telegraph route as well as killing prospectors on their way to the Montana mines. In January 1863, Connor took 300 men, chiefly cavalry, from Fort Douglas, Utah, and set out after the Shoshoni chief Bear Hunter. On January 27, Connor's troops reached Bear Hunter's village on the Bear River, near present-day Preston, Idaho. There they confronted about 300 warriors, who handily repulsed an initial frontal attack led by one of Connor's subordinates. After this defeat, Connor personally took command of a flanking attack, by which he managed to trap Bear Hunter and his warriors, catching them in murderous crossfire. Two hundred twenty-four Shoshonis, including Bear Hunter, lay dead the next morning. One hundred sixty women and children were taken prisoner, and substantial stores destroyed. Fourteen of Connor's men had been killed and 49 wounded. The battle was the principal encounter and climax of the Shoshoni War (more realistically called the Bear River Campaign) and prompted most of the Shoshoni and Bannocks to seek peace.

Connor also dealt harshly with the Utes and Gosiutes, who harassed travelers between Salt Lake City and Fort Ruby. During the summer and fall of 1863, Connor and Superintendent of Indian Affairs James D. Doty concluded a number of treaties with the Indians of Utah. During this period, too, Major Charles McDermit had his hands full patroling Paiute country in Nevada. Farther north, in Washington and Oregon, the Nez Percés signed a treaty in June 1863 and withdrew to their reservation, while the Western Shoshoni continued to harass emigrants traveling the Oregon Trail through southern Idaho. Colonel Reuben F. Maury led elements of the First Oregon Cavalry in patrols aimed at keeping the trail open. Maury's patrols, together with operations by the First Washington Territorial Infantry, mainly succeeded in policing the Western Shoshoni.

The Northern Paiutes—better known as the Snakes—were less easy to deal with. They rarely offered full-scale, formal resistance, but, as a former Indian superintendent observed, "Their stealthy presence is never indicated except by a consummated murder or robbery, while their parties are so small and so perfectly on the alert that pursuit is useless." The First Oregon Cavalry and elements of Colonel McDermit's command pursued the Snakes nonetheless, though to little avail. "*Ten good soldiers* are required to wage successful war *against one Indian*," observed J. W. Huntington, Oregon Indian superintendent. "Every Indian killed or captured has cost the government fifty thousand dollars at least."

## CHEYENNE—ARAPAHO WAR

In Colorado, the situation was different. There were no police actions, no fruitless pursuits, no halfway measures. When Governor John Evans failed to secure mineral-rich Cheyenne and Arapaho hunting grounds in exchange for reservations, he called upon Colonel John M. Chivington, military commander of the territory, to sweep the Indians out, even though, of all the Plains tribes, the Cheyenne and Arapaho had given the whites the least excuse for a fight. But, as the members of the federal peace commission concluded in a report issued some years later (January 7, 1868), white government needed little reason to fight. "Members of Congress understand the negro question," the report declared, "and talk learnedly of finance, and other problems of political economy, but when the progress of settlement reaches the Indian's home, the only question considered is, 'how best to get his lands.' "

Governor Evans had chosen the right man for the job he wanted done. A former Methodist minister, Chivington was known as the fighting parson, and his hatred of Indians was exuberant in its rabidity. He declared in an 1864 speech made in Denver that all Indians should be killed and scalped, including infants. "Nits make lice!" was the way he put it.

While the majority of Cheyennes were inclined toward

---

### THE DOG SOLDIERS

The Hotamitanio, or Dog Soldiers, were the most elite of various "soldier societies" common not only to the Cheyenne, but to the Plains tribes generally. By 1837, these militants had become a separate band within the Cheyenne tribe and, during the Cheyenne–Arapaho War, gained great renown—or notoriety, depending on one's point of view—for prowess in combat. Led during this period by Chiefs Tall Bull, Bull Bear, and White Horse, the Dog Soldiers repeatedly foiled attempts of peace chiefs, such as the hapless Black Kettle, to reach accommodation with the whites. Within the tribe itself, Dog Soldiers seem to have functioned as a kind of police force, possibly a mercenary police force in the service of a particular chief or group. It is possible that the name "Dog Soldier" is derived from a corruption of the name *Cheyenne* itself: from *chiens*, the French word for dogs.

---

peace, a militant faction, a group of young warriors known as the Hotamitanio, or Dog Soldier Society, provided Chivington with sufficient incidents for him to declare all the Cheyennes to be at war. He launched a number of attacks, which provoked Indian counter-erraids. To combat the crisis they had themselves created, Governor Evans and Colonel Chivington formed the Third Colorado Cavalry, composed of short-term, hundred-day enlistees drawn mainly from the territory's rough mining camps.

When winter came, however, a large number of Indians, led by Black Kettle, an older chief opposed to the youthful and tempestuous Dog Soldiers, were asking for peace. Through the sympathetic commander of Fort Lyon, in southeastern Colorado, Major Edward Wynkoop, they sought an audience with Governor Evans. Wynkoop announced this to the governor, who replied: "But what shall I do with the Third Colorado Regiment if I make peace? They have been raised to kill Indians, and they must kill Indians."

Nevertheless, Evans and Chivington met with the Cheyennes and Arapahos and told them that those Indians who wanted peace should "submit to military authority" by laying down their arms at a local fort. The Indians left the meeting and marched to Sand Creek, about 40 miles northeast of Fort Lyon, where they planned to talk with Major Wynkoop, who issued rations to them. The army, however, could not tolerate Wynkoop's humane attitude, and on November 5, one of Chivington's command, Major Scott J. Anthony, relieved Wynkoop as commander of the post. Anthony's first action was to cut the Indian's rations and to demand the surrender of their weapons. Apparently out of sheer meanness, he even ordered his men to fire on a group of unarmed Arapahos, who had approached the fort to trade buffalo hides for rations.

By the end of November, most of the Third Colorado had gathered at Fort Lyon. Black Kettle and his Cheyennes were still camped peacefully at Sand Creek, believing they had abided by Evan's and Chivington's order to submit to military authority and believing, above all, that they were at peace. Chivington deployed his 700-man force, which included four howitzers, around the camp. When three of Chivington's officers, Captain Silas Soule and Lieutenants Joseph Cramer and James Connor, protested that an attack on a peaceful village was murder and nothing but murder, Chivington barely restrained himself from striking Cramer. "Damn any man who sympathizes with Indians!" he roared. "I have come to kill Indians, and believe it is right and honorable to use any means under God's heaven to kill Indians."

The presence of a surrounding army alarmed Black Kettle's people. But the chief had faith in Wynkoop and

## BLACK KETTLE (c.1803–1868)

Black Kettle, a Southern Cheyenne chief called by his people Moketavato or Motavato, was renowned as a warrior who had fought against the Utes, Delawares, and others. During the Civil War years, however, he advocated peaceful relations with the whites, signed a treaty pledging peace in Colorado and along the Santa Fe Trail, and even visited President Abraham Lincoln in Washington, D.C.

When Colorado's territorial governor, John Evans, wanted to open the Cheyenne hunting ground to settlement and, especially, mining, he authorized a series of militia actions against the Indians, which brought Black Kettle and other chiefs to a council at Camp Weld, near Denver. At the council, Black Kettle and the others were told that if they relinquished their arms, camped near military outposts, and reported to them regularly, they would be safe from attack. Knowing that Major Edward Wynkoop—one of few officers sympathetic to the Indians—was in command of Fort Lyon, Black Kettle complied by leading 600 Southern Cheyennes (and some Southern Arapahos) to Sand Creek, near the fort. Just before this, however, Wynkoop had

been replaced by one of Chivington's men. On the night of November 28, 1864, Chivington deployed his Third Colorado Cavalry around the camp at Sand Creek and attacked at dawn of the following day.

Remarkably, Black Kettle managed to escape the wanton massacre. Even more remarkably, as the Cheynne–Arapaho War erupted around him, he persisted hopefully in counseling peace, signing the Treaty of Medicine Lodge in 1867, by which he and his Southern Cheyennes agreed to retire to a reservation in Indian Territory. Black Kettle, however, could control neither rapacious whites (who repeatedly violated the reservation) nor the younger Cheyenne warriors. When, on November 27, 1868, he learned of the presence of George Armstrong Custer and the Seventh Cavalry near his encampment on the Washita River, he fired a warning shot in the air and rode out to meet the yellow-haired commander. He hoped to avoid a fight. Instead, Custer's troops opened fire, killing him and his wife, and riding over their bodies as they commenced the brutal Battle of Washita.

in the honor of what he thought were Wynkoop's like-minded fellow soldiers. He sought to calm his people, and at the same time, to signify his loyalty and peaceful intentions, he hoisted an American flag *and* a white flag of truce over his tepee. In response, the troops opened fire and charged.

The unarmed Indians, warriors, old men, women, and children, ran in panic. Unspeakable atrocities were committed: Children's brains were beaten out with clubs, women were gutted like fish ("I saw one squaw cut open with an unborn child . . . lying by her side," reported Captain Soule), warrior corpses were castrated ("I saw the body of White Antelope with the privates cut off," reported Soule, "and I heard a soldier say he was going to make a tobacco pouch out of them"). Two hundred Cheyennes, two-thirds of them women and children, and nine chiefs were killed. Black Kettle escaped.

Far from disheartening the Indians, as Chivington had hoped, the Battle of Sand Creek galvanized their resolve to fight, as Southern Sioux, Northern Arapaho, and Cheyenne united in a spasm of savage raids during late 1864 and early 1865 called the Cheyenne–Arapaho War. Except for Black Kettle, who still desperately hoped for

peace, the chiefs gathered more allies for a quick strike against the military presence in Colorado.

On January 7, 1865, 1,000 Sioux and Cheyenne warriors massed south of Julesburg, Colorado, a settlement containing a stagecoach station, store, and warehouse, and guarded by modest Fort Rankin. The Indians sent a decoy party to draw out the company of Iowa Seventh Cavalry that garrisoned the fort. That stategem worked—until hotheaded youthful warriors attacked prematurely, betraying the trap. Captain Nicholas J. O'Brien was able to retreat to the fort, though with heavy losses (14 soldiers killed, in addition to four civilians). Failing to annihilate O'Brien's command, the Indians looted the town and held a council in which they decided to move north, to the Powder, Tongue, and Yellowstone rivers, where they would join forces with the Northern Sioux and other Cheyenne.

After the Julesburg raid, the army pursued raiding parties who were doing considerable damage along the Republican River. But these military efforts proved fruitless, and the Indians returned to Julesburg on February 2 to finish it off. Raiding continued as the Indians worked their way north. On February 4, 5, 6, and 8,

*Robert Lindneux, self-proclaimed artist-historian of the West, was born in New York in 1871 and died 99 years later in Denver. His 1936 depiction of the Sand Creek Massacre includes the American flag Chief Black Kettle raised above his tepee in a vain attempt to signal his allegiance and peaceful intentions. (Colorado Historical Society.)*

large bodies of warriors, numbering between 500 and 1,000, skirmished indecisively with much smaller army units in the vicinity of Forts Mitchell and Laramie. The raids were costly: 50 settlers killed, 1,500 head of cattle taken, buildings burned, large quantities of stores appropriated or destroyed.

Brigadier General Robert B. Mitchell attempted to organize an effective military response, but bad weather— flood waters, snow, bitter cold—made maneuvering nearly impossible. As Mitchell struggled with the elements, his superior, Major General Pope, drew up plans for a grand offensive, which called for the use of cavalry to carry out vigorous offensive operations while infantry regiments guarded and patrolled the mail and emigration trails. For the latter mission, Pope intended to use "Galvanized Yankees," Confederate prisoners-of-war who had been paroled on condition that they serve in the Union armies of the West. Pope's plans foundered in the same bad weather that plagued his subordinates; worse, Pope, an arrogant and outspoken man, ran afoul of Congress, which, disgusted by Sand Creek, was in the throes of a peace offensive. Facing

obstacles natural and political, Pope's grand campaign had little effect.

The peace offensive was by no means a permanent policy. The federal government vacillated between peace and war, so that, while Jesse H. Leavenworth, former colonel of Colorado Volunteers and presently Indian agent for the Upper Arkansas Agency, worked vigorously to hammer out a peace with the Comanches and Arapahos, Generals James H. Ford and Grenville M. Dodge fought them—as well as the Kiowas.

The pattern of Indian raiding and fitful military response came to a climax on July 26, 1865, when between 1,000 and 3,000 warriors massed to attack a cavalry unit guarding the Oregon-California Trail North Platte River crossing. On this day, Major Martin Anderson, commanding the Eleventh Kansas together with elements of two Ohio units at Upper Platte Bridge, 130 miles west of Fort Laramie, sent Lieutenant Caspar W. Collins with a detachment of 20 cavalrymen to help escort a wagon train past suspected Indian positions. The detachment was ambushed by hundreds of the waiting warriors. Miraculously, after close combat, all but Lieutenant Collins and four troopers made it back to the stockade. The Indians fared far worse, losing 60, with 130 wounded. Before retreating, they destroyed an army supply train and then withdrew for the fall buffalo hunt.

The attack provoked a sharp response from Brigadier General Patrick E. Connor, who dispatched a force of 3,000 into the Powder River country, destroying one Arapaho village and engaging the Sioux. It was again the weather, rather than military victory or defeat, that brought Connor's campaign—and the Cheyenne–Arapaho War—to an end. Premature winter storms forced Connor's withdrawal by the end of September, his men perilously close to starvation. By that time, too, Congress had more than moral objections to fighting Indians. The war that had been brought on by Chivington's action at Sand Creek had cost some $20 million and had produced no decisive results.

The end of the Civil War (May 26, 1865) released more men for western service—but only for the balance of their enlistments. These soldiers were not only temporary, but having enlisted to fight the Civil War, they were often resentful of being asked to risk their lives in the West. Significant numbers of the troops from the East were mutinous. As for Congress, weary of war in the East and the West, it acted to demobilize rapidly and that included quickly reducing troop numbers and military appropriations in the West. The army that faced the Indians in 1865 was small, poorly equipped, and seriously demoralized, receiving little support from the government and even less from the public.

# CHAPTER 23

## WARS ON THE PLAINS

### (1866–1869)

Although the end of the Civil War failed to bring a rush of reinforcements to the western frontier, it did make available for western service two aggressive commanders whose common philosophy of warfare had been forged in the conflict that just ended. William Tecumseh Sherman, as commander of the army's vast Division of the Missouri, and Philip H. Sheridan, commander of the Department of the Missouri (within Sherman's division), did not suffer from ambivalence about combat. During the Civil War, both had dramatically demonstrated a commitment to the doctrine of "total war," that is, warfare not limited to one army fighting another, but waged against the entire enemy population, soldiers and civilians alike, and intended not merely to achieve strategic victory, but to break the means and will of a people to make war. The swath of charred ruin Sherman left as a token of his "march to the sea" was the South's lesson in that doctrine.

Aggressive as he was, Sherman realized that it was one thing to wage "total war" with an army of a million and a half men, but quite another with a few thousand troops spread across the vastness of the West. Sherman craved a year or two of peace on the Plains in order to effect a transition between the disbanding volunteer forces that had borne the brunt of the Indian wars before and during the Civil War and the installation of the regular army. He also desperately needed time to whip his raw and poorly trained regiments into shape.

Accordingly, Sherman initially embraced the federal government's postwar mood of conciliation and approved of the series of treaties that were signed with the Plains tribes: the Kiowa, Comanche, Kiowa-Apache, Cheyenne, and Arapaho in the southern plains; the seven tribes of the Teton Sioux, and the Yanktonai Sioux in the northern plains. The irascible General John Pope,

having suffered through frustrating and abortive campaigns and the vagaries of federal Indian policy, harbored no illusions. "I do not consider the treaties lately made with the Sioux, Cheyennes, Arapahos, and Comanches worth the paper they are written on," he told General Sherman.

## WAR FOR THE BOZEMAN TRAIL

The peace was broken first in the north. While the Tetons had agreed in principle to withdraw from the vital Bozeman Trail and allow whites free passage on it, Chief Red Cloud feared that doing so would open his land to invasion. It was with doubt and caution that he went to Fort Laramie, in southeastern Wyoming, to negotiate terms with the peace commissioners there. In an extraordinary instance of bad timing, an infantry column commanded by Colonel Henry B. Carrington marched into the fort while the discussions were under way. Their mission, Red Cloud learned, was to build forts to protect the Bozeman Trail. "The Great Father sends us presents and wants us to sell him the road," Red Cloud observed, "but White Chief goes with soldiers to steal the road before Indians say Yes or No." Indignant, his suspicions fully confirmed, Red Cloud summarily refused not only to sell the trail and withdraw from it, but now warned that he would not allow whites even to use it.

After the failure of the peace conference, Colonel Carrington marched out of Fort Laramie on June 17, 1866, and went about the business of garrisoning three forts along the Bozeman Trail. Fort Reno was at the forks of the Powder River, and Fort Phil Kearny (his headquarters) was sited at the forks of Piney Creek. Leaving Wyoming and crossing

*The Indian artist Buffalo Meat (1847–1917) depicts a parley between warring Cheyennes and Pawnees. Indian warfare was hardly limited to combat with whites. Complex and changing alliances often pitted Indian against Indian. (Amon Carter Museum, Fort Worth, Texas.)*

into Montana, two companies under Captain Nathaniel C. Kinney established Fort C. F. Smith near the Bighorn River. Carrington prided himself on method and deliberation. He put his men to the task of building forts that were, in fact, far more elaborate than frontier conditions and the proximity of hostile Indians warranted—Fort Phil Kearny included 30 buildings and a bandstand. Red Cloud took advantage of Carrington's preoccupation by striking the forts before they were completed, forcing the troops into a desperate defensive posture.

Carrington turned a blind eye to the Indian harassment. Inflexible, even obsessive, he refused to deal aggressively and decisively with the Indians until the forts were completed. Until that time, he resolved to act defensively. If this blinded him to the Indian danger, it also meant that he refused to acknowledge the grumbling among his own officer corps. At last, one of Carrington's officers, Captain William J. Fetterman, fed up with cowering in a stockade fort, began boasting loudly that with 80 men he could ride through the entire Sioux nation. As winter closed in on Fort Phil Kearny, a steady supply of fuel became a matter of increasing priority, and while the fort was in many respects well situated, it was a considerable distance from sources of wood. On December 6, 1866, Indians attacked a wagon train hauling wood to the fort. Carrington chose his boastful captain and another officer, Lieutenant Horatio S. Bingham, to lead 30 cavalrymen in an effort to drive the Sioux west while he planned to cut the Indians off from behind with 25 mounted infantrymen.

*Chief Red Cloud, an Oglala Sioux, successfully resisted army efforts to defend the Bozeman Trail and keep it open to white travelers and settlers. (National Archives and Records Administration.)*

The tactics were sound enough, but the execution of the maneuver proved a disaster because the inexperienced soldiers panicked under attack and stampeded out of control. Lieutenant Bingham was shot through with arrows as he tried to rally the men, and Carrington, distracted by engagement with another band of Indians, never arrived to join forces with Fetterman's troops. All of the soldiers were forced to withdraw lamely to Fort Phil Kearny.

As for the Indians, they felt free to attack the wood train at will—and did so on December 21. This time, they massed between 1,500 and 2,000 warriors, who hid in ravines and along a ridge near the trail. Again, Carrington dispatched Fetterman to relieve the besieged train, warning him not to pursue the Indians beyond Lodge Trail Ridge, between the Big Piney Creek and the Bozeman Trail, but to remain on the wood road, drive the Indians off, and then retire. This time, Fetterman did not rely on raw recruits, but hand-picked a force of 49 experienced infantrymen. Lieutenant George W. Grummond—like Fetterman, no lover of Carrington—followed him out of the stockade with 27 cavalrymen. Captain Frederick H. Brown and two civilians came along just to see the fight.

Free at last from the timid restraints set by his commanding officer and leading a body of good and trusted men, Fetterman had no intention of following Carrington's order to keep to the wood road and do nothing more than relieve the wood train. He meant to move aggressively against the Sioux, not merely to defend a party of wood haulers. He marched his men away from the road and toward the Bozeman Trail, disappearing behind the Sullivant Hills.

Presently, echoes of heavy gunfire reached Carrington at the fort. He sent 40 infantry and dismounted cavalrymen under the bibulous Captain Tenodor Ten Eyck to assist Fetterman. Reaching the summit of the ridge, they saw hundreds of warriors. Along the road to Peno Valley, they discovered the naked and mutilated bodies of Fetterman and his command. There were 80 dead men counting Grummond's cavalry, precisely the number of soldiers Fetterman had said he needed to take him through the entire Sioux nation.

No one was left alive to tell the tale, but it was clear that the brash Fetterman had blundered into a trap set by a daring young Oglala Sioux warrior named Crazy Horse. He had led a small decoy party that lured Fetterman beyond Lodge Trail Ridge and into a valley of death. It was exactly the kind of fight favored in Indian tactics: ambush from concealment at close quarters and with overwhelming superiority of numbers. For the army, it was a stunning defeat and a bitter humiliation.

The Sioux did not repeat their triumph, however. In the so-called Hayfield Fight, on August 1, they attacked a group of hay cutters near another post of Carrington's command, Fort C. F. Smith. On August 2, they again struck out at woodcutters near Fort Phil Kearny in the Wagon Box Fight (called this because the soldiers took refuge behind a makeshift corral of wagon bodies, or boxes). By the time of these skirmishes, the army had replaced the cumbersome muzzle-loaded weapons Fetterman had used with much more efficient breach loaders. The Indians, stunned by the rapidity of the soldiers' fire, suffered substantial casualties, and withdrew. But they did not make peace.

## RED CLOUD (c.1822–1909)

Known among his people as Makhpíya-Lúta, this Oglala war leader was born near the forks of the Platte River in Nebraska. Orphaned at an early age, Red Cloud was raised by his maternal uncle, Chief Smoke, and quickly gained a reputation as a skilled and ruthless warrior in combat against the Pawnees and Crows. In 1841, Red Cloud took his uncle's side in a feud with the important Oglala chief Bull Bear, and at Fort Laramie, Red Cloud shot and killed the chief, an act that split the Oglalas for the next 50 years. Smoke's followers admired Red Cloud, and he acquired a large following, but he was not made chief of the divided tribe. Still, many saw him as the Oglalas' best warrior, and his counsel was sought on all important matters.

Red Cloud's greatest triumph against whites was his leaderships during the War for the Bozeman Trail, which may be considered the only western Indian war clearly won by the Indians. However, even after Red Cloud negotiated favorable terms in the Treaty of Fort Laramie, most Sioux regarded him as nothing more than an influential warrior and were concerned by his overweening ambition and his eagerness to take complete credit for the victory. After he traveled to New York and Washington, D.C., in 1870, many Sioux openly distrusted him, fearing that he was allowing himself to be co-opted by the whites. In 1871, when he settled at the Indian agency the government had named in his honor, only a fraction of the Oglala followed him—though that number steadily grew over time.

Red Cloud spent the remainder of his long life on agency land, perilously struggling to satisfy the deeply conflicting demands of whites and Indians alike. During the War for the Black Hills, Red Cloud counseled peace. Yet, after the Battle of the Little Bighorn, in which his son Jack and other Oglalas participated, government authorities accused Red Cloud of secretly aiding the hostiles and forced him to step down as leader of the Red Cloud Agency. In 1878, Red Cloud and his followers moved to the Pine Ridge Agency, but when Red Cloud fell into a dispute with Indian agent Trant Valentine McGillicuddy and requested his dismissal, it was Red Cloud who was unseated as chief of the Pine Ridge Agency.

Red Cloud acquiesced in the cession of the Black Hills and agreed to reduction of the Sioux reservation in 1889. For this, he became unpopular with many Sioux, and yet he was also abused by the whites who had authority over him. During the Ghost Dance Movement of 1890, Red Cloud, as usual, counseled peace, but, by this time, he lacked the influence necessary to control his warriors.

In his old age, Red Cloud became blind and ill. He was baptized in the Catholic faith a few years before he died in his government-built house at Pine Ridge.

## HANCOCK'S CAMPAIGN

Nor did the army *want* to make peace. In the wake of the Fetterman debacle, General Sherman telegraphed Ulysses S. Grant, the army's general-in-chief: "We must act with vindictive earnestness against the Sioux, even to their extermination, men, women, and children." Much of nonmilitary Washington, however, continued to favor conciliation. Throughout 1866 and 1867, the army loudly wrangled over policy with the Indian Bureau, which did not answer to the War Department. The chief issue was arms sales. The army, understandably, protested against arming hostile Indians, while the Indian Bureau argued that the Indians needed weapons in order to hunt; if they could not hunt, they could not feed themselves, and if they could not feed themselves, they would make war.

The War Department engineered a bill, introduced before the Senate on February 9, 1867, to transfer full authority over the Indians from the Department of the Interior to the Department of War. The bill came up against the report of a Senate investigative committee chaired by Wisconsin senator James R. Doolittle, which frankly assessed the root causes of Indian-white warfare and, recommending against the transfer of the Indian Bureau to the War Department, detailed military blunders and outrages (stressing Sand Creek) in the West:

The committee are of the opinion that in a large majority of cases Indian wars are to be traced to the aggressions of lawless white men, always to be found upon the frontier, or boundary line between savage and civilized life. Such is the statement of the most experienced officers of the army, and of all those who have been long conversant with Indian affairs. . . .

. . . [Indian warfare is] very destructive, not only of the lives of the warriors engaged in it, but of the women and children also, often becoming a war of extermination. . . .

While it is true many agents, teachers, and employés of the government are inefficient, faithless, and even guilty of peculations and fraudulent practices upon the government and upon the Indians, it is equally true that military posts among the Indians have frequently become centres of demoralization and destruction to the Indian tribes, while the blunders and want of discretion of inexperienced officers in command have brought on long and expensive wars, the cost of which, being included in the expenditures of the army, are never seen and realized by the people of the country. . . .

. . . weighing this matter . . . your committee are unanimously of the opinion that the Indian Bureau should remain where it is.

The War Department's bid for transfer of the Indian Bureau carried the House of Representatives but failed in the Senate, and another peace commission was sent into the field. Sherman had planned to dispatch Colonel John Gibbon with a force of 2,000 cavalry and infantry to punish the Sioux and Cheyennes of the Powder River country; this campaign would have to be tabled until the peace commission had (as Sherman was certain it would) failed. The peace commission was not, however, calling on the tribes of the central and southern plains—the Southern Cheyennes, the Southern Arapahos, Kiowas, and Oglala and Southern Brulé Sioux—so Sherman was not obliged to wait to campaign against these groups. He sent General Winfield Scott Hancock—an impressive Civil War commander, though new to Indian fighting— to do the job.

The Indians of this region at this time were neither unambiguously hostile nor friendly. They tended to be fragmented, the older leaders favoring peace and accommodation, the younger warriors restless and spoiling for a fight. Menacing words and minor raiding activity were common. Sherman was concerned. "If not a state of war," he observed of conditions on the southern and central plains, "it is the next thing to it, and will result in war unless checked."

On April 7, 1867, Hancock turned out 1,400 troopers of the Seventh Cavalry, the Thirty-Seventh Infantry, and

*This tepee hide, photographed about 1895, depicts a battle between Kiowas and U.S. soldiers. (National Archives and Records Administration.)*

the Fourth Artillery at Fort Larned, Kansas. He summoned a body of Cheyenne chiefs to the fort for a conference and to see for themselves the might of the U.S. Army. Bad weather delayed the meeting and resulted in a small turnout—two chiefs and 12 warriors—so Hancock decided to march a column of soldiers the next day to a combined Cheyenne and Sioux village in order to deliver his stern message to more chiefs. Doubtless recalling the treachery of Sand Creek, the women and children of the village scattered for the hills as they saw the soldiers approaching. Although Hancock instructed his principal field officer, Lieutenant Colonel George Armstrong Custer, commanding the Seventh Cavalry, to surround the village in order to prevent the men from escaping as well, by morning the lodges were all deserted.

"This looks like the commencement of war," Hancock dryly observed.

At 23, Custer had attained the rank of major general in the Civil War, earning a reputation as a brilliant, if erratic and egotistical cavalry commander. The flamboyant, yellow-haired "boy general" was, like many other officers, reduced in rank at the conclusion of the war. He was determined to recover his former glory by fighting Indians and fighting them unrelentingly. Acting on Hancock's orders, he led his Seventh Cavalry in hot pursuit of the fleeing Cheyenne and Sioux. From April through July, he and his men followed the chase, always in vain, as the Indians terrorized Kansas. Custer and the Seventh, exhausted, had to withdraw at last. What began as an offensive campaign became a series of desperate and futile attempts at defense—desperate and futile because 4,000 officers and men spread over 1,500 miles of major trails could hardly be expected to patrol the region effectively.

"Hancock's War" was yet another costly army failure and prompted a peace offensive on the southern and central plains to complement the peace activities in the north. Commissioners negotiated two sets of treaties, at Medicine Lodge Creek, Kansas, in 1867, and at Fort Laramie, Wyoming, the next year. The Medicine Lodge treaties established Cheyenne, Arapaho, Kiowa, Comanche, and Kiowa-Apache reservations in Indian Territory (present-day Oklahoma). The 1868 Fort Laramie treaties gave to Red Cloud most of what he had fought for, including the designation of the Powder River country as "unceded Indian territory," the establishment of a Great Sioux Reservation in all of present-day South Dakota west of the Missouri, hunting privileges outside the reservation "so long as the buffalo may range thereon in such numbers as to justify the chase" (which was to prove a significant proviso as white settlement drove the animals to near extinction), and the abandonment of the Bozeman Trail forts. The latter concession would appear a frank

admission of defeat in the War for the Bozeman Trail. And so, in the strictest sense, it was. However, by 1868, technology had intervened to make the Bozeman Trail far less of a prize than it had been in 1866. The transcontinental railroad was rapidly pushing west and, with each advancing mile, rendering the trail obsolete.

Like so many Indian-white treaties, the one signed at Fort Laramie on April 29, 1868, began hopefully enough:

From this day forward all war between the parties to this agreement shall forever cease. The Government of the United States desires peace, and its honor is hereby pledged to keep it. The Indians desire peace, and they now pledge their honor to maintain it.

And, like so many of these treaties, it did nothing at all to bring about the peace so solemnly pledged. In the treaty, the United States promised to punish any "bad men" (the actual language of the treaty) who might violate the agreement and do injury to the Indians. Similarly, the Indians promised to "deliver up" any "wrongdoer to the United States, to be tried and punished according to its laws." But, in reality, the Cheyennes were still sharply divided into a peace faction versus the Dog Soldiers, who would not brook confinement to any reservation. Together with elements of the Brulé and Oglala Sioux, Cheyennes, and Arapahos, the Dog Soldiers continued to raid throughout 1868 in western Kansas and eastern Colorado, killing a total of 77 settlers, wounding nine, and stealing a great deal of stock.

As for the Kiowas and Comanches, in February 1868, Indian Agent Jesse Leavenworth arrived at their new reservation in Indian Territory, only to find himself without the promised rations to give to the winter-hungry Indians. Outraged and desperate, several thousand Kiowas and Commanches engaged in raids on Texas, taking time out to terrorize Leavenworth and his agency as well as the agency of the peaceful Wichita Indians. For Leavenworth, the final straw came when Kiowa and Comanche raiders burned the headquarters of the Wichita Agency. Leavenworth left and tendered his resignation. Now there was absolutely nothing standing between the Indians and the citizens of Texas.

While the Kiowas and Comanches were raiding the southern plains, the Cheyennes began agitating for the guns and ammunition that the Medicine Lodge treaty had promised them. Tall Bull, a Dog Soldier chief, had led a raid on a neighboring Indian village, and the Indian Bureau was now fearful of issuing weapons. Repeated threats of war finally outweighed these fears, and the bureau yielded, commencing distribution. Unfortunately, a band of about 200 Cheyennes had not heard about the bureau's decision and raided settlements on the Saline

*Major General William Tecumseh Sherman (to the right of the white-bearded man) presides with commissioners over the signing of a treaty with Chief Red Cloud at Fort Laramie, Wyoming Territory, on April 29, 1868. Like most white–Indian agreements, the treaty promised much, but delivered little. (National Archives and Records Administration.)*

and Solomon rivers, killing 15 men, allegedly raping five women, burning ranches, and running off stock. As the peace factions of the Cheyenne as well as the Arapaho headed for the reservation in Indian Territory, the Dog Soldiers and other warlike factions renewed their raids throughout western Kansas and eastern Colorado.

## SHERIDAN'S CAMPAIGN

Sherman could not have been more pleased to have Phil Sheridan as his second in command in the west. The men saw eye to eye. As they had done against the South in the closing campaigns of the Civil War, they would now wage "total war" against the Indians. Sherman

spoke for them both when he declared: "These Indians require to be soundly whipped, and the ringleaders in the present trouble hung, their ponies killed, and such destruction of their property as will make them very poor."

Sherman was also greatly encouraged by the federal government's change of policy following the latest depredations of the Cheyenne. Since the various peace commissions had largely failed, the decision was now for an aggressive policy against hostiles, and it seemed certain that the entire Indian Bureau would be transferred to War Department control. Sherman was able to instruct Sheridan to "Go ahead in your own way and I will back you with my whole authority."

In consultation with Sherman, Sheridan decided that an aggressive winter campaign was necessary to deal most decisively and, indeed, cruelly with the hostiles. It was common Indian practice not to fight during the winter. This custom was accepted by military commanders and welcomed by beleaguered settlers thankful for reprieve and respite. Their food in short supply, the Indians were particularly vulnerable during the harsh winter months on the Plains. Sheridan declared:

If [a winter campaign] results in the utter annihilation of these Indians, it is but the result of what they have been warned again and again. . . . I will say nothing and do nothing to restrain our troops from doing what they deem proper on the spot, and will allow no mere vague general charges of cruelty and inhumanity to tie their hands.

Sheridan did not sit idly by awaiting the onset of the season. In the early autumn of 1868, he dispatched Major George A. Forsyth with 50 handpicked plainsmen to patrol settlements and travel routes. On September 17, the small company encountered 600 to 700 Dog Soldiers and Oglala Sioux in western Kansas. Forsyth's party took refuge on an island in the all-but-dried-up Arikara Fork of the Republican River. The only thing favorable about Forsyth's position was that his men were armed with repeating carbines, the rapid fire of which twice turned back the Indians' headlong charges.

Like previous militant Indian groups in the East and West, the Dog Soldiers believed in total abstinence from (peaceful) contact with whites. Indeed, on this occasion, one of the Cheyennes' most capable war chiefs, Roman Nose, was forced to restrain himself from joining the first two charges because he had broken his "protective medicine" by inavertently eating bread that had been touched by a metal fork—the "unclean" eating utensil

*Red Cloud (third from left) is shown here with members of a delegation some time after the Fort Laramie treaty but before 1876. The delegates include, to the chief's far right, Red Dog and Little Wound and, to his far left, American Horse (killed in 1876) and Red Shirt. John Bridgeman, an interpreter, is standing. (National Archives and Records Administration.)*

## SHERMAN AND SHERIDAN

A war-weary nation was quick to demobilize its vast Civil War army after Appomattox, so the end of the war did not release large numbers of troops to western service. However, the western command did inherit two formidable Civil War officers. William Tecumseh Sherman assumed command of the army's Division of the Missouri (which encompassed the Great Plains and included the Army's departments of the Missouri, Platte, Dakota, and Arkansas) in 1866. In 1869, when Ulysses S. Grant left the army to become president, Sherman became general of the army, with overall command of the western forces. One of his most trusted and aggressive Civil War-era subordinates, General Philip H. Sheridan, assumed command of the Department of the Missouri, replacing Winfield Scott Hancock.

Sherman (1820–91) was born in Lancaster, Ohio. Orphaned after his father's death in 1829, he was raised by his family's neighbor, Thomas Ewing. Sherman graduated from West Point in 1840 and saw service in the Second Seminole War and then the Mexican War. Like many young officers, he was dismayed by the dearth of opportunity in the army and resigned his commission in 1851. He became a banker in San Francisco in 1853 and prospered until a financial panic in 1857 brought about the collapse of the bank. He then practiced law briefly and unhappily in Kansas before deciding to return to the military. He did not, however, enter the regu-

lar army, but accepted instead a position as superintendent of the Louisiana State Military Academy (which later became Louisiana State University). As the country drew nearer to Civil War, Sherman resigned and visited Washington, D.C., intending to offer his services to the army, but, disgusted by the wholesale appointment of incompetent political hacks to important command positions, he set off for Saint Louis, where he very briefly headed a streetcar company. With the fall of Fort Sumter, Sherman felt he had no choice but to join the army again and accepted a commission as colonel.

Sherman was promoted to brigadier general of volunteers after the first Battle of Bull Run in July 1861, but his first important command, as head of the Department of the Cumberland, was disastrous. Accused of having exaggerated the weakness of his position, he was relieved in November 1861 and seemed to succumb to an attack of manic depression. Northern newspapers accused him of being insane. Struggling against military and public censure, Sherman redeemed himself at the Battle of Shiloh in April 1862. He was promoted to major general of volunteers and became Ulysses S. Grant's most trusted corps commander, playing important roles in the occupation of Memphis and the taking of Vicksburg (July 1863). After Vicksburg, Sherman was promoted to brigadier general in the regular army, and when Grant was named commander-in-

of whites. By the third charge, however, he could no longer resist and joined the fray—in the full knowledge that, in his contaminated state, it meant certain death. Sure enough, a bullet tore through his chest and killed him.

Badly shaken by the death of Roman Nose, the attackers broke off the third charge and, instead, did what Indian warriors generally disliked doing and executed poorly. They laid siege to the island. With half of Forsyth's company now dead or wounded, two messengers managed to slip through the Indian lines and travel 90 miles to Fort Wallace. A relief column arrived on the eighth day of the siege and drove off the Indians. The defenders, meantime, had been subsisting on their dead horses.

The winter campaign that Sheridan devised was three pronged. One column was to approach from Fort Bascom, New Mexico, another from Fort Lyon, Colorado,

and the third, under Custer, from Fort Dodge, Kansas. They would converge on the Indians' winter camps on the Canadian and Washita rivers, in Indian Territory. The yellow-haired commander led his Seventh Cavalry to a Cheyenne camp on the Washita, surrounded it, and on November 27, 1868, to strains of the famed regimental tune "Garry Owen," charged into the sleeping village, shooting down many Indians as they emerged from their tepees.

Custer was known for his impetuosity, which was in evidence on this occasion. He had charged the camp not only without reconnoitering, but also without knowing whom he was fighting. The 50 Cheyenne lodges now under attack belonged to Black Kettle, survivor of Sand Creek and an ardent advocate of peace. His people rallied as best they could, and the Seventh presently found itself under counterattack by warriors from nearby camps. Cus-

chief of the Union Army in early 1864, Sherman took over as commander in the West.

Sherman came into his own as a strategist during the Atlanta campaign (May–September 1864), executing a policy of what he called "total war"—combat directed not against military objectives alone, but at the civilian population as well, in order to destroy a people's very will to make war. Sherman ordered the evacuation of Atlanta and then burned it. From this point, he cut a fiery swath to the sea itself, thereby hastening the end of the war.

After the Civil War, Sherman introduced the concept of total war into the struggle with the Indians as well, ordering his commanders not merely to police the frontier, nor only to pursue and fight bands of warriors, but to attack and destroy Indian villages and stores of provisions. The officer to whom he entrusted the execution of his total war policy was Philip H. Sheridan (1831–88).

Born in New York and raised in Ohio, Sheridan entered West Point in 1848, but did not graduate until five years later because of a one-year suspension for fighting. He saw his first frontier duty in Texas and in the Pacific Northwest, where he fought in the Yakima War. Sheridan then served brilliantly in the Civil War, rising rapidly to the rank of major general and becoming commander of the Army of the Potomac's cavalry division, which was intrumental in cutting off Lee's Army of Northern Virginia and bringing about the surrender at Appomattox. After the war, Sheridan commanded the Division of the Gulf (1865–67) and was then given command of the Fifth Military District, which encompassed Texas and Louisiana. He held this post for only six months before President Andrew Johnson, concluding that Sheridan applied the principles of Reconstruction too harshly, caused his transfer to the West, where he replaced General Winfield Scott Hancock as commander of the Department of the Missouri.

Sheridan took Sherman's concept of total war to an effective extreme by conducting a series of winter campaigns with the aim of attacking Indians when they were at their most vulnerable. Sheridan's officers soon learned that such ruthless campaigns were almost as hard on soldiers as they were on the Indians.

Sheridan was promoted to lieutenant general in 1869 and given command of the Division of the Missouri when Sherman replaced Grant as commander-in-chief of the army. After campaigning in the Black Hills (1873–74) and against the Comanches, Kiowas, Southern Cheyennes, and Southern Arapahos in the Red River War (1874–75), and again against the Sioux in the Sioux War for the Black Hills (1876–77), Sheridan replaced Sherman as commander-in-chief of the army in 1883, from which office he directed General George Crook and, after him, Nelson A. Miles, in the long struggle against the Apaches under Geronimo. Sheridan was promoted to the rank of general of the army in 1888, the year in which he died.

ter, nevertheless, held his position, slaughtering 900 Indian ponies and setting tepees ablaze. At dusk, he marched his men toward the Indian camps downstream, as if he intended to attack them. Seeing this, the Indians broke off their counterstrike and prepared to defend the other camps. But it had been a ruse. At nightfall, Custer and the Seventh Cavalry quietly slipped out of the Washita Valley. The list of casualties was an ugly one: 5 soldiers killed and 14 wounded, plus 15 missing, whose bodies were discovered later. Among the 103 Indians killed, 93 were women, old men, and children—as well as Black Kettle, who had been cut down with his wife as they were riding double on a pony in a desperate attempt to forestall the attack.

Washita did, in fact, convince a substantial number of Indians to retire to the reservation. In the wake of the battle, Major Eugene Carr and Major Andrew Evans patrolled the plains north and west of the Washita, looking for parties of holdouts. On Christmas Day 1868, Evans discovered a Comanche village consisting of 60 lodges at Soldier Spring, on the north fork of the Red River, and a Kiowa camp a short distance downstream. Evans opened the attack with howitzers, forcing the Comanches to clear out of the village. With 300 troopers of the Third Cavalry, Evans entered the village, destroying it and its stores of dried buffalo meat and other provisions. Two hundred Comanches and Kiowas returned to counterattack, but withdrew after a daylong battle. His men exhausted and his horses spent, Evans could not pursue the retreating Indians. But he had done a lot of damage by destroying the winter provisions. Some of the Indians sought refuge among the Kwahadi Comanches, but most surrendered to Forts Cobb and Bascom.

Washita and Soldier Spring demonstrated how effective the winter strategy could be. There was, however, one serious drawback. Winter campaigning was almost as hard on the troops as it was on the Indians. Travel and supply during winter storms presented a logistical nightmare. It was not until March 1869 that Custer was again able to launch his Seventh against the Cheyenne, who had moved west into the Texas Panhandle. On March 15, 1869, at Sweetwater Creek, Custer discovered the villages of of Medicine Arrow and Little Robe. Reckless as he customarily was, this time he dared not attack, for he knew that the Indians held two white women hostage. Instead, he called for a parley, and during the talks seized three chiefs. He sent one back with surrender terms, demanding that the hostages be released or he would hang the other two. The Cheyennes complied and, even more, they lost their heart for fighting. They surrendered, with a promise to follow Custer to Camp Supply (and thence to their reservation) as soon as their ponies were strong enough to make the trip. Custer, whose own horses were dying for want of food and whose troops were exhausted, had little choice but to take them at their word; he and his command could not delay in returning to Camp Supply. For good measure, though, he kept the three hostages.

The Indians, however, did not report as they had promised. Worse, the Dog Soldiers, led by Tall Bull, did not stop fighting. They decided to join forces with the Northern Cheyennes in the Powder River country. On July 11, 1869, the Fifth Cavalry, commanded by Major Carr, and numbering in its rank a scout named William F. Cody—Buffalo Bill—came upon the Dog Soldiers' camp at Summit Springs, Colorado. With 250 troopers and about 50 Pawnee allies, Carr descended on the village. Surprise was complete—the Indians failed to discover the approach until the troopers were only 50 yards away. Tall Bull was killed, and the cavalry's victory was total, with far-reaching effects. The Dog Soldiers were finished in western Kansas, and the rest of the Cheyennes joined their brethren from Sweetwater Creek in retiring to the reservation.

Sherman and the army were heartened by success so long delayed. And they were cheered by yet another victory, that of Ulysses S. Grant in his bid for the presidency in 1868. With a military man in the White House, surely now the army would receive full support and an unambiguous mandate for its western mission.

# CHAPTER 24

## THE FATE OF "CONQUEST BY KINDNESS"

### The Snake War, the Modoc War, and the Red River War (1866–1875)

### GRANT'S PEACE POLICY

Although a military man was in the White House, hopes for a vigorous offensive mandate against the Indians were dashed. Even before his inauguration, Ulysses S. Grant announced a new policy of conciliation and peace—"conquest by kindness," Grant called it. After he assumed office, Grant commissioned Indian agents from among the most pacific group of people he could think of, the Quakers. One such agent was Lawrie Tatum, who left his Iowa farm to administer the Kiowa-Comanche reservation in Indian Territory. Big and hairless, he was called Bald Head Agent by his charges. Texans, however, soon found other names for him, as the reservation Indians, instigated by the Kiowa chief Satanta, stepped up their already frequent raids, now with the knowledge that all they had to do to escape punishment was retreat back into the reservation, from which the army was barred unless explicitly invited by the agent. Adding insult to injury, the Kiowas continued to draw government rations issued at Fort Sill, Indian Territory.

Despite the provisos of Grant's Peace Policy, the army had not been rendered powerless. To begin with, civilian agents were assigned only to the Central and Southern superintendencies; elsewhere, army officers served as agents. It was true that soldiers could not enter a reservation without the consent of the Indian agent, but it was also true that, while the Indian Bureau had absolute jurisdiction over Indians on the reservations, the army had authority over those beyond the reservations' confines and was, indeed, expected to deem such Indians hostile. In some ways, then, after initial shock and disappointment, the army high command realized that, if anything, it may have gained in power. Besides, the division between army and Indian Bureau jurisdiction was about to be rendered moot as transfer of the bureau from the Department of the Interior to the War Department was all but imminent.

Then opinion shifted yet again. On January 23, 1870, two squadrons of the Second Cavalry under Major Eugene M. Baker attacked a Piegan village in Montana. One hundred seventy-three Indians were killed, including 53 women and children. Sherman and Sheridan protested that the attack was in retaliation for various Piegan depredations, but the media persuaded the public and policy makers that the attack had been nothing less than a massacre. Not only was the transfer of the Indian Bureau blocked, but army officers were forbidden to hold positions as Indian agents. More church-related civilians, including additional Quakers, now filled the vacated posts.

The military commander at Fort Sill, Colonel Benjamin Grierson, gave Agent Lawrie Tatum great latitude in dealing with the Kiowas. Perhaps it was Grierson's indulgence that made it difficult for Sherman to believe all that he was hearing from Texas civilians. But the protests were loud, and Sherman decided to embark for Fort Sill on a tour of inspection. On May 18, 1871, Satanta, Satank, Big Tree, Eagle Heart, Big Bow, and about 100 Kiowa braves lay in ambush on Salt Creek Prairie, Texas. They let pass unmolested a small wagon train; for the medicine man had predicted a larger one would follow. Sure enough, a ten-wagon train followed late in the day. Only four of the train's 12 teamsters escaped massacre; the wagons were burned, and 41 mules were stolen. But the first, smaller train the Indians had allowed to pass harbored a much bigger prize than mules. It was the train carrying General William Tecumseh Sherman on his tour of inspection.

The general was appalled by Agent Tatum's inability to regulate his charges. The Texans, he now saw, had

## THE "PEACE POLICY"

The election of Ulysses S. Grant to the presidency in 1868 came at a time of great dissension between military and civilian leaders on the subject of Indian policy. The military felt hampered by humanitarian "do-gooders," while civilians accused the army of indiscriminate brutality and usurping civil authority. To the surprise and dismay of the army, Grant assumed office not as an ally of the military, but as an advocate of the humanitarian approach. While the president was not personally responsible for "Grant's Peace Policy"—which was not a single formal document, but a collection of directives—he approved and promoted it.

The object of the Peace Policy was "conquest through kindness" and emphasized civilian control of the Indian Bureau. The Grant administration sought the counsel of church groups, especially the Quakers, in nominating Indian agents and superintendents. A Board of Indian Commissioners was formed, consisting of philanthropists who served without pay; their mission was to oversee the disbursement of treaty appropriations, which had always been subject to inefficiencies, profiteering, and corruption. The Peace Policy also aimed at ending the traditional treaty system, by which Indian tribes were viewed as "domestic dependent nations" with which the United States had to negotiate as if dealing with sovereign foreign powers. Indians were to be concentrated on reservations, where they would be educated, Christianized, and taught to become self-supporting farmers.

Not all power was taken from the army by the Peace Policy. Only the Central and Southern Superintendencies—encompassing some of the Plains tribes—were staffed by church-nominated officials. All other superintendents and agents were military officers detailed to service with the Indian Bureau. More importantly, while the Indian Bureau was given sole jurisdiction over Indians resident on reservations, the army retained absolute authority over those beyond the reservations. Unless explicitly invited by an Indian agent, the army was not permitted to enter the reservations, but commanders were instructed to regard all Indians outside of the reservations as hostile.

The balance between the authority of the Indian Bureau and the military was tense and short lived. The Baker Affair of January 23, 1870 (Major Eugene M. Baker attacked a Piegan village, killing 173, of whom 53 were women and children), and the Camp Grant Massacre of April 30, 1871 (a Tucson vigilante group killed at least 86 Apaches who were under the protection of the army's Camp Grant; 29 children were sold into slavery), raised an outcry against the military, and for a time, liberal civilian forces gained control of Indian policy. Apache depredations, however, soon tipped the balance back in the other direction. Inconsistency of policy, which had characterized government-Indian relations for many years, was at its worst during the period of the Peace Policy as military and civilian authorities fitfully vied for control.

Despite the shifting back and forth, an overall trend is discernible. Problems with the Apaches steadily undermined the Peace Policy after 1873, but if the final collapse of the Peace Policy can be traced to any single event, it was the assassination of Brigadier General Edward R. S. Canby by the Modoc leader Captain Jack (Kintpuash) on Good Friday, April 11, 1873. The death of this respected and well-liked officer, a Civil War hero, outraged the army but, more significantly, enflamed public opinion against the Indians. The army was given a mandate to proceed aggressively, and the Peace Policy was brought to a bloody end by the Red River War of 1874–75.

---

been right. Moreover, even Tatum was about to have a change of heart. When he came to draw his rations on May 27, Satanta arrogantly boasted to Tatum about having led the Salt Creek massacre and then demanded additional arms and ammunition for even more raids. The Quaker agent decided that he was now more than willing to cooperate with the army. He requested Colonel Grierson to arrest Satanta, together with Satank and Big Tree.

Accordingly, the chiefs were summoned to the commander's quarters. They arrived with others, including the Kiowa war chiefs Stumbling Bear and Lone Wolf. In a moment of high drama, they confronted Sherman and Grierson, who stood on the building's porch. Satanta now boasted to Sherman that he had been responsible for Salt Creek. Sheman replied by announcing that he, Satank, and Big Tree were under arrest for murder.

At that moment, Satanta reached for a pistol concealed beneath his blanket, whereupon Sherman signalled, and the shutters of the commander's residence flew open. A squadron of black cavalrymen (Fort Sill was garrisoned by African-American troopers) trained their carbines on the Indians.

The talks continued until Stumbling Bear shot an arrow at Sherman. His aim was deflected by a soldier or another Indian. Lone Wolf pointed his rifle at the general, but Grierson seized the weapon, and the two tangled on the floor of the porch.

Bloodshed averted, Satanta, Satank, and Big Tree were shackled, loaded into wagons, and, under heavy escort, sent off to Texas. Satank, singing his death song, tore the flesh from his wrists and removed his handcuffs. Taking a penknife he had concealed, the Indian stabbed one of his guards in the leg. From the wagon behind the one carrying Satank, a soldier fired two shots, fatally wounding the chief in the chest. Satanta and Big Tree stood trial in a Texas state court, were convicted, and were sentenced to hang. In response to pressure from the Department of the Interior and from humanitarian

## BUFFALO

It is likely that several species of large bison were hunted by the earliest "Indians" who came to North America by way of an Ice Age land bridge from Asia. For Plains people, certainly, buffalo hunting had always been a way of life, and Plains Indian culture was intimately tied to the vast herds of this animal. The buffalo population reached its peak of about forty million during the seventeenth century, roaming the Great Plains from the Gulf of Mexico to the Candian woods, and from the Rockies in the West to the Mississippi River in the East; indeed, the earliest white travelers reported buffalo east of the Mississippi, in the Ohio Valley, Kentucky, Tennessee, and even into Virginia and the Carolinas.

Before the introduction of the horse among Plains tribes, hunting had been a laborious and time-consuming process. Once the Indians had acquired horses, however, hunting became highly efficient, and food and hides (for clothing as well as tepees) were plentiful. The role of the hunter became less a matter of brute labor than of consummate skill and courage on horseback. The skills acquired on the hunt were also readily transferable to war. The new efficiency meant greater leisure for the men, but added to the responsibilities of women, who had to dress and prepare the meat and the hides. Buffalo hunting forged strong bonds among women as well as among the hunters, who customarily organized themselves in closely coordinated bands of 30 or 40 men.

The leisure time gained from the more efficient hunt allowed for the elaboration of various aspects of Plains culture, including religion and ritual, promoted more complex and cooperative social organization among the hunters and among the women,

and also confirmed the Plains tribes in a nomadic existence as they followed the herds throughout the year. It was this nomadic feature of Plains culture that brought the Indians of the West into such irreconcilable conflict with the whites, whose own culture stressed containment, permanence of abode, and private ownership of clearly demarcated parcels of property.

Historians of the West frequently point out that the Plains Indian was not defeated by the U.S. Cavalry, but by the destruction of the buffalo. Early white explorers, fur traders, and emigrants freely hunted the herds for food. By the 1840s, the western fur market had largely given way to a rapidly growing market for buffalo hides, and soon more and more white hunters invaded the Plains. Prodigal as the white hunters were, killing many more animals than they could sell, it was not the hunting alone that reduced the herds. The system of emigrant trails, growing numbers of farms and ranches, and finally the ramifying network of western railroads divided buffalo country, disrupting the herds' migratory and grazing patterns. The railroads also brought even more hunters from the East, many of them out for "manly" sport, and from 1870 to 1883, the buffalo massacre was virtually unchecked. By the end of this period, the herds that once literally blackened the Plains had been hunted to the point of extinction. It is no accident that this period corresponds with the height of the Plains Indian wars and with the relentless confinement of the nomadic tribes to reservations. It is also no coincidence that a popular movement to preserve the buffalo began only at the turn of the century, after the Indian wars had ended.

groups, the sentences were commuted to prison terms. In 1873, responding to more pressure, the governor of Texas released Satanta and Big Tree.

If the release of the two chiefs was intended to placate the Indians into leaving the Texas frontier alone, it did not suceed. And despite the government's demonstration of its peaceful intentions, little was done to improve poor conditions on the reservations. Worse, the Plains were crawling with white buffalo hunters who were driving the animals to extinction, killing them for their hides alone. The buffalo was of paramount importance in Plains Indian culture. The herds were the Indians' chief source of food and clothing, and, as long as vast numbers of the animals ranged freely, the encroachment of ranchers and farmers was limited. The Indians of the Plains rightly saw that the herds were being exterminated, and they knew that, when the buffalo vanished, so would their traditional way of life.

By the summer of 1874, with Indians raiding the Texas Panhandle at will and with the reservation system in shambles, the army was given permission to carry its offensives into the reservations themselves. The Peace Policy had failed, and the Red River War was under way.

## THE SNAKE WAR

War was not confined to the Plains during this epoch of "conquest by kindness." The Northwest, scene of violence in the 1850s, erupted again. The first trouble was with the Yahuskin and Walpapi bands of the Northern Paiutes, popularly known as the Snakes, who inhabited southeastern Oregon and southwestern Idaho. During the Civil War years, they periodically attacked miners in the region and were the focus of ineffectual campaigns conducted by Oregon and Nevada Volunteers. With the end of the Civil War, the campaign against the Snakes fell to the First Cavalry and Fourteenth Infantry of the regular army, which, like the volunteer groups, enjoyed little success in neutralizing the chronic raids. The public raised an outcry against the army, which, in response, reorganized command in the area. The Second Battallion of the Fourteenth Infantry was reorganized into the Twenty-third Infantry, and Brevet Major General George Crook was dispatched to command it.

Unlike so many regular army commanders, Crook disdained military pomp and ceremony as well as orthodox field methods. He studied Indian combat practices carefully and did not hesitate to use them himself. He also made extensive use of Shoshoni auxiliaries. While cavalry commanders would not deign to trade their horses for lowly mules, Crook recognized that, as pack animals in rough terrain, the mule was far superior to the horse. He used these pack animals instead of the cumbersome wagon trains that slowed columns in pursuit of Indians.

The Snake War, which Crook waged between 1866 and 1868, was not a series of formal battles, but a virtually continuous pursuit and tireless guerrilla action. Crook wrote of the campaign with a spareness of words that was characteristic of this intense and introspective commander: "I took Captain Perry's company of the First Cavalry and left with one change of underclothes, toothbrush, etc., and went to investigate matters, intending to be gone a week. But I got interested after the Indians and did not return there [to Fort Boise] again for over two years." Vigorous and relentless, Crook inspired all the officers of his command to a similar degree of activity. During the two-year period, Crook and his officers engaged the Snakes at least 49 times and, more important, kept them on the run. By the middle of 1868, with 329 killed, 20 wounded, 225 captured, and their most revered chief, Pauline (or Paulina) dead, the Snakes indicated their willingness to make peace. Another hitherto hostile chief, Old Weawea, led 800 Indians to Fort Harney, in southeastern Oregon, on July 1, 1868, to talk to Crook.

The commander adopted the cruel, hard line he deemed most effective in dealing with Indians. Dead soldiers, he told Old Weawea, could be replaced instantly. Dead warriors, on the other hand, could be replaced only as children came of age. "In this way it would not be very long before we would have you all killed off, and then the government would have no more trouble with you." Exhausted, the Snakes got the message and many of them remained under the watchful eye of Fort Harney (from which they drew their rations) or retired to the Klamath and Malheur River reservations. Others remained at large, lying low, later to join the Bannocks and Cayuses in the Bannock War of 1878. Crook had effectively neutralized the Snakes just as Grant's Peace Policy was put into effect.

## THE MODOC WAR

Just south of Snake country, in the rugged Lost River valley of northern California and southern Oregon, the Modocs, a small tribe numbering between 400 and 500 people, still presented a threat. At the moment, they were trying to live in harmony with the miners who had come into the region, actively trading with them, which represented a substantial change in behavior. The Modocs were a hunting and gathering tribe, by nature aggressive, having terrorized white immigrants along the Applegate

Trail during the 1850s. But by the 1860s, under the leadership of Captain Jack (Kintpuash)—they wanted peace.

The single obstacle to peace was their unwillingness to accept life on a reservation, especially a reservation they were to share with the Klamath Indians who had, resenting intrusion into their land, made life unpleasant for the Modocs. The situation was all too common, since white administrators characteristically ignored differences among Indians as they tried to legislate and bully them into logistically convenient geographical divisions. Rather than suffer at the hands of the Klamaths, Captain Jack and his followers settled on the Lost River, near Tule Lake, getting their living for some seven years by trade with the neighboring white settlers. As the pace of white settlement increased during the late 1860s, pressure mounted for the Modocs' removal. In December 1869, Superintendent of Indian Affairs Alfred B. Meacham convinced Captain Jack to return to the reservation.

That move lasted only three months, when Captain Jack and 60 to 70 Modoc families returned to the Lost River. Thomas B. Odeneal, who succeeded Meacham as superintendent of Indian Affairs, recommended that the Modocs be removed to the Klamath reservation by force. On November 29, 1872, Captain James Jackson and Troop B, First Cavalry—three officers and 40 men—entered Captain Jack's camp and proceeded to disarm the Indians. A scuffle between a trooper and an Indian resulted in an exchange of fire. Jackson claimed that 16 Modocs had been killed; actually, only one had been killed and another wounded, while the troopers suffered one killed and seven wounded (one mortally). The army dignified the exchange by conferring on it the title of Battle of Lost River.

While Jackson was dealing ineffectually with Captain Jack and his followers, a vigilante group of ranchers attacked a smaller group of Modocs, followers of a man that the whites called Hooker Jim. The assault resulted immediately in the deaths of two whites and the wounding of another. Then, as Hooker Jim and his people rushed to join forces with Captain Jack, 14 more settlers were killed along the way. Now mustering 60 warriors in all, Captain Jack and Hooker Jim hid in the twisted, otherworldly landscape of the lava beds south of Tule Lake, a place the Indians called the Land of Burnt-Out Fires, and the whites came to refer to as Captain Jack's Stronghold.

On the night of January 16, 1873, Lieutenant Colonel Frank Wheaton deployed a force of 225 regular army troops and about 100 militiamen around Captain Jack's Stronghold. Preceeded by a howitzer barrage, he attacked at dawn. But Captain Jack's warriors were invisible among the lava flows and easily picked off troopers. Nine of Wheaton's men were killed, and 28 wounded.

Not only had the army failed to kill or capture any Modocs during the Battle of the Stronghold, but no soldier had even *seen* the enemy.

With his army unable to dislodge the Modocs by force of arms, and his peace policy under serious critical attack as a failure, President Grant appointed a peace commission to treat with the Modocs. For part of April and well into March 1873, the commissioners flailed about ineffectually with the Indians. At last, Brigadier General Edward R. S. Canby, commander of the Department of the Columbia (who had been instrumental in prosecuting the Navajo War in New Mexico a decade earlier), was given the authority to try his own hand at diplomacy. He formed a new peace commission consisting of himself, a Methodist preacher named Eleaser Thomas, former superintendent of Indian affairs Alfred B. Meacham, and another official, L. S. Dyar. Under a flag of truce, Canby began talks with Captain Jack by demanding unconditional surrender. The Indian replied by asking that he be given "this Lava Bed for a home. I can live here; take away your soldiers, and we can settle everything. Nobody will ever want these rocks; give me a home here."

What Captain Jack said was true. No white man would want the lava beds. But that was not the point, and Canby could not concede victory to the Modocs. Neither side backed down, and Jack withdrew to his camp. But he was confident that the general could be made to change his mind, and he urged the other Modocs to practice persistence and patience. However, most of them favored a quicker solution: Murder Canby and the other peace commissioners as a warning to all whites.

Captain Jack pointed out that the act would only result in more serious efforts at pursuit and, most likely, the annihilation of the Modocs. Berating Jack as a weak woman and coward, his most militant warriors goaded him into committing murder. "All who want me to kill Canby," Jack said to his warriors, "raise to your feet." When a majority did, Jack declared with resignation, "I see you do not love life nor anything else. . . . I will ask [Canby] many times. If he comes to my terms I shall not kill him."

On Good Friday, April 11, 1873, despite warnings from the well-intentioned Modoc wife of his interpreter, Edward Canby and the other three commissioners held council with Captain Jack. The general passed out cigars to all present and began the council by promising to take the Modocs to a good country. As he had told his fellow warriors he would do, Captain Jack answered each of the commission's demands with his own single demand: that he and his people be allowed to live in the lava beds.

Tempers on both sides flared. At one point, Hooker Jim donned Meacham's overcoat, which had been draped over the commissioner's saddle, strutted about in it, and asked, "You think I look like Meacham?"

*Donald McKay (leaning on the rock) led this group of Warm Springs Apache scouts, one of the units in pursuit of the Modocs. The photograph gives some suggestion of the barrenness of the Northern California lava bed country into which the Modocs had fled. Note the improvised military insignia on three of the scouts' hats. (National Archives and Records Administration.)*

In a bid to reduce the tension, the commissioner went along with the Indian's joke, offering Hooker Jim his hat. "Take it and put it on; then you will be Meacham."

"You keep a while. Hat will be mine by and by," Hooker Jim replied.

To Meacham, the threat was all too evident.

Canby, however, persisted, yielding nothing. He told Captain Jack that "only the Great Father in Washington" could withdraw the troops.

"I want to tell you, Canby," repeated Jack, "we cannot make peace as long as these soldiers are crowding me. If you ever promise me a home, somewhere in this country, promise me today. Now, Canby, promise me. . . . Now is your chance."

Meacham had had enough.

"General," he implored, "for heaven's sake, promise him."

Another Modoc, Schonchin John, leaped to his feet:

"You take away soldiers, you give us back our land! We tired talking. We talk no more!"

"Ot-we-kau-tux-e," Jack said: *All ready!*

He drew a pistol, pointed it at Canby's face and pulled the trigger. The hammer clicked, but the weapon failed to fire. Canby simply stared in astonishment as Captain Jack pulled the trigger again. This time there was a loud report, and Edward Canby fell back dead, the only general officer of the regular army killed in the Indian wars.

Meacham was wounded, and he and Canby were stripped, stabbed, and left to die (miraculously, Meacham recovered). Reverend Thomas was slain, but L. S. Dyar escaped without harm. Captain Jack and his warriors fled to the lava beds.

As Captain Jack had predicted, the murders only made the Modocs' situation much worse. Sherman, like the rest of the army officer corps, was outraged. "Any measure of severity to the savages will be sustained," he telegraphed General John M. Schofield, Canby's immediate superior. Colonel Alvin C. Gillem led two attacking infantry formations through the lava beds, pounding Modoc positions with howitzers and mortars from April 15th through the 17th. But most of the warriors eluded the massive attack.

The army refused to break off the pursuit. On April 26, Modoc warriors sighted a reconnoitering party of 5 officers, 59 enlisted men, and 12 Indian scouts under Captain Evan Thomas eating lunch in a vulnerable spot. With 22 braves, the leader, Scarfaced Charley, attacked, killing all 5 officers, 20 men, and wounding another 16. "All you fellows that ain't dead," Charley called out, "had better go home. We don't want to kill you all in one day."

The Modoc victories were taking their toll, not only in men but in morale. Yet, even in the face of these victories, the Modoc warriors were coming to realize that continued resistance would be ultimately futile. By the middle of May, with food and water scarce, the Modocs scattered. It remained for troops under Jefferson C. Davis (no relation to the former Confederate president) to hunt them down and bring the ringleaders to justice for the murder of Edward Canby. On May 28, assisted by Hooker Jim, who had been captured earlier, a cavalry detachment found Captain Jack, his family, and a number of followers. Hooker Jim convinced 37 warriors and their families to surrender, but Captain Jack refused to give up. Cavalry units were called in and sighted the leader's camp on May 29, but Captain Jack ran. They pressed the pursuit and, at last exhausted, the chief was overtaken on June 3. He and his family were hiding out in a cave, from which Captain David Perry persuaded him to emerge. Captain Jack and others identified as ringleaders—Boston Charley, Black Jim, and Schonchin John—were subsequently tried and hanged.

## THE RED RIVER WAR

Neither Canby nor Kintpuash was the principal casualty of the Modoc War. What fell hardest was Grant's Peace

*On Good Friday, April 11, 1873, Major General Edward R. S. Canby was shot and killed by Kintpuash, a Modoc leader better known to the whites as Captain Jack, while he was attempting to negotiate the removal of the Modocs to a reservation. Canby was the only general officer in the U.S. Army to die in the Indian Wars. (Library of Congress.)*

Policy. Back on the southern plains, the government's new policy of aggression was manifested in the Red River War. The parole of Satanta and Big Tree, combined with Indian outrage at inadequate agency rations, the white hunters' relentless assault on the buffalo, and other abuses, made conditions ripe for a major uprising.

In the spring of 1874, Kiowas, Comanches, and Cheyennes launched major raids: On June 27, Comanches and Cheyennes hit a white hunter village at Adobe Walls in the Texas Panhandle; on July 12, the Kiowa chief Lone Wolf ambushed Texas Rangers at Lost Valley. Throughout this period, warriors struck at ranchers and wayfarers in Kansas and Texas. Based on these depredations and the disintegration of the peace policy, Sherman secured

government authority to invade the reservations. On July 20, 1874, he telegraphed Sheridan to begin an offensive.

Sheridan and his lieutenants, Generals John Pope (commanding Kansas, New Mexico, and parts of Colorado and Indian Territory) and Christopher C. Augur (commanding Texas and part of Indian Territory), planned a campaign of convergence upon the Staked Plains region of the Panhandle, with columns closing in from Fort Sill, Indian Territory; Texas; New Mexico; and Kansas.

One of Pope's ablest field commanders, Colonel Nelson A. Miles, led eight troops of the Sixth Cavalry and four companies of the Fifth Infantry southward from the Canadian River into Indian Territory. Seven hundred seventy-four troopers encountered about 200 Cheyennes (soon augmented to about 600) as they approached the Staked Plains escarpment on August 30. The soldiers pressed the attack from one hill to the next, bringing Gatling guns and howitzers to bear at critical points, and alternating this pounding with infantry and cavalry charges. After a running battle covering 12 miles and lasting five hours, the Indians made a stand along the slopes of Tule Canyon. Although the Indians were exhausted and demoralized, Miles lacked the supplies to

*Chikchikam Lupatuelatko, known to the whites as Scarfaced Charley, was a Modoc warrior who surprised a party of U.S. Army pursuers as they ate lunch. After killing 25 out of 64 troopers, he called out to the survivors, "All you fellows that ain't dead had better go home. We don't want to kill you all in one day." (National Archives and Records Administration.)*

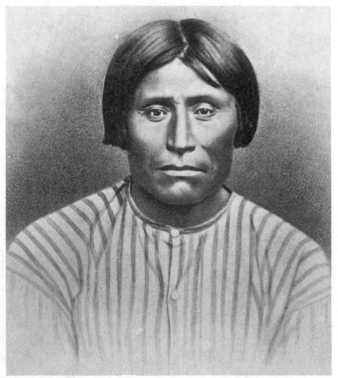

*After assassinating Edward R. S. Canby, Kintpuash ("Captain Jack") led his small tribe in resistance against removal to a reservation. Captured after a long, difficult, and costly pursuit on June 3, 1873, he was hanged soon afterwards. (National Archives and Records Administration.)*

## QUANAH PARKER (c.1845–1911)

Quanah Parker was the son of Peta Nocono, a Comanche chief, and Cynthia Ann Parker, who had been abducted by the Comanches when she was nine years old. Cynthia was adopted into the tribe, and as a teenager, she married Peta Nocono. From an early age, Quarah distinguished himself as a horseman and warrior. He also learned to hate the white man after Texas Rangers took his mother from him, forcibly returning her to relatives (she died four years later), and after the death of his father in combat. When Quanah's brother succumbed to a white man's disease, the young warrior joined the most aggressive of Comanche bands, the Kwahadi and, by 1867, was a war chief among them.

Under Quanah's leadership, the Kwahadi resisted confinement to a reservation and fought one of Sherman's ablest commanders, Ranald S. Mackenzie, in the Staked Plains region of the Texas Panhandle during September 1871. The following year, Mackenzie prevailed against the Kotsoteka Comanches, but the Kwahadis continued to resist. On June 27, 1874, Quanah was among the leaders of a massive attack by 700 warriors—Cheyennes, Kiowas, and Arapahos—against a small encampment of 28 white buffalo hunters at Adobe Walls on the South Canadian River. The battle turned out to be a disappointment to the Indians. Although they greatly outnumbered the hunters, they discovered that they were no match for the whites' new high-powered repeating rifles and were forced to withdraw with the loss of 15 warriors. Despite Adobe Walls, Quanah and others continued to raid. Soon, however, the relentless campaigning of the Red River War took its toll, and in June 1875, Quanah and his Kwahadis submitted to the reservation.

Unlike many Indian leaders confined to the reservation, Quanah became neither bitter nor desperate. Instead he adopted his mother's last name, and he learned English and Spanish. He became an influential spokesman for the Kwahadis in council with Indian agents and worked to improve the economic lot of the reservation Indians by carefully managing such remunerative resources as pasturage, grazing rights, and railroad rights-of-way. Quanah Parker soon earned a fine living as a rancher and rose to greater and greater prominence in reservation government. He served as a judge on the Court of Indian Offenses, and by 1890, he was recognized as chief of all the Comanche bands. In 1892, he was a principal negotiator with the Jerome Commission, which administered the Dawes Severalty Act, by which reservation lands were broken up and allotted to individual Indians. Quanah Parker became a familiar figure in Washington, D.C., to which he frequently traveled as a delegate on behalf of his tribe.

Whites pointed to Quanah Parker's beautiful home near Cache, Oklahoma, as an example of what a "cooperative" Indian might accomplish. Yet Quanah Parker did not "sell out" to white society. He worked toward the economic enfranchisement of the Indian, but he was not eager to back Indian Bureau educational programs, nor did he embrace Christianity. Indeed, his stubborn adherenece to polygamy (he had five wives) caused his dismissal from the Court of Indian Offenses in 1897, and he was instrumental in establishing what was to become (seven years after his death) the Native American Church. Among its sacraments is the use of peyote, which Quanah Parker advocated and popularized among Indians of the Plains, Southwest, Prairies, and Great Lakes.

press the attack any further. He withdrew for provisions, destroying abandoned Indian villages on the way.

Thus far in the campaign, a hellish drought had been as formidable an enemy as any human foe. On September 7, as Miles was still attempting to resupply his command, the drought ended abruptly in torrential rains. Rendezvousing with a force of 225 officers and men of the Eighth Cavalry under Major William R. Price, Miles struggled northward through a sea of mud in search of supply. But Kiowas and Comanches, some 250 warriors,

including Lone Wolf, Satanta, and Big Tree, attacked the army supply train on September 9, keeping it under siege for three days until the approach of Price drove them off. Miles, hampered by lack of supply, was unable to pursue.

General Augur's most capable field officer, Colonel Ranald S. Mackenzie, at the head of the Fourth Cavalry approaching from the southeast, had no such supply problems. During the night of September 26, 250 Comanches attacked Mackenzie's camp near Tule Canyon in an attempt to stampede the cavalry's ponies. But Mackenzie, anticipating such a maneuver, had taken the precaution of hobbling the animals and surrounding them with sentries. Unable to stampede the mounts, the warriors contented themselves with shooting at the troopers. Mackenzie struck back in the morning—his eight cavalry troops mustered 21 officers and 450 men—and drove the Indians off. Then, acting on information from Tonkawa scouts, he pressed on to Palo Duro Canyon, where he surprised a combined Kiowa-Comanche-Cheyenne village, routing the warriors there. Though he killed only three Indians, Mackenzie destroyed the village and all its provisions and took 1,424 Indian ponies. After selecting about 400 of the best mounts for his own men, he slaughtered the remainder. Into October, soldiers under the command of Colonel George P. Buell burned more villages. Miles and Price pursued a chief known as Gray Beard and his band of Cheyennes, failing to take the chief or kill his warriors, but destroying the village from which they fled—a camp of more than 100 lodges.

The Plains warfare that followed unfolded in the usual pattern of destruction and pursuit, destruction of homes and provisions that caused untold suffering, and pursuit that wore down Indian and soldier alike. What the army, practicing Sherman and Sheridan's doctrine of "total war," could not accomplish, the storms of a brutal Plains winter did. During the late fall and winter, their villages destroyed, their people cold and hungry, parties of Kiowas and Cheyennes straggled in to Forts Sill and Darlington to give themselves up and submit to life on the reservation. Satanta, together with Woman's Heart and other Kiowa war chiefs, surrendered at the Darlington Agency on October 7, 1874. The pace of surrender quickened as the winter wore on, and it continued into spring, when about 600 Kwahadi Comanches, yielding at last to Nelson A. Miles and the elements, consented to retire to a reservation. With a group of 407 defeated Kwahadis who reported to Fort Sill on June 2, 1875, came Quanah Parker, one of the most feared of the Comanche war chiefs—a leader who would henceforth work so hard to preserve the peace and ease the lot of his people that the U.S. Congress would eventually praise his public service.

With the southern plains essentially secured, Sheridan took the vital precaution of exiling 74 militant chiefs to Castillo de San Marcos, a former Spanish fortress in Saint Augustine, Florida. Satanta was consigned to crueler confinement in the Texas state penitentiary, from which he had been previously paroled. There on March 11, 1878, despairing in his captivity, he committed suicide by leaping from a window.

# CHAPTER 25

□

# THE NORTHERN PLAINS AND THE NORTHWEST

## The Sioux War for the Black Hills and the Pursuit of the Nez Percés (1876–1881)

As the wars on the southern plains smoldered, guttered out, and died, those on the northern plains fanned into flame. Various Sioux, Cheyenne, and Arapaho bands retired to the reservations, resigned to live on the government dole. Red Cloud and Spotted Tail (a Brulé Sioux) became leaders of these "reservation Sioux," locked into a seemingly perpetual contest with the Indian agency on the one hand and their own restless young warriors on the other. The reservations, always places of despair, were often places of violence as well.

Those groups that shunned the reservation—mainly the Oglala, Hunkpapa, and Miniconjou Sioux and factions of the Northern Cheyenne, as well as some Yankton, Teton, and Santee Sioux—remained openly and defiantly militant. Among them, Crazy Horse, an Oglala Sioux, and Sitting Bull, of the Hunkpapa Sioux, were gaining legendary status as warrior chiefs. Indeed, the very name of Sitting Bull had become among the Indians a word (as one white scout observed) for "all that was generous and great." In his forties during the 1870s, swarthy and broad-shouldered, with a penetrating gaze, Sitting Bull had nothing but contempt for his reservation brethren, who, he said, had made themselves "slaves to a piece of fat bacon, some hard-tack, and a little sugar and coffee."

## WAR FOR THE BLACK HILLS

Provoked by the inexorable white incursion into their lands, the Sioux of the northern plains raided settlements in Montana, Wyoming, and Nebraska. Sitting Bull, in particular, menaced survey parties laying out the Northern Pacific Railroad in 1873. A year later, George Armstrong Custer, leading a military expedition in the Black

Hills, discovered gold. Within another year—and in flagrant violation of the Treaty of Fort Laramie (April 29, 1868)—thousands of whites swarmed the Black Hills in search of ore. The army made some gestures of interference, but the high command was not about to incur popular censure for vigorously defending Indians against whites. The only real hope for a peaceful resolution of the crisis was government purchase or lease of the Black Hills. Accordingly, a commission chaired by Senator William Allison attempted negotiation, but as the ground most sacred to the Sioux people, the Black Hills were neither for rent nor for sale. At the end of 1875, therefore, the federal government dropped all pretext of fair dealing by issuing the tribes an ultimatum: Report to an agency and reservation by January 31, 1876, or be hunted and killed as hostiles.

The deadline came and went. Even if the Indians had decided to leave, they could hardly have done so on such short notice and in the middle of a cruel northern winter. Indian Bureau inspector E. C. Watkins had furnished "justification" for a campaign against the Sioux, citing various depredations committed by Sitting Bull and his followers. "The true policy, in my judgment," Watkins declared in a report, "is to send troops against them in the winter, the sooner the better, and *whip* them into subjection." And that is precisely what General Sheridan prepared to do with two of the kind of winter campaigns that had previously proven successful on the southern plains.

The first campaign, however, failed to get under way. Acting under General Alfred H. Terry's orders, Custer was supposed to lead his Seventh Cavalry westward from Fort Lincoln, at the junction of the Missouri and Heart rivers in present-day North Dakota, but was repeatedly foiled by heavy snow. General George Crook did lead 900 men out of Fort Fetterman, on the North Platte River

*Young-Man-Afraid-of-His-Horses, one of the most prominent among Oglala hostiles, a veteran of the Powder River fights and a strong follower of Red Cloud, is seen here, on January 17, 1891, less than three weeks after Wounded Knee, resigned to life on the Pine Ridge Reservation. (National Archives and Records Administration.)*

in Wyoming, on March 1, 1876, and, battling storms and cold, scoured the Powder River country for Indians. After three discouraging weeks, a trail was found, and Crook dispatched Colonel Joseph J. Reynolds with a large complement of cavalry—about 300 men—to attack a village of 105 lodges beside the Powder River.

Although taken by surprise, the Oglalas, under He Dog, and the Cheyennes, led by Old Bear, counterattacked so effectively that Reynolds was forced to withdraw back to Crook and the main column. Only one of Reynolds's squadrons had managed to penetrate the village, and another had seized the pony herd. But the first squadron had barely begun its work of destruction before

it was compelled to withdraw under the counterattack, and as for the ponies, the warriors managed to recover most of them.

With Reynolds in tow, Crook retreated to Fort Fetterman, where he brought charges against his subordinate for mismanaging both the attack and the retreat. General Sheridan ascribed Reynolds's poor showing to the weather and dismissed the charges. "General," Reynolds complained to Sheridan, "these winter campaigns in these latitudes should be prohibited. . . . The Month of March has told on me more than any five years of my life." Indeed, Crook's abortive winter campaign did little damage to the Indians; if anything, it galvanized

## GEORGE ARMSTRONG CUSTER (1839–1870)

George Armstrong Custer was born in New Rumley, Ohio, and was appointed to the U.S. Military Academy at West Point by Congressman John W. Bingham. His career at the academy was distinguished by two things: He accumulated a record number of disciplinary demerits, and he graduated in 1861 at the bottom of his class. But he did graduate at an opportune time for young officers—the opening months of the Civil War. Assigned to the Fifth Cavalry of the Army of the Potomac, he quickly impressed his commanders, including Phil Kearny and George McClellan, with his audacity, daring, and plain recklessness, rare commodities during the early, demoralizing months of the war. In 1863, Custer was breveted to the rank of brigadier general of volunteers, an extraordinary promotion that has been ascribed variously to politics or to clerical error, but was probably the deliberate work of General Alfred Pleasanton, who was looking for ways in which to inject life and spirit into the cavalry forces he commanded.

Custer was quickly dubbed the Boy General and participated in all the major battles of the Army of the Potomac, including the cavalry fight on the right flank at Gettysburg, which many authorities believe provided the "margin of victory" that enabled the North to win this pivotal battle. In 1864, Custer married the beautiful Elizabeth Bacon (whose autobiographical/biographical trilogy, written after the death of her husband, was responsible for much of the mythology that subsequently attached to Custer) and, at age 23, won promotion to the rank of major general in the regular army.

At the end of Civil War, as was the case with many officers, Custer reverted in rank. He served briefly as a captain but was soon promoted to lieutenant colonel and given command of the newly created Seventh Cavalry, assigned to duty under General Winfield Scott Hancock. Custer served as chief field commander during Hancock's Campaign (1867) but was court martialed for leaving his command without permission (he visited his wife) and for harsh treatment of deserters and overmarching his men. Convicted, Custer was suspended for one year, but was reinstated before the expiration of his sentence and led the brutal winter assault on Black Kettle's Southern Cheyennes in the Battle of Washita. The victory at Washita was highly controversial. To begin with, Black Kettle, who had endured the Sand Creek Massacre at the hands of Colonel Chivington in 1864, wanted nothing more than peace. Custer ignored this and proceeded with an attack that killed more than 100 Indians, the majority women and children. Moreover, when Custer was forced to withdraw under counterattack, he abandoned a contingent of 20 of his troopers, who were killed in ambush. From this point on, many of his officers questioned his judgment.

In 1873, Custer was part of an expedition exploring the Yellowstone River, and in 1874 he led an expedition into the Black Hills, which discovered gold and triggered a stampede of miners into this most sacred of Sioux territory. By 1876, the Sioux War for the Black Hills commenced, ending—for Custer—on June 25, 1876, at the Little Bighorn River, when his command was annihilated by Sioux forces under the command of Crazy Horse, Gall, and other prominent war chiefs.

"Custer's Last Stand" became the subject of popular literature, film, and more than 100 paintings and innumerable prints. Custer's role in the debacle has been interpreted as everything from tragic heroism to monumentally rash poor judgment, and Custer himself has been regarded as a valiant and audacious warrior and a cruel, reckless, self-aggrandizing martinet.

them into a large fighting force under the inspired leadership of Crazy Horse and Sitting Bull.

Late in the spring of 1876, Sheridan initiated another campaign of convergence: General Alfred Terry led a force from the east (including Custer and his Seventh), Colonel John Gibbon approached from the west, and Crook marched out of Fort Fetterman. They converged on the Yellowstone, even as the Indians were traveling that way. Early in June, at Rosebud Creek, the Indians held a religious ceremony known as a Sun Dance, at which Sitting Bull announced that he had seen a vision. It was of many, many soldiers "falling right into our camp."

On the morning of June 17, General Crook, with more than 1,000 men, halted for a rest at the head of the Rosebud. Crow and Shoshoni scouts attached to Crook's column sighted Sitting Bull's Sioux and Cheyenne as they descended upon Crook's position. The scouts gave sufficient warning to avert disaster, but even so, the Indians withdrew only after a sharp six-hour fight. Crook's column took severe punishment and was also forced to retreat. The battle was harder than most; more significantly, it was characterized by an unusual degree of coordination and unity of action on the part of the Indians, whose style of fighting customarily sacrificed cooperation to acts of individual heroism and prowess. Under the likes of Sitting Bull and Crazy Horse, these Plains warriors had become a militarily effective unit.

Following the Rosebud battle, the Indians established a camp. In the meantime, General Terry's column united with Colonel John Gibbon at the mouth of the Rosebud. Both men were unaware of Crook's retreat. The officers of both commands, including Custer, convened in the cabin of the Yellowstone steamer *Far West* to lay out a campaign strategy. They figured they would find the Sioux encampment on the stream that the Indians called the Greasy Grass and that white men called the Little Bighorn. What they had no notion of was the size of the camp. Augmented by the arrival of agency Indians who left the reservation for the spring and summer, the village now consisted of about 7,000 people.

The *Far West* plan called for Custer to lead his Seventh up the Rosebud, cross to the Little Bighorn, and proceed down its valley from the south as Terry and Gibbon marched up the Yellowstone and Bighorn to block the Indians from the north. In that way, Sitting Bull's forces would be caught between the two columns of a classic pincers movement.

On the morning of June 22, to the tune of "Garry Owen," the 600 men of the Seventh passed in review before Terry, Gibbon, and Custer. Shaking hands with his fellow officers, Custer set off to join his men. General Gibbon called after him: "Now, Custer, don't be greedy, but wait for us."

## THE BLACK HILLS

Standing Bull, a Teton Sioux chief, brought his people to the Black Hills—called by the Sioux *Paha Sapa*—in 1775. Over the next 40 years, the Tetons secured this region of present-day South Dakota, expelling the Kiowa in 1814. The Black Hills seemed to the Sioux a paradise and were regarded as a holy place, the home of *Wakan Tanka*, the Great Spirit. Darkly wooded, therefore "black," and watered by many beautiful rivers, *Paha Sapa* became the physical as well as spiritual center of Sioux life.

The first serious incursions into this region came in 1842 as wagons began to cross the Oregon Trail. The Fort Laramie Treaty of 1851 formally recognized Sioux ownership of some 60 million acres, but allocated the Powder River and Bighorn country, just west of the Hills, to other tribes. By 1862, Little Crow had accepted further reductions in Sioux land, and almost from sheer frustration, the Santee Uprising broke out in Minnesota and elsewhere. In 1866, the Black Hills were again invaded, this time by the Bozeman Trail. Red Cloud began the largely successful War for the Bozeman Trail in 1866, which ended with the 1868 Treaty of Fort Laramie, establishing the Great Sioux Reservation and designating the Powder River and Bighorn country "unceded Indian territory." This treaty held until George Armstrong Custer's 1874 expedition into the Black Hills discovered gold. The specially appointed Allison Commission sought to negotiate the purchase or lease of the Black Hills, but the Sioux refused to sell a region so sacred, and in 1876, the United States declared war on the Sioux.

The most famous battle of the Sioux War for the Black Hills was Custer's defeat and annihilation at the Little Bighorn. In the aftermath of the battle, Congress attached a rider to the Indian Appropriations Act, threatening to cut off all food and rations to the Sioux unless they not only ceded the Black Hills, but relinquished rights to all land outside of their permanent reservation. George Manypenny, a former commissioner of Indian Affairs, headed the commission that presented the congressional ultimatum to the Sioux. It was a choice between suicide and survival, and the Sioux chiefs agreed. An act of Congress, passed on February 28, 1877, gave the coercive agreement the force of law, and the Black Hills officially ceased to be the land of the Sioux.

The massacre at Wounded Knee in 1890 ended armed conflict between the Sioux and the United States. Almost from the beginning of the twentieth century, however, the battle for the Black Hills recommenced—not on the field, but in the nation's courtrooms. Today, the Black Hills still remain the subject of litigation and legislation.

"No," Custer replied, "I will not."

Seizing on this exchange and on Custer's well-deserved reputation as a brash and heedless fire eater, some historians have laid the blame for the Little Bighorn disaster entirely at the feet of the young colonel. But Gibbon's admonition was, in fact, jocular. It was never part of the *Far West* plan to join forces before engaging the Indians. The idea was for whoever made contact first to fight first, driving the Indians into the other half of the pincers; and it was assumed from the outset that Custer's highly mobile Seventh would be the first to make contact. It is true that Custer was supposed to follow the Rosebud beyond the point where the Indians' trail was expected to turn west, so that he would cross to the Little Bighorn valley south of the Indians' position, thereby insuring the enemy would be caught between the Seventh Cavalry and the forces of Gibbon and Terry. And it is true that Custer departed from the plan. He found the Indian trail, but it was much fresher than anticipated, which meant that the Indians were not in the upper valley of the Little Bighorn, but very close by. To continue up the Rosebud would carry the Seventh far from the Indians' position. Instead, Custer sent out scouts to follow the trail and locate the Indian village.

Custer planned to attack on June 26, the day Gibbon and Terry were scheduled to reach their position at the mouth of the Little Bighorn. On June 25, however, the scouts not only discovered a Sioux camp, but also warriors lurking nearby. Custer did not choose to amplify this intelligence. He made no attempt to ascertain the numbers of Indians involved. All he was certain of was the consequences of delay. If he waited even one day to attack, he believed, the Sioux would spot him and flee. Then this campaign, like so many others, would degenerate into days of weary, fruitless, thankless pursuit. The yellow-haired colonel decided to act now.

He led his men across the divide between the Rosebud and the Little Bighorn, dispatching Captain Frederick W. Benteen with three troops—125 men—to the south, in order to make sure that the Sioux had not moved into the upper valley of the Little Bighorn. As Custer approached the Little Bighorn River, he spotted about 40 warriors and sent Major Marcus A. Reno, with another three troops, after them. The plan was for Reno to pursue the warriors back to their village while Custer, with his remaining five troops, charged the village from the north. Custer had not actually seen the village, and he was maneuvering in entirely unfamiliar terrain. Neither Custer nor his commanding generals had any idea of how many warriors they were going up against. Later estimates put the number at anywhere from 1,500 to 6,000. Custer's combined strength was 600—and that had been split up.

*The best-known of Custer's Indian scouts at the Little Bighorn was Curly, a Crow whose flowing mane rivaled that of his commander, whom the Indians called Yellow Hair. (National Archives and Records Administration.)*

Reno's squadron of 112 men, in pursuit of those 40 warriors, was rapidly overwhelmed by masses of Sioux. He ordered his command to dismount and set up a skirmish line. When his left flank came under attack, he ordered a retreat to a cottonwood grove. Again, his position was infiltrated. He ordered his men to remount for a run to the bluffs across the river. By the time his troopers had reached this position, about 45 minutes after they had first engaged the enemy, their number had been reduced by about half.

In the meantime, Custer had ascended a bluff, had seen the vast Sioux encampment, and had seen Reno advancing for the attack. Custer called for his bugler, Giovanni Martini, and handed him a note to deliver to Captain Benteen, ordering him to bring the ammunition packs and join the fight.

Martini was the last surviving cavalryman to see George Armstrong Custer alive.

*John Mulvany's Custer's Last Rally (c. 1881) was the first of many white depictions of the debacle at the Little Bighorn. When the poet Walt Whitman saw it in New York in 1881, he pronounced it "altogether a Western phase of America . . . deadly, heroic to the uttermost; nothing in the books like it." (Library of Congress.)*

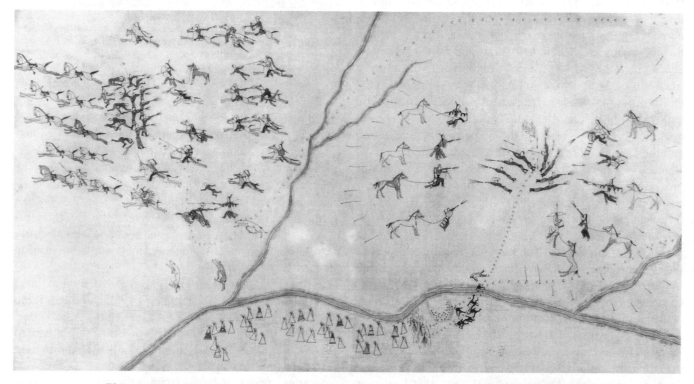

*This starkly schematic narrative depiction of the Custer fight is by White Bird, an Indian combatant. (Courtesy of The West Point Museum Collection, United States Military Academy, West Point, New York.)*

*Gall (also known as Pizi), a Hunkpapa chief, fought with Crazy Horse against Custer at the Little Bighorn. He was photographed at Fort Buford, North Dakota, in 1881. (National Archives and Records Administration.)*

Warriors led by a Hunkpapa chief named Gall surged across the Little Bighorn, pushing the troopers back. As Gall pressed from the south, Crazy Horse pushed in from the north. Within an hour, Custer and his men were dead.

Benteen, having received Custer's note, united with the remnant of Reno's command as it withdrew from the Little Bighorn Valley. When the sound of firing was heard, signifying that Custer was engaged, a number of officers wanted to ride off in his support. Reno refused, but some did go, only to return when warriors riding back from the Custer fight blocked their way.

The combined forces of Reno and Benteen—368 officers and men—dug in on the bluffs and fought off a daylong siege. On the next day, June 26, the siege was renewed, continuing until early afternoon. Finally, the

entire village moved off to the south as Generals Terry and Gibbon at last approached from the north. Casualties among the combined commands of Reno and Benteen were heavy. Far grimmer, of course, was the Custer battlefield, strewn with the naked and mutilated corpses of about 200 men. The body of Custer, found near his personal pennant—beside which he had taken his "last stand"—had been stripped naked. But the attackers in this one instance had refrained from scalping and mutilation.

The debacle of Little Bighorn moved Congress to increase army strength in the West by 2,500 cavalry privates. It also won for the military control of the Sioux agencies. Though controversial, Custer was, after all, young, dashing, and a hero of the Civil War. His death and that of his command gave the military in the West what it had long wanted: support from the civilian government. But the disaster also seemed to transform the army. Crook and Terry, both excellent officers, were demoralized, even unmanned by the Little Bighorn. They spent the rest of the summer of 1876 in desultory and mostly futile pursuit of Sioux, who had already scattered and headed east after the Custer fight.

One of Crook's officers, Captain Anson Mills, leading 150 Third Cavalrymen, did destroy a Sioux camp of 37 lodges on September 9 in the sharply fought Battle of Slim Buttes. Anson's attack scattered the Indians into the hills, from which they returned fire, pinning down the attackers until Crook arrived with the main column. The important war chief American Horse was killed in the battle.

But there was no follow-up to this engagement until November, when the able commander of the Fourth Cavalry, Ranald Mackenzie, won a significant victory in the Bighorn Mountains against a Cheyenne band led by Dull Knife and Little Wolf. With 1,100 troopers and Indian scouts out of Fort Fetterman, Mackenzie surprised a village of 200 lodges in a canyon of the Powder River's Red Fork on November 25. About 400 warriors defended the village in fierce combat, often hand-to-hand. By afternoon, however, Mackenzie took the village, destroyed provisions, and appropriated 700 fine ponies. He also found scalps, uniforms, and equipment, grim souvenirs of Custer's defeat at the Little Bighorn. Forty Cheyennes were slain in the battle, but far more suffered and died, provisionless and without shelter, in the $-30°$ F cold that followed the battle. Mackenzie lost one officer, five enlisted men, and sustained 26 wounded. Apparently, no record exists of the number of allied Indian scouts killed, although they had absorbed the first shock of the battle.

As great an asset as the Indian scouts were, they also had their own agenda, which was beyond the control of the military. Following Mackenzie's November 25 as-

## CRAZY HORSE (1841 or 1842–1877)

Born near present-day Rapid City, South Dakota, Crazy Horse (Tashunca-uitco) was the son of an Oglala Sioux medicine man and a Brulé wife, the sister of Spotted Tail. After his mother's death, Crazy Horse was raised by her sister, whom his father married, and he therefore spent time in both the Oglala and Brulé camps. Crazy Horse's childhood name was Curly, and his father bestowed his own name—Crazy Horse—on him when he was about sixteen, after the youth had related a dream that seemed to foretell his future greatness as a warrior. The name is better translated as "his horse is crazy."

The promise of Crazy Horse's dream was amply realized. He fought alongside Red Cloud in the War for the Bozeman Trail (1866–68) and was among those who annihilated William J. Fetterman and his command near Fort Phil Kearny in 1866. Following the Sioux triumph in the Bozeman conflict, Crazy Horse was made war chief of the Oglala and also commanded a following from among the Brulés and Northern Cheyennes. (Crazy Horse married a Cheyenne woman; he later took an Oglala wife as well.)

Crazy Horse rose to his greatest prominence during the Sioux War for the Black Hills (1876–77). When, on June 17, 1876, his force of 1,200 Oglalas and Cheyennes was attacked on the upper Rosebud by 1,300 troopers under General George Crook, Crazy Horse employed tactics that utterly baffled the white commander, who finally withdrew with serious losses. It was Crazy Horse who led the assault against George Armstrong Custer and his Seventh Cavalry at the Little Bighorn on June 25. Following the Little Bighorn fight, Crazy Horse led a brilliant campaign against one of the army's best commanders, Nelson A. Miles. Despite the warrior's skill, however, more and more Indians yielded to the unrelenting pressure of pursuit, and on May 5, 1877, Crazy Horse at last surrendered.

As part of the terms of his surrender, Crazy Horse was promised a reservation for the Oglala on the Powder River. When the reservation failed to materialize, Crazy Horse remained at the Red Cloud Agency, the discontented object of adulation from young warriors and of suspicion on the part of whites. General Crook, believing that Crazy Horse was fomenting an uprising, ordered his arrest. At Camp Robinson, in the northwest corner of Nebraska, the chief was killed by a bayonet thrust in a scuffle with soldiers and reservation policemen. The cause of the incident has never been accurately determined. Some reported that a jealous rival warrior deliberately pinioned the chief's arms as a soldier bayonetted him. Others reported that his death was an unfortunate accident.

---

sault, a delegation of Cheyenne, Miniconjou, and Sans Arc chiefs came to talk peace with Colonel Nelson A. Miles. They approached his Tongue River cantonment on December 16, only to be attacked by the general's Crow scouts, who killed five. Miles sent the Sioux the Crows' ponies as atonement and apology, but the incident had been enough to discredit the peace faction among the assembled Sioux, and the Indians harried the Tongue River cantonment throughout the balance of the month. In response, Miles took five companies of the Fifth Infantry and two of the Twenty-second—about 350 men and two artillery pieces—up the Tongue Valley in search of the hostiles.

In fact, the Indians *wanted* to be found; they were planning an ambush. But, as often happened, the young warriors could not be restrained from acting prematurely. On January 7, 1877, Miles's scouts captured a party of Cheyenne women and children. About 200 warriors attempted to recover them; they not only failed in this, they alerted Miles to the presence of a large party of warriors. Miles was prepared for the 500 Sioux and Cheyennes, led by Crazy Horse, who attacked his camp the next day. The Battle of Wolf Mountain was fought in a severe snowstorm, which hampered the attackers more than the soldiers, and when it was over, Miles was able to boast that he had "taught the destroyers of Custer that there was one small command that could whip them as long as they dared face it."

Actually, casualties were light on both sides. But, in the wake of tenuous indecision that followed the Custer debacle, the victory was significant. Once again, the peace faction among the Sioux and Cheyennes gained the ascendency. Unfortunately, Bear's Coat, as the Cheyennes called Miles, and other military commanders re-

*The skillful Cheyenne war chief Dull Knife met his match in the high-strung commander of the Fourth Cavalry, Ranald Mackenzie, who defeated him (together with Lone Wolf) in the Bighorn Mountains after fierce hand-to-hand combat on November 25, 1876. The army, severely shaken by the Custer debacle, badly needed the victory. (National Archives and Records Administration.)*

sponded to Indian peace feelers with nothing but stern demands for absolute and unconditional surrender. Sitting Bull decided to take his Hunkpapa Sioux north into Canada. The Miniconjous, Oglalas, Sans Arcs, and Cheyennes scattered. By mid-February, however, the army had softened its position somewhat and persuaded the important Brulé Sioux chief Spotted Tail to undertake a peace mission. By early April, large groups of Cheyennes surrendered to officials at the Indian agencies. Crazy Horse brought the Oglalas to the Red Cloud

Agency and surrendered there, dramatically throwing his Winchester to the ground.

The great Sioux War was not over yet, as 51 lodges of Miniconjous under Lame Deer, pledging never to surrender, made for the Rosebud to hunt buffalo. Miles gathered a squadron of Second Cavalry together with six companies of infantry and, on May 1, marched up the Tongue River in search of Lame Deer. Hampered by the slow-moving infantry, Miles took four cavalry troops west and, on May 7, acting on information from his scouts, he surprised Lame Deer's camp on a Rosebud tributary called Muddy Creek.

One of Miles's scouts, the Miniconjou Hump, until recently an adversary, persuaded Lame Deer and his head warrior, Iron Star, to give up. Shaken by the presence of Hump, the two Indians laid their rifles down and approached Miles and his adjutant, George W. Baird. The tension, however, was terrific; and when a scout rode up, drawing his rifle on Lame Deer and Iron Star, apparently intending nothing more than to keep them covered, the two Indians went for their own weapons. Lame Deer fired at Miles, who dodged the shot (which found its fatal mark in an unfortunate cavalryman behind him). The soldiers then opened fire and killed Lame Deer. Iron Star fell next. And so the Battle of Muddy Creek ended: 14 Sioux dead, including the chief and the head warrior; four enlisted men were also killed, and another seven of Miles's command wounded. The general pursued the fleeing Sioux to the Rosebud before returning to burn the village and appropriate the ponies.

Throughout the summer, a series of skirmishes followed, but the greatest threat to an uneasy peace was Crazy Horse, who proved restive on the reservation, an "incorrigible wild man, silent, sullen, lordly and dictatorial," as the Indian agent described him. Fearing that he would stir the reservation to revolt, General Crook ordered his arrest and confinement. Taken into custody on September 5, 1877, he was stabbed to death in a scuffle involving soldiers and Indians. It is unclear whether he had been mortally wounded by his own hand, the knife of another Indian, or a soldier's bayonet.

Later the same month, a delegation of chiefs, including Red Cloud and Spotted Tail, went to Washington, D.C., to persuade President Rutherford B. Hayes to set a new reservation for their people—the Oglala and the Brulé Sioux—in their traditional homelands. Followers of the slain Crazy Horse, however, left the reservation and drifted northward to Canada, to join Sitting Bull. The Northern Cheyennes reported to the Cheyenne and Arapaho Agency in Indian Territory during August 1877, but they hated the reservation and fared poorly on it during the winter of 1877–78. On September 7, 1878, Dull Knife and Little Wolf led 300 Northern Cheyennes in a break for the north. A combination of regular army troops and citizen volunteers pursued the fugitives in a military campaign that came to be called the Pursuit of the Northern Cheyenne.

As they fled with their people, the two chiefs fell to quarrelling, and the fugitive band was divided between them, Dull Knife's faction surrendering to soldiers at Camp Robinson on October 23, 1878, and Little Wolf's pressing northward. Dull Knife's group, held in the barracks at Camp Robinson, in the northwest corner of Nebraska, refused to return to Indian Territory. The camp commandant, Captain Henry W. Wessells, Jr., cut off all food and water in an attempt to force their departure south. After a week of thirst and starvation, the Indians made a break for it on the night of January 9, 1879. About one-half of Dull Knife's people were shot down, before the government, bowing to public pressure, granted the remainder their wish to live with the Sioux at the Pine Ridge Reservation in southwestern Dakota territory. Little Wolf and his faction kept ahead of the army through the long winter. Exhausted, they finally surrendered on March 29, 1879, at the Little Missouri River. Five years later, in 1884, the Tongue River Reservation was established in southeastern Montana, which gave the Northern Cheyennes a homeland they found livable.

Sitting Bull was the remaining loose end in the Sioux War. He was living in Canada with approximately 4,000 Hunkpapa, Oglala, Miniconjou, Sans Arc, and Blackfoot Sioux as well as a handful of Nez Percés. In October 1877, General Terry, with the cooperation of the North-West Mounted Police, located Sitting Bull in Canada and attempted to persuade him to come back to a reservation in the United States. Faced with winter famine and unwelcome by Canadian tribes who did not want to share with them the little game that was available, his Hunkpapas and members of the other tribes that had gathered around him were beginning to defect in small bands. But Sitting Bull rejected Terry: "You come here to tell us lies," he spat. "Go home where you came from." Within a few years, only 200 people remained with Sitting Bull. On July 19, 1881, he traveled with them to Fort Buford, northwestern Dakota Territory, where he surrendered.

## PURSUIT OF THE NEZ PERCÉS

The Nez Percés who had joined Sitting Bull in Canada— about 100 warriors and 50 women led by White Bird— were the last of the tribe who held out against confinement. They fled to Canada rather than surrender with Chief Joseph to Nelson A. Miles at the five-day Battle of Bear Paw Mountain (September 30–October 5, 1877).

*Sitting Bull, chief of the Hunkpapa Sioux, was among the most revered of Indian leaders. Uncompromising in his resistance to whites, he (with Crazy Horse, an Oglala Sioux) annihilated Custer and his command before he was defeated by Nelson A. Miles at the Battle of Wolf Mountain. (Library of Congress.)*

That engagement was the culmination of an incredible saga the army labeled the Pursuit of the Nez Percé.

The tribe became sharply divided into "treaty" and "nontreaty" factions after an 1863 gold rush prompted a revision of an earlier treaty that defined the boundaries of the Nez Percé reservation. The revised convenant excluded the mineral-rich lands from the reservation. Those Indians whose homes remained within the revised boundaries signed the treaty and agreed to sell the excluded lands; those who were dispossessed by the revision refused to sign. Prominent among the latter was the revered Chief Joseph, who repudiated the treaty and lived with his people in the Wallowa Valley, now technically be-

*This photograph of the Nez Percé agency in Idaho was taken in 1879, about two years after Chief Joseph, weary of being pursued, surrendered himself and his people to Colonel Nelson A. Miles. (National Archives and Records Administration.)*

yond the reservation. Few whites were interested in this particular area, however, and Joseph was left in peace. In 1873, two years after Joseph's death, President Grant even set aside part of the Wallowa Valley as a legitimate reservation.

About this time, however, Oregon settlers began to covet the land for grazing and pressured the Grant administration into reopening the tract to white settlement. Civil War hero Oliver O. Howard, a one-armed warrior known as the "praying general" because of his strong Christian and humanitarian leanings (among other things, he was the principal founder of Howard University in Washington, D.C.), was named head of a negotiating committee charged with convincing the nontreaty Nez Percés to vacate the disputed lands in return for compensation in goods and money.

Young Joseph, who had become chief after the death of his father, and another Nez Percé leader, Old Toohoolhoolzote, met with Howard between November 13 and 15, 1876, at Fort Lapwai, the reservation headquarters. While the general was sympathetic to their position—he agreed that Old Joseph had never sold the Wallowa Valley when the original treaty was revised—the conference broke down after the two Indian leaders refused to sell out now. Frustrated, Howard declared that the Indians had one month to move to the reservation or be driven off by force.

Young Joseph and the other chiefs knew that war would be fruitless. With their people, they marched off to the reservation. As usual, however, it was one thing for the chiefs to agree to the whites' terms and another for the tribe's young men to obey. On June 13 and 14,

*The Nez Percé chief Looking Glass would brook no surrender in the fight against army pursuers. Joseph, who saw the situation as hopeless, thought it time to stop fighting. Leaving a council with Joseph, Looking Glass was struck in the head by a stray bullet and killed. (National Archives and Records Administration.)*

while traveling to the reservation, some young warriors, fired up on liquor, killed four whites who were notorious for their ill treatment of Indians. Joseph and his brother Ollikut tried to persuade their people to explain to authorities that the killings had not been sanctioned by tribal council. But the nontreaty Indians decided to turn south toward the Salmon River. When news of the killings reached General Howard, he dispatched 100 cavalrymen under Captain David Perry out of Fort Lapwai. As the troopers made their way to the Camas Prairie, they learned of more depredations: the deaths of 15 more settlers.

The local settlers were in a panic and persuaded Captain Perry to make a forced night march to intercept the Nez Percés before they reached the mountains beyond the Salmon River. At dawn on June 17, Perry's exhausted command arrived at White Bird Canyon. Pursuant to Chief Joseph's counsel, a delegation of Nez Percés approached the soldiers under a flag of truce, intending to talk peace. Captain Perry had picked up a handful of

civilian volunteers, and unfortunately, these undisciplined men first encountered the truce party. Ignoring the white flag, they opened fire.

The result was disaster—not for the Indians, but for the troopers. The warriors shot well and relentlessly against Perry's front and both flanks. The civilians, who had started the battle, were the first to break and run, thereby exposing Perry's main body to enfilading fire. Many of Perry's men, little more experienced than the civilians, also broke and ran. Perry withdrew his men as best he could in a series of desperate defensive stands. When it was over, 33 men and one officer had been killed—one-third of Perry's command. No Nez Percés had died, though three had been wounded. For the army, it was a humiliating defeat and a bad start to the war with the Nez Percés.

In response, on June 22, Howard mustered about 400 men with the purpose of bottling up the Indians in White Bird Canyon. Local settlers convinced Howard that Chief

Looking Glass, whose village was near the forks of the Clearwater, was planning to join the hostiles. Since stationary Indians were more easily dealt with than those on the move, Howard sent Captain Stephen G. Whipple with two troops of cavalry and a brace of Gatling guns, together with a band of local volunteers, to surprise the village. Despite what the locals claimed, Looking Glass advocated neutrality. And, to his credit, Whipple did not intend to come in shooting, but planned first to parley.

To his discredit, he relinquished control of the situation to the civilian volunteers who, as usual, provoked a fight. On July 1, the regulars ended up using the Gatling guns against the village, sending 40 warriors and their families running and, what is worse, propelling the peacefully inclined Looking Glass straight into the camp of the hostiles.

Ten days of pursuit and attack followed, with the Indians gaining the upper hand and, at one point, on July 9

## CHIEF JOSEPH (c.1840–1904)

Chief Joseph, often called Young Joseph to distinguish him from his father, Joseph the Elder or Old Joseph, was born in the Wallowa Valley of Oregon. His Nez Percé name is variously transliterated as Heinmot Tooyalaket, In-mut-too-yah-lat-lat, Hin-mah-too-yah-lat-kekt, and Hinmaton-yalatkit, signifying "thunder coming from water over land." Old Joseph, himself a Christianized Indian, had his son baptized as Ephraim.

Old Joseph was among the Indians who, in 1855, concluded a treaty with Washington's territorial governor Isaac Stevens. Stevens violated the treaty almost as soon as he signed it, thereby provoking the Yakima War (1855–56), but Old Joseph kept the Nez Percés out of the conflict in the Northwest until 1861, when gold seekers pushed settlement into the Wallowa Valley. In 1863, government officials at the Lapwai Council proposed to revise the treaty of 1855, radically reducing the Nez Percé reservation. Those Nez Percés whose dwelling places lay within the revised boundaries signed the new treaty and agreed to sell the excluded land, while those whose land had been appropriated refused. Among these were Old Joseph and four other chiefs, whose bands became known collectively as the Non-Treaty Nez Percés.

Despite Old Joseph's defiant refusal to remove to the redefined reservation, whites were slow to invade the Wallowa Valley, and there was no attempt to oust the Non-Treaty Nez Percés by force. When Old Joseph died in 1871, Young Joseph became chief and continued his father's practice of passive refusal to move. Within a short time, however, white homesteaders pushed into the Wallowa Valley. Young Joseph protested, the Indian Bureau investigated, and President Grant established the Wallowa Valley as a reservation in 1873.

Young Joseph had triumphed and had done so peacefully.

Or so it should have been. As had happened so frequently in the past, the settlers simply ignored federal attempts to regulate them, settled wherever they wished, and then became a political constituency bent on forcing the government into changing the rules they had violated. In 1875, the president reversed his earlier decision and declared the Wallowa Valley open to settlement. General Oliver O. Howard was sent to negotiate with Young Joseph and the Non-Treaty Percés. Despite tribal pressure, Joseph unwaveringly counseled peaceful compliance, and his brother, the war chief Ollikut, leader of the militant faction among the Non-Treaty Nez Percés, backed him. Thus the Non-Treaty Nez Percés were on the verge of peace when, on June 12, 1877, a warrior named Wahlitits avenged the earlier death of his father at the hands of whites by killing four settlers. Other warriors, outraged at having to leave their land, killed 15 more. The die was cast, and Joseph decided that there was now no other choice than to support his warriors.

The pursuit of the Nez Percés began. It would cover some 1,700 miles and last—at great cost to the army and to the Indians—until October 5, when Chief Joseph surrendered to Nelson A. Miles, making a speech that, in its dignified emotion, seemed to summarize the whole tragic history of white-Indian conflict.

Joseph and 150 followers were consigned to the Colville Reservation in Washington. The chief's military adversaries, Oliver O. Howard and Nelson A. Miles, feeling a profound respect for Joseph and his people, worked on his behalf to regain the Wallowa Valley reservation, but they were unsuccessful, and Joseph died, in 1904, on the Colville Reservation. The physician who attended him gave the cause of death as a broken heart.

*Chief Joseph (also called Young Joseph) led his Nez Percés on an epic flight from the army and life on a reservation. After months of running, fighting, and suffering, Joseph surrendered to Nelson A. Miles. "Hear me, my chiefs!" he declared to Miles and his officers. "I am tired; my heart is sick and sad. From where the sun now stands I will fight no more forever." (National Archives and Records Administration.)*

and 10, holding a force of volunteers under siege at a place the would-be pursuers dubbed Mount Misery. The siege, while hard on the civilian volunteers, occupied the Indians long enough for Howard to bring his main force undetected to the rear of the Nez Percés. On July 11, the Battle of Clearwater began. Howard sacrificed the element of surprise when he began firing his artillery prematurely. The Indians maneuvered around Howard's position, surrounding him on three sides and turning what might have been a fast, decisive attack on an Indian village into a bloody two-day combat. Nevertheless, the Indians were at last driven from the field. Exhausted by the battle, Howard failed to pursue the scattering bands and, as a result, lost an opportunity to bring the war with the Nez Percés to an immediate conclusion.

Instead, weeks of fruitless pursuit followed. It was not until August 9 that the army again made contact with the Nez Percés, when Colonel John Gibbon, leading 15 officers, 146 enlisted regulars, and 45 volunteers, surprised a camp on the Big Hole River, Montana. Under the leadership of Looking Glass, the Indians quickly rallied and counterattacked, killing 2 of Gibbon's officers, 22 regulars, and 6 civilians, and wounding 5 more officers, 30 enlisted men, and 4 civilians. Indian losses were also heavy—at least 89 dead—but Gibbon was sent limping back to his station as the Nez Percés fled about 100 miles, killing 9 whites, seizing 250 horses, and raiding a wagon train before they entered the newly established Yellowstone National Park, where their presence provoked no little terror among the tourists.

Howard, along with the Seventh Cavalry, under Colonel Samuel D. Sturgis, gave chase, attempting to block the Indians' escape route. But the Nez Percés evaded both Howard and Sturgis. On August 19, 200 warriors skirmished with troopers on the Camas Meadows and made off with 150 army mules, killing one trooper and wounding seven. On September 13, the Seventh Cavalry engaged the Nez Percés at the site of present-day Billings, Montana, and once again, the army was bested, as Sturgis lost three men and had 11 wounded.

The Nez Percés sought haven among the Crows but soon discovered that Crow scouts had been fighting on the side of Howard. They determined, therefore, to press northward, to Canada, where they hoped Sitting Bull would welcome them as brothers. But first, Looking Glass counseled, the people needed rest, and believing they had left the soldiers far behind, the Nez Percés slowed their march. On September 30, they were camped just 40 miles south of the Canadian border, on the northern edge of the Bear Paw Mountains. There, with 350 to 400 men, Miles attacked. But the Indians had time to take up positions in a cutbank south and east of their camp, from which they were able to mow down 60 of

Miles's cavalrymen. The dashing commander pulled back and settled into a siege, which lasted through six snowy, miserable days, from September 30 to October 5. On the fourth day, General Howard arrived with a small escort, but wisely—and generously—left principal command to Miles.

During the siege, the Indians held council. Chief Joseph argued for surrender. Looking Glass and White Bird wanted to fight. The chiefs agreed at least to talk terms with the whites. On October 1, under a flag of truce, Joseph went to meet Miles to negotiate surrender terms. Talks broke down, and Miles decided to hold the chief hostage. But Lieutenant Lovell H. Jerome, apparently believing that the Indians were about to surrender, carelessly wandered into their lines and was seized, so that Miles was compelled to exchange Joseph for the errant lieutenant. On October 5, after another fruitless debate among Joseph, Looking Glass, and White Bird, Joseph again prepared to meet Miles. Leaving the council, Looking Glass was struck in the forehead by a stray bullet and killed.

Chief Joseph went to Miles and spoke with heart-wrenching eloquence:

I am tired of fighting. Our chiefs are killed. Looking Glass is dead. Toohoolhoolzote is dead. The old men are all dead. It is the young men who say yes or no. He who led on the young men [Joseph's brother, Ollikut] is dead. It is cold and we have no blankets. The little children are freezing to death. My people, some of them, have run away to the hills, and have no blankets, no food; no one knows where they are—perhaps freezing to death. I want to have time to look for my children and see how many of them I can find. Maybe I shall find them among the dead. Hear me, my chiefs! I am tired; my heart is sick and sad. From where the sun now stands I will fight no more forever.

Thus ended the epic pursuit of the Nez Percés. For three months, 800 strong, they traveled over 1,700 miles of extraordinarily rugged terrain, eluding the army at each turn. About 120 died on the trek.

After his retirement to the reservation, Chief Joseph spent many years petitioning the U.S. government for permission to return to the Wallowa Valley. Although he was earnestly aided in his efforts by his former adversaries, Miles and Howard, the land was never regained, and Joseph died on the Colville Reservation, Washington, in 1904.

# CHAPTER 26

# WARS AGAINST THE BANNOCKS, SHEEPEATERS, AND UTES

## (1878–1879)

### BANNOCK WAR

Buffalo Horn, an important chief among the Bannocks of Idaho, was much admired by Generals Oliver O. Howard and George Crook as well as Colonel Nelson A. Miles. He had served all of them as an able scout during the just-concluded war with the Nez Percés. Now Buffalo Horn gathered about him a significant following among the Bannocks and their neighbors, the Northern Paiutes (whose best-known leader was Winnemucca). Incursions of white settlement beginning in the mid 1870s were seriously depleting game and even camas roots, a staple that the Indians dug on Camas Prairie, 90 miles southeast of Boise, Idaho. The right to dig for these roots was guaranteed by a solemn treaty, but the settlers' hogs were destroying them. The reservation agencies, as usual, failed to supply sufficient rations to make up for the sparsity of game and roots.

General Crook was later asked: What caused the Bannock War?

"Hunger. Nothing but hunger," he replied.

On May 30, 1878, a Bannock shot and wounded two whites. The Bannocks, Shoshonis, and so-called Sheepeaters who lived on the Lemhi Reservation (and who were collectively called the Lemhis) and many of the 600 Bannocks who were enrolled at the Ross Fork, or Fort Hall, Agency in southeastern Idaho quickly reported to their agencies, fearful of punishment. Buffalo Horn, who commanded a following of about 200 warriors, including Northern Paiutes and Umatillas in addition to Bannocks, reacted differently.

Believing that he and his people were in for punishment regardless of what they did, Buffalo Horn decided to make the most of the situation by launching a raid in southern Idaho that resulted in the deaths of ten whites.

The rampage continued until June 8, when a party of civilian volunteers killed Buffalo Horn in a skirmish near Silver City, southwest of Boise, Idaho. Leaderless, Buffalo Horn's warriors rode to Steens Mountain, in Oregon, where they found Northern Paiutes who had followed a militant medicine man named Oytes and a chief known as Egan off the Malheur Reservation on June 5. The new alliance fielded about 450 warriors against a slightly larger number of soldiers led by General Howard, who dogged his quarry relentlessly, as if determined to make up for the mediocre performance of his First Cavalry in the pursuit of the Nez Percés.

Still, the army was willing to attempt a negotiated settlement before engaging in an all-out war. After all, no official, military or civilian, contested the Indians' right to the Camas Prairie, and, therefore, the whites were prepared to come to a parley with something to concede. Captain Reuben F. Bernard, commanding a troop of the First Cavalry, persuaded Sarah Winnemucca, daughter of the esteemed Paiute chief, to venture into the hostiles' Steens Mountain encampment and offer peace terms. War fever, however, had clearly infected Oytes and Egan, for Sarah Winnemucca and her father barely escaped with their lives.

Howard had little choice but to move against the camp, dividing his force into three columns. Oytes and Egan took their people off Steens Mountain and made for Silver Creek to the northwest. At this place, on June 23, Captain Bernard engaged the hostiles with three cavalry troops. The Indians broke and ran, taking up formidable defensive positions on the bluffs. Bernard decided that a close assault on such positions would be suicidal, so he did not offer chase. After a daylong exchange of fire at long range, the Indians made off at nightfall. Still, the Bannocks and Paiutes had been hurt.

At the Malheur Agency, which had been deserted and pillaged, General Howard mustered some 480 men to continue the pursuit of the remainder of the hostiles. His object was to prevent the Bannock-Paiute force from combining with other Indians in the region, including the Umatillas and Cayuses. From the end of June through the first week of July, the hostiles kept ahead of Howard, pausing only to skirmish with his troopers from time to time and to raid the luckless ranches that lay in their path. On July 8, Captain Bernard, now at the head of seven troops of cavalry, discovered the Indian position on high bluffs along Birch Creek near Pilot Butte. It would be a tortuous assault that would expose the columns to heavy fire. But, this time, Bernard would have to attempt it. Slowly, his columns drove the Indians to successively higher defensive positions, until the cavalry both flanked them and met them head-on. The Indians bolted, but by this time, Bernard's troopers were also spent and could not give chase.

Following the Battle of Birch Creek, Oytes, Egan, and their followers moved south, apparently to seek refuge and allies among the Nez Percés. Howard deployed his forces to block the hostiles, whereupon Oytes and Egan turned their people to the north again, in the direction of the Umatilla Reservation. Captain Evan Miles arrived at the reservation on July 12, leading a substantial force of infantry, artillery, and a troop of cavalry. His fear that the Umatillas would join forces with the Bannock-Paiute band was dispelled by the white flag the Umatillas displayed; they were only interested in observing the battle they knew was about to develop. It took place on July 13, though it was fought mostly at long range for the first six hours, until Captain Miles ordered an advance that pushed the hostiles into the mountains to the east. On the fifteenth, the Umatillas took an active role in the conflict. A party of them approached the Bannocks and Paiutes on pretense of joining them. Instead, they tricked Chief Egan into coming away from his warriors, and they killed him, presenting his scalp to Captain Miles as a trophy.

On July 14, six cavalry troops, formerly led by Captain Bernard and now with Lieutenant Colonel James W. Forsyth at their head, arrived at the Umatilla Agency. On the twentieth, they set out in pursuit of the hostiles. By this time, however, the Bannock-Paiute band had begun to disintegrate, with small groups of Northern Paiutes scattering across southeastern Oregon and the Bannocks moving back toward Idaho, causing destruction on their way. In response to the fragmentation of the enemy, Howard scattered the elements of his command along a front that stretched from Nevada to Idaho. By August, the Paiutes were caving in, and on the twelfth, Oytes surrendered. Many of the Bannocks followed a month

later, fighting their last engagement in Wyoming on September 12, 1878.

The struggle had been difficult and protracted, but neither side suffered catastrophic casualties: 9 troopers dead, 15 wounded; at least 78 Indians slain. Yet, it had been an exhausting, draining experience: "The campaign has been a hard, long, and expensive one," Howard reported. "Many of the troops have marched greater distances than during the Nez Percé war, and in all the services I have been called upon to render the government I have never known officers and soldiers to encounter and overcome greater obstacles."

Despite the finality of Howard's report, hostilities in Idaho were not yet concluded. Elements of the Bannocks who did not surrender took refuge among the Sheepeaters in the Salmon River Mountains of Idaho. Renegade Shoshonis and Bannocks, the Sheepeaters were, as a rule, neither friendly nor entirely hostile. But while the fugitive Bannocks were among them, either the Sheepeaters or their fugitive guests raided a prospectors' camp on Loon Creek, killing five Chinese miners in May 1879. Howard dispatched Captain Bernard with a troop of the First Cavalry and Lieutenant Henry Catley with 50 mounted Second Infantrymen, as well as 20 Indian scouts, to search out the murderers.

## SHEEPEATER WAR

The resulting "Sheepeater War" was waged against a handful of warriors, perhaps 35, but, as in the Modoc War and the Pursuit of the Nez Percé, the Indians' greatest ally and the bluecoats' most formidable foe was the terrain. As mentioned before, warfare against the Indians of the West consisted mainly of pursuit, and pursuit through the rugged wilderness of Idaho took its toll on officers, men, and animals as surely as enemy arrows and rifle fire.

Catley did not make contact with the Indians until July 29, when his command was ambushed by a mere 15 warriors. They bottled up his troopers in the canyon of the Big Creek, taking up a position on Vinegar Hill, from which they tried to burn him out. Catley defended himself by skillfully setting backfires and, abandoning all baggage and supplies, was able to sneak his 50 men out of the canyon. General Howard did not appreciate what he termed the lieutenant's "precipitate retreat before inferior numbers" and had Catley court martialed. His conviction for misconduct was subsequently overturned by presidential order.

On August 13, 1879, Bernard's cavalry joined Catley's infantry (now augmented by an additional 25 men and placed under the command of Captain Albert G.

*Western climate and terrain were often more formidable enemies than the Indians. The great western artist and illustrator Frederic Remington had a genuine feeling for the hard life of the cavalry trooper, as is evident in his* Cavalry in an Arizona Sandstorm *(c. 1889). (Amon Carter Museum, Fort Worth, Texas.)*

Forse) and the Indian scouts. They set out for the scene of Catley's defeat. On the nineteenth, the Umatilla scouts captured the contents of a Sheepeater camp—which included much that Catley had abandoned—but the warriors were nowhere to be seen. On the twentieth, the Sheepeaters attacked the army's supply train. They were driven off, but the soldiers were too exhausted to give chase. Howard called off the campaign as fruitless.

In September, Lieutenant Edward S. Farrow, who had commanded the scouts in the August campaign, set out again with the Umatillas. They captured two women and two children on September 21 and came upon an abandoned Sheepeater camp the next day. From one of the captured women they learned that the warriors were worn out and could not endure much more pursuit. Of course, neither could Farrow, but he kept up the pressure through the end of the month, when a four-day storm brought great misery to both sides. On October 1 and 2, 51 Sheepeaters and a few Bannocks surrendered to Farrow. Most of the Bannocks, however, disappeared, presum-

ably finding refuge on the Lemhi Reservation. The Sheepeaters were confined for the winter to Fort Vancouver, Washington, and subsequently placed on the Fort Hall Reservation in Idaho.

## UTE WAR

To the south of the Bannocks and Northern Paiutes was the country of their linguisitic relatives, the Utes of western Colorado and eastern Utah. As a result of silver strikes in the 1870s, miners were working the region intensely, always lusting after new territory to prospect. After wringing repeated cessions of land from the Utes, mining interests pressed for permission to invade what remained of their reservation in Colorado and to force the removal of the Utes to Indian Territory. In the meantime, in an effort to bring his charges rapidly under control, the Ute agent at White River, Nathan C. Meeker, was attempting to force these traditionally free-ranging people to take up wholly alien lives as sedentary farmers. He began his monomaniacal social experiment by demanding that the Utes begin plowing up their ponies' grazing land. When, on September 10, 1879, a Ute medicine man known as Johnson complained to Meeker that plowing the grazing lands would starve the horses, the agent replied: "You have too many ponies. You had better kill some of them."

In a context of unremitting demands on Indian rights and land, Meeker's stupid, egocentric, and arrogant words touched off a furious response. Either Johnson or a leader known as Chief Douglas threw the elderly Meeker out his own front door. The agent, who had been asking for military aid all through the tense summer, now became hysterical and telegraphed military authorities that he and the agency were in imminent peril. Major Thomas T. "Tip" Thornburgh, commanding a mixed unit of 153 infantry and cavalrymen supplemented by an additional 25 civilians, was ordered to Meeker's relief on September 16, 1879.

The news that troops had been summoned served only to stir the Utes to greater hostility. Meeker began to realize the magnitude of what he was provoking and asked Thornburgh to halt his column and approach the agency with only five soldiers for a parley. The major agreed, and the talks were arranged—but at the last minute Thornburgh decided it prudent to move 120 cavalrymen closer to the agency, just in case. The Utes, believing they were about to be attacked, confronted the soldiers on the trail on September 25. It was a tense face-off, and when the major's adjutant, Lieutenant Samuel A. Cherry, doffed and waved his hat—apparently in greeting—either an Indian or a soldier took it for a signal. A shot was fired, and the Battle of Milk Creek began as the Utes pressed the troops from the front and flanks.

Thornburgh was among the first slain, felled by a rifle bullet above the ear. The soldiers retreated across Milk Creek and took refuge behind their wagon train, which had been defensively circled up. By the end of this first day of battle, 11 bluecoats (including Thornburgh) lay dead and 23 were wounded; 23 Utes also were slain. The struggle settled into a weeklong siege, which ended only when two of the defenders were able to sneak through the Indian lines and summon reinforcements. On October 2, Captain Francis Dodge arrived with a unit of African American troopers but failed to break the siege (all of Dodge's ponies rapidly fell victim to Indian sharpshooters). Colonel Wesley Merritt arrived on October 5 with ample numbers of cavalry and infantry, and the Utes at last backed off.

All of this was too late for Agent Meeker. While the hapless Thornburgh command was enduring siege, Meeker and nine other agency employees had been killed and the agency buildings burned. Mrs. Meeker, her daughter, and another woman and her two children were taken captive. Generals Sherman and Sheridan, predictably, favored a vigorous campaign of punishment, even if it meant death for the captive women, and by this time, they had massed a sufficient number of soldiers—about 1,500—to do the job. However, Secretary of the Interior Carl Schurz, an Indian agent named Charles Adams, and a peace-counseling old Ute chief named Ouray managed to negotiate the release of the captives without further bloodshed by October 21.

During November and December of 1879, a commission of inquiry debated the justice of punishing the Utes, concluding, remarkably enough, that they had not intended to fight and should not, therefore, be held to blame. Twelve Ute men, however, were singled out for trial on charges of murdering Meeker and the others and committing "outrages" upon the captive women. The punishment of these individuals remained a thorny issue as a larger settlement with the Utes was concluded. By 1880, Chief Ouray consented to lead this proud tribe to reservations in eastern Utah and southwestern Colorado. To compensate the widows of Meeker and the other slain agency employees, Congress siphoned off a portion of an annuity trust fund established by treaty for the Utes. For most of the Utes, the transfer to the reservations was completed by 1881.

## CHAPTER 27

# THE APACHE EPOCH

## (1870–1886)

The Apache heritage, was one of raiding and warfare. Following the Apache Uprising during 1861 to 1863, there were several years of neither peace (the Apaches continually subjected their neighbors, American, Mexican, and Indian, to raids) nor of formal warfare. It was not until April 15, 1870, with the establishment of the military Department of Arizona, that the army fully confronted the Apache threat to settlement. The department's first commander, Brevet Major General George Stoneman, vitiated the army's purpose in creating the department when he established his headquarters not in Arizona, but on the California coast. He also sought to deal with the Apache in accordance with Grant's Peace Policy, by setting up a series of "feeding stations" for those Apaches who renounced raiding. Stoneman's remoteness from the scene, combined with his "benevolent" approach to what was at the time a military problem, brought accusations of spineless incompetence from outraged citizens—and influential newspaper editors—of Arizona.

Conditions were ripe for a citizen uprising. Lieutenant Royal E. Whitman, in charge of Camp Grant, a feeding station on the lower San Pedro River, was performing his assignment well, cultivating the trust and cooperation of Aravaipa and Pinal Apache. As far as local settlers were concerned, Whitman was doing his job too well. They believed that Camp Grant served as a sanctuary for Indians between raids, and on April 30, 1871, 148 citizens of Tucson attacked the Apache rancheria at Camp Grant, killing from 86 to 150 Indians, mostly women and children. Twenty-nine children were captured and sold into slavery.

The Camp Grant Massacre, as it came to be called, resulted in the replacement of General Stoneman by George Crook, who took command of the department in June 1871. President Grant wanted peace with the Apaches, and this is precisely what Crook hoped to achieve—except that he concluded a sound thrashing was necessary before peace negotiations could begin. This brought him into conflict with Vincent Colyer, Grant's secretary of the Board of Indian Commissioners, who compelled Crook to suspend operations until he had finished his negotiations. To his credit, Colyer made some inroads, but the citizens of Arizona continued to endure raids and terror. Crook issued an ultimatum to the Indians: Report to an agency by February 15, 1872, or be treated as hostile. This time, it was General Oliver O. Howard who overruled him by opening up another peaceful dialogue.

Neither Colyer nor, initially, Howard had any success in dealing with the legendary Chiricahua Apache leader Cochise, and without the participation of Cochise, there could be no genuine peace with the Apaches. Finally, late in 1872, Howard enlisted the aid of frontiersman Thomas J. Jeffords, known to be a trusted friend of the Chiricahua leader, to escort him to "Cochise's Stronghold," where he at last succeeded in hammering out a tentative and informal peace.

Or, at least, he created a situation in which some 5,000 Apaches and Yavapais (a tribe distinct from the Apaches, but often called Apache Mohaves) claimed peaceful intentions and began to draw rations from a newly organized system of reservations. In fact, from 1871 to 1872, Apache raids continued pretty much unabated. It was difficult to distinguish between Apache bands that professed peace in good faith and those that used the reservations as a cover for their outlawry. In any case, Arizona settlers were unwilling to make distinctions. They demanded that Crook and his soldiers be turned loose upon the Apaches, and they threatened to force the army's hand by staging another Camp Grant Massacre. Faced with citizen outrage and the realities of life in Arizona, the Indian Bureau at last authorized Crook to proceed—not to declare outright war, but to campaign systematically against the Apaches.

Crook applied all that he had learned in fighting the Paiutes in Oregon and Idaho. He stressed the use of Indian scouts and auxiliaries, mobility, and a dogged determination to pursue one's quarry until it was engaged and defeated. On November 15, 1872, Crook commenced his ambitious sweep through Arizona, a winter campaign that aimed at the concentration of hostile Apaches in the Tonto Basin, where they could be dealt with at once and en masse. It was a relentless operation: continual pursuit, about 20 actual engagements, 200 Indians killed—76 at the Battle of Skull Cave alone. (On December 28, 1872, 100 Yavapais were cornered in a cave in a wall of Salt River Canyon; heavy fire resulted in ricocheting bullets that caused many deaths.) But the most punishing aspect of the campaign was the pursuit. Kept constantly on the move, the Indians were forced repeatedly to abandon shelter and provisions. The Battle of Turret Peak, March 27, 1873, was the last straw. Under the command of Captain George M. Randall, elements of the Twenty-third Infantry surprised an Indian rancheria, killing 23. Throughout the spring and into the summer, Apaches

dejectedly reported to reservations. Even more significantly, Crook managed to keep the peace for four years—an unprecedented span in that volatile region.

As usual, in dealing with Indian relations, the federal government did not know when to stop. In 1875, officials decided to abolish the four separate reservations that had been established in Arizona and New Mexico and remove all of the Apaches to one large Arizona reservation, San Carlos. Cochise had died in 1874, and the Chiricahuas now lacked the leadership that might have kept them together in resistance. When they were ordered to San Carlos in 1876, about half went, and the remainder scattered into Mexico. The Warm Springs (Ojo Caliente) Apaches were ordered to the reservation the following year. Again, some scattered, some marched to San Carlos.

San Carlos was an awful place: barren, hot, disease ridden. The agency, predictably, provided insufficient rations and distributed poorly what little it had. In this place of discontent and misery, two militant leaders rose up, Victorio (a Warm Springs Apache chief) and Geronimo (a Chiricahua). Victorio made the first break from San Carlos on September 2, 1877, leading more than 300 Warm Springs Apaches and a few Chiricahuas out of the reservation. For a month, Victorio and his people resisted the pursuing soldiers but were finally compelled

*It was General Crook's policy to make extensive use of Indian scouts, including Apaches, some of whom were even drawn from the ranks of recently hostile bands. These Apache scouts are seen at drill on the parade grounds of Fort Wingate, New Mexico. (National Archives and Records Administration.)*

*No Indian warrior fared better against the army than the Chiricahua Apache called Goyahkla—better known by his Spanish name: Geronimo. One who rode with him called him "a true wild man." He led a long resistance in the Mexican-American borderlands. (National Archives and Records Administration.)*

to surrender at Fort Wingate, New Mexico. After the surrender, however, they were permitted to return to their homeland at Ojo Caliente, while the government debated their fate.

Within a year, the order came to return to San Carlos. Most did return, but Victorio, together with 80 warriors, headed for the hills and tried in vain to return to Ojo Caliente. In 1879, Victorio even attempted to settle with the Mescalero Apaches on their reservation, but it was not to be. On September 4, 1879, believing he was about to be arrested, Victorio led 60 warriors in a raid on the

camp of Troop E, Ninth Cavalry, at Ojo Caliente, killing eight soldiers, and stealing 46 ponies. Following this, an influx of Mescalero Apaches brought Victorio's strength to some 150 men, who set about terrorizing the Mexican state of Chihuahua, much of western Texas, southern New Mexico, and Arizona.

Mexican and American forces cooperated in pursuit of Victorio, who managed to elude them for over a year. By the fall of 1880, however, Victorio's warriors began to wear out. Colonel George P. Buell joined his regular infantry and cavalry with Mexican irregulars commanded by Colonel Joaquin Terrazas to run Victorio to ground in Chihuahua. As it became clear that they were about to make contact with the Indians, Terrazas summarily ordered Buell and his troops out of the country. The honor of destroying Victorio would belong to a Mexican officer.

During October 15–16, 1880, Terrazas engaged Victorio at the Battle of Tres Castillos in hand-to-hand combat, "man against man," as Terrazas reported, "the combatants wrestling with each other and getting hold of each other's heads." In this skirmish, the end of "Victorio's Resistance," 78 Indians died, including Victorio and 16 women and children. Those who escaped made their way back to New Mexico and eventually united with Geronimo in a last-ditch effort to escape confinement at the San Carlos Reservation.

Even among the Apaches, Geronimo—Goyahkla was his Indian name—was considered (as one warrior put it) "a true wild man." He rode with the Nednhi band of Chiricahua Apaches, whose homeland was in the Sierra Madre of Mexico. Geronimo was one of a number of Apache leaders who frequently gathered at the Ojo Caliente Reservation in New Mexico for the purpose of organizing raids.

When authorities realized that the reservation was functioning as a headquarters of resistance, it was ordered closed. Indian agent John P. Clum was dispatched to the reservation to oversee the removal of about 400 Warm Springs and Chiricahua Apaches to San Carlos and was supposed to rendezvous with eight troops of the Ninth Cavalry to facilitate the removal. The soldiers had not arrived by April 20, 1877, when Clum reached the reservation, which presented a serious problem, since Clum discovered that Geronimo was at Ojo Caliente, doubtless in the process of organizing violent resistance against the transfer to the hated San Carlos. Clum made a desperate decision. Backed up by a small force of Indian reservation policemen, he arrested Geronimo and 16 other leaders. The soldiers arrived two days later, only to find the Apache chief and his compatriots already in shackles.

After a year at San Carlos, Geronimo escaped to Mexico, but again returned to San Carlos in 1880, after being pursued by Mexican troops. During this second period of residence on the reservation, a prophet arose among the Apaches, Nakaidoklini, who preached the resurrection of the dead and a return to the halcyon days when the Apaches held sway across the Southwest. He trained celebrants of his religion to invoke the spirits by means of a dance, anticipating the Ghost Dance religion that, within the decade, would be introduced among the Sioux. Whites saw the religion of Nakaidoklini as dangerous and conducive to rebellion. On August 30, 1881, Colonel Eugene A. Carr, commanding Fort Apache, led 79 regulars, 23 White Mountain Apache scouts, and nine civilians to seek out Nakaidoklini at his village on Cibicu Creek and, as San Carlos Agent J. C. Tiffany put it, have him "arrested or killed or both."

Once they had the prophet in custody, Carr's troops set up camp outside the village. About 100 followers of Nakaidoklini attacked the encampment. The White Mountain scouts mutinied, killing their captain. A sergeant shot and killed Nakaidoklini, and Carr's command barely escaped the swarm of attackers. No sooner did the soldiers retire to Fort Apache than the Indians attacked them there. Newspapers carried panic headlines announcing that Carr's entire command had been butchered, and army regulars rushed into the San Carlos area from all over the Southwest. Since the Apaches had cut the telegraph lines, Carr was unable to communicate with the outside world until September 4. Sherman was relieved to learn that Carr had not been wiped out, but he was determined to end "this annual Apache stampede . . . and to effect that result will send every available man in the whole Army if necessary."

By the end of September, Naiche—son of Cochise—the Nednhi chief Juh, the Chiricahua leader Chato, and Geronimo, with 74 braves, were again heading for Mexico. On October 2, they fought off pursuing troops under the command of Major General Orlando B. Willcox, and then stole across the border, where they united with the survivors of the Battle of Tres Castillos. Word reached Willcox that the war leaders planned to enter the United States again in January 1882, to force the Warm Springs Apaches, led by Chief Loco, into an alliance. Willcox alerted all of his border patrols. But no incursion materialized until, suddenly, on April 19, 1882, an Apache war party, evading all patrols, stormed back to San Carlos, killed the reservation police chief, Albert D. Sterling, and compelled Loco, along with several hundred Indians, to return to Mexico with them. It was not a quiet ride back to the border; raiding killed between 30 and 50 whites.

Lieutenant Colonel George A. Forsyth, with five troops of the Fourth Cavalry and a unit of scouts, gave chase to no avail until April 23, when a patrol found the hostiles holed up in Horseshoe Canyon of the Peloncillos. Forsyth engaged the warriors, but they got away, after killing five troopers and wounding seven. Two troops of the Sixth Cavalry under Captain Tullius C. Tupper took up the chase, all the way into the Mexican state of Chihuahua, where, on April 28, they attacked. But the Apaches had dug into defensive positions that were so strong, Tupper merely exhausted his men as well as his ammunition without doing much damage.

Joined now by the main body of Forsyth's command, Tupper continued south in pursuit of the enemy. On April 30, Forsyth and Tupper encountered a unit of Mexican infantry commanded by Colonel Lorenzo Garcia. The colonel boasted that his men had succeeded in surprising the Apaches, who were distracted by having to defend against Tupper's pursuit, and had killed 78 and captured 33 women and children. Then the Mexican colonel ordered the American military out of the country.

The next blow was delivered on July 6, 1882, by a White Mountain Apache warrior named Natiotish, a militant partisan of the slain Nakaidoklini. He led a small force back to the San Carlos Reservation, where he killed the new police chief, J. L. "Cibicu Charley" Colvig, along with three of his officers. Following this, Natiotish led about 60 White Mountain Apaches in raids throughout the Tonto Basin. No fewer than 14 troops of cavalry fanned out in search of Natiotish. Near General Springs, between Fort Apache and Fort Verde, the White Mountain chief set an ambush, concealing his warriors at the edge of a narrow canyon. His plan was to annihilate a Sixth Cavalry column led by Captain Adna R. Chaffee as it rode through the canyon.

On July 17, however, Chaffee's scout, Al Sieber, discovered the ambush. Chaffee's column was reinforced by two troops from the Third Cavalry and another two from the Sixth, the captain deploying them so that they flanked the would-be ambushers. In the Battle of Big Dry Wash, Natiotish suffered losses estimated at 16 to 27 dead, with many more wounded. The survivors limped back to the reservation, and the White Mountain Apaches' days of raiding were thus ended.

Now the army faced only the Chiricahuas and the Warm Springs Apaches. Led principally by Geronimo, these were, however, formidable enough adversaries. The entire Natiotish episode prompted Sherman to relieve Orlando B. Willcox as commander of the Department of Arizona. Brigadier General George Crook, who had commanded the Department of Arizona from 1871 to 1875, when he left to command the Department of the Platte, was now returned to Arizona. Beginning in September 1882, Crook set about his task methodically. First, he worked with the new agent at the San Carlos

The "enemy." Apache prisoners photographed at Fort Bowie, Arizona, about 1884, at the height of the vigorous campaign against Geronimo and his followers, included many women and children. (National Archives and Records Administration.)

Reservation, P. P. Wilcox, to introduce a strong military presence onto the reservation. Crook recruited Indian scouts and informants, thereby infiltrating reservation cabals before they developed. Next, armed with a special reciprocal treaty signed with Mexico on July 29, 1882, Crook organized an expedition that would be authorized to penetrate far below the border to ferret out Geronimo in the state of Chihuahua.

First, however, Crook used Apache intermediaries to negotiate with the hostiles south of the border. The only response came in March of 1883, when two raiding parties hit Mexican and American targets. Geronimo and another warrior, Chihuahua, led a band through Sonora, appropriating stock, while Chato and the warrior Benito led another band into the United States. On March 21, 25 warriors rampaged through Arizona and New Mexico, killing 11 whites.

General Sherman ordered Crook into action, authorizing a move into Mexico. Immediately, Crook recruited 193 scouts from among the White Mountain Apaches.

With the scouts, commanded by Captain Emmet Crawford and Lieutenant Charles B. Gatewood, as well as a troop of the Sixth Cavalry under Chaffee and a supply train sufficient to sustain a protracted campaign, Crook pursued Apache raiders into the most remote reaches of Mexico's Sierra Madre. On May 15, 1883, the scouts attacked the encampment of Chato and Benito, killing nine warriors and destroying 30 lodges. It was a significant action, since the Indians had assumed that their wilderness position was undiscoverable and, in any event, impregnable. After this engagement, leaders, including Geronimo, came to parley with Crook. Only Juh remained at large.

In his talks with the Indians, Crook deliberately took the hard line that had served him well in previous negotiations with warrior leaders. He declared that the Mexicans as well as the Americans were tired of their "depredations" and that his mandate and intention was not to take them prisoner, but "to wipe them out." With the straight-faced guile of a good poker player, Crook announced that Mexican troops were now approaching and that the "best thing for them to do was to fight their way out if they thought they could do it. I kept them waiting for several days," Crook later reported. "Jeronimo and all the chiefs at last fairly begged me to be taken back to San Carlos."

Actually, only the Warm Springs Apaches—unwilling allies of the Chiricahuas in the first place—returned to San Carlos immediately. Geronimo and the other Chiricahuas did not arrive until March 1884. At that time, the reservation became full of unrest. General Crook had instituted many new rules to govern San Carlos, including a prohibition against a form of booze called tiswin. The Indians defied the ban in May 1885, and Geronimo, Naiche, Chihuahua, and the venerable chief Nana, with 134 others, bolted from the reservation and headed again for Mexico. Crook sent two forces into Mexico, one under Captain Crawford and Lieutenant Britton Davis (a troop of Sixth Cavalrymen and 92 scouts) and another led by Captain Wirt Davis and Lieutenant Matthias W. Day (a troop of Fourth Cavalry and 100 scouts), which crossed the Mexican border on June 11 and July 13, respectively. Crook also deployed about 3,000 troopers to patrol the border country in order to keep the Apaches from reentering the United States.

A long, frustrating pursuit developed, with Geronimo repeatedly eluding Crawford and Davis in Mexico and even slipping through Crook's wide net to cross into Arizona and New Mexico, where he terrorized the citizenry. In October 1885, Crook recalled Crawford and Davis to his Fort Bowie headquarters in Apache Pass. There he re-equipped them for another foray into Mexico. While this was under way, at the start of November, Josanie, brother of Chihuahua, led a mere handful of warriors, perhaps a dozen, on a four-week, 1,200-mile rampage through New Mexico and Arizona. Thirty-eight settlers were killed, and 250 horses stolen. After this, despite the presence of 3,000 U.S. cavalrymen and infantrymen in the region, he and his crew slipped back into Mexico without once engaging a soldier.

With confidence in his leadership ebbing and pressured *personally* by General Sheridan, Crook made a bold, defiant move. He sent Crawford at the head of two companies of scouts, White Mountain Apaches and *Chiricahuas*, so that some of the hunters were of the same band as the hunted. Moreover, except for two lieutenants, Crawford's command included no regular army personnel at all. Wirt Davis commanded his own scouts—solid San Carlos-resident Apaches—and a troop of cavalry. Crawford's command discovered the Apache camp on January 9, 1886, 200 miles south of the border, in Sonora. Geronimo and the others fled, and Crawford was left to destroy an abandoned camp. But, after running so long,

the renegades were tired and sent a squaw to Crawford's camp, with a message that Geronimo was prepared to talk about surrender. A conference was set for January 11.

On the morning of the eleventh, Captain Crawford was awakened by his sentries and told that troops were approaching. At first, Crawford believed it was another column of Apache scouts, and he yelled out to them in Apache. But the advancing soldiers opened fire—they were not scouts, but Mexican militiamen. Seeing this, Crawford climbed up a rock and waved a white handkerchief. "Soldados Americanos," he called out to the Mexicans. By way of response, there came another volley, and Emmet Crawford fell, mortally wounded. His scouts, enraged, traded fire with the Mexicans.

Although the Sonoran governor and the Mexican government later apologized for the "accidental" shooting of Crawford, it has never been clear just how accidental the attack was. Despite a treaty between the United States and Mexico, binding the two governments to cooperate in the pursuit of Geronimo, the Sonorans were never reconciled to the incursion of American soldiers onto their soil and liked even less the presence of Apache scouts, especially since the scouts often fell to looting and rustling. Moreover, the Mexican government paid the militiamen not a salary, but a bounty on scalps—and there was no way to tell whether a scalp had belonged to a hostile Apache or an Apache scout.

Although the peace conference was thus tragically postponed, it took place two days later at Canyon de los Embudos, on March 25, 1886. General Crook adopted his customary harsh demeanor. "I'll keep after you and kill the last one," he told Geronimo, Naiche, Chihuahua, and Nana, "if it takes fifty years." This time, he offered only one alternative to death: two years of exile in the East, removing Geronimo and the others from the country where they would always remain a danger.

After a long conference among themselves, the Apaches accepted. On the way to Fort Bowie, Arizona, the place agreed upon for the formal surrender, Geronimo encountered a whiskey peddlar and, always a hard-drinking man, indulged himself. Thus fortified, he bolted yet again, taking 20 men and 13 women with him. Compounding Crook's chagrin at this unhappy turn of events was a telegram from General Sheridan ordering him to retract the surrender conditions to which the Indians had agreed and to demand instead unconditional surrender. Exhausted, discouraged, and feeling morally unable to comply with Sheridan's order, General George Crook, one of a small handful of genuinely effective regular army Indian fighters, asked to be relieved of command.

Sheridan accepted his subordinate's resignation and dispatched another highly skilled commander, Nelson A.

Miles, who had fought in the Sioux Wars and was promoted to brigadier general in 1880, to take his place. In contrast to the unassuming Crook, the egotistical Miles disdained the use of Apache scouts. It would be regular army or nothing, and he sent a strike force under Captain Henry W. Lawton to run Geronimo to ground once and for all. Starting into Mexico on May 5, Lawton's men chased the Apaches through the whole summer of 1886, penetrating Mexico as far as 200 miles south of the border and traveling a total distance of 2,000 miles without once actually engaging the enemy. The pursuit took its

toll on Lawton's command (only one-third of the men who started with expedition stuck it out to the end), but was also hard on the Indians. By the end of August, Geronimo was again ready to talk.

Lieutenant Charles Gatewood accepted the hazardous assignment of venturing into Geronimo's camp, accompanied only by two Indian guides, to persuade the Apaches to accept what Crook had originally demanded, exile to a Florida prison until President Grover Cleveland might determine his ultimate fate. At first, Geronimo announced that he would accept confinement only at San

*Chiricahua Apache prisoners pose for a photograph beside the train that is carrying them to exile in a Florida prison, 1886. Geronimo is third from right in the front row. The soldiers perched in the vestibules between the cars are either smiling for the camera or can hardly contain their jubilation at having at last conquered Geronimo. (National Archives and Records Administration.)*

Carlos, but when Gatewood told him that all the Warm Springs and Chiricahua Apaches had already been moved to Florida, the dispirited warrior agreed to surrender—though he retained sufficient ego to demand that General Miles accept his surrender in person.

No one appreciated that demand more than the glory-loving Miles, who ceremoniously acknowledged Geronimo's capitulation and sent him out of Fort Bowie and on his way to Florida to the strains of ''Auld Lang Syne'' played by the regimental band. Eventually, the Chiricahuas and Warm Spring Apaches would be permitted to return to the West, but only as far as a reservation in Oklahoma. Geronimo died, at age eighty, at Fort Sill, Oklahoma, in 1909.

□

# GHOST DANCE AND WOUNDED KNEE

In 1886, as Geronimo surrendered to Brigadier General Nelson A. Miles, there were 187 reservations—181,000 square miles of land—in the United States, domiciling 243,000 Indians. The end of Geronimo's Resistance was, for the most part, the end of the American Indian wars.

It was not, however, the end of the killing.

While almost a quarter of a million American Indians were confined to reservations, not all of them had relinquished their identity and way of life. Sitting Bull, presiding over the Hunkpapa Sioux at the Standing Rock Reservation on the South Dakota-North Dakota border stubbornly refused to cooperate with the agent in charge and did all he could to avoid contact with the white world. Despite a number of government reports condemning and criticizing it, the reservation system of the 1880s showed little improvement over that of the 1860s and 1870s. While the Indian Bureau employed a number of dedicated and well-meaning men, the reservation system all too often operated as a corrupt and cruel machine that failed to maintain the Indians at a decent level of subsistence or to provide elementary sanitation.

Apportioned little more than hunger, disease, and despair, the reservation inmates held fast to a hope born of making renewed contact with their identity as Indians. There arose from the ashes of the 1880s a prophet, a Paiute shaman's son named Wovoka. He had spent part of his youth with a white rancher's family and had therefore imbibed white Christian as well as Indian religious traditions. Wovoka was moved to preach, and he told of a new world coming, one in which only Indians dwelled and in which buffalo were again plentiful. The generations of slain braves would come back to life in the new world, and all would live again, in bliss. To hasten this deliverance, Wovoka counseled, all Indians must dance the Ghost Dance and, most important, must observe ab-

solute peace. "Do no harm to anyone," Wovoka enjoined.

Soon, many of the western reservations were alive with Ghost Dancing. Among the Teton Sioux, however, Wovoka's commandment to peace was supressed. Worse, Short Bull and Kicking Bear, Teton apostles of the Ghost Dance religion, openly urged a campaign to obliterate the white man. They even fashioned a "ghost shirt," which, they said, was infallible armor against white men's bullets.

Even without the militant overtones, the dancing alone was enough to alarm white authorities. Pine Ridge Reservation agent Daniel F. Royer frantically telegraphed Washington in November 1890: "Indians are dancing in the snow and are wild and crazy. We need protection and we need it now." On November 20, 1890, cavalry and infantry reinforcements arrived at Pine Ridge and at the Rosebud Reservation.

Far from discouraging the Sioux under Short Bull and Kicking Bear, the army presence galvanized their resolve. About 3,000 Indians gathered on a plateau at the northwest corner of Pine Ridge called the Stronghold. Brigadier General John R. Brooke, commander of the Pine Ridge area, attempted to defuse the situation by sending emissaries to talk with the "hostiles." To Brooke's commanding officer, General Miles, such parleys were insufficiently decisive. Moreover, Miles knew that, whatever was about to happen, it was bound to be a culmination, the momentous end to the epic struggle between white and red for the American continent. He wanted in on it and, accordingly, decided to move his headquarters to Rapid City, South Dakota, in order to prosecute the campaign against the Ghost Dancers personally.

While Miles was preparing his move, Sitting Bull, most venerated of all Sioux leaders, began actively es-

*The key that had once identified these Crow prisoners has been lost, although it is known that they were photographed at the Crow Agency, Montana, in 1887. The Indians are dressed in their finery, and the soldiers are also turned out in their best uniforms, including, on three of the men, dress-white parade gloves. (National Archives and Records Administration.)*

pousing the Ghost Dance doctrine at Standing Rock Reservation. The agent in charge, James McLaughlin, was as level-headed as Pine Ridge's John Brooke was hysterical. He concluded that the old chief would have to be arrested and removed from the reservation—but not, under any circumstances, by a provocative force of soldiers. He would carry out the operation as quietly as possible, using the reservation's own Indian policemen.

General Miles did not accept this proposal. The arrest of Sitting Bull was a momentous event. It called for style, for showmanship. Accordingly, Miles contacted the greatest showman the West has ever known: Buffalo Bill Cody. He would convince Sitting Bull to step down and come along, quietly, meekly.

It was not an entirely bizarre idea. For a time, Sitting Bull had been a featured performer in Buffalo Bill's celebrated Wild West Show, and it was widely known that Cody was the only white man Sitting Bull trusted. But, for his part, Agent McLaughlin was appalled by the idea of importing a popular showman to carry out what should be an expeditious and dignified operation calculated not to enflame an already incindiary situation. When Buffalo Bill arrived at Standing Rock on November 27, 1890, McLaughlin arranged for him to be waylaid by the commanding officer of nearby Fort Yates, Lieutenant Colonel William F. Drum, who drank with Cody all night at the officers' club while McLaughlin worked behind Miles's back to have the showman's authority rescinded.

## THE GHOST DANCE

The Ghost Dance movement began in 1869 or 1870 when a Northern Paiute named Tävibo, from Mason Valley, near Virginia City, Nevada, began to preach among his fellow Paiutes that all white people would fall into holes in the gorund and be swallowed up, even as dead Indians would return to life and inherit the earth that the whites had lost. Tävibo said that he was in communication with the dead during trances, and he instructed his followers to induce a similar state in themselves by dancing the traditional circle dance of the tribes of the Great Basin while singing special chants that had been revealed to him. The Ghost Dance movement of 1870 was limited in extent and duration, spreading only to California, Oregon, and parts of Nevada, fading out when the prophecies failed to come to pass.

In 1889, the movement was suddenly revived when another Northern Paiute, Wovoka (c.1856–1932), was stricken with a fever during a total eclipse of the sun. He recovered and reported that, during his illness, he had been transported to the afterworld, where he had seen legions of dead Indians happily at work and play, and where the Supreme Being had told him to return to his people to tell them to love one another, to work, and to live in peace with the whites. The Supreme Being promised that, if they followed these injunctions faithfully, they would be reunited with the dead, death would cease to exist, and the white race would vanish. Through Wovoka, the Supreme Being gave his people songs and the Ghost Dance, by which they might help to bring the prophecy to realization.

Wovoka's preachings were a combination of the original Ghost Dance, traditional Indian religion, and Christian teaching. As a youth, Wovoka had lived with a white family named Wilson (local whites called Wovoka Jack Wilson) near Yerrington, Nevada. From them he imbibed the usual Christian teachings and, living in the same area as Tävibo, heard that prophet's message as well. (Uncredited legend holds that Wovoka was a son of Tävibo.)

The new Ghost Dance found no following among the Indians of California, who recalled with disappointment the earlier movement, but it spread rapidly through the Rockies and across the Great Plains, among the Sioux, Cheyennes, Comanches, Arapahos, Assinboins, Shoshonis, and other tribes. Interestingly, in the Southwest, where the Navajos and Apaches predominated, the Ghost Dance religion was actively shunned; these Indians had great fear of the spirits of the dead and had no desire to summon them.

Although Wovoka's message was explicitly pacific, Teton Sioux leaders of the Pine Ridge Reservation suppressed the injunction to live peacefully and used the Ghost Dance deliberately to foment an uprising. At Pine Ridge and elsewhere, special "ghost shirts" were fashioned of white muslin and decorated with the sun, moon, stars, and eagles or sage hens. The shirts, it was declared, offered protection against many dangers, especially bullets. The Ghost Dance spread through the Sioux reservations with increasing fervor and excitement, reaching fever pitch in the summer of 1890. White authorities were alarmed, and it became apparent that the Sioux reservations were on the verge of a general uprising.

The movement reached its tragic climax in the massacre at Wounded Knee, after which the Ghost Dance quickly disappeared from the Pine Ridge Reservation. Elsewhere, in scattered pockets, the movement lingered for a few years, but generally in its peaceful form, more an expression of forlorn hope than of vigorous belief.

---

It was a good plan. But what McLaughlin failed to consider was that the man had yet to be born who could drink Buffalo Bill under the table. In the morning, steady as ever, Cody set out for Sitting Bull's camp. McLaughlin arranged for some further delays—just long enough for the arrival of orders cancelling Cody's mission. The old showman, in great anger and disgust, set off for Chicago without seeing Sitting Bull.

As far as McLaughlin was concerned, Buffalo Bill had left the picture not a moment too soon. Matters were coming to a crisis, since Short Bull and Kicking Bear invited Sitting Bull to join them and their people at the Stronghold on the Pine Ridge Reservation. The agent decided that the time had come to move. He dispatched 43 reservation policemen on December 15 to arrest Sitting Bull before he could slip out of Standing Rock Res-

*The Ghost Dance religion spread rapidly among the reservation tribes, including the Arapahos, who are pictured performing the ceremonial dance. (National Archives and Records Administration.)*

*This view of the Pine Ridge Reservation was taken on November 28, 1890, shortly after Indian agent Daniel F. Royer telegraphed Washington: "Indians are dancing in the snow and are wild and crazy. We need protection and we need it now." (National Archives and Records Administration.)*

ervation. The officers deployed themselves around the old chief's cabin as Lieutenant Bull Head, Sergeant Red Tomahawk, and Sergeant Shave Head entered it.

The chief had been sleeping. "What do you want here?" he asked.

"You are my prisoner," explained Bull Head. "You must go to the agency."

Sitting Bull asked leave to put his clothes on.

By the time they emerged with Sitting Bull, a crowd had gathered. Catch-the-Bear called out to all assembled:

"Let us protect our chief." With that, he leveled his rifle at Lieutenant Bull Head, fired, and hit him in the side. The policeman spun about with the force of the impact, discharging his own weapon, pointblank, though perhaps accidentally, into the chest of Sitting Bull. Accident or not, Sergeant Red Tomahawk took it upon himself to finish the job. He shot Sitting Bull in the back of the head.

It was precisely the circus of horrors McLaughlin had been at pains to avoid. As the band of police officers tangled with Sitting Bull's people, the dead chief's horse,

## NELSON A. MILES (1839–1925)

One of the army's ablest commanders during the Indian wars, Miles was a clerk in a Westminster, Massachusetts, crockery store when Fort Sumter fell, signalling the beginning of the Civil War. He enlisted in the Twenty-second Massachusetts Infantry and rose in the ranks with the swiftness of a meteor. A staff officer under General O. O. Howard, he was wounded four times, received the Congressional Medal of Honor, and ended the war as a major general of volunteers. A skillful and courageous commander, he was also enormously egocentric, a tireless self-promoter, and possessed of a prickly personality. Put in charge of Jefferson Davis at the end of the war, Miles drew much public criticism for ignominiously clapping the ex-Confederate in shackles.

Like many other wartime officers, Miles was reduced in rank after the Civil War, and he became a colonel in the regular army, commanding the Fifth Infantry. Miles participated in the Red River War (1874–75) and served with particular distinction in the Sioux War for the Black Hills (1876–77). On January 8, 1877, he forced the surrender of Crazy Horse at the Battle of Wolf Mountain, and on May 7, 1877, at the Battle of Muddy Creek, he defeated the Miniconjou war leader Lame Deer. In the pursuit of the Nez Percés, it was Miles's regiment that finally forced Chief Joseph to surrender (October 5, 1877), and he was instrumental in the defeat of the Bannocks during the Bannock War of 1878. In 1879, Miles had to be restrained by federal officials from pursuing Sitting Bull into Canada.

Promoted to brigadier general in 1880, Miles fought in the Northwest as commander of the Department of the Columbia (1880–85), then assumed command of the Department of the Missouri (1885–86), and replaced General George Crook as commander of the Department of Arizona in 1886. Determined to succeed where Crook had failed in neutralizing Geronimo and the renegade Apaches, Miles deployed about 5,000 men to locate and capture the Apache leader and the 25 warriors who constituted his band of raiders at the time. Geronimo surrendered on September 4, 1886, and Miles immediately provoked controversy on two counts. To begin with, he went counter to President Grover Cleveland's instructions that Geronimo and the others be turned over to civil authorities to stand trial. Instead, Miles accepted their conditional surrender, personally pledging that they would not be hanged. While Miles was magnanimous in this regard, he indiscriminately packed off to prison at Fort Marion, Florida, a large number of Apaches, including those who had done nothing wrong and even some who had served the whites as loyal scouts. While the president, on the one hand, criticized Miles for exceeding his authority, General Crook and the Indian Rights Association, on the other, criticized him for meting out unjust punishment.

Miles weathered the controversy and was given command of the entire Division of the Missouri in 1890. In this post, he presided over the suppression of the Ghost Dance Uprising and the massacre at Wounded Knee and its brief aftermath. It was Miles who accepted the formal surrender of the Sioux on January 15, 1891, which symbolically ended the Indian wars.

Although his reputation had been damaged by the tragedy of Wounded Knee, Miles continued his military career, and in 1895 he was named commander in chief of the army. He saw his last major action in the Spanish-American War of 1898 and retired, a lieutenant general, in 1903.

## SITTING BULL (c.1831–1890)

Even people unfamiliar with Native American history know the name of Sitting Bull, chief and holy man of the Hunkpapa Sioux. He was born near the Grand River, close to the present-day town of Bullhead, South Dakota. His childhood name was Hunkesni, signifying "slow," but he proved himself as a hunter and warrior early in life, killing his first buffalo at age ten and counting his first coup in combat with the Crows four years later. He joined a warrior society, the Strong Hearts, of which he became leader at the age of 22 and conducted many raids against neighboring tribes.

Sitting Bull and the Hunkpapas were not involved in most of the early conflicts between whites and Sioux, since their lands were remote from the early white avenues and objects of migration. However, when Generals Henry Hastings Sibley and Alfred Sully pursued the Santee Sioux into the Dakotas in the aftermath of the Minnesota Santee Uprising of 1862–63, they violated Hunkpapa land. Sitting Bull and his Strong Heart followers responded by raiding and harassing the soldier columns during the summer of 1863 and fought against Sully in the Battle of Killdeer Mountain on July 28, 1864. A year later, Sitting Bull directed the siege of Fort Rice, and in September 1865 wreaked havoc on patrols along the Powder River.

Between this period and 1876, when the Sioux War for the Black Hills broke out, Sitting Bull, combining the qualities of holy man and warrior, assumed the role of spiritual and military leader of the resistance to invasion and to confinement on the reservation. During the Sioux War for the Black Hills, it was Sitting Bull who, in the course of a three-day Sun Dance, had a vision of soldiers falling dead from the sky into the Indian camp. The Battle of the Rosebud and the Battle of the Little Bighorn followed, on June 17 and 25, 1876.

While the destruction of Custer and his command temporarily stunned the army into inaction, by 1877 major offensives had been launched against the Sioux. Sitting Bull and his closest followers made for Canada, where they endured hardship and near-starvation conditions until July 19, 1881, when the venerable chief surrendered at Fort Buford, Dakota Territory.

Although Sitting Bull had been promised amnesty, he was unofficially imprisoned at Fort Randall, Dakota Territory until May 1883, when he was released to the Standing Rock Reservation on the present border of North and South Dakota. Between 1885 and 1886, he toured with Buffalo Bill Cody's famed Wild West Show. The showman and the Indian leader became respected friends, and Buffalo Bill presented Sitting Bull with a fine horse versed in a repertoire of show tricks. It was even Sitting Bull who conferred upon another of the Wild West Show's prize performers, Annie Oakley, the nickname by which she was best known to contempoary audiences, Little Sure Shot ("Watanya cicilia"). However, the dignified warrior soon tired of being a public spectacle and returned to the reservation.

Sitting Bull exercised great influence on the reservation Indians when the Ghost Dance movement threatened to break into a mass uprising in 1890. On December 15, 1890, reservation policemen attempted to arrest the chief at his cabin on Grand River. A fight with his followers broke out, and Sitting Bull, together with six followers, his teenaged son, and a half dozen policemen were killed. The old chief's body was hastily transported to the agency headquarters and buried without ceremony in quicklime. The "battle" of Wounded Knee two weeks later effectively squashed any impending uprising, but Sitting Bull, nevertheless, entered into Indian history and legend and into American popular culture.

which Buffalo Bill had presented to the Indian when he was part of the Wild West Show, was apparently stimulated in a familiar way by the noise of the crowd. He began to perform his repertoire of circus tricks.

Nelson A. Miles had one more important Ghost Dancer to contend with: Big Foot, the leader of the Miniconjou Sioux, who were living on the Cheyenne River. Ironically, the chief had personally given up the Ghost Dance religion; he came to the conclusion that it preached nothing but desperation and futility.

Miles did not know that Big Foot had renounced the Ghost Dance, and he was also unaware that Chief Red Cloud, a Pine Ridge leader friendly to the whites, had asked Big Foot to come to the reservation in order to use his influence to persuade the Stronghold party to surrender. All Miles heard was that Chief Big Foot was headed for the Stronghold. He assumed that he intended to join Short Bull, Kicking Bear, and the other hostiles, which Miles meant to prevent at all costs. Accordingly, he spread a dragnet across the prairies and badlands to intercept all Miniconjous and, in particular, Big Foot.

When a squadron of the Seventh Cavalry located the chief and about 350 followers on December 28, 1890, they were camped near a stream called Wounded Knee Creek. Big Foot, on a mission of reconciliation, was huddled miserably in his wagon, desperately ill with pneumonia. During the night of the twenty-eighth, more troops moved into the area, so that by morning 500 sol-

diers, under Colonel James W. Forsyth, surrounded Big Foot's camp. Four Hotchkiss guns—small, deadly howitzer-like cannon—were trained on the camp from the surrounding hills. Forsyth's mission was to disarm the Indians and take them to the railroad, so that they could be removed from the "zone of military operations." No one expected a fight.

The soldiers entered the camp and began to search for guns. Their intrusion and the arrogance with which they went about their task outraged a medicine man named Yellow Bird, who began dancing, and, as he danced, exhorted his people to resist, to fight. The ghost shirts they wore, he said, would protect them.

Black Coyote, whom another Indian described as "a crazy man, a young man of very bad influence and in

*Federal authorities feared that Sitting Bull, revered chief of the Hunkpapa Sioux and one of the greatest Indians leaders of the Plains, would mastermind a general uprising among reservation inmates. They, therefore, ordered his arrest, but a near riot broke out when the chief was taken into custody, and in the scuffle, he was killed. (National Archives and Records Administration.)*

*Sergeant Red Tomahawk was among the reservation policemen sent to arrest Sitting Bull. It was he who fired the shot that killed the chief. The photograph was taken in 1897 at Fort Yates, North Dakota. (National Archives and Records Administration.)*

*Big Foot, chief of the Miniconjou Sioux, was desperately ill with pneumonia when he was shot down during the massacre at Wounded Knee. (National Archives and Records Administration.)*

ans have seized upon to justify calling Wounded Knee a battle rather than a massacre—as it is more notoriously known.

After a round of hand-to-hand combat, the Indians began to flee. At this point, the Hotchkiss guns opened up on the camp, firing almost a shell a second at men, at women, at children.

"We tried to run," Louise Weasel Bear said, "but they shot us like we were buffalo."

It was over in less than an hour. Big Foot and 153 other Miniconjous were known to have been killed. So many others staggered, limped, or crawled away that it is impossible to determine just how many finally died. Most likely, 300 of the 350 who had been camped at Wounded Knee Creek lost their lives. The Seventh Cavalry had its casualties, too: 25 killed and 39 wounded, mostly from "friendly fire," to borrow a term from the twentieth-century war that spawned the massacre at My Lai, South Vietnam, sometimes compared to the "battle" of Wounded Knee.

Miles did not glory in Wounded Knee. On the contrary, he relieved Forsyth of command and ordered a court of inquiry. To Miles's chagrin, the court exonerated the colonel. Over the general's protests, General John M. Schofield—Miles's immediate superior—and the secretary of war reinstated Forsyth's command.

Wounded Knee prompted "hostile" and "friendly" Sioux factions to unite (though Chief Red Cloud protested against his people's participation) in a December 30 ambush of the Seventh Cavalry near the Pine Ridge Agency. Elements of the Ninth Cavalry came to the rescue, and General Miles subsequently marshaled 3,500 troops (out of a total force of 5,000) around the angry Sioux who had assembled 15 miles north of the Pine Ridge Agency along White Clay Creek. Slowly, patiently, Miles contracted the ring of bluecoats around the Indians, all the while urging their surrender and pledging good treatment.

It was becoming clear even to the most resolute that the cause was hopeless, and the union of Sioux factions at White Clay Creek was brief. With a formal surrender in the clear cold of January 15, 1891, four centuries of war between white man and red came to an end bitter and inglorious, suffused with exhaustion, sorrow, and shame.

fact a nobody," raised a Winchester above his head as the troopers were collecting weapons. He shouted that he had paid much money for the rifle, that it was his, that nobody was going to take it.

Soldiers crowded him, then spun him around. A rifle discharged. Perhaps it was Black Coyote's, perhaps not. It might have been accidental. It might have been deliberate. Few of the Indians were armed, but both sides opened fire. It is this fact that some later military histori-

*Most, perhaps all, of the participants in the "grass dance" photographed on August 9, 1890—members of Big Foot's band of Miniconjou Sioux—were killed on December 29 at the "Battle" of Wounded Knee. (National Archives and Records Administration.)*

*A great Sioux council, held at "Hostile Camp" on the Pine Ridge Reservation early in 1891, formally ended the Indian Wars. (National Archives and Records Administration.)*

# CHRONOLOGY

Wars between Indians and whites were rarely officially declared or officially concluded, and even when they ostensibly were, violence often preceded the official declaration and persisted after the official cessation of hostilities. Therefore, this chronology defines the span of any particular war by encompassing all of the conflicts traditionally associated with that war. It should also be noted that much white–Indian conflict was not part of any named war.

**1492**
**October 12**—Columbus sights present-day Watling Island in the Bahamas and claims the island for Spain. The next year, a garrison Columbus leaves at La Navidad clashes with island Indians, who wipe it out.

**1540–42**
A series of Spanish expeditions into the borderlands culminates with the explorations of Vásquez de Coronado, who travels as far as present-day Kansas, but most extensively in the great Southwest.

**1540**
In July, Coronado and his army demand the surrender of Hawikuh Pueblo. The town falls in less than an hour. By September, the Zuni and Hopi pueblo regions along the Rio Grande are subjugated.

**1541**
**May 8**—De Soto's expedition reaches the Mississippi River—the first Europeans to do so. That summer, after Coronado leaves the pueblo country to search the Great Plains for the legendary Seven Cities of Gold, an Indian rebellion is brutally and summarily put down.

**1565**
**September 8**—The first permanent European colony in what is now the United States is established at St. Augustine, Florida.

**1585**
**August**—The Roanoke Island colony is established.

**1590**
**August 17**—An expedition under John White reaches Roanoke and discovers that the colonists have vanished. The word *Croatoan* carved into a tree suggests that they may have fallen victim to the Croatan Indians.

**1598**
**April 30**—Don Juan de Oñate claims for Spain all of "New Mexico," a province stretching from Texas through California. Oñate aggressively colonizes the pueblo country.

**1599**
**January**—Of all the pueblos, only Acoma offers serious resistance to Oñate's troops. Acoma is brutally conquered in January.

**1607**
**May 13**—Jamestown, Virginia is founded.
**December**—Captain John Smith, captured by Indians of the Powhatan Confederacy, is sentenced to death, but (by his own report) is saved by the intercession of Pocahantas (Matoaka), Chief Powhatan's (Wa-hun-sen-a-cawh) daughter.

**1618**
Death of Powhatan. His anti-English half-brother, Opechancanough, becomes chief of the Powhatan Confederacy.

**1622–44**
*Powhatan War* in Virginia.

**1622**
**March**—*Powhatan War*. Servants of a Jamestown planter kill a prominent Powhatan Indian as revenge for having murdered their master. Opechancanough vows vengeance.
**March 22**—*Powhatan War*. Indians stage surprise attacks along the James River. Fourteen years of more or less continual warfare ensue.

**1632**
*Powhatan War*. Truce declared.

**1634**
**November 7**—Pequot representatives agree to hand over members of a tributary tribe guilty of the murder of Captain John Stone, a disreputable trader. They also agree to pay an exorbitant indemnity and cede vast tracts of land. The Pequot council fails to ratify the treaty.

**1636–37**
Period of the *Pequot War* in New England.

**1636**
**July**—*Pequot War*. Colonists renew their treaty demands of 1634. When another trading captain is killed off Block Island by Narragansetts or members of a tribe subject to them, Narragansett sachems offer reparations.
**August 25**—*Pequot War*. Massachusetts Bay Colony authorities dispatch a force to Block Island. They burn Pequot houses and destroy crops, inciting the Pequots to full-scale war.

**1637**
**May 22–24**—*Pequot War*. The Narragansetts and Eastern Niantics ally with the colonies.
**May 26**—*Pequot War*. Captain John Mason attacks a Pequot village at Mystic, Connecticut, killing 600–700 Indians there.
**July 13**—*Pequot War*. Connecticut and Massachusetts forces pursue survivors of the Mystic massacre, taking some 200 captives.

**1638–84**
Period of Iroquoian *Beaver Wars*.

**1638**
**September 21**—*Pequot War*. The war ends with the Treaty of Hartford. Many survivors are enslaved.

**1639–64**
Period of the *Dutch–Indian Wars*.

**1641**
*Dutch–Indian Wars*. Dutch livestock destroys Raritan Indian cornfields on Staten Island, provoking Indian retaliation. Governor Willem Kieft offers a bounty on Raritan scalps.

**1643**
**February**—*Dutch–Indian Wars*. The Mohawks, trading partners of the Dutch, attempt to extort tribute money from the Wappinger Indians, who flee and appeal to Kieft for protection. Kieft turns the Mohawks loose upon them.

**February 25–26**—*Dutch–Indian Wars*. Kieft sends Dutch soldiers to finish off the Wappinger refugees, mostly women and children, in a night of mayhem that becomes infamous as the "Slaughter of the Innocents." Appalled, various tribes wage war against the Dutch.

**October**—*Dutch–Indian Wars*. The Dutch hire English captain John Underhill to lead Dutch and English soldiers in a counteroffensive against the Indians.

### 1644

*Dutch–Indian Wars*. Indians lift their siege of New Amsterdam and agree to a peace.

**April 18**—*Powhatan War*. Old Opechancanough launches a devastating assault along the James River, killing 400–500 colonists.

### 1645

The United Colonies declare war on the Narragansetts, who quickly yield and pay a heavy tribute.

### 1646

**March**—*Powhatan War*. The Virginia assembly dispatches Captain Henry Fleet to negotiate peace with Opechancanough. Governor Berkeley leads an unauthorized raid and captures Opechancanough, who is killed.

**October**—*Powhatan War*. Virginia concludes a peace with Opechancanough's successor, Necotowance.

### 1649

**March 16**—*Beaver Wars*. Dutch-armed Senecas and Mohawks attack the Huron mission towns of Saint Ignace and Saint Louis.

**March 17**—*Beaver Wars*. Senecas and Mohawks attack Sainte Marie. By the end of the month, the Hurons abandon 15 towns.

**November–December**—*Beaver Wars*. Mohawks and Senecas attack the Tobaccos near Lake Erie, nearly annihilating them.

### 1650

**Late Autumn**—*Beaver Wars*. Iroquois launch a furious campaign against the Neutral Nation.

### 1651

**Spring**—*Beaver Wars*. Iroquois attack the Neutrals again.

### 1655

*Dutch–Indian Wars*. The so-called "Peach War" begins when a Dutch farmer kills a Delaware Indian woman for picking peaches in his orchard. Indian retaliation is followed by Dutch counterstrikes.

### 1656

**Winter**—*Beaver Wars*. Iroquois virtually annihilate French-allied Eries.

### 1659

**September**—*Dutch–Indian Wars*. Esopus Indians attack Wiltwyck (present-day Kingston, New York). Stuyvesant calls for a parley and treacherously murders a delegation of Esopus chiefs in their sleep. The Esopus capture eight Dutch soldiers and burn them alive. Fitful warfare ensues.

### 1660

*Dutch–Indian Wars*. Stuyvesant rounds up Indian children as hostages to extort "good behavior" from the various Delaware tribes.

### 1664

*Dutch–Indian War*. The Esopus finally yield to the Dutch, after Stuyvesant calls in his Mohawk allies to terrorize them.

**August 6**—King Philip (Metacom or Metaco-

met) is summoned to Plymouth Town to answer charges of plotting against Plymouth colony.

**October 4**—The English take possession of Dutch-held New Netherland and rename it New York.

### 1667

King Philip is again summoned to Plymouth to answer charges of plotting war.

### 1671

**April 10**—King Philip signs a document binding the Wampanoags to surrender their arms and acknowledge colonial authority.

### 1675

**July–August**—*Indian War of 1675–76*. A dispute between Maryland Nanticoke Indians and a Virginia planter leads to the murder of some Indians and a reprisal against whites, which escalates into war. Colonel John Washington and Major Isaac Allerton raise a 700-man militia, augmented by a 250-man force under Maryland Major Thomas Trueman.

**September**—*Indian War of 1675–76*. Major Trueman calls a parley with five Susquehannock chiefs and kills them.

**September–November**—*Indian War of 1675–76*. Susquehannocks withstand a siege at the junction of the Piscataway Creek and Potomac River. General raiding resumes. After 36 settlers have been killed, the Susquehannocks declare that (with approximately 10 common Englishmen killed for each of their chiefs slain), restitution has been made. Their offer of peace is rejected.

### 1675–76

**King Philip's War** in New England.

### 1675

**January 29**—*King Philip's War*. The dead body of John Sassamon, a Christianized Indian who had been spying on Philip for the colonists, is discovered.

**June**—*King Philip's War*. King Philip is implicated in the murder of Sassamon and hauled into court to answer charges. He behaves contemptuously.

**June 11**—*King Philip's War*. Wampanoags arm, and frightened settlers abandon some frontier towns. Massachusetts, Plymouth, and Rhode Island unite against Philip.

**June 21–23**—*King Philip's War*. Philip attacks Swansea and other frontier settlements.

**June 28**—*King Philip's War*. Benjamin Church and his troops are beaten at Miles's Bridge.

**July 1**—*King Philip's War*. Connecticut joins the other colonies in fighting Philip, who forges an alliance of his own with the Pocasset squaw-sachem Weetamoo.

**July 8**—*King Philip's War*. Benjamin Church leads 20 poorly-provisioned volunteers, who are attacked by some 300 Indians for six hours (the "Pease-field Fight"). They are eventually rescued by a river sloop.

**July 19**—*King Philip's War*. The Battle of Pocasset Swamp fails to dislodge the Wampanoags.

**August 24–25**—*King Philip's War*. The Battle of Hopewell Swamp, south of Deerfield, Massachusetts, results in an Indian retreat.

**August**—*King Philip's War*. War spreads to the upper Connecticut Valley, the Merrimac Valley, New Hampshire, and Maine.

**September 9**—*King Philip's War*. The United Colonies officially declare war and levy an army of 1,000, which does not muster until November and December.

**November 2**—*King Philip's War*. A treaty is concluded with the Narragansetts, but Con-

necticut resolves to prevent war with them by making a peremptory strike.

**December 18–19**—*King Philip's War*. Plymouth governor Josiah Winslow marches a 1,000-man army into a snowstorm to attack the stronghold of the Narragansett sachem Canonchet. In the Great Swamp Fight, 80 of Winslow's army die, including 14 company commanders, and about 600 Narragansetts—half of them women and children—are killed.

### 1676

**February 10**—*King Philip's War*. Lancaster, Massachusetts is raided.

**February 21**—*King Philip's War*. A 160-man militia force is defeated at Medfield, Massachusetts, which is partially destroyed.

**March 12**—*King Philip's War*. Clark's Garrison, Plymouth, is destroyed.

**March**—*King Philip's War*. Bostonians riot against friendly "praying Indians."

**March 29**—*King Philip's War*. Providence, Rhode Island is destroyed.

**April 21**—*King Philip's War*. Sudbury, Massachusetts, is attacked.

**May**—*Indian War of 1675–76/Bacon's Rebellion*. Virginia planter Nathaniel Bacon exploits public dissatisfaction with Governor Berkeley's policies in order to raise a private militia and attack the Susquehannocks. Bacon recruits Occaneechi Indian allies and betrays them.

**May 6**—*King Philip's War*. Captain Daniel Henchman sweeps through eastern Massachusetts.

**May 11**—*King Philip's War*. Plymouth Town raided.

**May 19**—*King Philip's War*. Captain William Turner attacks an Indian encampment at the Falls of the Connecticut. An Indian counterattack kills about 40 colonials, including Turner.

**May 26**—*Indian War of 1675–76/Bacon's Rebellion*. Berkeley posts Nathaniel Bacon as a traitor, arrests him, and takes his seat in the House of Burgesses. Bacon apologizes and is pardoned.

**June 12**—*King Philip's War*. Connecticut troops repel some 700 Indian warriors who attack Hadley, Massachusetts.

**June 23**—*Indian War of 1675–76/Bacon's Rebellion*. Bacon returns to Jamestown and threatens to open fire on the House of Burgesses unless it commissions him commander of all forces fighting the Indians. The Burgesses yield. Bacon attacks the friendly Pamunkeys.

**July**—*King Philip's War*. War with the Abnakis, Sokokis, and Pennacooks ends when the Pennacook sachem Wannalancet signs a treaty.

**July 2**—*King Philip's War*. At Nipsachuck, Rhode Island, John Talcott devastates a Narragansett band.

**July 3**—*King Philip's War*. Talcott kills 18 men and 22 women and children at Warwick.

**July 27–30** *King Philip's War*. One hundred eighty Nipmucks surrender at Boston.

**July 29**—*Indian War of 1675–76/Bacon's Rebellion*. Berkeley repeals Bacon's commission and again proclaims him a traitor. Many Virginia planters support Bacon and continue his indiscriminate war against the Indians.

**August 1**—*King Philip's War*. Benjamin Church and his men capture Philip's wife and son.

**August 6**—*King Philip's War*. Weetamoo, squaw-sachem of Pocasset and Philip's kin and ally, dies.

**August 12**—*King Philip's War*. Church's troops surround Philip, who is shot by an English-allied Indian named Alderman.

**September 13**—*Indian War of 1675–76/Bacon's*

*Rebellion*. Bacon returns to Jamestown, seizes the wives of Burgesses loyal to the governor, and uses them as shields while his men force Berkeley out of Jamestown.

**September 18**—*Indian War of 1675–76/Bacon's Rebellion*. Bacon burns Jamestown.

**October 18 or 26**—*Indian War of 1675–76/ Bacon's Rebellion*. Berkeley forces Bacon to a stand at Yorktown, where Bacon dies, not in combat, but of dysentery. Bacon's Rebellion comes to an end.

**1677**

**March**—*Indian War of 1675–76/Bacon's Rebellion*. A conference and treaty at Shackamaxon effectively ends the Indian War of 1675–76.

**1680**

*Beaver Wars*. The Iroquois launch a major war against the French-allied Indian bands living along the Illinois and Mississippi rivers.

**August 10**—*Popé's Rebellion*. Popé, from Tewa Pueblo, launches a general pueblo rebellion.

**August 19**—*Popé's Rebellion*. Santa Fe falls to Popé, who installs himself as dictator.

**1688–97**

*King William's War* is fought in New England; the *Abnaki War*, which began earlier, soon merges with it.

**1688**

*Popé's Rebellion*. Popé dies, leaving the pueblos in a chronic state of civil war.

**April**—*Abnaki War*. New York troops provoke war with the Abnakis. English settlers at Saco, Maine, take 16 Indians captive. The Abnakis respond with raids.

**September**—*Abnaki War/King William's War*. The English build stockades at North Yarmouth, Maine, but abandon them at the approach of the Abnakis. In fleeing, they encounter another band of Abnakis. An indecisive battle ensues.

**Autumn**—*King William's War*. Abnakis raid northern New England.

**1689**

*King William's War*. Louis de Buade, comte de Frontenac, becomes governor of New France and uses Indian allies as agents of terror.

*Popé's Rebellion*. Zia Pueblo is retaken by the Spanish.

**May 12**—*King William's War*. The War of the League of Augsburg erupts in Europe; in America, the conflict is already under way as King William's War, pitting the French and Abnaki Indians (of Maine) against the English and their Iroquois allies.

**July 25–26**—*King William's War*. La Chine, Quebec, is attacked by Iroquois. The demoralized French colonists retreat.

**Summer**—*King William's War*. Northern New England reels under French-aided Abnaki raids.

**1690**

**February 9**—*King William's War*. The French and their Indian allies attack Schenectady; killing 60 people.

**March 27**—*King William's War*. Frontenac attacks Salmon Falls, New Hampshire, killing 34 people.

**May**—*King William's War*. Fort Loyal (Falmouth, Maine) is attacked by Canadians and Abnakis. The garrison is massacred.

**May 11**—*King William's War*. Sir William Phips takes Port Royal, Acadia. Phips is assigned to invade Quebec, but fails.

**1691**

**September**—*King William's War*. The English call Benjamin Church out of retirement to defend Saco, Maine.

**November 29**—*King William's War*. The English make a truce with the Abnakis.

**1692**

*Popé's Rebellion*. The Spanish lay siege to Santa Fe, which surrenders.

*King William's War*. Despite the truce, Abnakis continue to raid.

**1693**

**January**—*King William's War*. The French and allied Indians move against Mohawk villages in New York.

**1695**

*First Pima Revolt*. Pimas of lower Pimeria Alta—present-day Sonora, Mexico, and southern Arizona—stage a short-lived revolt.

**1697**

**March 15**—*King William's War*. Abnakis raid Haverhill, Massachusetts.

**September**—*King William's War*. The Treaty of Ryswick ends the War of the League of Augsburg and winds down the conflict in America.

**1698 or 1699**

*King William's War*. Various western tribes, including the Ojibwas, defeat the Iroquois on the shores of Lake Erie.

**1702**

**May 4**—The War of the Spanish Succession is declared in Europe.

**September 10**—*Queen Anne's War*. The American phase of the War of the Spanish Succession, Queen Anne's War, begins.

**December**—*Queen Anne's War*. Five hundred colonists and Chickasaws attack Saint Augustine's fort; failing to breach it, they burn the town. A pattern of raid and counterraid develops throughout the South.

**1703**

**August 10**—*Queen Anne's War*. English settlers plunder the Maine house belonging to the son of Jean Vincent de l'Abadie, baron de St. Castin, touching off raids in northern New England.

**1704**

**February 29**—*Queen Anne's War*. Fifty French colonists and 200 Abnakis and Caughnawagas (French-allied Mohawks) descend on Deerfield, Massachusetts.

**July 1 and 28**—*Queen Anne's War*. Aged Benjamin Church terrorizes the Nova Scotia villages of Minas (July 1) and Beaubassin (July 28).

**August 18–29**—*Queen Anne's War*. French and Indians destroy the English settlement at Bonavista, Nova Scotia.

**July**—*Queen Anne's War*. Former South Carolina governor James Moore and a force of militia and Chickasaws virtually annihilate the Appalachees in western Florida.

**1710**

*Queen Anne's War*. Colonel Francis Nicholson and Admiral Sir Francis Hobby reduce Port Royal on October 16. The following summer, all Acadia falls.

**1711–13**

*Tuscarora War*

**1711**

**September 22**—*Tuscarora War*. Tuscaroras

raid New Bern and other North Carolina settlements. Raids by Tuscaroras, Corees, and other tribes follow.

**1712–33**

The *Fox Resistance* is fought against the French and their Indian allies.

**1712**

**March**—*Tuscarora War*. South Carolina sends military aid to North Carolina. Colonel John Barnwell attacks the stronghold of Tuscarora "King" Hancock. Barnwell withdraws and the North Carolina assembly orders him to return; he convinces Hancock to agree to a peace, then violates it by seizing Tuscarora prisoners and selling them into slavery.

**1713**

**March**—*Tuscarora War*. South Carolina's James Moore kills hundreds of Tuscaroras and captures some 400.

**July 13**—*Queen Anne's War*. The Treaty of Utrecht ends the War of the Spanish Succession and Queen Anne's War.

**1715**

**April 15**—*Yamasee War*. Yamasees, Catawbas, and other tribes attack settlements north of Savannah, Georgia, killing more than 100 settlers.

**June**—*Yamasee War*. South Carolina militia drives the Yamasees out of their villages.

**Fall**—*Yamasee War*. South Carolina's Charles Craven batters the Yamasees to the point of extinction.

**1716**

*Yamasee War*. South Carolina's Cherokee allies drive out remaining Yamasees and members of the Lower Creek tribe from territory northwest of Port Royal.

**1720–24**

*Chickasaw Resistance*. The Chickasaws defy a French ban on trade with the English. The French incite their Choctaw allies to raid Chickasaw settlements. The Chickasaws retaliate.

**1729**

*Fox Resistance*. The French and their Indian allies, chiefly Ojibwas, attack the Foxes.

**November 28**—*Natchez Revolt*. The Natchez attack Fort Rosalie, a French outpost. The Yazoo Indians join the uprising, but the French retaliate vigorously.

**1730**

*Fox Resistance*. The French and Ojibwas intensify attacks against the Foxes.

**1731**

The French build Fort Saint Frédéric at Crown Point. This, combined with the destruction of the Iroquois-allied Fox Indians, drives the Iroquois Confederation into an alliance with the English.

**1734**

*Chickasaw Resistance*. The French back Choctaw raids against the Chickasaws.

**1739**

**October 19**—*War of Jenkins's Ear*. England declares war on Spain; this conflict dissolves into the larger War of the Austrian Succession (called *King George's War* in America).

**1740–48**

*King George's War*. The American phase of Europe's War of the Austrian Succession (1740–48) was fought mainly by New England against the French and their Indian allies on the Nova Scotia peninsula.

**1740**

**January**—*War of Jenkins's Ear*. Aided by Creeks, Cherokees, and Chickasaws, Georgia's James Ogelthorpe invades Spanish Florida.

**May–July**—*War of Jenkins's Ear*. Ogelthorpe's forces besiege Saint Augustine.

**1742**

**June 9**—*War of Jenkins's Ear*. Ogelthorpe repels a major Spanish counteroffensive on Saint Simon's Island, Georgia, in the Battle of Bloody Marsh.

**1743**

*War of Jenkins's Ear*. Ogelthorpe makes a second attempt to capture Saint Augustine, fails, and withdraws from Florida.

**1745**

**June 16**—*King George's War*. After a long siege, Louisbourg, Nova Scotia, falls to the English.

**August**—*King George's War*. French provincials and Abnaki Indians begin to raid remote settlements in Maine.

**November 28–29**—French and Indians burn Fort Saratoga, New York.

**1746**

**August 20**—*King George's War*. Fort Massachusetts falls to French and Indians.

**August 25**—*King George's War*. Deerfield, Massachusetts, is successfully defended in the "Barrs Fight."

**1748**

**October 18**—*King George's War*. The Treaty of Aix-la-Chapelle ends the War of the Austrian Succession as well as King George's War.

**1749**

**March 27**—Ohio Company land grants rekindle enmity with the French and Indians.

**August**—Jacques-Pierre de Jonquière, marquis de La Jonquière, becomes governor of New France and begins a military build-up.

**1751**

**November 20**—*Second Pima Revolt*. Luis Oacpicagigua leads Pimas in a short-lived general uprising against the Spanish. Many Papagos, Sobaipuris, and Apaches join in the rebellion.

**1752**

**June 21**—Charles Langlade, a half-breed French Indian agent commanding Ojibwas, Potawatomies, and Ottawas, raids the Miami (Twightwee) "capital" of Pickawillany. Chief Memeskia is killed and the politically crucial trading post of George Croghan is destroyed. English colonial officials fail to respond, and for two years English trade in the Ohio Valley virtually ceases.

**July 1**—Ange Duquesne de Menneville, marquis Duquesne, becomes governor of New France and builds new forts to secure the Ohio country. He assembles an army of 2,200 men.

**1753–54**

Missionary Jean-Louis Le Loutre leads French resistance against the English in Nova Scotia, instigating Micmac Indians to raid British settlers.

**1753**

**August**—Lord Halifax moves England toward war by asserting claims to French-held Iroquois land.

**October 31**—Governor Robert Dinwiddie of Virginia sends 21-year-old George Washington to evict Captain Legardeur de Saint-Pierre, commandant of Fort LeBoeuf, from western territory claimed by Virginia.

**December 12**—Legardeur rebuffs Washington.

**1754–63**

*The French and Indian War*

**1754**

**January**—Construction begins on an English fort at the "forks of Ohio."

**April 17**—*The French and Indian War*. Captain Claude-Pierre Pecaudy de Contrecoeur captures the new English fort and renames it Fort Duquesne.

**May 28**—*The French and Indian War*. Washington surprises a 33-man French reconnaissance party, 10 of whom are killed in this first battle of the French and Indian War.

**June 19–July 10**—The Albany Congress fails to bring unity to the colonies.

**July 3–4**—*The French and Indian War*. French and Indians counterattack Washington, who surrenders after half his men are lost.

**1755**

**June 16**—*The French and Indian War*. Fort Beausejour, Nova Scotia, falls to the English.

**June 17**—*The French and Indian War*. Fort Gaspereau, Nova Scotia, falls to the English. By the end of the month, the British hold Nova Scotia, except for Louisbourg.

**July 7**—*The French and Indian War*. Major General Edward Braddock detaches a "flying column" of 1,500 men from his force to make the initial attack on Fort Duquesne.

**July 9**—*The French and Indian War*. French and Indians ambush Braddock's "flying column." Of 1,459 English officers and men engaged in the "Battle of the Wilderness," only 462 survive. Braddock dies.

**July 28**—*The French and Indian War*. Nova Scotia's Acadians are deported. The Micmacs, friendly neighbors of the Acadians, are finally dispossessed of their lands.

**September 8**—*The French and Indian War*. The French commander Jean-Armand, Baron de Dieskau, attacks William Johnson's forces. The important English-allied Mohawk chief Hendrick (Theyanoguin) is killed, but Dieskau is defeated.

**1756**

**March 27**—*The French and Indian War*. Indians, Canadians, and French regulars capture Fort Bull.

**May 11**—*The French and Indian War*. Louis Joseph, Marquis de Montcalm arrives in Canada to take charge of French and provincial forces.

**May 17**—*The French and Indian War*. England officially declares war on France.

**Late May**—*The French and Indian War*. Lieutenant Colonel John Bradstreet takes 1,000 men in 350 boats from Albany to Oswego to supply the imperiled Fort Oswego.

**July 3**—*The French and Indian War*. As Bradstreet and his men return from Oswego, 700 Canadians and Indians ambush his advance group of about 300. Outnumbered, Bradstreet and his troops defeat the attackers.

**August 11–14**—*The French and Indian War*. Montcalm takes Fort Oswego. The garrison is massacred.

**December**—*The French and Indian War*. William Pitt becomes British secretary of state for the southern department, with direct charge of American colonial affairs. He orders 2,000 additional troops to Nova Scotia.

**1757**

**August 4**—*The French and Indian War*. Major General Daniel Webb abandons Fort William Henry, leaving its defense to Lieutenant Colonel George Monro with 2,300 men, of whom only 1,100 are fit for duty at the time. Montcalm, advancing on the fort, commands 7,626 men, including 1,600 Indian allies.

**August 9**—*The French and Indian War*. Monro capitulates. He and his men, promised safe conduct, are massacred by the French-allied Indians.

**1758**

**July 1**—*The French and Indian War*. General James Abercromby, now in charge of American operations, assembles 16,000 troops for a march on Fort Ticonderoga (Fort Carillon). He sends ahead Bradstreet, who overpowers the fort's outer defenses and asks permission to press the attack. Abercromby insists on waiting for the main body of his troops. The delay gives Montcalm time to bring up reinforcements.

**July 8**—*The French and Indian War*. Abercromby ineptly attacks the reinforced Fort Ticonderoga and suffers a crushing defeat.

**July 26**—*The French and Indian War*. Louisbourg, Nova Scotia, falls to the British.

**August 27**—*The French and Indian War*. Fort Frontenac falls to Bradstreet.

**September 15**—*The French and Indian War*. A sortie of French and Indians issues from Fort Duquesne, overruns 800 Highlanders, and kills one-third of them. But Indian losses are also heavy, and many desert the French.

**October**—*The French and Indian War*. The Treaty of Easton returns to the Iroquois western lands ceded earlier, but prevails upon the Iroquois to grant the Delawares—hitherto French allies—the right to hunt and live on them. Iroquois are now firmly allied with the English, and the Delawares desert the French.

**October 12**—*The French and Indian War*. François-Marie Le Marchand de Lignery, commandant of Fort Duquesne, raids General Forbes's position at Loyalhanna, Pennsylvania, but is repelled.

**November 12**—*The French and Indian War*. Forbes repels a second raid.

**November 24**—*The French and Indian War*. Lignery blows up Fort Duquesne and withdraws to Fort Machault (present-day Franklin, Pennsylvania) to plan a counterattack. The English rename the ruins of Duquesne Fort Pitt and now control the gateway to the West.

**1759**

*The French and Indian War*. Pitt formulates a three-pronged strategy that includes the capture of Fort Niagara and reinforcement of Oswego, a strike through the Lake Champlain waterway into the Saint Lawrence Valley, and an assult on Quebec.

**April**—*The French and Indian War*. The Senecas, formerly inclined toward the French, propose to assist the English in reducing Fort Niagara.

**July–September**—*The French and Indian War*. Wolfe lays siege to Quebec City, defended by Montcalm.

**July 23**—*The French and Indian War*. Fort Niagara falls to the English.

**July 26**—*The French and Indian War*. Colonel Frederick Haldimand successfully reinforces Fort Oswego. The French abandon and blow up Fort Ticonderoga.

**July 31**—*The French and Indian War*. Jeffrey Amherst takes Fort Saint Frédéric.

**September 12–13**—*The French and Indian War.* After a long siege, Wolfe takes Quebec. Both he and Montcalm are killed.

**1759–62**
The *Cherokee Uprising* erupts along the southern frontier.

**1760**
**September 6**—*The French and Indian War.* Amherst and Murray take Montréal.
**September 8**—*The French and Indian War.* Governor Vaudreuil ·surrenders the province of Canada to the English.

**1761**
**February 22**—*The French and Indian War.* Jeffrey Amherst ends British gift-giving to the Indians, thereby aggravating discontent among the Iroquois.

**1762**
**Winter**—*Cherokee Uprising.* Cherokees cede much of their eastern land.

**1763–64**
*Pontiac's Rebellion.*

**1763**
**February 10**—*The French and Indian War.* By the Treaty of Paris, France cedes all of Louisiana to Spain and the rest of its North American holdings to Great Britain.
**April 27**—*Pontiac's Rebellion.* The Ottawa chief Pontiac holds a grand council, urging the Potowatomis and Hurons to join his Ottawas in an attack on Detroit.
**May 7**—*Pontiac's Rebellion.* Pontiac's first attempt to infiltrate Fort Detroit fails.
**May 8–9**—*Pontiac's Rebellion.* Pontiac attempts to enter the fort again. Failing this, he raids some settlers outside of the fort.
**May–September**—*Pontiac's Rebellion.* Fort Detroit endures a five-month siege.
**May 16**—*Pontiac's Rebellion.* Ottawas and Hurons take Fort Sandusky.
**May 25**—*Pontiac's Rebellion.* Fort Saint Joseph falls.
**May 27**—*Pontiac's Rebellion.* Fort Miami falls.
**June 1**—*Pontiac's Rebellion.* Fort Ouiatenon falls.
**Early June**—*Pontiac's Rebellion.* Fort Michilimackinac falls. Forts Pitt, Ligonier, and Bedford are all besieged, but hold out.
**June 16**—*Pontiac's Rebellion.* Fort Venango falls.
**June 18**—*Pontiac's Rebellion.* Fort Le Boeuf falls.
**June 20**—Joined by Ottawas, Hurons, and Ojibwas, the Senecas attack Fort Presque Isle (Erie, Pennsylvania).
**June 24**—*Pontiac's Rebellion.* Delawares demand the surrender of Fort Pitt. Acting on the orders of Amherst and Henry Bouquet, Simon Ecuyer presents Delaware chiefs with a handkerchief and two blankets from the fort's smallpox-ridden hospital. This act of "germ warfare" results in the withdrawal of the attackers and touches off an epidemic.
**August 5–6**—*Pontiac's Rebellion.* Henry Bouquet, leading a relief column to Fort Pitt, is ambushed by Delawares, Shawnees, Mingos, and Hurons. By tricking the Indians to fight in the open, Bouquet prevails after the closely fought Battle of Bushy Run.
**October 3**—*Pontiac's Rebellion.* Pontiac makes peace.
**October 7**—The Proclamation of 1763 reasserts the earlier Easton agreement, establishing a westward limit to white settlement.
**December 14**—*Paxton Riots.* Scottish-Irish Presbyterians from Paxton and Donegal, on the raid-wracked Pennsylvania frontier, kill six non-hostile Conestoga Indians in Lancaster County. Governor John Penn issues a proclamation of arrest for the mob, but it is ignored by frontier Pennsylvanians.
**December 27**—*Paxton Riots.* Lancaster County officials place the surviving Conestogas in a public workhouse to protect them. The "Paxton Boys" strike, killing 14 Conestogas while they kneel at prayer. The Paxton Boys march next on Philadelphia. Benjamin Franklin persuades the badly outnumbered Paxton Boys to go home.

**1764**
**September 7**—*Pontiac's Rebellion.* John Bradstreet engineers a sweeping treaty at Detroit, compelling Indians to submit to royal authority.

**1766**
**July 24**—*Pontiac's Rebellion.* Pontiac pledges loyalty to the English.

**1769**
*Pontiac's Rebellion.* Pontiac is assassinated.

**1773**
**May 29**—*Lord Dunmore's War.* Shawnee chief Black Fish sends braves to observe Virginia governor Lord Dunmore's surveying party. When surveyors cross the Ohio river into Shawnee country, Peshewa (Wild Cat) warns them back. He is shot dead.
**About June 11**—*Lord Dunmore's War.* In retaliation for the murder of Peshewa, Shawnees kill some of the surveyors.

**1774**
**April 30**—*Lord Dunmore's War.* Mingos are driven to war when the family of a principal chief, John Logan, is slaughtered by Daniel Greathouse and other members of Captain Michael Cresap's surveying party. Logan and others kill 13 Virginians in retaliation.
**May 15**—*Lord Dunmore's War.* The Shawnees' principal chief, Cornstalk, journeys to Fort Pitt (recently renamed Fort Dunmore) to negotiate a peaceful resolution to the conflict. Frontiersmen attack Cornstalk, his brother Silverheels, and Non-hel-e-ma as they return from the fort. Silverheels is fatally wounded, and all hope of peace is shattered.
**June 10**—*Lord Dunmore's War.* Lord Dunmore declares war.
**September 8**—*Lord Dunmore's War.* Dunmore's 1,500-man militia mobilizes. The plan is to go to Fort Pitt, descend the Ohio to its juncture with the Kanawha River, and rendezvous with Andrew Lewis, who is supposed to have recruited an additional 1,500 militiamen. The combined force is then to cross the Ohio and destroy the Shawnee villages.
**October 10**—*Lord Dunmore's War.* Cornstalk attacks Lewis, but is pushed back. Cornstalk is appalled by the poor performance of his Mingo, Delaware, and Wyandot allies. Lewis, enraged at Dunmore for failing to make the planned rendezvous, wants to press the war into the Shawnee villages, Dunmore's own forces are near mutiny.
**October 26**—*Lord Dunmore's War.* Dunmore prevails against Lewis, and Cornstalk's dispirited warriors prevail against him. A truce is declared.

**1775–83**
*American Revolution*

**1775**
**June 12**—*American Revolution.* Mohawks, Senecas, Cayugas, and Onondagas side with the British. Joseph Brant is named war chief of the Iroquois. The Oneidas and Tuscaroras side with the Americans.
**September 5**—*American Revolution.* Brant and Captain Gilbert Tice attack Major General Philip Schuyler's forces advancing on Montreal. Schuyler retreats.
**October 24–25**—*American Revolution.* Colonel Ethan Allen leads another assault on Montreal. Brant captures Allen and his men.

**1776**
**July 4**—*American Revolution.* Cornstalk abandons neutrality and throws in with the British.
**August**—*American Revolution.* American General Andrew Williamson, guided by Catawba scouts, destroys Cherokee villages.
**September**—*American Revolution.* Williamson, joined by North Carolina militiamen, drives the Cherokees toward Florida. Additional Virginia and North Carolina militiamen join the attack, and the British-allied Cherokees sue for peace.
**September**—*American Revolution.* Raiding by British-allied Indians is at its peak in frontier Virginia, Pennsylvania, and New York.

**1777**
**May–July**—*American Revolution.* Cherokees cede vast holdings of land to the Americans.
**March 18**—*American Revolution.* The Shawnee chief Black Fish attacks Harrodsburg, Kentucky, but withdraws because of bad weather.
**March 28**—*American Revolution.* Black Fish returns to Harrodsburg, but again is defeated by inclement weather.
**April 24–28**—*American Revolution.* Black Fish lays siege to Boonesboro, Kentucky, but withdraws.
**May 23–25**—*American Revolution.* Black Fish attacks Boonesboro again and withdraws.
**May 30**—*American Revolution.* Black Fish attacks a milking party near Saint Asaph. Settlers hold out for two days until Black Fish finally withdraws.
**Summer**—*American Revolution.* Wyandots, Mingos, Cherokees, and Shawnees raid the Wheeling area. American General Edward Hand recruits troops for an attack on a British–Indian supply depot near present-day Cleveland, Ohio.
**August 4**—*American Revolution.* Barry St. Leger commences artillery bombardment on Fort Stanwix and makes use of Indian snipers.
**August 6**—*American Revolution.* Joseph Brant, Indians, and Tories ambush American General Nicholas Herkimer. The Battle of Oriskany is a disaster for all concerned.
**August 16**—*American Revolution.* Americans defeat Hessian troops at the Battle of Bennington. The Hessians' Indian auxiliaries flee.
**August 22**—*American Revolution.* American General Benedict Arnold tricks Barry St. Leger into thinking that he is outnumbered. Some 500 to 600 warriors desert St. Leger, who hastily lifts the siege of Fort Stanwix.
**November 10**—*American Revolution.* Cornstalk, under a flag of truce, warns the Americans that, if Hand attacks, all the Shawnee and allied nations will retaliate. Despite the flag of truce, Cornstalk is captured and, on this date, killed. Shawnees intensify war against the Americans.

**1778**
**February 8**—*American Revolution.* The Shawnee chief Blue Jacket captures Daniel Boone, who is adopted by Black Fish. He does not escape—or chooses not to leave—until May, when he warns of an impending raid on Boonesboro.

**May**—*American Revolution*. Black Fish lays siege to Fort Randolph. The fort holds out and Black Fish withdraws, but Shawnee, Wyandots, Mingos, Delawares, Miamis, and some Kickapoos raid throughout the West.

**June 28**—*American Revolution*. Butler's Tory Rangers and 800 to 900 Delawares and Senecas (including Gu-cinge) descend on the Wyoming Valley.

**Early July**—*American Revolution*. George Rogers Clark takes the British fort at Kaskaskia and Cahokia.

**July 3**—*American Revolution*. Butler's Tory Rangers and Indian allies kill 300 Americans in the Wyoming Valley Massacre.

**September 8**—*American Revolution*. Black Fish lays siege to Boonesboro, which holds out.

**September 12**—*American Revolution*. Brant destroys German Flats.

**September–October**—*American Revolution*. Brant raids the valleys of the Neversink and Mamakating.

**September 21**—*American Revolution*. Pennsylvania militia sets out to destroy Susquehanna River Indian towns.

**October 2**—*American Revolution*. Colonel William Butler, of New York (not to be confused with the Tory Butlers), destroys Brant's headquarters town of Oquaga and other Indian towns.

**November 11**—*American Revolution*. Brant and the Seneca chiefs Little Beard and Gucinges attack Cherry Valley.

### 1779

**February 23**—*American Revolution*. Clark occupies Vincennes; Fort Sackville, the British outpost there, surrenders.

**April 21**—*American Revolution*. American-allied Oneida Chief Hanyerry helps destroy Onodaga, capital of the Iroquois Confederation.

**July 10**—*American Revolution*. The Continental Army and militiamen destroy Chillicothe, the Shawnee "capital," and mortally wound Chief Black Fish.

**August–September**—*American Revolution*. Sullivan and Clinton destroy much of Iroquoia.

**September 13**—*American Revolution*. Chief Hanyerry is slain.

### 1780

**Spring–Summer**—*American Revolution*. American Colonel Daniel Brodhead destroys Mingo, Wyandot, and Seneca towns. Mohawks, Senecas, and Cayugas push the American-allied Oneidas back to Schenectady.

**October 15**—*American Revolution*. Johnson, Brant, and the Seneca chief Cornplanter descend upon the Scoharie Valley, burning everything they encounter over the next few days and destroying a militia force of 130 men.

**October 19**—*American Revolution*. Patriot militia, augmented by Oneidas, drives Johnson and Brant out of Scoharie.

**June**—*American Revolution.*—Delawares, Hurons, Wyandots, Ottawas, Mingos, Ojibwas, Tawas, Miamis, and Potawatomis join with British and Canadian forces to invade Kentucky.

**June 22**—*American Revolution*. Ruddell's Station, Kentucky, falls; a massacre follows.

**August 8**—*American Revolution*. George Rogers Clark defeats Shawnees, Mingos, Wyandots, and Delawares at Piqua Town.

**October 7**—*American Revolution*. Cherokees, Chickamaugas, and Creeks raid American southern settlements until this date, when forces under John Sevier and Andrew Pickens devastate Indian settlements.

### 1781

**April**—*American Revolution*. Brant attacks Cherry Valley. American fortunes are at low ebb in New York when Colonel Marinus Willett is assigned command of the region. He quells raiding for most of the summer of 1781.

**October**—*American Revolution*. Willett defeats Tories, British regulars, and Indians under the command of Walter Butler, who is killed at Canada Creek. His death permanently ends raiding in western New York.

### 1782

**March 8–9**—*American Revolution*. American Colonel David Williamson massacres peaceful Indians at Gnaddenhutten, Ohio.

**May 25**—*American Revolution*. As the Gnaddenhutten massacre triggers Delaware vengeance, American Colonel William Crawford undertakes the "Second Moravian Campaign," destroying Moravian Indian, Delaware, and Wyandot towns.

**June 4–5**—*American Revolution*. Near Sandusky, Shawnees and Delawares rout Crawford's force and torture the colonel to death.

**August 19**—*American Revolution*. Brant and Simon Girty lead an ambush against Lincoln and Fayette counties, Kentucky; 70 Americans are killed and 20 captured or wounded.

### 1783

**September 3**—*American Revolution*. The Treaty of Paris formally ends the war.

### 1786–94
*Little Turtle's War*

### 1786

**January**—*Little Turtle's War*. U.S. negotiators, including William Butler and George Rogers Clark, meet with 300 Shawnees led by Kekewepellethe (Tame Hawk). Butler declares the Ohio country to be U.S. territory; Kekewepellethe counters that the land is Shawnee. Butler and Clark threaten war, and Kekewepellethe agrees to relinquish the entire Miami Valley. Other Shawnee bands and the Miamis repudiate the agreement and, led by Blue Jacket (Shawnee) and Little Turtle (Miami), they intensify raiding in the region.

**Fall**—*Little Turtle's War*. Clark leads a large militia force against the Shawnees, Miamis, and Ottawas, but the troops rapidly disband. Other militiamen, under Colonel Benjamin Logan, attack Shawnee villages on the Miami River.

**October**—*Little Turtle's War*. At Mackachack, a friendly Indian village, Logan's force is greeted by the aged and infirm Moluntha, whom Logan wrongfully accuses of participating in a four-year-old massacre at Blue Licks. Moluntha is summarily murdered, and Mackachack and other villages are burned. These acts prompt the Shawnees and many other tribes to all-out war.

### 1787

**July 13**—Congress passes the Northwest Ordinance.

### 1790

**September 30**—*Little Turtle's War*. General Josiah Harmar leads 1,133 poorly trained militiamen and 320 regulars from Fort Washington (present-day Cincinnati) to the Miami and Maumee region.

**October 19**—*Little Turtle's War*. Harmar's advance guard is routed, and Harmar withdraws.

**October 21**—*Little Turtle's War*. Harmar's rear guard is ambushed.

### 1791

**October 4**—*Little Turtle's War*. Arthur St.

Clair, governor of the Northwest Territory, leads a "punitive expedition" against the Shawnees and allied tribes.

**November 3**—*Little Turtle's War*. St. Clair encamps on a vulnerable plateau above the upper Wabash.

**November 4**—*Little Turtle's War*. Little Turtle and Blue Jacket rout St. Clair's camp from three directions, killing 623 officers and men, along with 24 civilian teamsters; 271 soldiers are wounded.

### 1792

**April**—*Little Turtle's War*. President George Washington replaces St. Clair with "Mad Anthony" Wayne.

### 1793

**August 15**—*Little Turtle's War*. The Shawnees reject new U.S. peace terms.

### 1794

**June 30**—*Little Turtle's War*. Twelve hundred warriors under Blue Jacket and Tecumseh rout one of Wayne's pack trains. Blue Jacket and Tecumseh, victorious, try to call off their warriors, but Ottawa and other Indian allies advance on Wayne's Fort Recovery, where they are repelled.

**August**—*Little Turtle's War*. Wayne builds two more advance posts, Fort Adams and Fort Defiance, the latter in the midst of abandoned hostile villages.

**August 17–20**—*Little Turtle's War*. In preparation for battle, Blue Jacket's warriors fast. However, Wayne pauses on August 17 to build Fort Deposit, where he caches all that is unnecessary for combat. It is August 20 before he resumes his advance. Many of Blue Jacket's now-famished warriors are out looking for food; those who remain are weak from hunger. Blue Jacket suffers a rout, and the British offer no aid. The Battle of Fallen Timbers ends Little Turtle's War and brings stability to the Old Northwest for the next 15 years.

### 1795

**August**—*Little Turtle's War*. The Treaty of Greenville establishes a "permanent" boundary of white settlement.

### 1803–1806

President Thomas Jefferson directs Indiana Territorial governor William Henry Harrison to acquire vast tracts west of the Greenville Treaty boundary. As Indian lands dwindle, the Shawnee warrior Tecumseh emerges as a powerful political force bent on forging an Indian union from the Great Lakes to the Gulf of Mexico.

### 1807

Tecumseh and his brother Tenskawatawa (the Prophet) establish Prophet's Town. Shawnee, Potawatomi, Ottawa, Winnebago, Ojibwa, and Wyandot leaders and warriors assemble there.

### 1808–11

The Sac chief Black Hawk responds to fraudulent land cessions by inciting his followers to repeated attacks on Fort Madison, near Saint Louis.

### 1808

**May**—As England and America drift toward the War of 1812, a British–Indian alliance is forged, with Tecumseh as key leader.

**1811**

**November 6**—William Henry Harrison takes advantage of Tecumseh's absence (he is unsuccessfully recruiting allies in the South) to attack Tippecanoe (Prophet's Town).

**November 7**—At the Battle of Tippecanoe, Harrison defeats Tenskawatawa, who is discredited as a prophet. Some tribes desert Tecumseh's cause.

**1812–15**

*War of 1812*

**1812**

**June 19**—*War of 1812.* The United States declares war on Great Britain.

**August 5**—*War of 1812.* Tecumseh ambushes 150 Ohio militiamen sent to escort a supply train. Hull sends 600 more men to escort the pack train, and, again, the party is ambushed. U.S. General William Hull withdraws.

**August 15**—*War of 1812.* The garrison at Fort Dearborn (present-day Chicago) surrenders and is massacred by Potawatomis.

**August 16**—*War of 1812.* General Hull surrenders Fort Detroit.

**September 5**—*War of 1812.* Zachary Taylor repels a Potawatomi attack on Fort Wayne. During this month other war parties attack Fort Madison near Saint Louis, Fort Harrison on the Wabash River, and the town of Pigeon Roost in southern Indiana. Most of the Old Northwest falls under Indian control.

**September 25**—*War of 1812.* British commander Henry Procter is informed (incorrectly) that 2,000 men under Harrison are on an intercept course with his forces. Tecumseh and Roundhead advise an ambush. Procter wants to wait. With the English and the Indians in disagreement, Procter withdraws, leaving Tecumseh and Roundhead with no choice but to withdraw as well. A chance to deal a crushing blow to Harrison's forces is lost.

**1813**

**January 21**—*War of 1812.* As Harrison prepares to move against Fort Malden by advancing across frozen Lake Erie, one of his subordinates, General James Winchester, starts off prematurely. At the Raisin River, just south of Detroit, 500 British regulars and 600 Indians attack. Only 33 of 960 Americans engaged escape.

**April 30–May 7**—*War of 1812.* Procter lays siege against Fort Meigs at the Maumee Rapids of the Ohio River, which Harrison successfully defends.

**July 21–23**—*War of 1812.* Fielding a combined army of 3,000, Procter attacks Harrison's principal supply depot, Fort Stephenson, but is held off spectacularly by Major George Croghan and only 150 men. The British–Indian alliance sours.

**August**—*War of 1812.* Harrison has rebuilt and enlarged the army, now fielding some 8,000 men.

**August 30**—*War of 1812/Creek Civil War.* During the War of 1812, the Creeks fight their own civil war, principally between a pro-American faction (the White Sticks) and a pro-British faction (the Red Sticks). William Weatherford (Red Eagle), a half-breed Red Stick, attacks Fort Mims, on the lower Alabama River, killing more than 400 settlers.

**September 10**—*War of 1812.* Oliver Hazard Perry destroys the British fleet on Lake Erie. The British abandon Fort Malden.

**October 5**—*War of 1812.* Harrison defeats Tecumseh and Procter at the Battle of the Thames. Tecumseh dies.

**November**—*War of 1812/Creek Civil War.* Andrew Jackson leads 5,000 Tennessee militiamen, 19 companies of Cherokee warriors, and 200 White Sticks in an offensive against the Red Sticks.

**1814**

**January**—*War of 1812/Creek Civil War.* Jackson destroys many Red Stick towns.

**March 27**—*War of 1812/Creek Civil War.* After the day-long Battle of Horseshoe Bend, some 750 of the 900 Red Stick warriors engaged lie dead. The Creek Civil War ends.

**December 24**—*War of 1812.* The Treaty of Ghent ends the War of 1812.

**1816**

**July 27**—*First Seminole War.* American forces attack "Negro Fort," held by Seminoles and fugitive slaves on Florida's Apalachicola River. The incident triggers Seminole raids.

**1817**

**November 20**—*First Seminole War.* An attack on Fowl Town, home of the Seminole chief Neamathla, officially begins the war.

**1818**

**April 12**—*First Seminole War.* Jackson and his allies attack the camp of Red Stick leader Peter McQuee, killing many.

**May 26**—*First Seminole War.* Jackson takes Spanish Pensacola, prompting Spain to cede Florida to the United States. The resulting influx of settlers overwhelms the Seminoles, who break off hostilities.

**1821–25**

William MacIntosh, a White Stick Creek claiming to represent Seminoles and Creeks, cedes 25 million acres. A majority of Creeks repudiate the cession.

**1829**

*Black Hawk War.* Black Hawk, chief of the Sac and Fox, returns from a hunting trip and finds that his lodge has been invaded by white settlers. He asks them to move. They ignore him, and the General Land Office announces that his land will be offered up for public sale.

**1830**

**May 28**—*Indian Removal.* President Andrew Jackson signs the Indian Removal Act.

**1831**

*Indian Removal.* The Choctaws remove to the West.

*Indian Removal.* Many Kickapoo warriors under Chief Kennekuk join forces with the Sac and Fox under Black Hawk.

**1832**

**April**—*Black Hawk War.* Black Hawk crosses the Mississippi with 2,000 men, women, and children, the "British Band" of the Sac and Fox. The Sac chief Keokuk opposes Black Hawk and alerts white authorities to his approach.

*Indian Removal.* Seminoles sign a provisional removal treaty, but, discovering fraud, rescind it.

**May 14**—*Black Hawk War.* Regular army and militia forces fruitlessly pursue Black Hawk. Major Isaac Stillman's force of 275 militiamen is camped just north of the mouth of the Kyte River. Stillman's men break out their whiskey ration. Black Hawk, encamped with about 40 warriors in advance of his British Band, decides that further resistance is futile. He sends three warriors under a white flag to Stillman's camp, and an additional five to

follow as observers. The three representatives enter the camp and announce that Black Hawk wants a parley. One of the militiamen sights the five Indians out on the prairie. Alarm spreads throughout the whiskey-charged battalion and, with neither orders nor order, men charge after the five Indians, killing two. Black Hawk musters his 40 warriors and routs the 275 well-armed militiamen in a "battle" instantly dubbed "Stillman's Run." In its wake, panic grips the frontier, and an emboldened Black Hawk renews his raids.

**Mid June**—*Black Hawk War.* White-allied Indians report that Black Hawk is lodged above Lake Koshonong. General Henry Atkinson now commands 3,400 men.

**June 15**—*Black Hawk War.* Overcautious, Atkinson fails to move, and President Andrew Jackson calls in Major General Winfield Scott. Around this time, Black Hawk attacks a fort on the Apple River near Galena, Illinois.

**June 28**—*Black Hawk War.* Atkinson moves out of Dixon's Ferry in pursuit of Black Hawk.

**July 22**—*Black Hawk War.* Neapope, Black Hawk's right-hand man, appears at militia Colonel Henry Dodge's camp with a surrender offer. Interpreters are absent, and Dodge fails to comprehend the proposal. Pursuit continues.

**August 1**—*Black Hawk War.* At the junction of the Bad Axe and Mississippi rivers, Black Hawk advises moving north to refuge among the Winnebagos. Instead, most of his people desperately try to cross the Mississippi. The majority are still on the east bank as the steamboat *Warrior* opens fire, killing 23 of the British Band. Black Hawk and a few of his followers flee northward.

**August 3**—*Black Hawk War.* Atkinson and Dodge's 1,300-man command arrives at the Bad Axe. Land forces and the *Warrior* kill many. About 200 Sacs and Foxes do reach the west band, but most are killed by white-allied Sioux.

**Late August**—*Black Hawk War.* The Winnebagos betray Black Hawk to white authorities. He is imprisoned for a year, then exhibited on a national tour.

**September 19**—*Indian Removal/Black Hawk War.* The Sacs and Foxes cede 6 million acres and agree to removal to Indian Territory by June 1, 1833.

**1832–34**

*Indian Removal.* The Chicakasaws accept removal.

**1832**

*Indian Removal.* The Cherokees protest persecution at the hands of Georgia by arguing their case before the Supreme Court, which finds in their favor. President Jackson refuses to enforce the court's decision.

**1835–42**

*The Second Seminole War*

**1835**

**Winter**—*Second Seminole War.* Osceola emerges as the central leader of the Seminole resistance.

**Late November**—*Second Seminole War.* Osceola and others kill Charley Emathla, a Seminole chief who has agreed to removal. The Second Seminole War commences.

**December**—*Second Seminole War.* The Seminoles name Osceola war chief and Jumper and Alligator as his seconds in command. With Philip (called King Philip), leader of the Seminoles east of Saint John's River, they coordinate an assault on white plantations.

**December 18**—*Second Seminole War.* The Battle of Black Point is fought west of the town of Micanopy.

**December 28**—*Second Seminole War.* Osceola kills Indian agent General Wiley Thompson. Elsewhere, Seminoles ambush a relief column under Major Francis Dade on its way to Fort King, killing 107 of 110 men.

**December 29**—*Indian Removal.* Jackson concludes a removal treaty with a tribal minority, deeming it binding on *all* Cherokees.

### 1836

*Indian Removal.* Most of the Creeks accept removal.

**January 1**—*Second Seminole War.* Osceola and Alligator ambush General Duncan L. Clinch's camp. Outnumbered three to one, Osceola forces Clinch to abort his offensive campaign.

### 1837

**October 21**—*Second Seminole War.* General Thomas Jesup violates a truce and takes Osceola prisoner.

### 1838

**January 30**—*Second Seminole War.* Osceola falls ill and dies in prison at Fort Moultrie, South Carolina.

### 1838–42

*Second Seminole War/Indian Removal.* Following Osceola's death, Alligator and Billy Bowlegs continue to lead the Seminole resistance. However, the number of Seminoles who accept removal steadily increases.

### 1838

*Indian Removal.* When only 2,000 Cherokees begin their journey west by the treaty deadline, a brutal roundup begins.

### 1838–39

*Indian Removal.* During the fall and winter, the Cherokees are marched off to Indian Territory along the "Trail of Tears."

### 1847

**November 29**—Cayuse Indians kill Oregon missionary Marcus Whitman and others.

### 1848

**February**—To avenge the Whitman massacre, Colonel Cornelius Gilliam leads 550 Oregon militiamen on an indiscriminate punitive expedition.

**March**—Palouse warriors attack Gilliam. Ten militiamen are wounded, and Gilliam dies of a self-inflicted wound.

**August 14**—The Federal government responds to the crisis in Oregon by creating the Oregon Territory.

### 1848–49

Militia groups wage a war of extermination against the "Digger Indians" of northern California.

### 1850–51

The *Mariposa War* breaks out when Miwoks and Yokuts rise against the miners who have invaded northern California.

### 1851

**November**—*Yuma and Mojave Uprising.* Antonio Garra, leader of a Yuma tribe called the Cupanga-kitoms, notifies San Diego County, California, authorities that his people will not pay taxes assessed them. With Garra, other Yuma leaders plan a general revolt.

**November 12–December 6**—*Yuma and Mo-*

*jave Uprising.* Lieutenant Thomas Sweeny sets up Camp Independence with about 100 men. The camp is besieged until December 6, when Sweeny withdraws.

**November 23**—*Yuma and Mojave Uprising.* Raiding is general in California, the most serious incident occurring on this day when Indians attack Warner's Ranch.

**December 25**—*Yuma and Mojave Uprising.* Major H. P. Heintzelman defeats a rebel Indian band at Coyote Canyon. Treaties are summarily concluded with this band.

### 1852

**March–April**—*Yuma and Mojave Uprising.* Operating out of Fort Yuma, on the California side of the Colorado, Heintzelman raids rebel villages.

**April 12**—*Yuma and Mojave Uprising.* Operating now in Baja, California, Sweeny burns two Cocopas villages, leading to the surrender of some 150 warriors, who agree to help fight the Yumas.

**August**—*Yuma and Mojave Uprising.* The Yumas ask for peace talks. Heintzelman approaches, however, with fixed bayonets. The Indians retreat, but request another parley.

**August 27**—*Yuma and Mojave Uprising.* The second parley results in a 10-day truce, which stretches into several weeks, as the Yumas evade negotiations.

**September 29**—*Yuma and Mojave Uprising.* Heintzelman surprises a band of Yumas near Blythe, California, who flee without offering battle.

**October 2**—*Yuma and Mojave Uprising.* The Yumas agree to permanent peace terms.

### 1853

**Summer**—Conflict with the Utes and the Jicarilla Apaches breaks out when ration distribution is stopped. Brigadier General John Garland, commanding the army's Department of New Mexico, authorizes military action.

### 1854

**March 5**—Lieutenant Colonel Philip St. George Cooke, commandant of Fort Union, defeats Jicarillas led by Lobo Blanco (White Wolf).

**March 26**—Jicarillas under Chacón kill 22 troopers in the Battle of Cieneguilla. Before the end of the month, with Kit Carson as a guide, Cooke pursues Chacón.

**April 8**—Indians ambush Cooke's column in the brief Battle of Rio Caliente.

**June 4**—Cooke's expedition surprises a Jicarilla camp of 22 lodges at the base of Fisher's Peak in the Raton Range.

**August 18**—High Forehead, a Brulé Sioux, shoots an arrow into the flank of an ox belonging to a Mormon wagon train. The owner of the ox puts in a complaint at Fort Laramie.

**August 19**—Lieutenant John L. Grattan is dispatched to arrest High Forehead. When he refuses to give himself up, Grattan opens fire on the Indian village, fatally wounding Chief Brave Bear. Brulé warriors, joined by Oglala Sioux, destroy Grattan's small band. General William S. Harney is sent to "punish" the Brulés.

**September 3**—Chief Little Thunder, successor to Brave Bear, gathers his band of 250, intending to surrender to Harney, who opens fire on the band, killing many.

**Fall**—Chacón surrenders.

**December 25**—Utes and Jicarillas descend on Pueblo, Colorado, killing 15 settlers. They raid and loot over the next several weeks.

### 1855

**January–February**—General John Garland sends

troops in a fruitless search of Utes for some two months.

**January 17–18**—Troops under Captain Richard S. Ewell and Captain Henry W. Stanton are attacked by Mescaleros. Stanton and a dragoon are killed.

**January 19**—Lieutenant Samuel D. Sturgis's troopers corner the Mescalero raiders, who offer to surrender. Claiming that he cannot understand them, Sturgis opens fire.

**April 25**—Volunteers attack 60 Jicarillas on the banks of the Purgatorie River, killing 6.

**April 28**—Volunteers and regulars kill 40 Indians in the Battle of Poncha Pass.

*Yakima War.* Isaac Stevens, governor of Washington Territory, concludes treaties binding Indians to relinquish their lands in exchange for a reservation. A stubborn minority, including the Yakima chief Kamiakin, refuses to sign. Twelve days after the last treaty is signed, Stevens opens the country to white settlement.

**August**—*Rogue River War.* Takelmas and Tututnis ("Rogue" Indians), who live near the Oregon-California border, kill 10 or 11 miners along the Klamath River. In retaliation, local whites kill some 25 Indians, touching off the Rogue River War.

*Yakima War.* A group of 5 braves led by Kamiakin's nephew, Qualchin, kills 6 prospectors. The local Indian agent, sent to investigate, is also killed. Pushed to premature action, Kamiakin threatens death to all whites who venture east of the Cascades.

**October 16**—*Rogue River War.* Captain Andrew Jackson Smith opens Fort Lane to Indian men, women, and children menaced by white mobs. Before he is able to admit all of the endangered Indians, settlers kill 23 "Rogue" Indians, including old men, women, and children.

**October 17**—*Rogue River War.* Indian war parties take revenge, killing 27 settlers in the Rogue Valley.

**December**—*Yakima War.* Colonel James Kelley leads a unit of militiamen into the Walla Walla homelands and agrees to a peace parley with Chief Peo-Peo-Mox-Mox. The chief secretly orders an attack and is killed as Kelley's command endures a 4-day siege.

### 1855–58

*Third Seminole War.* After a party of surveyors working in the Great Cypress Swamp vandalizes crops belonging to followers of the Seminole leader Billy Bowlegs, the Indians demand compensation or apology. Obtaining neither, they commence three years of sporadic raiding.

### 1856

**February 23**—*Yakima War.* Since the death of Peo-Peo-Mox-Mox, raids have been general. On this date alone, raids destroy more than 60 homes and leave 31 settlers dead.

**May 27–28**—*Rogue River War.* Takelma and Tututni chiefs agree to surrender at Big Meadows. Instead of surrendering, however, they muster some 200 warriors for an attack on Captain Andrew Jackson Smith's 50 dragoons and 30 infantrymen. Reinforcements arrive on the second day of battle, and the Rogues are routed.

**July**—*Yakima War.* A volunteer force defeats Walla Wallas and Cayuses in the Grande Ronde Valley. They sue for peace.

**August**—Cheyennes in search of hostile Pawnees stop a mail coach begging for tobacco. The driver panics and draws his revolver, takes an arrow in the arm before he can shoot, and makes for Fort Kearny. Captain Wharton dispatches Captain George H. Stewart to find the Cheyennes. The troopers attack, killing 10 and wounding another 10. Retaliatory raids commence.

**November**—The Navajo Indian agent disappears and is presumed dead. The Mogollons are blamed, and a punitive expedition is authorized. Unable to locate Mogollons, General Benjamin Bonneville attacks whatever Apache bands he encounters, including friendly Mimbres.

### 1857

**June 27**—In search of Mugollons, Dixon S. Miles attacks Coyotero Apaches.

**July 29**—Edwin V. Sumner's scouts report a band of 300 Cheyennes along the Solomon River. The warriors have washed their hands in a magic lake whose waters are supposed to protect them from bullets. When Sumner attacks with drawn sabers, the Indians run. Sumner gives chase for 7 miles.

### 1858

**May 15–16**—*Coeur d'Alene War*. About 1,000 warriors intercept a column of 158 men under Lieutenant Colonel Edward J. Steptoe near Spokane.

**May 17–18**—*Coeur d'Alene War*. The Indians attack, killing two officers. Steptoe's command escapes by night.

**July 7**—After an argument over grazing rights, Chief Manuelito leads Navajos in an attack on Fort Defiance.

**July 12**—A Navajo warrior murders the black servant of Major Thomas H. Brooks, commandant of Fort Defiance. Brooks demands that the Indians produce the murderer or suffer retribution.

**September 1**—*Coeur d'Alene War*. A punitive campaign commences against the Coeur d'Alenes, Kamiakin's Yakimas, and allied tribes. Colonel George Wright, with Nez Percé auxiliaries, defeats Kamiakin at the Battle of Spokane Plain. Kamiakin, injured, escapes.

**September 5**—*Coeur d'Alene War*. The Indians are again defeated at the Battle of Four Lakes.

**September 8**—Navajos fail to produce the servant's murderer. A nameless war commences with a punitive expedition to Canyon de Chelly, Arizona. The Navajos conduct retaliatory raids.

**October**—Fruitless expeditions are authorized against the Navajos. Little is accomplished.

### 1859

**March 8**—*Coeur d'Alene War*. U.S. Senate ratifies a treaty ending the war.

### 1860

Navajo raiding escalates.

**April 30**—A thousand Indian warriors attack Fort Defiance.

**May 4**—Fort Defiance is evacuated and abandoned. Brigadier General Edward R. S. Canby leads an offensive against the Navajos, resulting in the so-called Canby Treaty.

### 1860

**May**—*Paiute War (Pyramid Lake War)*. Traders at Williams Station, an overland mail stop along the California Trail, abduct and rape two Indian girls. Southern Paiutes rescue them, burn the station, and kill 5 whites.

**May 8**—*Paiute War (Pyramid Lake War)*. Responding to the Williams Station "massacre," a large and rowdy "army" of miners immediately assembles, then dissolves. A new force of 105 men makes its way to Pyramid Lake in Paiute country.

**May 12**—*Paiute War (Pyramid Lake War)*. Paiutes ambush the force, killing half its number.

**Late May**—*Paiute War (Pyramid Lake War)*. Militiamen and regulars defeat the Paiutes near the site of the ambush. The brief Paiute War ends.

**November**—*Apache Uprising*. John Ward, a rancher near Fort Buchanan, Arizona, is raided by a Pinal Apache band, which takes his stepson and rustles cattle. Ward tells the commander of Fort Buchanan that *Chiricahua* Apaches, led by Cochise, were responsible.

### 1861–65

*The Civil War.*

### 1861

**February 4**—*Apache Uprising*. Second Lieutenant George N. Bascom with 60 men is sent to recover Ward's stepson and the stolen stock. Bascom accuses Cochise. Cochise protests his innocence, escapes, and raids the Butterfield station, killing one employee and taking another prisoner. Cochise captures a small wagon train, killing 8 Mexicans and offering 3 Americans in exchange for the captives Bascom holds. He is refused.

**February 14**—*Apache Uprising*. Discovering the bodies of the 3 Americans, Bascom hangs his own prisoners. Cochise vows a war of extermination, and 25 years of warfare begins.

**July**—*Civil War*. As Confederate Lieutenant Colonel John R. Baylor prepares to take possession of Arizona Territory for the Confederacy, Chiricahua and Mimbreño Apaches, convinced that the Union soldiers have permanently withdrawn from the region, intensify their raids. Baylor authorizes a company of Arizona Rangers (July 18) to punish the Indians.

**August 1**—*Civil War*. Baylor takes possession of Arizona Territory for the Confederacy, proclaiming himself governor and ordering the Arizona Guards to exterminate "all hostile Indians."

**August–September**—*Civil War*. As the Canby Treaty has promised, a New Mexico volunteer regiment begins distributing rations to the Navajos at Fort Fauntleroy (Fort Lyon). Chief Manuelito runs a horserace against an army lieutenant. A fight breaks out, the soldiers close the gates of the fort, and attack the Indians, men, women, and children, killing 30 to 40, thereby touching off a series of Indian raids. Canby sends Kit Carson and volunteers to deal with the raids.

### 1862

**February 21**—*Civil War*. Confederate Henry Hopkins Sibley defeats the Union's Canby at Valverde, New Mexico. Sibley next takes Santa Fe and presses on to Fort Union.

**March 26–28**—*Civil War*. Union forces defeat Sibley at La Glorietta Pass.

**April 15**—*Civil War*. Colonel James Henry Carleton pushes the Confederates out of Arizona.

**June**—*Minnesota Santee Sioux Uprising*. A large group of Santee Sioux call on the Yellow Medicine Agency to receive the money and rations to which a treaty entitles them. The distribution is delayed.

**June 14**—*Minnesota Santee Sioux Uprising*. The Santee are again refused rations and money.

**July 15**—*Apache Uprising*. The van of Carleton's "California Column" is ambushed at Apache Pass by 700 warriors under Cochise.

**August 4**—*Minnesota Santee Sioux Uprising*. Mounted warriors break into the Yellow Medicine Agency warehouse but are repelled by a garrison detachment under Lieutenant Tim-

othy J. Sheehan, who persuades the local Indian agent to release some provisions.

**August 5–6**—*Minnesota Santee Sioux Uprising*. At a council with the Santees, prominent trader Andrew J. Myrick declares that if the Sioux are hungry, "let them eat grass."

**August 11**—*Minnesota Santee Sioux Uprising*. Indian agent Thomas J. Galbraith reneges on his pledge to distribute the Sioux's food.

**August 17**—*Minnesota Santee Sioux Uprising*. Four young Santee Mdewakanton men kill 7 whites, propelling the Santee chief Little Crow into full-scale war.

**August 18**—*Minnesota Santee Sioux Uprising*. Little Crow and a band of warriors attack Myrick in his store, kill him, and in a symbolic gesture, stuff his mouth with grass. Elsewhere, raiding is general.

**August 20**—*Minnesota Santee Sioux Uprising*. A war party of about 100 attacks New Ulm. Militiamen hold the warriors off until a sudden and severe thunderstorm prompts the Indians to break off the attack.

**August 21**—*Minnesota Santee Sioux Uprising*. Little Crow, with 400 warriors, attacks Fort Ridgely. The outnumbered defenders are saved by artillery.

**August 22**—*Minnesota Santee Sioux Uprising*. Little Crow again unsuccessfully attacks Fort Ridgely.

**August 23**—*Minnesota Santee Sioux Uprising*. Little Crow largely destroys New Ulm, but is driven off.

**August 27**—*Minnesota Santee Sioux Uprising*. The uprising is now general throughout Minnesota.

**September 2**—*Minnesota Santee Sioux Uprising*. Warriors under Big Eagle, Mankato, and Gray Bird attack the camp of Captain Hiram P. Grant, killing 22 troopers and wounding 60. A relief column under Colonel Samuel McPhail arrives, but is soon surrounded.

**September 3**—*Minnesota Santee Sioux Uprising*. The main body of Henry hastings Sibley's force relieves Grant and McPhail. The Indians withdraw from the Battle of Birch Coulee.

**September 23**—*Minnesota Santee Sioux Uprising*. Some 700 warriors prepare to ambush Sibley's column near Wood Lake, but reveal themselves prematurely. The Battle of Wood Lake scatters the Indians.

**September 26**—*Minnesota Santee Sioux Uprising*. Little Crow's army dissolves, and, on this date, Sibley accepts the surrender of some 2,000 hostiles.

**November 3**—*Minnesota Santee Sioux Uprising*. A military tribunal sentences 303 Santees to hang.

**December 6**—*Minnesota Santee Sioux Uprising*. President Abraham Lincoln overturns most of the execution orders, and 38 Indians hang.

### 1863

**January**—*Shoshoni War (Bear River Campaign)*. Colonel Patrick Connor leads 300 men in pursuit of the Shoshoni under Chief Bear Hunter.

**January 17–18**—*Apache Uprising*. Mangas Coloradas meets with Captain E. D. Shirland (serving with Brigadier General Joseph R. West) under a flag of truce. The chief is seized, delivered to West's camp, and assassinated.

**January 27**—*Shoshoni War (Bear River Campaign)*. Connor reaches Bear Hunter's village and engages 300 warriors, who repel a frontal attack led by a subordinate. Connor takes personal command of a flanking attack, killing Bear Hunter and 224 Shoshonis.

**Summer–Fall**—Connor and Superintendent of

Indian Affairs James D. Doty conclude a number of treaties with the Indians of Utah, but, in Nevada, Major Charles McDermit still patrols the troubled Paiute country. Farther north, in Washington and Oregon, the Nez Percés sign a treaty (June) and withdraw to their reservation, but the Western Shoshoni continue to harass emigrants. The Northern Paiutes—better known as the Snakes—conduct continual, small-scale raids and are pursued to little avail.

**June**—*Minnesota Santee Sioux Uprising.* Little Crow disappears with his son into Canada, where he is killed.

**July 24**—When the surgeon of the Minnesota Rangers is shot during a parley with Sisseton Sioux, Sibley opens fire with his artillery and routs the Indians.

**July 26**—Sibley presses the pursuit, burning villages.

**July 28**—Sioux warriors mass for a head-on attack at Stony Lake. Sibley parries the assault and resumes his pursuit.

**July 29**—Sibley, having killed some 150 Indian warriors, breaks off his pursuit.

**July 20**—*Navajo War.* The deadline set for Apache and Navajo removal to the Bosque Redondo reservation is passed. Kit Carson sets out to make war on the Navajo.

**September**—*Navajo War.* The first of the Navajos retire to the Bosque Redondo.

**September 3**—Sisseton chief Inkpaduta attacks Major Albert E. House, who summons reinforcements. The Battle of Whitestone Hill results in the deaths of 22 soldiers and 300 warriors.

**December 31**—*Navajo War.* Carleton orders a winter campaign against recalcitrant Navajos.

## 1864

**January 15**—*Navajo War.* Kit Carson declares the Canyon de Chelly Expedition ended.

**July 28**—Sully defeats Sissetons at the Battle of Killdeer Mountain.

**November 4**—*Cheyenne–Arapaho War.* Colonel John M. Chivington and Colorado Governor John Evans allow Chief Black Kettle and his peace-faction Cheyennes to camp near Fort Lyon for the purpose of negotiating a treaty.

**November 28**—*Cheyenne–Arapaho War.* By night, Chivington deploys his Third Colorado Cavalry around Sand Creek, including 700 men and 4 howitzers. The next day, his troops kill 200 Cheyennes.

## 1864–68

*Navajo War.* During this period, some 8,000 Navajos crowd into the reservation at the Bosque Redondo.

## 1865

**January 7**—*Cheyenne–Arapaho War.* One thousand Sioux and Cheyenne warriors mass south of Julesburg, Colorado. An attack on Fort Rankin fails, and the Indians loot Julesburg.

**February 2**—*Cheyenne–Arapaho War.* The army pursues raiding parties along the Republican River, but the Indians return to Julesburg and finish it off.

**February 4–6, 8**—*Cheyenne–Arapaho War.* Indians skirmish with army units near Forts Mitchell and Laramie.

**July 26**—*Cheyenne–Arapaho War.* Warriors mass to attack a cavalry unit guarding the Oregon-California Trail North Platte River crossing. Sixty Indians are killed and 130 wounded, but the attacks destroy an army supply train.

**August–September**—*Cheyenne–Arapaho War.* Connor dispatches a force of 3,000 into the Powder River country, destroying one Arapaho Village and engaging the Sioux.

## 1866

**June 17**—*War for the Bozeman Trail.* Colonel Henry B. Carrington builds 3 forts along the Bozeman Trail.

**December 6**—*War for the Bozeman Trail.* Indians attack a wagon train hauling wood to Fort Phil Kearny. Carrington's inexperienced soldiers panic and withdraw.

**December 21**—*War for the Bozeman Trail.* Crazy Horse masses 1,500 to 2,000 warriors in ambush. Carrington dispatches Captain William Fetterman to relieve another besieged wood train. Carrington orders defensive action only, but Fetterman takes the offensive. His command is wiped out.

## 1866–68

*Snake War.* Brevet Major General George Crook engages the Northern Paiutes—the so-called Snakes—of southeastern Oregon and southwestern Idaho at least 40 times in two years. By mid-1868, they make peace.

## 1867

**April 7**—*Hancock's Campaign.* General Winfield Scott Hancock summons Cheyenne chiefs to a conference. Bad weather results in a small turnout.

**April 8**—*Hancock's Campaign.* Disappointed, Hancock marches to a combined Cheyenne and Sioux village in order to deliver his stern message to more chiefs. The Indians flee. "This looks like the commencement of war," Hancock dryly observes.

**April–July**—*Hancock's Campaign.* Custer leads his 7th Cavalry in fruitless pursuit of fleeing Cheyenne and Sioux, who terrorize Kansas.

**August 1**—*War for the Bozeman Trail.* Indians attack hay cutters near Fort C. F. Smith. The "Hayfield Fight" ends in the Indians' withdrawal.

**August 2**—*War for the Bozeman Trail.* Sioux strike woodcutters near Fort Phil Kearny in the "Wagon Box Fight," but are forced to withdraw.

## 1868

**February**—*Sheridan's Campaign.* Failing to receive promised rations, Kiowas and Comanches raid Texas. At about the same time, Cheyennes raid settlements on the Saline and Solomon rivers.

**April 2**—*War for the Bozeman Trail/Hancock's Campaign.* The Treaty of Fort Laramie concedes to Red Cloud most of what he had fought for; however, the Dog Soldiers continue to raid.

**June 1**—*Navajo War.* A treaty restores the Navajos to their traditional homelands.

**September 17–24**—*Sheridan's Campaign.* George A. Forsyth, with 50 handpicked plainsmen, patrols western Kansas. On this date, the small company is attacked by 600 to 700 Dog Soldiers and Oglala Sioux. Forsyth is besieged for 8 days on an island in the Arikara Fork of the Republican River. The important Cheyenne chief Roman Nose is killed.

**Winter**—*Sheridan's Campaign.* Sheridan proposes a three-pronged winter campaign: one column will approach from Fort Bascom, New Mexico, another from Fort Lyon, Colorado, and the third from Fort Dodge, Kansas. They are to converge on the Indians' winter camps on the Canadian and Washita rivers, in Indian Territory.

**November 27**—*Sheridan's Campaign.* Custer attacks a peaceful Cheyenne camp on the Washita River. Among the 103 Indians killed in the attack, 93 are women, old men, and children—as well as Chief Black Kettle and his wife.

**December 25**—*Sheridan's Campaign.* Major Andrew Evans defeats Comanche and Kiowa warriors in the Battle of Soldier Spring. Most Indians involved surrender to Forts Cobb and Bascom.

## 1869

Ulysses Simpson Grant becomes president. To the dismay of the army, he advocates a Peace Policy toward the Indians.

**March 17**—*Sheridan's Campaign.* At Sweetwater Creek in the Texas Panhandle, Custer parleys with Dog Soldiers who hold two white women hostage. He seizes 3 chiefs and sends one back with surrender terms, demanding that the hostages be released or he will hang the others. The Cheyennes comply.

**July 11**—*Sheridan's Campaign.* Under Tall Bull, Dog Soldiers join forces with the Northern Cheyennes in the Powder River country. On this date, the 5th Cavalry, defeats the Dog Soldiers at Summit Springs, Colorado. Tall Bull is killed, and the Dog Soldiers retire to a reservation.

## 1871

**April 30**—*Apache Wars.* Local settlers, believing that the Army's Camp Grant (Arizona) serves as a sanctuary for Apaches between raids, kill 36 to 150 Apaches there, mostly women and children.

**May 18**—Satanta, Satank, Big Tree, Eagle Heart, Big Bow, and about 100 Kiowa braves ambush a wagon train on Salt Creek Prairie, Texas.

**May 27**—Satanta, Satank, and Big Tree are arrested. Satank is subsequently killed in an escape attempt. Satanta and Big Tree are tried, convicted, and sentenced to hang. The sentences are commuted to prison terms.

## 1872

**November 15**—*Apache Wars.* General Crook sweeps Arizona, aiming to concentrate hostile Apaches in the Tonto Basin.

**November 29**—*Modoc War.* The Modocs, a small northern California tribe, resist removal to Indian Territory. On this date, a small force of soldiers enters the camps of the Modoc leader Captain Jack and proceeds to disarm the Indians. A scuffle results in an exchange of fire that the army calls the Battle of Lost Rivers. At about the same time, a group of ranchers attacks a smaller group of Modocs, followers of Hooker Jim. Two whites are killed. Then, as Hooker Jim and his people rush to join forces with Captain Jack, they kill 14 more settlers. Now, mustering 60 warriors, Captain Jack and Hooker Jim hide in the Lava Beds south of Tule Lake.

**December 28**—*Apache Wars.* Seventy-six Yavapais Apaches die at the Battle of Skull Cave in Salt River Canyon.

## 1873

**January 16–17**—*Modoc War.* Lieutenant Colonel Frank Wheaton fails to dislodge the Modocs.

**March 27**—*Apache Wars.* The Battle of Turret Peak results in 23 Apache deaths. Many report to reservations.

**April 11**—*Modoc War.* Captain Jack kills General Edward R.S. Canby at a council.

**April 15–17**—*Modoc War.* Colonel Alvin C. Gillem pounds Modoc positions with howitzers and mortars for three days. Most of the warriors elude the massive attack.

**April 26**—*Modoc War.* Warriors under Scarfaced Charley attack one party of pursuers, killing 5 officers, 20 men, and wounding another 16—over half the contingent.

**May 28**—*Modoc War.* Assisted by Hooker Jim, who has been captured earlier, a cavalry detachment finds Captain Jack, his family, and a number of followers. Captain Jack refuses to give up.

**June 3**—*Modoc War.* Captain Jack surrenders. Along with Boston Charley, Black Jim, and Schonchin John, he is tried and hanged.

**1874**

**June 27**—*Red River War.* Comanches and Cheyennes attack white hunters at Adobe Walls in the Texas Panhandle.

**July**—*Sioux War for the Black Hills.* Custer's 7th Cavalry, on an expedition in the Black Hills, discovers gold. Thousands swarm over this sacred Sioux territory.

**July 12**—*Red River War.* The Kiowa chief Lone Wolf ambushes Texas Rangers at Lost Valley.

**July 20**—*Red River War.* Sherman telegraphs Sheridan to commence a major offensive.

**August 30**—*Red River War.* Nelson A. Miles wages a 5-hour battle over 12 miles before Cheyennes make a final stand along the slopes of Tule Canyon. Miles wins the day.

**September 9–12**—*Red River War.* Some 250 Kiowas and Comanches, including Lone Wolf, Satanta, and Big Tree, attack an army supply train, keeping it under siege for 3 days until Major William R. Price drives them off.

**September 26**—*Red River War.* Comanches attack the Tule Valley camp of the 4th Cavalry under Colonel Ranald Mackenzie.

**September 27**—*Red River War.* Mackenzie drives off the Comanches, then routs a Kiowa-Comanche-Cheyenne village at Palo Duro Canyon.

**October 7**—*Red River War.* Satanta and other Kiowa war chiefs surrender.

**1875**

*Sioux War for the Black Hills.* Federal authorities attempt to negotiate the sale or lease of the Black Hills, but the Sioux refuse.

**June 2**—*Red River War.* Quanah Parker, feared Comanche war chief, surrenders.

**1876**

*Apache Wars.* Apaches are ordered to San Carlos Reservation in Arizona. Warfare is renewed.

**January 31**—*Sioux War for the Black Hills.* Authorities set this date as the deadline by which the Sioux must report to the reservation.

**June 17**—*Sioux War for the Black Hills.* Sioux and Cheyennes, led by Sitting Bull, attack General George Crook's column of more than 1,000 men at the head of the Rosebud.

**June 25**—*Sioux War for the Black Hills.* Custer's scouts discover a Sioux camp and warriors lurking nearby. Rather than wait another day, as the battle plan calls for, Custer attacks, sending Captain Frederick W. Benteen with 125 men south, to make sure that the Sioux have not moved into the upper valley of the Little Bighorn. He sends Major Marcus A. Reno, with another 125 men, after some 40 warriors he has sighted. Custer will charge the Sioux village with the balance of his cavalry. Reno's squadron is quickly overwhelmed. After dispatching his bugler to fetch Benteen, Custer rides to Reno's aid. Custer's entire command is killed by warriors under Gall and Crazy Horse. The remainder of Reno's command, now joined by Benteen's—368 officers and men in all—withstand a siege that stretches into the next day.

**September 9**—*Sioux War for the Black Hills.* Captain Anson Mills, 3rd Cavalry, destroys a Sioux camp in the Battle of Slim Buttes. The war chief American Horse dies.

**November 13, 15**—*Pursuit of the Nez Percé.* The Nez Percés, under Young Joseph, refuse to leave their Wallowa Valley homeland for the reservation.

**November 25**—*Sioux War for the Black Hills.* Ranald Mackenzie defeats a Cheyenne band under Dull Knife and Little Wolf.

**December 16**—*Sioux War for the Black Hills.* Chiefs who come to talk peace with Miles are attacked by Crow scouts. Miles's cantonment falls under attack throughout the balance of the month.

**1877**

**January 8**—*Sioux War for the Black Hills.* Sioux and Cheyennes, led by Crazy Horse, attack. The Battle of Wolf Mountain is fought in a severe snowstorm. Sitting Bull takes his Hunkpapa Sioux into Canada; the Miniconjous, Oglalas, Sans Arcs, and Cheyennes scatter.

**Mid-February**—*Sioux War for the Black Hills.* The Brulé Sioux ask for peace.

**Early April**—*Sioux War for the Black Hills.* Large groups of Cheyennes surrender. Crazy Horse surrenders.

**April 20**—*Apache Wars/Victorio's Resistance.* Indian agent John P. Clum arrests Geronimo at the Ojo Caliente Reservation. Consigned to the hated San Carlos reservation, Geronimo escapes after a year, is pursued by Mexican troops, and returns to San Carlos.

**May 7**—*Sioux War for the Black Hills.* Miles surprises Lame Deer's Miniconjou Sioux camp on Muddy Creek. Lame Deer and his head warrior, Iron Star, decide to surrender, but panic when they believe a scout is taking aim at them. Shots are fired, both Lame Deer and Iron Star die, and the Battle of Muddy Creek is fought.

**June 13–14**—*Pursuit of the Nez Percé.* While traveling to the reservation as ordered, a group of young warriors kills 4 whites. This convinces the nontreaty faction of Nez Percés to turn south, away from the reservation and toward the Salmon River. General O.O. Howard pursues.

**June 17**—*Pursuit of the Nez Percé.* Captain David Perry reaches White Bird Canyon, where he is approached by Nez Percés under a flag of truce. Civilian volunteers ignore the flag and open fire. One-third of Perry's command dies.

**June 22**—*Pursuit of the Nez Percé.* Captain Stephen G. Whipple surprises the village of Chief Looking Glass.

**July 1**—*Pursuit of the Nez Percé.* Looking Glass is inclined to neutrality, and Whipple approaches for a parley. Civilians under his command open fire, a battle follows, and Looking Glass turns hostile.

**July 9–10**—*Pursuit of the Nez Percé.* Ten days of pursuit and engagement follow the attack on Looking Glass's village.

**July 11–12**—*Pursuit of the Nez Percé.* The bloody Battle of Clearwater drives the Indians from the field.

**August**—*Pursuit of the Northern Cheyennes.* The Northern Cheyennes report to the reservation.

**August 9**—*Pursuit of the Nez Percé.* Colonel John Gibbon surprises a camp on the Big Hole River, Montana. Looking Glass counterattacks, inflicting heavy losses. The Nez Percés are pursued for some 100 miles.

**August 19**—*Pursuit of the Nez Percé.* Some 200 warriors engage in a skirmish with troopers on the Camas Meadows.

**September 2**—*Apache Wars/Victorio's Resistance.* Victorio, an influential Apache leader, makes a break from San Carlos on this date, leading more than 300 Warm Springs Apaches and a few Chiricahuas. The Indians evade soldiers for a month before they finally surrender.

**September 13**—*Pursuit of the Nez Percé.* The

7th again engages Nez Percés, at the site of present-day Billings, Montana, and, once again, is bested.

**September 30–October 5**—*Pursuit of the Nez Percé.* The Indians camp 40 miles south of the Canadian border. Miles lays siege.

**October 5**—*Pursuit of the Nez Percé.* Looking Glass is killed, and Chief Joseph surrenders to Miles at the Battle of Bear Paw Mountain.

**September 5**—*Sioux War for the Black Hills.* During his arrest, Crazy Horse is stabbed to death in a scuffle.

**1878**

**May 30**—*Bannock War.* After a shooting incident, Bannock chief Buffalo Horn, with a following of about 200 warriors, leads raids in southern Idaho.

**June 5**—*Bannock War.* The militant medicine man Oytes and Chief Egan lead a group of Northern Pauites off the Malheur Reservation.

**June 8**—*Bannock War.* Civilian volunteers kill Buffalo Horn in a skirmish near Silver City. His warriors ride to Steens Mountain, Oregon, where they join the followers of Oytes and Egan.

**June 23**—*Bannock War.* Oytes and Egan evade Captain Reuben F. Bernard after a day-long battle.

**Late June–Early July**—*Bannock War.* General Howard pursues Bannock–Paiute hostiles.

**July 8**—*Bannock War.* Captain Bernard defeats the Indians at the Battle of Birch Creek.

**July 13**—*Bannock War.* Captain Evan Miles fights it out with the Bannocks and Paiutes, pushing the hostiles into the mountains to the east.

**July 15**—*Bannock War.* Umatillas approach the Bannocks and Pauites on pretext of joining them. They kill Chief Egan and present his scalp to Miles as a trophy.

**August 12**—*Bannock War.* Oytes surrenders.

**September 7**—*Pursuit of the Northern Cheyennes.* Dull Knife and Little Wolf lead 300 Northern Cheyennes off the reservation. Regular army troops and volunteers pursue.

**September 12**—*Bannock War.* The Bannocks fight their last engagement in Wyoming.

**October 23**—*Pursuit of the Northern Cheyennes.* Dull Knife and Little Wolf quarrel, and the fugitive band divides. Dull Knife's faction surrenders at Camp Robinson on this date, while Little Wolf presses northward.

**1879**

**January 2**—*Pursuit of the Northern Cheyennes.* Dull Knife's group refuses to return to Indian Territory. The Camp Robinson commandant cuts off food and water in an attempt to force their departure.

**January 9**—*Pursuit of the Northern Cheyennes.* After a week of thirst and starvation, Dull Knife's group makes a break. Half are killed before the government grants the remainder their wish to live with the Sioux at Pine Ridge.

**March 29**—*Pursuit of the Northern Cheyennes.* Little Wolf surrenders.

**May**—*Sheepeater War.* Sheepeaters (renegade Shoshonis and Bannocks) raid a prospectors' camp. Captain Bernard and Lieutenant Henry Catley search for the raiders.

**July 29**—*Sheepeater War.* Catley's 50-man command is ambushed by 15 Indian warriors. Catley escapes with his troopers, but General Howard courtmartials Catley for ''precipitate retreat before inferior numbers.''

**August 20**—*Sheepeater War.* Sheepeaters attack the army's supply train. They are driven off, but the soldiers are too exhausted to give chase. Howard calls off the campaign.

**September**—*Sheepeater War.* Lieutenant Edward S. Farrow (who had commanded the scouts in the August campaign) sets out again with Umatilla Scouts.

**September 4**—*Apache Wars/Victorio's Resistance.* Ordered to return to San Carlos, Victorio and his followers attempt to settle with the Mescalero Apaches on their reservation. On this date, Victorio leads 60 warriors in a raid on the camp of Troop E, 9th Cavalry at Ojo Caliente. Victorio terrorizes the Mexican state of Chihuahua, much of western Texas, southern New Mexico, and Arizona.

**September 10**—*Ute War.* Nathan C. Meeker, the zealous agent at the White River reservation in Colorado, menaced by his charges, telegraphs military authorities for aid.

**September 16**—*Ute War.* Major Thomas T. "Tip" Thornburgh is ordered to Meeker's relief.

**September 25**—*Ute War.* Thornburgh agrees to talk with the Utes, but a gesture of greeting is mistaken for a threat, and shots are fired. The two-day Battle of Milk Creek begins.

**September 25–October 5**—*Ute War.* The Battle of Milk Creek becomes a siege. Reinforcements are too late to save Thornburgh.

**October 1–2**—*Sheepeater War.* Fifty-one Sheepeaters and a few Bannocks surrender. Most of the Bannocks disappear.

## 1880

**Fall**—*Apache Wars/Victorio's Resistance.* Colonel George P. Buell unites his regular infantry and cavalry with Mexican irregulars commanded by Colonel Joaquin Terrazas to run Victorio to ground in Chihuahua. As the combined forces close in, Terrazas orders Buell and his troops out of the country.

**October 15–16**—*Apache Wars/Victorio's Resistance.* Terrazas kills Victorio at the Battle of Tres Castillos.

## 1881

**July 19**—Sitting Bull leaves Canada and surrenders at Fort Buford, Dakota Territory.

**August 30**—*Apache Wars/Geronimo's Resistance.* During his second period at San Carlos, Geronimo is influenced by a prophet named Nakaidoklini, who preaches Indian supremacy and separation from the whites. On this date, Colonel Eugene A. Carr, commanding Fort Apache, seeks out Nakaidoklini at his village on Cibicu Creek. The prophet is arrested, Carr's column is attacked, and a sergeant shoots and kills Nakaidoklini.

**October 2**—*Apache Wars/Geronimo's Resistance.* Naiche—son of Cochise—Juh, Chato, and Geronimo, with 74 braves fight off pursuing troops and steal across the border, where they unite with the survivors of the Battle of Tres Castillos.

## 1882

**April 19**—*Apache Wars/Geronimo's Resistance.* An Apache war party storms back to San Carlos, kills the reservation police chief,

and compels the Warm Springs Apaches to join the resistance.

**April 23**—*Apache Wars/Geronimo's Resistance.* Lieutenant Colonel George A. Forsyth engages the Apaches at Horseshoe Canyon.

**April 28**—*Apache Wars/Geronimo's Resistance.* Cavalry pursues Geronimo into the Mexican state of Chihuahua.

**April 30**—*Apache Wars/Geronimo's Resistance.* Forsyth joins Captain Tullius C. Tupper, but encounters a Mexican infantry unit, which orders them out of the country.

**July 6**—*Apache Wars/Geronimo's Resistance.* Natiotish, a militant partisan of the slain Nakaidoklini, leads a small force back to the San Carlos Reservation, where he kills the new police chief and 3 officers. He leads raids throughout the Tonto Basin.

**July 17**—*Apache Wars/Geronimo's Resistance.* The Battle of Big Dry Wash ends raiding by White Mountain Apaches.

**July 29**—*Apache Wars/Geronimo's Resistance.* The U.S. and Mexico conclude a treaty authorizing troops of either nation to cross the border in pursuit of Geronimo.

## 1883

**March**—*Apache Wars/Geronimo's Resistance.* Geronimo and Chihuahua raid Sonora, while Chato and Benito conduct raids in the United States.

**March 21**—*Apache Wars/Geronimo's Resistance.* An expedition commanded by Captain Emmet Crawford and Lieutenant Charles B. Gatewood penetrates Mexico.

**May 15**—*Apache Wars/Geronimo's Resistance.* Crawford's scouts attack the encampment of Chato and Benito. Geronimo parleys with Crook; only Juh remains at large.

## 1884

**March**—*Apache Wars/Geronimo's Resistance.* Geronimo arrives at San Carlos this month and foments unrest.

## 1885

**May**—*Apache Wars/Geronimo's Resistance.* Geronimo, Naiche, Chihuhua, and Nana, with 134 others, bolt from the reservation and head for Mexico.

**June 11**—*Apache Wars/Geronimo's Resistance.* Captain Crawford and Lieutenant Britton Davis cross into Mexico.

**July 13**—*Apache Wars/Geronimo's Resistance.* Captain Wirt Davis and Lieutenant Matthias W. Day cross into Mexico. Crook also deploys some 3,000 troopers to patrol the border country.

**October**—*Apache Wars/Geronimo's Resistance.* Crawford, Day, and the two Davises pursue Geronimo for months in vain. Crook recalls them.

**November**—*Apache Wars/Geronimo's Resistance.* Despite Crook's border patrol, Josanie, brother of Chihuahua, leads a dozen warriors on a 4-week rampage through New Mexico

and Arizona. Crook sends Crawford back into Mexico.

## 1886

**January 9**—*Apache Wars/Geronimo's Resistance.* Crawford discovers the Apache camp in Sonora. Geronimo and the others flee, but send a message saying they are prepared to surrender.

**January 11**—*Apache Wars/Geronimo's Resistance.* On this, the day set for surrender, Crawford's camp is attacked by Mexican militiamen. Crawford is killed.

**March 25**—*Apache Wars/Geronimo's Resistance.* General Crook himself accepts Geronimo's surrender. On the way back to San Carlos, Geronimo once again bolts. Crook resigns and is replaced by Nelson A. Miles.

**May 5**—*Apache Wars/Geronimo's Resistance.* Miles sends a strike force under Captain Henry W. Lawton to run Geronimo to ground. After a summer-long chase, Geronimo finally surrenders on September 4.

## 1890

**November 20**—*Ghost Dance Uprising.* Cavalry and infantry reinforcements arrive at the Pine Ridge and Rosebud reservations to counter an uprising that has developed around the "Ghost Dance" religion preached by the prophet Wovoka. Some 3,000 Indians gather on a plateau at the northwest corner of Pine Ridge called the Stronghold.

**November 27**—*Ghost Dance Uprising.* Buffalo Bill arrives at the Standing Rock Reservation to convince his former Wild West Show star Sitting Bull to help avert an uprising. Indian agent James McLaughlin, preferring to arrest Sitting Bull quietly, delays Buffalo Bill and rescinds his authority.

**December 15**—Reservation policemen move in to arrest Sitting Bull. A riot develops, and Sitting Bull is killed.

**December 28**—*Ghost Dance Uprising.* A squadron of the 7th Cavalry locates Chief Big Foot and about 350 Miniconjous near a stream called Wounded Knee Creek. The chief is on his way to the Stronghold to counsel the rebellious Sioux to surrender. The military, however, believes that he is on his way to join the Ghost Dance Uprising.

**December 29**—*Ghost Dance Uprising.* Five hundred soldiers, under Colonel James W. Forsyth, surround Big Foot's camp. The soldiers enter the camp and begin to disarm the Indians, a scuffle develops, and soldiers rake the camp with powerful Hotchkiss guns. The "Battle" of Wounded Knee claims perhaps 300 lives, including that of Big Foot.

**December 30**—*Ghost Dance Uprising.* The 7th Cavalry is ambushed near the Pine Ridge Agency. Elements of the 9th Cavalry come to the rescue, and General Miles marshals 3,500 troops around the angry Sioux.

## 1891

**January 15**—*Ghost Dance Uprising.* The Sioux formally surrender at White Clay Creek.

# BIBLIOGRAPHY

Adair, James. *The History of the American Indians: Particularly Those Nations Adjoining to the Mississippi, East and West Florida, Georgia, South and North Carolina and Virginia; Containing an Account of Their Origin, Language, Manners, Religious and Civil Customs, Laws, Form of Government, Punishments, Conduct in War and Domestic Life, Their Habits, Diet, Agriculture, Manufactures, Diseases and Methods of Cure, and Other Particulars, Sufficient to Render it a Complete Indian System. . . .* London: Edward and Charles Dilly, 1775. Reprint. New York: Promontory Press, 1974.

Adams, Charles Francis. *Three Episodes of Massachusetts History: The Settlement of Boston Bay; The Antinomian Controversy; A Study of Church and Town Government.* Boston: Houghton Mifflin, 1892.

Adams, Ramon F. *Burs Under the Saddle: A Second Look at Books and Histories of the West.* Norman: University of Oklahoma Press, 1964.

————. *More Burs Under the Saddle: Books and Histories of the West.* Norman: University of Oklahoma Press, 1978.

Allen, Ethan. *The Narrative of Colonel Ehtan Allen.* Edited by Brooke Hindle, Facsimile of 1807 ed. New York: Corinth Books, 1961.

Altshuler, Constance Wynn. *Chains of Command: Arizona and the Army, 1856–1875.* Tucson: Arizona Historical Society, 1981.

Ambrose, Stephen E. *Crazy Horse and Custer: The Parallel Lives of Two American Warriors.* Garden City, N.Y.: Doubleday, 1975.

Anderson, Gary Clayton. *Little Crow.* St. Paul: Minnesota Historical Society Press, 1986.

Anderson, Latham. "Canby's Services in the New Mexican Campaign." In *Battles and Leaders of the Civil War,* edited by Robert Underwood Johnson and Clarence Clough Buel. Vol. 2. New York: Thomas Yoseloff, 1956.

Anderson, Mabel Washbourne. *The Life of General Stand Watie.* Pryor, Okla.: Mayes County Republican, 1915.

Andrews, Charles M. *The Colonial Period of American History.* 1934–38. Reprint. New Haven: Yale University Press, 1964.

Andrews, Charles M., ed. *Narratives of the Insurrections, 1675–1690.* New York: Barnes and Noble, 1943.

Andrews, Matthew Page. *Tercentenary History of Maryland.* Chicago: Clarke, 1925.

Andrist, Ralph K. *The Long Death: The Last Days of the Plains Indians.* New York: Macmillan, Collier Books, 1969.

Anonymous. *Mrs. Huggins, the Minnesota Captive.* 1864. Reprinted in Washburn, vol. 86.

Anonymous. *Our Great Indian War. The Miraculous Lives of Bill (Mr. Wm. Rhodes) Decker and Miss Marion Fannin.* 1876. Reprinted in Washburn, vol. 86.

Ashbaugh, Don. *Nevada's Turbulent Yesterday.* Los Angeles: Westernlore Press, 1963.

Askins, Charles. *Texans: Guns and History.* New York: Winchester Press, 1970.

Athearn, Robert G. *Forts of the Upper Missouri.* Englewood Cliffs, N.J.: Prentice-Hall, 1967.

Austerman, Wayne R. *Sharps Rifles and Spanish Mules.* College Station: Texas A & M University Press, 1985.

Axelrod. Alan. *Art of the Golden West: An Illustrated History.* New York: Abbeville Press, 1990.

Axtell, James. *The European and the Indian: Essays in the Ethnohistory of Colonial North America.* Oxford and New York: Oxford University Press, 1981.

Bachman, Van Cleaf. *Peltries or Plantations: The Economic Policies of the Dutch West India Company in New Netherland, 1623–1639.* Baltimore: Johns Hopkins University Press, 1969.

Bailey, Lynn R. *Long Walk.* Los Angeles: Westernlore Press, 1964.

Bakeless, John. *Daniel Boone: Master of the Wilderness.* New York: William Morrow, 1939.

Babour, Philip L. *The Three Worlds of Captain John Smith.* Boston: Houghton Mifflin, 1964.

Bass, Althea. *Cherokee Messenger.* Norman: University of Oklahoma Press, 1936.

Beal, Merrill D. *"I Will Fight No More Forever": Chief Joseph and the Nez Percé War.* Seattle: University of Washington Press, 1963.

Bearss, Edwin C., and Arrell M. Gibson. *Fort Smith, Little Gibraltar on the Arkansas*. Norman: University of Oklahoma Press, 1969.

Berry, Don. *A Majority of Scoundrels: An Informal History of the Rocky Mountain Fur Company*. New York: Harper's, 1961.

Beverley, Robert. *The History and Present State of Virginia, in Four Parts. . . .* London: R. Parker, 1705.

Billington, Ray Allen. *The Far Western Frontier 1830–1860*. New York: Harper & Brothers, 1956.

Black Elk. *Black Elk Speaks: Being the Life Story of a Holy Man of the Oglala Sioux*. Translated by John G. Neihardt. New York: William Morrow, 1932.

Black Hawk. *Black Hawk: An Autobiography*. Edited by Donald Jackson. Ubana: University of Illinois Press, 1955.

Boatner, Mark M., III. *The Civil War Dictionary*. 1959. Reprint. New York: Vintage, 1988.

Bourke, John G. *An Apache Campaign in the Sierra Madre*. New York: Scribner's, 1958.

———. *On the Border with Crook*. New York: Scribner's, 1891.

Bradford, William. *Of Plymouth Plantation*. Edited by Samuel Eliot Morison. New York: Modern Library, 1967.

Brady, Cyrus Townsend. *Indian Fights and Fighters*. 1904. Reprint. Lincoln: University of Nebraska Press, 1971.

Brandon, William. *Indians*. New York: American Heritage; Boston: Houghton Mifflin, 1985.

Brill, Charles J. *Conquest of the Southern Plains*. Oklahoma City: Privately printed, 1938.

Brodie, Fawn. *No Man Knows My History: The Life of Joseph Smith*. New York: Knopf, 1945. Revised ed., 1971.

Browder, Nathaniel C. *The Cherokee Indians and Those Who Came After*. Hayesville, N. C.: Browder, 1973.

Brown, Dee. *Bury My Heart at Wounded Knee: An Indian History of the American West*. New York: Holt, Rinehart & Winston, 1970.

———. *Fort Phil Kearny: An American Saga*. New York: Putnam's, 1962.

Brown, Mark H. *The Plainsmen of the Yellowstone*. New York: Putnam's, 1961.

Browne, J. Ross. *Letters, Journals and Writings*. Edited by Lina Fergusson Browne. Albuquerque: University of New Mexico Press, 1969.

Carrington, Frances. *My Army Life and the Fort Phil Kearny Massacre*. Philadelphia: Lippincott, 1911.

Catlin, George. *North American Indians*. Edited by Peter Matthiessen. New York: Viking Penguin, 1989. [Reprint ed. of *Letters and Notes on the Manners, Customs and Condition of the North American Indians Written During Eight Years' Travel (1832–1839) Amongst the Wildest Tribes of Indians of North America*, 1841.]

Clum, Woodworth. *Apache Agent: The Story of John P. Clum*. Boston: Houghton Mifflin, 1936.

Cokran, David H. *The Cherokee Frontier*. Norman: University of Oklahoma Press, 1969.

Condon, Thomas. *New York Beginnings: The Commercial Origin of New Netherland*. New York: New York University Press, 1968.

Connell, Evan S. *Son of the Morning Star*. San Francisco: North Point Press, 1984.

Connor, Seymour V., and Jimmy W. Skaggs. *Broadcloth and Britches: The Santa Fe Trade*. College Station: Texas A & M University, 1977.

Coupler, Charles J., ed. *Indian Treaties, 1778–1883*. New York: Interland, 1972.

Covey, Cyclone, trans. and ed. *Cabeza de Vaca's Adventures in the Unknown Interior of America*. New York: Macmillan, 1967.

Craner, Verner. *The Southern Frontier, 1670–1732*. Ann Arbor: University of Michigan Press, 1929.

Crook, George. *Autobiography*. Norman: University of Oklahoma Press, 1946.

Debo, Angie. *A History of the Indians in the United States*. Norman: University of Oklahoma Press, 1977.

DeVries, David Pietersz. *Short Historical and Journal notes of several Voyages made in the four parts of the World, namely, Europe, Africa, Asia, and America*. 1655. Reprinted in Cornell Jarey, ed., *Historic Chronicles of New Amsterdam, Colonial New York, and Early Long Island*. First Series. Port Washington, N.Y.: Ira J. Friedman, n.d.

Dippie, Brian W. *The Vanishing American: White Attitudes and U.S. Indian Policy*. Middletown, Conn.: Wesleyan University Press, 1982.

Dodge, Richard Irving. *The Plains of the Great West and Their Inhabitants, Being a Description of the Plains, Game, Indians &c. of the Great North American Desert*. Facsimile of 1876 ed.. New York: Archer House, 1959.

Donnell, F. S. "The Confederate Territory of Arizona, as Compiled from Official Sources," *New Mexico Historical Review* 17, no. 2 (April 1942).

Driver, Harold E. *Indians of North America*. 2d ed., revised. Chicago: University of Chicago Press, 1969.

Eccles, W. J. *France in America*. New York: Harper and Row, 1972.

Eckert, Allan W. *The Conquerors*. Boston: Little, Brown, 1970.

———. *The Frontiersmen*. Boston: Little, Brown, 1967.

———. *Twilight of Empire*. Boston: Little, Brown, 1988.

———. *The Wilderness War*. Boston: Little, Brown, 1978.

Edmunds, R. David. *The Potawatomis: Keepers of the Fire*. Norman: University of Oklahoma Press, 1978.

Ehle, John. *Trail of Tears: The Rise and Fall of the Cherokee Nation*. New York: Anchor Books/Doubleday, 1988.

Ellis, Richard N. *General Pope and U.S. Indian Policy*. Albuquerque: University of New Mexico Press, 1970.

Emerson, Everett. *Letters from New England: The Massachusetts Bay Colony, 1629–1638*. Amherst: University of Massachusetts Press, 1976.

Estergreen, M. Morgan. *Kit Carson: A Portrait in Courage*. Norman: University of Oklahoma Press, 1962.

Faulk, Odie B. *Crimson Desert: Indian Wars of the American Southwest*. New York: Oxford University Press, 1974.

———. *Destiny Road: The Gila Trail and the Opening of the Southwest*. New York: Oxford University Press, 1973.

———. *The Geronimo Campaign*. New York: Oxford University Press, 1969.

Faust, Patricia L., ed. *Historical Times Illustrated Encyclopedia of the Civil War*. New York: Harper and Row, 1986.

Fehrenbach, T. R. *Lone Star: A History*

*of Texas and the Texans.* New York: Macmillan, 1968.

Filler, Louis, and Allen Guttmann, eds. *The Removal of the Cherokee Nation: Manifest Destiny or National Dishonor?* Boston: Heath, 1962.

Finger, John R. *The Eastern Band of Cherokees, 1819–1900.* Knoxville: University of Tennessee Press, 1984.

Fleischmann, Glen. *The Cherokee Removal, 1838.* New York: Franklin Watts, 1971.

Flint, Timothy. *Biographical Memoir of Daniel Boone.* 1833. Reprint ed. edited by James K. Folsom. New Haven, Conn.: College and University Press, 1967.

Ford, John Salmon. *Rip Ford's Texas.* Austin: University of Texas Press, 1963.

Foreman, Grant. *Indian Removal: The Emigration of the Five Civilized Tribes of Indians.* Norman: University of Oklahoma Press, 1932.

Frost, Lawrence A. *The Custer Album: A Pictorial Biography of General George A. Custer.* Norman: University of Oklahoma Press, 1964.

Gibson, Arrell M. *The Chickasaws.* Norman: University of Oklahoma Press, 1971.

Gilbert, Bil. *God Gave Us This Country: Tekamthi and the First American Civil War.* New York: Anchor/Doubleday, 1989.

Goetzmann, William H. *Army Exploration in the American West, 1803–1863.* New Haven: Yale University Press, 1959.

———. *Exploration and Empire.* New York: Knopf, 1966.

*Great Law of Peace of the Longhouse People, The.* Mohawk Nation at Akwesasne, N.Y.: White Roots of Peace, 1971.

Gregg, Josiah. *Commerce of the Prairies.* 1844. Reprint ed. edited by David Freeman Hawk. Indianapolis and New York: Bobbs-Merrill, 1970.

Griffiths, D., Jr. *Two Years' Residence in the New Settlements of Ohio, North America.* Facsimile of 1835 ed. Ann Arbor, Mich.: Readex Microprint, 1966.

Grinnell, George B. *The Fighting Cheyennes.* Norman: University of Oklahoma Press, 1956.

Gurko, Miriam. *Indian America: The Black Hawk War.* New York: Crowell, 1970.

Hagan, William T. *The Sac and the Fox Indians.* Norman: University of Oklahoma Press, 1958.

Hall, Martin Hardwick. *Sibley's New Mexico Campaign.* Austin: University of Texas Press, 1960.

Hart, Herbert M. *Old Forts of the Southwest.* New York: Bonanza, 1964.

Hartley, William, and Ellen Hartley. *Osceola: The Unconquered Indian.* New York: Hawthorn Books, 1973.

Hassrick, Royal B. *The Sioux: Life and Customs of a Warrior Society.* Norman: University of Oklahoma Press, 1964.

Heard, Isaac V. D. *History of the Sioux War and Massacres of 1862 and 1863.* New York: Harper and Brothers, 1864.

Heidenreich, Conrad. *Huronia: A History and Georgraphy of the Huron Indians, 1600–1650.* Toronto: McClelland and Stewart, 1971.

Hoffman, Charles Fenno. *A Winter in the West.* 2 vols. Facsimile of 1835 ed., Ann Arbor, Mich.: Readex Microprint, 1966.

Hoig, Stan. *The Sand Creek Massacre.* Norman: University of Oklahoma Press, 1961.

Hollon, W. Eugene. *Frontier Violence: Another Look.* London, Oxford, and New York: Oxford University Press, 1974.

Hubbard, William. *The History of the Indian Wars in New England from the First Settlement to the Termination of the War with King Philip, in 1677.* Facsimile of 1865 reprint of 1814 ed. New York: Kraus Reprint Co., 1969.

Hunter, John Dunn. *Memoirs of a Captivity among the Indians of North America from Childhood to the Age of Nineteen. . . .* 1824. Reprint. Edited by Richard Drinnon. New York: Schocken, 1973.

Hyde, George. *Red Cloud's Folk: A History of the Oglala Sioux Indians.* Norman: University of Oklahoma Press, 1937.

———. *A Sioux Chronicle.* Norman: University of Oklahoma Press, 1956.

———. *Spotted Tail's Folk: A History of the Brulé Sioux.* Norman: University of Oklahoma Press, 1961.

Irving, Washington. *Astoria; or Anecdotes of an Enterprise Beyond the Rocky Mountains.* 1836. Reprint. Edited by Edgeley W. Todd. Norman: University of Oklahoma Press, 1964.

———. *A History of New York.* 1809. Reprint. Edited by Edwin T. Bowden. New Haven, Conn.: College and University Press, 1964.

———. *A Tour on the Prairies.* 1835. Reprint. Edited by John Francis McDermott. Norman: University of Oklahoma Press, 1956.

Jackson, Helen Hunt. *A Century of Dishonor.* 1881. Reprint. Minneapolis: Ross & Haines, 1964.

Jennings, Francis. *The Ambiguous Iroquois Empire: The Covenant Chain Confederation of Indian Tribes with English Colonies.* New York: W. W. Norton, 1984.

———. *Empire of Fortune: Crowns, Colonies, and Tribes in the Seven Years War in America.* New York: W. W. Norton, 1988.

———. *The Invasion of America: Indians, Colonialism, and the Cant of Conquest.* New York: W. W. Norton, 1976.

Johnson, Amandus. *The Swedish Settlements on the Delaware: Their History and Relation to The Indians, Dutch and English, 1638–1664.* Philadelphia: University of Pennsylvania Press, 1911.

Josephy, Alvin M., Jr. *The Civil War in the American West.* New York: Knopf, 1991.

———. *The Indian Heritage of America.* New York: Knopf, 1970.

———. *The Nez Percé Indians and the Opening of the Northwest.* New Haven: Yale University Press, 1965.

Josephy, Alvin M., Jr., and the editors of Time-Life Books. *War on the Frontier: The Trans-Mississippi West.* Alexandria, Virginia: Time-Life Books, 1986.

Kerby, Robert Lee. *The Confederate Invasion of New Mexico and Arizona, 1861–1862.* Los Angeles: Westernlore Press, 1958.

King, Duane. *The Cherokee Indian Nation: A Troubled History.* Knoxville: University of Tennessee Press, 1979.

*King Philip's War Narratives.* Facsimiles of *The Present State of New-England, with Respect to the Indian War* (1675), *A Continuation of the State of New-England; Being a Farther Account of the Indian War* (1676), *A New and Further Narrative of the State of New-England, Being a Continued Account of the Bloody Indian War* (1676), *A True Account*

*of the Most Considerable Occur-
rences that Have Hapned in the
Warre between the English and the
Indians in New-England* (1676), and
*The War in New-England Visibly
Ended* (1677). Ann Arbor, Mich.:
Readex Microprint, 1966.

Lamar, Howard R. *The Reader's Encyclopedia of the American West.* New
York: Crowell, 1977.

Lavender, David. *Bent's Fort.* Garden
City, N.Y.: Doubleday, 1954.

———. *The Great West.* Boston: Houghton
Mifflin, 1987.

———. *Land of Giants: The Drive to the
Pacific Northwest, 1750–1950.* Lincoln: University of Nebraska Press,
1958.

Lazarus, Edward. *Black Hills, White Jus-
tice: The Sioux Nation Versus the
United States, 1775 to the Present.*
New York: HarperCollins, 1991.

Leonard, Zenas. *Narrative of the Adventures of Zenas Leonard.* Facsimile of
1839 ed. Ann Arbor, Mich.: Readex
Microprint, 1966.

Mahon, John K. *History of the Second
Seminale War: 1835–1842.* Gainesville: University of Florida Press,
1967.

———. *The War of 1812.* Gainesville:
University of Florida Press, 1972.

Marshall, S. L. A. *Crimsoned Prairie:
The Indian Wars.* New York: Scribner's, 1972.

Mather, Cotton. *Magnalia Christi Americana,* Books 1 and 2. 1702. Reprint.
Edited by Kenneth B. Murdock.
Cambridge: Belknap Press of Harvard University Press, 1977.

Mayhall, Mildred P. *The Kiowas.* Norman: University of Oklahoma Press,
1962.

Mooney, James. *The Ghost-Dance Religion and the Sioux Outbreak of 1890.*
Washington, D.C.: Smithsonian Institution, 1896.

Moulton, Gary E. *John Ross: Cherokee
Chief.* Athens: University of Georgia
Press, 1978.

Murray, Keith A. *The Modocs and Their
War.* Norman: University of Oklahoma Press, 1959.

Nash, Roderick. *Wilderness and the
American Mind.* Revised ed. New
Haven and London: Yale University
Press, 1967.

Nichols, Edward J. *Zach Taylor's Little
Army,* Garden City, N.Y.: Doubleday, 1963.

Nuttall, Thomas. *A Journal of Travels
into the Arkansa Territory, during
the Year 1819.* Facsimile of 1821 ed.
Ann Arbor, Mich.: Readex Microprint, 1966.

Nye, W. S. *Plains Indian Raiders.* Norman: University of Oklahoma Press,
1968.

Oehler, C. M. *The Great Sioux Uprising.*
New York: Oxford University Press,
1959.

Olson, James C. *Red Cloud and the Sioux
Problem.* Lincoln: University of Nebraska Press, 1965.

Oswalt, Wendell H. *This Land Was
Theirs: A Study of the North American Indian.* New York: John Wiley,
1966.

Parker, Watson. *Gold in the Black Hills.*
Norman: University of Oklahoma
Press, 1966.

Parkman, Francis. *The Conspiracy of
Pontiac and the Indian War after the
Conquest of Canada.* 2 vols. Boston:
Little, Brown, 1874.

———. *France and England in North
America: A Series of Historical Nar-
ratives.* 4 vols. Boston: Little,
Brown, 1875.

Prucha, Francis Paul. *The Great Father:
The United States Government and
the American Indian.* Lincoln: University of Nebraska Press, 1984.

Prucha, Francis Paul, ed. *Documents of
United States Indian Policy.* 2d ed.,
expanded. Lincoln: University of Nebraska Press, 1990.

Quinn, David B., ed. *North American
Discovery Circa 1000–1612.* New
York: Harper and Row, 1971.

Reedstrom, E. Lisle. *Apache Wars: An Illustrated Battle History.* New York:
Sterling, 1990.

Rich, E. E. *The History of the Hudson's
Bay Company, 1670–1870.* London:
Hudson's Bay Record Society, 1958–
59.

Ridgely, Joseph V. *William Gilmore
Simms.* New York: Twayne, 1962.

Robinson, Doane. *A History of the Dakota
or Sioux Indians.* Minneapolis: Ross
& Haines, 1956.

Robinson, Elwyn B. *History of North Dakota.* Lincoln: University of Nebraska Press, 1966.

Sabin, Edwin L. *Kit Carson Days (1809–
1868).* Chicago: A. C. McClurg, 1914.

Sandoz, Mari. *Crazy Horse: The Strange
Man of the Oglalas.* New York:
Knopf, 1942.

———. *Hostiles and Friendlies.* Lincoln:
University of Nebraska Press, 1959.

Sanford, Paul. *Sioux Arows and Bullets.*
San Antonio, Tx: Naylor, 1969.

Satz, Ronald N. *American Indian Policy
in the Jacksonian Era.* Lincoln: University of Nebraska Press, 1975.

Sauer, Carl Ortwin. *Sixteenth Century
North America: The Land and the
People as Seen by the Europeans.*
Berkeley: University of California
Press, 1971.

Schellie, Don. *Vast Domain of Blood: The
Camp Grant Massacre.* Los Angeles:
Westernlore Press, 1968.

Scott, James L. *A Journal of a Missionary
Tour through Pennsylvania, Ohio,
Indiana, Illinois, Iowa, Wiskonsin,
and Michigan.* Facsimile of 1843 ed.
Ann Arbor, Mich.: Readex Micro-
print, 1966.

Seymour, Flora. *Indian Agents of the Old
Frontier.* New York: Appleton-
Century, 1941.

Sheehan, Bernard W. *Savages and Civil-
ity: Indians and Englishmen in Colonial Virginia.* Cambridge: Cambridge
University Press, 1980.

Simms, William Gilmore. *The Yemassee:
A Romance of Carolina.* 1835. Re-
print. Edited by Joseph V. Ridgely.
New Haven, Conn.: College and
University Press, 1964.

Slotkin, Richard. *Regeneration through
Violence: The Mythology of the
American Frontier, 1600–1860.* Mid-
dletown, Conn.: Wesleyan University
Press, 1973.

Slotkin, Richard, and James K. Folsom,
eds. *So Dreadfull a Judgement: Puritan Responses to King Philip's War,
1676–1677.* Middletown, Conn.: Wesleyan University Press, 1978.

Smith, Page. *A New Age Begins: A People's History of the American Revolution.* New York: Viking Penguin,
1976.

Smith, William, Jr. *The History of the
Province of New York; Volume One:
From the First Discovery to the Year
1732; Volume Two: A Continuation,
1732–1762.* 1757, 1830. Reprint.
Cambridge: Harvard University Press,
1972.

Sonnichsen, C. L. *The Mescalero Apaches.*
Norman: University of Oklahoma
Press, 1958.

Stewart, Edgar I. *Custer's Luck.* Norman:
University of Oklahoma Press, 1955.

Sturtevant, William C. *Handbook of*

*North American Indians*. Washington, D.C.: Smithsonian Institution Press, 1978- .

Swanton, John R. *The Indian Tribes of North America*. Washington, D.C.: Smithsonian Institution Press, 1952.

Tatum, Lawrie. *Our Red Brothers and the Peace Policy of President Ulysses Grant*. Philadelphia: Winston, 1899.

Thrapp, Dan L. *The Conquest of Apacheria*. Norman: University of Oklahoma Press, 1967.

Trelease, Allen W. *Indian Affairs in Colonial New York*. Ithaca, N.Y.: Cornell University Press, 1960.

Turner, Katherine C., ed. *Red Men Calling on the Great White Father*. Norman: University of Oklahoma Press, 1951.

Tuska, Jon, and Vicki Piekarski. *The Frontier Experience: A Reader's Guide to the Life and Literature of the American West*. Jefferson, N. C.: McFarland, 1984.

Tyler, Lyman S. *A History of Indian Policy*. Washington, D.C.: U.S. Government Printing Office, 1973.

Underhill, Ruth M. *Red Man's America: A History of Indians in the United States*. Chicago: University of Chicago Press, 1971.

Utley, Robert M. *Frontier Regulars: The United States Army and the Indian, 1866–1890*. New York: Macmillan, 1973.

———. *Frontiersmen in Blue: The United States Army and the Indian, 1848–1865*. New York: Macmillan, 1967.

———. *Indian Fights: New Facts on Seven Encounters*. Norman: University of Oklahoma Press, 1966;.

———. *The Indian Frontier of the American West 1846–1890*. Albuquerque: University of New Mexico Press, 1984.

———. *The Last Days of the Sioux Nation*. New Haven: Yale University Press, 1963.

———. *With Crook at the Rosebud*. Harrisburg, Penn.: Stackpole, 1956.

Utley, Robert M. and Wilcomb E. Washburn. *Indian Wars*. New York: American Heritage; Boston: Houghton Mifflin: 1977.

Vestal, Stanley. *Sitting Bull: Champion of the Sioux*. Boston: Houghton Mifflin, 1932.

Waldman, Carl. *Atlas of the North American Indian*. New York: Facts on File, 1985.

———. *Who Was Who in Native American History: Indians and Non-Indians from Early Contacts through 1900*. New York: Facts on File, 1990.

*War of the Rebellion: A Compilation of the Official Records of the Union and Confederate Armies, The*. Washington, D.C.: U.S. Government Printing Office, 1880–1901.

Washburn, Wilcomb E. *The Indian in America*. New York: Harper & Row, 1975.

———. *Red Man's Land/White Man's Law: A Study of the Past and Present Status of the American Indian*. New York: Scribner's, 1971.

Washburn, Wilcomb E., ed. *The Garland Library of Narratives of North American Indian Captivities*. 311 titles in 111 vols. New York: Garland, 1976–78.

Wellman, Paul I. *Death on the Prairie: The Thirty Years' Struggle for the Western Plains*. 1934. Reprint. Lincoln: University of Nebraska Press, 1987.

White Bull, Joseph. *The Warrior Who Killed Custer. . . .* Translated and edited by James H. Howard. Lincoln: University of Nebraska Press, 1968.

Whitford, William C. *Colorado Volunteers in the Civil War: The New Mexico Campaign in 1862*. Boulder, CO: Pruett Press, 1963.

Williams, Harry T. *Lincoln and His Generals*. New York: Grosset and Dunlap, 1952.

Williams, John. *The Redeemed Captive Returning to Zion: or, a Faithful History of Remarkable Occurrences in the Captivity and Deliverance of Mr. John Williams*. 1853. Reprint. Cambridge and Boston: Applewood Books, 1987.

Wright, John S. *Letters from the West; or a Caution ot Emigrants*. Facsimile of 1819 ed. Ann Arbor, Mich.: Readex Microprint, 1966.

Wyeth, John B. *Oregon; or a Short History of a Long Journey from the Atlantic Ocean to the Region of the Pacific by Land*. Facsimile of 1833 ed. Ann Arbor, Mich.: Readex Microprint, 1966.

# INDEX